The Israeli Economy, 1985–1998

The Israeli Economy, 1985–1998

From Government Intervention to Market Economics

Edited by Avi Ben-Bassat

The MIT Press
Cambridge, Massachusetts
London, England
The Maurice Falk Institute for Economic Research in Israel

This book was set in Times New Roman on 3B2 by Asco Typesetters, Hong Kong, and was printed and bound in the United States of America.

Library of Congress Cataloging-in-Publication Data

Mi-Me'oravut Memshaltit le-Kalkalat Shuk. English
The Israeli economy, 1985–1998 : from government intervention to market economics / edited by Avi Ben-Bassat.
p. cm.
Includes bibliographical references and index.
ISBN 978-0-262-02518-8 (hc. : alk. paper)—978-0-262-52784-2 (pb.)
1. Israel—Economic policy. 2. Israel—Economic conditions. 3. Structural adjustment (economic policy)—Israel. I. Ben-Bassat, Avi. II. Title.
HC415.25 .M574 2002
330.95694′054—dc21 2002016532

The MIT Press is pleased to keep this title available in print by manufacturing single copies, on demand, via digital printing technology.

In Memory of Professor Michael Bruno
teacher and leader
July 30, 1932–December 26, 1996

Dedicated also to Maggie (Margalit) Eisenstadt, 1942–1999, who was the publications editor at the Falk Institute for over twenty years and worked closely with Michael Bruno. She edited and translated some of the chapters in this volume.

Contents

Preface: Michael Bruno—Teacher and Leader ix
Introduction xiii
Contributors xv

1 **The Obstacle Course to a Market Economy in Israel** 1
Avi Ben-Bassat

I **FISCAL POLICY**

2 **Reducing the Relative Size of Government in Israel after 1985** 61
Michel Strawczynski and Joseph Zeira

II **MONETARY POLICY AND THE INFLATIONARY PROCESS**

3 **A Monetary Labyrinth: Instruments and the Conduct of Monetary Policy in Israel, 1987–1998** 85
Joseph Djivre and Daniel Tsiddon

4 **The Disinflation Process in Israel in the Past Decade** 129
Nissan Liviatan and Nathan Sussman

5 **Israeli Inflation from an International Perspective** 157
Stanley Fischer and David W. H. Orsmond

III **REFORMS IN THE FINANCIAL MARKET**

6 **Reform in the Israeli Financial System and the Flow of Funds of Publicly Traded Manufacturing Firms** 189
Asher A. Blass and Oved Yosha

7 **Pension Fund Reform** 221
Avia Spivak

8 **Liberalization in the Capital Account of the Balance of Payments** 243
Daniel Gottlieb and Mario I. Blejer

IV **REFORMS IN THE GOODS AND SERVICES MARKETS**

9 **The Import-Liberalization and Abolition of Devaluation Substitutes Policy: Implications for the Israeli Economy** 281
Yoram Gabai and Rafael Rob

10 Structural Changes in the Israeli Public Utilities—The Reform That Never Was 309
Reuben Gronau

V IMMIGRATION AND THE LABOR MARKET

11 Integration of Immigrants from the Former Soviet Union in the Israeli Labor Market 349
Zvi Eckstein and Yoram Weiss

12 The Flexibility of the Israeli Labor Market 379
Yael Artstein

VI GROWTH, BRANCH STRUCTURE, AND INCOME DISTRIBUTION

13 Capital Accumulation, Productivity, and Growth in the Israeli Economy 423
Zvi Hercowitz

14 Structural Change and the Emergence of Israel's High-Tech Sector 445
Moshe Justman

15 The Rise of Earning Inequality 485
Momi Dahan

Index 519

Preface

Michael Bruno—Teacher and Leader

I first met Michael when I was a student, in the late sixties. To us students, he symbolized the Perfect Economist, a role model in the fullest sense of the word. This was not so much because Michael was the best lecturer, but because of his concern about and activities on behalf of his students and the problems of the Israeli economy. He never confined himself to building complex models on the blackboard the way professors tend to do; rather, he was an economist who was immersed in each and every aspect of his profession—developing growth models, studying the problems of the Israeli economy, frequently being involved in policymaking, teaching, and later, extensive international activities. Whichever path he chose, he always reached the top.

Michael stamped his love of and dedication to the Israeli economy on his students. He encouraged us to write our graduate and Ph.D. theses on issues related to the Israeli economy. Remember that in those days the available databases were poor, and rising to this challenge often called for constructing them from scratch. It was Michael who established the principle (used by the Research Department of the Bank of Israel) that a researcher's job is not merely to use existing data but also to expand and enrich them by creating new databases. As a model teacher, he practiced what he preached in his doctoral thesis on the inter-relationship between production inputs and output. To complete this research, Michael had to create a completely new database, which together with his measurement methods, formed the foundation of ongoing input-output data series, produced first at the Bank of Israel and then at the Central Bureau of Statistics.

The public at large came to know Michael mainly through his involvement in economic policy. Indeed, there is no stage in his extraordinary career in which Michael was not involved in economic policymaking. He never secluded himself in an academic ivory tower; he was never satisfied with purely scientific or teaching tasks. Michael answered every call to join the effort to formulate Israel's economic policy, and sometimes did not even wait for the call. His CV shows gaps of less than two years between his various endeavors in connection with pivotal issues in Israeli economic policy. It all began, as we know, with his work at the Bank of Israel's Research Department, where he served as joint-director (with Zvi Sussman and Eliezer Sheffer) in the first half of the sixties. It continued when Michael joined the Hebrew University. One important landmark was 1967, in the immediate aftermath of the Six Day War, when Michael headed a team charged with planning the economic future of the occupied territories. After the Yom Kippur War, Michael headed the Economic Policy Team; in 1975, he was a member of the Tax Reform Commission; and two years later, he was appointed economic advisor to Finance Minister Yehoshua Rabinowitz.

Of the long list of Michael's accomplishments, his crowning achievement was without doubt his contribution to Israel's stabilization policy in 1985. At that time, the economy was at the height of a ten-year crisis: we had galloping inflation at hundreds of percent annually, an almost intolerable external debt (80 percent of GDP), and virtually zero economic growth. Many efforts had been made to extricate the economy from this crisis. They all failed. Some of these failures only made things worse, serving to deepen the general air of malaise.

Michael was one of several key figures whose efforts resulted in the 1985 stabilization plan. His collaborators came from the academic world (notably, Eitan Berglas and Nissan Leviatan), the research department of the Bank of Israel (headed by Mordechai Frenkel), and the Treasury (headed by Emanuel Sharon). Together, they formulated what at the time was a daring and innovative emergency plan that combined orthodox and heterodox policy instruments. There was no shortage of doubters and skeptics, especially among fellow economists, regarding the heterodox part of the plan. It took a person of outstanding professional authority to "sell" the plan, not only to politicians and the public, but also to the professional economic community. This was Michael's unique gift: he worked tirelessly, putting his professional reputation at stake, to convince the prime minister, other ministers, the Histadrut leadership, and his colleagues, that the plan could work. Even after the plan was approved by the government, a massive campaign had to be waged to explain the plan to the public at large, to convince people who were tired of repeated flops that this was the right way out of the crisis. Michael's credibility was a crucial element in the plan's eventual success.

No one today has any doubt that the plan was a great success in all economic respects; my personal belief is that it also made a real contribution to raising the flagging national spirit—it drew the entire nation out of apathy and gloom into a new era of hope.

The plan's early success was extremely fragile. Its long-term success required tenacity, determination, and, above all, credibility. Michael Bruno's appointment as governor of the Bank of Israel one year after the stabilization plan was launched was a key factor in bolstering the plan and ensuring its future success. As governor, Michael worked consistently and creatively to ensure the plan's success. In spite of the fact that a central element in the plan itself was a stable exchange rate, he did not hesitate to adopt a floating rate within a limited band three years later, when the fixed rate appeared to have run its course.

Michael believed that internal and external economic stability was merely the foundation upon which the economy as a whole should be built—economic growth through structural reform. These reforms aimed at reducing the government's share and involvement in the economy, and promoting competition in all sectors of the economy. Early on in his term as governor, Michael appointed teams to look into various aspects of Israel's structural economic problems and propose reforms. During this period, the government's involvement in Israel's capital market was reduced, many constraints on monetary policy were removed, discrimination among economic agents was abolished, and monetary tools were improved. The money and capital markets gradually opened up to international capital movements. Michael did not confine himself to the specific spheres related to his official duties as governor. As economic advisor to the government, he advocated structural changes in other sectors as well. Many of his proposals met strong opposition, but Michael was not one to avoid a confrontation; always pleasant and agreeable, he was also determined and resolute in the pursuit of his policy.

Michael's activities in bringing about structural change culminated in the plan for the absorption of immigrants from the former Soviet Union. This plan, too, bears Michael's particular creative stamp. As with the inflation crisis, this wave of immigration stimulated a lively public debate on the appropriate absorption policy that should be pursued. Many economists believed that it would prove impossible to absorb a million new immigrants within a fairly short period of time without resorting to government-initiated enterprise. Michael led those economists who believed the economy was sufficiently robust to absorb most of these immigrants in the business sector, leaving the government to handle public services, funding subsistence for immigrants until they found employment, resolving market failures, and creating conditions amenable to business-sector growth. The government heeded Michael's advice, which soon bore fruit. Today, ten years after the wave of immigration started, the absorption plan has proved a success, although some problems remain unsolved.

Michael also made a major contribution to strengthening the Bank of Israel's position as the institute entrusted with Israel's monetary policy and the governor's authority as economic advisor to the government. He was appointed governor not long after the bank shares crisis, when the Bank of Israel's reputation had suffered a serious blow, and morale was very low. Michael immediately set out to repair the damage. As governor, he excelled at management—he was both demanding and considerate. His professional and administrative talents, together with his winning personality, enabled him to lead the Bank's personnel, at all levels, into a fresh phase of creativity and dedication. He not only put the Bank back on its feet; he led it to new heights of professionalism and prestige both in Israel and abroad.

Five years have passed since Michael raised the idea. Today, the economic restructuring seems to have become even deeper. Inflation has been eradicated, high-tech industry has taken up a significant place in the economy and is leading the economic growth, and the global ranking of Israel's economy has improved immeasurably.

Michael made an enormous contribution to these achievements. The Israel Prize awarded to him in 1994 for economic research expresses the country's appreciation of his work.

After retiring from the Bank of Israel, Michael became chief economist of the World Bank. In this capacity, he investigated the economic ills of Third World and Eastern European countries and helped to formulate recovery plans for these countries. The World Bank also recognized his talent in translating theory and empirical research into policy advice. His experience as the mastermind and executor of a successful stabilization program helped to boost his authority and credibility in various countries as an economic advisor for the World Bank.

Michael's last dream was to set up the Don Patinkin School of Economics. One of his ambitions was that this school would promote research on the Israeli economy at the Falk Institute. His first project was to have been a comprehensive study of structural change in the Israeli economy during the eighties and the nineties. In spite of his failing health, he plunged wholeheartedly into this project, but tragically did not live to see it take off.

After his death, the Falk Institute assumed responsibility for launching the project, seeing it through, and dedicating it to Michael's memory.

The loss we suffered when Michael was taken from us is enormous; we have lost not only a great teacher and a courageous leader, but also a close friend.

May he rest in peace.

Avi Ben-Bassat

Introduction

In the twelve years between the 1973 Yom Kippur War and the 1985 economic stabilization program, the Israeli economy was immersed in deep crisis: The growth rate declined substantially, foreign debt increased steadily, and inflation rose from year to year, soaring to annual rates of few hundred percents. By profoundly altering fiscal and monetary policies, the 1985 stabilization program resulted in an abrupt, steep decline of inflation, and in higher growth rates. The prolonged crisis that preceded the 1985 stabilization also helped transform policymakers' economic perceptions, from belief in pervasive government intervention into reluctant acceptance of a much greater role for market forces.

The different chapters in this book describe in detail the economic pass that Israel took since 1985, a pass that led to a profound transformation of its economy, from one dominated by heavy government intervention, into a vibrant, market-oriented, open economy. This pass entailed a steep downsizing of government and a series of structural reforms that increased market stability and efficiency, namely,

1. introducing fiscal discipline and enhancing central bank independence,
2. reducing government intervention in the primary factors markets—capital, labor, and finance,
3. enhancing competition in markets that were previously monopoly-dominated.

Following this pass, the Israeli economy in the late 1990s was transformed to such an extent that it would hardly be recognized by one who knew it only until 1985. For example, the share of government expenditure in GDP declined from 77 percent to 55 percent; government involvement in directing credit fell from 65 percent of credit volume to only 5 percent; and the tight control of the foreign-exchange market was almost eliminated. As a result of increased competition, the real price of a one-minute phone call from Israel to the U.S.A. dropped by 80 percent.

The economic developments in Israel during the period under review were also greatly influenced by the geopolitical processes of the time, such as the disintegration of the Soviet Union and the subsequent mass immigration to Israel and the peace process with Israel's neighbors.

In this book, the authors analyze not only the favorable impact of the various reforms enacted in Israel since 1985 on growth, employment, inflation, the balance of payments, and the rapid expansion of high-tech industry, but also evaluate the price of these reforms in terms of greater income inequality. They also discuss the problems that remain unresolved.

Acknowledgments

This book is dedicated to the late Michael Bruno, who in 1996 initiated the research project whose outcome is here reported. This research project was sponsored and organized by the Maurice Falk Institute for Economic Research in Israel. The participating researchers came from the Hebrew University, Tel Aviv University, Ben-Gurion University of the Negev, Tel Aviv-Yafo Academic College, the Bank of Israel Research Department, and the International Monetary Fund. The academic steering committee was composed of Elhanan Helpman, Giora Hanoch, Shlomo Yitzhaki, Leo Leiderman, Joram Mayshar, Stanley Fischer, and Avi Ben-Bassat. Members of the steering committee and the two directors of the Falk Institute, Shlomo Yitzhaki and Joram Mayshar, and the outgoing chair of the Falk Institute's board of directors, Meir Heth, helped to direct the project and contributed useful comments. The researchers were helped by a large group of research assistants: Evgeny Agronin, Yael Amit, Gil Avnimelech, Avivit Bar-Eliezer, Gadi Berko, Ravit Ben-David, Yaron Buchnik, Eldad Brick, Mimi Cohen, Alex Dozortsev, Gilad Fernandez, Anat Kahana, Erez Kapitolnik, Smadar Katz, Vladimir Lipschitz, Artur Lokomet, Renat Lokomet, David Lombrozo, Vadim Marmer, Ariel Resnick, Josiah Rotenberg, Ron Stern, Maria Tripolski, and Amit Yatov.

Many people have provided helpful comments on the drafts that were presented to the public at two public conferences, the first held in January 1999, and the second in June 1999, as part of the annual meeting of the Israeli Economic Association.

The late Maggie Eisenstadt, publications editor at the Falk Institute, worked tirelessly to edit some of the chapters and to organize the conferences. Maggie, who passed away in September 1999, was a wonderful colleague and an exceptional professional editor, totally devoted to her work. Her memory will remain in our hearts.

Ronit Ashkenazi invested much effort and skill in preparing the book, organizing the conferences, and administering the financial aspects of the research project; Ziva Litvak contributed in the administrative effort during the early stage of the project; Naftali Greenwood translated several chapters from the original Hebrew; and Karine Gabay helped with the graphs.

The budget steering committee included Freddy Wieder, Meir Heth, Dov Lautman, Eytan Sheshinski, and the directors of the Falk Institute. The research was funded by the Bank of Israel, the National Insurance Institute, the Association of Banks, the Caesarea Edmond Benjamin de Rothschild Foundation, the Koret Foundation, and Teva Pharmaceutical Industries.

I am grateful to the donors and to everyone who took part in the project.

Avi Ben-Bassat
Jerusalem

Contributors

Yael Artstein
The Academic College of Tel-Aviv–Yaffo

Avi Ben-Bassat
Department of Economics, The Hebrew University of Jerusalem

Asher A. Blass
Research Department, Bank of Israel

Mario I. Blejer
Department of Economics, The Hebrew University of Jerusalem
International Monetary Fund

Momi Dahan
School of Public Policy, The Hebrew University of Jerusalem

Joseph Djivre
Research Department, Bank of Israel

Zvi Eckstein
The Eitan Berglas School of Economics, Tel Aviv University
Centre for Economic Policy Research

Stanley Fischer
Citigroup, Inc.

Yoram Gabai
The Maurice Falk Institute for Economic Research in Israel

Daniel Gottlieb
Bank of Israel

Reuben Gronau
Department of Economics, The Hebrew University of Jerusalem

Zvi Hercowitz
The Eitan Berglas School of Economics, Tel Aviv University
Bank of Israel

Moshe Justman
Ben-Gurion University of the Negev

Nissan Liviatan
Research Department, Bank of Israel

David W. H. Orsmond
International Monetary Fund

Rafael Rob
Department of Economics, University of Pennsylvania

Avia Spivak
Ben-Gurion University of the Negev

Michel Strawczynski
Research Department, Bank of Israel

Nathan Sussman
Department of Economics, The Hebrew University of Jerusalem

Daniel Tsiddon
The Eitan Berglas School of Economics, Tel Aviv University
Centre for Economic Policy Research

Yoram Weiss
The Eitan Berglas School of Economics, Tel Aviv University

Oved Yosha
The Eitan Berglas School of Economics, Tel Aviv University

Joseph Zeira
Department of Economics, The Hebrew University of Jerusalem

The Israeli Economy, 1985–1998

1 The Obstacle Course to a Market Economy in Israel

Avi Ben-Bassat

1.1 Introduction

The structure and performance of the Israeli economy have changed substantially since the 1985 Economic Stabilization Program. The changes embrace all areas of economic policy, geopolitical background conditions, and the economy's performance. This chapter profiles the changes in each of these areas, analyzes them and their interrelations, and suggests lessons for the future on the basis of the analysis.

In 1985, the Israeli economy was on the verge of an extremely severe crisis. The annual inflation rate exceeded 400 percent, GDP was hardly growing, and the net external debt came to 80 percent of GDP. The state of the economy is totally different today. Since the stabilization program, GDP has been growing by 4.5 percent on annual average, the inflation rate in 1998 fell to a single-digit level, price stability has been achieved since then, and the external debt has fallen to 10.9 percent of GDP (table 1.1).

Macroeconomic indicators do not express the full effect of the structural changes. As we will see, the principal markets—such as capital, foreign-currency, and labor—and the structure of industry also underwent important changes. Government intervention in the markets of production factors and finance was significantly reduced, and deregulation has made the markets more competitive. The structure of main industry groups has become more intensive in trade and services at the expense of all other industries, including manufacturing. The nature of manufacturing, too, has changed profoundly; the share of human-capital–intensive civilian high-tech industries has been growing steadily and that of defense and traditional industries has been diminishing.

The dramatic change in economic developments is mainly the result of a profound change in the economic thinking of policymakers and has also been influenced by regional and global geopolitical processes.

The implementation of the Economic Stabilization Program in July 1985 halted the severe economic deterioration that was triggered by the Yom Kippur War. The program included many measures—first and foremost, the elimination of the government's budget deficit and a peg of the exchange rate aimed at anchoring prices. The stabilization program restored stability in the economy and extricated it from the crisis, but it also marked a turning point in the economic approach of the two large political parties: from an economy in which government is deeply involved, directly and indirectly, in almost all areas of economic activity, to an economy increasingly based on market forces. It took a broad national consensus to implement

Table 1.1
Israel: Basic Economic Data

	1984	1999
Mean population (million)	4.2	6.1
Israeli persons employed (million)	1.4	2.1
GDP (NIS billion, 1999 prices)	215.6	417.4
Per capita GDP ($'000s, current prices)	6.2	16.5
Unemployment rate (percent)	5.9	8.9
Inflation rate (during year, percent)	444.9	1.3
Export ($ billion)	10.5	39.3
Import ($ billion)	15.3	47.5
Net foreign debt (percent of GDP)	79.6	10.9
General government expenditure (percent of GDP)	72.4	54.4
General government deficit (percent of GDP)	14.5	4.8

the budget cut and, a fortiori, to alter the existing economic regime. Indeed, the establishment of a national unity government in 1984, which ruled until 1991, helped to realize the turnabout in economic policy and consolidate the new economic policy. Thus, the new doctrine was continued even after the change of governments.

The purpose of the new policy was to make the growth process more sustainable—to achieve price stability and eliminate the current account deficit of the balance of payments—important conditions for the sustainability of growth. According to this approach, sustainable growth must emerge from the business sector. Thus, the role of government in the economy had to be reduced to free up resources for the business sector's growth. To facilitate this process, the government had to take a host of actions aimed at enhancing the efficiency and stability of the business environment. This included structural reforms in the major markets, a reduction of government involvement in directing the use of economic resources, and strengthening of competition in largely monopoly-controlled markets. These reforms were to improve resource allocation; lower the costs of important inputs such as labor, credit, electricity, fuel, and communications; and thereby improve business sector profitability and its incentive to invest and expand.

The share of general government expenditure in the GDP was sharply diminished; within ten years, it declined by an impressive 20 percent of GDP, freeing up extensive resources for the business sector. The composition of the budget was also revised to support growth of the business sector, as infrastructure investments expanded and government involvement in allocating production factors, by means of capital subsidies and taxes on labor, contracted greatly.

Although the beginnings of structural reforms to reduce government involvement in various markets were visible in the stabilization program itself, real change began in 1987. The reforms were implemented more slowly in Israel than in other countries and, even though fourteen years have passed since the restructuring began, the process has not yet been completed. For the most part, the macroeconomic reforms have by and large been carried out and have improved functioning of the financial and capital market, the foreign-currency market, and foreign trade. However, the microeconomic aspects of reform that aim to enhance competition in industries controlled by monopolies still need to be accomplished. The entry of competitors in the telecommunication market—cellular-telephone service and international calls—has been very successful and has helped to bring about a substantial fall in prices. However, other areas of infrastructure—electricity, fuel, refineries, ports, aviation, water, and public transit—remain monopolistic, and the government has settled for regulating rates in some of these industries in a more rational manner.

Geopolitical processes have been no less important. First, the disintegration of the Soviet Union caused a mass Jewish immigration to Israel that expanded the economy and enriched it with human capital. The newly established Eastern European countries opened up their trade with Israel. The second related political factor that left its imprint on the economy is the peace process. The peace accords reduced the effectiveness of the Arab boycott, allowed Israel to access new markets, mitigated Israel's security risks, and encouraged foreign investment in Israel.

The downsizing of government, the structural reforms, and the peace process have helped to accelerate economic growth, particularly in the business sector. Thus, the business sector's share in GDP has grown steadily since the stabilization program, from 59 percent in 1984 to 67 percent in 1998. However, that growth and the rise in standard of living have come at a price—greater inequality in income distribution.

This chapter describes changes in fiscal and monetary policy, structural reforms, political processes, and their implications on resource allocation, growth, the balance of payments, and inflation. The chapter also analyzes the Israeli reform process from an international perspective and discusses the obstacles that Israel faces on its way to a market economy.

1.2 Budget Policy Reform

The Size of Government

Between the Yom Kippur War and 1985, general government spending claimed a decisive share of economic resources, 77 percent of GDP on average. The desired size

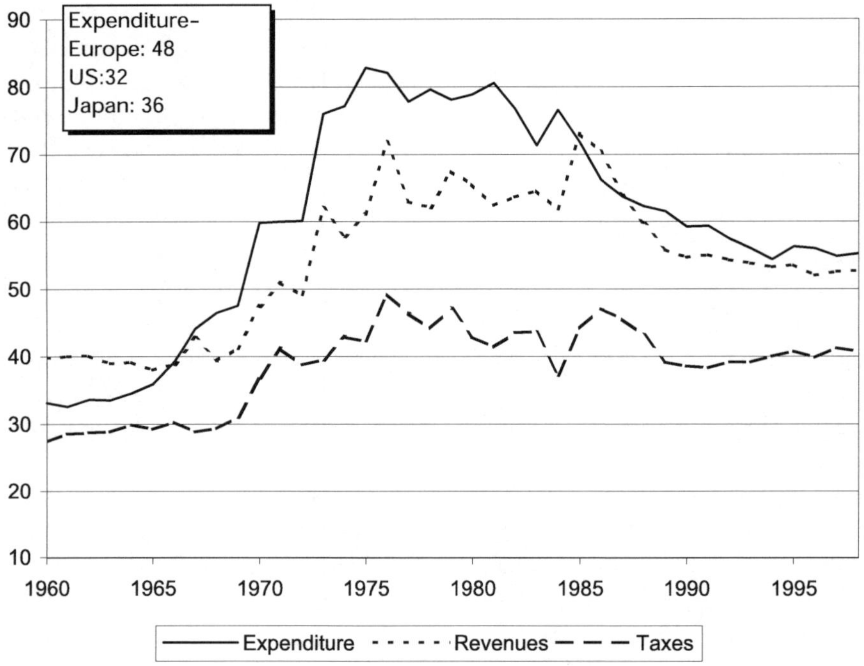

Figure 1.1
General-Government Expenditure and Tax Burden in GDP, 1960–1998
(Percent)

of government expenditure relative to GDP and the nature of services offered by the government to the public are a matter of normative decision. Although Western economies differ among each other in their approach to this question, the relative size of government is much smaller in all Western countries than in Israel (figure 1.1). Furthermore, although government involvement in economic affairs has always been extensive in Israel, until 1967 the share of government expenditure in GDP was only 35 percent, rather small in comparison with other countries. The government's share began to rise steeply after the Six Day War (1967), following the increase in defense expenditure, and escalated further after the Yom Kippur War.

Such a scale of expansion does not leave much space for the business sector to develop. An increase in government expenditure eventually necessitates a corresponding increase in the tax burden and leaves the business sector with fewer available production factors. The high income tax penalizes the propensity to work and thus impedes employment growth. Fixed investment becomes less profitable and, accordingly, the business sector's capital stock is drained and capital utilization lowered.

Indeed, the tax burden (measured as share of taxes in GDP) rose considerably, from 28 percent in the early 1960s to 44 percent in the crisis years. However, since the added taxes did not suffice to cover the extra spending, the general-government deficit widened and reached a huge size—14 percent of GDP, on average, in 1974–1985. Consequently, the public debt got out of control, and price stability was undermined as well.

The composition of the financing of government expenditure is secondary in importance to the development of GDP of the business sector; its main effect is on the transmission channels between fiscal policy and business-sector GDP. This is certainly the case if one accepts the Ricardian equivalence theorem, which postulates that the public perceives the financing by means of bond issues as a future tax. Even if we disregard this approach, we find that proportional increases in government expenditure had a restraining effect on business-sector growth, partly by increasing the tax burden and partly by expanding the budget deficit. The increase in the general-government budget deficit may have stimulated economic activity in the short run but eventually led to higher inflation, increased economic uncertainty, and higher interest rates, all of which hampered investment demand and economic growth in the business sector.[1] For the same reasons, a reduction of government expenditure would set the opposite processes in motion, that is, accelerate growth of business-sector GDP and increase its share.

The Economic Stabilization Program that was implemented in July 1985 proved to be a turning point for the economy. It eliminated the government deficit in one stroke and prompted a gradual downscaling of general-government expenditure in terms of share of GDP. This process lasted until 1994. The proportion of average general-government expenditure was 21 percent of GDP lower in 1994–1998 than in 1980–1984. Although the share of general-government expenditure declined perceptibly, the tax burden contracted only by a negligible 1.1 percent of GDP. The sources freed up were used for two purposes—mitigating the government's dependency on foreign unilateral transfers and lowering the budget deficit.

Most central-government spending abroad is for defense imports, and the lion's share of the reduction in government expenditure was based on lowering defense expenditure, mainly for imports. Concurrently, foreign assistance for the financing of new defense procurements decreased, as did the repayment of loans previously taken to finance weapons imports. Foreign assistance to the government of Israel has remained constant in dollar terms since 1986, but its share in GDP has declined by 7 percentage points, much like the decline in government spending abroad (see table 1.2). This decrease in the government's dependency on external sources enhanced certainty that the proportional decline in government expenditure would be sustainable; it also lessened the risk of a balance-of-payments crisis.

Table 1.2
General-Government Expenditure and Income, 1980–1998 (Percent of GDP, current prices)

	Domestic		Foreign currency		Total deficit
	Expenditure	Income	Expenditure	Income	
1980–1984	65.8	51.5	10.9	12.1	+13.2
1985–1989	55.6	51.2	9.5	13.4	+0.6
1990–1993	52.5	46.2	5.5	8.3	+3.6
1994–1998	51.6	47.6	3.8	5.2	+2.6
(1980/84)–(1994/98)	−14.2	−3.8	−7.1	−7.0	−10.6

Source: Central Bureau of Statistics.

The total decrease in the general-government budget deficit from the early '80s to the later '90s was 10.6 percent of GDP. In the first years after the stabilization program (1985–1989), the total general-government budget was nearly in balance. In the early 1990s, however, it became necessary to expand the deficit temporarily to absorb the mass immigration from the former Soviet Union. To make sure that the deviation would remain temporary, the government initiated a law that required it to reduce the deficit gradually starting in 1992 and to balance the budget by 1995. However, already in 1993, the target for 1995 was relaxed, requiring only a reduction in the share of the deficit over time. At first, the government adhered to these targets and actually overshot them. In 1995–1996, however, the deficit deviated significantly from the planned path—a development that was corrected in 1997. Notwithstanding the volatility of the deficit, overall the government's fiscal discipline seems to have improved substantially. Support for this impression may be found in the interrelationship between the reduction of expenditure and the lowering of the rate of taxation in GDP. Strawczynski and Zeira (in this volume) tested government spending and taxes for cointegration and found a significant change from weak to strong budget discipline after the stabilization program. The statistical tests also showed that the lag between the change in expenditure and the change in taxes has been decreasing over time. Legislation that forbade the government to "print money," that is, to borrow from the central bank, also helped to strengthen fiscal discipline and to create a clear division of responsibilities between the government and the Bank of Israel.

In sum, we see that the main paths of transmission between downscaling government and letting the business sector expand ran along two axes—greater economic certainty and stability. Those were achieved by a smaller government deficit and less reliance on foreign assistance. The contraction of the tax burden, in contrast, was minimal.

Composition of the Budget

The composition of the budget also had several important implications for the expansion of the business sector: (a) The privatization process shifted a rising share of general-government expenditure to the business sector (see Strawczynski and Zeira in this volume), as reflected in a gradual and steady proportional increase in general-government purchases from the business sector, for example, for cleaning services, printing, health care, and contract labor. The share of purchases (in 1995 prices) in total civilian general-government consumption climbed from 13.1 percent in 1980–1984 to 26.3 percent in 1994–1998, whereas the share in defense consumption was unchanged. The increase in procurements from the business sector during that time contributed 2.6 percent to the increase in its share in GDP.[2]

(b) Infrastructure investments are of fundamental importance for business-sector growth because they act as a complementary production factor in business activity. However, the budget shortage during the crisis years led to a preference of the present over the future. As a result, general-government sources for intrastructure investments declined significantly, and therefore impaired growth and productivity. Since the stabilization program, however, the share of general-government investments began to rise again, from 2.5 percent of GDP in the early 1980s to 3.6 percent in 1994–1998 (figure 1.2). Bergman and Merom (1993) and Dahan and Strawczynski (1993) found a significant positive effect of infrastructure investments on business-sector GDP supply. Lavie and Strawczynski (1998) found that government investments in road infrastructure made a favorable contribution to the growth of business-sector GDP by improving productivity but did not have a complementary effect on the expansion of capital and labor factors.

1.3 Structural Reforms—The Full Half of the Glass

Intensive government involvement in managing the Israeli economy is as old as the economy itself. The first indications of change in the economic regime came into sight in the mid-1960s with an import liberalization, trade agreement with the European Common Market, and elimination of multiple exchange rate practices. In the early 1970s, the Interest Ordinance, which had subjected nonindexed interest rates to an administrative cap, was abolished. Thus, the approach that favored the directing of nonresidential investments by officials gave way to more rational investment-support criteria, in the course of which economic evaluation became more important. After the Yom Kippur War, however, public expenditure rose perceptively, especially for defense purposes but also for transfer payments. Rearmament and a more

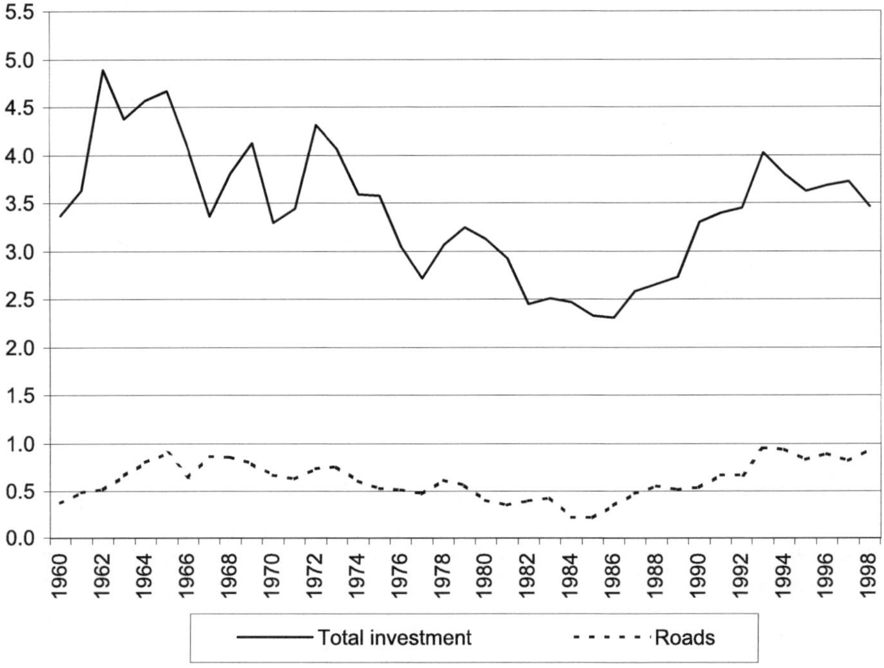

Figure 1.2
Infrastructure Investments, 1960–1998
(Percent of GDP, current prices)

generous social-service policy, without a parallel increase in state revenues, caused a rapid expansion in the government deficit. As a result, the downtrend in government intervention that had been evident in the early 1970s was halted, and the situation was even worsened. The process of de facto nationalization of the supply of funds in the capital-market intensified, and the sources were used to finance government deficits, expand direct support, and provide credit benefits for the business sector. As the balance of payments worsened, nontariff import barriers also proliferated in various and sundry ways. Thus, on the verge of the stabilization program, the government was deeply involved in economic activities.

Only after the stabilization program went into effect in 1985 did policymakers realize that stabilizing the economy was not enough and that to reignite growth, structural reforms that would move Israel toward a market economy were needed. The success of the stabilization program helped its procreators to persuade the political system and the public that this second stage in healing the economy was crucial. At first, a few reformatory steps were taken, mainly concerning financial markets, but soon a broad and clear conception took shape, first at the Bank of Israel and afterwards at the Ministry of Finance as well.[3]

Financial Reforms—Money, Capital, and Foreign-Currency Markets

Until the mid-1980s, Israel's financial system fell far short of the essential conditions for perfect competition. One of the main reasons for the lack of competition was massive government intervention in all segments of the financial market—the money market, capital market, and international capital flows in both directions. Another factor is the oligopolistic structure of the financial intermediation system.

The government intervened in all activities in the market—raising capital, allocating it, and determining returns. The arguments for government intervention were diverse and varied over time. Until 1973, the main goal was to strengthen population growth in development towns in areas of high national priority, subsidizing housing for immigrants and young couples, and attaining economic targets in the business sector, such as exports and fixed investments, whereas the financing of the government's deficit was of secondary importance. However, the steep increase in the government deficit after the Yom Kippur War in 1973 led to a turning point in both the magnitudes and the goals of the intervention. After 1974, the government used administrative measures to channel most private savings to government bonds in order to finance its huge budget deficit at a lower price than competitive conditions would allow.[4]

The government used a host of tools to control financial markets and dictate its priorities—administrative barriers, exceptionally high liquidity ratios, credit quotas and exemptions from them, restrictions on international capital flows, discriminatory tax rates and subsidies. The financial market was virtually nationalized, and excess regulation made the market very complicated and cumbersome.

Heavy and persistent government intervention in the financial markets had distorted resource allocation. For example, the government allocated "directed credit" for exports in accordance with the rate of increase in export and imposed ceilings on credit for other purposes. Furthermore, interest rates on loans for exporters were subsidized. The preference for exports boosted the financial sources available for this use relative to other goals, such as the manufacture of import substitutes, even though both activities contribute toward narrowing the import surplus and increasing growth. Thus, efficiency in resource allocation was impaired and, for this reason, so was the growth rate. Another striking example—until the late 1970s, the government raised loans from the public in which the principal and interest were pegged to the Consumer Price Index and, concurrently, granted nonindexed loans for favored purposes.

The variety of prohibitions and exceptions to them, the broad spectrum of controled interest rates, and the range of tools that the government used to control the market brought about a complicated market structure, impaired its efficiency, and increased the costs of financial intermediators and their regulators. This was reflected in a positive trend in average interest.

The government's heavy-handed intervention impaired the efficacy and efficiency of monetary policy at two levels. First, the provision of unrestricted credit for certain purposes reduced the basis on which monetary policy could operate. For example, export credit, which accounted for one-third of total short-term credit, expanded automatically with export growth. This forced the Bank of Israel to attain its targets by applying policy on a smaller monetary base or, alternatively, to retreat from its original monetary goals. Second, the government's intervention in the financial and capital markets led to a chain reaction of problems. An attempt to solve one problem created a new one.

Thus, the financial system became a labyrinth of regulations. In 1977, for example, a foreign-currency liberalization was instituted despite large budget and balance-of-payment deficits. In the absence of appropriate macroeconomic conditions, policymakers were afraid that the reform would trigger a large capital flight; therefore, they offered the public a government-backed deposit in domestic currency, indexed to the exchange rate (Patam accounts) as an alternative to investing abroad. The share of Patam in liquid assets (the M4 aggregate) climbed to 22 percent within several months of its debut, continued to rise gradually afterwards, and peaked at 66 percent in late 1984. Thus, the proportion of nonindexed assets, on which the management of monetary policy is based, decreased dramatically. Another example was the government policy in the bond market. In 1977–1982, the government stabilized real bond yields to mitigate the risk of holding bonds and, thereby, to reduce the price it had to pay for capital. This policy entailed the sale and purchase of bonds for considerations that were extraneous to the conduct of monetary policy, thereby weakening the Central Bank's control of the monetary base.[5] Furthermore, a sizeable share of nontradeable government bonds was issued to institutional investors at subsidized interest rates. Thus, the size of the free bond market was severely limited and the possibility of open market operations was thwarted. These developments contributed to the loss of monetary control and the high inflation process in 1974–1985.

After the stabilization program, especially from early 1987 on, the government gradually reduced its involvement in the domestic financial and capital market to eliminate restrictions on cross-border capital flows and to enhance competition among financial intermediators. There exist strong substitution effects among the various segments of the financial system, and the degree of interdependence between them is high. However, each of these markets has unique attributes. Therefore, we first describe the reform in each segment and then examine the combined effect of the measures in making Israel's financial markets more competitive and efficient.

Money-Market Reform The financial-market reform was meant to eliminate restrictions that had distorted the assets-and-liabilities portfolios of households and businesses and to enhance the effectiveness of monetary policy. The reform included dozens of individual measures that may be categorized into several groups:

1. The Bank of Israel stopped using liquidity ratios as a tool of monetary policy. Accordingly, the ratios were lowered gradually to a level consistent with business liquidity ratios. The differences among ratios were also greatly reduced. Because a liquidity ratio is like a tax, it widens the spreads between credit and deposit interest rates. Variance in liquidity ratios creates discriminatory tax rates and distorts asset portfolios and, therefore, credit portfolios as well. In 1987, liquidity ratios ranged from 32 percent for domestic-currency deposits to 84 percent for deposits in denominated foreign currency or indexed to exchange rates (figure 1.3). Today, liquidity ratios on all types of deposits are 3–6 percent.

2. When the stabilization program went into effect, Patam deposits indexed to the exchange rate and backed by a government commitment became unidirectional; they could be redeemed but not newly created. Instead of Patam, the banking system was allowed to accept deposits indexed to the exchange rate (Patsam) and to lend to the public on their basis. The result—a decrease in Patam deposits and an increase in Patsam deposits—reduced government involvement in the market of indexed assets.

3. All term limitations on maturities on assets and liabilities indexed to the Consumer Price Index or the exchange rate were lifted.

4. All quotas on foreign-currency credit and bank guarantees were abolished.

5. All directed-credit arrangements were abolished. These arrangements had created a preference for exports, imports of special goods—equipment, fuel, and animal fodder—and assistance for industries in distress. Actually, directed credit began to contract in 1982.

6. As the plethora of restrictions on the financial market was eliminated, two new monetary policy tools were developed—monetary loans and deposits, and issue of Treasury bills. The Bank of Israel used these two tools to control domestic interest rates.

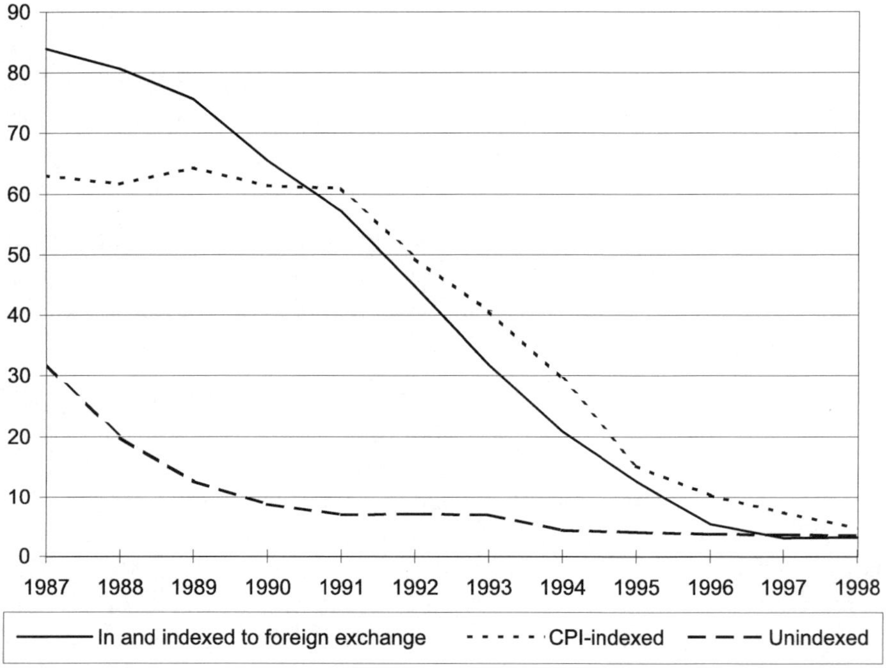

Figure 1.3
Liquidity Ratios for Deposits, End of Year, 1987–1998
(Percent)

Capital Market Reform By 1987, the government had taken several administrative actions that resulted in a de facto nationalization of a very large share of the public's middle- and long-term savings. The elimination of the government's budget deficit removed the main motive for the nationalization of private savings. This development, coupled with the change in the government's economic credo, marked the beginning of gradual reform in the composition of assets and liabilities of the public, institutional investors, and the business sector.

1. All institutional investors—provident funds, pension funds, and advanced-training funds—were required to invest most funds under their management in government bonds. The proportion was 80 percent in the 1960s, but escalating budget deficits raised the share to 93 percent in 1976. A similar requirement was imposed on banks' saving plans. In April 1987, the government began to change course by lowering the compulsory rate of investment in government bonds for all institutional investors except pension funds. The proportion today is 40 percent (figure 1.4). This deregu-

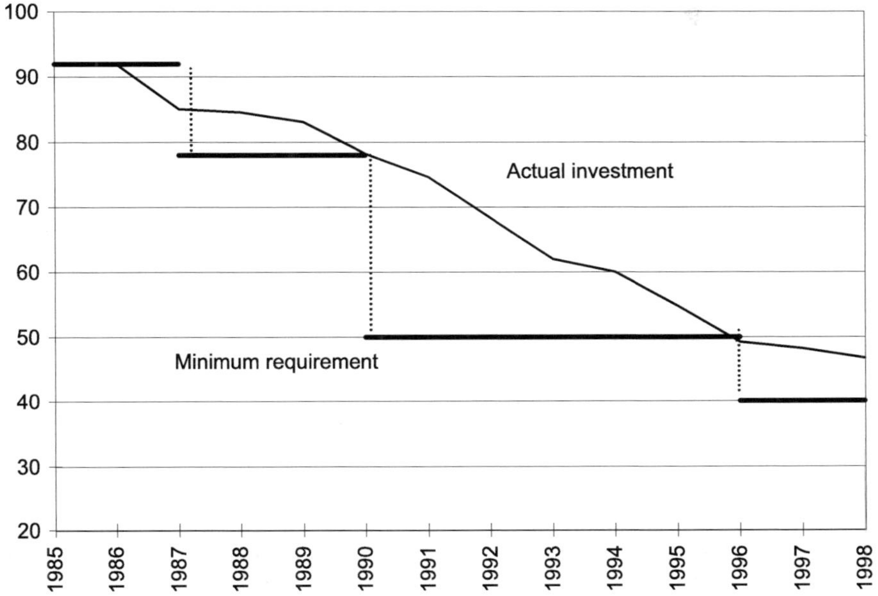

Figure 1.4
Share of Government Bonds in Portfolio of Provident Funds—Compulsory and Actual, 1985–1998 (Percent)

lation reduced the share of such bonds in institutional investors' portfolios. Because the adjustment was gradual, the new restrictions did not have a binding effect during most of this time. Today, the gap between the share of government bonds and the investment requirement is 7 percent.

2. Until the reform, corporate bond issues were prohibited except with government authorization, which was very rarely given. In 1987, the private sector was given a general permit to issue bonds. Additionally, the tax laws applying to corporate and government bonds were equalized.

3. Most government bonds issued to institutional investors were nontradeable and paid interest at a preferential rate. This deprived the Israeli free market of tradeable assets and made it susceptible to considerable volatility. Since mid-1985, the government has issued nontradeable bonds only to pension funds and for life-insurance plans. Consequently, the share of tradeable bonds in total internal debt climbed steadily, from 16 percent in 1986 to 51 percent in 1998.

4. In 1995, the government decided to revise the pension-fund industry comprehensively. Existing (henceforth, "old") pension funds were not allowed to accept new

members, and new funds were given a lower level of government support and required to maintain actuarial balance (Spivak, in this book). However, the method of support, for both old and new funds, was left unchanged, that is, the government continued to subsidize pension funds by providing them with nontradeable bonds that paid higher-than-market interest.

Subsidization of pension funds by means of preferred bonds perpetuates the absence of these funds from the capital market. The removal of such an important component from the capital market distorts the interest rate that would bring national savings and firms' demand for these savings into equilibrium. For this reason, it may impair the desired level of savings and investment in the economy at large. The issuance of earmarked bonds to pension funds also creates risks in managing the state budget and carries the hazard of government involvement in the economy. The law of diminishing budget deficits, in its original version, required the government to cut its budget deficit gradually until a balanced budget would result within four years.[6] Therefore, after fiscal consolidation will have been achieved, the government's undertaking to provide pension funds with special bonds will leave the government with unnecessary funds. The government might thus be tempted to increase public expenditure and retreat from its strategy of a diminishing deficit. Alternatively, the government may resume its superfluous function as a financial intermediator—borrowing from pension funds and lending to the business sector. The only way the government can avoid these problems is to refrain from recycling tradeable bonds that have matured, but in this case the tradeable bonds market will shrink and eventually disappear. Such an outcome would derail the economy from the reform path it has followed since the stabilization program, and it would mark a significant retreat from the process of capital-market and budget reform.

The establishment of new pension funds did not help to restructure this industry, which remains highly centralized. The new funds are even more centralized than the old ones (Spivak, in this volume). The main reason for the industry's oligopolistic structure is its high entrance barriers.

Foreign-Currency Market Reform

LIBERALIZATION OF CAPITAL FLOWS The first attempt to carry out a sweeping liberalization in the foreign-currency market took place in 1977. The liberalization was carried out amidst grave economic problems—huge budget and balance-of-payments deficits, spiraling inflation, and a large public and external debt. Consequently, this liberalization attempt failed. Eventually, the government not only repealed it but also, within a few years, made foreign exchange control much stiffer than it had been shortly before the liberalization.

The lesson of the 1977 failure was learned well. It took until 1985, after the government invoked a far-reaching economic recovery program, to launch the second attempt to institute freedom of transaction in foreign currency. The government decided to liberalize foreign-currency activity gradually and to study continually the implications of measures already carried out. The liberalization of capital flows has substantive advantages for an economy—it allows for investment to exceed national savings; it creates the possibility of reducing portfolio risk for households and firms by diversifying the assets portfolio; it makes the financial and capital markets more competitive; and it enhances discipline in macroeconomic policy. However, the utility an economy may gain from these advantages entails risks. Integrating the domestic capital market into international markets exposes the domestic foreign-currency market to speculative attacks and makes the economy much more vulnerable to external shocks. Such shocks may have negative effects because financial markets often overreact in both directions. Furthermore, when Israel began to liberalize, the economy was characterized by two factors that placed the stability of the liberalization at exceptional risk. First, given that inflation spreads between Israel and its trading partners were rather large, there was an unusually high probability of speculative runs on the currency. Second, the public debt was still very high. Furthermore, policymakers were worried that the possibility of overseas investment after many years of a ban on such activity might generate a large capital outflow as the public sought to diversify its assets portfolio.

The choice of gradualism meant that the elimination of restrictions had to be sequenced. The sequence was dictated by three main criteria:

- Restrictions against the activity of the business sector, on both liabilities and assets, should be eliminated before restrictions pertaining to households and institutional investors, because this sequence would have a greater effect on GDP growth.
- Restrictions on capital inflow should be eliminated before restrictions on capital outflow. Given that the limited competition in the banking system is reflected chiefly in credit, competitive capital inflows would make a greater contribution. Additionally, the limitation of foreign-currency sources and the level of the internal debt made it necessary to give capital inflow a higher priority.
- Restrictions on individuals should be eliminated before restrictions pertaining to institutional investors, because most internal debt was invested with institutional funds.

The liberalization of international capital flows began in 1987 and was completed in 1998. The restrictions that were left in effect pertain to overseas investment by institutional investors and forward transactions (Gottlieb and Blejer, in this volume).

DEVELOPMENT OF THE EXCHANGE-RATE REGIME The exchange-rate regime is closely related to the intensity of the liberalization of capital flows. It is true that the use of the exchange rate as a peg for prices is advantageous in a small economy. However, since the liberalization of capital flows aggravates the volatility of foreign-currency demand and supply, considerable foreign reserves are needed to defend the exchange rate. A floating exchange rate facilitates liberalization of capital flows even without large reserves.

The process of enhancing the flexibility of the exchange-rate regime began in 1989. The inflation differentials between Israel and its trading partners generated expectations of frequent currency depreciation and, consequently, waves of speculation in the foreign-currency market. Because the exchange rate was defended mainly by means of the lending rate, the Central Bank's interest rate became severely volatile. To attenuate the speculative attacks, a changeover to a target zone regime—a horizontal band at first, a crawling band later on—was set in motion gradually. Furthermore, the band was broadened commensurate with the easing of restrictions on international capital flows, from 3 percent in either direction from the midpoint in 1989 to 15 percent in either direction in 1997. However, although the characteristics of the regime changed several times, only the changeover from a fixed exchange rate to a horizontal band in 1989 was found to be statistically significant.[7]

The transition to a crawling band was meant to reduce the business sector's uncertainty about the expected annual rate of change in the exchange rate and to mitigate the speculative attacks. Therefore, the Bank of Israel intervened not only at the boundaries of the band but also within the band (until May 1995) to keep the exchange rate from deviating far from the midpoint. However, since the main goal of the exchange-rate policy was inflation control, the intervention skewed the progression of the rate downward (Ben-Bassat, 1995). The preference of the inflation target over the maintenance of business-sector profitability gained strength in the middle of 1995, when the Bank of Israel stopped intervening within the band and predicated its anti-inflation policy on very high interest rates. These rates, in turn, caused the exchange rate to sink to the bottom of the band. This approach was also much in evidence in October 1998, when the Bank of Israel responded to the international financial crisis by raising the lending rate steeply to restrain inflation expectations that had risen sharply in response to the rapid currency depreciation that occurred.

Competition in the Banking System The Israeli banking system is characterized by an oligopolistic structure, that is, control of most countrywide financial activity by a small number of major banks. For example, about two-thirds of total assets in the banking system are concentrated in the hands of the two largest banks (Hapoalim and Leumi), and some 80 percent are held by the three largest. Because the large banks also own banking subsidiaries, the industry is even more concentrated in terms of the share of large banking groups in it. International comparison shows that Israel has one of the highest rates of banking concentration in the Western world. This phenomenon can hardly be attributed to the utilization of economies of scale since banking in most small Western countries, such as Belgium, Denmark, and Norway, is much less concentrated than in Israel. Furthermore, Rothenberg (1994) found that the optimum size of an Israeli bank falls in the range of 9 to 12 percent of the market.

Small industrial countries have two additional sources of competition in the financial and capital market that are negligible in Israel. First, they have many substitute financial intermediators to banks, such as brokers, insurance companies, and pension funds. Second, they have a substantial share of foreign banks, and the banking system in the European Communities is quite close to being one big financial market. Additionally, banks in Israel offer the broadest spectrum of services known to exist in world banking. It includes all capital-market activities including management of provident funds, which are part of Israel's pension system. The banks' share in the Israeli pension system is exceptionally large even in European terms, where universal banking is practiced. Israel's two largest banks also controls numerous nonbanking corporations that generate a rather large fraction of GDP.[8] Notably, no other Western country has such a broad range of activities coupled with such a concentrated structure. This breadth of activities creates potential conflicts of interest and, therefore, dampens competition. Because financial intermediation by means of provident and mutual funds is an alternative to classical bank activity, competition is narrowed when banks control these funds (Yosha, 1993). The banks' control of nonbanking enterprises creates a captive market; therefore it, too, impairs competition and creates an entrance barrier (Ben-Bassat, 1996; Bebchuk et al., 1997; *Report of the Committee of Examination on Bank Holdings in Nonbanking Corporations*, 1995). The absence of pension funds in the bond and stock markets also narrows competition in the financial and capital market relative to the standard in developed countries.

In recent years, several decisions to enhance competition in this industry have been made, but few have been carried out. Bank Leumi was forced to sell off Union Bank, and first steps toward splitting of nonbanking corporations controlled by banks were taken.

There are several indications that the structure of Israel's banking system is not competitive. For a lengthy time, this structure caused an exceptionally large spread between credit interest and deposit interest (figure 1.8). Samet and Elias (1994) found a significant correlation between interest spreads and the degree of concentration in

Israel. Recently, Yosha and Ribon (1998) showed that the deposit market is competitive but that the credit market operates in a noncompetitive environment. Moreover, the exploitation of conflicts of interest[9] would not be possible were the system competitive. The banking system has become somewhat more competitive in recent years, but because this is due to financial-system reforms at large, we will discuss its dimensions and causes in the next section.

Indicators of Success of the Financial Reforms Assets and liabilities interrelate in substitutionary or complementary ways, albeit in varying intensities. Therefore, each reform measure affects a broad spectrum of assets and liabilities as well as the overall matrix of yields. It is difficult to isolate the relative contribution of each of the many measures described above in enhancing competition and efficiency in the financial and capital market. However, the main factors in these developments are described in the presentation of the main results.

The reform measures have significantly revised the composition of finance in the business sector and among homebuyers. First, direct government involvement by means of directed credit and earmarked deposits decreased drastically—from 65 percent in 1985 to only 5 percent in 1998. Directed credit declined steeply in the mortgage market as well, from 72 percent in 1986 to 26 percent in 1998 (figure 1.5). Because the freeing up of uses of provident funds made more unrestricted sources available to mortgage banks, the proportions of credit offered to households were raised; the share of dwellings financed with unrestricted credit only climbed from 20 percent in 1984 to 60 percent in 1998.

The decrease in the general-government budget deficit and the contraction of central-government involvement in resource allocation freed up considerable resources for unrestricted uses. The composition of uses also changed significantly due to the elimination of the many restrictions that had applied to borrowers and lenders. The main trend in the composition of private-sector financing is the replacement of government-directed credit and government deposits for credit (table 1.3) with unrestricted credit and domestic and foreign share issues. Similar trends are visible in industrial finance (Yosha and Yafeh, 1995; Blass and Yosha, chapter 6). The reforms as a whole have animated a powerful dynamic in the composition of finance as a function of trends in source yields and risks.[10]

Before the reform, there were large interest spreads among near-substitute assets, among alternative liabilities, and, especially, among uses. Many forms of tax discrimination and subsidies were eliminated, and the removal of many restrictions narrowed interest spreads in all pairings of sources and uses. Several main examples follow:

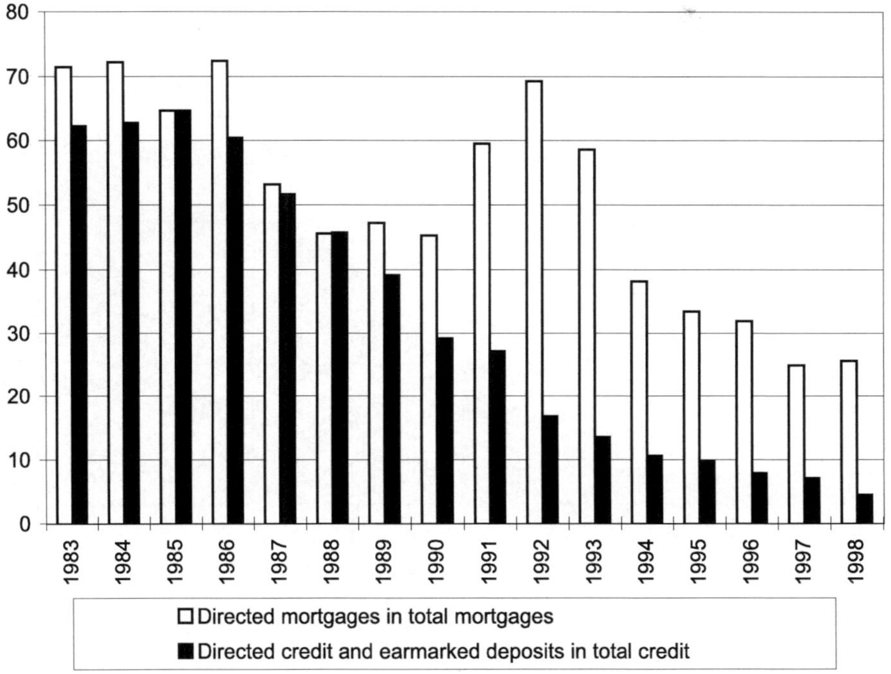

Figure 1.5
Share of Government-Directed Credit, 1983–1998
(Percent)

Table 1.3
Composition of Private-Sector Finance, 1980–1998 (Percent)

	Issue of bonds			Change in credit			
	Domestic shares	Shares abroad	Bonds, net	Unrestricted	Directed and ear-marked deposits	Direct from abroad	Total
1980–1984	19.5	0.0	2.4	24.0	38.8	15.4	100
1985–1989	9.6	0.0	30.9	99.6	−31.1	−8.9	100
1990–1993	38.7	3.0	−3.9	112.3	−49.2	−0.9	100
1994–1998	15.8	9.3	−6.9	82.8	−8.3	7.4	100

Source: Bank of Israel, *Annual Report*.

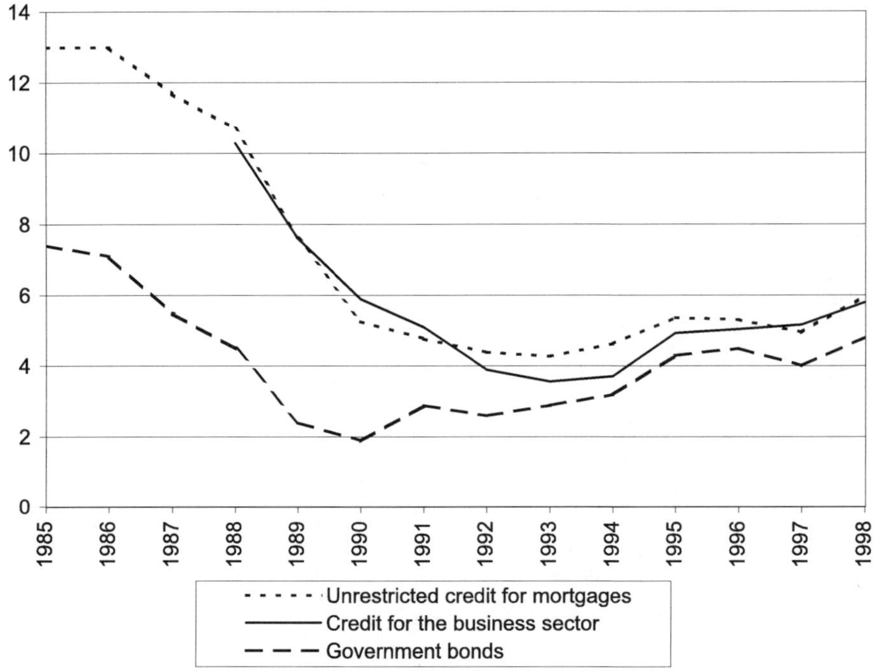

Figure 1.6
Long-Term Credit and Government Bonds Interest, 1985–1998
(Percent)

Foremost, the spread among different uses of the same type of credit was narrowed. For example, the interest rate on credit from abroad in 1985 ranged from 8.3 percent for borrowers in the preferred group to 33.8 percent for loans that were subject to administrative ceilings.[11] This spread was totally eliminated. There were also large spreads among households that qualified for mortgages from government deposits and households that took unrestricted credit for the same purpose.

The significantly preferential treatment that the government awarded itself in the capital market made capital much cheaper for government than for other uses. For example, the spread between interest on unrestricted mortgages and interest on government bonds contracted from 5 percentage points in 1985–1988 to only 1 percentage point in 1995–1998 (figure 1.6). Much the same happened to the spread of yields between CPI-indexed unrestricted credit and government bonds.

The right to borrow abroad lowered the interest rate on domestic bank loans in foreign currency to the LIBOR rate. The interest spread between these two sources of

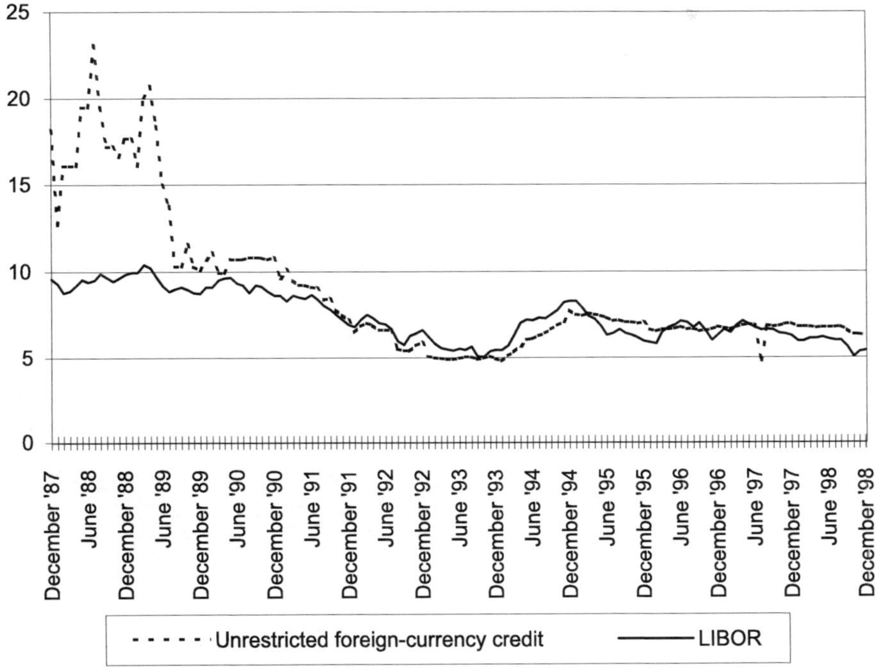

Figure 1.7
Domestic Cost of Foreign-Currency Credit and LIBOR Interest Rate, 1987–1998 (Percent)

credit plummeted from 8 percent in 1987–1988 to 0.4 percent in 1997–1998 (figure 1.7).

The interest spread that best reflects the contraction of government involvement and the enhancement of competition in the financial and capital market is that between short-term domestic-currency credit and domestic-currency deposits. This spread contracted gradually from 44 percentage points in 1987 to 8.5 percentage points in 1993 and has been stable since then (figure 1.8). Almost all the financial-reform measures had a contractionary effect on interest spreads—lowering of the liquidity ratio, freeing up of sources by the government; elimination of administrative restrictions in domestic currency that focused mainly on credit, partial deconcentration of the banking system (see Elias and Samet, 1994), the splitting of nonbanking enterprises from the two largest banks, and the liberalization of capital flows.[12] The decrease in interest spreads also reflects an upturn in competitiveness in the

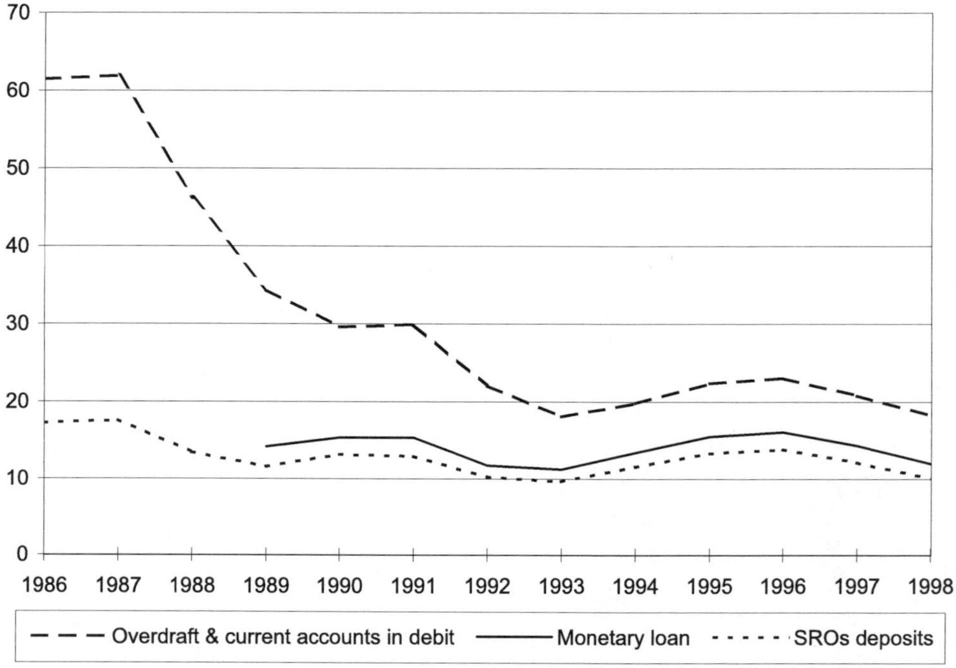

Figure 1.8
Interest in Unindexed Domestic-Currency Activity, 1986–1998
(Percent)

banking industry. Yosha and Ribon (1999) found that although both the deposit market and the credit market were characterized by less than perfect competition in the 1989–1996 period, the degree of uncompetitiveness declined steadily during that time.

The correction of imperfections in the financial and capital market has also enhanced the effectiveness of monetary policy. The transmission mechanisms between policy measures and financial markets have improved, as reflected in a gradual strengthening of the correspondence between changes in interest rates set by the Bank of Israel and changes in banks' borrowing and lending rates (Djivre and Tsiddon, in this volume).

Summarizing this chapter, it should be noted that the financial reforms had many additional favorable implications that may be gauged by studying the other chapters in this book.

Taxation and Subsidization of Production Factors and Goods

Since the 1950s, the government has been intervening in the allocation of production factors in many ways. Two of the most important budget-related ways were subsidization of capital (mainly in priority areas) and taxation of labor. This policy contributed to the establishment of excessively capital-intensive enterprises, harmed employment, and wasted foreign-currency sources. The Encouragement of Capital Investments law was enacted mainly to support employment in areas of national priority, but the many forms of discrimination built into the law—among production factors, industries, purposes of output, citizenship, and so forth—weakened its efficacy. Additionally, because R&D subsidies are awarded without regional differentiation, high-tech industries are concentrated in the large cities of the country where highly qualified labor is more easily avaliable, whereas traditional and capital-intensive industries have gravitated to priority areas in the periphery (Schwartz and Razin, 1992). Because the technology chosen in each industry was also more capital-intensive in priority areas than in the center of the country, investments there contributed less to employment than they could have without the discriminatory government intervention. Moreover, these industries base themselves on unskilled labor, which, due to severe competition with developing countries, is barely profitable and fails to provide stable employment.

The rate of subsidy in total industrial investment has hardly changed since 1983 and has ranged from 8.5 percent to 11.5 percent (Ben-Bassat and Melnick, 1998). Unsurprisingly, despite the many incentives given to investors, the share of priority areas in employment has not increased since 1980.

The most important amendment to the law of Encouragement of Capital Investments was enacted in late 1995 to reduce the rate of grants in priority areas. The grant rate has been cut back gradually since then—from 38 percent of the approved investment in high priority areas and 20 percent in the lower priority areas to 20 percent and 10 percent, respectively.

Action to reduce discrimination between labor and capital began in 1987 when the employers' payroll tax was lowered from 7 percent to 4 percent. The tax was further cut to 3 percent in 1991 and finally eliminated a year later. Similarly, employers' social security contributions on employees' account were reduced from 15.5 percent of employees' wages in 1985 to 5 percent in 1997.

These measures, as a whole, did much to reduce the discrimination between acquisition of plant and equipment and hiring of labor; they also mitigated discrimination among uses. The support for goods (mainly for export) declined by 5 percent of GDP between the early 1980s and the second half of the 1990s. Capital benefits

Table 1.4
Taxation and Subsidization of Production Factors, Products, and Consumption, 1980–1998 (Percent of GDP)

	Business sector				Households		
	Employers' tax and social security*	Capital subsidy	Production subsidy***	Total	Transfer payments	Commodities subsidy****	Total
1980–1984	6.0	2.9	5.9	2.8	9.3	4.0	13.3
1985–1989	4.3	1.3	3.0	−0.1	11.1	1.9	13.0
1990–1993	3.1	2.8**	1.8	1.4	11.5	1.2	12.7
1994–1998	2.3	1.7	0.8	0.2	12.3	1.0	13.3
(1980/84)–(1994/98)	−3.7	−1.2	−5.2	−2.6	3.0	−3.0	0.0

* Including social security contributions by employers on account of employees. In 1992, the employers' tax was abolished for businesses; thus, the tax in 1994–1998 is that paid by general government.
** Including subsidization of contractors during the period of mass immigration from the former Soviet Union.
*** Including export subsidies, credit benefits, R&D, and miscellaneous.
**** Basic commodities and housing services.
Source: Central Bureau of Statistics.

(grants and credit) decreased by 1.2 percent of GDP and payroll taxes (employers' tax and social security contributions) decreased by almost 4 percent of GDP (see table 1.4). Figure 1.9 shows clearly that total subsidization of the business sector resulting from a combination of reduced subsidization and tax cuts declined by 2.6 percent of GDP during this time. Even more important is the decrease in both the rate of subsidization of capital and the rate of taxation on labor; thus, discrimination among production factors decreased sharply. This helped to reduce distortions in resource allocation, stimulate employment, and enhance business-sector productivity.

The method of support for consumers also changed: Subsidization of basic goods, awarded irrespective of individuals' income, were significantly reduced and replaced with transfer payments to households. Notably, most transfer payments were given without income or standard-of-living tests. The two measures offset each other (table 1.4).

Restructuring of the Labor Market

Since the early 1990s, the characteristics of the labor market and the wage-setting mechanisms have undergone many changes. Most of the changes stem from exogenous shocks and long-term domestic economic trends following the stabilization program; a few are the results of regulatory policy.

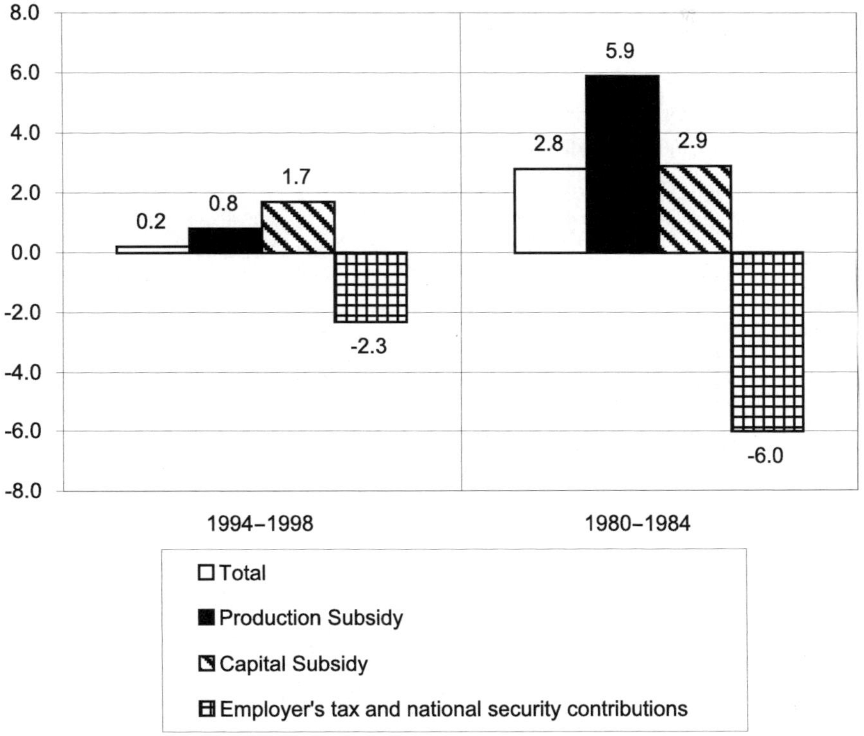

Figure 1.9
Taxation and Subsidization of Production Factors and Goods in the Business Sector (Percent of GDP)

Two exogenous shocks—immigration from the former Soviet Union (FSU) and terrorist attacks that occasioned an influx of foreign workers—made the most important impacts to the increased flexibility of the labor market. These events share several characteristics and are interrelated. Both pertain to national goals, that is, immigrant absorption and replacing Palestinian labor, which had become a growing security risk. In both cases, the economy was given access to an almost intinitely large supply of labor from abroad, willing to work even for extremely low wages. The second important change was the decline in the Histadrut's (the General Federation of Labor) power. This process began in the early 1980s, when industry structure shifted toward human-capital and technology intensive sectors, which are more open to the global market. The phenomenon became much more powerful after the stabilization program, as Israel moved toward a market economy with increasing momentum. Another factor that contributed to the increasing flexibility of the labor market was the grave failure of Histadrut-owned enterprises (Artstein, in this volume). The decline of the Histadrut's importance is manifested in a significant decline in membership and a proportional increase in hiring by personal contracts and through labor contractors, all without union representation.

There were few changes in regulatory policy pertaining to the labor market, and not all of them helped make this market more flexible. The major changes were the following:

1. The Cost-of-Living Allowance (COLA) arrangement was modified several times after the stabilization program to bring down the rate of automatic wage adjustment. Schiffer (1997) shows that the marginal rate of wage protection achieved by the COLA fell from 68 percent at its peak period to 42 percent in 1986–1989 and 36 percent thereafter. Several studies, however, have found that the decrease in automatic indexation created alternative, market-driven compensation mechanisms (Kleiman, 1989; Artstein and Sussman, 1992).

2. The most substantive change in labor-market regulation was a toughening of unemployment compensation eligibility terms and of rules pertaining to the unemployed. According to Artstein (1997), unemployment compensation has a perceptible positive effect on wages in all industries and prolongs the duration of unemployment (Ribon, 1990). These findings support the approach that advocates a short term of unemployment compensation, as exists in Israel in contrast to the European labor market.

3. In April 1987, the Knesset enacted a law that set the minimum wage at 45 percent of the national average wage. Ten years later, the legislature raised it to 47.5 percent. This change has diminished wage elasticity to employment and, therefore, may be detrimental to employment. However, since compliance with the law is rather poor (Flug and Kasir, 1993 and Gottlieb, 2000), the effect of the law on market flexibility has been minimal.

4. Employers' contributions to social security were lowered substantially in two phases—from 15.5 percent employees' wages in 1985 to only 2.4 percent in 1995. In 1997, the rate was raised to 5 percent. The reduction of payroll taxes helps to stimulate employment because taxation of employment is harmful to producers' profitability, demand for labor, and labor-market flexibility.

The increased flexibility of the labor market was reflected in two instances. First, between 1989 and 1995, the economy created jobs for half a million immigrants and nonimmigrants (augmenting employment by 35 percent). In addition, 140,000 foreign workers joined the economy, replacing 70,000 Palestinian laborers. Furthermore, the immigrants found work more quickly than any economic institute had predicted and even helped to lower the unemployment rate among nonimmigrants. Thus, the unemployment rate declined by 2.6 percentage points between 1989, before the mass immigration of the 1990s had started, and 1996. Second, real wages in the business sector declined by 5 percent between 1989 and 1994, almost solely due to the changes in the composition of employment (Artstein, in this volume), a recomposition that was strongly supported by the process of rapid growth. In 1997 and 1998, although rapid growth was halted, wages again rose swiftly despite a steep increase in the unemployment rate. The influx of foreign workers made only the wages of poorly paid unskilled workers more elastic, and at the price of greater inequality in income distribution and increased social tension (Kleiman et al., 1999). This shows that the structure of the labor market (especially in the public sector) still has mechanisms that reduce flexibility such as automatic wage drift and linkages in the wage structure among sectors and occupations, to name only two.

Reforms in the Market for Goods and Services

Competition in the market for goods and services was enhanced in three channels. The most efficient way to create competition in tradeable goods in a small economy is by exposing domestic manufacture to competing imports. Even this does not assure perfect competition because of exclusive distribution agreements, concentration in imports, and control by local manufacturers of importing goods that are supposed to compete with them. Opening the economy to imports does not resolve the lack of competition in the market for goods that are not traded in international markets. This is especially true for government-owned, monopolistic, infrastructure. In these areas, it is necessary to restructure the domestic market and create competition, or at least to set price regulation and control mechanisms until the restructuring is complete. The third channel is the prevention of cartels in production and retailing.

Import Liberalization Israel's trade policy is predicated on its reciprocal tariff-reduction agreements with the European Community and the United States. The agreements with the European Community were signed in 1965–1975 and were fully applied by 1989; the agreement with the U.S. was signed in 1985 and fully implemented by 1995. With respect to other countries, protective barriers based mainly on tariffs were established. In the early 1980s, however, there was a significant retreat from the process of liberalization in a wide variety of aspects. The most severe of them was a set of nontariff barriers against imports from "third countries," those with which Israel had no trade agreements. The number of customs items that were subjected to nontariff barriers—such as compulsory licensing, compulsory marking in Hebrew, and the like—climbed by 68 percent. Liberalization vis-à-vis Europe and the United States also retreated, as evidenced in measures meant to bypass the agreements, such as duties on financial and nonfinancial transactions (1–3 percent) and imposition of purchase taxes in ways that discriminated against imports relative to domestic manufacture (Gabai and Rob, in this volume). The tariff-reduction process stipulated in the agreements did continue, the effective rate of protection declining from 28.2 percent in 1982 to 15.7 percent in 1987 (Halevi, 1994). This, however, was partly offset by the expansion of nontariff barriers. Furthermore, the composition of foreign trade became severely distorted. Trade was diverted from relatively inexpensive sources, from which imports were severely restricted, to expensive sources, foremost Europe. Thus, foreign-currency sources were wasted, and the level of consumer prices was pushed upwards.

Trade liberalization, similarly to the liberalization in the capital and financial markets, was implemented by a gradual approach. The measures taken to liberalize imports may be categorized in four main groups:

1. 1989–1993—elimination of discriminatory import purchase taxes.

2. 1990–1992—elimination of duties on foreign travel, purchase of foreign currency, and imported services.

3. 1991–1993—elimination of compulsory licensing for imports of industrial goods. In 1990, all nontariff barriers on imports from "third countries" were abolished and replaced with relatively high tariffs (20–75 percent). In 1992, a phased process of lowering these tariffs was started, and in 2000, they were to range between 8 and 12 percent. In 1995–1998, a similar process for agricultural products was set in motion.

4. Export subsidies, by means of exchange-rate insurance and preferential interest on credit, were phased out.

The implementation of these measures has moved the Israeli economy toward nearly total exposure to foreign trade. The nontariff barriers have been eliminated; tariffs are very low on average and have much smaller variance (table 1.5). This policy has had several favorable implications. The price of goods for which protection was significantly lowered (clothing and footwear) declined by 19 percent between 1991 and 1998 relative to the index of tradeable goods at large. The import penetration rate of industrial goods at large climbed from 25 percent to 30 percent. Many distortions in the composition of trade have been corrected; in industries in which the elimination of nontariff barriers in trade with "third countries" was dominant, the share of these countries in imports climbed from 16.2 percent to 22.3 per-

Table 1.5
Effects of the Foreign-Trade Reform, 1990–1998

	1990–1991	1995–1996
Average rate of import taxation	11.0	8.1*
Range of tariffs	0–30	0–20
Share of "third countries" in imports:		
in which only nontariff barriers were lowered	16.2	22.3
in which nontariff barriers and purchase taxes were reduced	16.9	8.3
Price index of metal, footwear, and clothing relative to total tradeable goods	100	81*
Share of import penetration in industry	25	30**
Average rate of concentration in industry	33.8	29**

* 1998.
** 1994.
Source: Gabai and Rob (in this volume) and Bank of Israel, *Annual Report*.

cent. In contrast, in industries in which the elimination of discriminatory purchase taxes was more important than the elimination of nontariff barriers, the share of Europe and America climbed while that of "third countries" declined from 16.9 percent to 8.3 percent.

Public Services All firms in this sector (except for public transportation) that provide infrastructure services have a monopolistic status, and are fully or partly government-owned. Examples are the supply of electricity, water, port services, communications, and the oil refineries. These industries have a strong effect on the general productivity and profitability of the business sector, because most of their outputs are intermediate goods and services in other industries' production processes. In the past, the industrial organization of most infrastructure services around the world was monopolistic because they were believed to have economies of scale. The concern that these companies would reduce output and raise prices prompted many countries to place them under government ownership. This was intended to avoid monopolistic exploitation of consumers. Excessive profits, insofar as the monopoly generated them, would enrich the government revenues and allow the government to provide more services or cut taxes.

In practice, the main beneficiaries of the excessive profits of monopolistic infrastructures were their employees and not the public at large. Organized labor in these industries took advantage of its ability to disrupt economic life to channel much of the monopolies' surplus earnings into its pocket. Governments, ever fearful of strikes in vital services, succumbed to labor's excessive wage demands. Thus, the wages of employees of monopoly infrastructures exceed by far those of other workers in the business sector. In 1996, for example, the wages of transport and communications workers exceeded the national average wage by 30 percent and those in electricity and water by 100 percent (Gronau, in this volume). Fortunately the public's high sensitivity to excessive wage demands in the government sector limits the absorption of excess profits by means of wage increases. Nevertheless, the public sector employees sometimes enhance their welfare by reducing work effort and productivity and by pressuring the company to overhire. For example, the Shorer Committee, which looked into telephone rates (1993), reported that even in the company's view, headcount could be trimmed by 20 percent with no detriment to service. The Gronau Committee (1996) found that headcount per production-capacity unit at the oil refineries in 1992 was 60 percent over the Western European average. Public ownership also contributed to price gouging by suppliers of other equipment and services to the monopolistic infrastructures.

In addition to distorting the scope and price of inputs, the monopolies implemented a set of prices that reflected cross-subsidization of services and led to the distortion of efficient allocation of economic resources. For example, consumers with variable demand for electricity subsidized fixed-demand consumers. Intensive users of telephone services subsidized those who made few calls, and international dialers subsidized local dialers. At the ports, imports subsidized exports, and expensive import cargoes subsidized less expensive import cargoes.

The damage to efficiency and the distortions in relative prices created pressure for competition in monopolistic infrastructures by admitting new companies in the market (in communications and transport, for example) or by splitting existing companies into several competing companies (in electricity, refineries, and ports, for example). An important lesson of the Israeli experience is that firms should be privatized only after competition is created. Notwithstanding numerous plans, only the communications industry has been made more competitive among a few players, first in cellular telephone and added-value services and, afterwards, in international dialing. The privatization process in these fields did help reduce prices of dialing services considerably.

The obstacles in the path to competition in these industries generated pressure for interim solutions—rationalization of the pricing system and control of future pricing developments. In regulating prices, the guidelines were to base rates on the producer's costs in each product, eliminate cross-subsidization, and create a price-adjustment mechanism for the future, based on the behavior of input prices and on a price-reduction coefficient that takes company efficiency measures into account. The

Table 1.6
Privatization of State-Owned Enterprises, 1985–1998 ($ millions)

	State-owned enterprises	Banks	Total
4/1986–3/1990	328	0	328
4/1990–6/1992	514	230	743
7/1992–6/1996	1,228	1,246	2,474
7/1996–8/1998	636	2,659	3,295
1986–1998	2,696	4,135	6,840
Proportion sold to controlling investors	41	37	39

Source: Report of the Government Companies Authority.

efficiency-enhancement coefficient was based on an estimation of excess inputs in the base year, the company's scale economies, and foreseen technological changes in the industry. In other words, the price-setting method was revised from cost-plus to a price ceiling (Gronau, in this volume).

Privatization of State-Owned Enterprises In 1985, 160 companies, most of them very small, were under government ownership. About 90 percent of the employees of state-owned enterprises are concentrated in the ten largest firms. In 1983, the country's four largest banks joined the state-owned enterprises in the aftermath of the bank share crisis. In 1985—the year in which privatization was declared an important goal—8.6 percent of persons employed in the business sector worked for state-owned enterprises.

The privatization process has been advancing very slowly. Since it began, $2.7 billion in equity of state-owned enterprises and $4.1 billion in bank shares have been sold to the public (table 1.6). Only 40 percent of the shares sold resulted in the transfer of state control to private hands. For the rest, the sale of shares amounted to nothing more than raising capital. Furthermore, the sale of control in the monopolistic infrastructures has not yet begun due to obstacles in the process of making these industries more competitive and, mainly, due to resistance from labor.

1.4 Geopolitical Factors

The disintegration of the Soviet Union and the change in regime there affected the Israeli economy in two ways—the authorities' attitude toward Jewish emigration to Israel and the access given to Israel by Eastern European markets that had been off-limits to Israel since 1967.

Immigration from the former Soviet Union began in 1990, and from that time until 1997, 710,000 immigrants, mostly from those countries, boosted the Israeli population by 16 percent. Some 53 percent of the immigrants were of working age and about half of their labor-force participants had practiced an academic or management occupation before their immigration, as against 8 percent among the nonimmigrant Israeli labor force. This is an exceptional rate compared to any other country. The immigrants' high human capital enhanced the economy's growth potential but also created hardship among the immigrants in the process of their absorption in occupations that did not always correspond to their schooling.

Despite the magnitude and complexity of the problem, the government decided not to intervene directly in creating jobs for the immigrants; instead, this task was left to market forces. The government's role had two focal points—providing public goods (such as education, health, and infrastructure investment) as warranted by the vigorous increase in population; and creating conditions that would accelerate business-sector growth and allow the business sector to hire most immigrants. This concept is a direct continuation of the approach that Israel adopted in the Economic Stabilization Program.

Mass immigration from the former Soviet Union caused private and public demand to expand steeply. The government reinforced this trend by granting immigrants a subsistence allowance in their first year in the country and by financing and subsidizing their purchase of housing. On the supply side, the government encouraged the business sector to create jobs by reducing employers' labor costs, subsidizing the newly hired for a limited period of time, sponsoring vocational training, streamlining the Employment Service, and refining the unemployment-compensation system. It also awarded credit subsidies for new investments and made progress in implementing structural reforms. Overall, however, the government policy to expand demand was exaggerated, and its actions to expand supply were rather weak relative to plans (Ben-Bassat and Melnick, 1999). It is especially important to note that the government did not seize the unique opportunity of immigrant absorption as a stimulus in order to complete the structural reforms.[13]

All in all, the immigrant absorption exceeded all expectations. Within six years, most immigrants found employment, and their unemployment rate today resembles that of nonimmigrants. Eckstein and Weiss (in this book) found that by dividing immigrants into three occupational categories—academic, white collar, and blue collar—one finds that the gaps between their original occupations and their Israeli occupations have been narrowing rapidly, especially among the young (those in the 26–40 age cohort). However, studies that classified immigrants by a broader range of occupations found that the degree of the adjustment from original occupation to current occupation in Israel is slack and even worse than among previous immigration waves (Flug and Kasir, 1996; Ofer, Flug, and Kasir, 1997). The average wage of immigrants in their first stage of absorption in Israel is some 40 percent lower than that of nonimmigrants with similar occupational and demographic characteristics. The gap is shrinking gradually and is expected to narrow to 16 percent by the end of a twenty-five-year period, but no full convergence is expected (Eckstein and Weiss, in this volume). Furthermore, married immigrants were found to have higher wages than unmarried immigrants with similar traits, and their wages also increased more quickly.

The second geopolitical process that has left its imprint on the economy is peacemaking. The peace negotiations that began after the Gulf War reached a climax with the signing of peace agreements with the Palestinians and with Jordan. Pursuant to these agreements, it was increasingly believed that the Middle East conflict was about to end. The signing of the agreements in itself lessened Israel's perceived security risk and, therefore, enhanced motivation to do business with Israel. But the serious terrorist attacks in 1996 and the subsequent peacemaking uncertainty show how fragile the achievements are.

It is difficult to isolate the effects of the peace process on Israel's economic strength in the first half of the 1990s, and the effects of the destabilization of the process since 1996, because other dramatic political changes and the structural reform process occurred simultaneously. Furthermore, the interdependence between these factors are of utmost importance. However, one may point to several fields in which the peace process had a strongly favorable effect on developments. Inbound tourism doubled between 1990 and 1995. The peace agreements also contributed to a substantial expansion of net foreign investment in existing companies, new companies, and financial assets—from $100 million in 1990 to $2.5 billion in 1998. Israel's country rating as reflected in the *Institutional Investor* index was substantially improved between 1985 and 1998—from rank sixty-four to forty-one. According to other sources, the improvement was even greater (see Gottlieb and Blejer, in this volume). Consequently, Israel's risk premium in international borrowing contracted. The peace agreements also weakened, though did not officially abolish, the effectiveness of the Arab boycott on Israeli products. This prompted new markets, mostly in the Far East, to begin trading with Israel; accordingly, Israel's foreign trade expanded greatly, especially its exports (see table 1.9). The peace agreements and the belief that they would expand to the entire region also evoked expectations of a future decline in defense expenditure, thereby making it possible to reduce the GDP share of government expenditure further.

The staggering peace process since 1996 has reduced the economic gains that the process had set in motion at its beginning.

1.5 Results of the Policy

The turnabout in economic policy and its geopolitical background conditions ramified results but also claimed a price. In this section, we observe four main fields from a bird's eye perspective—growth and composition of GDP, balance of payments, inflation rate, and income distribution.

GDP, Its Composition, and Productivity

The economic policy and geopolitical changes prompted an acceleration of GDP growth along several tracks on both the demand and supply sides. Until 1989, this acceleration of growth was powered by a policy that expanded GDP supply of the business sector. Crucial factors in this expansion between 1985 and 1989 were the budget policy and disinflation. As stated, this policy operated along three paths: (1) It enhanced economic certainty about the elimination of the general-government budget deficit and the contraction of dependency on foreign aid; (2) the expected long-run tax rate declined as a result of the fiscal consolidation, although the actual reduction in tax rates was insufficient; and (3) infrastructure investments increased. The government also carried out a series of reforms that reduced costs in the business sector, corrected distortions in relative production factor prices, and improved production factor allocation. Consequently, the annual growth rate of GDP climbed from 2.9 percent in 1980–1984 to 3.8 percent in 1985–1989. The uptrend in GDP of the business sector was even swifter (table 1.7).

The period between the stabilization program and the onset of immigration was not homogeneous. The first three years were marked by very rapid growth; a two-year slump followed. In part, the transition from boom to bust reflected the price of the freezing of the exchange rate and the exceptionally high real interest rate in the first years of stabilization. It also reflected a delayed response to structural problems in the business sector that became exposed in the aftermath of the stabilization program—inefficiency that stemmed from commodity and capital subsidies, cheap credit, administrative protection, bailouts for bankrupt enterprises, and wage rigidity (Bruno and Meridor, 1991), occasioned by institutional arrangements in setting wages and unemployment compensation. All these factors entailed recovery plans that involved layoffs and cutbacks in production in the short term.

Table 1.7
Sources and Uses, 1980–1998 (Average annual percent change)

	Sources				Uses			
	GDP	Business GDP	Imports of goods and services	Total sources = Total uses	Private consumption	Public consumption	Gross domestic investment	Export value in domestic market
1980–1984	2.9	3.3	2.5	2.8	3.6	1.6	−0.2	4.8
1985–1989	3.8	4.9	3.5	3.7	5.9	−0.3	−0.3	5.6
1990–1993	5.5	6.6	11.8	7.6	7.0	4.1	18.2	5.7
1994–1998	4.6	5.3	6.4	5.2	5.8	2.0	2.1	8.8
(80/84)–(94/98)	1.7	2.0	3.9	2.4	2.2	0.4	2.3	3.9

Source: Central Bureau of Statistics.

In 1990, two additional processes that expanded both domestic demand and GDP supply got under way. Immigration from the Former Soviet Union greatly expanded private and public demand, on the one hand, and labor supply, on the other. It also helped to make the labor market more flexible and restrain wages in the business sector, thereby making immigrant absorption relatively swift and easy. The government's goal of steering immigrants mainly to the business sector prompted it to sustain the structural-reform process.

Peace negotiations with the Palestinians also helped stimulate demand by improving Israel's country risk rating in international markets. These processes accelerated the annual growth rate further. Because some of the acceleration reflected a one-time adjustment, the growth rate began to decline in the middle of 1996. In 1997–1998, the economy entered a slowdown as a result of several factors—preference of the inflation target over the growth target. Fiscal and monetary policies were strongly tightened, and coincided with cyclical factors. However, supply-side indications show that, even after the main impetus of the immigration wave had been exhausted, Israel had a potential growth rate of about 4 to 5 percent per annum.[14]

Between the stabilization program and 1998, GDP of the business sector climbed more swiftly than overall GDP by about 1 percent per year. Thus, the share of business-sector GDP rose steadily from 59 percent in 1984 to 67 percent in 1998 (figure 1.10).[15] The increase in the share of the business sector in GDP since 1960 illuminates the importance of structural reforms for business-sector growth. In the 1960s, two background conditions that were important for business-sector growth—relatively small government expenditure and low inflation—were prevalent. However, since government involvement in the economy was extremely high, the proportional growth

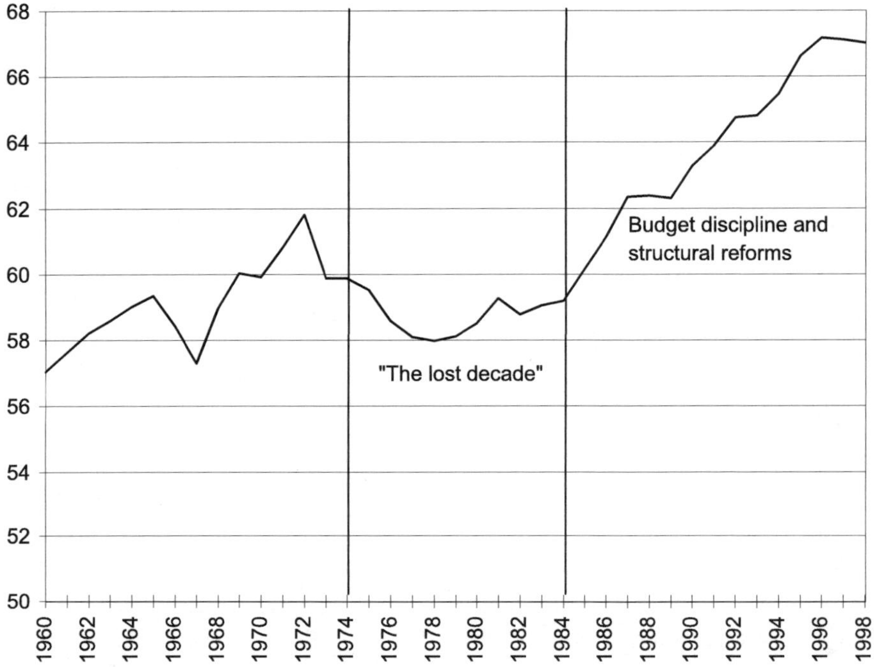

Figure 1.10
Share of the Business Sector in GDP, 1960–1998
(Percent)

of the business sector in GDP was moderate during this time. In the crisis years (1975–1985), the share of the business sector actually decreased. After 1985, in addition to downscaling its share in GDP and stabilizing the economy, the government embarked on a gradual transition to a market economy. This transition had an especially strong effect in accelerating the growth rate of business-sector GDP, allowing the share of this sector to climb more rapidly than in the 1960s.

As the business sector expanded, the composition of its activity changed substantially. Two phenomena stand out in the industry-group composition of the business sector: The first is the long-term downtrend in agriculture, construction, electricity and water, and (since the late 1970s) manufacturing. The contraction of these industries was rapidly substituted by an expansion in services and trade, which together accounted for 50 percent of business-sector product in 1998. A similar trend is occurring in all industrialized countries. The second phenomenon is unique to the Israeli economy and is of utmost importance. Since the second half of the 1980s, the composition of industry has been experiencing a structural change, as civilian high-tech industries have been accounting for a rising share of production, exports, and investment from domestic and foreign sources. This reflects a change in the composition of Israel's advanced industries, and this, too, should be credited largely to the economic restructuring that has been occurring since the stabilization program (see Justman, in this volume). Due to the downsizing of Israel's defense budget and the decrease in global demand for military equipment, demand for the output of the defense industries has declined severely. However, the most important point in the turnabout that defense manufacturing has experienced was the government's strategic decision in 1987 to discontinue the Lavie aircraft project. These changes prompted the defense industries to move to civilian outlets for their output, but they did not manage to revise the composition of production significantly and had to shed much of their staff. The twenty-nine enterprises that had previously sold 10 percent or more of output to the defense system dismissed thirty thousand workers between 1986 and 1996. Thus, personnel with advanced technological schooling and vast experience became available in the private sector. They were joined by higher-education graduates in the sciences in the 1990s—a group that previously had found work mainly in the military industries—and by immigrants from the Former Soviet Union. Thus, hundreds of new projects came into being, and some recorded impressive economic success. Some of these projects were based on unique knowledge that had been developed at the military industries. The liberalizations in financial markets and foreign trade helped these industries to establish marketing systems abroad, create cross-border partnerships, and benefit from cheap sources of finance. For example, investments by venture-capital funds escalated from one hundred million dollar per year in the early 1990s to roughly one billion dollar in 1999.

Israel had one of the world's highest rates of total factor productivity growth (4.4 percent per year) until 1972, but in the crisis years, this indicator plunged to 0.5 percent per year. Productivity made a considerable recovery after the stabilization program, but after 1990 the total productivity growth rate fell again to nearly zero. The National Accounts statistics indicate that average productivity in 1992–1998 was actually negative at about half a percent per year; data based on developments in nonresidential industries point to about 1 percent productivity per year. Be this as it may, the productivity trend in the 1990s is genuinely puzzling. The negligible improvement is very surprising because previous waves of immigration were noted for their high productivity and, especially, because the current wave is endowed with abundant human capital.

Some trace the explanation to measurement problems. Justman (in this volume) notes that productivity in agriculture, communications, electricity, and water increased impressively and that the decline in productivity focuses on construction, services, and manufacturing. In his opinion, there are measurement problems in the first two industries mentioned, leaving only the productivity decline in manufacturing in need of explanation. In his estimation, the substantial upturn in the share of advanced industries has created a significant downward bias in the measurement of productivity. On the one hand, he argues that investments in human capital and in research and development are recorded as current expenditure instead of investment; on the other hand, sale of equity in high-tech companies to nonresidents is not recorded as an output, even though, in fact, it is part of the exports of these industries. In the estimation of Hercowitz (in this volume), and Hercowitz, Lavie, and Melnick (1998), the decrease in productivity in the 1990s is related to the massive intake of new equipment that has an embodied component of high technology. Since the adoption of these technologies initially entails learning expenses, it results in poor productivity.

The accelerated growth was accompanied by a secular rise in inequality in the income distribution. Economic inequality has been rising steadily since the mid-1970s and, in recent years, has exceeded the level in the United States, which characteristically exhibits the highest inequality among developed countries. Dahan (in this volume) notes that the increase in income inequality stems mainly from changes in the return on human capital and is not caused by greater inequality in the possession of human capital. In the 1990s, the wages of the highly trained workers have grown more steeply than those of the poorly trained, and the wages of the managerial occupations improved with particular vigor. The increase in the relative return on schooling coincides with an uptrend in the proportion of well-trained persons in the population. This indicates that demand for persons with higher schooling has outpaced its supply in the past decade. Perhaps, too, as the number of persons with higher schooling increased, schooling quality also became more diverse, and therefore, inequality among people whose schooling only seems to be equal expanded.

A massive increase of transfer payments was necessary to correct this trend. These developments emphasize the urgency to adopt policies aimed at narrowing economic inequality in the labor market. The main way to achieve this goal is to narrow schooling gaps among population groups—especially between Mizrahi ("Oriental") Jews and those of European-American origin, and between the Muslim and Jewish populations.

Balance of Payments

The balance of payments, like other indicators, improved perceptibly in the first five years after the stabilization program. Exports expanded more rapidly than imports,

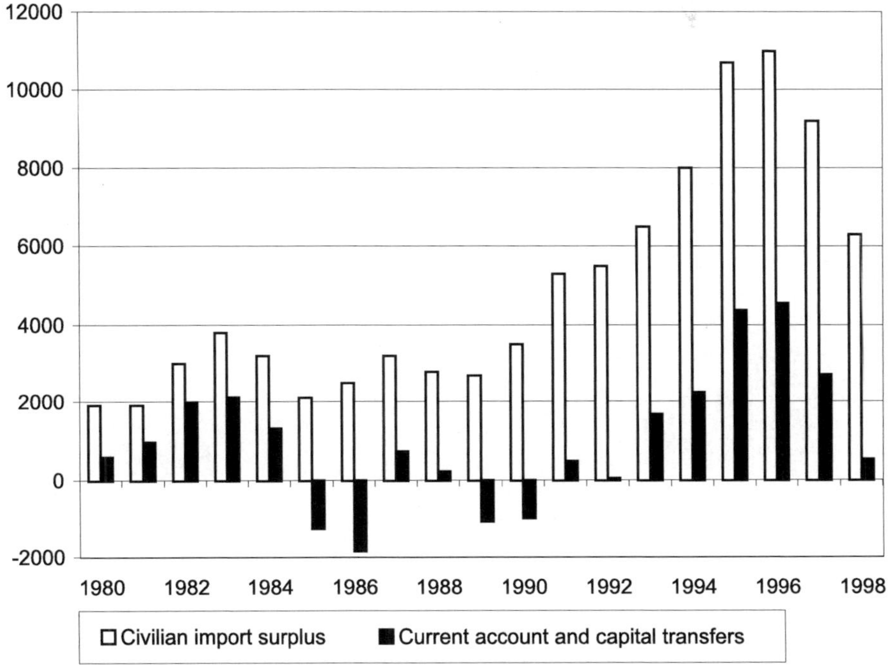

Figure 1.11
Import Surplus and Current-Account Deficit, 1980–1998
($ millions)

and the import surplus declined in dollar and GDP terms (figure 1.11 and table 1.8).[16] Since 1990, however, several exogenous and endogenous processes have been causing trade and the import surplus to increase significantly. The most dramatic change is the collapse of the Soviet regime and the onset of Jewish immigration to Israel. Immigration led to strong growth in private and public consumption, residential and nonresidential investments, and GDP supply. However, since the growth of domestic demand outpaced GDP supply, the import surplus widened. Although civilian public expenditure increased, its share in GDP declined between 1980–1984 and 1994–1998 by 10.7 percentage points. This decrease was offset by a 10.9 percentage-point increase in private consumption. However, the strong increase in investments—by 5.4 percent of GDP—was reflected in a similar increase in the import surplus (table 1.8). The widening import surplus was also manifested in real currency appreciation. These two processes were able to occur because of a strong upturn in private unilateral transfers by immigrants and United States government credit guarantees to the government of Israel.

Table 1.8
Domestic Uses and Import Surplus, 1980–1998 (Percent of GDP)

	Domestic uses				
	Private consumption	Public consumption	Thereof: domestic	Gross domestic investment	Import surplus*
1980–1984	51.3	45.6	38.3	18.7	11.2
1985–1989	55.2	39.6	33.4	15.9	9.1
1990–1993	57.8	34.5	30.7	22.4	13.9
1994–1998	62.2	30.0	27.5	24.1	16.2
(80/84)–(94/98)	10.9	−15.6	−10.7	5.4	5.0

*The change of base year in computing price indices every few years creates discrepancies in the relative prices of sources and uses. Accordingly, sources and uses are not identical in 1995 prices. The largest deviation occurred in 1980–1984, at 4.4 percent of GDP.
Source: Central Bureau of Statistics.

The components of Israel's international trade were affected not only by the trend in domestic GDP supply and demand but also by geopolitical developments and by reforms in foreign trade and other fields. The downfall of the Communist regimes in Eastern Europe opened these markets to Israel for the first time since the Six Day War (1967). Consequently, exports to Eastern Europe expanded in 1989–1991 by 34 percent on annual average,[17] as against an increase of 7 percent per year in exports to Western Europe and the United States (table 1.9). The peace process weakened the effectiveness of the Arab boycott and opened new markets in Asia—mainly in the Far East—to Israeli trade. As a result, in 1992–1996, exports to these countries expanded by 18 percent per year beyond the increase in exports to Western Europe and the United States. These two political turning points contributed 4.2 percent per year to the growth of exports in 1992–1996 and about 1 percent per year in 1989–1991.[18]

The restructuring of the economy made a perceptible contribution to both imports and exports. The foreign trade liberalization in the 1990s exposed domestic manufactures to competing imports mainly from Asian and Eastern European countries, and indeed, imports from these countries expanded much more rapidly than imports from the rest of the world (table 1.9). Presumably, imports were also affected by the peace process and the changes in regime in Eastern Europe. Evidence of the effect of the liberalization, however, may be found in the continued rapid growth of imports from these countries even in 1997–1998, while imports from other countries did not increase at all. This is almost definitely the result of the continued reduction of tariffs on imports from "third countries."

Table 1.9
Foreign Trade, by Region, 1989–1998 (Average annual percent change)

	Imports				Exports				
	Total	From countries with trade agree-ments*	Rest of Europe	Asia, incl. Japan	Total	From countries with trade agree-ments*	Rest of Europe	Asia, incl. Japan	Global trade
1989–1991	7.1	6.5	21.9	11.0	7.3	6.7	31.4	7.3	5.8
1992–1996	11.8	11.0	23.3	15.6	11.8	8.5	35.3	26.6	6.8
1997–1998	1.8	−0.2	24.6	9.4	10.4	12.5	7.9	1.1	6.5

* European Union, EFTA, and North America.
Source: Central Bureau of Statistics.

The contribution of the structural changes as a whole stands out in the trend of exports to Western Europe and the United States. Although Israel had free trade area agreements with these countries before the liberalization, exports to these destinations expanded more quickly than global trade by 2.3 percent on annual average in the 1990s.

Another favorable effect is reflected in greater openness to foreign trade. This openness increased steadily in the 1960s and 1970s, halted in the first half of the 1980s, and resumed with greater strength after the stabilization program. The combined share of imports and exports in GDP has been climbing rapidly—from 60 percent in 1980–1984 to 81 percent in 1994–1998.

On the eve of the stabilization program, net external debt had reached 80 percent of GDP, and the economy was on the brink of a balance-of-payments crisis. The economic recuperation and, mainly, the cutting of the general-government budget deficit gradually narrowed the external debt to 35 percent of GDP in 1989 (figure 1.12). However, mass immigration entailed large absorption outlays, especially in residential and nonresidential investment. At the beginning of the process, it was believed that much of this investment would be financed from foreign sources and that this would add twenty-three billion dollar to the current-account deficit in 1990–1995. The loans needed to finance this increase were expected to increase the share of external debt in GDP by 9 percentage points. However, the actual current-account deficit was much smaller than these expectations because the import surplus was unexpectedly small and transfers by immigrants were unexpectedly large (Ben-Bassat and Melnick, 1998).[19] From the onset of the mass immigration until 1998, the current-account deficit came to $15.6 billion (figure 1.12). Notably, not all of the increase in the current-account deficit can be traced to immigrant absorption; some

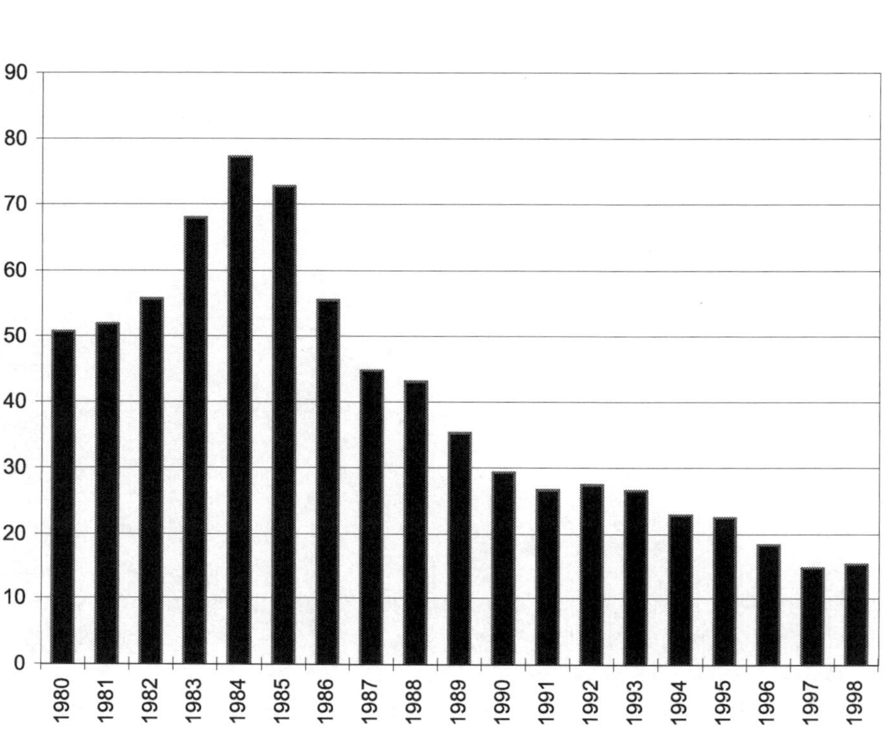

Figure 1.12
Net External Debt, 1980–1998
(Percent of GDP)

of it originates in a deviation from budget policy in hiring, and, especially, in wages. Because GDP growth outpaced the increase in the outstanding foreign debt even during the era of immigrant-absorption, the share of net external debt in GDP continued to fall and came to 15.5 percent in 1998.

Inflation

The stabilization program lowered the annual inflation rate immediately from about 400 percent to around 18 percent. Since then, disinflation has followed a stepwise pattern with relatively small variance around each step (Liviatan and Melnick, 1998). The first step was crossed in 1992, when the inflation rate fell to 9–10 percent. The second step occurred in 1997, the inflation rate falling to 5–6 percent. Notably, stabilization programs in most high-inflation countries did not lower inflation to a single-digit level in one step. Fischer and Orsmond (in this volume) analyzed nine countries' attempts and found that only in Croatia did inflation fall immediately to a single-digit level; it took two years for this to occur in Argentina and Brazil and five years on average in other countries.

Developments in the pace of price increases in Israel correspond closely to the exchange-rate policy and the intensity of demand pressures. In the stabilization program, the exchange rate was chosen as the main nominal anchor,[20] because of the high proportion of tradable goods in the economy, and because many domestic transactions, nonfinancial and financial, were denominated in foreign currency. However, as the economy put the rapid-inflation period behind it, the main effect of the exchange rate focused on anchoring the prices of tradable goods; prices of non-tradable goods, in contrast, were affected largely by the intensity of demand pressures (Ben-Bassat, 1995). Both steps of disinflation had several factors in common. First, both featured a decrease in import prices and a slowdown in currency depreciation, which caused the increases in prices of tradable goods to decelerate. Second, both corresponded to an upturn in unemployment (Liviatan and Sussman, in this volume). Notably, Lavie and Sussman (1997) found a significant correlation between inflation and unemployment in the short term.

Several factors converged in the steep decrease in inflation in 1992 (see figure 1.13). A slowdown in prices of imported raw materials and currency depreciation helped slow the rate of increase in prices of tradable goods. However, the main turning point occurred in the prices of nontradable goods. This turnabout is primarily a response of the mass immigration from the former Soviet Union that began in 1990. At first, the immigrants boosted domestic demand, mainly for housing. The short-term housing shortage led to a considerable increase in housing prices, which was contained by the ensuing increase in supply. However, the immigrants' dominant impact on the inflation rate occurred on the supply side.

As the immigrants gradually joined the labor market, growth and employment accelerated but the unemployment rate climbed to a peak of 11.2 percent in 1992. By 1990, this development severely dampened nominal wage increases in the business sector and, in fact, caused the real wage to decline. Moreover, the immigration helped to make the responses of wage and employment in the labor market more flexible. It also affected the inflation process in indirect ways (Sussman and Liviatan, in this volume). The concern that immigrant absorption would disrupt the budget permanently led to legislation that required the government to lower its budget deficit gradually, thereby toughening fiscal discipline and improving its credibility. This concern, among other things, also led to greater foreign economic assistance in the form of U.S. government loan guarantees, which facilitated long-term restraint of prices of tradable goods by means of real currency appreciation.

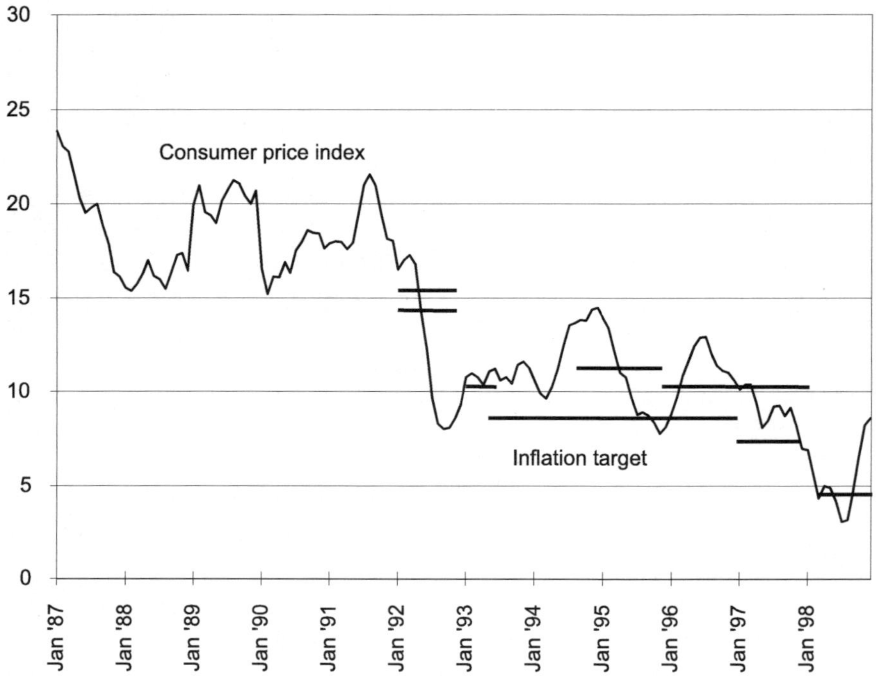

Figure 1.13
Inflation Rate and Inflation Target, 1987–1998
(12-month rate of change, percent)

The second turning point, like the first, was related to the behavior of global prices and the policy that drove the economy into high unemployment. In 1994, inflationary pressures mounted due to an exceptional rise in civil-service wages that resulted in an increase in the budget deficit. In response, the Bank of Israel raised the interest rate substantially and thereby halted the negative price implications of the budget overrun. However, monetary restraint remained tight even after the government corrected the deviation of the deficit trajectory in 1997. The combination of fiscal and monetary restraint caused the unemployment rate to rise and began to leave its imprints on the pace of price increases. The adoption of such a contractionary mix of policy measures convinced the public that the government and the Bank of Israel were more determined than in the past to give disinflation priority over employment targets. This policy was assisted by a slowdown in the pace of increases of prices of tradable goods—which was partly exogenous, resulting from a decline in import prices, and partly endogenous, as a consequence of lowering the slope of the crawling band from 4 percent to 2 percent.

The disinflation did not level off at that point because the protracted monetary restraint had triggered a large capital inflow and boosted the business sector's foreign-currency position to some fifteen billion dollars. There was concern that lowering the interest rate would cause a capital outflow, currency depreciation, and price increases. Djivre and Tsiddon (in this volume) mention another aspect of this phenomenon. In their estimation, the potential for inflationary pressure upon the easing of monetary restraint was created due to the overexpansion of the money base relative to the M1 aggregate and the perceptible increase in banks' deposits with the Bank of Israel.

1.6 Structural Reforms—The Empty Half of the Glass

The structural-reform process that aimed to reduce government involvement in the markets and enhance competition has been continuing for fourteen years and has not yet been completed. To assess the reasons for the slow pace of movement toward a market economy, we will compare Israel with other countries and analyze the motives for the reforms, the decision-making process, and the obstacles that have kept the process from completion.

International Comparison

The following comparison of the pace of reforms in various countries is based mainly on the economic freedom index developed by the editors of the annual publication *Economic Freedom of the World.* This index is made up of twenty-five quantitative indicators that characterize seven main fields—state budget, monetary policy, financial markets, foreign-currency market, foreign trade, goods market, and economic legislation.

The indicators show that global economic freedom began to climb in the mid-1970s. At first, the increase occurred only in the industrial countries and several countries in Asia. Since the mid-1980s, a large majority of countries worldwide have been moving toward a market economy, and at an accelerating pace (table 1.10).

The industrial countries made strong progress in economic freedom even though they had more freedom than other countries to begin with. This is especially evident when one calculates the pace of progress toward a market economy as a share of the remaining potential.[21] However, the greatest progress between 1985 and 1987

Table 1.10
Average Economic Freedom of the World,* 1985–1997 (Score on scale of 10)

	1985**	1990	1997
Industrialized countries	7.3	8.3	8.6
Europe and Middle East***	4.1	5.0	6.4
South America	3.8	4.9	6.7
Asia	4.8	5.5	6.7
Worldwide	6.7	7.6	8.1
Israel	3.3	4.4	6.0

* Weighted in the GDP of each country in 1995 dollars.
** The 1985 freedom indicators were adjusted to a new definition based on the relationship among indicators according to the various definitions in 1990.
*** Semi-industrialized countries in Europe (not including Eastern Europe).
Source: Economic Freedom of the World.

occurred in semi-industrialized countries that had lower degrees of economic freedom, such as New Zealand, Portugal, Spain, Greece, and most countries in South America (table 1.11). Israel, too, which until 1985 had rested almost at the bottom of the market-economy ladder, has experienced momentum in economic freedom, but in the pace of this momentum, Israel falls short of the semi-industrialized countries and most countries in South America.

Motives and Timing of Reforms

Many researchers (Bates and Kruger, 1993; Pereira, 1993; Williamson, 1994; et al.) note that the stimulus for reforms seldom occurs when economic achievements are satisfactory. Furthermore, large-scale reforms were carried out in the aftermath of severe balance-of-payments crisis or were prompted by an exceptional upturn in inflation. An economic crisis creates a climate of urgency and greater receptiveness to a policy turnabout. It encourages those affected to learn from economies that have performed well over time and encourages the affected country to import the economic structure and policies that prevail in industrial countries (Harberger, 1993). At the initial stage of recovery, this influence is especially evident in budget and monetary policy because the measures most urgently needed to emerge from the crisis are in those fields. The success of the stabilization policy may convince the public that the reform measures should be extended to domains related to the economic system, that is, reducing government involvement in resource allocation and introducing competition in monopolistic industries. These actions are much harder to carry out because they affect strong pressure groups that have benefited from the existing system. Therefore, economic leaders in several countries have exploited crises to

Table 1.11
Development of Economic Freedom in Selected Countries, 1985–1997

	Improvement in score, percent of potential*		Global ranking**	
	1985–1990	1990–1997	1985	1997
New Zealand	63.0	52.9	36	3
Portugal	18.4	45.2	49	29
Greece	15.8	44.4	60	37
Spain	15.3	40.5	31	26
Argentina	24.4	75.0	86	6
Peru	14.1	62.5	97	33
Bolivia	35.6	38.9	70	26
Costa Rica	44.6	27.6	54	20
Chile	38.5	30.0	43	20
Nicaragua	−2.1	52.7	96	47
Mexico	28.6	31.6	58	39
Ecuador	18.4	39.6	74	42
Brazil	13.5	25.0	87	68
Honduras	−5.2	26.2	24	44
Colombia	3.6	18.9	65	65
Venezuela	8.8	9.3	39	54
Uruguay	−12.5	23.3	13	29
Israel	16.0	29.4	84	59

* $(R_t - R_{t-1})/(10 - R_{t-1})$, where R_t expresses the economic freedom index for year t.
** The country's ranking divided by the number of countries and multiplied by 100.
Source: Economic Freedom of the World.

bundle the most essential and urgent corrections, those pertaining to fiscal and monetary policy, with reforms in specific industries (Rodrik, 1994), even if the latter reforms could be postponed. This tactic mitigates the resistance of pressure groups by presenting the new policy to the public en bloc. At times of crisis, pressure groups are forced to give up their advantages because otherwise the economic stabilization measures, which correspond to their own interests, will not be carried out. Tommasi and Velasco (1995) cite the experience of Argentina in 1995 as an example of packaging especially tough reforms in the fields of pensions, labor-market elasticity, and privatization of banks under the umbrella of a new stabilization policy. Furthermore, many countries that did not implement reforms in conjunction with their stabilization programs rushed to do so immediately afterwards.

In Israel, the severe economic crisis in the first half of the 1980s provided the motive for the stabilization program. Unlike many countries, however, Israel did not exploit the crisis to promote economic structural reforms concurrently. A few structural actions were taken in the stabilization program itself, such as issuing provident funds with tradable bonds instead of earmarked bonds. Real change, however, did not begin until early 1987, when the first phases of reform in the capital market were carried out (Ben-Bassat, 1991). There are several possible explanations for Israel's approach. First, Israel was one of the first countries to apply a heterodox policy to stabilize its economy. Because this approach was controversial at the time, one can understand that Israel found it difficult to carry the war to an additional front concurrently. Furthermore, structural change was not needed to lower the inflation rate. It was important to win the first battle before launching another one. Second, to assure rapid and sustainable disinflation and to create price synchronization, the program included a three-month price and wage freeze; afterwards, too, 90 percent of goods and services remained price-controlled, as against 25 percent before the stabilization program. The controls were lifted gradually, and in early 1998 the percent of price-controlled goods returned to its original level. Such intensive use of price control is inconsistent with reforms that aim to strengthen market mechanisms. Significant deregulation of prices is needed before the importance of the reforms can be presented convincingly.

Even when Israel began its reform process, it did so gradually and very slowly. South American countries made structural reforms along with or shortly after stabilization programs and, more importantly, applied many of the reforms within three to seven years (see also Tommasi and Velasco, 1995). In Israel, in contrast, the process has been going on for fourteen years and has not yet been accomplished. Even though economists disagree about the optimum pace of reforms, Israel's pace is exceptionally slow. Sachs (1994) and others believe that reforms are most efficient when implemented rapidly because this allows for greater saving on the expenses of adjusting the economy to the new situation. Furthermore, according to this view, it is the only possible strategy from the political standpoint. Martinelli and Tommasi (1993) reinforce this approach by explaining that gradualism would cause those who gain from the first reforms to thwart subsequent reforms because they would infringe on their interests. Some dispute these two claims. Desai (1995) and Gavin (1993) believe it is actually rapid implementation that boosts adjustment expenses, unemployment, and, consequently, opposition to the reforms. Several researchers (Wei, 1992, and Dewatripont and Ronald, 1994) argue that gradual implementation increases the probability of completing the reforms because each success in applying them enhances the government's credibility and, therefore, the public's support for the continuation of the process. In Israel, the gradual approach seems to have bolstered support for the transition to a market economy. All the measures carried out thus far have had favorable results for both the business sector and households. Furthermore, the group that might be harmed by future reforms has been contracting gradually.

Edwards (1992) considers gradualism important when the reforms are interdependent or where there are prerequisites for implementing them. In the Israeli case, one may note two markets in which the sequence of actions was important. Cutting the budget deficit reduced government capital-raising and, for this reason, diminished the government's motivation to intervene in the capital market and facilitated the elimination of restrictions on the composition of institutional investors' uses. A smaller budget deficit and a lower inflation rate were also crucial for foreign-currency liberalization. The experience of the 1977 liberalization showed that the foreign-currency reform would be doomed to failure without a prior solution of macroeconomic problems.

Accomplishments to Date

As stated, although the economic restructuring began long ago, the process has not yet been completed. By and large, macroeconomic reforms in the financial markets have been carried out; most reforms meant to enhance competition in monopoly-controlled industries have remained on paper. The extent of implementation of reforms thus far is a consequence of the degree of harm to the interests of various groups and the power of the lobbies that support them. To illustrate this, I have ranked the reforms—those programmed and those carried out—by these criteria.

Reforms That Improve Citizens' Welfare This group is composed of all measures that reduce the public's tax burden, directly or indirectly, by eliminating administrative barriers and therefore are not opposed. It includes many of the financial reforms, such as repeal of duties and taxes on imports of goods, services, and capital; lowering of liquidity ratios for financial assets; permission to sell assets and credit indexed to the CPI or the exchange rate; liberalization of international capital flows; and permission to issue corporate bonds.

Reforms That Contain Mutually Offsetting Benefits and Burdens The offset may not be total and is definitely not total for the individual economic unit, but it greatly reduces opposition to the implementation of reforms. For example, the issuance of earmarked bonds for provident funds was terminated while the compulsory investment in government bonds was downsized. The capital subsidy was reduced as payroll taxation was lowered. Directed credit was eliminated along with restrictions on borrowing overseas and the capital-inflow surcharge—measures that in any case wiped out the built-in subsidy in directed credit.

Reforms Harming Weak Lobbies This group includes the package of foreign-trade reforms—exposure of domestic manufacture to imports from "third countries," elimination of discriminatory purchase taxes, and elimination of the export subsidy that exchange-rate insurance had provided. Apparently, in this field, too, compensation was given by shifting or widening the crawling band. However, because the exchange rate was practically set by the market in between the boundaries of the band, this did not provide real compensation. Those harmed by these reforms were manufacturers and some merchants. This lobby lost much of its power after the stabilization program went into effect; in fact, it failed in most of its struggles. In addition to its failure to slow the import liberalization (except in the textile and lumber industries), it failed to effect change in the causes of greatest concern to it, the interest-rate and exchange-rate policies.

Reforms Harming Strong Lobbies Israel's two strongest economic lobbies are the development towns (new towns in priority areas) and the Histadrut. These lobbies have had greater success than others in preventing or impeding reforms. Many committees have proposed substantial cutbacks in investment grants for priority areas and their replacement with investments in physical, educational, and cultural infrastructure. However, the development-town lobby managed to impede these changes for a lengthy period of time. The lowering of capital grants did not begin until late 1995.

The lobby of owners of capital and the Histadrut, which derives most of its strength from the large labor unions, have managed to obstruct all attempts to tax capital gains and interest and have even prompted the government to retreat somewhat from the capital-market reform by means of the pension arrangements that were concluded in 1995. The Histadrut also prevented legislation that would have made the labor market more flexible, eliminated wage indexations among groups of workers, and downscaled automatic wage drift. Other countries also find labor-market reform one of the most difficult reforms to carry out.

Reforms Harming Very Strong Lobbies The most severe difficulties came to light in the attempt to create competition in monopolistic infrastructures, because the harm inflicted in this case is more specific and the potential loosers are the economy's most powerful groups. In South American countries, too, progress was slowest in this field (Edwards, 1995). In Israel, the main success in this regard was attained in the communications industry, which is gradually becoming more competitive. Technological changes in communications have supported the government's efforts to promote structural change in this industry; evidently the main reason for the success of this reform is daring to struggle with the labor union. In banking, too, the government managed to effect several changes, foremost in prohibiting control of nonbanking corporations by banks. This prohibition forced the two largest banks to split several

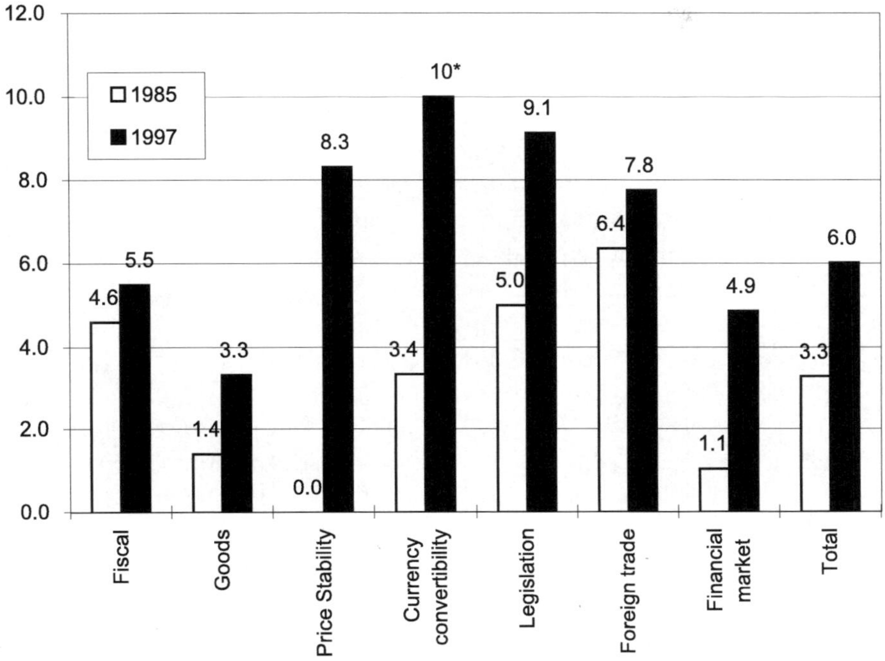

Figure 1.14
Development of Economic Freedom in Israel, 1985, 1997
(Score on scale of 10)
* 1998's rank
Source: J. Gwaertney and R. Lawson, *Economic Freedom of the World.*

companies that they had controlled. However, other changes, especially the splitting of provident funds, still remain only on paper.

In all other monopolistic infrastructures (electricity, fuel, refineries, ports, aviation, and public transport), the government has not managed to create competition and has settled mainly for installing a more rational basis for price control. The successful experience with the communication industry shows that the concern about the exploitation of labor's strength to idle crucial services in order to stop the reforms was overstated.

Summing up, figure 1.14 shows Israel's progress in each field of economic freedom. The greatest progress was attained in price stability, from a score of 0 to 8.3; in currency convertibility, in which the score climbed from 3.4 to 10, in the financial markets;[22] and in economic legislation, from 5.0 to 9.1. Progress was also attained in budget policy and policy towards improved competition in goods markets, but in these fields much room for improvement remains.

1.7 Summary and Lessons

In 1974–1984, Israel applied policies that cost it a decade of economic development and placed the internal and external strength of its economy at risk. The policymakers eventually learned the lessons of these failures and within the framework of the 1985 Economic Stabilization Program, corrected the main policy errors that had caused the downslide. After the stabilization program was implemented, a new economic approach took shape, was applied in most years since then, and has achieved a success worth imitating. There have been deviations from the path, for which a heavy price was paid, but these are exceptions that prove the rule. Just as we managed to learn from our errors, it is also important to reconstruct the policy that led to success for the Israeli economy and for others.

After the economy was stabilized in 1985, the policymakers set growth of business-sector product as their main economic target. To attain it, they downscaled government gradually and freed up sources for the use of the business sector. A lengthy series of measures meant to create a comfortable economic environment for investments and growth assured the absorption of labor and capital by the business sector. To bring this about, structural reforms in main markets reduced government involvement in directing resources to specific uses and made many markets more competitive. Monetary policy also supported the growth process by making the financial and capital markets more flexible, maintaining relative stability, and significantly lowering the real interest rates that followed the stabilization program.

This was a very successful recipe in most respects. Business-sector GDP expanded vigorously, the inflation rate dropped, the external debt declined perceptibly, and the Israeli economy became much more attractive in international markets. These trends were strongly reinforced by mass immigration from the former Soviet Union and by the peace process. However, economic inequalities among population groups have continued to widen.

In late 1994, the economy began to deviate from the positive trajectory that it had been following for a decade. Wages and workers in the public sector severely exceeded desired levels, and, in their wake, the budget deficit grew. The attempt to impede the negative effects of the budget breach by means of a tight monetary policy had some curative effects at first. However, the persistence of high interest rates even after the budget deficit was corrected did much to decelerate growth and raise unemployment, mainly due to currency appreciation that reduced export growth. The downward momentum accelerated in the middle of 1996 as monetary restraint was joined by fiscal restraint, uncertainty in the peace process, financial crises abroad, and a slowdown in the implementation of structural reforms.

The favorable experience in 1985–1994 should guide us when we choose a policy strategy for the years to come. The way to return to a trajectory of sustainable growth is to complete the efforts begun during that decade. The main provisions of this policy should be the following:

Budget Policy

• Because Israel still has a higher government-to-GDP ratio than industrialized countries, action to lower the ratio should continue. In other words, government spending may increase in the future but should grow more slowly than GDP. This will free up sources for sustainable growth of business-sector product.

• By lowering the ratio of general-government expenditure to GDP, it will also be possible to reduce the average tax burden. However, a tax reform that abolishes exemptions for preferred groups is needed; in order to expand the tax base and, thereby, make it possible to lower tax rates further.

• It is essential to maintain a low fiscal deficit and to keep the deficit on its long-term downward path. However, the expenditure policy should not be modified in either direction due to cyclical changes in tax collection (the automatic stabilizer).

• The composition of the budget should support the growth target by reserving a larger share for investments in education, vocational training, and transport infrastructure. These investments will not only boost the growth rate but also respond to specific problems such as intergroup gaps in education, inequality in income distribution, and road congestion.

Monetary Policy

• The real interest rate is much higher than a growth-supportive level. However, the protracted high-interest policy has caused the currency to appreciate and exposed the business sector to a large foreign-currency position. If the interest rate is cut rapidly, an aberrant currency depreciation may ensue, and stability may be undermined. To escape the trap into which monetary policy has fallen, the interest rate should be lowered cautiously but more quickly than the Bank of Israel has lowered it thus far, both because the state of the economy requires preference of the growth target and because the current high unemployment rate will ease the inflationary pressures of currency depreciation.

Structural Reforms

• *Overview:* The economy is structured much differently today than it was on the eve of the stabilization program. Government involvement in the various markets has decreased perceptibly, and economic competitiveness has risen. However, the implementation of reforms has been slower in Israel than in other semi-industrialized countries and has not yet been completed. The main macroeconomic reforms implemented have been those pertaining to financial markets, while most reforms meant to enhance competition in monopoly-controlled industries have remained on paper. The completion of the structural reforms will make resource allocation more efficient, lower consumer prices and producer costs, enhance business-sector profitability, and expand investments and growth.

• *Capital market:* There has been much progress in reforming the financial markets but important measures must still be taken. All government intervention in the composition of investments of provident and pension funds should be phased out, for example, compulsory investment in government bonds and the issuance of preferential nontradeable bonds for pension funds. All intervention that is not meant to enhance stability impairs competition and efficiency in the capital market and provides no return. All forms of discriminations in taxation of yields on different assets should also be abolished and replaced with a uniform tax rate on all assets yields for all savers.

• *Labor market:* The wage-setting mechanisms should be made more flexible in various ways, for instance, reducing automatic wage indexation between occupations and groups of workers, greatly reducing automatic wage drift and job ranks that do not correspond to employees' performance, and so forth. Because these increments create a floor on which the rate of wage increase is applied, they hinder disinflation or, alternatively, exacerbate unemployment.

• *Centralized industries:* Many industries, especially in infrastructure, are characterized by absence of competition (electricity, refineries, domestic calls, ports, public transport, etc.) or limited competition (banking and insurance). Nevertheless, Israeli governments have done very little to change this situation, mainly because the required measures would create struggles with labor and management in these enterprises. The fact that several communication industries have been made more competitive without disruption of industrial labor relations shows that the fear of labor's reaction is exaggerated. In almost all these industries, there are plans to enhance competition by splitting up active companies or allowing new players to enter the industry under license, depending on industry structure. It is important to apply these plans promptly. After each industry has become competitive, the state-owned enterprise that operates in it should be privatized.

Many of these measures can help to lower unemployment and expedite growth by themselves, but some are interdependent. If one is adopted while the other is rejected, the desired results will not be fully achieved. Furthermore, the measures have positive correlations that will enhance the contribution of each when the program is carried out in full. En bloc implementation of this program will put the economy back on a growth path without disrupting internal and external stability.

Notes

I thank Yael Amit and Ariel Resnick for devoted and outstanding research assistance. I am also indebted to Elhanan Helpman, Meir Heth, and Shlomo Yitzhaki for helpful comments.

1. The rapid acceleration of inflation caused loss of welfare in additional fields, e.g., an increase in sources devoted to anti-inflation defenses, impairment of tax-system functioning, and obscuring of transparency in many businesses (Kleiman, 1984; Merom, 1987).

2. Strawczynski and Zeira, ibid., note that this increase exceeded the contribution of privatization to GDP of the business sector.

3. The Bank of Israel began to formulate a far-reaching reform plan in August 1986. The details of the working teams' analyses and recommendations appear in many internal memoranda. For a broad description of the recommended concept, see Bank of Israel (1988).

4. For a survey of government involvement in the capital market up to the reform, see Blum and Peterman (1987).

5. For a far-reaching discussion of the monetary policy and its institutional arrangements during the crisis period, see Sokolar and Cukierman (1989).

6. The law was amended several times. According to its most recent version, the central-government budget deficit must be pared to 1.5 percent of GDP by 2001.

7. The smaller the coefficient of variation of the exchange rate and the greater the coefficient of variation of foreign reserves and interest rate, the less volatile is the exchange rate (Ben-Bassat, 1995). For the purpose of the discussion above, the 1995 tests were adjusted to the end of 1998. Since May 1995, the Bank of Israel has intervened in the foreign-currency market by means of the interest rate when the exchange rate is within the band and directly when the exchange rate approaches the boundaries of the band.

8. See *Report of the Committee of Examination on Bank Holdings in Nonbanking Corporations*, 1995.

9. Conflicts of interest in the banking system were widely exploited until 1983. They are documented at length in *Report of the State Commission of Investigation on the Regulation of Bank Shares* (the "Bejski Report," 1986). A recently published study by Ber, Yafeh, and Yosha (1999) points to exploitation of conflicts of interest in the 1990s as well.

10. For a detailed analysis of the sources of funding, the use to which they were put, and correlations among them, with respect to 250 companies traded on the Tel Aviv Stock Exchange in 1990–1997, see Blass and Yosha (in this volume).

11. See Sokoler and Cukierman (1989), table 8.

12. See Yosha and Ribon (1998).

13. It is usually easier to carry out structural reforms at times of crisis or exceptional national events, because then far-reaching economic programs are more favorably received. (See also section 6.)

14. See *Bank of Israel Annual Report*, 1997, pp. 32–33.

15. The share was calculated in constant prices because the estimate is meant to test proportional changes that derive from real factors and not from relative prices.

16. The import surplus began to shrink in 1977. In GDP terms, it contracted from 16.2 percent in 1973–1979 to 11.2 percent in 1980–1984.

17. Notably, the extent of trade with Eastern European countries was very low at the point of origin.

18. The uptrend in exports to Asia and Eastern Europe slowed considerably in 1997–1998 because of the economic crises that beset many countries in these areas.

19. The Israel Central Bureau of Statistics adopted the IMF definitions in 1988. Therefore, it charges immigrants' transfers to the capital account instead of the current account. This makes the current-account deficit greater. Because capital transfers do not create external debt, the new definition dismantles the relationship between the current-account deficit and the added increment in external debt, which is crucial for the analysis presented here. See *Bank of Israel Annual Report*, 1998, p. 150.

20. Fischer and Orsmond (in this volume) note that all countries that attempted to bring down high inflation initially based themselves on the exchange rate as a nominal anchor.

21. Henderson (1998) suggests that the pace of progress be examined on the basis of the relationship between the change in each country's actual score and the highest possible score (10).

22. Notably, in 1998, much progress was achieved in making the sheqel convertible and by increasing the share of privately owned banks with the privatization of Bank Hapoalim. Accordingly, the author adjusted the score in view of the accepted indicators in the original study.

References

Artstein, Yael. "Wage Rigidity in Israel: Institution vs. Market Forces." The Eitan Berglas School of Economics, Tel Aviv University, Working Paper no. 35–97, 1997a.

———, and Zvi, Sussman "Wage Dynamics in Israel: Market Forces and Spillover Effects." *Applied Economics* 24 (1992): 969–979.

Bank of Israel, Research Department. "One Million Immigrants—An Absorption Program." Jerusalem, 1991.

Bank of Israel, *Annual Report*, 1997, 1998.

Bank of Israel. "Plan to Reinstate Growth and Slow Inflation." Jerusalem, 1988. (Hebrew)

Bates, Robert H., and Anne O. Krueger. *Political and Economic Interactions in Economic Policy Reform.* Oxford: Basil Blackwell, 1993.

Bebchuk, Lucian Arye, Louis Kaplow, and Jesse M. Fried. Concentration in the Israeli Economy and Bank Investment in Commercial Companies. Harvard University Discussion Paper no. 209, 1997.

Ben-Bassat, Avi. "Capital Market Reform in Israel." *Bank of Israel Economic Review* 65 (March 1993): 17–30.

———. "The Inflation Target in Israel: Policy and Development." In *Targeting Inflation*, edited by Andrew G. Haldane (pp. 15–48). London: Bank of England, 1995.

———. "The Implications of Banking-Nonbanking Conglomerates on the Real and Financial Sector." *Banking Quarterly* 135 (September 1996): 74–87. (Hebrew)

Ben-Bassat, Avi, and Rafael Melnick. "Immigration and Growth 1990–1995—The Plan and Its Results." *The Economic Quarterly* 45 (December 1998): 647–678. (Hebrew)

Ber, Hedva, Yishai Yafeh, and Oved Yosha. "Conflict of Interest in Universal Banking: Evidence from the Post-Issue Performance of IPO Firms." Bank of Israel, Research Department, Discussion Paper no. 97.05, 1997. Also forthcoming in *Journal of Monetary Economics.*

Bregman, Arie, and Arie Marom. "Growth Factors in the Israeli Business Sector (1958–1988)." Bank of Israel, Research Department, Discussion Paper 93.03, 1993. (Hebrew)

Blass, Asher A. "Performance and Market Structure of Provident Funds: 1987–1994, *The Economic Quarterly* 43, no. 2 (1998): 260–279.

Blass, Asher A., and Yishai Yafeh. "Vagabond Shoes Longing to Stray—Why Foreign Firms List in New York." Bank of Israel, Research Department, Discussion Paper no. 98.02, 1998.

Blum, Liora, and Silvia Peterman. "Government Involvement in the Israeli Capital Market—Survey and Guidelines for Reform." *The Economic Quarterly* 131 (February 1987): 855–864. (Hebrew)

Bruno, Michael, and Liora Meridor. "The costly Transition from Stabilization to Sustainable Growth." In *Lessons of Economic Stabilization and Its Aftermath*, edited by M. Bruno, S. Fischer, E. Helpman, N. Liviatun and M. Meridor (pp. 241–275). Cambridge: MIT Press (1991).

Bruno, Michael. *Crisis Stabilization and Economic Reform.* Oxford: Clarendon Press, 1993.

Cukierman, Alex, and Mariano Tommasi. "Why Does It Take a Nixon to Go to China?" Harvard University, 1994. Mimeo.

Dahan, Momi, and Michel Strawczynski. "General-Government Budget and Economic Growth in Israel." *Bank of Israel Survey* 70 (1993): 27–40. (Hebrew)

Desai, Padma. "Beyond Shock Therapy." *Journal of Democracy* 6 (April 1995): 102–112.

Dewatripont, Mathias, and Gerard Roland. "The Design of Reform Packages under Uncertainty." ECARE, Brussels, 1994. Mimeo.

Elias, Riki, and Tsippi Samet. "Structure of the Israeli Banking System, Level of Competition, and Their Impact on the Financial Spread in Non-Indexed Local-Currency Activity." *Issues in Banking* 12 (November 1994): 27–48. (Hebrew)

Edwards, Sebastian. *Crisis and Reform in Latin America: From Despair to Hope.* Oxford: Oxford University Press, A World Bank Book, 1995.

———. "The Sequencing of Structural Adjustment and Stabilization." ICEG Occasional Paper 34, 1992.

Flug, Karnit, and Nitsa Kasir. "Minimum Wage Law Compliance In the Business Sector." Bank of Israel, Research Department, Discussion Paper 94.12, 1994. (Hebrew)

———. "Short-Run Absorption of the Ex-USSR Immigrants in Israel's Labor Market." In *Immigration and Integration in Post-Industrial Societies*, edited by Naomi Carmon (pp. 107–126). London: Macmillan Press, 1996.

Flug, Karnit, Nitsa Kasir, and Gur Ofer. "Absorption of Soviet Immigrants into the Israeli Labor Market: Occupational Substitution and Retention." In *Immigrants: Liability or Asset*, edited by Naomi Carmon (pp. 279–377). Haifa: The Technion—Israel Institute of Technology, 1997.

Gavin, Michael. "Unemployment and the Economics of Gradualist Reforms." Columbia, 1993. Mimeo.

Gottlieb, Daniel. "Compliance to the Minimum Wage Law and its Enforcement in Israel." *Quarterly Israeli Review on Taxation*, 28, 110, (September 2000): 65–84.

Gronau, Reuben. *Report of the Committee for Regulation of Telecommunications Rates* ("The Gronau Committee Report"), September 1998. (Hebrew)

Gwaertney, J., and Robert Lawson. *Economic Freedom of the World*, Fraser Institute, various annual reports.

Halevi, Nadav, ed. *Israeli Import Policy and the Exposure of Industry to Competition.* Jerusalem: The Maurice Falk Institute for Economic Research in Israel, 1994. (Hebrew)

Henderson, D. "The Changing Fortunes of Economic Liberalism: Yesterday, Today and Tomorrow." The Institute of Economic Affairs, 1998.

Kleiman, Ephraim. "Indexation in the Labor Market." In *The Israeli Economy: Maturing Through Crises*, edited by Yoram Ben-Porath (pp. 302–319). Cambridge, Mass.: Harvard University Press, 1996.

Kleiman, Ephraim, et al. "Foreign Workers In Israel." In *The Growth-Resumption Policy*, edited by Avi Ben-Bassat (pp. 47–68). Sixth Economic Conference, Israel Democracy Institute, 1999. (Hebrew)

Lavie, Yaakov, and Michel Strawczynski. "The Influence of Policy Variables and Immigration on Business-Sector GDP Supply and Its Components, Production Factors, and Productivity: Israel, 1960–1995." Bank of Israel, Research Department, Discussion Paper 98.07, 1998. (Hebrew)

Lavie, Yaakov, and Nathan Sussman. "The Phillips Curve and its changes 1965–1996." In *Inflation and Disinflation in Israel*, edited by Leo Leiderman (pp. 315–346). Jerusalem: Bank of Israel, Research Department, 1999. (Hebrew)

Liviatan, Nissan, and Rafael Melnick. "Inflation and Disinflation by Steps in Israel" In *Inflation and Disinflation in Israel*, edited by Leo Leiderman (pp. 347–376). Jerusalem: Bank of Israel, Research Department, 1999. (Hebrew)

Martinelli, Cesar, and Mariano Tommasi. "Sequencing of Economic Reforms in the Presence of Political Constraints." IRIS Report no. 100, University of Maryland, 1993.

Report of the Committee of Examination on Bank Holdings in Nonbanking Corporations, 1995. (Hebrew)

Report of the State Commission of Investigation of Bank-Share Regulation (the "Bejski Report"), 1986. (Hebrew)

Razin, Eran, and Dafna Schwartz. "Evaluation of Israel's Policy of Dispersion of Industry in View of Changing Conditions." *The Economic Quarterly* 153 (December 1992): 236–273. (Hebrew)

Ribon, Sigal. "Factors that Affect the Duration of Unemployment of Persons Entitled to Unemployment Compensation." Bank of Israel, Research Department, Discussion Paper 90.09, 1990. (Hebrew)

Ribon, Sigal, and Oved Yosha. "Financial Liberalization and Competition in Banking: An Empirical Investigation." Tel Aviv University and Bank of Israel, 1998. Mimeo.

Rothenberg, David. "Optimal Structure of the Israeli Banking System—Theory and Practice." *Issues in Banking* 12 (November 1994): 47–79. (Hebrew)

Sachs, Jeffrey D. "Life in the Economic Emergency Room." In *The Political Economy of Policy Reform*, edited by John Williamson, 503–523. Washington D.C.: Institute for International Economics, 1994.

Schiffer, Zalman. "The Rise and (Partial) Fall of Indexation in Israel." Bank of Israel, Research Department, Discussion Paper 97.07, 1997. (Hebrew)

Shorer, Doron. *Report of the Committee for Regulation of Bezeq Rates* (the "Shorer Committee Report") 1993. (Hebrew)

Sokoler, Meir, and Alex Cukierman. "Monetary Policy In Israel and Its Institutional Arrangements: Past, Present and Future." *The Economic Quarterly* 139 (1989): 371–425. (Hebrew)

Tommasi, Mariano, and Andres Velasco. "Where Are We in the Political Economy of Reforms?" New York University, 1995. Mimeo.

Wei, Shang-Jin. "Gradualism versus Big Bang: Speed and Sustainability of Reforms." Harvard, December 1992. Mimeo.

Williamson, John, ed. *The Political Economy of Policy Reform*. Washington, D.C.: Institute for International Economics, 1994.

Williamson, John, and Stephan Haggard. "The Political Conditions for Economic Reforms." In *The Political Economy of Policy Reform*, edited by John Williamson (pp. 525–596). Washington, D.C.: Institute for International Economics, 1994.

Yosha, Oved. "Privatising Multi-Product Banks." *Economic Journal* 105 (November 1995): 1435–1453.

Yosha, Oved, and Yshai Yafeh. "The Capital-Market Reform and Its Impact: Analysis from an 'Industrial Structure' Angle." Research Department, Bank of Israel, Discussion Paper 95.07, 1995. This source provides a synoptic discussion of the two approaches and their implications. (Hebrew)

I FISCAL POLICY

2 Reducing the Relative Size of Government in Israel after 1985

Michel Strawczynski and Joseph Zeira

2.1 Introduction

This chapter analyzes the dynamics of fiscal policy in Israel in recent decades. It identifies and tries to explain the two major changes in fiscal policy following the stabilization program of 1985—a sharp decline in the public sector deficit and a gradual decline in the relative size of the public sector in Israel. These changes have followed a long period in which both the share of government and public deficit have been very high, following the wars of 1967 and 1973. Our analysis yields four main conclusions. The first is that fiscal discipline increased substantially after 1985. The second is that reduction of the relative size of government has been achieved mostly by reduction of defense expenditure and of subsidies to the business sector. The third conclusion is that defense reduction can be attributed to two main causes—the decline in intensity of the Israeli-Arab conflict, and a sharp change in economic behavior of the defense sector after 1985, which has become more frugal. The fourth conclusion is that reduction of these government activities had some fiscal cost, as the rise of unemployment and poverty after 1985 caused an increase in welfare transfers.

We begin with a broad survey of the public sector since 1960. Its expenditure increased dramatically in the years 1967–1973, from less than 35 percent of GNP to more than 75 percent of GNP, and remained at this high level until 1985. This increase was triggered by the intensification of the Israeli-Arab conflict during those years. The deficit was also high at an average level of 15 percent of GNP. After 1985 we observe a clear change in direction, with expenditure decreasing to a current size of 55 percent of GNP. During the same period, public income has declined as well, but with a lag, so that the deficit has been sharply reduced immediately after 1985. The decline in deficit and expenditure can also be appreciated from an international perspective. Whereas before 1985, the relative size of the Israeli public sector was the highest in the world, in the early nineties it became close to European countries like Italy, France, the Netherlands, and Germany.

We turn next to examine statistically the relationship between public expenditure and public income. A cointegration analysis of expenditure and income shows that they become more cointegrated after 1985, when lags of adjustment to one another become shorter. This result is interpreted as an indication for stronger fiscal discipline after 1985, which also helps in bringing the deficit down. We also conduct a specific test for a change in cointegration after 1985 and show that such a change is indeed significant. We briefly discuss the reasons for greater fiscal discipline after

1985, among them the Law of No-Printing of 1985 and the Budget Deficit Reduction Law of 1991.

We then turn to analyze the relative reduction of expenditure after 1985. We first observe that the decline has occurred primarily in three expenditures—defense, subsidies to the business sector, and interest payments. Subsidies to the business sector were reduced immediately in 1985, as price subsidies were slashed down as part of the stabilization program. The following liberalization process further reduced transfers to the business sector. Interest payments relative to output have gradually declined since 1985 as a result of the decline of debt, due to low deficits after 1985. Of the three reductions, the largest has been in defense, which fell by more than 10 percent of GNP.

We next examine defense expenditure reduction in more detail. One possible explanation of that reduction could simply be rapid output growth. From 1985 to 1998, real output doubled in Israel, while defense costs went down from 20.1 percent to 9.2 percent of GNP; that is, the absolute decline in defense costs has been moderate. But this does not solve the puzzle, because economic growth is also accompanied by higher wages, with technical progress and thus with more advanced weapon systems. That should have raised defense costs substantially, and we explore why this did not happen. We find that throughout the period defense costs were strongly correlated with three main variables—defense expenditure of the neighboring Arab countries, defense expenditure of the U.S., and the relative price of defense in Israel. We also find that this correlation changed significantly after 1985. The main change has been in price elasticity, which increased significantly after 1985. We, therefore, observe a sharp change in the economic behavior of the defense sector in 1985, toward greater cost awareness and a greater tendency to reduce expenditure.

Finally, we analyze the only expenditure that has increased relative to output after 1985, namely, transfer payments to households. We find that three main variables can explain most of the changes in transfer payments—the share of people above the age of sixty-five in the population, the rate of unemployment, and income inequality. We find that the rise of transfer payments can be accounted for by aging, rising unemployment, and higher inequality since 1985.

These conclusions point to three main trends in fiscal policy in the last two decades. The first is a significant increase in fiscal discipline, the result of the trauma of the period of loss of fiscal control and high inflation (1973–1985). The second trend is a serious trimming down of the defense sector, which has been enabled by a worldwide trend in defense expenditure reduction, coupled with a decrease in the level of the Israeli-Arab conflict, and greater economic discipline in the defense sector. The third trend is a reduction in the intervention of government in the economy. This liberalization led to reduction of transfers to the business sector. But it also in-

Table 2.1
Public Expenditure, Income, Deficit and Debt: 1960–1998 (% of GNP, not including health tax after 1995)

Years	1960–1966	1967–1972	1973–1984	1985–1989	1990–1992	1993–1996	1997–1998
Expenditure	34.6	53.0	78.2	65.1	58.7	54.9	53.6
Income	39.2	45.1	63.6	64.6	54.7	52.4	51.1
Taxes	29.0	34.3	43.4	43.8	38.6	39.1	39.5
Deficit (−)	4.6	−7.9	−14.6	−0.6	−4.0	−2.5	−2.5
Net debt	52.3	62.1	114.8	139.6	111.9	93.9	89.5

Source: Bank of Israel.

creased unemployment and inequality in Israel, which raised transfers to households. Hence, the liberalization process had a mixed effect on fiscal policy.

The chapter is constructed in the following way. In section 2.2, we present a general survey of government reduction in Israel. In section 2.3, we analyze the dynamic interrelationship between public expenditure and income. Section 2.4 is an examination of those components of expenditure that have contributed to the aggregate reduction. Section 2.5 is an analysis of changes in defense costs, and section 2.6, an analysis of changes in transfer payments. In section 2.7, we summarize our findings.

2.2 General Trends in Fiscal Policy in Israel

The aggregate variables of fiscal policy in the years 1960–1998 are presented in table 2.1 and figure 2.1. The variables are public expenditure, public income, taxes, public deficit, and public debt as shares of GNP. The distinction between public income and taxes is important due to large overseas donations and intergovernmental transfers, mostly from the U.S.[1] Table 2.1 describes averages of these fiscal variables within subperiods.[2]

The subperiods in table 2.1 follow the main events of the time. The years 1960–1966, prior to the Six Day War, are characterized by relative stability in the Israeli-Arab conflict and by a high growth rate, which slowed down during the 1965–1966 recession. The years 1967–1972 are years of increasing conflict with the Arab world, beginning with the Six Day War, occupation of land from Egypt, Jordan, and Syria, and followed by a war of attrition with Egypt, Syria, and the Palestinians throughout most of the period. These are also years of high growth rates, spurred by increased military spending and increased labor supply from the occupied territories. The years 1973–1984 follow the peak of the Arab-Israeli conflict and are also high inflation years. The Yom Kippur War against Egypt and Syria was costly both in terms of

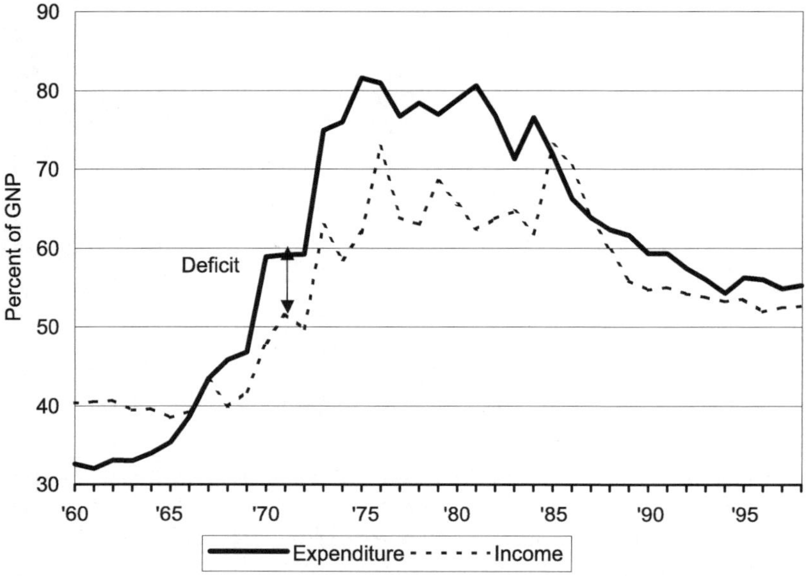

Figure 2.1
Expenditure, Income, and Deficit of the Public Sector, 1960–1998

human life and economically, and it led to a costly arms race throughout the seventies. This is also a period of high inflation and low economic growth. The stabilization program of July 1985 reduced the annual rate of inflation from more than 400 percent to an average of 20 percent. The years 1985–1989 are therefore years of stabilization, which end in a recession in 1988–1989. These are also the years of the first Palestinian uprising. In 1990 a large wave of immigration from the former Soviet Bloc began, which started a period of high economic growth. The years 1990–1992 mark the immediate absorption of the immigration wave. In 1993–1996 economic growth was further spurred by the peace process, which was revitalized by the Oslo Accords in September 1993. In the years 1997–1998, the economy entered a recession, led by a reduction in investment due to various reasons.

As shown in table 2.1 and figure 2.1, the public sector increased significantly after 1967, peaked between the years 1973 and 1985, and has been gradually reduced since then. Since 1985, public expenditure has been reduced by more than 23 percent of GNP. This enabled a reduction of deficit from 15 percent to 3 percent of GNP, that is, by 12 percent of GNP. It also made possible a reduction of income by more than 11 percent of GNP, which includes a reduction of the tax burden by 4 percent of GNP and also a reduction of aid from the U.S. relative to GNP.[3]

It is important to note that though expenditure reduction was gradual, the reduction of deficit was immediate.[4] Deficits remained relatively low since 1985, despite the large exogenous shocks during this period, such as mass immigration and peace agreements. The immediate reduction of deficit was achieved in 1985 and 1986 both by reducing expenditure by 10 percent of GNP and by increasing income by a similar amount. This was achieved by the special one-time U.S. aid package of $1.5 billion and by the recovery of tax collection after the stabilization.[5] The reduction of expenditure did not lead to immediate reduction of taxes, which remained high at a level of 45 percent of GNP in 1985–1988. Only in 1989, when expenditure reduction was already secured, taxes were reduced to 39 percent of GNP.

These observations show that in addition to reduction of its relative size, the public sector also adopted a much higher fiscal discipline after 1985. In section 2.3, we test this hypothesis more systematically. The increase in fiscal control can be explained as a result of the trauma from the loss of fiscal control and high inflation in the years 1973–1985. Fiscal discipline was helped by two important acts of legislation—the Law of No Printing of 1985 and the Budget Deficit Reduction Law of 1991. The first law passed in September 1985 as part of the stabilization program. It prohibits the Bank of Israel from lending money to the government to finance its deficit, and it puts lower bounds on the government's accounts in the Bank. As a result, deficits are now financed by borrowing from the public and abroad and not by monetary injections. This has contributed significantly to fiscal discipline.[6] The second law further restricted the central government by setting a future path of diminishing deficits. The original law from 1991 set a target of zero domestic-budget deficits within a number of years. In later years, it was softened, and it was recently rephrased in terms of the overall deficit instead of domestic deficit.[7]

The decline in the public sector can be further appreciated when presented from an international perspective. Prior to 1985, the relative size of the public sector was the highest in the world.[8] In the early nineties, it was within the range of many European countries. We have compared the relative size of public sectors, more precisely, sums of central and local governments in Israel and in Organisation for Economic Cooperation and Development (OECD) countries in the years 1993–1996. We have found that central and local government in Israel (51.5 percent of GDP) was much smaller than in Sweden (68.8 percent); close to that of Italy (49.1 percent), Germany (51.2 percent), France (52.7 percent), and the Netherlands (52.4 percent); and larger than in the U.S., U.K., Japan, and Spain. A word of caution applies. In some countries, like Italy and France, the government provides full pension, unlike in Israel, where pension funds are to a large extent private. A comparison of tax rates yields similar results. In 1994 taxes in Israel were 40.0 percent of GDP, while the average in

EU countries was 42.5 percent, and the average in OECD countries was 38.5 percent.[9] This brief international comparison indicates that the public sector in Israel became close to major European countries in the early nineties.

Concerning taxation, the main changes since 1985 have been a decline of direct taxation and increase in indirect taxation. This has been due mostly to two increases in the rate of value added tax (VAT), in 1985 and in 1991. Income tax and national insurance (social security) payments declined after the stabilization mostly in 1989, when income tax rates were lowered.[10] An international comparison of the structure of taxes with OECD countries shows that Israel has the lowest level of direct taxes relative to GDP and the highest level of indirect taxes.[11]

The decline of the public sector is reflected not only in size reduction, but also in its mode of operation. One of the most dramatic processes since 1985 has been a gradual privatization, both of public companies and public services and activities. While the privatization of public companies received much public attention, the process of privatization of public activities, also known as "outsourcing," has received less attention although it is of larger magnitude. Privatization of services means that more public services are purchased from private suppliers rather than produced by public employees.

Data on privatization of services is not available, but we can get some indirect quantitative estimate to this process. We break up public civilian consumption net of depreciation costs into labor inputs and purchases as a crude measure of the scope of the process.[12] In 1980 labor costs amounted to 83 percent of civilian consumption, while purchases were 17 percent. Since then, labor costs have declined to 72 percent in 1998, while purchases have increased to 28 percent of civilian consumption. This large increase gives an indication of the scale of privatization of services. To comprehend the size of this increase, note that civilian public purchases have increased by 2.5 percent of GNP since 1980.

2.3 Fiscal Discipline

In section 2.2, we raise the hypothesis that fiscal discipline increased substantially after 1985, based on the observation that deficits have been low since 1985 and that taxes were reduced only in 1989, after several years of expenditure reduction. In this section, we test the hypothesis of greater fiscal discipline after 1985, by performing a cointegration analysis of the variables expenditure and income. Such an analysis examines how close the two variables follow one another and at what speed one adjusts to changes in the other.

Table 2.2
Expenditure and Income: Johansen Cointegration Test (5% significance critical values in parentheses)

	1960–1998		1980–1998		1986–1998		1987–1999*	
	Lags	F-statistic	Lags	F-Statistic	Lags	F-Statistic	Lags	F-Statistic
E-I	5	20.0 (20.0)	4	34.9 (20.0)	1	21.0 (20.0)		
E-T	5	23.9 (20.0)	4	31.8 (20.0)	2	34.8 (20.0)		
EQ-IQ							10	21.5 (20.0)

* 1987:02–1999:01.

We use two data sets. The main one includes annual data of total (domestic and foreign) expenditure and income of the public sector, in the period 1960–1998 (source: Central Bureau of Statistics). The second set is used mostly to corroborate our main results, and it consists of quarterly cash data of total domestic expenditure and income of the central government, from the second quarter of 1987 to the first quarter of 1999 (source: Accountant General in the Ministry of Finance).[13] The variables are real, deflated by the Consumer Price Index. We use the following notation for variables:

- E—Total Annual Public Sector Real Expenditure
- I—Total Annual Public Sector Real Income
- T—Total Annual Public Sector Real Income, excluding Unilateral Transfers
- EQ—Quarterly Domestic Real Expenditure of the Central Government
- IQ—Quarterly Domestic Real Income of the Central Government

As a first step, we perform a Johansen Cointegration test, which serves two important goals. First, it checks for existence of cointegration, namely, a long-run relationship, between income and expenditure. Second, it reveals the structure of lags in this relationship, which is crucial for understanding how expenditure adjusts to income and vice versa. The results are shown in table 2.2.

The most striking result in table 2.2 is that the lag structure between expenditure and income becomes shorter with time.[14] In the whole period (1960–1998), cointegration between expenditure and income is obtained using a five-year lag structure, both for total income and for income excluding unilateral transfers (mostly taxes). Such a long lag means that expenditure and income practically do not react to each other. In the subperiod 1980–1997, cointegration improves and the lag shortens to four years. Finally, in the more recent period (1986–1998), the lags shorten to one and two years for total income and income excluding unilateral transfers, respectively. This pattern of lags can be interpreted as follows: the closer we get to the present, the shorter the period of adjustment of income to changes in expenditure. This trend is observed also for taxes, which react within shorter lags than total income in all subperiods. The economic meaning of these statistical findings is that fiscal discipline increased significantly after 1985.

The cointegration test for quarterly data for the recent subperiod supports the annual results, as it shows that cointegration is obtained after ten periods, that is, two years and a half, which is roughly consistent with the result obtained for annual income excluding unilateral transfers.

The weak cointegration for the whole period together with the result of shorter lags in more recent periods lead us to the hypothesis that fiscal discipline changed significantly after 1985. Consequently, the second step in the analysis is to test cointegration allowing for a regime shift after 1985. For this purpose, we use the methodology developed by Gregory and Hansen (1996).[15] Results are presented in table 2.3. Note that we test both for causality from expenditure (E) to taxes (T) and vice versa. Because unilateral transfers are considered to be more exogenous than taxes, we examine only causality from total income (I) to expenditure. Furthermore, in the test for total income in table 2.3, cointegration is obtained only when accounting for a regime change in 1984 instead of 1985, because unilateral transfers increased sharply in that year.

The results of table 2.3 support our hypothesis of a regime shift from low to high fiscal discipline.[16] In all three tests, the ADF is higher than the critical value at 1 percent significance, and coefficients have the expected signs. Moreover, while in the first period (1960–1984), the coefficient of expenditure was unsustainable in the long run (1.52), the regime shift (−0.61) allows for a sustainable behavior of the public sector expenditure, because the sum of coefficients turns to be 0.91. A similar picture is obtained in the other tests, of tax adjustment to expenditure, and of expenditure adjustment to total income (i.e., including unilateral transfers). In the former test, the sum of coefficients is 1.06, whereas in the latter, it is 1.

2.4 Which Expenses Were Reduced?

Section 2.3 shows that fiscal discipline increased dramatically after 1985. Greater fiscal discipline obviously played an important role in reducing the relative size of the public sector in Israel. When ability to tax is limited, deficit reduction can be

Table 2.3
A Shift in Coefficients after 1985
(Sample period: 1960–1998, standard errors in parentheses)

Variable	E-T	T-E	E-I
C	−5,718	4,797	−4,599
	(2,266)	(1,508)	(2,171)
I			1.26
			(0.04)
E		0.64	
		(0.02)	
T	1.52		
	(0.05)		
D85	34,773	−32,197	−11,727
	(8,421)	(7,579)	(10,175)
D85*T	−0.61		
	(0.09)		
D85*E		0.42	
		(0.06)	
D85*I			−0.26
			(0.09)
ADF	−5.67	−6.15	−5.49
Critical value (1 percent)*	−5.47	−5.47	−5.47
AdjR^2	0.98	0.99	0.99
D.W.	1.87	1.74	2.17
Error correction	$d(E)$	$d(T)$	$d(E)$
C	2,336	1,808	2,992
	(1,172)	(808)	(1,264)
RES(−1)	−0.52	−0.74	−0.67
	(0.17)	(0.16)	(0.23)
D(E(−1))	0.19	0.02	0.39
	(0.16)	(0.10)	(0.22)
D(I(−1))			−0.19
			(0.23)
D(T(−1))	0.27	0.45	
	(0.22)	(0.15)	
AdjR^2	0.28	0.39	0.14
D.W.	2.05	2.07	1.92

*Critical values for regime shifts according to Gregory and Hansen (1996).

Table 2.4
The Composition of Public Expenditures: 1980–1998 (% of GNP)

Years	1980–1984	1985–1989	1990–1992	1993–1996	1997–1998
Public Consumption	39.0	33.4	29.4	28.0	28.0
Defense	20.7	16.1	12.3	9.8	9.2
Administration services	4.8	4.4	3.7	3.3	3.1
Education	7.4	7.2	7.5	8.5	9.2
Health	3.6	3.5	3.7	4.5	4.6
Welfare services	2.4	2.2	2.2	2.0	2.0
Public investment	2.5	2.4	3.3	3.8	3.4
Transfers	33.9	28.7	25.9	23.2	22.2
Transfers to households	8.6	10.1	11.2	11.7	12.9
Transfers to the business sector	12.8	6.1	5.9	4.3	2.7
Finance expenses	12.5	12.4	8.8	7.2	6.6

Source: Bank of Israel (1999), Table 5-A-4.

achieved mostly by expenditure reduction. But the question still remains as to what enabled reduction of expenditure. We turn to this question in the following sections. In this section we present a survey of the various components of public expenditure. This will help us find which were the main elements of expenditure reduction.

Table 2.4 presents a breakup of public expenditure into its components and examines how these have changed during the eighties and the nineties. We first break up public expenditure into public consumption, public investment, and transfers. We then further split public consumption into security, public administration, education, health, and welfare services.[17] We also break up transfers into transfers to households, transfers to the business sector, and finance costs, namely, interest payments. Note that transfers to the business sector are of three types—price subsidies to a large group of consumption goods, which increased significantly during the inflationary period, subsidies to credit and investment projects, and export subsidies. The results are portrayed in figure 2.2 as well.

A close examination of table 2.4 reveals that the decline in public expenditure can be attributed to three main items:

1. The share of defense expenditure in output declined significantly after stabilization from a level of 21 percent to less than 10 percent of GNP in recent years. This decline is analyzed in the next section, but we can already point to a number of factors that enabled it. One is peace with Egypt. Second, there has been a serious attempt to reduce defense costs and operate in a more economic fashion since 1985. One example is the cancellation of the Lavi project in 1987.

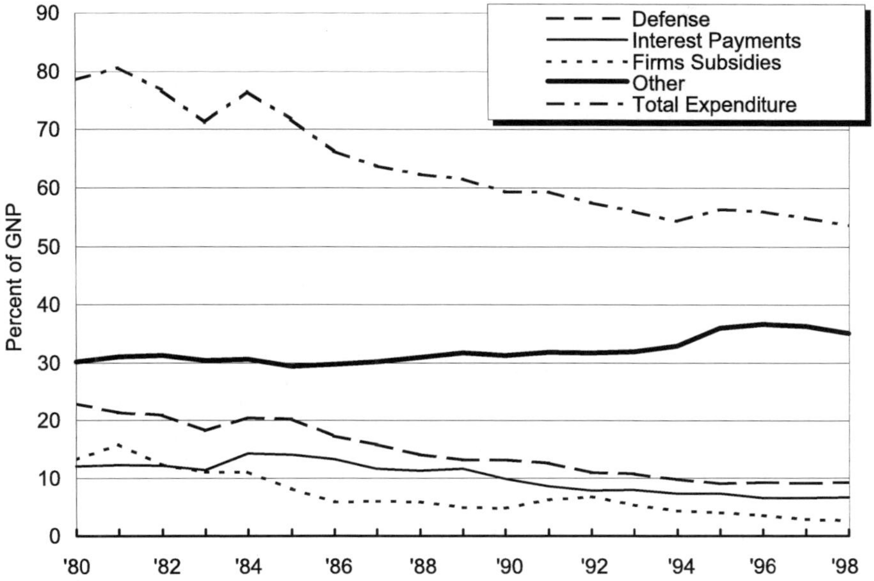

Figure 2.2
Expenditure Composition

2. Subsidies to the business sector decreased significantly. In 1985 the government slashed subsidies to consumption goods as part of the stabilization program and further reduced them later on. Export subsidies and credit subsidies were reduced later as part of the liberalization of trade and capital markets. Thus, transfers to the business sector declined throughout the period. They increased only once, in 1991 and 1992, when the government subsidized housing on a large scale for the wave of immigration then taking place. But this episode was short and did not affect the overall decline in transfers to the business sector, as shown in table 2.4.

3. Interest payments have declined significantly since 1985 as a direct result of deficit reduction since the mid-eighties. Public net debt, which reached a risky level of 157.6 percent of GNP in 1985, declined after the stabilization and reached a level of 89.6 percent of GNP in 1998. As a result, interest payments declined as well.

Not all components of public expenditure have declined since 1985:

1. The largest increase has been in transfers to households, namely, in welfare payments. This increase is discussed in section 2.6, where we examine if it represents a

change in policy, or only a reaction to demographic and economic developments, like aging of the population, rise of unemployment rates, and higher inequality.

2. Other areas in which expenses were reduced in 1985, but later increased during the early nineties are education, health, and investment in infrastructure. These increases reflected a policy change of the Rabin government of 1992–1996. Note that Israel's infrastructure was quite neglected until then. The need to improve it and adjust it to the large increase in population was acute by the early nineties.

A similar picture appears when we examine the role of the different units of the public sector in expenditure reduction. The central government reduced its relative expenditure significantly, while the other branches of the public sector increased their expenditure relative to output. Indeed, the types of costs that led expenditure reduction, namely, defense, interest payments, and subsidies to the business sector, are all under the responsibility of the central government.

2.5 Explaining the Reduction in Defense Costs

In this section, we examine more carefully the reduction in the relative size of defense expenditure, which has been a key factor in public expenditure reduction. In order to understand the dynamics of defense expenditure, we perform a cointegration analysis, which tests the existence of a long-run relationship between this variable and a set of explanatory variables. Our variables are the following:[18]

• ISRAEL—defense expenditure of Israel—is the dependent variable.

• RIVALS—defense expenditure of neighboring Arab countries—is the sum of defense expenditures of Egypt, Syria, and Jordan, which are the main military adversaries of Israel.[19] Our a priori hypothesis is that there is a positive relationship between defense expenditure of Israel and that of its rivals.

• PD_PFF—the relative price of defense expenditure—is a composite price index of government defense consumption in Israel. The coefficient of this variable provides an indication of the elasticity of defense demand in Israel. Caution in this interpretation is required, given that price changes may reflect changes in quality as well. Note that this price index is composed of both wages in the defense sector and prices of military equipment.

• USA—defense expenditure of the U.S.—measures the defense expenditure of an important ally and arms supplier. The two expenditures are both complements and substitutes for obvious reasons. We cannot ex-ante tell which effect dominates.

• TREND is a time trend, which may act as a substitute for the quality of military equipment, mostly due to technical progress.

• Periodical and Political Variables, which are represented by dummies for different periods, include periods of various defense ministers. The main variable examined is the period following 1985, in order to test whether there has been a structural change in the behavior of the defense sector after the stabilization.

All variables are real, in constant dollar prices. The source of data on military expenditure is the U.S. Arms Control and Disarmament Agency (ACDA).[20] The sample period is 1966–1997.[21] The data on military prices is derived from the Israeli Central Bureau of Statistics.

Table 2.5 presents the results of the cointegration analysis. The basic equation includes defense expenditure of the neighboring Arab countries and of the U.S., the price index (PD_PFF) and a time trend. The coefficients are significant and with the expected signs, but cointegration is rejected at the 5 percent level. This lack of cointegration leads us to the next step in the analysis, which is to test for a regime shift after 1985, since a similar shift is found is section 3 with respect to total public expenditure. Another finding that leads us to test for a regime shift is the relatively high price elasticity found in the basic regression. Using the methodology of Gregory and Hansen (1996), the second regression in table 2.5 presents the test of the hypothesis of a change in *all* coefficients after 1985 through an interaction variable (d85), which takes the value *0* before the stabilization plan and *1* afterwards. The result indicates that after allowing for the regime shift, cointegration cannot be rejected at the 5 percent significance level.

The regression with regime shift also shows that the coefficients changed significantly after 1985. First, the positive correlation between defense expenditures in Israel and neighboring countries disappears after 1985. This is a direct result of the peace with Egypt and the Gulf War.[22] Second, the negative effect of the USA disappears after 1985 and becomes positive. Most importantly, price elasticity rises dramatically. Whereas previous to 1985, defense costs were insensitive to price changes according to regression (2) in table 2.5, after 1985 they are strongly negatively related to price. One interpretation is that this is a result of greater fiscal discipline, and that the defense sector became much more cost and price aware. Another possible (and complementary) interpretation is that given the general trend of reduction in defense expenditure, a decision was made to substitute quantity for quality, both in equipment and personnel. Such substitution contributes to the negative correlation between price and quantity. Regression (3) repeats the same exercise for domestic defense expenditure (ISRAEL_D) and presents similar results.

Table 2.5
Defense Expenditure
(Sample period: 1966–1997, standard errors in parentheses)

Independent variable (in levels or in first differences)*	Cointegration equations dependent variable				Error correction equation dependent variable
	log(ISRAEL)		log(ISRAEL_D)	ISRAEL_Y	d(log(ISRAEL))
Equation	(1)	(2)	(3)	(4)	
C	6.03	15.67	11.09	32.34	0.03
	(4.15)	(4.56)	(3.28)	(3.82)	(0.03)
Log(RIVALS)	1.22	0.82	0.79		0.56
	(0.19)	(0.36)	(0.24)		(0.30)
Log(PD_PFF)	−0.95	−0.12		−9.47	0.65
	(0.66)	(1.19)		(9.85)	(0.43)
Log(USA)	−1.03	−1.19	−0.80		−0.27
	(0.32)	(0.29)	(0.22)		(0.81)
Trend	0.02	0.06	0.04		
	(0.01)	(0.02)	(0.01)		
Log(RIVALS)*d85		−1.19	−1.21		
		(0.32)	(0.22)		
Log(PD_PFF)*d85		−2.50		0.35	
		(1.20)		(11.73)	
Log(USA)*d85		0.73	0.80		
		(0.24)	(0.17)		
Log(PDD_PFF)			0.94		
			(0.94)		
Log(PDD_PFF)*d85			−1.02		
			(0.85)		
RIVALS_Y				0.71	
				(0.13)	
USA_Y				−4.54	
				(0.74)	
RIVALS_Y*d85				−0.36	
				(0.21)	
USA_Y*d85				5.64	
				(0.96)	
d85				−30.53	
				(5.22)	
Residuals(−1)					−0.73
					(0.21)
Adj R^2	0.63	0.81	0.87	0.88	0.31
D.W.	1.01	1.56	1.28	1.82	1.71
ADF	−3.96	−6.23	−6.26	−6.14	
*Critical value***	−4.43	−6.00	−6.00	−6.00	

* In the cointegration equations—levels; in the Error Correction equation—first differences.
** The critical value in equation 1 is based on Davidson and MacKinnon (1993). In the equations with a regime shift (eq. 2 to 4), they are based on Gregory and Hansen (1996).

In regression (4) in table 2.5, we replace the absolute defense variables by the share of defense expenditure in GNP. Clearly, this regression does not include the trend variable, given that in the long run the share of defense expenditure in GNP has no trend. In this regression as well, cointegration is not rejected. Finally, we present the error correction equation, which strengthens the case for cointegration, because the lagged value of the residuals is significant, and its coefficient is negative between zero and minus one, as expected.

Regression (4) in table 2.5 enables us to answer our initial question, What enabled the large reduction in the relative size of defense costs since 1985? We use the coefficients of this regression and find that 32.1 percent of the decline can be attributed to a reduction in defense costs of neighboring Arab countries. The reduction of American military costs accounts for 30.6 percent of the decline in Israeli defense costs, and 37.3 percent are due to higher prices of defense, namely, higher price elasticity. The large impact of the USA variable is of great interest here, due to its large effect. A possible interpretation is that in the nineties we observe a global trend in defense reduction, due to the end of Cold War, which is captured by our USA variable. This trend reduced defense exports from Israel and thus contributed to the decline of defense industries, which are part of defense costs.

Finally, we also examine whether additional political variables have affected defense expenditure, by adding dummy variables for periods during which different defense ministers held office. Note that these variables reflect not only different defense ministers, but also specific events that have occurred in each period, such as the large costs of implementing peace with Egypt during Weitzman's period (1977–1981). We do not present the results of these regressions here but report that most variables are insignificant. Overall, these political variables seem to contribute to the analysis much less than the post-stabilization variable (d85).

2.6 The Rise of Welfare Transfer Payments

As shown in section 2.4, transfer payments evidence an opposite trend to the decline in public expenditure, and their share in GNP has risen since 1985. In this section, we try to gain some understanding of this increase in welfare transfers. We examine to what extent it can be viewed as a response to demographic and economic changes, like aging, rising unemployment, or rising inequality. The source of data is the Central Bureau of Statistics and the National Insurance Institute.

The variables we analyze are the following:

- TR—total real current transfers to households—is the dependent variable. It is used both in per capita terms (TR_P) and as a share of GNP (TR_Y).

• POP65—the share of people over sixty-five years old in the population—is the main demographic variable. It is included due to the importance of old-age transfers. Another demographic variable is the percent age of families with four children or more (FAM4). Clearly, we expect positive coefficients on these variables.

• LOG(Y_P)—log of real GDP per capita—is the main economic variable we use. A rise in income raises transfers, which can be viewed as a normal good. Hence, the coefficient should be positive.

• U—the rate of unemployment—is our second macroeconomic variable. Although one may think that this variable is stationary, and as such should not be included in cointegration analysis, we find that similarly to OECD countries, the rise in unemployment in Israel has been quite persistent.[23] Hence, we add U as a potential candidate for explaining the persistent increase in transfers.

• BOT_TOP—the income ratio of the bottom-to-top quintile—measures income inequality. An additional measure is MEAN_MEDIAN—the ratio between the mean and median income. Two opposite forces are expected to play a role. An increase in inequality due to greater poverty increases welfare payments. This has been shown to prevail in OECD countries.[24] At the same time, increased inequality might be correlated with less social solidarity and with increased political pressure to reduce taxes, which finance transfers. We expect the variable BOT_TOP to represent the first force, and MEAN_MEDIAN to represent the second force.

The results of the analysis are presented in table 2.6. The first regression is performed for the longest period for which data is available—1960–1997—but uses only demographic variables, due to missing data on some economic variables in the years 1960–1970.[25] Interestingly, this is the only equation in which we cannot reject cointegration, a result that is strengthened by the error-correction equation. We find that both old age population and four-children families have significant effects. Concerning four-children families it seems that the choice of the period is crucial: whereas this variable is significant throughout the entire period, in the regressions covering the period after the seventies, it is not significant. One possible explanation for this result is the statutory change in children allowances, which followed the Ben-Shachar Committee in 1975.

The other regressions are restricted to the period 1970–1997 and include both economic and demographic variables. In regression (2), the coefficient of BOT_TOP is not significant at the 5 percent level, probably because it is correlated with both the share of elderly (65+ years old) in the population and the unemployment rate. The coefficient of the variable MEAN_MEDIAN is negative as expected, reflecting increasing opposition of taxpayers to transfers.

Table 2.6
Current Transfers
(Standard errors in parentheses)

Sample	1960–1997			1970–1997	1960–1997
Independent variable (in levels or first differences)*	Dependent variable		Cointegration equations		Error Correction
	log(TR_P)			TR_Y	
	(1)	(2)	(3)	(4)	d(log(TR_P))
C	−8.65 (0.78)	−1.29 (0.90)	2.67 (0.15)	−4.79 (2.46)	0.05 (0.01)
FAM4C	0.06 (0.03)				0.04 (0.02)
POP65	4.12 (0.22)	0.36 (0.05)	0.40 (0.04)	3.20 (0.21)	1.74 (0.49)
TREND	0.01 (0.00)				
BOT_TOP		−2.19 (1.52)			
MEAN_MEDIAN		−2.46 (0.81)	−1.31 (0.46)	−10.11 (2.88)	
U		0.012 (0.007)	0.011 (0.007)	0.20 (0.07)	
LOG(Y_P)		1.09 (0.31)	0.81 (0.27)		
DUM85					−0.19 (0.02)
Residual(−1)					−0.24 (0.14)
Adj R^2	0.99	0.97	0.97	0.93	0.42
D.W.	1.04	1.77	1.48	1.75	1.66
AEG**	−4.38	−3.88	−3.67	−3.68	
Critical Value 5 percent	−4.12	−4.72	−4.42	−4.12	

* In the cointegration equations—levels; in the error correction equation—first differences.
** Augmented Engle-Granger statistic, according to Davidson and MacKinnon (1993).

In regression (4), the dependent variable is transfers as a percent of GNP. This regression is also used as the basic specification for a nonreported analysis that introduces additional political variables, such as different periods of the Knesset, as fixed effects. None of these political variables is significant, except for the negative effect of the first national unity government (7.84–11.88). This government implemented the stabilization program, which included some erosion of transfers. The result, that additional political variables have a weak effect on transfers, does not mean that changes in transfers have not been a result of political processes. It just raises the possibility that policy changes have reacted to demographic and economic changes and were endogenous to a large extent.

2.7 Concluding Comments

This paper examines the long-run dynamics of fiscal policy in Israel. We explore both the aggregate behavior of the public sector, and specific components of expenditure. We find that since 1985 there has been a continuous reduction in the size of the public sector together with much tighter fiscal discipline. These two results are of course strongly related. On the one hand, expenditure reduction helps in balancing the budget, and, on the other hand, deficit reduction after 1985 reduces public debt and interest payments and thus accounts for some expenditure reduction.

An examination of the components of the share of public expenditure in GDP reveals that most changes have been in three areas—defense; subsidies to the business sector and interest payments, which declined; and welfare transfers to households, which increased. We identify three main processes behind these changes. The first is the decline in the intensity of the Israeli-Arab conflict; the second is the greater fiscal discipline after the trauma of the inflation years; and the third is the process of liberalization of the Israeli economy after 1985.

The reduction of the level of the Israeli-Arab conflict during these years has been very significant despite a few fluctuations. The peace agreement with Egypt, the Madrid process, the Oslo Accord, and peace with Jordan mark significant steps in the process of reducing the level of hostility, which has made possible a significant reduction in defense expenditure.

The second process is tightening fiscal discipline after 1985. This has led to low deficits since 1985, and as a result to a reduction of debt to output ratio. This reduced interest payments, one of the three costs reduced since 1985. Tighter fiscal discipline had a strong effect on defense expenditure as well. As we have shown, cost awareness of the defense sector increased significantly after 1985, which helped in expenditure reduction. Another effect of tighter fiscal discipline has been reduction in subsidies to the business sector, such as price subsidies, and credit and export subsidies.

Note, that the reduction of subsidies to the business sector was not motivated by fiscal prudence only, but can also be viewed as part of an ongoing process of liberalization, in which the government reduces its active role in production and allocation. This is the third process that has shaped fiscal policy since 1985. Although this process reduced some costs, such as subsidies to goods, exports, credit, and investment, it has had an opposite effect on other costs. Liberalization has social ramifications such as higher inequality and higher unemployment, although they are caused by other factors, like immigration, as well. As a result, welfare payments have increased, as we show.

We would like to end by trying to draw some conclusions on possible future trends in fiscal policy in Israel. Given the high fiscal discipline, the tax burden can be reduced only after more expenditure reductions. Reducing expenditure significantly seems unlikely when we look at the three locomotives of cost reduction—defense, interest payments, and subsidies to the business sector. The ability to reduce the relative size of defense seems limited as it is already below 10 percent of GNP, and the peace process is still far from completion. Subsidies to the business sector are already very small—2.6 percent of GNP in 1998. Interest payments can be further reduced if the deficit is kept small and if the relative size of debt keeps shrinking. However, transfer payments might continue to rise, due to increased inequality and increased unemployment. Hence, further significant reductions of expenditure can be achieved only through reductions in areas like education, health, and welfare. Such changes involve major debates about Israel as a welfare state.

Notes

We are grateful to Avi Ben-Bassat for his help, advice, and support. We thank Michael Beenstock, Leo Leiderman, and Gur Ofer for very useful comments. Anat Kahana, Smadar Katz, and Vadim Marmer supplied us with excellent research assistance, and Avisar Cohen helped generously with data. We are grateful to them all. Thanks are also due to the Falk Institute and the Bank of Israel for financial support.

1. Transfers from the U.S. began in the early seventies, and increased significantly after 1973. In 1985–1986, Israel received an additional transfer of $1.5 billion to support the stabilization program. Since then, aid has been stable at an annual level of $3 billion. In the early sixties, Israel received substantive aid from Germany, as part of the reparation agreement from 1952.

2. As of 1995, there is a new health tax, which is approximately 1.5 percent of GNP. It is deducted in table 1 from both income and expenditure, for the sake of comparison with previous periods.

3. Because U.S. aid has remained at three billion dollar since 1985, its real value has declined since then, and, more importantly, its size relative to GNP has fallen dramatically from 8.6 percent of GNP in 1987 to 3.5 percent in 1998.

4. The impact of fiscal consolidations has been studied extensively in recent years. A recent contribution is Alesina and Ardagna (1998).

5. This is a clear demonstration of the Tanzi-Oliviera effect in reverse.

6. Some claim that the government can still circumvent the No Printing Law, by borrowing from abroad and exchanging the foreign currency by the Bank of Israel. Such loopholes must of course be closed.

7. A detailed description of the history of this law can be found in Dahan and Strawczynski (1999).

8. See the *World Development Report 1984* of the World Bank, pp. 268–269.

9. See State Revenue Administration (1997).

10. For further discussion of the fiscal consequences of rapid growth in these years, see Ben-Bassat and Melnick (1998) and Hercowitz and Strawczynski (1998).

11. See State Revenue Administration (1997).

12. We use civilian consumption and exclude military consumption for two reasons. First, defense can be much less privatized than the rest of the government. Second, defense purchases are highly influenced by defense prices, which increase significantly over time.

13. In order to remove credit movements from cash data during the period 1987–1991, we used seasonality coefficients on credit operations. We thank Avisar Cohen for providing us the data on credit operations.

14. The procedure for computing the number of lags is based on computing likelihood ratios (LR) for successive increases in the number of lags. We report the minimal number of lags that passes consecutively two LR-Tests.

15. We are grateful to Michael Beenstock for referring us to this methodology.

16. In nonreported regressions, we dealt with the possibility of additional regime shifts, mainly during the sixties. However, the single period in which the slope coefficient of the regime shift was significant is after 1985.

17. In this table, we deduct the health tax from expenditures for the sake of comparison.

18. There are many combinations of explanatory variables, which can be candidates for a cointegration vector. Beenstock (1998) performs a cointegration analysis with additional combinations of variables.

19. We have not included Iraq in this variable, given that Iraqi defense expenditures are to a large extent affected by events independent of the Israeli-Arab conflict, like the Iran-Iraq war. Controlling for that would have over complicated the analysis.

20. Arms Control and Disarmament Agency (ACDA) data is expressed in constant U.S. dollars (using implicit GNP price deflators and the official exchange rate in the base year). The data is not adjusted for differences in purchasing power parity due to the difficulty of calculating specific military price indices. The data on Israel is from ACDA, to assure consistency with the other data. We found that it corresponds to the data of the Central Bureau of Statistics almost completely.

21. Data for 1998 was not available at the time of writing. As for historical data, because data on defense expenditure in the fifties is not available, we begin our sample when defense expenditure begins to rise in Israel, just before the Six Day War in 1967.

22. Ideally, we should test such a change in the year of the peace agreement with Egypt. However, the methodology of Gregory and Hansen (1996) requires the use of a dummy variable for the *whole cointegration vector*. Because we are interested in examining changes in economic behavior in 1985, we have chosen the year 1985 for a potential time for regime change.

23. In fact, testing for the degree of integration shows that this is a unit-root variable.

24. Alesina and Perotti (1997).

25. The reason is twofold: First, data on income inequality is not available for the sixties; second, unemployment benefits constitute a relevant variable only after the seventies.

References

Alesina, Alberto, and Silvia Ardagna, "Fiscal Adjustments: Why They Can Be Expansionary." *Economic Policy* 0 (October 1988): 489–545.

Alesina, Alberto, and Roberto Perotti, "The Welfare State and Competitiveness." *American Economic Review* 97 (December 1997): 921–939.

Bank of Israel, *Annual Report*, 1998. Jerusalem: The Bank of Israel, 1999.

Beenstock, Michael, "Country Survey XI: Defence and the Israeli Economy." *Defence and Peace Economics* 9 (1998): 171–222.

Ben-Bassat, Avi, and Rafi Melnick, "Immigration and Growth in Israel in 1990–1995: Plan and Results." *The Quarterly Economic Review* 45 (December 1998): 647–676. (Hebrew)

Dahan, Momi, and Michel Strawczynski, "Fiscal Policy and Inflation in Israel." In *Inflation and Disinflation in Israel*, edited by Leo Leiderman (pp. 23–71). Jerusalem: The Bank of Israel, 1999.

Davidson, Russel, and James G. MacKinnon, *Estimation and Inference in Econometrics*. Oxford: Oxford University Press, 1993.

Gregory, Allen W., and Bruce E. Hansen, "Residual-based Tests for Cointegration in Models with Regime Shifts." *Journal of Econometrics* 70 (January 1996): 99–126.

Hercowitz, Zvi, and Michel Strawczynski, "On the Cyclical Bias of Government Spending." Discussion Paper Series 98.06, Research Department, Bank of Israel, 1998.

MacKinnon, James G., "Critical Values for Cointegration Tests." In *Long-run Economic Relationships*, edited by Robert F. Engle and Clive W. J. Granger, 267–276. Oxford: Oxford University Press, 1991.

International Monetary Fund, *Government Finance Statistics Yearbook*. Washington D.C.: International Monetary Fund, 1998.

Roubini, Nuriel, and Jeffrey Sachs, "Political and Economic Determinants of Budget Deficits in the Industrial Economies." *European Economic Review* 33 (May 1989): 903–933.

State Revenue Administration, *Annual Report*, 1997. Jerusalem: Ministry of Finance, 1998.

The World Bank, *World Development Report*, 1984. Washington D.C.: The World Bank, 1984.

II MONETARY POLICY AND THE INFLATIONARY PROCESS

3 A Monetary Labyrinth: Instruments and the Conduct of Monetary Policy in Israel 1987–1998

Joseph Djivre and Daniel Tsiddon

3.1 Introduction

Since the establishment of the State of Israel in 1948, the Israeli economy has experienced waves of monetary, fiscal, and foreign exchange turmoil. After a long period of fairly rapid growth, the Israeli economy experienced rising inflation and increasing fiscal deficits following the Yom Kippur War at the end of 1973. The two oil shocks affected adversely economic activity, and the economy entered a period of high inflation and low growth with recurrent crises in the foreign exchange market. It is not until 1985, after the economy was hit by hyperinflation that the government initiated a serious stabilization program that reduced the inflation rate to less than 20 percent per annum.

Other than general rules, however, little was known about the proper conduct of monetary policy. Up until the stabilization program, monetary policy had been subordinated to the budget deficit financing requirements. The effort to lower the cost of the budget deficit financing led to financial repression. This repression was reflected in the imposing of quantity, price, and maturity restrictions on financial transactions as well as direct allocation of credit to the private sector by the government. Moreover, as a result of prolonged and volatile inflation, the domestic-currency nonindexed segment of the capital market was underdeveloped, thereby limiting the choice of monetary instruments at the disposal of the Israeli central bank (The Bank of Israel, hereafter *BoI*). Thus, monetary policy during the period following the stabilization program was conducted by the BoI in a highly regulated and financially underdeveloped environment with a highly centralized and, because of the inflationary experience, highly skilled financial sector. Mistakes of the monetary authorities were to be exposed and exploited almost immediately, and the efficacy of the monetary authority was to be challenged routinely.

In a way, the analysis of the conduct of monetary policy in Israel during the period surveyed is that of an everlasting effort to learn. Although monetary policy is always and everywhere conducted in an uncertain and changing environment, in Israel, the lack of basic know-how, together with the changing institutional environment typical of a postinflationary era, made learning much harder. The monetary authority had to cope not only with a strong banking sector and large exogenous shocks, but also, perhaps predominantly, with the understanding of the behavior and efficiency of monetary instruments during a period of structural changes following the gradual liberalization of financial markets.

This work focuses on the conduct of monetary policy and its rationale and on interdependence in the evolution of the money markets, of the monetary policy and instruments and of the exchange rate regime. Our analysis indicates the existence of considerable interdependence between the choice and efficiency of the various monetary instruments, on the one hand, and the structure of financial markets, on the other. We also show later that the competition-enhancing liberalization of capital flows erodes the monopoly power of banks, narrowing the interest rate spread between bank-deposit and lending-interest rates and thereby enhancing the efficacy of the transmission of monetary policy.

A quantitative assessment of the evolution of monetary aggregates shows a considerable surge in liquidity. This surge in liquidity may be attributed to decreasing inflation expectations, lack of monetary instruments of relatively long maturity, and accommodation of the increase in the demand for liquid assets arising from the aforementioned structural changes. This accommodation may be traced to the scant attention paid to the evolution of market interest rates and wide monetary aggregates, the BoI emphasizing instead the evolution of M_1 and short-term interest rates. Our interpretation is supported by the results of econometric estimation, which show that the relation between the short-term interest rate targeted by the BoI and market interest rates changed during the period surveyed. As a result of this change, the BoI interest rate ceased to provide an accurate indicator of the liquidity of the money market.

The observed expansion of the wider monetary aggregates is not by itself inflationary. However, the relative expansion of the monetary base that accompanied it entails "an inflation potential" because it may support the growth of monetary balances after monetary tightening is relaxed. A similar inflation pressure may arise from the monetization of domestic currency liabilities accumulated by the BoI in the context of the monetary tightening after 1994.

The prevention of the aforementioned monetization requires the absorption of some of the excess liquidity, which may be created following the relaxation of monetary tightening, using if need be the foreign currency reserves accumulated by the BoI.

This work continues as follows: In the second part, we present briefly the institutional setting prevailing in the pre- and poststabilization periods and the monetary instruments used to conduct monetary policy. Then we describe the evolution of this setting, and that of the monetary instruments and policy with emphasis on their interdependence. The third part contains a quantitative survey of the evolution of monetary instruments and aggregates, bank credit and interest rates. In this part, we also put forward a hypothesis concerning this evolution based on the institutional

Table 3.1
Selected Indicators of the Israeli Economy (In percentage points)

Period	The budget deficit (+) of the public sector/GDP	The inflation rate*	The inflation coefficient of variation	The public sector domestic debt—GDP ratio**	The share of directed credit in total credit***
1964–1970	3.0	5.8	2.3		
1971–1980	13.9	55	1.1		69
1981–1984	12.8	254	1.0	90	59
1985–1986	−2.5	176	2.1	111	62
1987–1988	1.1	17	0.6	100	53

All percentage points have been rounded at the first decimal point except the budget deficit and one-digit inflation rates.
* Annualized rate of monthly average
** Since 1983
*** Since 1973

and policy changes described in the previous sections. In the fourth part, we provide an econometric estimation of the changing link between interest rates on monetary instruments and bank deposit and credit interest rates. In the last part, we offer our conclusions.

3.2 The Institutional Setting and Main Monetary Instruments

The Structure of the Monetary Framework during the Stabilization Era

The monetary framework during the disinflation era (1985) as well as directly after it was characterized by a little developed capital market in general and its nonindexed segment in particular. Two reasons may account for this underdevelopment. First and foremost, the three-digit inflation rates and inflation uncertainty that prevailed in Israel during the first half of the eighties were not conducive to such a development (table 3.1). Second, a monopolistic banking sector was slow to promote the development of markets that could induce competition.

The financing requirements of the budget deficit gave rise to financial repression whose objective was to lower the government's cost of funds by preventing competition in the capital and in the money markets.[1] This repression encompassed almost every segment of the money, bond, bank deposit, and credit markets and was based on regulations restricting financial transactions. The rationale behind these restrictions was to prevent competition in the raising of funds by limiting the investment outlets of domestic lenders and by restricting the entrance of additional borrowers in

Table 3.2
The Investment Requirements on Government Bonds* (In percentage points)

	Saving schemes indexed to the CPI		Saving schemes indexed to the exchange rate		Pension funds		Provident funds	
Year	Required ratio	Actual ratio	Required ratio	Actual ratio	Required ratio	Actual ratio	Required ratio	Actual ratio
1983	83		100		92		92	
1987	55	57	85	85	92	92	78	85
1988	55	57	65	70	92	94	78	86

* See Ben-Bassat (1990).

the local capital market. They included the high reserve requirements on both domestic and foreign currency denominated deposits. The former were instrumental in imposing low interest rates upon lenders, whereas the latter secured a supply of foreign currency at a low cost to the public sector. Additional restrictions included, among others, the need of government authorization of debt offerings by the business sector at the stock exchange, severe controls on capital flows, and direct government involvement in the allocation of credit to the private sector, which narrowed the scope of monetary policy.[2] Beyond this partial list, mandatory investment requirements on government bonds were also imposed on large segments of the market (table 3.2).[3]

The years that followed the stabilization plan witnessed the tightening of some of the aforementioned restrictions in an effort to enforce a disindexation of the financial markets. While these additional restrictions meant to prevent the automatic monetary accommodation of nominal shocks, they intensified the inefficient allocation of resources in the economy and allowed the limited credibility of the stabilization plan to be reflected in extremely high ex-post real interest rates.

Until 1987, the BoI based its monetary policy on instruments in the form of regulations restricting financial transactions such as credit and interest rate ceilings, tax on capital imports, and the regulation of access to directed credit (Cukierman and Sokoler, 1989) and on more conventional monetary instruments too. The latter included (1) *The monetary loan*, which was practically demand-determined because of its perfectly elastic supply until November 1987 at relatively low interest rates; (2) *reserve requirements* and exemptions thereof; (3) *interest on reserve requirements* paid by the BoI to mitigate the tax burden entailed in such requirements and prevent disintermediation (Offenbacher 1988).[4] (4) *open market operations*—Until 1985, the BoI managed the yield on government bonds leading to an automatic monetization of the budget deficit. The market for nonindexed Treasury bills (Makam), however, remained underdeveloped and was characterized by short-term maturities rendering their use in the conduct of monetary policy practically impossible.

The underdevelopment of capital markets and the high degree of regulation limited the scope of financial intermediation, which made the coexistence of enough banks to sustain interbank competition impossible.[5] This noncompetitive structure of the banking sector gave rise to wide spreads between deposit and lending rates, supporting the government's effort to reduce the cost of funding its budget deficit.

In order to compete with the government in the raising of funds, commercial banks in Israel intervened in the stock market to secure a minimal return on holdings of bank shares, inciting also their clients to invest on their shares. This ill-conceived plan of concerted bank share manipulation culminated in a stock market crash in October 1983 in whose aftermath the banking sector was practically nationalized affecting adversely the motivation for competition-inducing measures. This bailing out of the banking sector and its high concentration was considered by the public as an indicator of the existence of a tacit government insurance against bank failure of the form "too big to fail." This assessment led to a mispricing of risk and of the cost of capital, accentuating at the same time the problems of moral hazard involved in bank activity.

It must have become clear to the reader that the consideration of any structural change in the Israeli capital market prior to 1987 was futile. Between the government's need to finance its budget deficit and the highly monopolistic system of commercial banks, interests were simply too strong.

The Evolution of Monetary Instruments and Targets after 1987

The Government Budget-Deficit Cut as a Catalyst for Structural Changes in the Money and Capital Markets The evolution of the monetary policy in Israel in the nineties was characterized by two interdependent developments: (a) the gradual transition from a fixed exchange rate regime to a floating exchange rate with a widening over time exchange rate band, and (b) the transition from using the exchange rate as a nominal anchor to the use of the BoI interest rate as the main short-term monetary target and the inflation rate as the medium and long-term monetary target.

The evolution of monetary policy in general and of its targets and instruments in particular was influenced by two major changes, which followed the stabilization program of 1985. A cut of the public sector budget deficit, which secured the consistency between the macroeconomic fundamentals and the disinflation policy, and the granting of independence to the BoI in defining and carrying out the monetary policy. The cut in the budget deficit weakened the government's motivation to

Table 3.3
The Evolution of the Domestic Debt (Annual average, in percentage points)*

Period	The Public Sector Domestic debt/GDP	Negotiable** debt	Total*** debt
1984–1985	104		
1986–1987	104	37	
1988–1991	102	60	81
1996–1998	82	46	62

* All percentages have been rounded at the first decimal point.
** The share of the negotiable government debt in the stock market capitalization.
*** The share of the total government debt in the stock market capitalization augmented by the stock of non-negotiable domestic government debt.

subordinate monetary policy to the financing requirements of the budget deficit leading to the formal decoupling of monetary policy from fiscal policy. The BoI independence was based on legislation forbidding the financing of the government budget deficit through credit from the central bank (money printing).

Moreover, the fall in the budget deficit gross domestic product (GDP) ratio from 14.5 percentage points in 1984 to a budget surplus of 1.6 percentage points between 1985 and 1987 and its relatively small size thereafter also weakened the government's motivation to monopolize the Israeli capital market. This allowed a loosening of the government's grip over the local capital market through a series of competition-enhancing measures (table 3.3).

We will relate here only to the general spirit of this competition-enhancing process, which started around April 1987. It consisted in the gradual lifting of the restrictions whose aim had been the strengthening of the government's monopsonistic power in the capital market and the consequent lowering of the budget deficit financing cost. The lifting of restrictions consisted in the gradual relaxation of the investment requirements imposed on saving schemes and institutional investors, regarding the share of government bonds in their portfolio, in the suspension of the government's approval of bond offerings by the business sector and of the tax discrimination against bonds issued by the business sector (Ben-Bassat, 1990). At a later stage (1990–1992), these liberalization measures were extended to capital inflows and to the gradual reduction of the reserve requirements on bank deposits.

The liberalization measures had two major effects on the structure of the capital markets and the banking sector, which affected the conduct of monetary policy: (a) they contributed to the development of financial markets through which the effect of monetary policy is transmitted to the rest of the economy and, in particular, to the shaping of the various channels of the monetary policy transmission mechanism; (b) they created markets offering alternatives to bank deposits and credit, whose interest rate elasticity increased, thereby weakening the banks' rent extraction ability. A massive exploitation of the potential offered by the liberalization of the domestic capital market took place in the context of an expansionary monetary policy between 1992 and 1993. It was expressed in an unprecedented wave of public offerings in the Tel-Aviv stock exchange (TASE).[6] Moreover, the ability of the business sector to hold foreign currency denominated bank deposits in Israel and abroad, already at the relatively early stages of the liberalization process, also eroded the banks' monopsony power over bank deposits. This outcome was strengthened further by the deepening of the treasury-bill market (Makam) and by the gradual development, at a later stage of a market for nonindexed government bonds with longer maturities.[7] In a similar manner, the raising of credit in foreign currency and abroad and later on of capital in foreign stock markets may be considered as a complementary measure eroding the banks' monopolistic position in the underwriting market and in the supply of credit.

These liberalization measures thus contributed to the convergence of the banking sector to more competitive pricing practices. We show later that this convergence strengthened the response of the banking-sector interest rates to changes in the BoI interest rates and affected the transmission of the changes in the interest rates from the monetary instruments to the bank interest rates.

The ordering in the process of liberalization of capital flows whereby precedence was given to inflows over outflows of capital, to the business sector over the households, to real direct investments over financial investments and, in general, to long-term flows over short-term flows, reflected the authorities' concentration on the stability of the foreign exchange market.[8] A possible destabilization of this market when the exchange rate served as a nominal anchor for the economy could inflict a severe blow to the macroeconomic stability of a small and open economy like Israel. These fears were apparently due to the substantial potential of capital exports by households, in light of their accumulation of domestic currency denominated financial wealth over the years.[9] The timing of the first major liberalization measures after the success of the stabilization plan (1990) provides additional insight into the authorities' apprehension with respect to the liberalization process. The gradual liberalization of the capital account contributed to the deepening of the foreign exchange market, which made possible at a later stage the transition to a floating exchange rate, within a crawling exchange rate band, without drastic changes in the exchange rate.

The only remaining major restrictions to this date on capital outflows refer to the quantitative restrictions imposed on the foreign investments of institutional investors

Table 3.4
The Reserve Requirements on Selected Bank Deposits (Monthly average during the period, in percentage points)*

				Foreign currency deposits			
	Domestic currency deposits			Current Accounts		Fixed-Term Deposits	
Period	Current Accounts	Weekly Deposits	3-month deposits	Residents	Tax exempted	Residents	Tax exempted
1981–1984	45	40	13	96	10	88	10
1985–1987	49	37	18	100	10	100	10
1988–1991	18	12	7	100	13	100	10
1997–1998	6	3	3	6	6	3	3

* All percentages have been rounded at the first decimal point.

(provident and pension funds and life insurance plans) and to the tax discrimination against financial investments abroad and against investments in foreign currency at the home market. On such investments, there exists a 35 percent tax on capital gains and on income from interest. Shares of Israeli firms, which are traded in foreign stock markets, are tax-exempted. This tax discrimination constitutes an effective restriction on capital outflows. In particular, the share of foreign investments in the portfolio of provident funds was around 1 percent at the end of 1998, whereas the still existing quantitative restrictions foresee an investment ceiling equal to 5 percent of their assets' worth.

Another change with far-reaching consequences for the conduct of monetary policy was the dramatic reduction of the reserve requirements on banking deposits (table 3.4).[10] This reduction in reserve requirements covered both domestic and foreign currency denominated bank deposits. This step was instrumental in the narrowing of the interest rate spread between bank rates on domestic currency denominated credit and deposits and affected the transmission of changes in the monetary policy to the market interest rates.

The reduction in the reserve requirements on foreign currency denominated deposits, which were substantially higher than those on domestic currency deposits, increased the substitutability between currencies and opened a window for a foreign currency denominated credit supply expansion. This potential was indeed exploited by the business sector, allowing for the shift from domestic currency denominated credit to foreign currency denominated credit, which followed the tightening of monetary policy in the second half of 1994.

The difference between the reserve requirements on resident and nonresident or new-immigrant foreign currency deposits is striking. Because higher reserve requirements imply lower interest rates on these deposits, this difference seems to reflect the different interest rate elasticity of supply between these two categories of depositors. This difference arose, apparently, from the fact that unlike residents, tax-exempted depositors could costlessly shift to foreign markets.

The gradual reduction of reserve requirements on bank deposits was also accompanied by the suspension of reserve requirements that had been imposed on bank credit. The suspension included a 1 percent reserve requirement on domestic currency denominated nonindexed bank credit (in April 1990) and a 100 percent reserve requirement on CPI-indexed credit (in November 1991).

The Structure of the Financial Intermediation Sector and of the Capital Market and the Choice of Monetary Instruments As part of the stabilization program, the adoption of the exchange rate as the nominal anchor for the economy and the establishment of a fixed exchange rate regime was based on the daily intervention of the BoI in the foreign exchange market. The effect of this intervention on the money market was partially or totally sterilized through changes in the monetary loan. The monetary loan constituted the main monetary instrument until 1996, and through it, the BoI affected directly the volume of the liquid domestic currency resources that could serve the commercial banking sector as reserves and as sources for credit expansion.

The monetary loan may be differentiated into two categories—the monetary loan at the discount window and the loan at the monetary auction.[11] The monetary loan at the discount window is a loan given separately to each individual bank at interest rates that start from a minimum interest rate announced by the BoI and increase gradually with the loan quantity, thus forming an upward-sloping, steplike supply function. The interest rate at the highest window has been determined at a prohibitive level since December 1987. While the interest rate at a given window is the same for all banks, the amounts available to the same bank at different windows or to different banks at the same window are not of the same size. The interwindow difference in the size of the monetary loan reflects policy considerations whereas the interbank difference at the same window reflects the fact that the loan at each window is proportional to the share of the individual bank in the reserve requirements on domestic currency denominated deposits of the banking sector as a whole.[12] This arrangement allowed the BoI to differentiate among the various commercial banks according to their size.

The monetary auction to commercial banks, which was initially conducted on an irregular basis (December 1987) and later on a regular weekly basis (January 1989–July 1996) was followed at a later date by the daily auction (December 1990–January

1997). The monetary auction was a sealed bid auction in which the BoI determined a minimum interest rate and the auctioned quantity of liquid funds was allocated sequentially to the highest bidder. The amounts of the loans were determined by the bidder, in multiples of one million new Israeli sheqels (NIS), and the auction was repeated until the whole auctioned quantity was absorbed by the banking system. The single bank could bid at different interest rates so that it might end up at the closure of the auction with monetary loans at different interest rates. If there were an excess demand for liquid assets at the lowest interest bid at the auction, then the remainder of the auction was allocated among the various bidders in proportion to their ex-ante demand at this interest rate.

This choice of monetary instruments was made because of the existing restrictions on the use of alternative instruments. In working through open market operations, the BoI faced two important constraints concerning the use of treasury bills (*Makam*) for the day-to-day conduct of the monetary policy. The stock of *Makam* was rather low compared to the monetary base, and the BoI depended on the government for the issue of new T-Bills.[13]

The stock of T-bills (*Makam*) relative to the monetary base was indeed low (9.1 percent in 1986–1987) because of the high reserve requirements and the underdeveloped treasury-bill market due to high inflation. As a result, the purchase in the open market of treasury bills would have been rather inefficient in bringing about a monetary expansion, especially in view of the considerable intramonth volatility of government absorption and injection relative to the monetary base.[14] This vacuum was partly filled by the process of gradual reduction of the high reserve requirements on bank deposits, which started in the beginning of 1987. The BoI dependence upon the government can be traced to the existence of ceilings on the volume of treasury bills whose upward adjustment required government action (until 1995).

As a result, the BoI had to work directly through the commercial banks, especially if it wished to maintain a relatively tight control over the development of monetary aggregates, which requires a relatively stable monetary multiplier. This may have also been the reason for its initially preferring large banks over small ones, as it is indicated by the fact that the loan at the discount windows was the only monetary loan until the introduction of the weekly auction on a regular basis (1989). This policy may have increased the efficiency of monetary policy given the highly concentrated banking sector. It worked however in exactly the opposite direction in a dynamic context, retarding the convergence process of the banking sector to competitive pricing and its response to changes in monetary policy.

The governor of the BoI used moral suasion in the second half of 1989 to limit the monopoly power of the banking system. Additional competition-enhancing measures were tried down the road, such as the weekly monetary auction to the nonbanking sector (June 1990–April 1995) and the aforementioned daily auction to the banks.

These measures failed, however, to increase substantially interbank competition for a number of reasons: (a) The monetary auctions to the nonbanking private sector were held through the intermediation of commercial banks, which reduced their competition-enhancing potential; (b) it transpired that the conduct of the monetary loans was conducive to the tacit collusion among commercial banks. Djivre and Tsiddon (1996) show that when a commercial bank's demand for liquidity increased, it preferred to raise its demand for the monetary loan at the discount window and rise to a higher individual interest rate bracket than to bid up the interest rate at the daily monetary auction. Such a reaction could have affected the cost of liquidity to the rest of the banks had the latter decided to respond, possibly leading to a price war and to the collapse of the informal banking cartel.

As time passed, the reduction in the reserve requirements on bank deposits, on the one hand, and the deepening of the treasury bill market, on the other, led to an increase in the importance of the treasury bills as a monetary instrument, especially after the tightening of monetary policy in mid-1994. Still, the BoI continued to use the monetary loan as its main instrument for the conduct of monetary policy. The reason may be traced to the aforementioned restrictions on the adjustment of the treasury-bill ceiling until 1995. After this date, the rate of automatic semi-annual adjustment of the bill ceiling (the highest occurring between the rate of inflation and the rate of growth of M_1 during the past six months) seems to have constituted a binding restriction relative to the absorption needs of the BoI at that time. These needs were reflected in the almost complete depletion of the stock of the monetary loan and the gradual suspension of all the auctions, and led to the introduction of the commercial bank deposit auctions at the BoI in June 1996.[15] These auctions were initially held on a weekly basis for three-month deposits. In February 1997, March 1997, and January 1998, auctions for one-month, one-week, and daily deposits respectively, were introduced. These auctions were still held until the end of 1999 whereas the three-month deposit auction was suspended in April 1998.[16]

The deposit auctions constituted the mirror image of the monetary loan auctions in the sense that the BoI set a maximum interest rate (instead of a minimum rate in the loans) and the deposits of the lowest bidder were accepted sequentially by the BoI, until the quantity auctioned was exhausted. These auctions constituted nonnegotiable debt issued by the BoI, which provided an inexhaustible source of monetary instruments for sterilization. The sterilization needs originated in the policy of exchange rate management within the exchange rate band alongside the tightening of monetary policy since mid-1994, which was followed by an unprecedented expansion of foreign currency denominated bank credit to finance domestic activities. This credit expansion gave rise to an excess supply of foreign currency at the prevailing exchange rate, absorbed by the BoI through sterilized intervention in the foreign exchange market.

The Interdependence between Changes in the Exchange Rate Regime, the Monetary Policy, and Its Instruments and Targets This section shows how the inconsistencies between the monetary targets and instruments and the exchange rate regime led to an increasing flexibility of the latter as a macroeconomic consistency-inducing mechanism.

The adoption of a fixed exchange rate regime as part of the stabilization program of 1985 had as an objective the synchronization of the public's inflation expectations with the disinflation of the stabilization plan. In the beginning, the exchange rate was fixed with respect to the U.S. dollar (until July 1986) and later on with respect to a currency basket.[17] The choice of the exchange rate as the nominal anchor was considered as appropriate because of the extended currency substitution due to the high inflation and a developed indexation system to the exchange rate especially in the context of price-fixing and updating. Bestowing macroeconomic consistency upon the stabilization program was necessary for its success. This was achieved partially by the aforementioned cut of the government budget deficit and a 1.5 billion dollar loan from the U.S. government, which provided foreign currency resources to finance the daily intervention of the BoI in the foreign exchange market, and thus support the fixed exchange rate regime. The macroeconomic consistency of the components of the stabilization program was only partial, and the foreign exchange market experienced until the end of 1991 speculative attacks on the BoI foreign currency reserves. These attacks originated in the systematic real appreciation of the exchange rate arising from continued inflation, on the one hand, even though at dramatically lower rates than in the past, and the initially fixed exchange rate, on the other. The unsustainability of the real exchange rate appreciation gave rise to devaluation expectations precipitating the speculative attacks. The need to cope with these attacks imposed changes in the structure of the monetary loan at the discount window and in the exchange rate regime.

The wish to prevent a complete monetary accommodation to devaluation expectations led in December 1987 to the setting of the interest rate at the highest interest rate bracket at a prohibitive level. Until that date, the upward-sloping supply of liquidity at the discount windows became perfectly elastic at a low interest rate, relative to the rate of inflation, allowing the automatic monetary accommodation of the devaluation expectations at the initial stage of the speculative attack. This policy could allow the attack to gain momentum before the BoI became conscious of it and raised interest rates. An altogether perfectly inelastic supply schedule could have been more efficient in dealing with devaluation expectations in the short run, but it could have penalized, for instance, other shocks or structural changes that might have not warranted higher interest rates, such as positive shocks to the demand for money. In this respect, the upward slope of the monetary loan at the discount window may be considered as a mechanism allowing an optimal adjustment of the monetary policy to shocks when it is unclear on impact whether these shocks should be followed by a change in monetary policy.

The first changes, which were introduced in the exchange rate regime, aimed at reducing the frequency of the speculative attacks by limiting the extent of real exchange rate appreciation. These changes included the introduction of an horizontal exchange rate band in January 1989, which was widened later and culminated in the introduction of a crawling exchange rate band in December 1991. The slope of this band reflected the forecast inflation differential between Israel and its major trading partners. The adoption of the crawling exchange rate band may be attributed to the horizontal band's inability to accommodate indefinitely the inflation differential between Israel and its main trading partners. The daily sterilized intervention of the BoI in the foreign exchange market continued in spite of the changes in the exchange rate regime. This policy implied an informal narrow exchange rate band, within which the exchange rate fluctuated, and an interest rate smoothing policy.[18] In this context, the wider formal exchange rate band played the role of an escape clause during crises.

The variety of shocks whose origin could not be identified in real time, especially during the first transition years of the period surveyed, led the BoI to adopt multiple monetary instruments and short-term targets in addition to the exchange rate (interest rates, foreign currency reserves, and quantitative targets for the monetary aggregates). It is only when the inflation rate fell to around 10 percent per annum and the stability of the exchange rate was guaranteed that short-term interest rate targets and medium and long-run binding inflation targets were adopted. The inflation targeting was adopted for the first time by the government for 1994, following the implicit inflation targeting implied by the slope of the crawling band since the end of 1991 (table 3.5). Clearly, without the fall in the inflation rate and the end of the recurrent speculative attacks, the adoption of inflation targets would have been less efficient and the use of the short-term interest rate targeting could have been reflected in an automatic short-run accommodation of the devaluation expectations.

The desired level of the interest rate by the BoI had also served to derive the required changes in the stock of the monetary loan prior to 1994, but the exchange

Table 3.5
Inflation Targets in Israel (Annual rates)

Year	1992*	1993*	1994	1995	1996	1997	1998	1999	2000–2001
Inflation target	14–15	10	8	8–11	8–10	7–10	7–10	4	3–4

* Forecast inflation.

rate had always remained the main intermediate target.[19] Under the policy of exchange rate management within the band and interest rate smoothing, the monetary aggregates were determined endogenously. Their deviation from a predetermined range over time was considered, however, an indicator requiring the reassessment of monetary policy.

The later use of the interest rate on the monetary instruments, whose supply is controlled by the BoI, as a short-term target by the BoI had also some drawbacks: (a) Because of the absence of interbank competition in the allocation of the monetary loans, the short-term interest rate targeting prevented the BoI from differentiating between the demand for liquidity by commercial banks out of regular business considerations or because of liquidity problems. (b) The announcement of the precise change in the interest rate on the monetary loan by the BoI served the commercial banks as a focal price on which they based their tacit collusion on the monetary loan interest rate determination. The formal adoption of the interest rate by the BoI as a short-term intermediate target was accompanied by the narrowing of the spread between the monetary loan and the interbank interest rates. The narrowing of this spread and the observed fall in the intramonth variance of the interest rate at which the daily monetary auction was cleared imply a reduced interbank competition in the market for liquidity (Djivre and Tsiddon, 1996). (c) The change in the relation between the interest rate on the monetary loan and the interest rates on bank credit and deposits following the liberalization of capital flows made the former an inaccurate indicator of monetary conditions. This was due to the fact that changes of a given size in the interest rate on the monetary loan affected the market and the bank interest rates differently over time; these rates constitute a more appropriate indicator of monetary conditions.

The new targets of monetary policy and its tightening after 1994 made necessary the gradual augmenting of the exchange rate regime flexibility. These measures, whose aim was to bestow compatibility between monetary policy targets and instruments, included the widening of the crawling exchange rate band in June 1995, the suspension of the BoI intervention in the foreign exchange market in March 1996 and the introduction of an ever-widening exchange rate band in June 1997 (table 3.6). However, as long as prices are affected by changes in the exchange rate, the

Table 3.6
Changes in the Parameters of the Exchange Rate Band

Period	Bandwidth around midpoint	Slope of upper bound	Slope of lower bound
3.1.89–1.3.90	3 percent	0	0
2.3.90–17.12.91	5 percent	0	0
18.12.91–9.11.92	5 percent	9 percent p/a	9 percent p/a
10.11.92–26.7.93	5 percent	8 percent p/a	8 percent p/a
27.7.93–31.5.95	5 percent	6 percent p/a	6 percent p/a
1.6.95–18.6.97	7 percent	6 percent p/a	6 percent p/a
19.6.97–5.8.98	increasing	6 percent p/a	4 percent p/a
6.8.98–	increasing	6 percent p/a	2 percent p/a

adoption of inflation targets restricts the higher potential volatility of the exchange rate implied by a wide band to the very short run. Otherwise, a protracted deviation of the exchange rate from the course that is compatible with the inflation target risks jeopardizing its attainment.

The gradual but increasing flexibility of the exchange rate regime allowed to cope with the vulnerability of short-horizon inflation targets, like the annual targets set in Israel, to inflation shocks. This was achieved by exploiting the interest rate effect on the evolution of the exchange rate to counter the inflation shocks. Moreover, the enhanced exchange rate flexibility facilitated its exploitation in disinflating through a protracted monetary tightening, in line with the government's engagement to achieve low one-digit inflation rates by 2001. The switching to a free float within the exchange rate band was reflected in a higher exchange rate volatility, which weakened the transmission of changes in the exchange rate to the price level and contributed to the stability of the foreign exchange market by raising the exchange rate premium (table 3.7).

The suspension of the sterilized intervention by the BoI in the foreign exchange market also slowed down the accumulation process of domestic currency denominated liabilities by the BoI. Between December 1994 and February 1996, the BoI accumulated 7.1 billion dollars through its interventions in the foreign exchange market, turning from a net creditor of 8.3 billion NIS to the private sector in Israel to a net debtor of some 10 billion NIS in March 1996. This development led, apparently, to the aforementioned change in the regulations concerning the issue of treasury bills in 1995 and to the suspension of the BoI intervention in the foreign exchange market.

Moreover, after the appreciating exchange rate hit the band's lower bound, the sterilized intervention by the BoI in the foreign exchange market was renewed. Be-

Table 3.7
The Cumulative Distribution of the Daily Changes in the Exchange Rate* (Rates of change in percentage points and in absolute terms)

	The daily rate of change versus the currency basket		
Period	Smaller than 0.2%	Smaller than 0.4%	Smaller than 0.6%
1989–1990	61.3	87.2	95.7
1991–1994	81.2	94.6	99.0
1995–1998**			
Subperiod 1	64.6	87.0	94.5
Subperiod 2	83.5	91.1	93.7
Subperiod 3	54.5	78.2	89.1

* The observations corresponding to discrete devaluations following realignments have been excluded.
** Subperiod 1 is the period of sterilized intervention between December 1994 and February 1996. Subperiod 2 is the period of sterilized intervention at the the band's lower bound during the following periods: August 1996–October 1996, January 1997–June 1997 and January 1998. Subperiod 3 is the period of pure float within the band.

tween August 1996 and June 1997 (and January 1998), the BoI intervened in the foreign exchange market to support the band's lower bound.[20] The purchases of foreign currency by the BoI during this period amounted to 8.7 billion dollars, and the accumulated purchases since the end of 1994 reached the amount of 15.8 billion dollars. The domestic currency net liabilities of the BoI (including T-bills) reached some 38 billion (10.8 percent of gross domestic product [GDP]) in May 1997. The continued sterilized intervention of the BoI at the band's lower bound triggered the further augmenting of the exchange rate regime flexibility in June 1997. In particular, the flattening of the slope of the lower band may be considered as an effort to push the exchange rate back into the band.

The accumulation of domestic currency liabilities by the BoI since 1994 may create a fiscal burden in the domestic budget of the consolidated public sector if the BoI does not use its foreign currency denominated assets to reduce its domestic currency denominated liabilities. Such a burden is consistent in the long run with higher inflation for reasons similar to those pointed out by Sargent and Wallace (1981) and by Liviatan (1983) for a closed economy. In this context, the switch to a free float within the exchange rate band was also instrumental in mitigating the risk of long-run inflation pressures by eliminating the accumulation of domestic currency denominated liabilities through sterilized intervention. This implies that the aforementioned long-term inconsistency between sterilized intervention and long-run low inflation targets could have been avoided altogether had the BoI not intervened in the foreign currency market, say, prior to March 1996 and after August 1996, following an earlier transition to a pure float.

It transpires from this analysis that the introduction of the auction for commercial bank deposits at the BoI violates the economic reasoning of the law prohibiting the financing of the budget deficit through money printing. This prohibition basically defines that the government budget deficit will be financed by issuing debt and implies that the debt redemption will not be backed by money printing. However, the fact that the BoI losses arising from the servicing of its domestic currency debt is not included in the budget deficit and that the debt itself is not considered as part of the government debt implies that the BoI liabilities are backed by money printing. As a result, the introduction of the auction for commercial bank deposits at the BoI as an instrument for absorbing the monetary injection, entailed in its foreign currency purchases, has deferred but not eliminated the inflation threat.

The credibility of inflation targeting bestowed upon the more flexible exchange rate regime stability that might have been otherwise absent. More precisely, the transition to a more flexible exchange rate regime might have been perceived by the public as offering an opportunity for inflating to stimulate economic activity. Such a perception may lead to a higher inflation equilibrium out of considerations similar to those pointed out by Barro and Gordon (1983). The adoption of inflation targets and the government's engagement to secure the convergence of the economy to low one-digit inflation rates by 2001 seem to have prevented the public from misinterpreting the transition to a more flexible exchange rate regime as a pretext for inflating. This credibility-enhancing effect may be attributed to policy measures such as the legislation starting in 1991, that defined a declining course for the government's budget deficit. These measures may be traced to an effort to assure that the fiscal expansion entailed in the absorption of the emigration wave in the beginning of the nineties would be transitory, leading at a later stage to the adoption of a conscious policy of budget deficit reduction. The initial government decision has undergone several changes since 1991, and deviations have been observed in both directions from the declared targets. However, the basic concept of the gradual budget-deficit reduction trend has been retained and followed in practice.

What Is Next?

The liberalization of capital flows was almost complete by May 1998 with the exception of restrictions on investments of households. The low taxation revenues from foreign currency investments and from investments abroad suggests that the aforementioned tax discrimination against household investments abroad is not suspended lest the rising share of foreign assets in the public's stock of wealth destabilizes the foreign exchange market. In this context, the setting of an inflation target with an horizon longer than a year may contribute to the completion of the liberalization of capital outflows, by weakening the adverse implications of an exchange rate depreciation on attaining the inflation target.

The fear of the exchange-rate depreciation supported by a rising demand for foreign currency to finance the shift in the composition of the public's asset portfolio arises from the assumption that the BoI will not intervene in the foreign exchange market. Another way of severing the link between the change in the public's asset portfolio on the one hand and the inflation rate on the other is the gradual lifting of the remaining restrictions on capital flows combined, possibly, with sales of foreign currency to slow down the rise in the exchange rate. According to this approach, the tax discrimination will first be eliminated from the foreign investments of the various institutional investors and will be accompanied by the gradual lifting of the quantitative restrictions on their foreign investments. Eventually, the elimination of tax discrimination will also be extended to the households' direct investments in the foreign financial markets. In this context, the elimination of tax discrimination implies only the equalization of effective tax rates, which should not be made necessarily at a zero tax rate.

The economic implications of the liberalization of capital flows are equivalent to the competition-enhancing entrance of foreign financial intermediaries in the Israeli capital market. Its completion is therefore a necessary step for enforcing the competitive pricing of the cost of capital in Israel, thereby achieving an efficient allocation of resources in the domestic capital market. In this context, a possible rise in the share of foreign assets in the public's stock of wealth should be regarded as an inevitable outcome of the completion of the liberalization.

It is reasonable to assume that the completion of the liberalization of capital outflows will also affect the channels of transmission of the monetary policy by affecting the relation between the market interest rates, on the one hand, and those on the various monetary instruments, on the other. As a result, the focusing of monetary policy on the interest rate on these instruments may only mislead the monetary authorities with respect to the actual impact of changes in the monetary policy on the economy. Under these circumstances, the use of market interest rates and monetary aggregates as monetary indicators is warranted.

3.3 The Evolution of Monetary Instruments and Aggregates, Bank Credit, and Interest Rates

In this section, we will provide a brief quantitative analysis of the main monetary instruments, liquid monetary aggregates, bank credit, and various interest rates during the period surveyed. In our analysis, we will differentiate among three subperiods—the first between 1987 and 1990, the second between 1991 and 1994, and the third between 1995 and 1998.

The first subperiod was characterized by the stabilization of the inflation rate around 20 percent per annum, a policy of exchange rate management, starting with a fixed exchange rate regime and shifting later on to a horizontal exchange rate band. This subperiod was also characterized by the gradual relaxation of some of the restrictions on indexed credit (to the CPI and to foreign currency) on foreign currency deposits on the investment requirements on government bonds imposed on institutional investors and saving schemes in the domestic capital market.

The second period was characterized by the stabilization of inflation around 10 percent per annum. From the policy point of view, this period was characterized by the most important competition-enhancing measures in the Israeli capital market. These measures included the acceleration of the liberalization of the capital flows and, especially, capital imports, the introduction of monetary auctions as an interbank competition-enhancing instrument in the allocation of liquidity by the BoI, and the adoption of the crawling exchange rate band. Toward the end of the period, a binding inflation targeting was also adopted.

The third subperiod was characterized by the tightening of monetary policy, which started in the second half of 1994, a shift to a floating exchange rate regime within the crawling band, and the relinquishment of the exchange rate as a formal nominal anchor. The liberalization of capital flows was extended to capital outflows, even though some restrictions on household investment abroad are still in place.

The Monetary Instruments and Aggregates and the Bank Credit

We shall present here a quantitative analysis of the development of the major monetary instruments, the monetary loan, the treasury bills, and the auction of commercial bank deposits at the BoI.

Monetary Instruments[21] The development of the *monetary loan* during the period surveyed constitutes the mirror image of the exchange and interest rate smoothing policy in the context of the aforementioned policy of sterilized interventions in the foreign currency market (table 3.8 and figures 3.1 and 3.2).

In this way, the monetary loan witnessed a gradual expansion during periods in which the BoI sold foreign currency to the public and a contraction during periods of foreign currency purchases by the Israeli central bank. The growth of the monetary loan accelerated after August 1988 and reached its apex in November 1994.

Table 3.8
The Stock of Monetary Instruments—Monetary Basis Ratio (Percentage points)*

Period	Loan at the discount windows	The weekly auction	The daily auction	The auction to the public	T-Bills	The deposit auction
1987–1990	24	26	1	14	33	
1991–1994	27	52	61	26	81	
1995–1998	10	6	17	1	144	166

* All percentages have been rounded at the first decimal point.

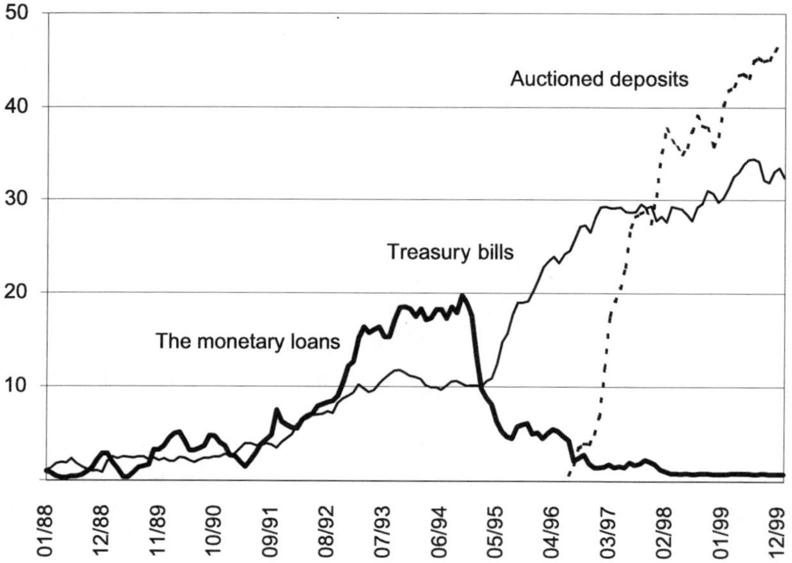

Figure 3.1
The Evolution of the Major Monetary Instruments
(Monthly data, billions of NIS)

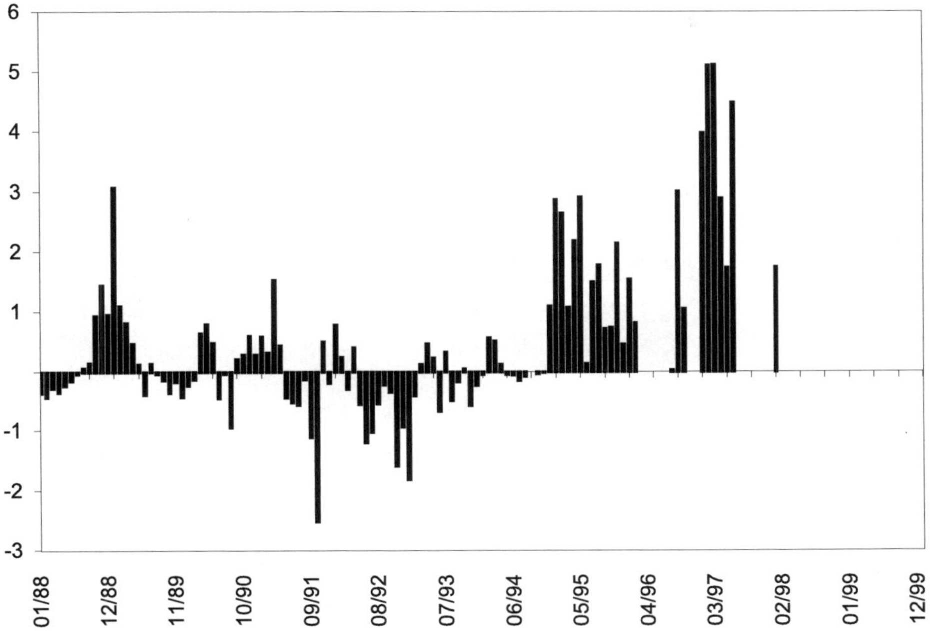

Figure 3.2
Purchases of Foreign Currency by the BoI
(Monthly data, billions of NIS)

The rise in the relative weight of monetary auctions in the monetary loan after 1991 reflects an effort to increase interbank competition in the allocation of liquid funds to the banking sector without, however, much success (Djivre and Tsiddon, 1996). The contraction of the monetary loan characterized primarily the period of tight monetary policy after 1994.

Treasury-Bills (Makam) Stock was small in the beginning of the first subperiod relative to the monetary base, but it increased later on. The BoI encouraged the public to hold T-Bills during the first years of the period surveyed as substitutes for interest-bearing deposits. This policy was reflected in the gradual rise of the private nonbanking sector's share in the holdings of T-Bills from around 50 percent at the end of 1987 to 89 percent in December 1991.

The stock of the treasury bills was 1.5 times higher than the monetary base in 1998, compared to only 9.1 percent during the years 1987–1988. The substantial growth of the stock of treasury bills took place mainly during the third subperiod

(1995–1998), and the reasons have been pointed out elsewhere in the present paper. The stock of treasury bills reached some 23.4 billion I.S. in 1998 (6.1 percent of GDP).

Auctions for Commercial Bank Deposits Auctions for commercial bank deposit at the BoI were introduced during the third subperiod and increased substantially during the first half of 1997. This happened after the exchange rate hit the lower bound of the exchange rate band and the BoI was constrained to renew its sterilized interventions in the foreign exchange market. After June 1997, the position of the exchange rate inside the band allowed the BoI to suspend its daily intervention in the foreign exchange market, with the exception of January 1998, when the exchange rate hit the band's lower bound again. Given the tight monetary policy implemented at the time, the stock of the auctioned bank deposits reached in 1998 the daily average of 46.8 billion NIS (11.2 percent of GDP). Out of this stock, 70 percent had an average maturity lower than four days.

The increase of the net liabilities of the BoI, including T-bills and the monetary loan, reached on the same date the amount of 62.7 billion NIS (16.4 percent of GDP). The increase in these net liabilities by 6.4 GDP between June 1997, after the suspension of the sterilized intervention policy of the BoI, and December 1999 provides an indicator of the inflation potential contained in the domestic currency liabilities accumulated by the BoI after the reduction of short-term interest rates.

The substantial growth of the stock of *Makam*, which we have documented here, allows the BoI to save on treasury bills, simultaneously raise the stock of the auctioned deposits, and use the former in the context of open market operations as its main monetary instrument. Given the failure of auctions to increase interbank competition, such a measure may prove to be competition enhancing, given that more agents are involved in open market operations than in the various auctions. The effectiveness of such a measure may be increased if it is accompanied by the suspension of the monetary loan at the discount window.

The Monetary Base, Monetary Aggregates, and Bank Credit The evolution of the *monetary base*, during the two first subperiods, was affected by two processes working in opposite directions. On the one hand, the reduction of the reserve requirements on bank deposits led to a contraction of the monetary base. On the other hand, the economy's growth and the expansion of interest-bearing nonindexed deposits led to its expansion. Because of the changes in the reserve requirements, it is difficult to provide an estimate of the potential inflation pressures entailed in the monetary base expansion. A simple calculation, based on the extrapolation of the rate of growth of

Table 3.9
The Rate of Growth of the Monetary Base and its Major Components (Percentage points)*

Period	The M_1 component	The interest bearing deposits**	The monetary base M_0
1987–1990	23.2	33	31
1991–1994	14.0	32	22
1995–1998	17.3	24	21

* All percentages have been rounded at the first decimal point.
** The bank deposits with maturity up to one year.

M_o between two consecutive changes in the reserve requirements, indicates a substantial growth of the monetary base even after 1994. This growth is at a rate beyond the rate consistent in the long run with a low one-digit inflation rate (table 3.9).

The Monetary Aggregates and the Bank Credit The M_1/GDP ratio fluctuated between 5 and 6 percent during the whole period under consideration in contrast to the interest-bearing domestic currency denominated deposits. These grew substantially during the whole period under consideration both with respect to the GDP and in absolute terms (figure 3.3 and table 3.10)

In view of the constant M_1/GDP ratio, it is not surprising that the fast rate of growth of the wider monetary aggregates has not yet been reflected in inflation pressures because it is the growth of money balances used in the purchase of goods, which has inflationary implications. As a result, the rate of growth of the monetary base, which is systematically higher than that of M_1 may provide only an indicator of the inflationary potential.

The data indicate that the monetary expansion between 1991 and 1994, which started in the second half of 1992, refers mainly to the growth of the liquid monetary aggregates and, to a lesser extent, to the bank credit (figure 3.4). The substantial differential between the rate of growth of M_2, on the liability side of the banks' balance sheet, and the rate of growth of the bank credit, on their asset side, implies that the fast expansion of the interest-bearing deposits reflects a shift of the public from long maturity assets to short maturity assets. This shift is corroborated by the data, which show a rise in the ratio of interest-bearing deposits to GDP and a fall in the corresponding ratio of the saving schemes and the foreign currency denominated and indexed deposits (figure 3.3).

The credit growth between 1992 and 1993 reflects mainly a credit expansion related to the financing of stock purchases in the primary market,[22] which culminated in November 1993. This process is reflected in the evolution of the twelve-month rate of growth of bank credit, which experienced a sharp increase in November 1993,

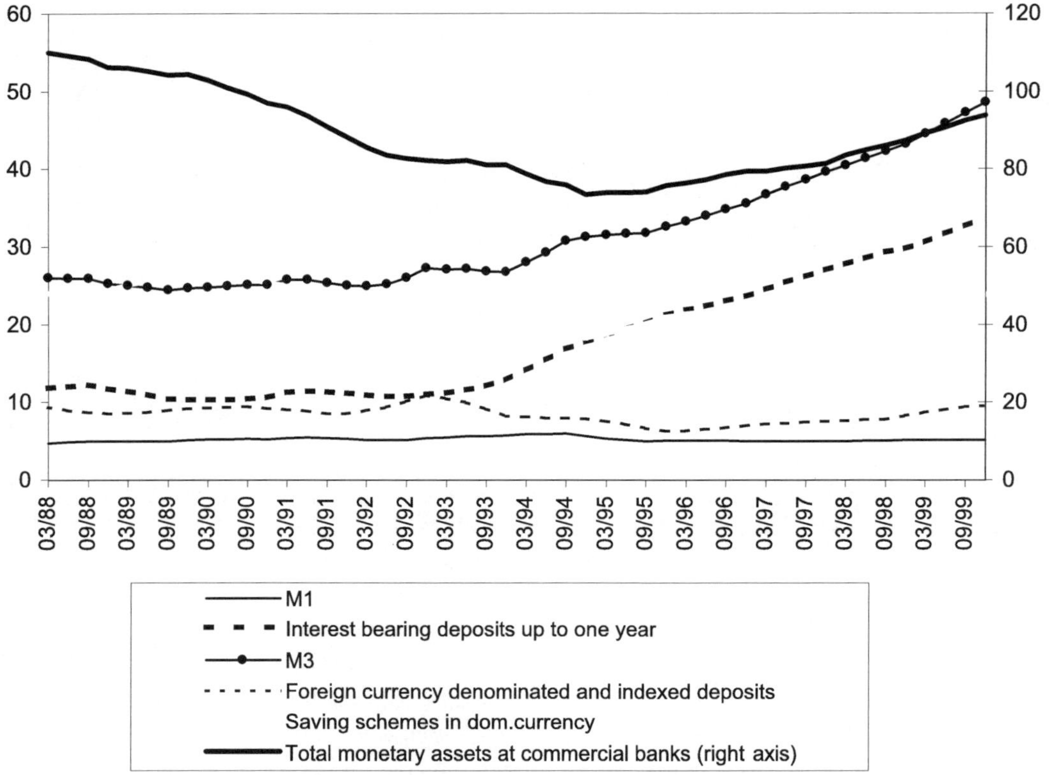

Figure 3.3
The Ratio of Selected Monetary Aggregates to GDP
(Quarterly data, percentage points)

followed by a sharp fall a year later. The wave of public offerings in the middle of a boom in the TASE, the stock index rose by 250 percent between January 1992 and January 1994, bears witness to a bubble in the asset market alongside a monetary expansion. These developments may provide an explanation for the tightening of the monetary policy by the BoI in the second half of 1994, after the inflation rate deviated during the first half of the year from the inflation target set for the first time for that year. After netting out the extreme expansion of bank credit during the last quarter of 1993 it is possible to discern an acceleration in bank-credit expansion between September 1993 and March 1995.

The bank credit expansion was more moderate since 1995 than in the previous subperiods and reflected, mainly, the expansion of the foreign currency denominated

Table 3.10
The Growth of the Monetary Aggregates and Bank Credit (Average annual growth rates during the period in percentage points)*

Period	M_1	Fixed term deposits	Foreign currency denominated and indexed deposits	M_3**	Total bank credit***	Domestic currency denominated credit****	Foreign currency denominated credit
1987–1990	32	27	16	23	25	53	27
1991–1994	19	37	18	28	20	33	28
1995–1998	12	27	18	23	19	22	37

* All percentages have been rounded at the first decimal point.
** M_3 does not include T-bills and deposits related to stock subscriptions. M_3 is equal to: M_1 + Fixed term domestic currency denominated deposits + Foreign currency denominated and indexed deposits. All deposits are for a term up to one year. Source: The Monetary Department, Bank of Israel.
*** The data on total bank credit include directed and earmarked credit but do not include mortgage credit. Source: The Supervisor of the Banks, Bank of Israel.
**** The domestic currency denominated credit includes credit indexed to the CPI. The differentiation between indexed and nonindexed credit in NIS started only from 1990. The foreign currency denominated and indexed credit does not include credit from abroad.

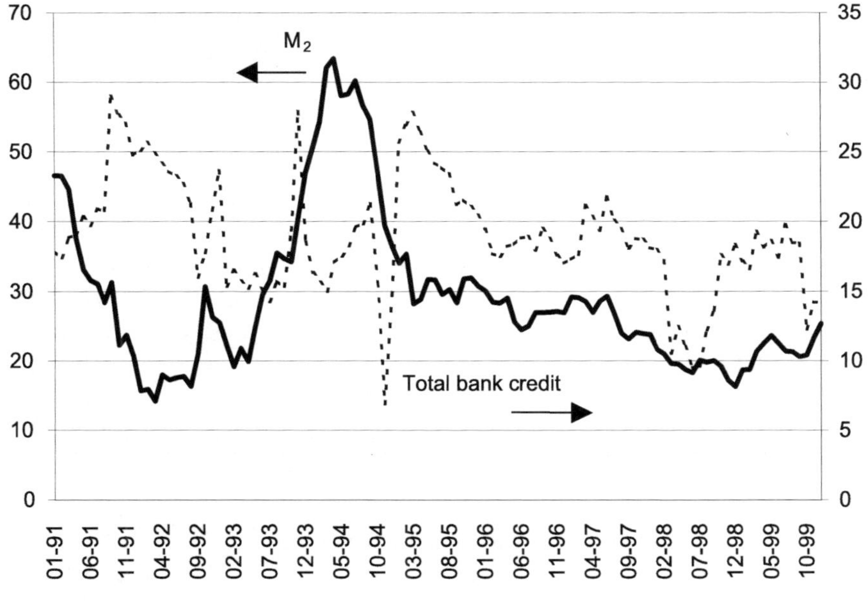

Figure 3.4
The Rate of Growth of M_2 and Bank Credit during the Past Twelve Months (Percentage points)

Table 3.11
The Range of the Rates of Growth of Monetary Aggregates and Bank Credit, 1992–1994 (12-month moving average in percentage points)*

	The maximum rate of growth	The minimum rate of growth
M_1	38 (March 1994)	−3 (November 1994)
Bank credit to the private sector**	29 (September 1994)	7 (November 1994)
Interest-bearing bank deposits		
Up to one week	81 (April 1994)	−14 (December 1994)
One week to three months	122 (September 1994)	−1 (March 1992)
Three months to one year	163 (December 1994)	−5 (February 1993)

* All percentages have been rounded at the first decimal point.
** See footnote 3 to table 3.10.

and indexed credit after the tightening of the monetary policy in the second half of 1994. Still, this expansion seems to have been faster than the rate, which would have been implied by the substitution of bank credit in domestic currency for foreign currency–denominated and indexed credit, leading to a rise in the bank credit-GDP ratio from 65 percent at the end of 1994 to 78 percent at the end of 1998. After 1994, the growth of the liquid monetary aggregates, which are wider than M_1, followed a pattern similar to that of the commercial bank credit. This pattern consisted in a rise of their ratio to GDP in spite of the slowdown in their rate of nominal growth (table 3.10, figure 3.3) relative to the previous subperiod.

The changes in the composition of the liquid monetary assets of the private non-financial sector reflect the effect of the lifting of the restrictions on foreign currency indexed and denominated deposits. These liberalization measures led to the expansion of these deposits between 1990 and 1993 at the expense of the domestic currency denominated deposits. This trend was reversed with the tightening of the monetary policy after 1994. The weight of domestic currency denominated non-indexed deposits up to one year in the total short-term deposits fell from 54 percent at the end of 1990 to 42 percent in the first half of 1993 and rose again after 1994 stabilizing around 70 percent since 1997. The corresponding weights for foreign currency denominated and indexed short-term deposits are 6, 32, and 20 percent. Money balances, M_1, exhibit a gradual falling trend during the period surveyed, reaching some 11 percent of the total liquid monetary assets of the nonbanking private sector in December 1998 as compared to some 26 percent at the end of 1990.

A stabilization has also been observed in the composition of the commercial bank credit since the second half of 1997. In the composition of commercial bank credit, the main change has been the increase in the relative weight of the foreign currency

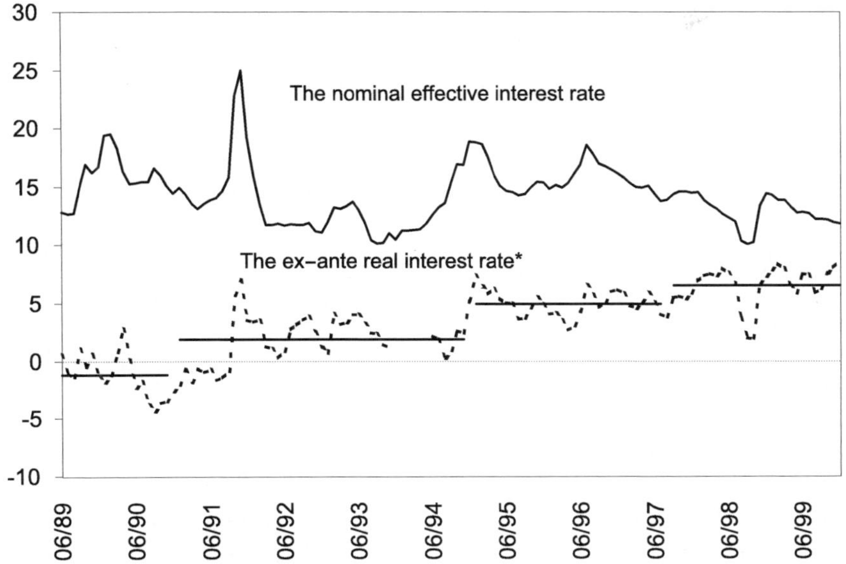

Figure 3.5
The Monthly Interest Rate at the Marginal Discount Window
(Annual rates in percentage points)
* The inflation expectations series is available from June 1989. Between December 1993 and May 1994, the maturity of government bonds did not allow the derivation of these expectations.

denominated and indexed credit following the monetary tightening after 1994. Its weight in total commercial bank credit increased from 18 percent in January 1994 to 32 percent in December1998 at the expense of the nonindexed domestic currency denominated bank credit whose relative weight fell during the same period from 50 percent to 38 percent.

A striking point requiring explanation, is the process of monetary expansion during the period 1992–1994 and the process of liquidization of the public's portfolio, which continued even during the period of monetary tightening. We relegate this discussion to a later section.

The Evolution of the Interest Rates and of the Interest Rate Spreads

The differentiation of the period surveyed into three subperiods also fits the evolution of the real ex-ante interest rate on the monetary loan and bank deposits. These interest rates were negative during the first subperiod, around zero or slightly positive between 1991 and 1994, and strictly positive thereafter (figure 3.5 and table 3.12).

Table 3.12
The Evolution of Selected Real Ex-ante and Ex-post Interest Rates (Period averages in percentage points)

	Overdraft lines of credit		Deposits up to one week		The marginal rate at the discount windows	
Period	Ex-ante	Ex-post	Ex-ante	Ex-post	Ex-ante	Ex-post
1989–1990*	10.9	13.0	−4.2	−3.8	−1.2	−0.7
1991–1994	10.2	8.8	−0.3	−1.3	1.9	0.8
1995–1998	11.1	12.1	3.0	4.0	5.3	6.3

* The data on inflation expectations are available from June 1989.

The real interest rate on the monetary loan reached an average level higher than 5 percent per annum after 1994, the ex-post real rate being even higher.

The nominal interest rate at the discount windows fell substantially between 1987 and 1989 as a result of rapid disinflation. It stabilized around 15 percent per annum until the end of 1991, and was reduced further between 1992 and 1994, following an additional drop in the annual inflation rate (figure 3.6). The monetary tightening after 1994 was reflected in higher nominal and real interest rates on the monetary loan. The former was reduced after 1997, whereas the latter remained still high after that date.[23] The nominal interest rate on short-term bank deposits and on overdraft lines of credit followed a similar path between 1987 and 1998. The rise in the real interest rate on the monetary loan at the discount windows between 1991 and 1994 reflects the fall in the inflation rate beyond the decline of the BoI interest rates. In contrast, the higher real interest rate after 1994 is primarily the result of a higher level of nominal interest rates.

The interest rate spread between debit and credit interest rates, which has been calculated here as the interest rate differential between overdraft lines of credit (*Hahad*) and interest on up to one week deposits (*Pahak*), fell from 50 percentage points in 1987 to 19 percentage points in 1990. This spread continued to narrow until 1994 and stabilized thereafter between 8 and 9 percentage points per annum (figure 3.7a–c).

A simple but crude way of neutralizing the effect of the downward trend of the BoI interest rate on the spread is to calculate the ratio between interest rates on bank credit and bank deposits. Because the BoI interest rate appears in both the numerator and the denominator of the calculated ratio as a product component, the effect of changes in the BoI interest rate may thus be mitigated.[24]

The results of such a calculation indicate that this relative spread exhibits during the period under consideration similar evolution patterns to the traditional interest

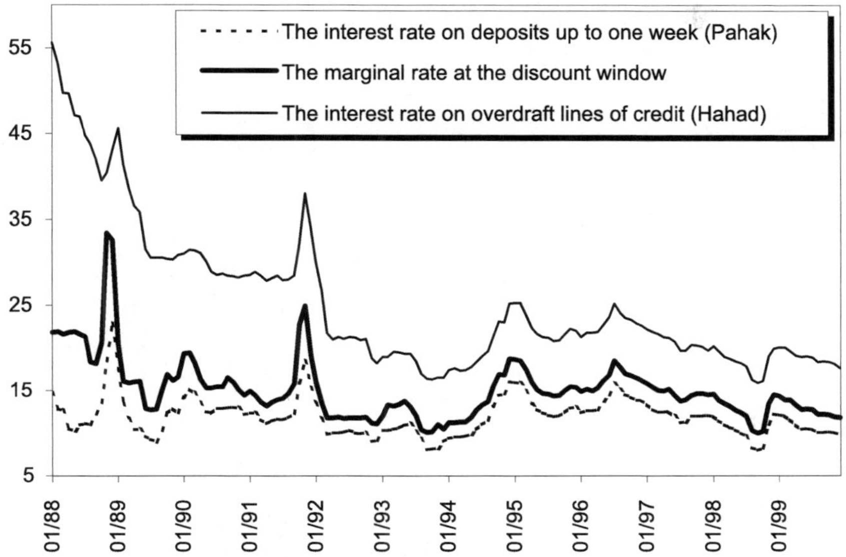

Figure 3.6
Selected Effective Nominal Interest Rates
(Monthly data in percentage points)

rate spread (figure 3.7). It seems, therefore, that the data provide, at first glance, support for the hypothesis that the contraction of the nominal interest rate spread arose not only because of the downtrend of the interest rate on the monetary loan between 1987 and 1994 but also because of additional factors.

We have also calculated separately the debit and credit interest rate spreads as the interest rate differential between the corresponding bank interest rates and the nominal marginal interest rate on the monetary loan. The evolution of these spreads indicates that the contribution of the interest rate on deposits to the narrowing of the spread was restricted mainly to the first subperiod.

The effect of the interest rate on bank credit on the narrowing of the spread continued, however, until the years 1993–1994.

The different patterns exhibited by the interest rates on deposits and bank credit suggest a segmentation between these two markets. This segmentation may explain the simultaneous use of different monetary instruments by the BoI on either sides of the money market, supplying liquidity on the one hand to the banking sector through the monetary loan and absorbing liquidity through open market operations using T-Bills.

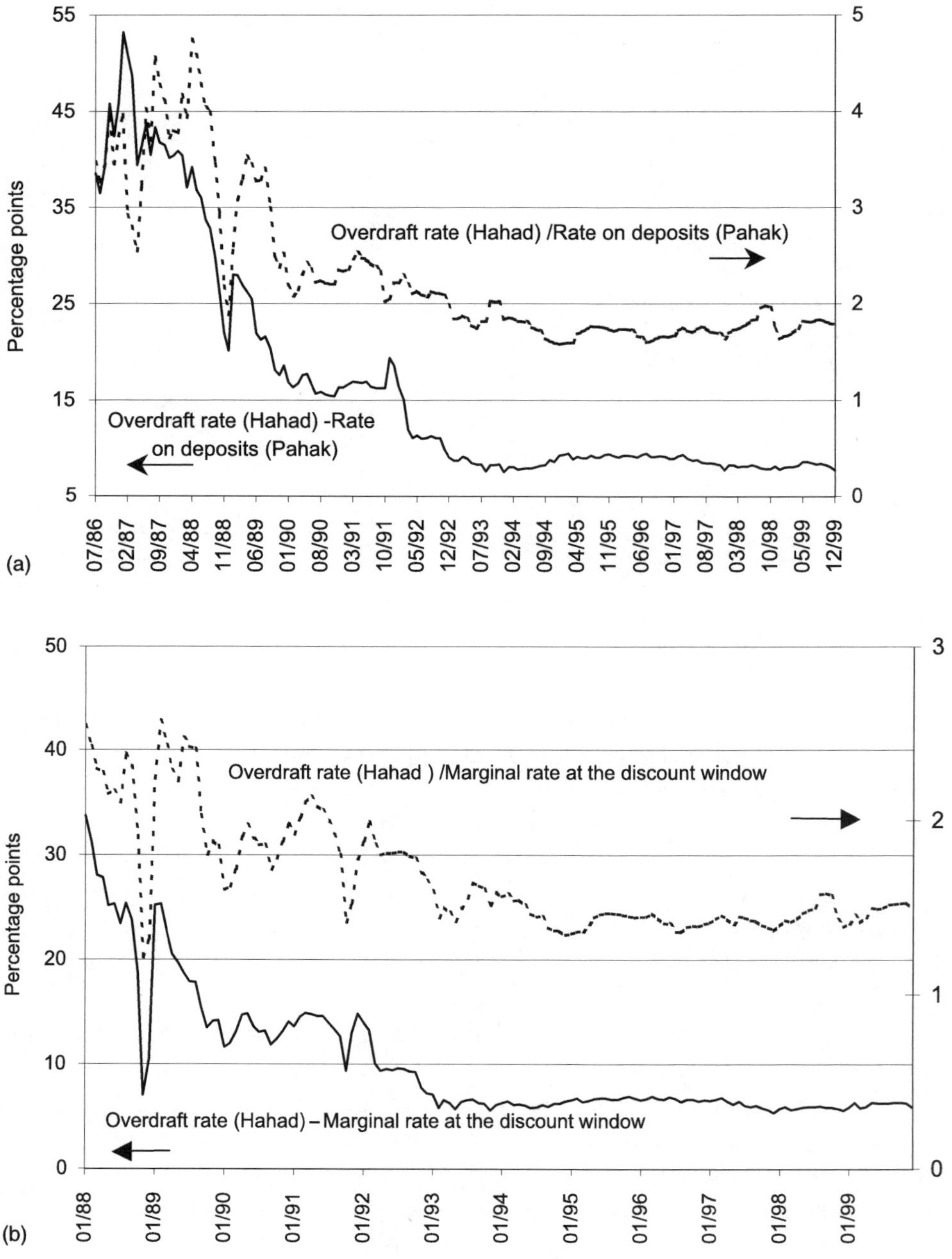

Figure 3.7
(a) The Interest Rate Spread. (b) The Spread between the Overdraft Interest Rate and the Rate at the Discount window
(Monthly data)

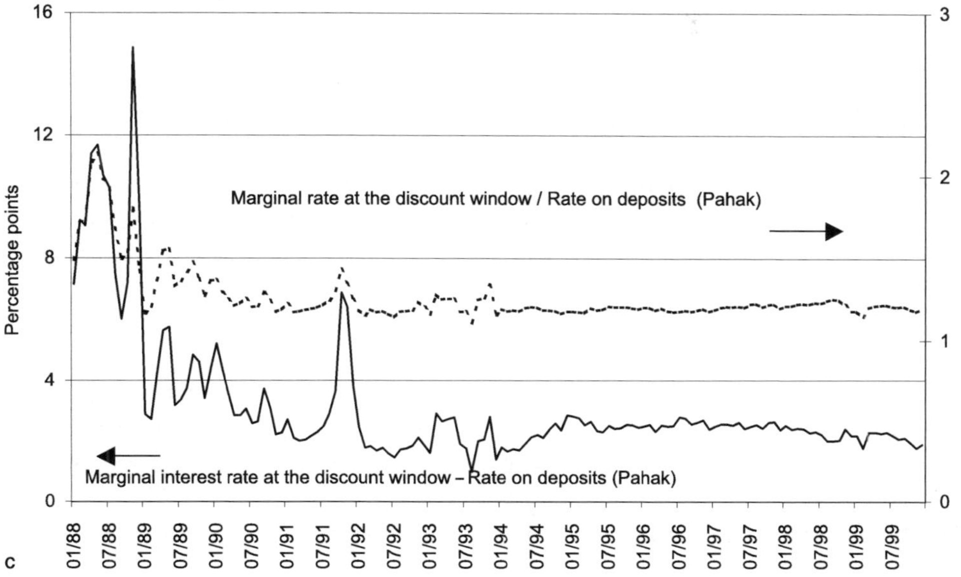

Figure 3.7c
The Spread between the Marginal Rate at the Discount Window and the Rate on Deposits up to One Week
(Monthly data)

Summary and Interpretation of the Data

This section summarizes the picture one gets from the data and presents a hypothesis concerning the factors that gave rise to the observed pattern of evolution of the data. The data indicate that the stock of monetary instruments has been characterized by extreme changes, the BoI turning from a net creditor of the private sector to a net debtor between 1987 and 1998. This change may be attributed to the combination of a tight monetary policy and a policy of sterilized intervention in the foreign exchange market. Although M_1 remained relatively constant, the period surveyed was also characterized by an expansion of the monetary aggregates, which are wider than M_1 and by an endogenous and relatively fast growth of the monetary base, which implies a "liquidization" of the public's portfolio. The growth rate of the monetary base was higher than low one-digit inflation rates, after one accounts for sustainable long-term real GDP rates of growth (between 4 and 5 percent per annum).

The real interest rate on the monetary loan underwent a transition from low and even negative levels to positive interest rates increasing over time (after 1991). This trend was shared by the interest rate on bank deposits.

The narrowing of the interest rate spread between bank interest rates on credit and deposits may be attributed to the decreasing interest rate on the monetary loan and to additional factors as well. As such, factors may be tentatively considered an increasingly competitive pricing of credit and deposits by the banking sector induced by liberalization in the domestic capital market and capital flows.

In view of the far-reaching changes described above, it does not seem appropriate to limit the discussion about monetary policy to the analysis of the evolution of short-term interest rates on the monetary instruments. If the same BoI interest rates give rise to different interest rates on credit and deposits over time, then it is impossible to characterize the monetary policy, ignoring the structural changes in the money markets.

Our interpretation of the facts is based to a large extent on the structure of the banking sector and its evolution, and on the structural arrangements and regulations in the capital markets and in capital flows. Every one of these factors was influenced by the rest, and all together affected the transmission mechanism of the monetary policy and the use of the monetary instruments, thus affecting the evolution of the monetary aggregates as well.

The tightening of monetary policy is generally expected to be reflected in a contraction of the bank reserves, which are held against the reserve requirements on the various bank deposits, the reserve requirements being inversely related to the liquidity of the deposits. This contraction of the reserves is consistent in equilibrium with a shift to interest-bearing deposits with longer maturities and lower reserve requirements. In a growing economy, monetary tightening is not expected to be expressed in a monetary base contraction but rather in a slowdown of its rate of growth.

In contrast to this process, the period surveyed was characterized by a substantial growth of the monetary base after the tightening of the monetary policy, which was even greater than that of money balances, M_1, after 1994.

This relatively high rate of growth of the monetary base implies an expansion of the interest-bearing deposits at a rate higher than the one arising from the parallel slowdown in the expansion of money balances because of the monetary tightening.

The transition of an economy with highly developed indexation arrangements from a high inflation rate to a low two-digit inflation and later on to one-digit inflation and to macroeconomic stability will be sooner or later accompanied by a shift of the public to nonindexed deposits. However this shift in Israel was not limited to a substitution between bank deposits with the same maturity, but entailed also a shift from long term indexed deposits to short-term interest-bearing nonindexed deposits documented in the previous section. An additional factor, which contributed to this liquidization of the public's portfolio, may be traced to the increasing leverage of the nonbanking private sector, expressed in a higher bank credit-GDP ratio over the years.

If such an expansion of the monetary aggregates arises from an increase in their demand because of a fall in inflation, then it does not constitute an inflation threat. This is not necessarily the case, however, if this expansion is due to structural changes in the fundamental financial relations. Under these conditions, the relation between the interest rate on monetary instruments and the market interest rates changes. As a result, the short-term interest rates on the monetary instruments do not constitute a reliable indicator of the liquidity in the money market because over time they affect the market interest rates differently. The narrowing spread between bank interest rates on credit and on deposits arising from these very structural changes may therefore be ignored and automatically accommodated when monetary policy focuses on monetary instrument interest rate smoothing or targeting.

In this context it seems that the narrowing of the spread between interest rates on liquid bank deposits and interest on the monetary loan was reflected in an increased supply of funds to the banking sector. This shift was also supported by the gradual contraction of the government domestic debt-GDP ratio, because of the cut in the government budget deficit. The simultaneous narrowing of the corresponding spread on the debit side led, apparently, to an increase in the demand for bank credit. In other words, an accommodative monetary policy to the aforementioned narrowing of the interest rate spread led to an expansion of the bank credit alongside a shift of the public from financing the government's budget deficit through long-term indexed bonds to supporting the aforementioned expansion of bank credit through short-term non-indexed deposits. The effective restrictions on capital outflows because of the tax discrimination between domestic and foreign financial investments contributed to this liquidity-enhancing process, by preventing the export of capital by households following the liberalization in the Israeli capital market and its subsequent structural change.

A monetary expansion after a liberalization in the capital markets and in capital flows, which is followed by an excessive expansion of bank credit and a rise in asset prices, as it happened in Israel between 1992 and 1993, is a frequent phenomenon in many countries. Such episodes characterized the Japanese economy in the eighties and the Swedish economy in the second half of the same decade and the economies of Southeast Asia in the second half of the nineties. The correction of asset prices involves also sometimes the destabilization of the financial system, which financed this asset price boom through bank credit.[25]

The rapid growth of the monetary base during the period surveyed, and especially its growth after 1994, which was faster than that of M_1, and the dramatic increase of the BoI domestic currency denominated net liabilities may be considered as factors entailing an inflation potential. This potential could be realized following the relaxation of monetary tightening. The fast growth of the interest-bearing deposits instead of M_1 may be considered, therefore, as a deferment of inflation and not as its permanent elimination.

In spite of the considerable spread between interest rates on domestic and foreign currency denominated and indexed credit, the capital inflows fueled by interest rate differentials did not get out of control. This was due, apparently, to a parallel increase in the risk premium, which counterbalanced the interest rate spread. This rise in the risk premium may be attributed to several factors. The most important among them are the rise in the exchange rate depreciation volatility, the risk augmenting higher share of the foreign currency liabilities of the private nonbanking sector in its total liabilities and the increasing uncertainty concerning the ability of the BoI to persist with its sterilized intervention policy if the exchange rate hits again the band's lower bound. The renewal of the policy of sterilized interventions in the foreign exchange market by the BoI is expected to increase the uncertainty in this market, because of the long run unsustainability of such a policy due to its inconsistency with the existing low inflation target. This unsustainability contributes to the creation of expectations of a further widening of the exchange rate band or of an interest rate reduction along the lines imposed by the markets in some European countries in the autumn of 1992.

In spite of the fact that transparency increases in general policy efficiency, a certain ambiguity concerning the intermediate targets of the monetary policy with respect to the evolution of the exchange rate seems to be useful sometimes. In view of the fact that this ambiguity affected mainly the short-term considerations of capital imports, it worked as a stabilizing "Tobin-tax."

3.4 The Bank Interest Rates and the Interest Rate on the Monetary Loan: An Econometric Estimation

In this section, we will document, on the basis of an econometric estimation, the change in the relation between the interest rate on the monetary loan, on the one hand, and the interest rates on bank credit and deposits, on the other. We approach this issue following the conception, which has characterized this paper, namely, that the transmission mechanism of the monetary policy depends on the structure of the capital market in general and of the banking sector in particular.

Our estimation shares characteristics with previous empirical work on the behavior of commercial banks in Israel by Geva et al. (1988), Elkayam (1991), Elias and Samet (1992), Elias (1992), and, more recently, Ribon and Yosha (1998).

Their empirical findings confirm the hypothesis that the spread between the interest rates on bank credit and deposits is an increasing function of the interest rate on the monetary loan. Moreover, according to Elias (1992), until the liberalization in capital markets and capital flows, the interest rate on bank deposits was closer to its perfect competition paradigm than the interest rate on overdraft lines of credit. A similar finding has also been reported by Ribon and Yosha (1998).

We examine here directly the dependence of two bank interest rates, the interest rate on deposits up to six days (*Pahak*) and the interest rate on overdraft lines of credit (*Hahad*) on the marginal interest rate at the discount window and its evolution over time. We have estimated separately the relation between credit and deposit interest rates on the one hand and the marginal interest rate at the discount window on the other. We avoided the direct estimation of the relation between the spread of these two bank interest rates and the interest rate on the monetary loan. The use of the spread would have rendered difficult the identification of different evolution patterns over time between the two aforementioned bank interest rates and the marginal rate at the discount window. We chose short-term bank interest rates for our estimation because the bank credit and deposits over time should also account for the risk of interest rate changes effectuated by the central bank. Because such a premium does not remain necessarily constant over time, our estimation results could have suffered from omitting this unobserved and changing premium over time had we used longer term bank interest rates The estimated regression equations have been specified as follows:

The bank interest rate on overdraft lines of credit (Hahad)

$$i_{Hahad} = A_1 + B_1 * i_{ML} + C_1 * Z_1 + u_t \tag{3.1}$$

The bank interest rate on bank deposits (Pahak)

$$i_{Pahak} = A_2 + B_2 * f(i_{ML}) + C_1 * Z_1 + e_t \tag{3.2}$$

These two equations have been derived from the first-order conditions of a profit-maximizing monopolistic (monopsonistic) bank in the context of a single period model. The variable i_{ML} in the two estimated regression equations measures the marginal effective interest rate on the monetary loan at the discount windows. In the case of interest-bearing deposits, $f(i_{ML})$ is equal to the same marginal interest rate adjusted for the reserve requirement ratio and for the interest rate paid by the BoI on a tranche of these reserve requirements during part of the surveyed period.

The vectors of explanatory variables Z_1 and Z_2 include indicators of economic activity, foreign interest rates, and a proxy for bank commissions. We have also included in this vector the lagged value of the dependent variable in order to account for the gradual adjustment of the bank interest rates to the changes in the interest rate on the monetary loan at the beginning of the period surveyed.

In the context of our single period model the i_{ML} and the $f(i_{ML})$ coefficients in the estimated regressions should converge to unity as a result of the increasing interest rate elasticity of the supply of deposits and of the demand for credit.[26] More precisely, our using the lagged dependent variable as a regressor implies that the aforementioned convergence to unity should refer to the B_1 and B_2 coefficients adjusted so as to account for the lagged dependent variable on the right-hand side of the regression equation.[27]

In turn, the coefficients of the remaining regressors should converge to zero, given that changes in these variables cannot under perfect competition affect the bank interest rates if the supply of liquidity is perfectly elastic within the reserve accounting month, as we have assumed here.

Our estimation of the two regression equations was based on the rolling regression methodology. We used monthly data from January 1988 to December 1998. The sample size of the rolling regressions included twenty-four monthly observations. The estimation was made following the 2SLS procedure.

The estimation results indicate that the pricing of bank deposits was initially (1988–1990) closer to the perfect competition paradigm than the pricing of the overdraft bank credit. Indeed, the coefficient B_2 adjusted for the lagged response of the bank interest rates to changes in the interest rate on the monetary loan was close to unity. The similarly adjusted B_1 coefficient was higher than unity, implying a monopolistic pricing of the overdraft credit. This result may be attributed to the existence of alternative markets to that of domestic currency denominated bank deposits at an earlier stage than that at which similar alternatives existed for bank credit in domestic currency. As relatively close substitutes to short-term interest-bearing deposits, we may consider the T-Bills (Makam). Indeed, the BoI encouraged the public to hold T-Bills during the first years of the surveyed period as substitutes to interest bearing deposits.

The estimation results indicate also that the pricing of bank deposits and overdraft credit underwent two major changes. There was an acceleration in the adjustment of the bank interest rates to changes in the interest rate on the monetary loan. This acceleration was reflected in the convergence of the coefficient of the lagged dependent variable to zero. At the same time, the "unadjusted" B_1 and B_2 coefficients converged gradually to unity (figures 3.8a–b). The convergence was faster for overdraft credit than for deposits, and its timing (1990–1992) coincides with that of the lifting of the major restrictions on foreign currency denominated and indexed credit.[28]

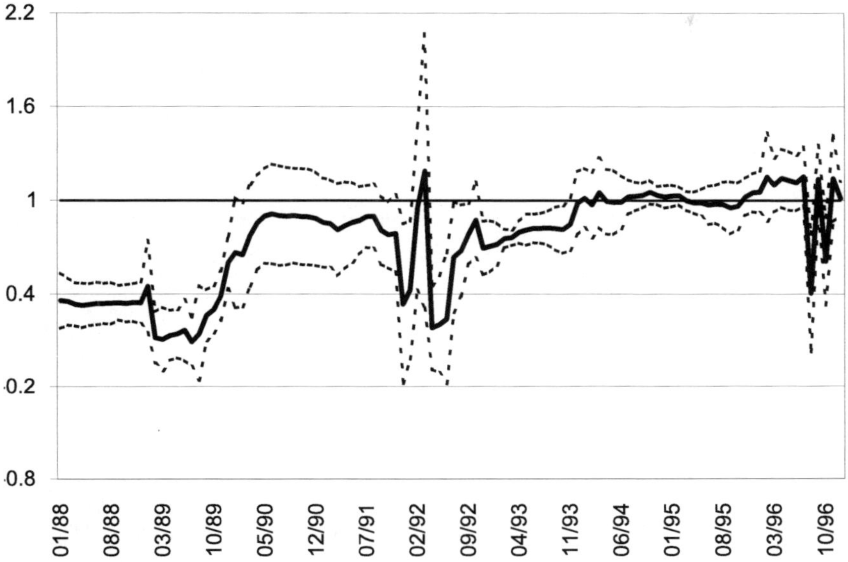

Figure 3.8a
The Estimator of the B_1 Coefficient ± 2 S.E

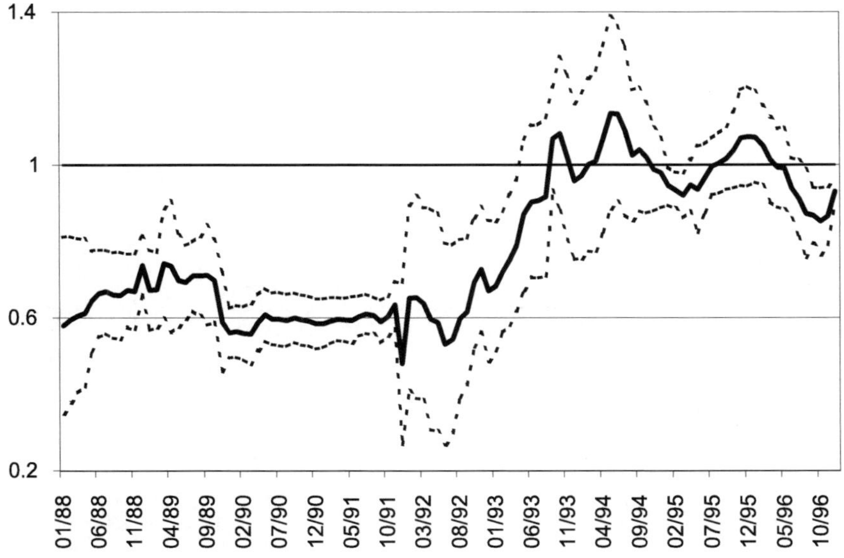

Figure 3.8b
The Estimator of the B_2 Coefficient ± 2 S.E

The estimation results show also that the variance of the estimated coefficients B_1 and B_2 fell substantially after 1993–1994, implying a rising efficiency of the monetary policy in the determination of the short-term interest rates of the banking sector (figure 3.9).

The timing of the fall in the variance of B_1 coincides with the fall in the variance of the interest rate on the monetary loan in the daily auction and in the daily interbank trade for liquidity (Djivre and Tsiddon, 1996). Contrary to the observed convergence of the B_1 and B_2 coefficients to unity over time, their decreasing variance could be considered as an indicator of concerted action by commercial banks casting some doubts over our interpretation of the results as indicating greater interbank competition. This, in spite of the fact that the coefficient of the proxy for bank commissions was not statistically different from zero, a result which could be formally considered as a rejection of the hypothesis of a shift to two-part tariff pricing by commercial banks.

The convergence of the coefficients of the remaining regressors to zero is not complete, and it is impossible to discern in the data a convergence trend.

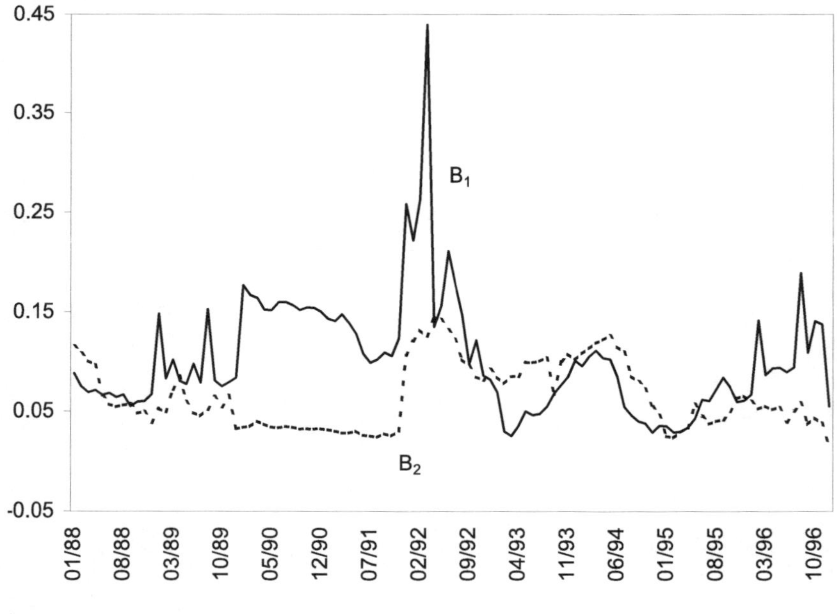

Figure 3.9
The Standard Error of the B_1 and B_2 Estimators

3.5 Summary

This chapter has focused on the conduct of monetary policy and its rationale, and on the coevolution of money markets, monetary policies, and instruments and the exchange rate regime. It is shown that this coevolution was shaped by the gradual liberalization of capital markets and capital flows, as well as by changes in the exchange rate regime.

We show how underdevelopment of the domestic capital market led to the use of the monetary loan as the main monetary instrument, instead of the competition-enhancing open market operations. This choice delayed, in turn, the interbank competition in the allocation of liquidity by the BoI. We proceed to show how the resolution of inconsistencies between the monetary targets and instruments and the exchange rate regime led eventually to an increasing flexibility of the latter as a macroeconomic consistency-inducing mechanism.

We also identify the liberalization process as the major competition-enhancing factor in the financial markets. The development of financial markets and investment opportunities weakened the monopolistic power of the Israeli banking system, allowing the gradual convergence to competitive pricing of bank credit and deposits in spite of the still high concentration of the banking sector. This convergence was reflected in a change in the relation between the bank interest rates and the interest rate targeted by the BoI, and it is corroborated by the results of an econometric estimation. This change implies that the use of the interest rate on the monetary instruments as the unique short-term target of monetary policy during periods of structural changes may lead to the automatic monetary accommodation of the narrowing of the interest rate spread, which usually accompanies the structural change. We attribute partly to such an accommodation the liquidization process of the public's asset portfolio, which was observed during the surveyed period. We consider as additional factors supporting this process the fall in the domestic debt-GDP ratio, the fall in the inflation rate, and the effective restrictions on capital outflows, which limited the change in the public's portfolio composition to domestic assets only.

In spite of the liberalization of capital flows and especially of inflows, the capital imports arising from the tightening of the monetary policy did not get out of control. This may be attributed to, among other things, an increase in the exchange rate depreciation risk and the uncertainty about possible changes in the exchange rate regime or in the monetary policy stance. This higher-risk premium worked as a "Tobin-tax" on short-term capital flows.

During the past decade, the monetary policy in Israel has achieved a very important accomplishment, successful disinflation. Two important policy developments also contributed to this achievement: (a) the introduction of fiscal discipline reflected in the gradual reduction of the government budget deficit, and (b) the independence of the BoI.

Nevertheless, the monetary policy has still left unresolved an important issue. It seems that the liquidization of the public's portfolio and the systematic expansion of the monetary base that accompanied it entail some inflationary potential, which may be realized with the relaxation of monetary tightening. These two factors may constitute the driving force behind a protracted price-level adjustment following the relaxation of monetary tightening. This inflation-inducing mechanism is related to, among other things, the fact that the redemption of the BoI domestic currency debt is backed by money printing in the context of a free float of the exchange rate. It may therefore be desirable to design an alternative mechanism whereby the redemption of this central bank debt and its servicing do not involve money printing by including the fiscal burden of the monetary policy in the budget deficit, which is targeted by the government so as to avoid the consequences of the "unpleasant monetary arithmetic" (Sargent and Wallace 1981).

Measures to bring about a relative contraction of the monetary base and an absorption of the commercial bank deposits at the BoI following the relaxation of the monetary tightening may contribute to future price stability. The gradual lifting of the remaining restrictions on capital outflows and the ensuing change in the composition of the public's wealth may contribute to the mitigation of the potential inflation pressures, if they are followed by liquidity-absorbing sales of foreign currency by the BoI.

Notes

We would like to thank Akiva Offenbacher and Zeev Ziolti of the monetary department of the Bank of Israel for their useful comments. We also thank Alex Dozortsev, Vadim Marmar, and Ron Stern for their excellent research assistance, and assume the responsibility for any mistakes. The views expressed in this paper are those of the authors and do not represent the opinion of their respective institutions.

1. For details concerning the government's involvement in the capital market, see Blum and Piterman (1987) and Yafeh and Yosha (1998).

2. The restrictions on capital flows were temporarily suspended in the context of the failed liberalization of 1977. See Gotlieb and Blecher (in this volume), Bufman and Liederman (1995), and Sussman (1992).

3. The fact that the investment on government bonds sometimes exceeded the investment requirements indicated the severity of underdevelopment of capital markets (table 3.2). According to Blum and Pitterman (1987), the policy of yield smoothing was discontinued earlier, in 1983.

4. This tranche was initially substantial (70 percent of the total reserve requirements on current deposits and higher for fixed-term deposits) and decreased over time until its elimination in October 1991 for current deposits and in December 1994 for fixed term deposits. After December 1994, the reserve requirements on bank deposits was determined on the basis of their time horizon irrespective of indexation.

According to the new regulations, the reserve requirement on deposits up to six days is 6 percent, and from one week to one year, it is 3 percent. On deposits beyond one year, there are no reserve requirements.

5. According to Heth (1991), the number of banking institutions fell drastically over time. In 1990, there were twenty-six banking institutions in Israel compared to fifty-two in 1962. The Herfindal index shows that the Israeli market for deposits and bank credit was consistent with the existence of three banks in these markets. According to Yafeh and Yosha (1998), the situation has not changed much since then. Ribon and Yosha (1998) have found that deposit and credit pricing by Israeli banks has become more competitive over time.

6. The net public offerings of the business sector reached the amount of 3.2 billion NIS in 1992 (3.9 percent of market capitalization) and 7.4 billion in 1993 (4.9 percent of market capitalization) compared to 1 billion in 1991. After a long period of inaction following the collapse of stock prices in 1994, public offerings were renewed only in 1997.

7. These bonds include floating interest rate bonds (Gilon), is set every six months (every quarter for ten-year maturities), and fixed coupon bonds (shahar), the first with maturities up to ten years (in April 1999) and the second up to five years (in August 1998).

8. For details concerning the liberalization of capital flows, see the Bank of Israel Annual Reports and those of the Controller of Foreign Exchange at the BoI between the years 1990 and 1998, and Gotlieb and Blecher (2001), in this book.

9. An investment of one percent out of the portfolio of institutional investors (provident and pension funds and life insurance plans) in foreign markets corresponded to 7.2 percent of the foreign currency reserves of the BoI in 1990, 10 percent in 1992, and 3.4 percent in December 1999.

10. In Israel, the reserve computation period and the reserve maintenance period, the "liquidity month" are identical. The "liquidity month," which since November 1987 constitutes the shortest period of monetary planning, is made up by "liquidity weeks" during which commercial banks can experience, since December 1998, reserve deficits of up to 40 percent of their reserve requirement. Commercial banks, however, have to fulfill on a monthly average their reserve requirements; otherwise, they are supposed to pay high fines in the form of prohibitively high interest rates on their reserve deficits. The identity between reserve maintenance and reserve computation period introduces an element of uncertainty in the management of bank reserves. To mitigate this problem, the banks are allowed to register funds they raise in the interbank market at the previous day's value.

11. For a more detailed description of monetary loans, see Djivre and Tsiddon (1996). A more detailed description of the loan at the discount windows appears in Offenbacher (1988).

12. Since January 1998, the reserve requirements on foreign currency denominated deposits of residents are held in NIS.

13. The *Makam* are zero-coupon government bonds, which are issued solely for the implementation of monetary policy, and they are not used to finance the government budget deficit. Otherwise, a monetary expansion through the use of *Makam* would imply that the BoI finances the government budget deficit through money printing, which is forbidden by law. The interest on the *Makam* is actually paid by the BoI.

14. The monthly average of the maximum cumulative government injection and absorption in 1986 was 11.8 and 14 percent of the monetary base, respectively, and in 1987, it was equal to 10.5 and 13.3 percent, respectively.

15. Prior to the introduction of the deposit auctions, the Boi used a swap facility between NIS and U.S. dollars for sterilization purposes (August 1995). Since August 21, 1997, these swap auctions ceased to be used as an active monetary instrument. Their stock is simply renewed at the level of 1.4 billion dollars.

16. The first two auctions are still held on a weekly basis while the third one is held on a daily basis. The interest rate paid on these deposits by the BoI is floating, and it is adjusted during the term of the deposit if there are changes in the monetary policy during this period.

17. The first basket was instituted on 1.8.1986 and was changed on June 5, 1995, and on April 30, 1996. The basket consists of a fixed number of units of each of its five constituting currencies, the U.S. dollar, the Deutsche mark, the British pound, the French franc, and the Japanese yen.

18. See Djivre (1993) and Hadj Hiye (1993).

19. The first press release by the BoI on monetary policy containing the change in the interest rate was communicated on August 29, 1994.

20. More precisely, the BoI intervened in the foreign exchange market during the following periods—August 1996–October 1996, January 1997–June 1997 and January 1998.

21. We survey here only the main monetary instruments. In addition to these, the BoI used also the aforementioned swap auctions, foreign currency call and put options, swaps between treasury bills and government indexed bonds, the BoI absorbing the indexed bonds, and forward purchase agreements for treasury bills.

22. This credit expansion may be traced to a special arrangement existing at that time in Israel. According to this arrangement, an amount equal to the worth of the stocks ordered in the primary market by each individual investor had to be deposited a day prior to the public offering in a special bank account, allowing the calculation of the rate of monetary expansion net of the stock subscription effect. A similar breakdown does not exist, however, for bank credit. This arrangement was followed in spite of the fact that the deposited amount would constitute ex-post, because of the oversubscriptions, a multiple of the value of the stocks, which were actually allocated to the investors. This arrangement, which was later abolished, created excess demand for bank nonindexed credit on the eve of the public offering.

23. The interest rate used here is the interest rate at the highest discount window (the marginal rate). The monetary loan at the discount windows constitutes the only interest rate available on a monetary instrument during the entire period surveyed, thus allowing the use of a single indicator on whose basis it is possible to characterize the evolution of monetary policy.

24. It is possible to show in the context of a single period model of a profit-maximizing bank that the spread between credit and deposit interest rates is an increasing function of the interest rate targeted or controlled by the central bank. This is true both under perfect competition and monopolistic bank behaviour.

25. See, for instance, Englund (1999) and Ademirguc et al. (1998).

26. Under the assumption that the BoI sets the interest rates on the monetary loan during the surveyed period, the first-order conditions imply that $\mathrm{i}_{\mathrm{ML}} = i^{*}_{Hahad}(1 + 1/\eta)$, where η is the interest rate elasticity of the demand for overdraft credit. In view of the interest rate smoothing policy followed by the BoI before adopting the short-term interest rate, targeting policy, this assumption is not far from reality during this period either. As the interest rate elasticity of the demand for credit increases the "adjusted" B_1 coefficient in the first regression equation converges to unity from above. For similar reasons, the "adjusted" B_2 coefficient converges to unity from below. The coefficients in diagrams 3.8a–3.9 are the "unadjusted" coefficients estimated by the regressions.

27. To simplify the exposition we do not report here the detailed estimation results concerning the regression coefficients of the lagged dependent variables.

28. The dates on the x-axis of diagrams 3.8a and 3.8b indicate the beginning of the sample period, which includes also the twenty-three consecutive months.

References

Ademirguc-Kunt, Asli, and Enrica Detragiache. "Financial Liberalization and Financial Fragility." Working Paper 83, IMF, Washington, D.C., 1998.

Ben-Bassat, Avraham. "The Inflation Target in Israel: Policy and Development." In *Targeting Inflation*, edited by Andrew Haldane. London: Bank of England, 1995.

Ben-Bassat, Avraham. "The Reform in the Capital Market, Targets and Initial Results." *The Bank of Israel Economic Review* 65 (July 1990): 43–57. (Hebrew)

Bertola, Giuseppe, and Ricardo Caballero. "Target Zones and Realignments." *American Economic Review* 82 (June 1992): 520–536.

Blass, Asher, and Richard Grossman. "A Harmful Guarantee?" *International Review of Law and Economics* 16 (December 1996): 461–472.

Blass, Asher, and Oved Yosha. "The Reform in the Israeli Financial System and the Flow of Funds of Publicly Traded Manufacturing Firms" (in this volume)

Blum, Liora, and Silvia Pitterman. "The Government Intervention in the Israeli Capital Market—Survey and Reform Outlines." *The Economic Quarterly* 131 (February 1987): 855–864. (Hebrew)

Bufman, Gill, and Leonardo Leiderman. "Financial Reform in Israel: A Case for Gradualism." In *Financial Opening: Policy Lessons for Korea*, edited by Rudiger Dornbusch and Y. Park. Seoul, Korea Institute of Finance, 1995.

Cukierman, Alex. "The End of High Israeli Inflation: An Experiment in Heterodox Stabilization." In *Inflation Stabilization*, edited by Michael Bruno, Duido Di Tella, Rudiger Dornbusch, and Stanley Fischer. Cambridge: MIT Press, 1988.

Cukierman, Alex, and Meir Sokoler. "Monetary Policy and Institutions in Israel: Past, Present and Future." *The Economic Quarterly* 139 (January 1989): 371–426. (Hebrew)

Djivre, Joseph. "The Exchange Rate Band in Israel and the Bank of Israel Daily Intervention in the Foreign Exchange Market." Unpublished. Jerusalem: Bank of Israel, The Research Department, 1993. (Hebrew)

Djivre, Joseph, and Sigal Ribon. "Monetary Policy, the Output Gap and Inflation—The Case of Israel." Discussion Paper, 00.09. Jerusalem: Bank of Israel, The Research Department, 1999.

Djivre, Joseph, and Daniel Tsiddon. "The Efficiency of the Monetary Auction and of the Monetary Loan at the Discount Window." Discussion Paper 96.07. Jerusalem: Bank of Israel, The Research Department, 1996. (Hebrew)

Elias, Riki. "The Behaviour of the Interest Rate in the Sheqel Non-Indexed Sector." Discussion Paper 92.05. Jerusalem: Bank of Israel, Bank Supervision Department, 1992. (Hebrew)

Elias, Riki, and Tsipi Samet. "The Structure of the Israeli Banking Sector, the Extent of Competition and their Influence on the Interest Rate Spread on the Non-Indexed Sector." Discussion Paper 92.04. Jerusalem: Bank of Israel, Bank Supervision Department, 1992. (Hebrew)

Elkayam, David. "The Influence of the Monetary Policy on the Interest Rate Spread in the Non-Indexed Shekel Sector between 1986 and 1990." Discussion Paper 91.16. Jerusalem: Bank of Israel, Research Department, 1991. (Hebrew)

Englund, Peter. "The Swedish Banking Crisis: Roots and Consequences." *Oxford Review of Economic Policy* 15 (Autumn 1999): 80–97.

Geva, David, Tsipora Samet, and David Ruthenberg. "An Analysis of the Interest Rate Spread in the Shekel Non-Indexed Sector in the Banking System in Israel." *Banking Review* 77 (March 1988): 3–13. (Hebrew)

Gottlieb, Daniel, and Mario Blejer. "Liberalization in the Capital Account of the Balance of Payments." In this volume.

Haj-Yehia, Mohamed S. "The Exchange Rate Policy of the Bank of Israel 1985–1992." Discussion Paper, 93.06. Jerusalem: The Hebrew University, The Maurice Falk Institute, 1993. (Hebrew)

Heth, Meir. "The Banking Sector in Israel: Activity Characteristics and Lessons from Crises." Jerusalem Institute of Israel Research, 1994. (Hebrew)

Krugman, Paul. "A Model of Balance of Payments Crises." *Journal of Money Credit and Banking* 11 (August 1979): 311–325.

Liviatan, Nissan. "Inflation and the Composition of Deficit Finance." In *Global Econometrics*, edited by F. Gerard Adams and Bert G. Hickman. Cambridge, Mass.: MIT Press, 1983.

Offenbacher, Akiva. "Short-Run Monetary Control in Israel." *Bank of Israel Economic Review* 65 (March 1993): 31–65.

Ribon, Sigal, and Oved Yosha. "Financial Liberalization and Competition in Banking: An Empirical Investigation." Discussion Paper 99.05. Jerusalem: Bank of Israel, The Research Department, 1999.

Sargent, Thomas, and Neil Wallace. "Some Unpleasant Monetarist Arithmetic." *Federal Reserve Bank of Minneapolis Quarterly Review* 9, no. 1 (Fall 1981): 1–17.

Sussman, Oren. "Financial Liberalization: The Israeli Experience." *Oxford Economic Papers* 44 (July 1992): 387–402.

Yafeh, Yishay, and Oved Yosha. "Financial Markets Reform. Patterns of Corporate Finance, and the Continued Dominance of Large Banks: Israel, 1985–95." *Economic Systems* 22 (June 1998): 175–199.

4 Disinflation Process in Israel in the Past Decade

Nissan Liviatan and Nathan Sussman

4.1 Introduction

The 1985 stabilization program in Israel was a watershed in the inflation process in this country and is rightfully considered as the most important event in our inflationary history.[1] When inflation was brought down from over 400 percent to around 20 percent in that program, it was not expected that the process of convergence to international levels of inflation would take fifteen years and remain a major problem for macroeconomic policy. The history of inflation in the post-1985 period is not lacking in episodes of decline in inflation, which raised hopes of quicker convergence to European rates, but which turned out to be premature. However, there was one sharp reduction of inflation to a sort of plateau of 10 percent around 1992, which has been the second big event in Israel's inflation history and which has not been reversed. An enigmatic development in the disinflation process took place in the last quarter of 1997 when inflation appeared to have dropped to a plateau of around 5 percent and stayed there for about a year, but then jumped up again as a result of a speculative attack in the foreign exchange market, again leaving observers in doubt as to where we stand in the inflation process. At the time, it was not clear whether this was a shock to the price level or to inflation, but in hindsight, it turned out to be a price shock. We therefore take the view, which we shall elaborate later, that the inflation plateau actually fell at the end of 1997, thus beginning an era of single-digit inflation in Israel.

The stepwise reduction of inflation can be viewed as part of a long-term downward trend. Inflation expectations, as derived from bond market data are around 2 percent for the coming twelve months, and this is no doubt different than the inflation environment of the late eighties. In this paper, we shall analyze the inflation process in the past decade, examining the long-term trend along with medium-term and short-term developments.

Analytically, we can decompose the disinflation process in Israel into three components. First, there is the long-term underlying trend of the reduction of inflation to Organization for Economic Co-operation and Development (OECD) levels, which is not observable in year-to-year developments. Then there are the medium-term developments, which have been characterized by inflation remaining on a sort of plateau[2] or step, of which there have been three since 1985, with one break occurring around 1992 and another at the end of 1997 (figure 4.1). Last, there are the short-term inflation dynamics within each plateau.

Our procedure for analyzing the disinflation process is to examine each of these three components and the interaction between them. In this framework, we have to

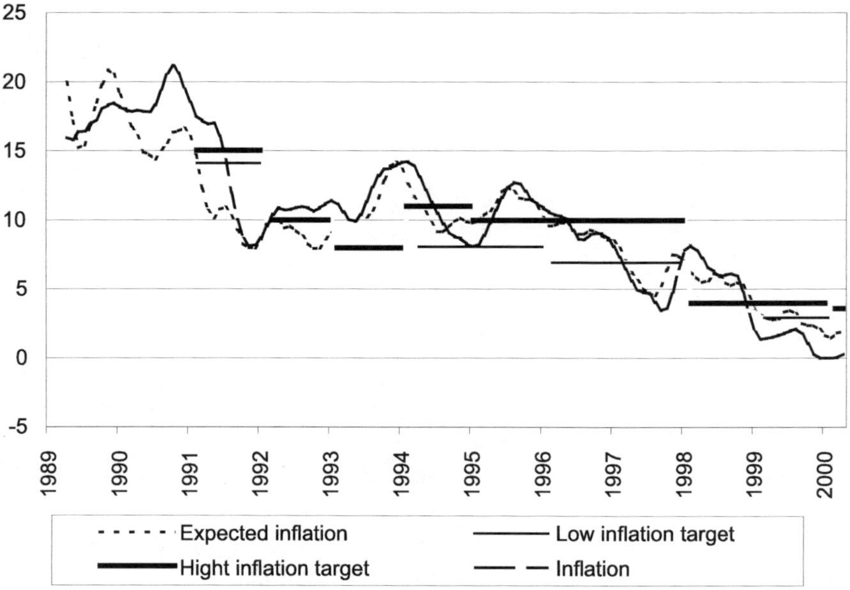

Figure 4.1
Expected Inflation Derived from the Capital Market, Inflation, and Inflation Target

address a number of questions. A key question is why has the disinflation process been so lengthy. Why have other countries in a lower stage of economic development been more successful in reducing inflation than Israel? Is this related to the role of fiscal and monetary policies in affecting the trend as well as the public's reaction to these policies? Has fiscal policy been too lax, or monetary policy too tight, and if so, in what way? What was the role of external shocks on the disinflation dynamics, and how did they interact with the domestic policies? Finally, what are the implications of the history of the past decade for future policies? Clearly, for most of these questions there is no clear-cut answer. In these cases, we shall attempt to state a balanced view of the considerations involved.

4.2 The Declining Long-Term Trend

Fiscal Discipline

The drastic reduction of the fiscal deficit so as to stop the increase in the public debt was the cornerstone of the 1985 stabilization program, and adherence to this com-

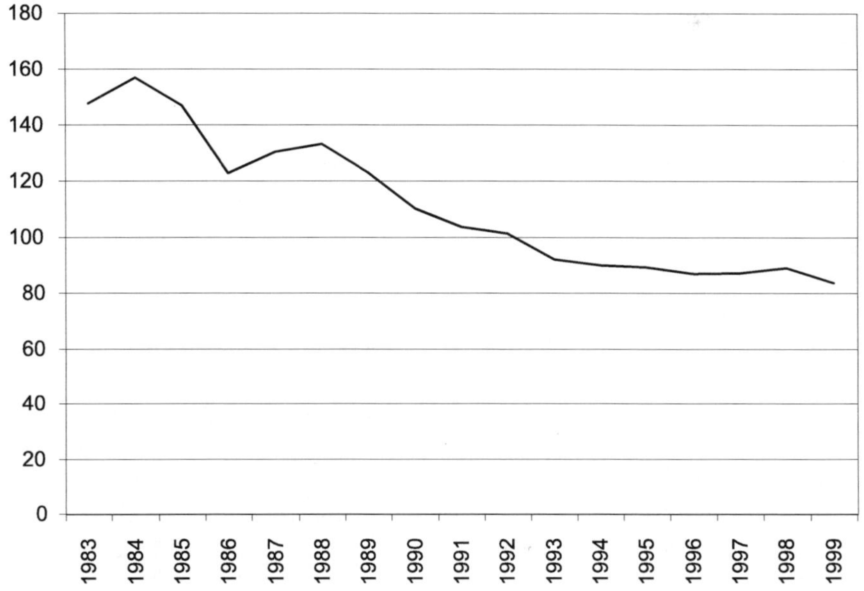

Figure 4.2
Ratio of Public Debt to GDP

mitment over the years, with some inevitable deviations, continued to be the cornerstone of the long-term reduction in inflation. Indeed, the ratio of public debt to GDP continued to decline as a result of low fiscal deficits and the secular growth of the economy. The behavior of this ratio is perhaps the clearest indication of the change that has taken place in the macroeconomic environment as a result of the 1985 stabilization (figure 4.2).

This commitment has been put to the test a number of times and has proved to be robust. When the absorption of the immigration wave from the former Soviet Union in the early nineties required an increase in the fiscal deficit, the government initiated a law of reduction of the deficit over time in order to signal that the increase in the deficit was a temporary phenomenon. When the deficit deviated from the law in 1994–1995, the correction came very soon with the change of government in 1996. An additional test came with the recession that developed in the economy during the middle of the latter year. The issue was whether the concept of the deficit for the purpose of the law should be modified to mean a "structural (cycle-adjusted) deficit" so as to let the automatic stabilizers mitigate the effects of recession. In spite of sensible economic arguments in favor of the latter modification, the argument for preserving credibility won the day, and the deficit target continues to be stated in terms of the actual deficit.

Nominal Anchors

The 1985 stabilization embraced the principle that disinflation must be based both on fiscal discipline and a nominal anchor; that is, fiscal policy alone is not capable of anchoring inflation, at least not in the medium term. This principle has been maintained throughout the disinflation process although the actual nominal anchors have changed over time. Initially, the program was based on a peg of the exchange rate to the U.S. dollar, then to a basket of currencies. The peg to the exchange rate was made flexible in 1989 with the introduction of an exchange rate band that widened over time, and in 1991 the Bank of Israel introduced the sliding exchange rate band. A basic change with regard to the nominal anchor took place in the early nineties when the Bank of Israel adopted a regime of inflation target (following a similar trend in some other countries) without abolishing the exchange rate band—a move that caused some inconsistencies. In general, the inflation target followed a declining path that was supposed to reflect a consensus between the Bank of Israel and the Treasury about the path of the nominal variables. It appears that the constant attention to the nominal anchors in their different forms played an important role in preserving the long-term decline of inflation. In this respect, the Bank of Israel played a major role in putting disinflation at the top of its priorities, and pursuing this issue relentlessly in spite of continued opposition within and outside the government. This attitude of the Bank brought about, over time, not only a revision of the government's view on the issue of disinflation, but also that of the public at large, so that at present, price stability has become a political asset.

The Decline in World Inflation

The past decade witnessed a reduction of inflation both in the industrial countries but also in the traditional inflationary economies of the developing world, especially those of Latin America (the so-called chronic inflation economies of which Israel was part). The tendency to converge to the low-inflation standards of the OECD[3] was not only because of the recognition of the benefits of low inflation, but mainly because of the acceptance of the economic model of the industrial countries as the superior development model (the change of conception was strongly influenced by the debt crisis of the eighties and the collapse of the centrally planned economies). Thus, low inflation became part of accepting a package deal, which included many market-oriented reforms, a process that has been supported by the international organizations such as the International Monetary Fund (IMF) and the World Bank. This change of attitude toward world inflation strongly influenced policymakers and public opinion in Israel, especially because deviations from the world trend tended to become more costly in terms of the rating of the economy for foreign investors and in terms of trade transactions.

Why Has Disinflation Been So Slow?

This is the natural question to ask in light of the above characterization of the process. We may add to the foregoing comments the fact that Israel's inflation was an outlier compared with other countries in its category of income per capita, which can certainly be viewed as a deficiency in policies or in the underlying social structure.

We may suggest a number of factors that may have some bearing on this question. One reason could be the fact that although fiscal discipline has been fairly satisfactory in terms of the public-sector deficit, it has not been accompanied by fundamental fiscal reforms and massive privatizations such as in Argentina. The process of establishing credibility in fiscal conservatism has taken place through an effort of persisting with low deficits and dealing with deviations by various ad hoc measures. But we must note that the size of the public sector as measured by the ratio of expenditures to GDP stopped declining since the early nineties, which undermines the credibility of persistence with low fiscal deficits.

Recent literature stresses the view that in order for the fiscal adjustment to be effective, it is not enough to manage the fiscal deficit; one should also ensure that we have a proper "fiscal consolidation" that is based on a cut in permanent expenditure items in the budget (such as wages and transfer payments) and not on a reduction in public investment in infrastructure or on an increase in the rate of taxation. This is relevant not only for attaining the growth potential but also to the disinflation process, because it enhances the credibility in the sustainability of low fiscal deficits (this is over and above its indirect contribution to disinflation via growth, according to the inflation tax model).

In Israel, the main source of fiscal consolidation has been the cut in subsidies in the early stage of the 1985 stabilization and the secular decrease in expenditures on defense (from over 20 percent of GDP in 1985 to around 10 percent in 1998). However, the latter process was exhausted around 1994, and along with it, the reduction of the share of public expenditure in GDP came to a stop and the weight of taxes has even increased in recent years. One may assume that the lack of progress in the process of fiscal consolidation has been one of the factors that slowed down the course of disinflation.

Another reason for the slow disinflation is related to the fact that traditionally, the importance of further disinflation and its pace, following the sharp drop of inflation in 1985, was subject to debate, which is not very surprising given that the basic indexation mechanisms in the economy survived the 1985 stabilization. This was especially the case in the mid-90s when the basic inflation plateau dropped to around 10 percent, and particularly when it entered the single-digit range. After all, there is no consensus amongst economists about the payoff of reducing inflation in the single-digit range (for example from 8 percent to 4 percent) whereas the costs may be considerable. This led to a series of open disagreements between the more aggressive disinflation stance of the Bank of Israel vis-à-vis the Treasury.

As a result, the Bank of Israel was constrained in implementing persistent tough monetary policies. Until recently, whenever tougher monetary policy encountered difficulties in the form of recession or appreciation, it tended to retreat to some compromise. Thus, in the early stages following the 1985 stabilization, the government implemented a full peg to the U.S. dollar and then to a basket of currencies, but the recession that became evident in 1988 along with an appreciation led to a flexibilization of the exchange rate regime. The new exchange rate regime included an adjustable exchange rate band, which turned in 1991 into a sliding one. The upward slope of the mean value of the band in effect acknowledged the existence of a fairly high level of basic inflation.

Later, within the framework of the inflation target regime, one may observe a very gradual approach in setting the parameters of the target, with the exception of the target set in 1998. Monetary policy has been quite aggressive in dealing with upward deviations from the target, but as shown in figure 4.3, tended to compromise after some time. In this figure, we see how the real interest rate on the monetary loan was increased sharply at the end of 1994 and in early 1996 (in response to surges in inflation), but then, following a favorable response of inflation, the tight interest rate policy was relaxed. Only in 1999 and 2000 did the Bank of Israel maintain high real interest rates in the face of a decline in inflation. Thus, for almost the entire nineties, the nominal anchors in their various forms did not signal an uncompromising attitude to disinflation.

In this respect, Israel differs from the southern members of the European Community who were more successful in reducing inflation in the nineties in the single-digit range and at a lower cost in terms of recession. The relative success of the latter economies can be explained by their strong motivation to fulfill the requirements of the Maastricht convergence criteria in order to reap numerous benefits from joining the European Monetary Union (EMU). They could then take full advantage of these side benefits to reduce inflation at relatively low cost, which they could not do when

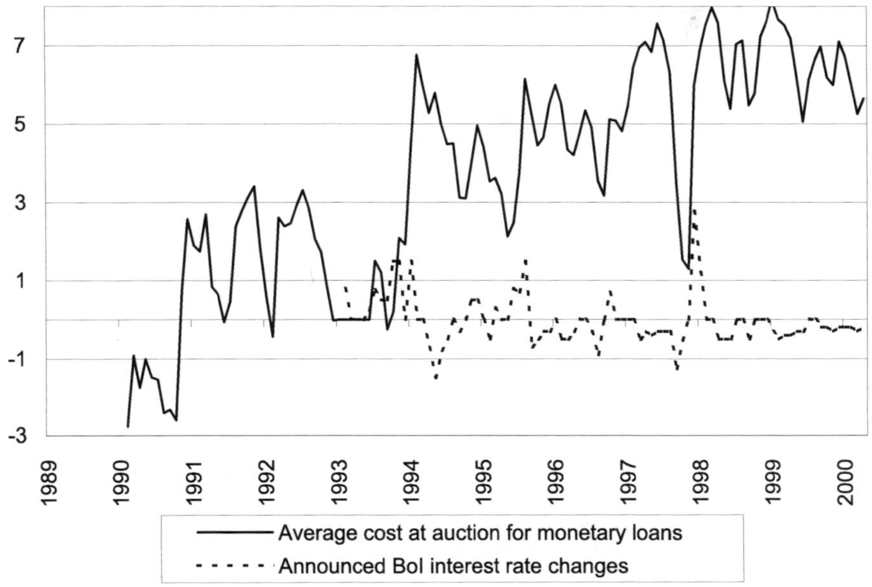

Figure 4.3
Real Interest Rate

the issue was confined to disinflation as such. A recent study[4] of the disinflation in Spain shows clearly that the "sacrifice ratio" of disinflation decreased drastically when the policy was carried out in the context of the strategy of joining the EMU, with a similar effect of the "credibility shock" in Portugal and Italy. Israel has been attempting to behave as if it, too, had the above payoffs whereas, in fact, it is not clear at all whether the comparison is relevant.

4.3 Medium-Term Dynamics (the Inflation Steps)

The economic analysis of the shift from higher to lower inflation steps is a fundamental aspect of the process of disinflation in Israel. However, before we go into this, it is important to provide statistical support for this step-function process. We follow and extend the statistical principles of Liviatan and Melnick (1998), focusing on the 1992 step, given that from a statistical standpoint, the recent 1997 step is too short to show up clearly in the formal analysis, although it is extremely important to analyze it from the economic perspective, as we shall do later.

Table 4.1
Stochastic Properties of Nominal Variables: 1987–1997

Variable	Inflation	Inflation	Inflation ex. housing and fruits	Monetary anchor	Imported inflation	Nominal wage	Nominal wage
Sample	1987–1997	1989–1997	1989–1997	1987–1997	1987–1997	1987–1997	1989–1997
Assumption	Trend	Trend	Trend	Trend	Trend	Intercept	Trend
ADF statistic	−3.25	−3.96	−4.39	−5.76	−6.86	−5.45	−8.96
1% significance	−5.11	−5.48	−5.48	−5.27	−5.11	−4.33	−5.48
5% significance	−3.93	−4.08	−4.08	−3.44	−3.41	−2.76	−4.98

A Quantitative Analysis of the Inflation Steps

As a preliminary observation, we note that the series of inflation has not followed the same statistical pattern as the nominal anchors, which are closely connected with it in the long run. To show this, we conducted an Augmented Dickey-Fuller unit root test, using annual data, to examine the stochastic properties of the series.

We find (table 4.1) that the inflation-rate series for the entire sample (1987–1997) has a unit root that is different from the stochastic properties of the nominal anchors. In particular, the nominal anchors are trend stationary—are stationary around a declining trend. The finding of stationarity in the "policy" variables is expected. It is the finding of a unit root in the inflation series that merits closer examination, as it indicates that inflation is perhaps governed by a different process.[5] Thus, an explanation of the inflation process necessarily requires the inclusion of additional (real or break) variables that explain the apparent persistence of inflation in the medium run at a given plateau in face of the declining trends in its nominal anchors.

The finding of a unit-root process for inflation in the annual data lends support to the "steps" theory of inflation (Liviatan and Melnick, 1998), which we discuss below. A formal approach to testing the "step" hypothesis is by conducting an endogenous break test (Perron, 1989)

$$Y_t = \beta_0 + \beta_1 Y_{t-1} + \beta_2 \text{TREND} + \beta_3 D_{long} + \beta_4 D_{pulse} + \sum_{i=1}^{k} \beta_{i+4} \Delta Y_{t-i}$$

where D_{long} is a dummy variable that takes the value zero at all times prior to time t and the value one from that time onwards, and D_{pulse} is a dummy variable that takes the value one at time t and zero at all other times.[6] This test is performed iteratively on all the data points in the series where the dummy variables are moved forward one observation at a time. The most significant break is selected, and then the test is performed on the remaining observations until a second break is found and so forth. The break test was estimated with annual data.

The table shows that inflation had a significant break in 1991 or 1992, depending on the definition of inflation employed. The finding of a break captured by the long dummy is consistent with the finding of stationarity after allowing for the break in the level of inflation. This finding lends support to the "step" hypothesis.[7] The wage anchor had a break very early on in the sample, which is related to the 1988 recession and to the gradual response of the real wage to the immigration wave that started in 1990. The monetary anchor and the imported inflation anchor did not exhibit any significant break during the period. Taken together, the results confirm the hypothesis that the stochastic properties of the inflation rate as well as its break cannot be explained by similar properties of the nominal anchors' series and suggests that other factors to be discussed later played a significant role in generating this step process.

We have carried out a similar statistical analysis, which is reported in an earlier version of this paper, using monthly data. This analysis confirms the basic features of the annual study and brings out some new features. Thus, the 1992 break in inflation was preceded by a break in inflation expectations as derived from the bond market, and the same is true of nominal wage inflation. Thus, inflation exhibited some rigidity, which had to be broken by some special developments about which we shall speculate shortly.

The First Inflation Step (1985–1991)

Following the big step-reduction in inflation in 1985, inflation landed on a step of about 18 percent to 20 percent annually. Inflation seemed to have a life of its own as it was not affected by the periods in which the exchange rate was fully pegged. A possible explanation for this step is that the big payoff for policymakers is in the reduction of inflation from extreme rates, and there is not much that can be gained from a reduction from moderate to low inflation rates. Because this is realized by the public, it can form a basis for an equilibrium in the framework of a policy game.

Most of the energies in this period were devoted to consolidating the big cut in the fiscal deficit and keeping inflation from flaring up again. The 1988–1989 recession was one of the consequences of the efforts to keep inflation down by using the exchange rate anchor as a disinflation instrument. However, the government's readiness to bear this cost and its determination not to bail out firms in financial distress signaled a change in the rules of the game and helped to exit the period of price controls without reigniting inflation.

The 1992 Break

The break to a lower plateau of about 10 percent took place around 1992. In line with our earlier, more formal analysis, both inflation and inflation-expectations dropped to around 9 percent in that year. Similarly, interest on short-term loans dropped sharply in that year. Inflation continued around this level, with ups and downs, for approximately another six years. It is important to note that this step-reduction in inflation (unlike the 1985 step) was not the result of any conscious effort by the government; that is, the reduction was not associated with any specific stabilization program. It should be acknowledged that at the current state of research, it is not possible to explain fully the turning point of 1992 by a single approach. Accordingly, we shall address the issue from some alternative points of view.

The Immigration Shock One prevalent approach maintains that the main shock was the surge of massive immigration from the former Soviet Union in 1990, which led not only to a reduction in real wages through unemployment, but also to a flexibilization of labor market rigidities and the weakening of the powerful nationwide trade union organization (the Histadrut). The immigration shock affected the disinflation process through additional indirect channels. Thus, the law of the gradual reduction of the fiscal deficit, which is considered an important contribution to the reduction of long-term inflationary expectations, was indirectly related to the immigration wave because it was intended to signal that the increase in the deficit, which was related to the absorption of the immigrants, was of a temporary nature. One should also note the role played by U.S. guarantees for international borrowing in connection with the absorption of the immigrants, which facilitated disinflation by stabilizing the external position of the economy.

The view that it was the supply shock of the immigration wave that was the main trigger for the reduction of inflation is supported by our earlier analysis and by the decline in the rate of growth of nominal wages in the business sector. This decline started with the beginning of the surge of immigration in 1990 and continued till inflation stabilized on the lower plateau.

The Phillips Curve A related approach, by Lavi and Sussman (1999), which focuses on the labor market and monetary policy, uses a dynamic simulation of the Taylor (1994) model (to be explained more fully later) that succeeds in capturing the 1992 break with remarkable success. The variables that are used in this model to explain the path of inflation are the lagged values of the real ex-post interest rate (on loans), unemployment, and immigration into the country.[8] Thus, this model suggests that the main players in the 1992 break were the developments in the labor market (indirectly related to the immigration wave) and the conservative monetary policy of the Bank of Israel, as well as the decline in the demand stimulus of immigration which took place at that period.

The Fiscal Impulse Yet another approach by Dahan and Strawczynski (1997) stresses the role of the fiscal factor in the 1992 break by applying a version of the Alesina-Perotti (1996a, 1996b) model of fiscal consolidation. According to this view, a continued negative fiscal impulse (properly defined) is likely to cause a reduction in the inflation trend on a long-term basis. In their application of this procedure, the authors estimate and subtract the direct public expenditures related to the absorption of the immigrants, assuming that these should be considered as temporary (and thus are irrelevant for the "continued" fiscal impulse). According to the stated criterion, the authors find that 1991 qualifies as a break in the inflation series. In spite of the possible bias that may result from the above adjustment in public expenditures, we view this finding as lending more support for the importance of the fiscal factor in the step decline of inflation of 1991–1992.

Tight Money We should note that monetary policy played a supporting role in this process. Because the pace of the reduction of the Bank of Israel's interest rate on its monetary loan was slower than the pace of disinflation, we witnessed an increase in the real interest rate. In addition, there was a sharp temporary increase in the Bank's interest rate in late 1991 to fight off a speculative attack against the currency. Thus, Bufman and Leiderman (1998) stress the role of monetary policy that brought about a change in real interest rates from negative to positive levels in causing the 1992 step.

Multiple Equilibria and the Critical Mass Approach The above descriptions still leave open the question of why the reduction of inflation took the form of a step reduction rather than a more gradual path along with the path of the nominal wage rate. The view taken in Liviatan and Melnick (1998) is one of a multiple equilibrium situation in which a sufficiently strong shock can change the basic inflation plateau. A similar approach is taken by Bufman and Leiderman (1998). Toward 1992, there was an accumulation of changes all of which worked in favor of a reduction of inflation—the fall in wages, increase in unemployment, initiation of the law of the reduction in the fiscal deficit, U.S. loan guarantees, introduction of the sliding exchange rate band, slow reduction in the Bank of Israel's interest rate, and drop in import prices in 1991. It appears that the weight of all these factors was sufficient to move the basic inflation level to a new lower position. We shall refer to this interpretation as the "critical mass approach."

Table 4.2
Results of Endogenous Break Tests on Nominal Variables

Variable	Inflation	Inflation ex. housing and fruits	Monetary anchor	Imported inflation	Nominal wage
Break date	1991	1992	None	None	1988
Break type	$\beta_3 < 0$	$\beta_3 < 0$			$\beta_3 < 0$
Significance (t-value)	−3.77*	−4.04			−4.62
Stationarity	Yes	Yes			Yes
Trend	No	No			Yes

* Excluding the trend variable. The t-statistic with trend is −1.76.

The 1997 Step Reduction

It seems that another step reduction in inflation took place toward the end of 1997, when inflation dropped unexpectedly to around 5 percent and stayed at about that rate for a whole year. The fact that inflation and expected inflation fell dramatically below the lower limit of the inflation target range (figure 4.1) took everyone, including the Bank of Israel, by surprise. Accordingly, the government's inflation target was reduced from the range of 7 percent to 10 percent in 1998 to 4 percent for 1999, which looked as an attainable objective without the need to tighten further the monetary policy stance.

Again a Critical Mass of Factors There were several reasons that led to the view that the sharp reduction of inflation in the end of 1997 marked another step reduction of inflation with long-term implications, similar to the one observed in 1992. One of the main reasons for this growing conviction came from the fiscal side; for the first time in recent years, the new finance minister, Yaakov Ne'eman, endorsed the strategy of the tight monetary policy pursued by the Bank of Israel under the leadership of Jacob A. Frenkel. Even as recession intensified, the Treasury maintained fiscal discipline. (Recall that in the 1992 step, the fiscal stance was strengthened by the passing of the law of deficit reduction). Second, the disinflation process received a boost from the decrease in import prices (recall that a similar phenomenon occurred prior to the 1992 step). Third, the slope of the floor of the exchange rate band (the appreciated part) was reduced from 4 percent to 2 percent annually; because the exchange rate was very near the floor, this enabled a faster disinflation potentially (recall that the introduction of a sliding band in December 1991 had a similar effect). Fourth, most econometric models, except that of Lavi and Sussman (1999), to which we shall return later, failed to capture the drop in inflation in that episode, which underscores the discontinuous shift. Fifth, the period preceding the drop of inflation

Table 4.3
Contribution of Real and Nominal Values to the Disinflation of 1995

	Average levels over period				
	Inflation	Predicted inflation	Percent explained	Unemployment	Real interest rate
1991:4–1993:3	12.4%	11.6%	93%	10.9%	2.9%
1996:4–1998:3	7.5%	7.7%	103%	7.1%	3.0%
	Contribution to change in inflation				
	Constant	Change in Unemployment	Change in real interest rate	Change in Immigration	
1991:4–1993:3	50%	24%	1%	26%	
1996:4–1998:3	40%	30%	28%	1%	

Based on quarterly data using the following reduced form of Taylor's model: $\Delta(\text{inflation}) = -0.0055500265 - 1.905994{*}\Delta(\text{unemployment}(-2)) - 0.50290134{*}\Delta(\text{Real interest rate } (-1)) + 1.7342257{*}\Delta(\text{immigration}(-1))$.

in the recent step was characterized by a significant increase in the number of foreign workers in Israel, which had some similar effects on the flexibilization of the labor market as in the big immigration wave of the early nineties, which exerted a fundamental effect on disinflation in that period. Finally, we note that world inflation decreased in the nineties, and this trend should at some point spill over to Israel as well. Thus, it appears that the sharp reduction in inflation at the end of 1997 had many common elements with the 1992 step, and is consistent with the "critical mass approach" that we mentioned in connection with the latter step.

In table 4.3, we provide a summary of the relative importance of the factors that affected the two inflation steps according to the Lavi and Sussman (1999) approach, which is based on the rates of change of the variables. We average these rates of change over a two-year period that centers on the break quarter. It can be seen that the constant term (which in terms of a difference equation measures the trend in the levels) captures close to one half of the change. In spite of this, it shows clearly that the role of the real interest rate increased impressively in the second break, while the important role of unemployment remained rather similar, and the immigration factor practically disappeared.

The Setback: A Price Shock or an Inflation Shock? In the event, the apparent step reduction received a setback, at least temporarily, by a devaluation caused by a shock of speculative demand for foreign exchange in October 1998, following the crisis in Russia and the sharp reduction of the Bank of Israel's interest rate, which raised the CPI inflation for 1998 to 8.6 percent. The Bank of Israel countered this shock with a hike of interest rates (of four percentage points) without intervening in the foreign exchange market. This pacified the assets markets and stabilized them. Thus, inflation expectations for the coming year (measured on the basis of capital market data) dropped from 8 percent in September 1998 to 2 percent today and various forecasts made by private sources estimate the coming twelve-months inflation in the range of 2 percent. These figures suggest that the basic inflation rate has indeed fallen. This is of course not independent of the public's perception that the Bank of Israel will not relax its tough stand on inflation. One may infer from the reaction of the capital market and the public that indeed the basic inflation rate has fallen.

The question of whether there was a step reduction of inflation of a more permanent nature at the end of 1997 is critical for the assessment of the long-term inflationary trend in Israel. Therefore, we will devote further analysis to this issue, in spite of the speculative nature of some of our remarks (which cannot be avoided in view of the short time span in question).

The very fact that the Bank of Israel succeeded in stabilizing the shock of the October 1998 devaluation with a relatively small increase in the interest rate is an indication that the basic financial environment is stable and amenable to monetary policy. It is instructive, in this context, to note the various economic arguments (as, for example, in Furman and Stiglitz, 1998) that try to explain why raising the interest rate may be counterproductive in stabilizing the exchange rate in a crisis situation (for example, the rise in interest rates may increase the risks of bankrupcy, which will entail bailouts and put strains on the exchange rate). This evidently did not happen in Israel. On the research level, the application of the "continuous fiscal impulse" approach of Dahan and Strawczynski indicates that the tight fiscal policy in 1997 qualified this year as being potentially a turning point in the inflation path.

There are, however, some considerations that mitigate the above optimism. We must first mention the fact that the stepped up disinflation has taken place in an environment of growing unemployment. It is argued that this movement along the Phillips curve may be reversed when the economy returns to more normal conditions. Although this argument cannot be shrugged off, we should note that in the course of the disinflation process, a movement along the Philips curve can be turned into a downward shift *of* the curve as policymakers enhance the credibility in their disinflation commitment, which might well be the case in Israel.

Another argument, which is currently subject to public debate, is related to the alleged increase in the vulnerability of the economy to external shocks. It is claimed

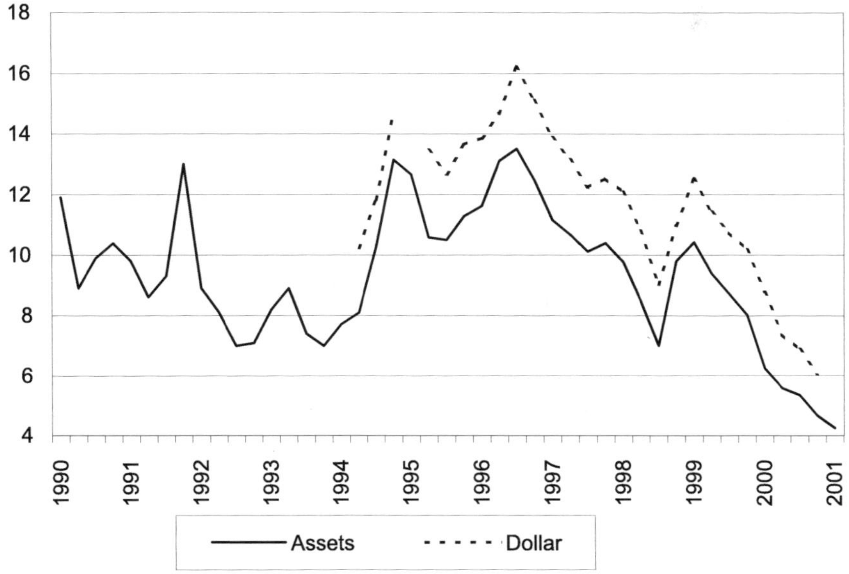

Figure 4.4
Interest Rates* Spread (without devaluation)
* Foreign interest rates on basket of currencies.

that this resulted from the portfolio shifts connected with the capital inflows in recent years, which may have inflationary consequences as in October 1998. This issue is of considerable importance, and we shall analyze the issues involved in the following section.

A Digression on Portfolio Shifts and Vulnerability Figure 4.4 shows that since the end of 1994, there has emerged a significant spread between domestic and foreign interest rates (with or without adjusting for the rate of devaluation with respect to the USD or the basket of currencies). This was the beginning of the period when the strategy of the Bank of Israel shifted effectively to the inflation target regime, which started with an implementation of tight money and a hike in domestic interest rates. In addition to the increase in the interest rate spread, we may assume that the public internalized the shift of regimes and understood that the probability of devaluation decreased significantly (given that the expected continuation of tight money will tend to appreciate the exchange rate). This was especially the case because the exchange rate was pushed by monetary policy and by exogenous inflows toward the floor of the exchange rate band (figure 4.5), which reduced the likelihood of devaluation for

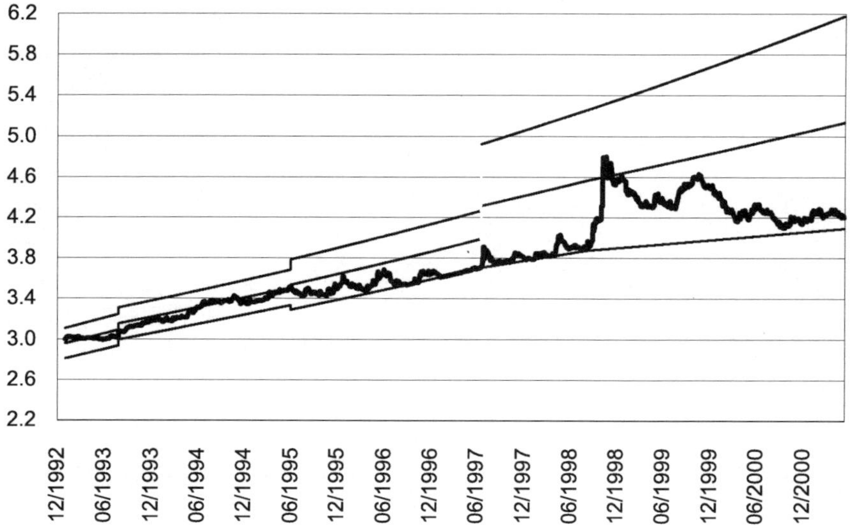

Figure 4.5
NIS Exchange Rate against the Currency Basket

the short run. As a result, it became more profitable to borrow abroad and shift the short-term asset portfolio to sheqel deposits (figure 4.6), which yield relatively high returns. This shift appears very dramatically in the stock of dollar-denominated short-term loans (figure 4.7), which started to rise very steeply at the beginning of 1995, rising from about five to close to twenty billion USD by mid-1998 (which is about equal to the stock of foreign exchange reserves of the Bank of Israel).

A related way of looking at the effects of sterilized intervention is though the changes in the balance sheet of the Bank of Israel. Sterilized intervention entailed the reduction in the monetary loan outstanding of the Bank of Israel since agents preferred to borrow abroad rather than at the Bank. As the monetary loan to the commercial banks disappeared, the Bank of Israel started to sell deposits to these banks. The balance of these operations, which increase the exposure to foreign exchange risk, is reflected to a large extent by the contraction of the net domestic credit (NDC), which can be derived indirectly by subtracting the foreign exchange reserves from the monetary base. Figure 4.8 shows that NDC started to contract (indicating tight money) in 1995, with the more dramatic contraction taking place in 1997.

The changes in portfolio that followed from the tight monetary policy presumably increased the vulnerability of the economy to external shocks. This implies that the initial disinflationary effect of tight money through the channel of exchange rate appreciation created problems later on, given that one must pay for excess appreciation

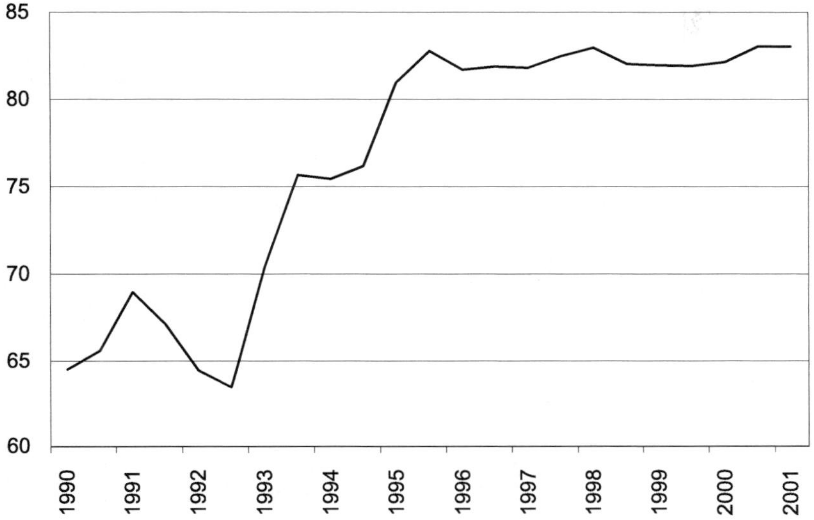

Figure 4.6
Percentage of Nonlinked Assets in the Total Assets (M3)

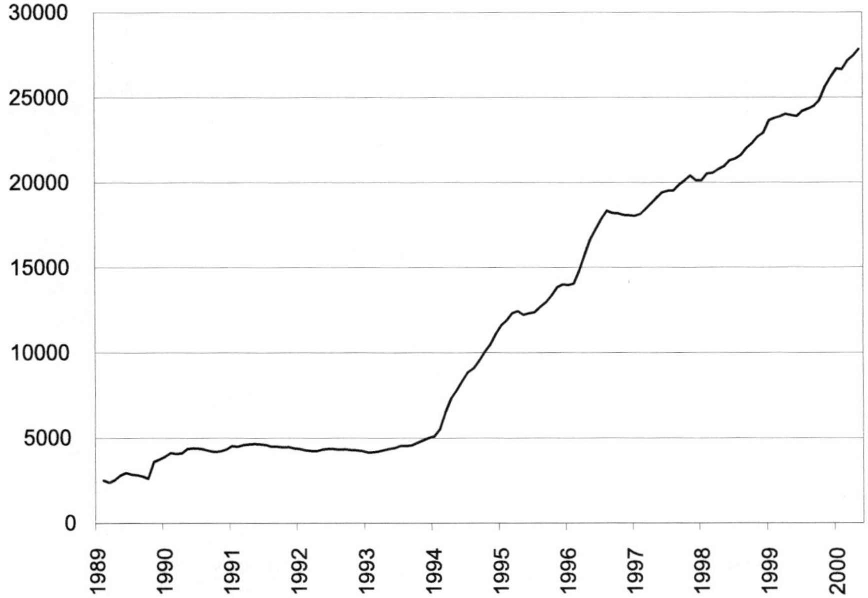

Figure 4.7
Foreign Currency Denominated Loans (millions of dollars)

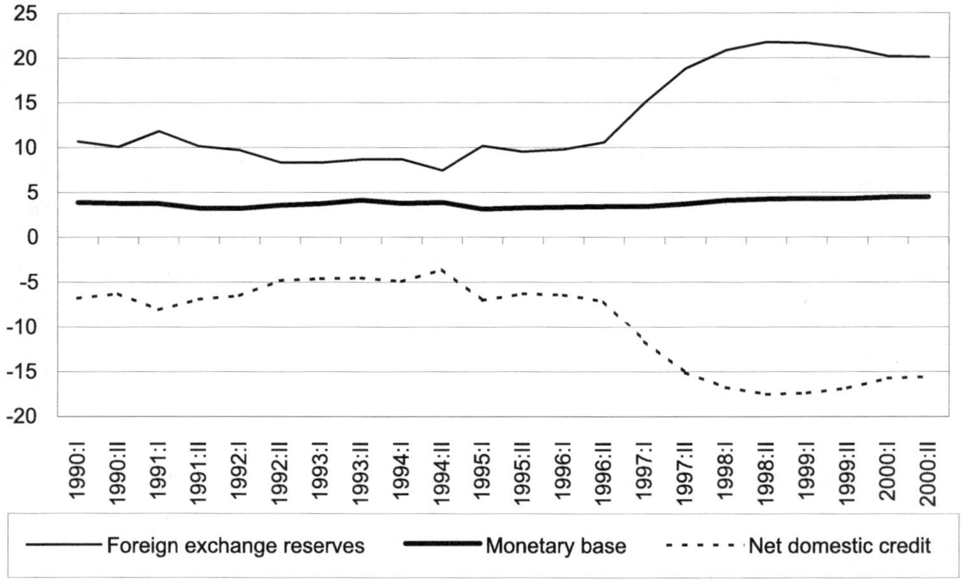

Figure 4.8
Monetary Base, Foreign Exchange Reserves, and Net Domestic Credit (% of GDP)

eventually with increased vulnerability to devaluation in the future. A small adverse external shock may result in a big devaluation, which seemed to be the case with the October 1998 devaluation, which was in turn passed on to inflation.

The growing exposure of the business sector to exchange rate risk since 1994 is documented in the Annual Review for 1988 by the Department of Foreign Exchange Supervision of the Bank of Israel. Thus, the open position of this sector increased from five billion USD at the end of 1994 to fifteen billion in August 1998 as a result of the reasons stated earlier.[9] According to the Review, the fact that there has recently been greater internalization of the exchange rate risk by the business sector, which increased its hedging activities through the options market, did not reduce the vulnerability substantially.

It should be noted that the increased vulnerability is basically the result of the inconsistency between the inflation target and the exchange rate band when the floor of the band becomes an effective constraint. From this point of view, a more flexible exchange rate regime would be effective in reducing the financial vulnerability. Indeed, the width of the exchange rate band has been increased on various occasions and has recently become about 30 percent wide. However, the widening of the band was implemented almost entirely through raising the ceiling of the band (i.e., the depreciated limit), whereas the effective limit was the floor, as a result of tight monetary policy and the increase in long-term foreign investment. From this point of view, the October 1998 devaluation alleviated the situation by enabling the exchange rate path to rise above the floor of the band.

4.4 Monetary Policy in the Short Run

Having discussed the long-term trend and the medium-term inflation steps, we turn to make a few remarks about the short-term dynamics. We refer to short-term dynamics as the developments within a given inflation step, which divides the period under consideration into three subperiods, with one dividing line being around 1992, and another around the end of 1997. We shall focus, however, on the developments in the post-1992 period, because it is more relevant for current policy concerns. In addition, we shall deal mainly with monetary and exchange rate policies because the main action in the short run comes from this side; as is well known, the fiscal policy is less flexible over short periods of time.

Inflation Targeting

The fundamental change concerning short-term monetary policy has been the change in the conception about the role of the interest rate. Until 1994, the interest rate was used to defend the exchange rate band against speculative attacks, and thus supported *indirectly* the disinflation process (which was anchored to the exchange rate); the conception changed after 1994 to one in which the interest rate is to be employed to deal *directly* with inflation regardless of the state of the exchange rate within its band.

The change of strategy was related to an increase of inflation in 1994, following a period of lax monetary policy in 1993, and in the absence of pressures on the exchange rate. These developments indicated that the exchange rate by itself did not provide a sufficiently tight anchor for inflation in the short run and that the interest rate should come into play to deal directly with deviations of inflation from target. Thus, the interest rate became the main policy instrument of the Bank of Israel to deal with short-term problems. The change in strategy is reflected clearly in figure 4.3 above that shows the break in the path of the real interest rates after 1995.

Monetary Policy Proved Effective

In general, monetary policy proved to be quite effective in restraining short-term deviations of inflation from its target. As shown in econometric studies, the tightening of monetary policy tends to reduce inflation with a lag of about two quarters.[10] The transmission mechanism involves the exchange rate channel, which operates through the appreciation of the currency with a relatively short lag and through the influence of the rise in the real interest rate on aggregate demand, which works with longer lags.[11]

Figure 4.1 describes the behavior of inflation, inflationary expectations in relation to inflation targets. In conjunction with figure 4.3, which shows the behavior of Bank of Israel's and interest rates on loans, it suggests that until the end of 1997 the Bank of Israel used tight money to fight off two big deviations from target (in 1994 and 1996) with some relaxation when inflation responded in the desired way. This scenario repeated itself in 1998 after the surge of inflation following the October 1998 devaluation, when inflation was brought back to the vicinity of the new target by a tightening of monetary policy. As noted before, this suggests that the monetary system is basically stable and that this stability increased with the growing credibility of the Bank of Israel.

The presumed increase in the risk premium as a result of the portfolio shift, which increased the vulnerability of the economy, created a constraint on the ability of the Bank of Israel to reduce its interest rate in response to a independent step reduction in inflation. This was reflected since 1998 in the phenomenon of a declining interest rate spread, following the reduction of the Bank of Israel's nominal interest rate, along with an increasing *real* interest rate following the step reduction of inflation in the end of 1997. The reason is that an unexpected drop in inflation that raises the real interest rate does not affect directly the arbitrage condition relating the domestic and foreign interest rates. The fact that a four-percentage-points hike in the Bank of Israel's interest rate was required to stop the speculative attack in October 1998 provides some idea about the size of the risk premium. The limitation that this imposes on the ability of the Bank of Israel to cut nominal interest rates can be rectified only by implementing policies that enable the business sector to allocate its portfolio over time so as to reduce its exchange rate risk.

4.5 The Cost of Disinflation

The Gross Trade-offs in Recent Years

We noted that since 1994 the Bank of Israel has maintained a tight monetary policy according to various criteria, but there is still no consensus about its contribution to growing unemployment. The reason is that the latter has also been influenced by other important factors such as the downturn of the business cycle associated with the slowdown in the immigration wave, the difficulties encountered in the peace process, and the tightening of fiscal policies since 1996, which was needed to restore external balance.

The *gross* relationships (without distinguishing between the contribution of the various factors to the recession) between the real interest rate, unemployment (or the slowdown of growth), and inflation are quite clear. Thus, the real interest rate on the monetary loan (both ex-ante and ex-post) of the Bank of Israel increased by about three percentage points between 1996 and the first half on 1998, and at the same time, unemployment increased by 2.3 percentage points (to about 9 percent), while the rate of growth of the economy decelerated from 4.7 percent in 1996 to 2.7 percent and 2 percent in the following two years. Again, between 1996 and the first half of 1998, both actual and expected Consumer Price Index (CPI) inflation fell by about six percentage points (to 4.5 percent annually in the first half of 1998). This suggests a trade-off in recent years between inflation and unemployment of about 2.6 to 1 (and a somewhat higher trade-off in terms of the output gap if we assume that 4.5 percent growth is the normal rate); however, as we noted, so far there has not been found a reliable way of allocating the observed trade-offs between the different factors that contributed to the recession.[12]

When one considers the cost of disinflation, one must compare it with an alternative course of action. Unfortunately, we are unable to quantify a reliable counterfactual. From the point of view of an alternative policy, one has to consider the dangers of an external crisis erupting as a result of a less conservative monetary policy. From the same perspective, is not conservative monetary policy more conducive for foreign direct investment and therefore to sustainable growth? One cannot ignore the general sentiment in an environment of financial turmoil in the world capital markets that the name of the game has become financial stability rather than full employment, and tight money seems to be in line with the former. It is for this reason that the implementation of tight fiscal and monetary policies in a recessionary environment did not give rise to greater public opposition.

Given that the authorities decided to embark on a disinflation process, we may ask whether the resultant real interest and the unemployment rates are exceptionally high, indicating that in some sense the disinflation strategy is inefficient. Using an international comparison as our standard, it appears that the disinflation cost and the stringency of monetary policy has by no means been excessive, as is indicated by a presentation in the Annual Report for 1988 of the Monetary Department of the Bank of Israel (pp. 14–15), which reviews the disinflation experiences of Italy, Canada, Finland, Ireland, Spain, Norway, and New Zealand.

The Dynamics of Inflation, Unemployment, and Interest Rates

Statistically, the evolution of inflation is "explained" quite well by unemployment and the real interest rate, but we have to keep in mind that the latter two variables are not independent (though we can show that Granger causality goes from the interest rate to unemployment). We demonstrate this relationship using the Lavi-Sussman framework, which is based on the Taylor-type model (see appendix for a detailed description).

This model consists of three equations—a version of the IS equation (with the "unemployment gap" replacing the output gap), a Phillips curve, and a reaction function of the central bank. A reduced form of this model relates the changes in inflation to changes in expectations, lagged changes in unemployment, and lagged changes in the real interest rate (an additional variable relevant for the early nineties is the lagged rate of immigration). Figure 4.9 shows that the reduced form equation of this model (corresponding to equation 6 in the appendix) aptly captures the two inflation steps of 1992 and 1998. These results indicate that unemployment and tight money played major roles in the turning points of the disinflation process.

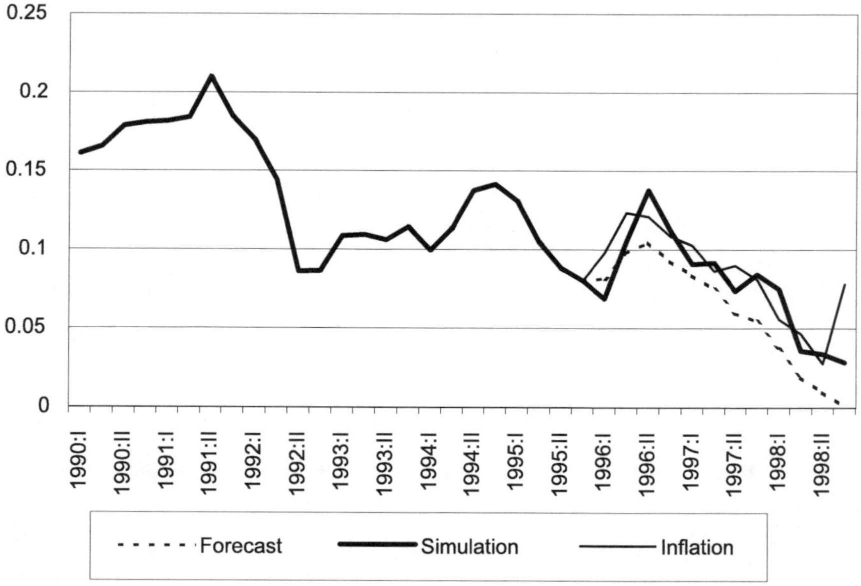

Figure 4.9
Inflation Forecast and Simulation according to the Lavi-Sussman Model

4.6 Summary and Conclusions

The review of disinflation in Israel in the past decade reveals that the process can be viewed from three aspects—the downward trend, the step reductions in inflation, and the dynamics within steps. The declining trend has been influenced by adherence to fiscal discipline, by the continued attention to nominal anchors, and by the reduction in world inflation. Fiscal discipline has been institutionalized by the "law of deficit reduction," and its credibility has been enhanced by correcting deviations from the law. The main developments in the monetary sector have been the gradual flexibilization of the exchange rate regime and the shift to the inflation target regime, with the Bank of Israel's interest rate as the main instrument of monetary policy.

The main break in inflation after 1985, from about 20 percent to 10 percent, took place around 1992, and was related to a large extent to the immigration wave from the former Soviet Union in the context of other favorable developments that created a critical mass for a sharp drop in inflation. Another break occurred at the end of 1997 and was related mainly to the tight fiscal and monetary policies that were accompanied by a significant increase in unemployment, which was related in part to other factors such as the reduction in the rate of immigration and difficulties in the peace process. The statistical analysis reveals that the inflation series, which followed a stepwise pattern, behaved in a different way than the inflation anchors such as the money stock, import prices, and nominal wages that followed a trend stationary process.

We analyze short-term policies primarily in the context of the post-1992 step and especially since 1994, when the monetary policy started to use the interest rate policy in a more aggressive manner to keep inflation in line with the inflation targets set by the government. We conclude that monetary policy was successful in performing this role; however, the inconsistency of the inflation target regime and the commitment to the exchange rate band resulted in an increase in the vulnerability of the economy to external shocks through an induced change in the public's and the central bank's portfolios. An example of this vulnerability has been the reaction of the economy to the devaluation in October 1998, which cast some doubts on the robustness of the reduction of the inflation plateau that was observed in 1998.

Both the inflation steps and the short-term movements of inflation are explained reasonably well by a Taylor version of the Phillips curve in which the changes in inflation are related to changes in unemployment and to changes in the (ex-post) real interest rates after allowing for the short-term effects of immigration. The gross data indicate a positive correlation in recent years between the real interest rate and unemployment, but the growth of the latter has been affected by other factors as well.

Having said this, we state that a more lenient monetary policy would have its own risks, especially with the growing financial turmoil in the world.

We turn now to suggest a number of policy implications and dilemmas that emerge from our analysis. As a preface to this discussion, we should note that the inconsistency between the inflation target, tight monetary policy, and the exchange rate band—borne out by the deviation of the path of inflation from the path of its nominal anchors—reflected a basic contradiction related to the lack of consensus about the desired pace of disinflation. Thus, the political system in Israel has not entrusted the change of the parameters of the exchange rate band to the Bank of Israel, as the change of these parameters can be performed only with the consent of the Treasury, which had traditionally different views about the pace of disinflation, echoing views prevalent in some sectors of the economy. The fact that the Bank of Israel could not manipulate the floor of the exchange rate band led to sterilized intervention and increased vulnerability. We may suppose that the whole disinflation process would have worked more smoothly, unlike the stepwise manner reflected in its breaks, had Israel reached a consensus about the process, as has been the case in Europe in the context of joining the EMU.

In the context of policy implications, it is important to stress the role of fiscal tightness in reducing inflation not only in the long run, but also in bringing about reductions of the inflation plateau in the medium term. Thus, both the sharp reductions in the inflation steps in 1992 and 1997 were associated with a strengthening of the fiscal commitment.

Monetary policy proved to be an effective tool in restraining short-term deviations of inflation from target, and thus, seems to have justified the strategy of using the interest rate on the Bank of Israel's funds as the major monetary policy instrument. However, the continued use of a high interest rate policy, under the constraint of the floor of the exchange rate band, required sterilized intervention, which induced opening up positions in foreign currency. This resulted in increased vulnerability both of the private sector and the Bank of Israel to devaluation risks, which raised over time the likelihood of inflationary shocks. It is doubtful whether the accumulation of foreign exchange reserves by the central bank in the course of this process did in fact increase the protection of the economy against financial crises, because it was offset by the increased vulnerability resulting from the portfolio shifts. Thus, the initial successes of monetary policy in reducing inflation quickly through the appreciation channel has to be balanced by the later adverse cumulative effect of increased vulnerability.

The conclusion is that tight money may be counterproductive if it is used on a continued basis and not confined to the prevention of occasional deviations of inflation from target. This statement should be qualified by the consideration that a continued tough stand of monetary policy may succeed in "bending" inflationary expectations and shift the economy to a more favorable equilibrium. But this involves a gamble that may not pay off.

Following the October 1998 devaluation, the exchange rate has been raised above the floor of the exchange rate band, as was the case prior to 1995. In a way, we may be back to square one. But the situation is different in two respects. On the one hand, the exchange rate band is much wider now; on the other hand, the vulnerability of the system is greater, not only because of the domestic side but also because the financial world is less stable. With the present initial conditions, it would seem desirable to diffuse gradually the dangers arising from the so-called sheqel mountain and the external open positions. It is also suggested that one should refrain from using high interest rate policies for extended periods in order not to generate another round of sterilized intervention, which will exacerbate further the financial vulnerability of the economy.

Our analysis shows that unemployment exerts a strong deflationary effect, in the form of a downward movement along a given Phillips curve. However, does the social cost involved guarantee a lasting decrease in inflation? In the standard framework of Phillips curve analysis, the answer is negative, unless inflationary expectations change in the course of this process. Again, in the context of multiple equilibria, this is a possibility that should be reckoned with, as is suggested by the step reductions in 1992 and 1997.

The increase in the real interest rate exerts a disinflationary effect directly through its effect on the exchange rate, on domestic demands, and, indirectly, through its effect on unemployment. But, again, what are the odds that the effect on inflation will be a lasting one? Our study of the 1992 step suggests that the main long-term influence of the rise in real interest rates was in the context of locking in a step-reduction of inflation that occurred as a result of other factors and only partly as a result of tight money. A similar phenomenon took place in the 1997 step when the inflation target was reduced to 4 percent. Thus, the use of tight money seems to be especially effective in the long-term perspective when it is used to lock in step reductions of inflation that may be influenced partly by other developments.

Appendix

Adaptation of Taylor's (1994) Model for the Israeli Economy Based on Lavi and Sussman (1999)

In Taylor's model, short-term analysis of the Phillips curve incorporates the central bank, which uses the nominal interest rate as a mechanism for attaining the inflation and employment targets. Because changes in nominal interest rates can cause changes in real interest rates, the short-term policies of the central bank have real effects, in particular, on unemployment. Two changes will be made in the original model: First, it will be simplified by assuming that the central bank only maintains the inflation target, which is not unreasonable in the Israeli context. Second, in order to avoid the issue of natural unemployment rates, a difference equation derived from the model will be used.

The model contains three equations: (1) the aggregate demand equation, which is negatively related to the real interest rate (equation 4.1); (2) the short-run Phillips curve, which assumes a negative correlation between unemployment and inflation (equation 4.2); and (3) an equation for the behavior of the central bank (equation 4.3).

$$U_t - U_N = \beta(i_t - \pi_t - r^*) + u_t \tag{4.1}$$

$$\pi_t = \pi_t^e - \alpha(U_{t-1} - U_N) + e_t \tag{4.2}$$

$$i_t = \pi_t^e + h(\pi_t - \pi^*) + r_t^f + v_t \tag{4.3}$$

Where i is equivalent to the rate of nominal interest set by the central bank, r^* is the equilibrium rate of the real interest rate, and r^f is the real interest rate, for which the central bank assumes that there is no deviation from the inflation target (π^*) in the short run. The deviations u_t reflect demand shocks, that is, fluctuations in the aggregate demand curve.

Substituting for the interest rate from equation 4.3 into equation 4.1 we obtain:

$$U_t - U_N = \beta(\pi_t^e - \pi_t) + \beta h(\pi_t - \pi^*) + \beta(r^f - r^*) + \beta v_t + u_t \tag{4.4}$$

The rate of actual unemployment correlates positively with the deviation of inflation from the target due to the countercyclical policy of the central bank, and with the deviation in the real interest rate. Using equation 4.2 and substituting the lagged rate of inflation for the deviation in expected inflation, the following equation is obtained:

$$U_t - U_N = \alpha\beta(U_{t-1} - U_N) + \beta h(\pi_t - \pi^*) + \beta(r_t^f - r^*) + \beta(v_t - e_t) + u_t \tag{4.5}$$

The negative correlation between current and past unemployment derives from the central bank's countercyclical policy with respect to the inflation rate.

Equation 4.5 can be combined with equation 4.2 and differenced to obtain the following difference equation:

$$\Delta\pi_t = \Delta\pi_t^e - \alpha^2\beta\Delta U_{t-2} - \alpha\beta\Delta\pi_{t-1} - \alpha\beta\Delta r_{t-1}^f + \mu_t \tag{4.6}$$

The short-term difference equation indicates that changes in inflation rates are derived from changes in lagged inflation, the real interest rate, which is set by the central bank, as well as from demand and supply shocks, changes in expectations, and changes in the inertia factors.

Notes

1. See Bruno (1993).
2. Liviatan and Melnick (1998).
3. The declared intention of the government is to attain the OECD inflation levels by 2001–2003.
4. Sobczak (1998).
5. It is possible to show that in a subsample from 1989 to 1997, inflation (especially inflation excluding housing fruits and vegetables) can be characterized as almost a trend stationary stochastic process.
6. Under the assumption that there is a one-time change in the mean of a unit root process, $\beta_1 = 1, \beta_2 = 0$, $\beta_3 = 0$, and $\beta_4 \neq 0$, because a "shock" will tend to persist. Under the alternative hypothesis of a permanent one-time break in a trend stationary series, $\beta_1 < 1, \beta_2 \neq 0, \beta_3 \neq 0$, and $\beta_4 = 0$.
7. A finding of a unit root with a break would suggest that some one-time shock permanently altered the course of the inflation process.
8. We should note that the estimating equation on which this analysis is based is also consistent with a simpler formulation of the Phillips curve, where the relevant interest rate is indeed the market rate and not the central bank's rate. Thus, if the supply of output is a function of the real wage and the demand is a function of the market real interest rate (the IS curve), then we can derive a similar estimating equation by equating supply and demand and using a wage-based Phillips curve. In addition, we have to assume that the rate of change of the interest rate is proportional to the deviation of its current level from its long-run equilibrium.
9. The evaluation of the above report of the process that has led to the increased vulnerability is similar to ours: "The exposure of the business sector to a devaluation increased quickly, according to our estimate, since the end of 1994, especially in the course of 1995 and in the first half of 1997, as a result of borrowing in foreign exchange for sheqel uses. This took place against the background of restrictive monetary policy in the process of disinflation, which created a large interest rate spread between the sheqel and foreign exchange, against the background of a relatively narrow band, and intervention of the Bank of Israel in the foreign exchange market within the band (till February 1996); these factors, together with the improvement in the basic current account, reduced very considerably the probability of devaluation." Report, *op. cit.*, p. 19. We should add that the measurement of the exposure to exchange rate risk is complicated both conceptually and practically, as explained in the above report.
10. See Bufman and Leiderman (1997).
11. See Djivre and Ribon (1998).
12. A regression of changes in unemployment on lagged change in the real interest rate (using alternative definitions) for the whole of the nineties does not yield a good in-sample prediction of the path of unemployment in recent years. The reason seems to be that the statistical estimation is blurred by the dominance of other factors, such as immigration, in the early nineties. The same regression yields good in-sample prediction if the estimation is confined to the 1996:1–1998:4 period. Even though picking the subperiod that yields good results is doubtful from the point of view of statistical principles, it does suggest that the role of the real interest rate in explaining unemployment gained importance in recent years.

References

Alessina, Alberto, and Roberto Perotti. "Budget Deficits and Budget Institutions." IMF Working Paper no. 96/52, 1996.

———. "Fiscal Adjustment in OECD Countries: Composition and Macroeconomic Effects." IMF Working Paper no. 96/70, 1996.

Bruno, Michael. *Crisis Stabilization and Economic Reform.* Oxford: Clarendon Press, 1993.

Bufman, Gil, and Leo Leiderman. "Monetary Policy and Inflation in Israel." Bank of Israel, Research Department, Working Paper no. 98.04, 1998.

Dahan, Momi, and Michel Strawczynski. "Fiscal Policy and Turning Points of Inflation." Bank of Israel, The Research Department, Working Paper no. 97.04, 1997.

Djivre, Joseph, and Sigal Ribon. "The Impact of Monetary Policy on the Output Gap and Inflation—The Case of Israel." Bank of Israel, The Research Department, Working Paper, 1998.

Furman, Jeffrey, and Joseph Stiglitz. "Economic Crises: Evidence and Insights from East Asia." *Brookings Papers on Economic Activity* 2 (1998): 1–114.

Lavi, Yaakov, and Nathan Sussman. "The Phillips Curve and Its Changes, 1965–1996." In *Inflation and Disinflation in Israel*, edited by Leo Leiderman (pp. 315–346). Jerusalem: Bank of Israel, 1999. (Hebrew)

Liviatan, Nissan, and Rafi Melnick. "Inflation and Disinflation by Steps in Israel." Bank of Israel, The Research Department, Discussion Paper no. 98.01, 1998.

Sobczak, Nicolas. "Disinflation in Spain: The Recent Experience." IMF Working Paper no. 98/106, 1998.

Taylor, John B. "The Inflation/Output Variability Trade-off Revisited." In *Goals, Guidelines and Constraints Facing Monetary Policymaking*, Proceedings of a Conference held in June 1994, Federal Reserve Bank of Boston, 1994.

5 Israeli Inflation from an International Perspective

Stanley Fischer and David W. H. Orsmond

5.1 Introduction

In its fifty-year history, Israel has undergone almost the full range of inflation experiences, including periods of low inflation in the 1950s and 1960s, double-digit inflation in the 1970s, triple-digit inflation through the mid-1980s, then back to a prolonged period of moderate double-digit inflation after the 1985 stabilization program, and, finally, achieving low single-digit levels in recent years. The only missing experiences are those of deflation and genuine hyperinflation, although the high inflation of the mid-1980s is often described as a hyperinflation.

The Israeli inflationary experience and its successful 1985 stabilization program have been extensively compared with the experiences of other countries (see, for example, Bruno, et al., 1988, 1991; Bruno, 1993). The main focus of this paper is on the poststabilization period. In particular, we compare Israel's experience of moderate inflation and eventual disinflation with those of other countries to draw conclusions for both Israeli policy and the disinflation process in general.

The paper is organized as follows. In the second section, we provide a brief overview of Israel's long-term inflation history. This sets the context for the description in the third section of Israel's struggle during the poststabilization period to disinflate from moderate to low single-digit levels. In the fourth section, we summarize lessons on the disinflation process that have emerged from experiences in other countries. The lessons are drawn in reference to nine countries, three of which moved from high to low inflation levels without an intervening period of moderate inflation, three of which experienced moderate inflation for a period and then lowered inflation to single-digit levels, and three of which were for a long time stuck with moderate inflation. Drawing on these general lessons, we analyze in the fifth section why it proved so difficult to tame inflation in Israel. In the final section, we address institutional issues that will help determine whether Israel is able to sustain the current low inflation levels.

5.2 Rising Inflation Pressures and Stabilization, 1951–1985

Figure 5.1 plots (on a logarithmic scale) the inflation rate in Israel during the last half-century. After rising briefly in the early 1950s to a peak of 60 percent per annum as previously controlled prices were deregulated and the exchange rate was devalued, inflation remained below 10 percent for virtually the entire period until the 1970s.

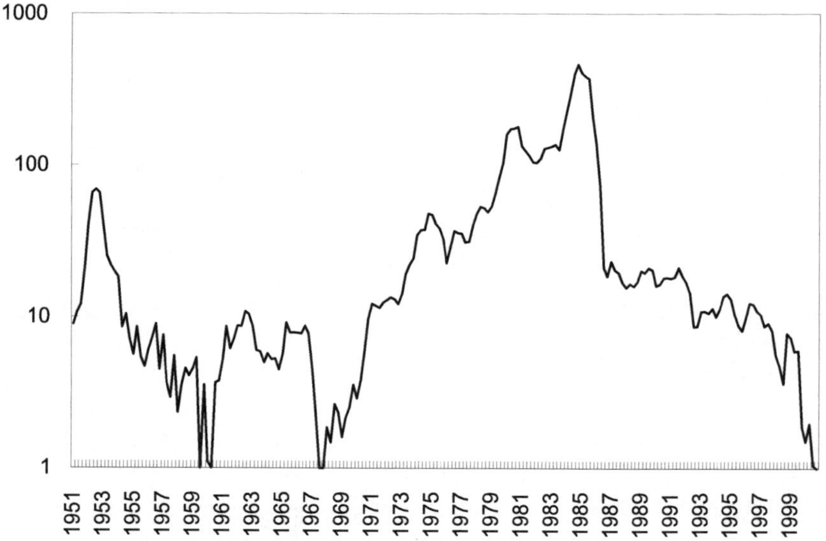

Figure 5.1
Israel: Overall Inflation, 1951–2000
(In percent; four-quarters-to rate)

This was the period of Israel's miracle economic growth, which averaged 10 percent per annum until 1965, when, in the face of an increasing external deficit and rising inflation, policy turned sharply contractionary, and a recession began that reduced inflation to close to zero and raised the unemployment rate to more than 10 percent.

The restrictive fiscal and monetary policies were reversed at the end of 1966. Although the Six Day War resulted in a large increase in government spending,[1] it also, in effect, increased the labor force, as Palestinians began to be employed in Israel, and inflation, although rising, continued low through the end of the 1960s. Growth, too, returned to the former miracle rates. The pace of inflation then rose rapidly, first to double-digit levels in the early 1970s as expansionary policies continued, to annual rates that averaged 35 percent in 1974–1977, then to rates around 125 percent in 1980–1983, and, finally, to annual rates that peaked at over 450 percent in 1984–1985.

The initial rise in inflation to levels that were more than 30 percent per annum was linked to the sudden slowdown in annual growth to just 3 percent, itself a function of the first oil price shock in 1973, the Yom Kippur War (after which military expenditure increased by 10 percent of GDP, partly financed by increased foreign aid), the failure to adjust other fiscal expenditures to reflect the slower pace of growth and hence of revenues, and the rapid growth in real wages even as total productivity in the business sector declined. Inflation then accelerated after 1977 as the nominal anchors in the economy were weakened with the introduction of a real exchange rate rule, liquid foreign exchange (*Patam*) accounts that decreased the demand for sheqel-denominated assets, and other policies that limited the Bank of Israel's (BoI) control over the monetary base.[2] In response, efforts to reduce inflationary pressures were either pursued for too short a period (nine months in 1979), or focused on price and wage controls rather than on a lasting fiscal retrenchment (1982–1983), an approach that provided at best a brief respite.

The famous mid-1985 stabilization program represented a comprehensive attack on the root causes of high inflation in Israel. It was based on the following components:

- The high fiscal deficit—which had been at the core of both the excess demand conditions for nearly twenty years and the rising public debt level—was substantially reduced through a cut in subsidies for basic foods, transport, and export credits, reductions in defense spending, the imposition of new taxes including a temporary surcharge on self-employed income, and increased foreign aid. The fiscal deficit fell from 13 percent of GDP in 1984, to less than half that level in the second half of 1985, and the budget was in surplus by 1986.

- The effectiveness of monetary policy was enhanced: The Bank of Israel (BoI) restricted the growth of credit by raising reserve requirements and the real discount rate on deregulated bank lending; the minimum term for dollar-indexed (*Patam*) deposits was raised to one year; a new central bank law in 1986 forbade borrowing from the BoI to finance the budget except for bridging loans within the fiscal year; and the tradeability of government bonds was improved.

- The exchange rate was devalued by 25 percent at the start of the program, and partially unified for exporters and importers. To anchor price expectations, the rate was fixed to the U.S. dollar at NIS 1.5 per dollar, conditional on maintaining an "appropriate" level of wages.

- Backed by the solid adjustment in the macroeconomic fundamentals, an incomes policy was used to reduce inflationary inertia. Backward-looking wage indexation was temporarily suspended, replaced with a flat increase in nominal wages by 14 percent in August and 12 percent in September, designed to compensate for the initial devaluation and inflation, with further wage increases delayed until December. The prices of virtually all (90 percent) goods and services were frozen for three months after an initial 17 percent increase. The extensive indexation of financial assets was not altered.[3]

- The credibility of the stabilization program was enhanced by large-scale U.S. financial aid to help finance the fiscal deficit and guarantee balance of payments viability ($1.5 billion over two years, or over 3 percent of GDP per year), and by the withdrawal from Lebanon in the same month the Knesset voted on the stabilization package. Patinkin (1993) argues that the withdrawal from Lebanon increased the government's policy credibility by showing its ability to deliver on controversial policies.

As a result of these aspects, the twelve-month inflation rate fell quickly from 450 percent in mid-1985 to 20 percent by the start of 1986. Indeed, Israel's stabilization program remains one of the most successful on record.

5.3 Israel's Experience with Moderate Inflation, 1986–2000

There have been three distinct inflation periods in Israel since the stabilization program in 1985—the first from 1986–1991, when annual inflation was around 15–20 percent; the second from 1992 to mid-1997, when annual inflation hovered around 10 percent; and the third from mid-1997 onwards, when inflation fell rapidly to recent levels around 2 percent although there was a temporary spike in inflation at the end of 1998 due to the effect on the price level of the large depreciation. Economic indicators for the poststabilization period are shown in table 5.1 and figures 5.2 and 5.3.

The Initial Poststabilization Inflation Plateau, 1986–1991

Reinflationary pressures were evident after mid-1986. In large part, these were caused by the nominal and real wage increases conceded in the early phases of the program and their accommodation by monetary policy, which was looser than originally envisioned as credit growth exceeded its target. While real interest rates were initially high in the deregulated segment of bank borrowing—6–7 percent per month in mid-1986—this segment constituted only a small share of total credit, and real rates were much lower for the large directed credit segment. By the end of 1986, real rates in the deregulated lending segment had fallen to the still excessively high level of 2 percent per month (Leiderman, 1993).

Demand pressures increased as monetary restrictiveness was relaxed. The early success of the stabilization program—increases in foreign reserves and the rapid decline in inflation without an initial output cost—led to the perception that "now was the time to grow," meaning now was the time to relax restrictive policies (Bruno and Piterman, 1988). Reflecting this view, marginal income taxes were reduced, and investment incentives were increased, whereupon the *domestic* fiscal deficit (which abstracts from foreign assistance) deteriorated in each quarter from mid-1986, rising from 1 percent of GDP in 1986 to 4 percent of GDP by 1988. The *foreign* fiscal deficit also increased after 1986 with the conclusion of the extraordinary U.S. financial assistance.

Demand pressures were sustained by increases in real wages. After contracting by 7 percent in 1985, real business wages increased 9 percent in 1986 and 8 percent in 1987; indeed, real business sector wages returned to their prestabilization level within nine months of the start of the program, and public sector wages within twelve months, levels that had been regarded before the stabilization as too high. This increased pressure on nontradeable prices (figure 5.2)—most price controls had been removed by March 1986—and squeezed profitability levels, especially in the tradeable sector. With the looser-than-envisioned monetary policy, a deteriorating fiscal position, and high real wage growth, there was only a very gradual decline in the rate of increase in underlying nontradeable prices after the initial success.[4]

Tradeable goods price increases were tied to the NIS/$ peg. Initially, the decline in the U.S. dollar in the second half of 1985 against other major currencies imparted an inflationary boost to the overall price index—which helped offset the impact on competitiveness of the increase in nominal wages and hence in nontradeable prices—but there were important counteracting pressures from the simultaneous decline in world oil prices. After the peg was set in terms of a currency basket in August 1986, competitiveness began to be eroded and with it profitability. At the same time, the interaction of the fixed exchange rate with the loose fiscal, monetary, and wage policies noted above supported a consumption boom—a common feature in exchange rate based stabilization programs (Calvo and Vegh, 1990, 1991; Bufman and Leiderman, 1995)—which was reflected in a sharply deteriorating current account position. Faced with these pressures, the authorities devalued the currency by 10 percent in January 1987.

In response to the squeeze on profitability and some structural reform in the business sector, inflation pressures began to slow again beginning in mid-1987. Monetary policy was then significantly relaxed, with real interest rates turning negative, and the automatic stabilizers acted to increase the fiscal deficit. At the end of 1988, the exchange rate was again devalued, and the fixed rate regime was replaced with a horizontal band, which was then adjusted four times in a two-and-a-half year period. These adjustments were made in response to speculative flows associated with the ongoing inflation premium vis-à-vis Israel's trading partners, which ensured that a correction would have to be undertaken, albeit by an unknown magnitude at an

Table 5.1
Israel: Economic Indicators, 1980–1999 (In percent; unless otherwise indicated)

	GDP	Inflation Rate				Money		Real Wage Index		
			Nontradeable							
	Growth rate	Overall	Total	Partial*	Tradeable	Growth of M1	Interest**	Overall	Business	Profits***
1980	3.6	132.9	—	—	—	96.7	—	77.5	80.1	13.7
1981	4.7	101.5	—	—	—	91.3	—	85.5	88.4	17.1
1982	1.4	131.5	136.3	140.6	117.1	109.2	—	85.3	89.8	14.8
1983	2.6	190.7	191.8	201.2	197.2	139.9	—	90.4	93.9	12.4
1984	2.2	444.9	438.2	402.1	455.0	353.7	—	90.1	93.0	14.5
1985	4.4	185.2	202.1	206.6	160.4	246.1	—	82.0	86.7	11.9
1986	3.6	19.6	23.5	30.0	13.8	112.7	−11.1	88.4	94.5	4.7
1987	6.2	16.1	17.8	24.4	13.1	49.5	15.3	95.4	102.1	3.3
1988	3.4	16.4	20.3	20.6	10.0	11.3	5.1	101.1	107.0	5.9
1989	1.3	20.7	24.8	23.3	14.2	44.4	−5.4	99.8	105.3	6.8
1990	6.2	17.6	20.8	17.3	12.3	30.6	−1.0	98.8	103.8	9.5
1991	5.9	18.0	20.2	16.3	14.0	13.8	−3.9	95.8	98.3	13.6
1992	6.7	9.4	9.7	11.8	8.8	32.0	−0.6	96.9	100.1	15.4
1993	3.3	11.2	13.7	9.5	6.5	27.9	0.3	97.5	100.4	13.2
1994	7.0	14.5	17.9	10.6	9.0	7.7	1.6	100.0	100.0	10.2
1995	6.8	8.1	8.4	9.5	7.7	15.1	4.6	102.2	100.6	10.7
1996	4.6	10.6	12.0	11.8	8.3	20.4	4.7	103.8	102.1	8.0
1997	2.9	7.0	7.7	7.9	5.8	11.3	5.0	106.3	105.7	6.1
1998	2.2	8.6	8.6	8.1	8.7	12.2	7.3	108.6	108.8	5.7
1999	2.2	1.3	2.3	3.9	−0.1	20.4	6.7	110.6	112.5	4.1

* Excludes housing, fresh fruit, and vegetables (HFV).
** Nominal discount interest rate annualized, deflated by overall ex-post CPI. Data are similar if the BoI's price expectations series is used (this series is only available after 1989).
*** Real rate of return on net capital.
**** Operational general government balance as reported in Bank of Israel, *Annual Report*.
***** An increase is an appreciation. Index 1995 = 100.
****** Civilian imports and exports prices, excluding capital services and diamonds. Index 1995 = 100.
Sources: IMF, *International Financial Statistics*; Bank of Israel, *Annual Report* 1999; and authors' calculations.

Table 5.1 (continued)

Employment		Fiscal/GDP****				Current Account		Reserves	
Growth	Jobless Rate	Overall	Domestic	Debt/ GDP	REER*****	Millions U.S. dollars	Percent of GNP	Mths. of imports	Terms of trade******
1.1	4.8	−13.3	−12.8	—	92.4	−878	−4.2	—	—
2.0	5.1	−17.5	−17.0	—	93.8	−1360	−6.0	3.1	91.6
1.4	5.0	−12.7	−10.8	—	98.2	−2255	−9.5	3.5	95.9
3.2	4.5	−6.5	−8.9	125.2	106.8	−2370	−8.9	3.1	102.8
1.4	5.9	−14.5	−19.4	148.2	100.4	−1571	−6.3	2.6	99.5
−0.7	6.7	1.0	−6.5	157.7	97.2	990	4.3	3.1	99.0
1.4	7.1	3.9	−1.0	147.2	94.8	1302	4.5	3.8	103.7
2.6	6.1	0.1	−4.5	123.3	92.5	−1406	−4.1	3.7	101.9
3.5	6.4	−2.6	−4.0	129.6	101.5	−830	−1.9	2.8	107.1
0.6	8.9	−5.5	−7.9	132.4	102.5	213	0.5	3.6	105.9
2.1	9.6	−4.8	−7.6	122.3	100.1	161	0.3	3.5	103.0
6.1	10.6	−4.7	−7.9	109.8	102.0	−1314	−2.3	3.3	106.7
4.2	11.2	−4.9	−8.1	103.5	99.4	−980	−1.5	2.5	105.6
6.1	10.0	−4.6	−6.3	101.3	98.2	−2560	−3.9	2.8	105.7
6.8	7.8	−3.5	−4.6	92.5	99.2	−3387	−4.6	2.6	103.0
5.0	6.8	−4.8	−5.9	89.9	100.0	−5197	−6.0	2.7	100.0
2.4	6.6	−5.5	−6.6	89.7	105.9	−5434	−5.8	3.3	103.0
1.4	7.5	−4.1	−5.4	88.3	113.3	−3514	−3.6	3.8	105.4
1.5	8.6	−3.6	−5.0	88.3	109.9	−842	−0.9	6.7	107.5
3.1	8.9	−4.8	−5.5	87.8	105.7	−2601	—	5.9	108.4

unknown time. (Box 5.1 outlines the various exchange rate regimes of the post-stabilization period.)

The first phase of the poststabilization period ended around 1991, as the heavy immigration from the former Soviet Union continued, and as it became clear that the adjustable peg system with a band was not sustainable. The immigration was a major boon to the Israeli economy: Its impact on economic performance was enhanced by the market-friendly absorption policies implemented by the government, and especially by the agreement to allow new immigrants to work at below-union scale wages. The immigration thus put downward pressure on business-sector wages as unemployment increased (through an increase in the supply of labor) by 4 percentage points to $10\frac{1}{2}$ percent in 1991, and enhanced labor market flexibility; it also added to demand pressures by requiring spending for settlement costs and the housing sector.

By 1991, the twelve-month rate of inflation stood at 18 percent, only marginally below the rate achieved five years earlier.

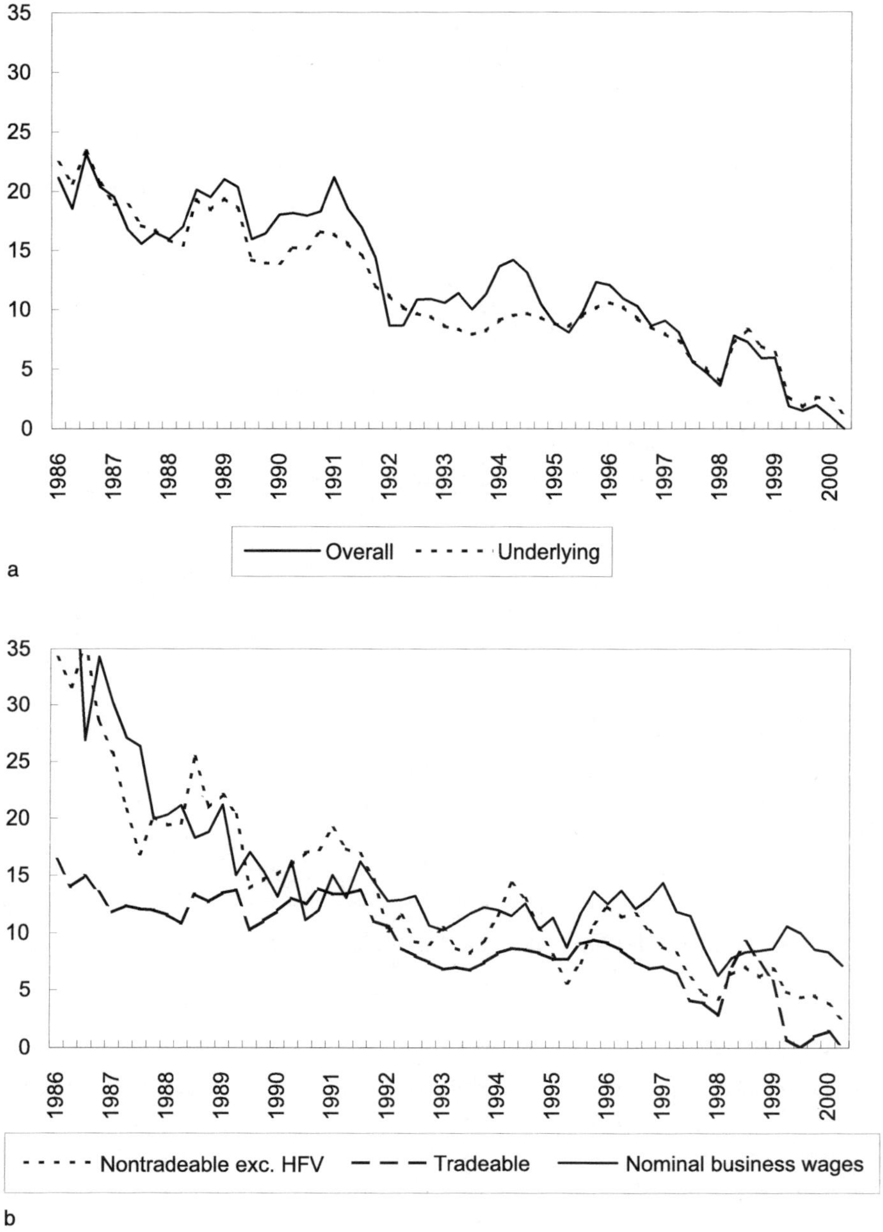

Figure 5.2
Israel: Inflation Indicators, 1986–2000. (a) Overall and underlying inflation. (b) Tradeable, nontradeable, and wage inflation.
Note: Underlying inflation excludes housing, fresh fruits, and vegetables.

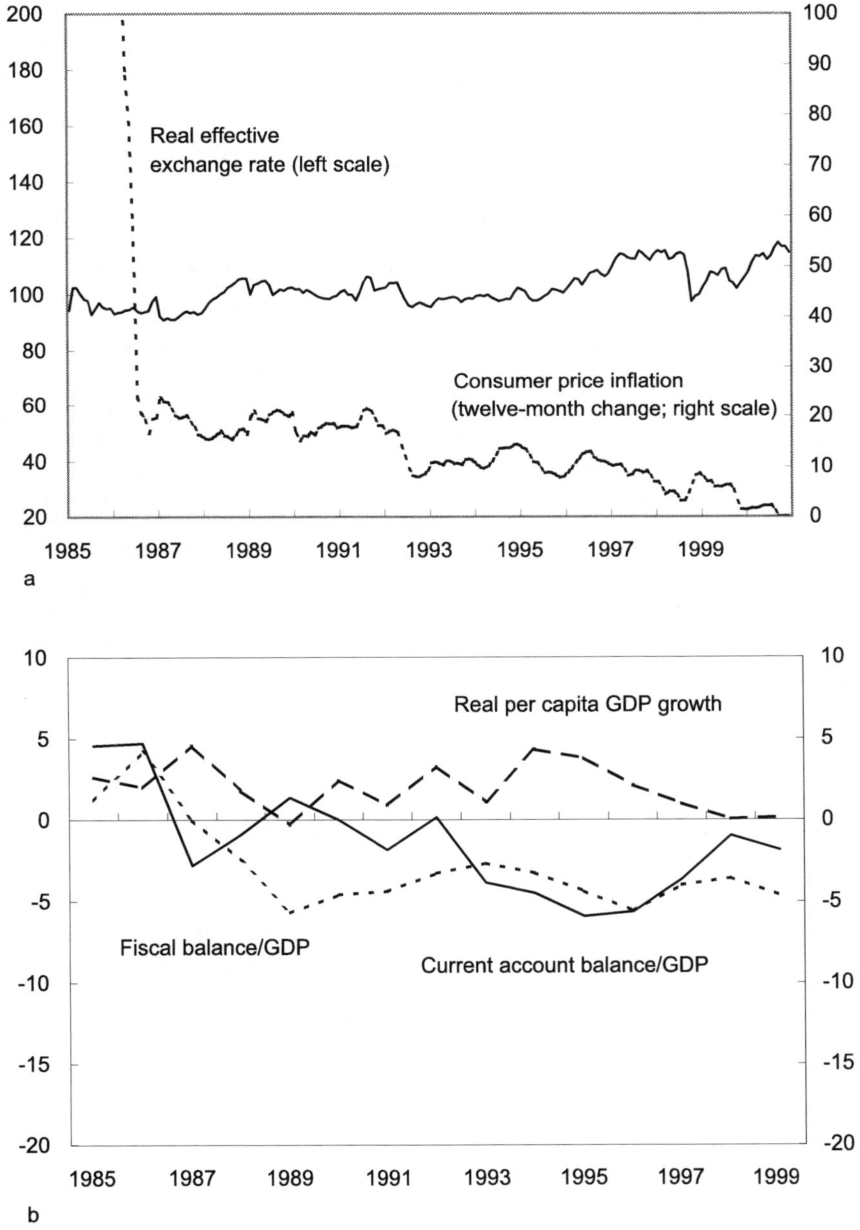

Figure 5.3
Israel: Macroeconomic Indicators, 1985–2000. (a) Inflation and REER level. (b) Growth rate, fiscal, and current account balances

Box 5.1
Israel: Exchange Rate Arrangements, 1980–2000

Real exchange rate rule (April 1979–September 1982): Exchange rate adjusted to follow a rough real exchange rate rule against a currency basket.

Tablita (September 1982–October 1983): Monthly exchange rate change limited to 5 percent.

Floating exchange rate (October 1983–July 1985): Floating regime after 23 percent devaluation.

Fixed exchange rate (July 1985–December 1988): Fixed rate initially against the U.S. dollar after 25 percent up-front devaluation in late June and early July. Rate set at NIS 1.5 per U.S. dollar. Peg switched to a currency basket instead of the U.S. dollar in August 1986, and a devaluation was undertaken in January 1987 (10 percent).

Horizontal exchange rate band (January 1989–December 1991): Devaluation of 13 percent to a midpoint of NIS 1.95 per currency basket unit, within an exchange band of ±3 percent in January 1989. Midpoint and band devalued with a midpoint of NIS 2.07 per currency basket unit in June 1989. Midpoint shifted to NIS 2.19 per currency basket unit with width of the band expanded to ±5 percent in March 1990. Midpoint shifted to NIS 2.41 in September 1990, and then to NIS 2.55 in March 1991.

Crawling exchange rate band (December 1991–present): Initially devaluation of 3 percent with midpoint of 2.63 moving at 9 percent per annum thereafter with a width of ±5 percent. Devaluation of 3 percent with midpoint at 2.93 with rate of crawl adjusted to 8 percent per annum in November 1992. Devaluation of 2 percent with midpoint at 3.15 with rate of crawl adjusted to 6 percent per annum in July 1993. Devaluation of 0.8 percent with midpoint at 3.54 with rate of crawl left at 6 percent per annum but width of the band expanded to ±7 percent in May 1995. Shift in the depreciated limit by 14 percent with rate of crawl of the depreciated limit left at 6 percent per annum, but rate of crawl of the appreciated limit lowered to 4 percent per annum in July 1997. Rate of crawl of the appreciated limit lowered to 2 percent per annum in August 1998.

The Second Inflation Plateau, 1992–1996

As the exchange rate regime shifted to a crawling peg with a bandwidth of ±5 percent, inflation fell to around 10 percent in 1992, and for several years thereafter remained around this level, the result initially of a decline in the rate of increase of tradeable goods prices, and of the supply-side effects of lower wage increases. The initial reduction in tradeable prices reflected a 6 ½ percent decline in U.S. dollar import prices in 1991–1992 due to the appreciation of the dollar against other major currencies. The continuation of the lower rate of inflation resulted from the ongoing moderation in wages, the easing of housing price pressures as the number of new immigrants started to slow after 1992, and some tightening of monetary and fiscal policies.[5]

These lower inflation levels were by and large sustained in the period 1993–1996. Annual tradeable price inflation remained relatively constant at 8 percent, and underlying nontradeable inflation at around 10 percent. In contrast, housing and fruit and vegetable prices showed a very high level of volatility.

In part, the consolidation of inflation at lower levels reflected important steps taken in 1991–1992 to enhance the credibility and effectiveness of the policy framework. First, the 1991 Budget Deficit Reduction Law aimed to provide some assurance that the expansion in fiscal spending associated with the immigrant inflows was temporary. Under this law, a four-year domestic deficit[6] retrenchment path was outlined, the targets of which fell from 6 percent of GDP in 1992 to fiscal balance by 1995 (Bufman and Leiderman, 1999; Dahan and Strawczynski, 1999). The actual domestic deficit undershot these targets in both 1992 and 1993.

Second, as already noted, in December 1991, the mechanics of the nominal anchor were changed. A forward-looking crawling exchange rate band was introduced, with the rate of crawl based on the projected differential between inflation in Israel and abroad. Gradually, as the width of the band was increased from ± 5 percent to ± 7 percent—partly to accommodate capital account liberalization—interest rate policy switched from being used in support of the exchange rate regime to achieving the inflation target itself.[7] However, the official inflation targets set for the new monetary regime were not very ambitious (between 7–10 percent during this period), and there was little progress on disinflation. After moderating in 1993, nontradable price pressures accelerated sharply in 1994 in response to a premature easing of monetary policy starting in mid-1993, a consumption boom as new immigrants were absorbed into the labor force, the confidence imparted by the peace process, and a sharp increase in housing and especially fruit and vegetable prices. In the face of these pressures, rather than being tightened, fiscal policy was eased, including a 16.5 percent increase in public sector wages at the end of 1994. The domestic deficit subsequently exceeded its target (3.2 percent of GDP in 1995, compared to a target of 2.75 percent), and the current account began to deteriorate.

With the inflation target achieving increased operational significance, monetary policy was tightened sharply during the second half of 1994, with a 4.5 percentage point increase in the nominal bank rate, and nontradeable inflation pressures eased in 1995. A premature easing of monetary policy during 1995 and substantial fiscal expansion in 1996 (the domestic deficit was 4.7 percent of GDP, compared to a target of 2.5 percent) led to further inflationary pressures and a deterioration in the current account deficit during 1996. Monetary policy was again tightened, and this time it was kept restrictive.

The sharp increase in interest rates implied by the combination of loose fiscal and tight monetary policies, as well as the initiation of the peace process and relatively open capital account, led to heavy capital inflows from early 1995. These inflows resulted from direct and portfolio foreign investment, government borrowing under the U.S. loan guarantee program, as well as foreign currency credit from banks as the business sector perceived the costs of such borrowing would be lower than for borrowing in sheqels.[8] As the exchange rate appreciated to the lower bound of the band, monetary policy became seriously overburdened: The BoI was required to intervene to defend the band and to sterilize the inflows to protect the inflation target.[9] In this environment, although monetary policy was used to offset the rising inflationary pressures caused by demand pressures, and hence consolidated inflation at annual rates around 10 percent, further advances in disinflation proved elusive.

Single-Digit Inflation, 1997–2000

At the end of 1996, the government announced a new policy package, including a front-loaded fiscal retrenchment path that aimed to reduce the overall fiscal deficit to 1.5 percent of GDP by 2001, and for the first time set a medium-term inflation target (but not path) for 2001 equal to the average of the OECD countries (operationally taken to be 4.5 percent). Almost immediately thereafter, with the ongoing tight monetary policy and associated low economic growth, actual trends indicated that the 1997 deficit target of 2.8 percent of GDP would be exceeded.

In mid-1997, the new minister of finance announced a fiscal package that in the end proved sufficient to achieve the 1997 deficit target,[10] and at the same time, the depreciated limit of the exchange rate band was widened significantly. With fiscal and monetary policy now both restrictive, the weak activity level (especially investment) and rising unemployment level, a real appreciation of the sheqel, and initiation of some structural reforms that lowered prices (e.g., in the telecommunications sector), inflation pressures moderated rapidly after mid-1997. One year later, the twelve-month inflation rate was 4 percent, well below the official target of 7–10 percent. In mid-1998, the 1999 target was set at 4 percent, and there was a sharp decline in nominal interest rates in the wake of the declining inflation trend.

Following the Russian crisis and world contagion in August–September 1998, the sheqel depreciated sharply in the second half of 1988 as foreign and domestic agents reassessed the risks associated with their earlier unhedged foreign borrowing.[11] The risk of renewed inflationary pressures was met forcefully with a 4 percentage point increase in official interest rates; the ongoing containment of fiscal policy and the impact of the depressed economy on the current account helped to consolidate this monetary response. The BoI chose not to intervene by selling foreign exchange, relying rather on the interest rate increase and private sector responses to it to reverse the depreciation. The inflation rate rapidly returned to annual levels around 4 percent; output growth remained depressed and unemployment high. By 2000, inflation had fallen sharply to around 1 percent per annum, undershooting the inflation target range for the year of 3–4 percent.

5.4 Lessons from Other Countries' Experiences with Disinflation, 1985–1999

We report here on the conclusions of comparative studies of the disinflation process, particularly for countries that have been stuck for a period with moderate inflation (drawing mainly on Dornbusch and Fischer, 1993, and Burton and Fischer, 1998). To provide a context for the subsequent comparative analysis of Israel's disinflation experience, we summarize experiences in nine countries—three that moved from high to low inflation levels without a period of moderate inflation (Argentina, Brazil, Croatia), three that experienced moderate inflation for a period and then reduced inflation to low levels (Chile, Egypt, Greece), and three that also experienced a period of moderate inflation and at the time of writing still had inflation levels around 10 percent per annum (Colombia, Hungary, Mexico). The main macroeconomic series for these nine countries are shown in figures 5.4–5.6. A summary of critical features that affected each countries' success in reducing inflation is presented in table 5.2; their respective experiences are described in greater detail in Burton and Fischer (1998) and in Fischer and Orsmond (2001). The experiences of these nine countries, and others, suggest the following interrelated generalizations.

Stabilizing inflation at low single-digit levels can take a long time.

After a stabilization program was launched, it typically (but not always) took a considerable time to attain a low level of inflation. Indeed, of the nine countries discussed here, Croatia was the only country that reduced inflation to low single-digit levels almost immediately following the start of the stabilization program. Two countries took around two years (Argentina, Brazil), but the others took much longer (on average around five years) to achieve this result, in part due to the lack of forcefulness in their disinflation policies. This result suggests the need for policymakers to be prepared from the outset to persevere with anti-inflation policies if their goal is indeed to achieve and then to sustain a low inflation level.

A sustainable fiscal balance is critical to the maintenance of low inflation. Accordingly, fiscal retrenchment is generally necessary to lower demand pressures and ensure the maintenance of low inflation.

The establishment and maintenance of a sound fiscal position is a necessary, though not sufficient, condition to reduce inflation to low levels.[12] All countries that man-

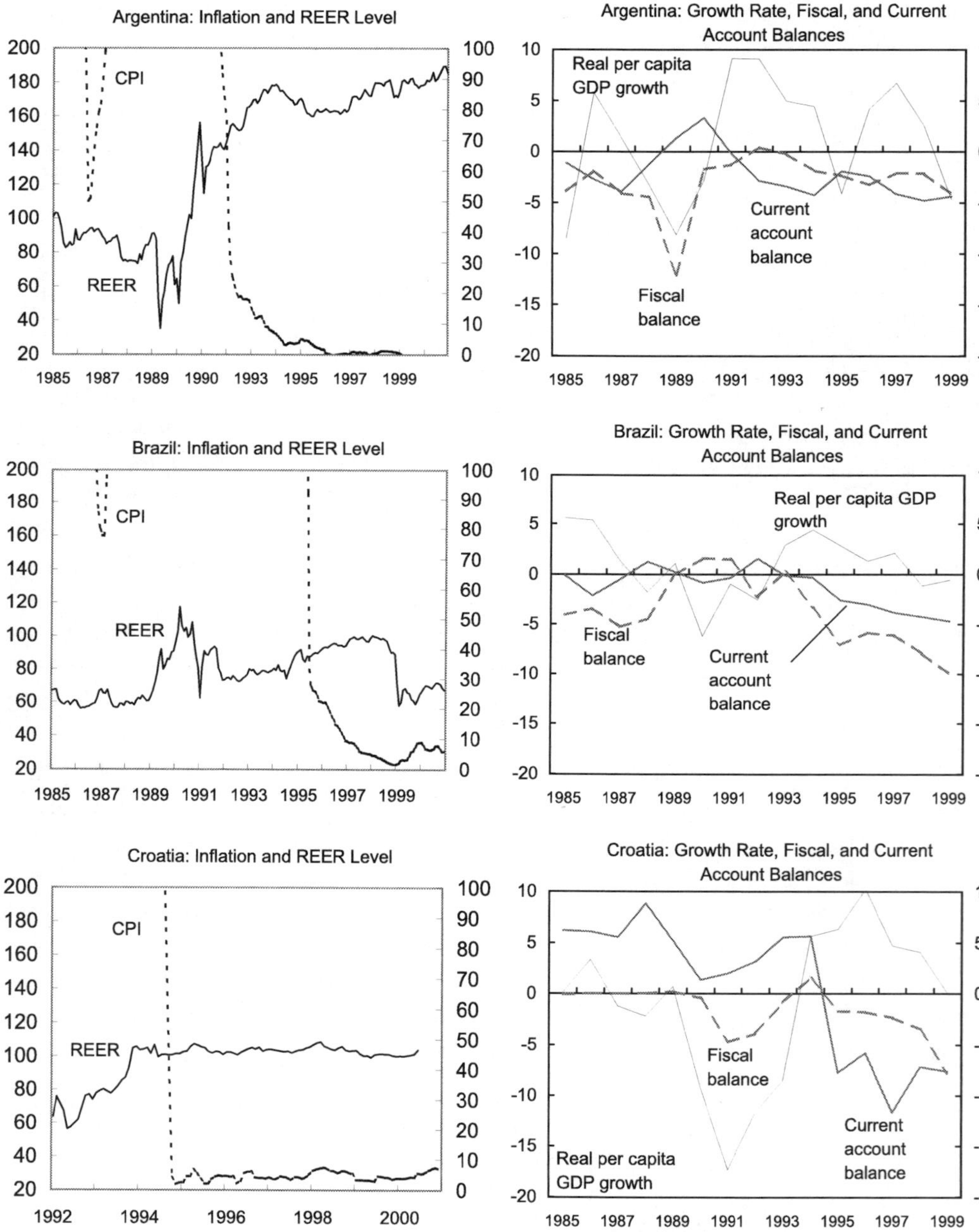

Figure 5.4
Argentina, Brazil, and Croatia: Macroeconomic Indicators, 1985–2000
(REER index, 1990 = 100; CPI 12-month change; balances in percent of GDP)

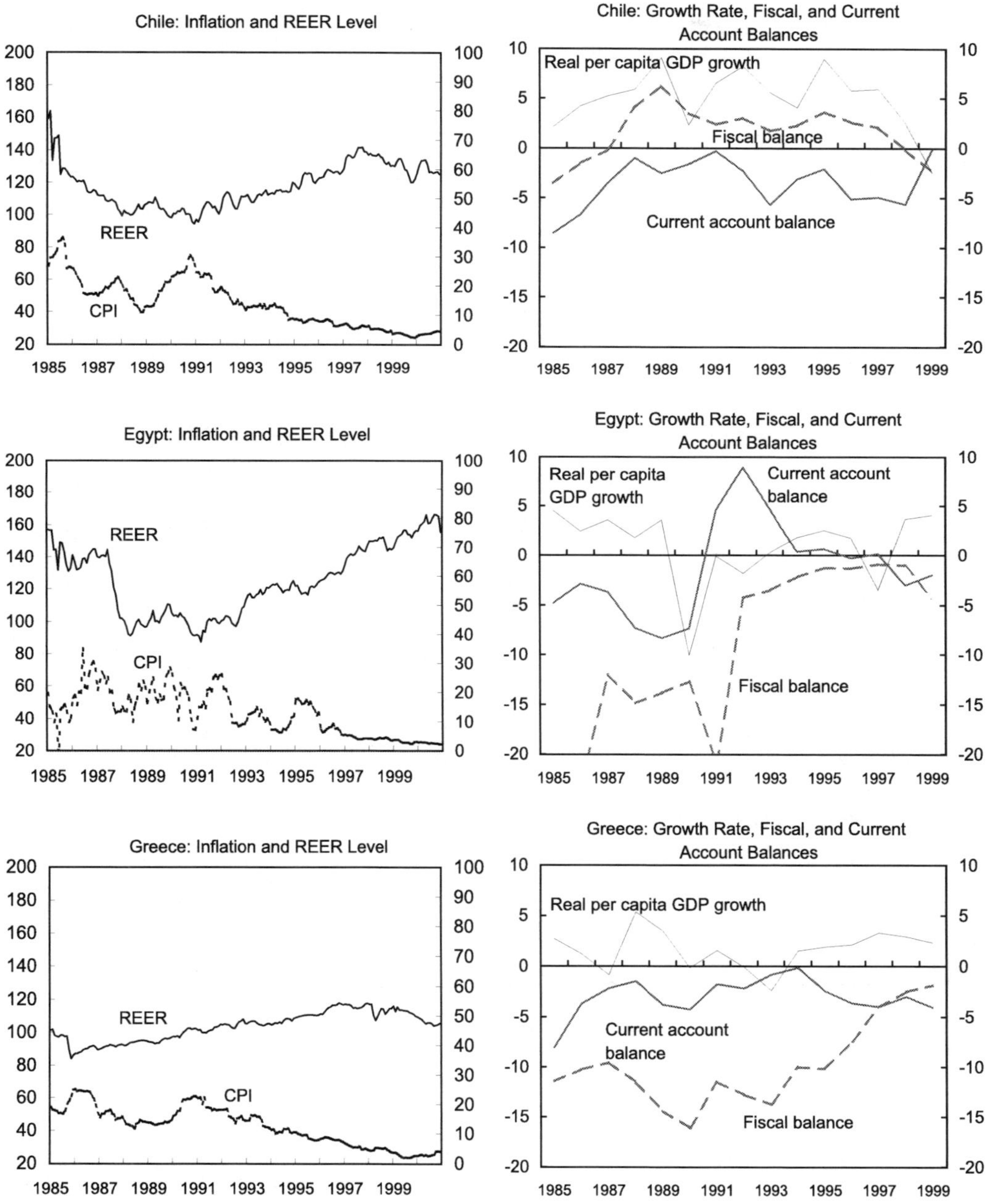

Figure 5.5
Chile, Egypt, and Greece: Macroeconomic Indicators, 1985–2000
(REER index, 1990 = 100; CPI 12-month change; balances in percent of GDP)

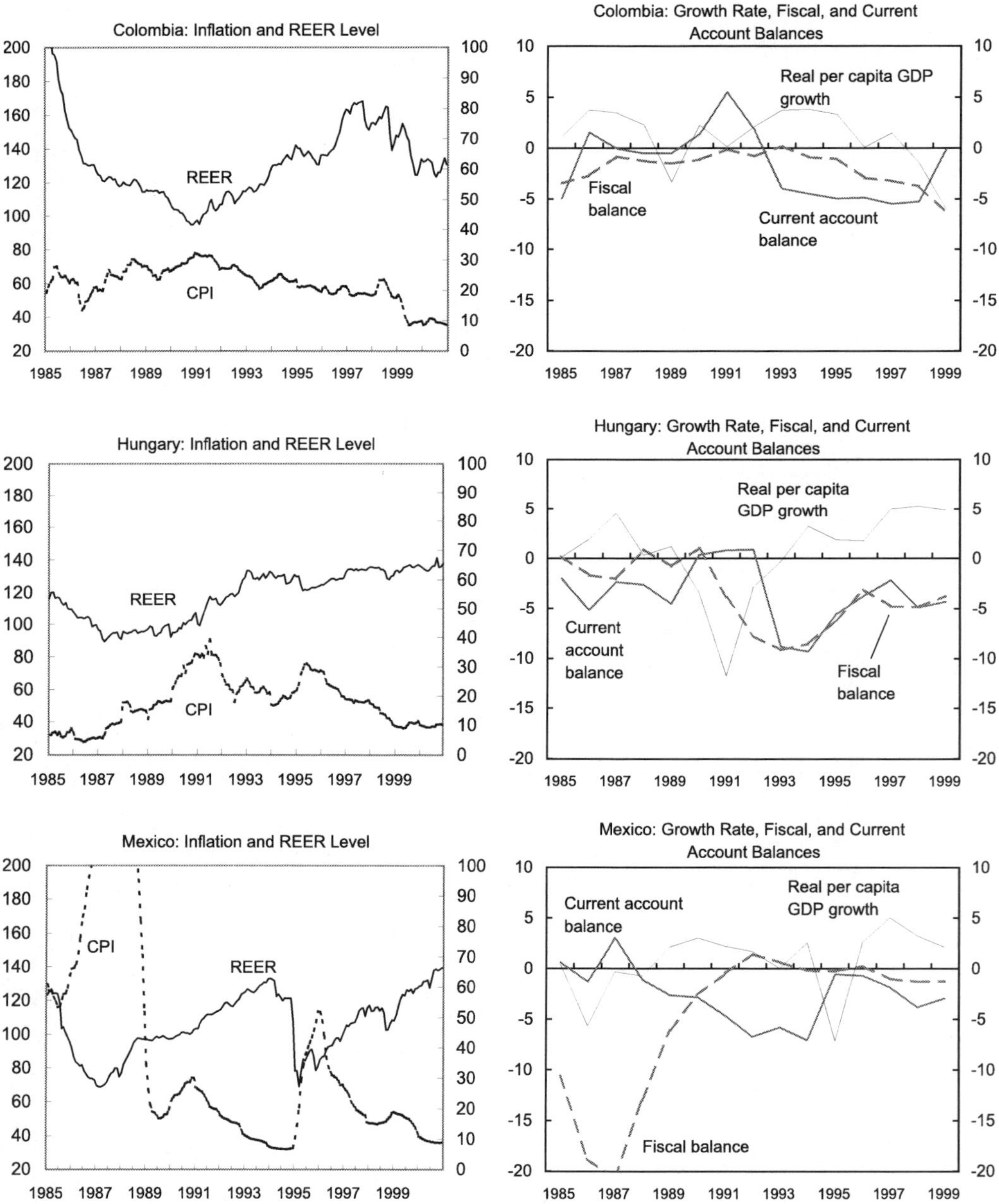

Figure 5.6
Colombia, Hungary, and Mexico: Macroeconomic Indicators, 1985–2000
(REER index, 1990 = 100; CPI 12-month change; balances in percent of GDP)

aged to tame inflation had either already reduced fiscal imbalances (such as Argentina, Brazil, Chile) or made a major fiscal effort from the outset of the stabilization program (such as Croatia and Egypt). Achieving an initial fiscal adjustment was not, however, by itself sufficient to sustain low inflationary pressures. In some countries, the fiscal position was relaxed soon thereafter because structural fiscal issues were not adequately addressed (Brazil, for example, which did not forcefully address the pension system and intergovernmental relations, in contrast to the effort to address key aspects of structural fiscal reform in other countries, such as in Greece), while in other countries nonfiscal issues were largely responsible for ongoing inflation levels (Mexico and, initially, Colombia). Countries that started with a large fiscal deficit and reduced it only slowly experienced a lengthy disinflation process (Hungary, Greece).

Efforts to reduce nominal rigidities in order to lower the costs of inflation inertia during stabilization programs can be helpful. Price and wage controls can prove useful, especially in helping reduce the initial output costs of disinflation, though they are at best temporary measures—designed to reduce the output costs of the disinflation—and hence the disinflation effort needs to be backed by sound macroeconomic fundamentals. Steps taken during the stabilization period to enhance labor market flexibility also assist in the stabilization effort, including the modification or abolition of wage indexation.

Efforts to break inflation inertia, if backed by a sustained adjustment in the fundamentals, reduced the time it took to disinflate. Official wage and price freezes or slowdowns—particularly in the public sector—were a feature in all the countries that reduced inflation without becoming stuck at moderate levels. Countries that banned wage indexation at the outset of the program disinflated more quickly without becoming stuck at moderate levels (Argentina, Brazil, Croatia, and, initially, Mexico), although other rigidities in the labor market sometimes implied a heavy cost in terms of employment (Argentina). Two countries continued in practice with wage indexation—Chile, where inflation fell only gradually (even against the background of weak labor market conditions), and Colombia, which still has a rather high inflation level.

Exchange rate anchors lower inflation pressures rapidly, but the real exchange rate appreciation that typically follows threatens medium-term balance-of-payments stability.

Virtually every country that tried to disinflate initially relied on the exchange rate as the nominal anchor. Success in reducing inflation rapidly and at low output cost with

Table 5.2
Selected Countries: Policy and Other Factors in Inflationary Process

	Fiscal policy	Exchange rate policy	Monetary policy	Capital inflows
Countries that reduced high inflation rapidly				
Argentina	Deficit reduced prior to stabilization program; initially tight position thereafter until fiscal impulse during 1992–1994; thereafter, fiscal structural weaknesses addressed but not eliminated	Currency board at outset of stabilization program	Supporting role; remonetization and fall in interest rates as inflation rate declined. Tightened with outflows due to the currency board regime	Inflows with return of earlier capital flight, remonetization, and privatization. External events prompted later outflows as well
Brazil	Small operational surplus at outset of stabilization; inadequate fiscal structural reforms; fiscal stance subsequently weakened	Anchor role with the exchange rate initially subject to a floor; later crawling peg at less than the ensuing inflation	Loosening in fiscal stance placed increasing burden on monetary policy	Substantial inflows, exacerbated by imbalance between monetary and fiscal policy. External events and domestic policies prompted later outflows
Croatia	Slow fiscal consolidation	Exchange rate peg with an unannounced narrow band; ten percent depreciation last two years	Supporting role	Significant inflows after investment grade; capital controls imposed
Countries that experienced moderate inflation and then reduced it to low levels				
Chile	Central government fiscal surplus from late 1980s until 1997	Initially discrete depreciations in context of a crawling arrangement; thereafter, backward-looking real rule within a band, which appreciated on several occasions to help reduce inflation; free float in 1999	Targets real interest rates to control domestic expenditures. Policy generally directed toward reducing inflation	Large throughout 1990s; capital controls imposed and later suspended when outflow pressures began
Egypt	Loose fiscal policy finally addressed and then remained at lower levels	Pegged throughout as nominal anchor	Supporting role; effectiveness increased with financial sector deregulation	Episodes of large inflows; offset by sterilized intervention and capital controls

Table 5.2 (continued)

Indexation	Incomes policy	Relative price adjustment	Other
Indexation of local currency wage and financial contracts banned	Freeze on public sector wages, pensions and prices for nine months	Up-front depreciation, adjustments in domestic prices, at outset of stabilization program	Wide-ranging structural reforms to improve competitiveness including tariff reform; inflexibilities remain in the labor market, and unemployment is high
Backward indexation for less than one year eliminated by denominating wages, prices, and financial transactions in the new unit of account	Following introduction of new currency, wages to remain fixed during contract period. Public prices fixed	Prior denomination of prices and wages in unit of account designed to avoid relative price misalignments	Wide-spread reform, but important areas remain to be adequately addressed, such as social security
State sector wage and pension indexation abolished at outset of stabilization program	Some initial steps to control wage growth for public sector employees	Not a major factor. Most prices implicitly indexed to exchange rate before stabilization	Enterprise restructuring encouraged through privatization and financial control; not fully successful
In practice, still widely used in labor and financial sectors	Not a factor	Not a significant factor	Wide-ranging structural reform prior to program; central bank made more independent; positive shocks to terms of trade-affected inflation
Not a factor	Not a factor	Not a factor	Wide-ranging structural reforms

Table 5.2 (continued)

	Fiscal policy	Exchange rate policy	Monetary policy	Capital inflows
Greece	Loose fiscal policy gradually tightened after 1990; structural issues started to be addressed but more required	Crawling band anchor after 1994; ERM participant since early 1998 and entry into euro area from 2001	Supportive role; effective with financial sector deregulation	Large inflows of official assistance; capital account liberalization
Countries that experienced moderate inflation which is still around 10 percent per annum				
Colombia	Not a major factor initially; loosening after 1995	Crawling band with preannounced rate of crawl after 1994; large depreciation in 1998; peso was floated after September 1999	Supporting role	Large inflows led to imposition of capital controls
Hungary	Loose fiscal policy gradually tightened after 1995	Shift from ad hoc adjustments to crawling band as an anchor in 1995; rate of crawl gradually lowered	Initially loose, then supportive of tight fiscal stance	Hindered disinflation in 1995–1996 leading to maintenance of capital controls and sterilization
Mexico	Major factor behind initial stabilization; influenced later changes in inflation performance	Initially fixed for one year, then crawling peg then band; increasingly used as nominal anchor until the end of 1994; flexible since	Main tool for reducing inflation in 1995–1996	Inflows major factor in early 1990s; outflows triggered crisis at end of 1994

an exchange rate peg depended on the accompanying fiscal and monetary measures. In particular, as the anchor became perceived as credible, wage and nontradeable price inflation pressures moderated. However, residual rigidities and entrenched expectations typically led to a period of real appreciation of the exchange rate. Thus, maintenance of the inflationary gains from the initial stabilization often required a subsequent fiscal or monetary tightening to bring inflation down further.

This pattern did not hold in a few countries: In particular, there was no real appreciation in Croatia which ended inflation almost overnight. This unusual achievement is probably due to the fact that at the outset of the program, virtually all prices were linked to the deutsche mark, which was used as the peg. In Hungary, a narrow band backed by tight fiscal and monetary policies and strong output growth as a consequence of earlier structural reforms managed to contain the real appreciation.

Table 5.2 (continued)

Indexation	Incomes policy	Relative price adjustment	Other
Wages formally deindexed but in practice still widely used	Restriction of wages in public sector	Not a factor	Start to structural reform on a wide front related to ERM and euro area entry
Backward-looking wage indexation	Voluntary social pact introduced in 1995; limited effectiveness	Not a major factor	Deeply entrenched inflation expectations
Minor factor; no formal wage indexation	Restriction of wages in state enterprises in 1995 and flexible labor markets	Important factor	Wide-ranging structural reforms providing large productivity gains
Important factor prior to 1987; replaced later with social pact	Important factor under the social pact that set a convergence path for wages, selected public prices, and the exchange rate	Administered price increases minor factor	Wide-ranging structural reform prior to the program; ongoing weak banking sector

In most other countries, however, the real exchange rate appreciated, typically by around 30–50 percent, which soon called into question the sustainability of the current account position. Subsequent movements away from pegs to crawling bands accommodated at least part of the ongoing domestic-foreign inflation differential (Greece). Countries that allowed their exchange rate to fully offset these differentials—moving to a backward-looking real exchange rate rule as in Chile or the recent floating exchange rate used in Mexico—weakened the nominal anchor, leading to more gradual disinflation. Real exchange rate rules also ran the risk of transforming one-time changes in the price level into permanent changes in the rate of inflation (Bufman and Leiderman, 1999). At the same time, such rules reduced the likelihood of subsequent balance of payments crises during the disinflation effort.

In countries where the capital account is open, policies need to adjust to capital inflows that threaten the maintenance of low inflation levels, and to capital outflows that threaten balance of payment sustainability. In economies that use an exchange rate peg as the nominal anchor and faced capital inflows, fiscal tightening is, on balance, a better choice than a relaxation of monetary policy, sterilization, and/or recourse to price or quantity-based capital controls.

All the countries detailed here experienced capital inflows, and most, also, subsequent outflows, both of which complicated the disinflation process. These inflows result from the combination of relatively high domestic interest rates to fight inflation with the appreciation of the currency typical in an exchange-rate based stabilization. In some cases, the high interest rates were clearly the consequence of an excessively expansionary fiscal policy, in which case fiscal adjustment could be undertaken. In other cases, the inflows reflected remonetization of the economy or simply increased investment opportunities, including from privatization.

In managing such inflows, the exchange rate peg regimes that were useful in anchoring expectations in the initial stages of adjustment programs could later prove a liability. In the absence of exchange rate flexibility, fiscal policy had to be tightened, although this could prove politically difficult for some countries. The alternatives to fiscal tightening under an exchange rate peg were not especially effective. Monetary loosening was inconsistent with the goal of bringing inflation down further; sterilization was costly, ineffective over the medium term, and stored up future problems by causing an increase in the open foreign exchange position of the private sector, which increased vulnerability; and imposing controls on short-term flows typically lengthened maturities rather than reduced the magnitude of the total inflows. Similarly, the countries that were most successful in addressing outflows were those that aggressively increased and sustained the restrictiveness of monetary policy, although this implied a willingness to endure a potentially large shock to the real sector, which was not always viewed as credible (Brazil, Mexico).

Structural reform is important to provide a base for strong and sustainable growth, which also assists in the maintenance of low inflation, including by preventing noncompetitive pricing behavior by protected firms.

The countries that grew rapidly were often those that had the most far-reaching structural reform programs (Argentina, Chile, Hungary), whereas those where growth has recently slowed typically undertook relatively weaker structural reforms, at least in some important areas (Brazil, Croatia, Colombia). Some structural reforms, such as a reduction in import tariffs, had the potential to lower price pressures, whereas a lack of reform could lead to price and wage inflexibilities. Typically, these reforms were most likely to succeed if they were initiated at the outset of the program when political support was high.

Positive favorable shocks can be used to reduce inflation (opportunistic disinflation), and it is important to respond forcefully to adverse shocks.

All countries experienced external shocks during their disinflation efforts. Several were able to take advantage of positive shocks—such as improvements in the terms of trade—to make further inroads into inflation (Chile). It was important that external negative shocks—usually transmitted via capital flight—were dealt with forcibly if the disinflation effort were not to be lost (Argentina, Mexico, Brazil in 1994).

Signals of a government's resolve to lower inflation via changes in institutional arrangements can have an important effect on underlying inflation pressures.

Several countries changed the institutional framework in ways that enhanced the authorities' inflation-fighting credibility, such as the use by Argentina of a currency board arrangement, Chile's move in 1991 to make the central bank more independent, and Greece's commitment to join the ERM and euro area, all of which were effective in reducing inflationary pressures.

Finally, stabilization from high inflation levels supports economic growth, and there is little evident output cost of disinflating from moderate inflation levels either.

In the countries reviewed here, growth did not decline and usually accelerated following the initiation of the stabilization program, and then remained strong for several years thereafter.

5.5 Explaining Israel's Disinflation Experiences

We now return to the discussion of Israel, analyzing the disinflation period from the perspective of the lessons that emerge from the experiences in other countries. Clearly, in Israel, *stabilization of inflation to low single digits has taken a long time.* In large part, this has simply reflected a lack of political consensus on the need to pursue single-digit inflation. Although the far-ranging and bold initial stabilization program led to a sharp reduction in inflation from very high levels in 1985, the effort to continue the disinflation effort—meaning, in practice, persistence with tight fiscal and monetary policies—waned thereafter.

After the initial success in lowering inflation, the next sustainable decline in inflation had more to do with exogenous factors associated with immigration levels and world commodity prices than deliberate policy decisions to reduce inflation. The conclusion that there was little political support for further disinflation is supported by the official inflation targets for the period 1993–1998, all of which lay between 7–10 percent, and both monetary and fiscal policies were relaxed prematurely during this time. It was only after both fiscal and monetary policies were tightened in 1997 and the government set a medium-term inflation target for 2001 (but not a target path) and low inflation targets for 1999–2000 that were treated seriously by the BoI, that further advances on reaching and sustaining low inflation levels were made.

Reflecting this lack of consensus to disinflate quickly or at all, the *fiscal deficit has periodically been loosened*, which complicated the stabilization effort. Indeed, the fiscal deficit was relaxed almost immediately after the 1985 stabilization program began. Some credibility may initially have been gained by the introduction of the 1991 Budget Deficit Reduction Law—with a target end point of budget balance—but this was not lived up to. The 1996 fiscal retrenchment law set a front-loaded medium-term profile, but with a less ambitious target point than under the previous program (an overall deficit of 1.5 percent of GDP by 2001).[13]

Not only has periodic fiscal slippage had its impact on the credibility of the disinflation effort—it is hard to view the 16.5 percent public sector wage increase granted in 1994 as consistent with the official inflation target in that year of 8 percent—it has also implied that most of the disinflation effort has depended on restrictive monetary policy, a costly policy mix in terms of its impact on growth and complications from capital inflows. It is only recently that the fiscal sector has contributed more substantially to the disinflation effort. As for the composition of the fiscal accounts, expenditure has continually been curtailed on defense and subsidies, although there is room for further strengthening, including tax reform. Pressing areas to ensure a sustainable medium-term fiscal position include further reform of the health sector and the pension system.

Direct measures to reduce inflation were not a major part of the stabilization effort, except at the outset of the program, when they were politically important. Beyond the initial wage freeze, which was soon relaxed, and price controls for the first six months—which did play an important role in securing public support for the stabilization program and were effective in helping reduce inflation at a low initial cost in terms of unemployment—there was no strong effort to contain inflation inertia. Wage indexation was maintained, and real wages returned rapidly to their prestabilization levels. This rapid increase in real wages at the outset of the program was, in essence, blessed by the government-agreed wage agreements made within two months of the start of the program; Bruno and Piterman (1988) argue that the increases reflected a lack of faith by firms in the government's initial resolve to deliver price stability and hence in the willingness to limit large nominal increases.[14] In any event, the consequence was to undo much of the initial real adjustment achieved through the incomes policy aspects of the stabilization program, implying that an increased emphasis would have to be placed on the other (orthodox) components of the program if the disinflation effort were to be sustained. Thereafter, it was not until the exogenous increase in immigration levels that the wage-setting process became more flexible. In recent periods, further labor market rigidities have been added, including the lowering of the backward-looking inflation threshold above which a COLA is paid, and the linking of, and then increase in, the ratio of the minimum wage to the average wage.

The *exchange rate regime* has in stages shifted toward greater flexibility during the disinflation process. Given the ongoing domestic-foreign inflation differential, the government's resolve to protect the price anchor aspects of the stabilization policy was tested early in the period following the 1985 stabilization program. The initial devaluation in 1987, and the subsequent changes to the horizontal band between 1988–1991, clearly signaled to the private sector that this nominal anchor had been weakened in order to keep the real exchange rate roughly constant and to thereby protect the balance of payments, at a time when there was no alternative and transparent anchor in place.[15]

This problem has gradually been resolved as a forward-looking inflation target has gained credibility and inflation has declined. The increased reliance on inflation targeting as a nominal anchor has been combined with a gradual exit from the exchange rate anchor, but the slow pace of the exit led to periodic conflicts as to whether the exchange rate or the inflation target was the dominant anchor. The credibility of the inflation target was enhanced by the firm monetary response to the initial price level effects of the depreciation at the end of 1998, and private-sector inflation expectations fell back to levels close to the 1999–2000 targets.

Large capital inflows from 1995 through mid-1997 in response to the loose fiscal/tight monetary policy mix complicated the disinflation process and led to a sharp real appreciation of the exchange rate. The response of monetary policy—sterilized intervention—was not sustainable over the medium term, but managed for a period to contain inflationary pressures. The consequence, however, was a rapid buildup in the open foreign exchange position of the private sector—given that the BoI was the counterpart for the inflows—which increased vulnerability, and which contributed to the sharp depreciation and inflation impulse when the risk of open foreign exchange positions was reassessed at the end of 1998.

Outside of extensive financial sector reform, which improved the effectiveness of monetary policy, *far-reaching structural reforms were not a major part of the initial stabilization effort, nor has there been a consistent emphasis on structural reform subsequently.* The lack of widespread structural reform, which could have contained prices in noncompetitive sectors, precluded a potential downward pressure on the price level that could have aided disinflation (Ministry of Finance, 1998). The privatization program was begun late and has had a heavy focus on changing ownership of the government-owned banking sector without, thus far, corresponding efforts to increase competition in financial services. The most positive development has been the increasing competition in the telecommunications sector, where prices have declined sharply. Remaining areas for reform include, inter alia, the labor market, reform of the capital market including the pension system and taxation of financial income, increasing competition in goods markets, and reducing the size of the (large) government sector.

Turning to the other lessons that emerge from the international experience of disinflation, Israel was particularly successful in capitalizing on several *positive external shocks.* These included the decline in oil prices at the early stages of the stabilization program, the flexibility added to the labor market during the high immigrant inflows, and later declines in import prices. The government has frequently endeavored to *build credibility by signaling its policy resolve* such as by its announcement of the two medium-term fiscal retrenchment paths, and the announcement of a medium-term inflation target, although the actual effect of these measures in lowering inflation is difficult to determine given that in each case the resolve of the government was not fully believed. Finally, the *link between disinflation and growth has been mixed.* The initial disinflation effort was achieved at no immediate cost to growth, although this came later as the initial consumption boom faded. Recent disinflation efforts took place during a significant growth slowdown, in part a reflection of the previous poor policy mix, as well as the unwinding of extraneous factors.

5.6 Strategy for the Future

By the start of 2000, the goal of moving Israeli inflation to the low levels of the better performing industrial countries had been reached. Consolidating this achievement will require an appropriate policy environment, the elements of which should include: (1) fiscal policy restraint, with further consolidation of the underlying fiscal position; (2) monetary policy aimed toward sustaining the recent low inflation levels; and (3) bold structural reforms to move the economy to its potential level of growth as soon as possible. To bolster these policies, the inflation experiences of Israel and the other countries studied here suggest the need for changes in institutional arrangements to provide the best chance of sustained low-inflation levels and improved economic performance.

Central Bank Operational Independence and Policy Goals

International experience suggests that the achievement and maintenance of low inflation and sustained growth is more likely if monetary policy has the primary goal of maintaining low inflation, and if the central bank is given the operational independence to achieve its goals. The inflation target itself can be specified by the government. The inflation experience of Israel, especially that prior to the stabilization program, indicates the cost of not providing the BoI with the independence to use the instruments of monetary policy toward the inflation goal, and using monetary policy to support goals for which it is not well suited. The Levin Committee recommendations on the appropriate policy objectives and operational practices for the BoI offer a suitable approach.

Inflation-Targeting Regimes

The worldwide experience with inflation targets is brief—mainly restricted to the 1990s—and hence the most effective mechanisms under such a regime are still being tested. Nonetheless, theory suggests that to be most effective at guiding monetary policy (which acts with a lag) and to enhance certainty for the private sector, the inflation targets should be set over the medium term (two or more years ahead) rather than on a year-to-year basis as currently in Israel.[16] The adoption of such a framework would increase the ability of the central bank to maintain low inflation on average, while taking account of whatever short-run tradeoffs might exist between inflation and economic activity. Further, most inflation-targeting countries (such as Australia, Canada, New Zealand, and the United Kingdom) have at least the operational (if not the actual) inflation target based on underlying rather than overall inflation, so that monetary policy is not hostage to fluctuations in volatile prices. Such a shift would contribute to the success of monetary policy in Israel, which has in the past tended to respond to short-term fluctuations in prices of fruits and vegetables and housing.[17] Note too that the experience to date suggests that although the monetary authorities need not have goal independence, they must have a reasonable degree of instrument (operational) independence to meet the inflation goal (Debelle and Fischer, 1994).

Consistency of Inflation-Targeting Regime with Exchange Rate and Other Policies

Although Israel for some time operated with inflation targets in a crawling peg exchange-rate regime, it is clear that there may well be conflicts between these two approaches to monetary policy. The question then arises as to which should have primacy when a conflict arises. Typically, the conflict occurs when inflation is low and the real exchange rate appreciated, with the current account deficit becoming uncomfortably large (Masson, et al., 1997). At that point, there may be a short-run trade-off between the current account and inflation targets: An expansionary monetary policy (cut in interest rates) will temporarily produce a real depreciation. Given that such a tradeoff is typically very short-term—especially in Israel—the real answer to the dilemma lies in the area of fiscal policy. Hence, in general, particularly in economies open to international capital flows, the inflation target should predominate, and the exchange rate should be allowed to become flexible.

Fiscal Policy Framework

Several countries such as Australia, New Zealand, and the United Kingdom have recently adopted formal fiscal policy frameworks, stressing the transparency of the fiscal accounts and the setting of medium-term policy goals; Argentina has also just completed a transparency report in line with the IMF's Fiscal Transparency Code. Israel was among the first in this decade to adopt a medium-term fiscal policy framework, but the credibility of the initial framework was undermined by the failure to follow it. Such a framework can nonetheless reinforce inflation and other economic performance, both by constraining potential occasional fiscal policy excesses, and by informing private-sector expectations of future economic policy.

Notes

1. The overall public sector balance turned from a surplus of 6 percent of GNP in the early 1960s to a deficit of almost 10 percent of GNP at the start of the 1970s due to a sharp increase in military (after the 1967 war), social (education, health, and welfare), and subsidy expenditures.

2. In particular, the opening of the capital account in 1977–1979, which compromised efforts to control the money supply, the ongoing expansion of export credits (control over which was in part the responsibility of the Ministry of Finance), official steps to stabilize the price of government bonds on the secondary market to lower the cost of borrowing, and maintaining a low discount rate so that large fiscal borrowing did not crowd out private sector activity.

3. There were labor protests immediately following the announcement of the stabilization program, which initially included a wage freeze. Negotiations resulted not only in the wage adjustments for August and September, but also in an agreement that wages would increase in December, January, and February by 4 percent per month plus a COLA payment of 80 percent of the excess of inflation above 4 percent per month. New wage negotiations would begin in April 1986.

4. The price index for underlying nontradeable prices excludes the prices of housing and fresh fruit and vegetables, which have been very volatile in the poststabilization period.

5. The U.S. guarantee in 1992 on future government foreign borrowing may have also lowered inflationary pressures by providing some assurances of future current account sustainability and reducing borrowing costs (Liviatan and Sussman, 2001).

6. Recall that this is the *operational*, i.e., inflation-adjusted, deficit.

7. If credible—a critical assumption, and a critical goal of monetary policy—an inflation-targeting regime can serve as a transparent guide to monetary policy and coordination device in the wage- and price-setting process and formation of the public's inflation expectations; see Bufman and Leiderman (1999).

8. Foreign exchange credit increased from 7 percent of GDP in 1994 to 23 percent of GDP by 1998; sheqel-denominated credit as a share in GDP increased from 54 percent to 57 percent in this period.

9. From 1995 to mid-1997, the BoI purchased around fifteen billion dollars (as compared with reserves of seven billion dollars at end 1994), which was sterilized through the monetary-deposit facility provided to commercial banks.

10. Although the overall deficit target as a share in GDP was met, the domestic deficit exceeded its target and the foreign surplus was larger than expected. The latter reflected high foreign earnings from official reserves, the level of which increased sharply as the BoI intervened after 1995 to defend the exchange rate band in the face of large capital inflows. The cost to the BoI of sterilizing capital inflows, incurred via interest payments to commercial banks that place funds at the BoI, is not reflected in the definition of BoI profits used in the fiscal accounts.

11. Interestingly, and as in many other countries, the recent strong and rising FDI flows were not affected by this reassessment.

12. Note though that nominal deficits would typically decline along with inflation, as nominal interest rates decline.

13. And it should be noted that this is the operational or inflation-adjusted deficit, which includes only the real component of interest payments on domestic government debt.

14. It was not until almost four years after the initiation of the program that the COLA was switched from a quarterly to a semiannual payment, indicating the lack of credibility expressed by the private sector in the sustainability of the stabilization effort (Leiderman, 1993).

15. This is not to criticize the decision not to prevent the real exchange rate from appreciating excessively, which was amply justified—merely to emphasize the lack of alternative policies to maintain pressure to reduce inflation.

16. Although it is sometimes argued that the BoI in practice operates with a medium-term path in mind, this lack of transparency for private-sector decision making undermines much of the point of an inflation-targeting regime.

17. See Orsmond (1998) for further details. It is sometimes suggested that the data series in Israel are too short for reliable seasonal adjustment and the creation of an index of underlying inflation; however, operating with an imperfect index would be better than ignoring the problem entirely.

References

Bruno, Michael. *Crisis, Stabilization, and Economic Reform: Therapy by Consensus.* Oxford: Clarendon, 1993.

Bruno, Michael, and Sylvia Piterman. "Israel's Stabilization: A Two Year Review." In *Inflation Stabilization: The Experiences of Israel, Argentina, Brazil, Bolivia, and Mexico,* edited by Michael Bruno et al. (pp. 3–47). Cambridge, Massachusetts: MIT Press, 1988.

Bruno, Michael, et al. *Inflation Stabilization: The Experiences of Israel, Argentina, Brazil, Bolivia, and Mexico.* Cambridge, Massachusetts: MIT Press, 1988.

Bruno, Michael, et al. *Lessons of Economic Stabilization and Its Aftermath.* Cambridge, Massachusetts: MIT Press, 1991.

Bufman, Gil, and Leonardo Leiderman. "Israel's Stabilization: Some Important Policy Lessons." In *Reform, Recovery, and Growth: Latin America and the Middle East,* edited by Rudiger Dornbusch and Sebastian Edwards (pp. 177–222). Chicago: Chicago University Press, 1995.

———. "Monetary Policy Strategies for Disinflation: Lessons from Recent Experiences in Transition Economies and Israel." In *Central Banking, Monetary Policies, and the Implications for Transition Economies,* edited by M. I. Blejer and M. Skreb (pp. 215–270). Boston: Kluwer, 1999.

Burton, David, and Stanley Fischer. "Ending Moderate Inflation." In *Moderate Inflation: The Experience of Transition Economies,* edited by Carlo Cottarelli and György Szapáry (pp. 15–96). Washington, D.C.: International Monetary Fund, and Budapest: National Bank of Hungary, 1998.

Calvo, Guillermo, and Carlos Vegh. "Credibility and the Dynamics of Stabilization Policy: A Basic Framework." IMF Working Paper 90/110, 1990.

———. "Exchange Rate Based Stabilization under Imperfect Credibility." IMF Working Paper 91/77, 1991.

Dahan, Momi, and Michael Strawczynski. "Fiscal Policy and Inflation in Israel." In *Inflation and Disinflation in Israel,* edited by Leonardo Leiderman. Jerusalem: Bank of Israel, 1999.

Debelle, Guy, and Stanley Fischer. "How Independent Should a Central Bank Be?" In *Goals, Guidelines, and Constraints Facing Monetary Policymakers,* edited by J. Fuhrer (pp. 195–221). Federal Reserve Bank of Boston Conference 38, 1994.

Dornbusch, Rudiger, and Stanley Fischer. "Moderate Inflation." *World Bank Economic Review* 7 (January 1993): 1–44.

Fischer, Stanley, and David W. H. Orsmond. "Israeli Inflation from an International Perspective." In *The Israeli Economy, 1985–1998: From Government Intervention to Market Economics,* edited by Avi Ben-Bassat (pp. 165–203). Jerusalem: Am-Oved, 2001. (Hebrew)

Leiderman, Leonardo. *Inflation and Disinflation: The Israeli Experiment.* Chicago: University of Chicago, 1993.

Liviatan, Nissan, and Nathan Sussman. "Disinflation Process in Israel in the Past Decade." In *The Israeli Economy, 1985–1998,* edited by Avi Ben-Bassat (pp. 135–164). Jerusalem: Am-Oved, 2001. (Hebrew)

Masson, P. R., M. A. Savastano, and Sunil Sharma. "The Scope for Inflation Targeting in Developing Countries." IMF Working Paper 97/130, 1997.

Ministry of Finance. *State Budget Proposal for the Fiscal Year 1998.* Jerusalem.

Orsmond, David W. H. "Volatility of Interest Rates in Israel." In *Israel: Background Studies.* IMF Staff Country Report SM/98/24, 1998, pp. 29–48.

Patinkin, Don. "Israel's Stabilization Program of 1985; or, Some Simple Truths of Monetary Theory." *Journal of Economic Perspectives* 7 (Spring 1993): 103–128.

III REFORMS IN THE FINANCIAL MARKET

6 Reform in the Israeli Financial System and the Flow of Funds of Publicly Traded Manufacturing Firms

Asher A. Blass and Oved Yosha

6.1 Introduction

Following the stabilization program of 1985, and over a period of several years, a series of reform measures were introduced that affected virtually all segments of the Israeli financial system. The reforms were designed to reduce government involvement in financial markets, increase international capital mobility, and promote competition in the banking industry and the development of the Tel Aviv Stock Exchange (TASE). Later on, attempts were made to reduce potential for conflict of interest within the highly universal bank conglomerates, while serious efforts were made to privatize the banks and other state-owned enterprises.

A substantial body of research has attempted to assess the success of these reforms. Ben-Bassat (1993) focuses on the reduction in government involvement in financial markets, Bufman and Leiderman (1995) on the process of international financial liberalization, Blass and Yafeh (2001) on initial public offerings (IPOs) of Israeli firms in New York, Yafeh and Yosha (1998) on the involvement of banks in corporate financing decisions, and Ribon and Yosha (1999) on competition in deposit and loan markets. Closely related are Yosha (1995) on issues related to bank privatization; Blass (1996) and Blei (1998), respectively, on the performance of bank-managed investment funds; Ber, Yafeh, and Yosha (2001) on conflicts of interest in bank lending, underwriting, and fund management; Blass (1999) on the extent to which the TASE index reflected fundamentals during the price run-up of 1992 and 1993; and Ber (1998) on how bank (or bank-affiliated) shareholders affect firm performance. The survey by Blass, Yafeh, and Yosha (1998) evaluates the impact of the reforms on corporate governance in Israel. These studies are described in more detail in the next section.[1]

Overall, external funding opportunities for Israeli firms improved with many firms raising equity financing on TASE or abroad. Were these funds put to "good use?" According to the 1994 Bank of Israel Report (p. 40), the funds raised in equity offerings on TASE contributed to the surge in investment in the 1990s.[2] By contrast, some have argued that the IPO wave in the early 1990s provided managers with easy money that was abused and directed toward speculative financial investments. Neither claim has been substantiated with systematic microdata analysis, a task we undertake here.

While the government's role in capital markets has been reduced, increasing attention has been devoted to the roles (still) played by Israeli banks in the financial system, and in funding investments in particular. Yafeh and Yosha (1998) studied this question using manufacturing industry aggregate data, concluding that although reduced, bank dominance is still substantial. The unique firm-level dataset that we construct allows us to explore the role of banks as providers of financing during the equity offerings wave in a more systematic manner. We can determine whether firm characteristics—exogenous, such as firm age, or potentially endogenous, such as profitability and geographic location—are associated with particular forms of financing or investment patterns, and whether certain forms of financing are correlated with particular types of investment. Because we have data regarding government funds obtained by individual firms, we can evaluate which types of firms benefited the most from government assistance.

To address these issues, we construct year-by-year flow of funds charts for about two hundred manufacturing firms traded on the TASE for the years 1990–1997. For each firm, we compute the ratios of internal funds, debt, equity, and government financing as fractions of total sources and, similarly, the ratios of capital expenditure, investments in inventory, working capital, securities, and cash, as well as dividend payouts as fractions of total uses. We also compute Tobin's q for each firm on a year-by-year basis. Both flow of funds charts and Tobin's q have never before been calculated in Israel at the firm level, and not in any meaningful sense at the aggregate level either. The flow of funds data permit us to carry out a firm-level analysis of the correlation between financing sources—equity financing, bank credit, and retained earnings—and various uses.[3]

In the next section, we present and discuss the recent studies on the reforms in the Israeli financial system. In the third section, we describe the sample and the construction of the variables we use in the empirical analysis; in the final section, we present the empirical results and conclude.

6.2 The Reform in the Israeli Financial System

The Financial System before the Reform

Government Involvement in Capital and Credit Markets The Israeli financial system prior to the reform was characterized by heavy government involvement. For all intents and purposes, the government set the cost of capital and determined its allocation. It issued special subsidized and illiquid bonds to pension and provident funds, life insurance companies, and banks, so that most of the public's savings were channeled to the government through purchase of these bonds.[4] The value of these bonds was considerably larger than the value of all traded corporate bonds, many of which were issued by government-owned utilities (table 6.1). Because the real return on

Table 6.1
Domestic Government Debt, Corporate Bonds, and Stock Market Values, 1985–1998* (As percent of GDP)

Year**	1. Net domestic govt. debt	2. Govt. credit to households and firms	3. Of which: Cumulative value of govt. subsidized mortgages (from 1992)	4. Gross domestic govt. debt (4) = (1) + (2)	5. Bank of Israel debt excluding Makam***	6. Liquid govt. bonds including Makam	7. Estimated earmarked govt. non-liquid debt (7) = (4) − (5) − (6)	8. Corporate bonds	9. Stock market value****
1985	107	13	—	120	28	15	77	2	14
1986	109	15	—	123	22	17	85	3	14
1987	94	12	—	106	12	23	71	4	14
1988	100	13	—	113	12	30	71	5	5
1989	105	13	—	118	10	40	68	7	8
1990	100	16	—	115	11	38	66	7	9
1991	88	15	—	104	8	44	52	7	11
1992	79	16	3	95	4	47	44	6	22
1993	76	18	6	94	3	47	44	6	36
1994	70	17	7	87	2	41	44	5	19
1995	70	16	8	86	3	44	40	4	23
1996	73	16	9	89	5	45	39	3	20
1997	80	16	10	96	13	45	38	3	27
1998	83	16	10	98	14	45	40	3	26

* The figures in column 3 are not adjusted for changes in interest rates, while those in column 5 are adjusted and reflect market values.
** End of year (December 31st)
*** Makam are bills (with maturities up to one year) issued by the Bank of Israel.
**** Net of government owned shares and double counting due to cross-holdings of equity.

these bonds was subsidized and guaranteed, the government set the de facto long-run rate of return on saving. A central reason for this type of government intervention was the need to finance the huge budget deficit.

The government also intervened in credit markets. Most corporate credit was government "directed" credit, that is, subsidized and distributed via the banking system. Economic theory and anecdotal evidence suggest that as a result, capital was allocated inefficiently; many profitable endeavors could not obtain funding whereas some nonprofitable, but politically appealing projects were allocated funds. Since investors did not bear the full opportunity cost of capital, many firms overinvested in physical capital.

Government financing crowded out nongovernment financing in the private sector: Mortgages were rationed by the government according to criteria designed by politicians and civil servants; firms were not permitted to issue bonds without explicit authorization from the Treasury and the Knesset. In practice, privately owned firms issued virtually no bonds, and rarely used the stock market as a vehicle for raising equity capital. Indeed, the TASE in the mid- and late 1980s was small and illiquid.

The 1983 Bank Share Crisis The government's role in the capital market was enhanced following the bank share crisis of 1983. In October of that year, the government became the effective owner of most of the banking system. Bank stocks traded on TASE, constituting about 17 percent of the public's financial portfolio, had been regarded for some time as virtually riskless. These stocks collapsed following a long period of bank intervention in which most banks bought and sold their own shares, smoothing fluctuations and pushing share prices up.[5] During the collapse, bank shares lost approximately 40 percent of their value. The government (in part for political reasons) decided to purchase the bank stocks from the public at (shaved) precrash prices, becoming the owner of most of the banks' equity. There are different opinions regarding the extent of government involvement in bank management since 1983.[6] Currently, the government is in the process of reprivatizing the banks. Some (e.g., Sarnat and Szpiro 1992) have argued that as a result of the crash, investors lost confidence in the TASE as a vehicle for long-term savings, which, of course, made it more difficult for firms to raise funds on the exchange. There is no disagreement, however, that the bank share crisis was a traumatic event that prepared the ground for the reforms.

The Banking System The commercial banks are extremely dominant in the Israeli financial system. They are universal, managing mutual and retirement provident funds and controlling subsidiaries that specialize in activities such as underwriting, brokerage, or mortgage origination. Moreover, banking concentration is very high.

In the early 1990s, the combined assets of the two largest banks constituted almost three quarters of total bank assets (with the five largest banks controlling over 95 percent of these activities), while the Herfindahl index in local currency nonindexed bank deposits and credit was about 0.25. This is high by international standards, although in some European countries concentration in banking is also high.[7] The combination of concentration, universality (multiproduct banking),[8] and restrictions on international capital mobility strengthens potential distortions due to market power.[9]

The Reform and Its Consequences

A dramatic decline in the government budget deficit took place in the mid-1980s, which was almost a precondition for the reform in the financial system given that it was no longer vital for the government to attract most of the public's savings to finance the deficit.

Relaxation of Investment and Financing Restrictions Concurrent with the fiscal consolidation in the mid-1980s, the government stopped selling special subsidized bonds to the provident funds, which, in turn, were allowed to allocate a greater share of their holdings to nongovernment securities. Similarly, over time, banks were no longer required to deposit depositors' funds with the Treasury, and were permitted to extend loans directly to the business sector with little government intervention. In addition, corporations were allowed to issue bonds without explicit Treasury approval. Many foreign-currency restrictions were removed, and access to capital markets abroad was eased. In particular, firms were allowed to raise equity capital on overseas stock exchanges and to borrow from foreign banks. Table 6.2 displays the change in the aggregate financing patterns of the manufacturing sector as a consequence of the reform. The reduction of directed credit, the lack of development of the corporate bond market, and the increased reliance on overseas equity financing are clearly visible.[10]

Equity Finance and the IPO Wave The early 1990s witnessed a sharp increase in the use of equity finance by Israeli firms. During the early 1990s, the number of traded manufacturing companies increased from about 100 in 1990 to about 250 in 1995. Annual trading volume doubled between 1992 and 1993, exceeding $30 billion, after having grown by a factor of ten from 1988; and market capitalization as a fraction of GNP increased from 7 percent in 1984 to 46 percent in 1992 (Blass 1999).[11] As a consequence of the reform, corporate stocks trading volume increased relative to that of government bonds.[12]

Table 6.2
Components of External Finance in Manufacturing
(Flow, December 1998 prices, million NIS)

		Stock exchanges				Ministry of Industry and Trade	
			TASE				
Year	Total 1 + 5 + 10	Total 1 = 2 + 3 + 4	Equity 2	Bonds 3	Foreign exchanges 4	Total 5 = 6 + 7 + 8 + 9	Capital grants and exercise of guarantees 6
1985	5,594	399	129	0	270	3,263	268
1986	9,495	871	168	703	0	4,357	1,733
1987	12,405	809	483	89	236	4,497	1,545
1988	6,247	393	310	83	0	3,906	1,031
1989	1,489	971	734	227	10	3,857	861
1990	8,279	898	589	221	88	3,724	1,141
1991	6,449	2,326	968	159	1,199	3,327	944
1992	9,105	4,795	2,449	148	2,198	3,909	1,357
1993	11,458	5,953	3,264	42	2,647	3,142	1,530
1994	11,186	3,535	2,323	0	1,211	2,734	1,492
1995	8,986	2,449	667	0	1,782	3,048	1,937
1996	13,511	5,418	357	0	5,061	2,888	1,919
1997	12,909	4,304	928	39	3,337	2,762	1,761

One reason for the IPO wave was that provident funds, which no longer offered subsidized government bonds, sought alternative investment opportunities, raising the demand for equity. In 1988, the share of corporate stocks in the funds' portfolio was under 2 percent, increasing to over 10 percent by 1994. The mutual funds were even larger net purchasers of stocks. Because they had not been subject to the restrictions that applied to the provident funds, and because all along they were never issued subsidized bonds, we can conclude that the demand for stock was affected by factors other than by reforms enacted from above. Nonetheless, Yafeh and Yosha (1998) claim that as a result of the reform, stock market financing became a viable method of raising external funds for Israeli firms, but qualify this conclusion by stressing that the extent to which stock market financing is an *independent* alternative to bank financing is less clear given the still dominant role of banks in the financial system.

Blass and Yafeh's (2001) study of Israeli IPOs in New York illustrates the success of the reform in liberalizing financial markets. Although most new shares were sold in Israel and listed on the TASE, many Israeli corporations, mostly in electronics and software, chose to issue and list their stock on U.S. exchanges, primarily the NASDAQ (usually instead of, and occasionally in addition to the TASE).[13] By 1995,

Table 6.2 (continued)

	Ministry of Industry and Trade			Credit			
Year	R&D grants net of royalties 7	Export subsidies 8	Other (mostly marketing grants) 9	Total 10 = 11 + 12 + 13	Directed (government) credit 11	Domestic bank credit 12	Credit from banks abroad 13
1985	256	2,739	1	1,932	734	972	226
1986	440	2,158	26	4,267	1,448	2,288	530
1987	406	2,496	51	7,100	1,776	4,485	839
1988	418	2,390	66	1,948	−1,283	3,104	128
1989	423	2,520	51	−3,339	−3,171	−217	49
1990	481	2,061	41	3,658	−5,777	9,502	−68
1991	593	1,672	117	797	−6,448	7,374	−129
1992	719	1,669	164	401	0	814	−414
1993	767	672	173	2,363	0	2,710	−346
1994	910	125	207	4,917	0	4,993	−76
1995	934	13	164	3,489	0	3,587	−98
1996	889	12	68	5,205	0	4,843	362
1997	957	3	41	5,843	0	5,484	358

the number of NASDAQ-listed Israeli firms nearly equaled the number of all other foreign firms combined (excluding Canadian companies). Blass and Yafeh find that Israeli firms issuing equity in New York are young, high-tech, and export-oriented with few tangible assets, compared to firms issuing equity on the TASE. In comparison to Tel Aviv IPOs, pre-IPO shareholders relinquish a larger portion of their equity in the U.S., whereas postissue returns are higher. They suggest that this reflects costs associated with listing in the U.S. that successful firms are willing to incur as a credible signal of quality to investors.[14]

The Banking System Ribon and Yosha (1999) study the effect of the reform on competition in the banking industry, asking whether banks lost market power despite the fact that commercial banking per se has remained highly concentrated. They estimate "conduct parameters" for the nonindexed local currency deposits and loans markets, finding that the market for bank loans is less competitive than the market for bank deposits, and that in both markets the hypothesis of perfect competition is rejected. To address their main question—the effect of financial liberalization on competition in banking—they allow the conduct parameters in both markets to vary over time, finding a large and statistically significant increase in competition in both markets from 1986 to 1993. However, they point out that fees and commissions on nonindexed local currency deposits and loans as well as spreads and fees in other bank activities (e.g., foreign currency denominated deposits and loans) might have increased, so that it is premature to conclude that commercial banking had become substantially more competitive.

As mentioned earlier, despite the IPO wave, the banking system is still dominant in the provision of financing, mainly in the form of credit. Indeed, in 1992–1994, bank credit expanded at an annual average rate of 33 percent (compared to less than 20 percent nominal GDP growth), and during 1995–1997, at an average rate of 20 percent (compared to less than 15 percent nominal GDP growth).

Reducing Banks' Involvement in Capital Markets: The Brodet Committee As mentioned, banks in Israel are overwhelmingly universal and own large amounts of the equity of firms, directly as well as via bank-managed investment funds. The banks were heavily involved in IPOs on the TASE, both as underwriters and as buyers (mainly through investment funds).

The combination of bank universality and market concentration (in banking and in the retirement provident-funds sector) has raised concern that bank conglomerates are excessively powerful, and that the diversity of activities (in combination with market power) might involve conflicts of interest. In 1995, the blue ribbon Brodet Committee studied this issue in depth, and recommended as follows: (1) No banking firm will control a nonbank entity, and by the end of 1998, a bank will hold at most 20 percent of the voting equity of such firms; (2) the proportion of bank-appointed directors to the board of a nonbank firm will not exceed the bank's equity holding in the (nonbank) firm; (3) Bank Hapoalim will divest its equity stakes in one of two powerful industrial conglomerates—Koor and Clal. These recommendations were legislated and implemented almost according to schedule.

Ber (1998) studies the issue of bank holdings of large equity blocks in nonfinancial firms. She outlines the advantages—assistance during financial distress, informed underwriting, and better monitoring of firm managers.[15] On the other hand, bank shareholding of nonfinancial firms can also lead to distortions. For example, a bank's fund management subsidiary might purchase shares of a company, part of whose equity is owned by the parent bank, even if it were not in the best interest of the funds that it manages. That would be especially true in a public offering of stock where the bank will have an incentive to use investors' money to support a higher offering price for the shares that it owns. Furthermore, banks' credit operations can lead to conflicts of interest with its underwriting, fund management, and investment advisory roles. For example, a bank concerned that a company to which it loaned funds is about to default might persuade the company to issue stock through its underwriting subsidiary, knowing that its fund management subsidiary would purchase some of these shares. The bank would thereby effectively transfer the credit risk associated with a bad loan on to investors in its fund management subsidiaries.

Ber, Yafeh, and Yosha (2001) bear directly on this issue. They find that Israeli IPO firms whose equity was underwritten by a bank-affiliated underwriter when the same bank was also a large creditor exhibited better than average postissue *accounting* performance, and interpret this as evidence that Israeli banking conglomerates use their superior information regarding client firms to float the stock of successful firms ("cherries").[16] On the other hand, the *stock* performance of such firms during the first year following the IPO is considerably lower than average. This is interpreted as overpricing; namely, investors paid too much for bank underwritten IPOs. In this respect, bank underwritten IPOs are "lemons," not "cherries." The main conclusion from the study is that there are indeed conflicts of interest in the combination of bank lending, underwriting, *and* fund management.

This conclusion is consistent with Blass' (1996) examination of performance and structure of the forty-one largest provident funds, most of which were managed by the five largest banks, between 1987 and 1994. Average annual returns were lower than the average market return in each of three main investment categories. The performance from 1990 through 1994 was even worse: The average annual return was 1.2 percent in real terms. It seems that the funds were poor market-timers as well as poor selectors of individual securities.[17]

The Road to Competitive Capital Markets in Israel

Several impediments continue to block the development of competitive capital markets in Israel. As described above, a small number of commercial banks, not yet fully privatized, provide virtually all bank credit. Blass, Yafeh, and Yosha (1998) argue that the reforms, which reduced the government role as a financial intermediary, have actually increased the banks' role in allocating credit and, consequently, enhanced their influence. As mentioned above, banks also operate as merchant banks and, through pyramidal structures of ownership, own large segments of manufacturing, construction, insurance, and services. Until the late 1990s, there was virtually no new entry into commercial banking, neither by foreign banks nor by other entities. Finally, direct household holdings are minimal whereas two thirds of capital market assets are held by institutional investors such as pensions, life insurance programs, and bank-managed provident and mutual funds; see Blass, Yafeh, and Yosha (1998).

The need to limit the ties between the provident and mutual funds and the commercial banks—in light of the high concentration in the provident fund industry, the cross-price effect that exacerbates monopolistic price distortions, the poor performance of the funds, and potential conflicts of interest—has been emphasized beginning with the Bejsky commission report, set up in the aftermath of the bank share crisis. Yosha (1995) studies the issue, taking into account the trade-off between competition and economies of scale and scope. He finds that were the funds to be spun-off, the potential efficiency losses would be minor compared to the gains from enhanced competition.

To conclude our description of the postreform financial system, we would like to mention the stock price bubble on TASE. Blass (1999), first published in early 1994 (before the bubble burst), noticed the apparent divergence in 1992 and 1993 between stock prices and (then) current fundamental factors such as earnings and cash flow. He considered two explanations for the rapid increase in stock prices, each of which was then found to be implausible. First, the peace process or other developments may have led investors to believe that Israeli firms were facing new and extraordinary growth opportunities. It was difficult to find evidence to support that proposition. Similarly, while a decline in the required return on equity could have explained the increase, there was little evidence that the required return declined to levels that would support the stock price increase. The bubble exploded in early 1994, and prices remained low for much of the next two to three years.

We turn to the microlevel analysis of financing and investment patterns of publicly traded manufacturing firms. Our database allows us to "test" the conjecture that before the stock market crash, firms issued equity on the TASE mainly to benefit from inflated prices, and that they subsequently "squandered" these funds.

6.3 Empirical Analysis: Dataset Construction

Sample and Data Sources

Our sample consists of about two hundred Israeli manufacturing firms that are listed on TASE.[18] We follow the sample from 1990 to 1997. Almost two thirds of these firms went public during the 1990s, whereas most of the firms who had been listed prior to that issued more stock during the last few years, particularly in 1992–1993.[19]

For each firm, we collected data from four key sources: (1) financial statements obtained mostly from a Compustat-type database ("Dukas") compiled by the TASE from annual reports; (2) stock price data; (3) prospecti submitted by firms issuing equity (IPOs or seasoned offerings); and (4) flow statements compiled by the Bank of Israel Research Department from annual reports. We also collected data on geographic location and firm age (mostly from prospecti).

Financial Statements Data The Dukas database contains information on all TASE-listed securities. Because firms that go public are required to provide financial statements for two years prior to the IPO, our sample includes pre-IPO data for such IPOs (more than half of the sample).

Stock Price Data The TASE provides daily data for all securities listed on the exchange. The data include prices, number of shares outstanding, year of IPO, and dividend information. The data have been accumulated by the Bank of Israel Research Department.

Prospecti We collected data from prospecti submitted to the Securities Authority in Israel (and the Securities Exchange Commission in the U.S.). Because most firms issued equity during the 1990s, either for the first time as IPOs, or as a seasoned offering, the data are available for the overwhelming majority of firms.

Flow Statements The Bank of Israel Research Department has collected annual reports for listed firms and entered by hand the "consolidated flow statement" (not contained in Dukas) that decomposes the change in a firm's balances into flows derived from operating activities, investment activities, and financing activities (broken down into up to fifty subentries). This information allows us to construct flow of funds for each firm-year in the sample. For each observation, we compute various sources, uses, the ratios of these sources and uses to total sources, as well as profitability ratios.[20]

Removing Outliers We removed from the sample firm-year observations in which we identified inconsistencies between the Dukas database and flow statements entered by hand.[21] We also removed firms that were extreme outliers in terms of the average (over time) of one or more source ratio, use ratio, or profitability ratio.[22] In our analysis, we use both time-averaged firm-level data and year-by-year panel data. Whenever year-by-year data are used, we further remove year-by-year outliers in terms of one or more source ratio, use ratio, or profitability ratio,[23] and firm-year observations for which total sources were negative. When time-averaged data are used, we further remove firms for which there are only one or two observations (nine firms), as well as firms for which the time-average of total sources was negative (thirteen firms). In tables 6.3–6.4 and 6.8–6.11, the procedure for year-by-year data was adopted, whereas in tables 6.5–6.7 the procedure for time-averaged data was adopted.

Descriptive Statistics The number of firms each year ranges from 117 in 1990 to 188 in 1995. They are on average twenty-seven years old. One fifth of all firms are located exclusively in development areas, which, for simplicity's sake, are defined in our analysis as firms located in telephone area codes 06 and 07, whereas several other firms have plants located in development areas and other areas ("multiplant" firms). Average size (total assets in real terms) does not vary much over the sample years, and profitability peaks in 1992 and then declines over the next three years, rebounding in 1997. Leverage does not exhibit sharp variations over the sample period. (For reasons of space, we do not provide a table.)

Constructing Flow of Funds In order to summarize the information contained in the flow statements, we combined the approximately fifty types of entries provided in the statements into twelve broader groups. Six—internally generated cash, net stock issues, net bond issues, net increase in other debt, government capital grants, and deferred taxes—can be viewed as alternative sources of capital; six others—capital expenditure and increase in inventories, working capital (other than inventory), securities, cash or cash equivalents, and dividend payments can be viewed as uses.

SOURCES Internally generated cash is calculated by adding depreciation (a noncash expense) to net income and then further adding and subtracting several additional components. These include expenses, such as deferred employee benefits, and revenue, such as unrealized gains on marketable securities, that are included in the calculation of net income but do not involve cash flows. Although internally generated cash is by far the largest source of funds, representing more than half of all sources, it is apparently less dominant than in other countries (See Shin and Stultz (1998), Board of Governors of the Federal Reserve, *Flow of Funds Accounts*, and OECD *Financial Statistics* 1997).[24]

The role of equity issues—defined as total proceeds received from floatation of common stock, convertible bonds,[25] and warrants as well as proceeds received from exercise of warrants and options—is relatively high, representing almost one quarter of all funds. Table 6.3 depicts the large year-by-year variation in stock issues. In 1992 and 1993, stock issues represented more than a third of all funding, but in 1995, they represented 8 percent of funding, rebounding in 1997. Much of the fluctuation can probably be explained by Israeli managers' attempts to time their issues. Indeed, that behavior would be consistent with Asquith and Mullins' (1986) finding that stock is more likely to be issued in the United States after stock prices have risen.

The role of corporate bonds issues has been negligible throughout the entire period (table 6.3). When the reforms were implemented beginning in the 1980s, it was assumed that a vibrant corporate bond market would develop as a consequence of the government's exit from credit markets. From 1985 to 1989, corporate bond issues became, in fact, a more important source of finance, growing from 2 to 7 percent of

Table 6.3
Flow of Funds in Publicly Traded Manufacturing Corporations—Average Sources, 1990–1997
(December 1998 prices, million NIS; fraction of total in space brackets; standard deviation in parentheses)

	Average for year ending 1990	Average for year ending 1991	Average for year ending 1992	Average for year ending 1993	Average for year ending 1994	Average for year ending 1995	Average for year ending 1996	Average for year ending 1997	Average for all years and all firms
Internally generated cash	26.4 [0.966] (72.2)	29.7 [0.931] (87.3)	25.0 [0.490] (71.8)	26.1 [0.478] (68.9)	23.9 [0.543] (58.5)	31.9 [0.447] (72.8)	30.4 [0.389] (66.7)	27.8 [0.529] (58.0)	27.7 [0.530] (69.5)
Net stock issues	5.4 [0.196] (18.0)	7.3 [0.230] (23.5)	20.1 [0.392] (83.4)	18.5 [0.339] (31.7)	12.0 [0.272] (29.4)	5.9 [0.084] (38.4)	9.5 [0.121] (39.3)	16.2 [0.308] (57.8)	12.2 [0.230] (45.9)
Net bond issues	0.02 [0.007] (1.7)	−0.03 [−0.001] (0.3)	1.80 [0.035] (10.0)	1.94 [0.036] (20.7)	−0.05 [−0.001] (1.9)	−0.11 [−0.001] (1.2)	2.25 [0.030] (32.1)	0.18 [−0.003] (1.2)	0.75 [0.014] (14.4)
Net increase in other debt	−4.70 [−0.172] (36.0)	−7.78 [−0.243] (42.9)	−0.77 [−0.015] (34.0)	4.84 [0.088] (216.6)	5.85 [0.132] (162.9)	26.94 [0.378] (48.2)	28.35 [0.363] (164.7)	4.66 [0.088] (49.2)	8.18 [0.154] (109.7)
Development grants	1.5 [0.054] (6.6)	1.9 [0.059] (10.8)	3.2 [0.063] (22.0)	3.0 [0.056] (19.7)	2.5 [0.055] (15.5)	6.4 [0.089] (44.6)	7.6 [0.097] (53.1)	3.3 [0.063] (24.0)	3.8 [0.072] (29.8)
Deferred taxes	−1.2 [−0.045] (9.1)	0.8 [0.024] (8.0)	1.8 [0.034] (10.0)	0.1 [0.002] (7.4)	−0.1 [−0.002] (4.8)	0.2 [0.002] (10.0)	−0.1 [−0.001] (7.9)	0.7 [0.013] (7.9)	0.3 [0.006] (8.3)
Total sources	27.2 (56.2)	31.9 (72.8)	51.2 (155.1)	54.6 (152.7)	44.0 (88.3)	71.1 (307.7)	78.0 (280.9)	52.5 (111.8)	53.0 (183.2)
Number of firms	117	146	175	183	182	188	174	169	1334

GDP (table 6.1).[26] In recent years, however, very few firms have raised funds through corporate bonds, and as seasoned bonds matured, the relative size of the market declined. Today, it is no larger than it was before the reforms.

Some have argued that it is unlikely that the corporate bond market will become significant as long as the commercial banks are as dominant as they are today. Table 6.3 indicates that bank debt has been an important source of funding for publicly traded manufacturing firms; still, the role of bank debt for these firms is considerably smaller than for the manufacturing sector as a whole (i.e., for publicly traded and privately held firms).[27]

The numbers in table 6.3, for 1992–1993 and 1995–1996, reveal a striking pattern: Firms that took advantage of the 1992–1993 expansion of the TASE to raise external funds in the form of equity drastically reduced their reliance on bank debt. By contrast, in 1995–1996, when equity funding on the exchange was low, bank debt rebounded, suggesting that bank debt and public equity financing are substitutes.

The role of debt—mostly short- and long-term bank debt—is relatively small compared to most Western countries and has fluctuated dramatically. In 1990 and 1991, companies on average paid down substantial portions of their debt, a phenomenon almost never observed in Western economies, but, as indicated above, in other years, firms increased their debt dramatically. A potential explanation is that many companies have relatively rigid investment programs so that when profits drop they make up the shortfall by borrowing, and when market conditions allow them to issue equity, they use the proceeds to pay off debt instead of increasing investment.

We are able to identify two sources of government funding in our data. Government investment grants (development grants) represent 7 percent of all funding, peaking at 9 to 10 percent in 1995 and 1996. By contrast, the deferral of tax liabilities to the government (usually through accelerated depreciation allowances) averaged less than 1 percent of all sources, peaking at 3.4 percent in 1992.[28] These figures on government assistance (i.e., grants and tax deferrals) understate the extent of government subsidy because R&D grants, marketing subsidies, and tax benefits other than tax deferrals (e.g., benefits to firms with foreign ownership) are not recorded as separate entries in the flow statements.[29] Instead, such items are included in the overall revenue pool, thereby inflating after-tax profits.[30]

USES Capital expenditures include investments (net of sales) in property, plants, and equipment. From 1990 through 1997, 54 percent of all sources were devoted to capital expenditures (table 6.4). These expenditures increased significantly during most of the 1990s (in real terms but not as a percent of total uses) before declining in 1997. We compared the rates of growth according to our data and those reflected in the

Table 6.4
Flow of Funds in Publicly Traded Manufacturing Corporations—Average Uses, 1990–1997
(December 1998 prices, million NIS; fraction of total in space brackets; standard deviation in parentheses)

	Average for year ending 1990	Average for year ending 1991	Average for year ending 1992	Average for year ending 1993	Average for year ending 1994	Average for year ending 1995	Average for year ending 1996	Average for year ending 1997	Average for all years and all firms
Capital expenditure	14.0 [0.510] (30.6)	19.5 [0.613] (56.9)	21.2 [0.413] (67.8)	27.6 [0.502] (84.7)	26.4 [0.598] (47.9)	43.4 [0.610] (130.6)	45.0 [0.577] (147.8)	24.5 [0.468] (51.2)	28.7 [0.540] (118.9)
Investment in inventory	1.5 [0.056] (12.0)	1.0 [0.031] (10.7)	4.6 [0.090] (11.3)	6.2 [0.114] (19.5)	6.5 [0.146] (18.7)	8.2 [0.115] (18.7)	8.0 [0.101] (33.2)	−1.3 [−0.025] (17.4)	4.6 [0.087] (60.7)
Investment in working capital	0.9 [0.033] (20.7)	6.0 [0.187] (19.9)	−0.5 [−0.010] (33.9)	5.2 [0.095] (17.4)	4.6 [0.105] (21.8)	1.7 [0.023] (24.3)	4.9 [0.062] (20.2)	6.8 [0.130] (24.8)	3.8 [0.070] (30.8)
Investment in securities	3.1 [0.113] (18.2)	0.2 [−0.005] (13.5)	7.0 [0.135] (25.1)	5.9 [0.105] (14.0)	1.1 [0.025] (19.0)	5.0 [0.071] (89.8)	2.4 [0.031] (49.9)	1.8 [0.034] (9.60)	3.4 [0.064] (55.3)
Investment in cash and cash equivalents	1.4 [0.052] (25.1)	1.6 [0.051] (31.8)	13.0 [0.253] (45.0)	5.7 [0.103] (41.0)	1.4 [0.031] (17.9)	5.4 [0.076] (30.8)	11.4 [0.146] (40.0)	14.2 [0.271] (36.6)	7.0 [0.133] (45.9)
Dividends	6.4 [0.234] (28.2)	3.8 [0.121] (17.5)	6.0 [0.118] (17.8)	4.2 [0.077] (14.0)	4.1 [0.093] (14.3)	7.2 [0.101] (17.3)	6.2 [0.079] (11.7)	6.3 [0.120] (13.5)	5.5 [0.104] (21.3)
Total uses	27.5 (52.8)	31.9 (60.2)	51.3 (117.4)	54.9 (113.3)	44.1 (65.6)	71.0 (224.3)	78.0 (213.0)	52.5 (86.0)	53.0 (183.3)
Number of firms	117	146	175	183	182	188	174	169	1334

two Central Bureau of Statistics (CBS) databases—the Industry and Crafts Surveys and the National Accounts Data.[31] Although the CBS methodologies and definitions are different from ours (as well as being different among themselves), and the weights of different industries are not the same, the general trends in the two CBS databases are consistent with our data, exhibiting sharp increases in the early years, and then recording a slowdown in 1996 and 1997.

Investment in inventory is defined as outlays for raw materials not yet used in the production process plus the net change in the stock of finished goods. This item is not included as an expense in the calculation of net income and, therefore, needs to be subtracted from net income in order to calculate flows from operations. Investment in inventory represents on average about 9 percent of all uses.

Investment in working capital (other than inventory) is defined as an increase in current assets, such as trade accounts receivable, less current liabilities, such as trade accounts payable. Sales recorded on the income statement might overstate (or understate) actual cash receipts given that part of the proceeds from sales might not be received by the end of the year. An offsetting effect occurs if payments for materials and services used in production are delayed, in which case accounts payable will increase, and that increase needs to be added to net income. Investment in working capital represents 7 percent of all uses, with considerable variation over time.

Investment in securities is defined as a net purchase of publicly traded securities and mutual funds. Six percent of all funds are devoted to this item. Here too, the year-by-year variation is large. In 1992 and 1993, 13 and 10 percent, respectively, of funds were devoted to these investments, mostly due to the large amounts of cash raised in the form of equity during these years.

Thirteen percent of all funds were devoted to investment in cash and cash equivalents such as short-term deposits. In 1992 and 1997, more than a quarter of funds were allocated to cash and cash equivalents, whereas in 1994, cash balances were not increased.

Ten percent of all funds (or about one fifth of internally generated cash) are paid out as cash (dividends). The variation over time subsequent to 1990 is relatively small compared to some of the other uses, suggesting that dividend smoothing may take place in Israel, as in other countries.

SOURCE, USE, AND PROFITABILITY RATIOS For each firm-year observation, we compute the ratios of internally generated cash, net stock issues, net bond issues, net increase in other debt, government capital grants, and deferred taxes as fractions of total sources and, similarly, the ratios of capital expenditure, investments in inventory, working capital, securities, and cash, as well as dividend payouts as fractions of total uses. We also calculate standard profitability ratios such as net profits to sales and net profits to equity.

Calculation of Tobin's q We measure *average* Tobin's q as the market value of assets divided by their replacement value. Replacement values are calculated assuming that fixed assets and inventories appreciate at a rate equal to that of the Consumer Price Index (CPI). The market value of assets equals the market value of common equity plus the value of debt. The latter is calculated as the replacement value of assets less the sum of the book value of common equity and (CPI adjusted balance sheet) deferred taxes and employee benefits. Tobin's q so calculated rises dramatically in 1992 and 1993, reflecting the stock price run-up in those years, and then declines precipitously to an average of 0.93 in 1996. In 1997, however, market conditions improved, and market value becomes as large as replacement value.

Tobin's q estimated in this way may be understated because price increases of equipment (representing most fixed assets) since the mid-1980s have been substantially lower than the increases in the CPI so that replacement costs are actually lower than implied by the CPI.[32] This is because the real appreciation of the sheqel over the years has resulted in price increases of imported capital goods typically lower than the overall rate of inflation.[33] The overstatement of replacement costs (and the understatement of q) should be greater the older the vintage of firm equipment, and the larger the share of fixed assets in firm total assets. Furthermore, the effect could be stronger in the latter years of the sample, as the cumulative effect of the sheqel's appreciation grew over time. In our analysis, we attempt to correct for such measurement difficulties.

6.4 Empirical Analysis: Firm-level Financing and Investment Patterns

The literature on the determinants of investment often assumes that financing sources are either exogenous or precede investment decisions, and mostly focuses on capital expenditure to the exclusion of other uses of funds.[34] We study the overall mix of both sources and funds without presuming a particular line of causality. As a consequence, most of our analysis is mainly descriptive. Nevertheless, several interesting findings emerge.

We conduct three experiments. First, we regress the source ratios (the ratio of each source to total sources), separately, on firm characteristics, and similarly for uses. The regressions are Generalized Least Squares (GLS), and the weighting is by total sources (in constant prices).[35] Second, we compute the simple correlations of pairs of source and use ratios (one source and one use each time). We carry out these computations both as a "panel" of firm-years, and cross-sectionally, averaging the observations for each firm over the sample period. Last, we conduct a somewhat more structured estimation of potential determinants of firm-level investment flows.

In the first two analyses we use both time-averaged firm-level data and panel data, since the year-by-year panel observations are "noisy." Indeed, it is plausible that investment decisions in a particular year are affected by the amount of resources available and by financing decisions (credit obtained from a bank, IPO funds) in previous, or even subsequent years. The analysis with time-averaged data is also important for determining whether long-term financing such as equity funding is associated with particular forms of investment. Moreover, for approximately 240 firm-year observations, both total sources and total uses were *negative* (even though for most of these firms, over time, average total sources and uses are positive), as some firms in certain years lost money and returned debt, and stayed afloat by reducing inventories and liquidating cash balances. For such firms in those years, the source ratios as defined cannot describe how activities are actually financed (instead, they depict how firms wind down their activities).[36] As mentioned above, we did not include these firm-year observations in the year-by-year analysis. It is worth recalling, however, that for other questions such as cash management (the revealed firm-level demand for money) or inventory fluctuations—issues that we plan to pursue in future work—the inclusion of these firm-year observations in a year-by-year analysis may be germane.

The panel regressions include time-fixed effects (time dummies). Their inclusion controls for aggregate fluctuations in output as well as other macroeconomic conditions such as interest rates. All the regressions, panel as well as with time-averaged data, include industry dummies, firm age, geographic location, and profitability variables.

Tables 6.5 and 6.8 display regressions of source ratios on firm characteristics. The year-by-year analysis (table 6.8) indicates that large firms rely more on internal funds and development grants, and less on stock offerings. The result regarding equity funding holds in the time-averaged data as well (table 6.5). Overall, profitable firms rely less on external funds and more on internally generated cash.

A quite striking, albeit not surprising, finding is that firms in development areas very strongly rely on government grants, whereas firms in the greater Tel Aviv area tend to rely on bond issues and other debt. Two stories come to mind. The first is that firms in the periphery obtain all the cash they need through government assistance, and find no use for external funding. Alternatively, this finding may reflect an "easy life" approach on the part of underwriters and banks, who prefer to market the securities of and lend to firms in the Tel Aviv area rather than take the trouble to do

Table 6.5
Factors Affecting Average 1990–1997 Flow of Funds: Sources*
(Each column is a GLS regression of the corresponding ratio to total sources using firm-level data averaged over time; t-statistics in parentheses)

	Internally generated cash	Net stock issues	Net bond issues	Net increase in debt	Development grants	Deferred taxes
Size (total assets—Dec. 1998 million NIS)	−0.007 (−0.191)	−0.047 (−3.789)	0.0003 (0.121)	0.054 (1.416)	0.007 (2.008)	−0.007 (−1.870)
Profitability (operating profits/sales)	0.506 (1.393)	−0.367 (−2.959)	0.010 (0.374)	−0.220 (−0.578)	0.021 (0.584)	0.048 (1.188)
Net profits/Equity	0.049 (0.460)	−0.056 (−1.515)	−0.007 (−0.927)	0.023 (0.206)	−0.008 (−0.782)	−0.0009 (−0.075)
Industry dummies	YES	YES	YES	YES	YES	YES
Greater Tel Aviv area**	0.066 (0.486)	−0.135 (−2.907)	0.027 (2.687)	0.017 (0.124)	0.003 (0.225)	0.020 (1.362)
Development areas***	0.068 (0.545)	−0.035 (−0.841)	−0.001 (−0.133)	−0.201 (−1.536)	0.126 (9.862)	0.043 (3.108)
Multi-plant firms****	−0.078 (−0.539)	−0.087 (−1.759)	−0.001 (−0.139)	0.126 (0.827)	0.013 (0.929)	0.027 (1.685)
Age	0.012 (3.650)	−0.0011 (−1.046)	−0.0006 (−2.701)	−0.009 (−2.713)	−0.0004 (−1.312)	−0.0003 (−1.046)
R^2	0.161	0.345	0.180	0.128	0.630	0.142

*Weighted by total sources. Number of observations: 234.
**A dummy variable that equals 1 if firm is located in area codes 03, 09, and 0 otherwise.
***A dummy variable that equals 1 if firm is located in area codes 06, 07, and 0 otherwise.
****A dummy variable that equals 1 if firm has plants in more than one region, and 0 otherwise. Area codes 02, 04, 08 are the control region.

business with firms in the periphery where monitoring is harder, relationship building is more difficult, and bankruptcy risk is higher.

The coefficients of the year dummies in the year-by-year analysis (not shown) indicate that the role of external financing (relatively to the base year 1990), particularly debt, increased sharply beginning 1992, which is consistent with the following scenario. In the late 1980s and 1990, firms retired debt, funded through enhanced profitability following restructurings. Beginning in 1991–1992, firms relied to a greater degree on external sources to fund their activities, on equity from 1992 to 1994, and increasingly on bank debt since 1995.[37]

An analogous exercise is performed for uses. The results are displayed in tables 6.6 and 6.9. From table 6.9, it can be seen that on a year-by-year basis, large firms invest more in equipment and less in working capital and cash, suggesting perhaps that they are less concerned with building buffer stocks of liquid assets. Not consistent with

Table 6.6
Factors Affecting Average 1990–1997 Flow of Funds: Uses*
(Each column is a GLS regression of the corresponding ratio to total uses using firm-level data averaged over time; t-statistics in parentheses)

	Capital expenditure	Investment in inventory	Investment in working capital	Investment in securities	Investment in cash and cash equivalents	Dividends
Size (total assets—Dec. 1998 million NIS)	−0.023 (−0.912)	−0.006 (−0.322)	−0.011 (−0.468)	0.017 (0.800)	0.024 (0.890)	−0.0003 (−0.030)
Profitability (operating profits/sales)	−0.269 (−1.030)	−0.173 (−0.868)	−0.121 (−0.514)	−0.088 (−0.400)	0.429 (1.584)	0.222 (2.269)
Net profits/Equity	0.004 (0.059)	0.085 (1.431)	0.070 (0.980)	−0.004 (−0.064)	−0.169 (−2.096)	0.014 (0.495)
Industry dummies	YES	YES	YES	YES	YES	YES
Greater Tel Aviv area**	0.230 (2.360)	−0.192 (−2.582)	0.062 (0.702)	−0.038 (−0.461)	−0.069 (−0.686)	0.007 (0.200)
Development areas***	0.502 (5.605)	−0.063 (−0.920)	−0.168 (−2.063)	−0.032 (−0.421)	−0.230 (−2.461)	−0.010 (−0.319)
Multi-plant firms****	0.221 (2.108)	−0.060 (−0.760)	0.061 (0.645)	0.015 (0.170)	−0.207 (−1.902)	−0.030 (−0.749)
Age	0.0028 (1.165)	−0.0022 (−1.211)	−0.0030 (−1.397)	−0.0004 (−0.230)	0.0008 (0.322)	0.0021 (2.366)
R^2	0.253	0.090	0.100	0.036	0.266	0.219

*Weighted by total sources. Number of observations: 234.
**A dummy variable that equals 1 if firm is located in area codes 03, 09, and 0 otherwise.
***A dummy variable that equals 1 if firm is located in area codes 06, 07, and 0 otherwise.
****A dummy variable that equals 1 if firm has plants in more than one region, and 0 otherwise. Area codes 02, 04, 08 are the control region.

this interpretation is their higher investment in securities. Profitable firms pay out a larger share of funds as dividends, as can be seen in both tables 6.6 and 6.9. Although it might seem intuitive that profitable firms would invest relatively more in fixed assets, and hence grow more rapidly, the results do not provide support for this proposition. However, it is not clear a priori that growth should be skewed toward capital expenditures, at the expense of inventories or working capital. Firms in development towns invest in fixed assets but not in working capital. Older firms tend to pay dividends. The panel data year dummies do not exhibit any meaningful time pattern, fluctuating from year to year.

Table 6.7 displays correlations of sources and uses using firm-level data averaged over time, weighted by total sources. These correlations do not control for many relevant variables, nor do they establish causality. Still, some interesting results

Table 6.7
Flow of Funds: Correlation of Sources and Uses, 1990–1997*
(Firm-level data averaged over time; P-values in parentheses)

	Capital expenditure	Investment in inventory	Investment in working capital	Investment in securities	Investment in cash and cash equivalents	Dividends
Internally generated cash	0.178 (0.0062)	−0.098 (0.132)	−0.180 (0.006)	−0.067 (0.303)	0.066 (0.310)	0.188 (0.004)
Net stock issues	0.083 (0.201)	0.006 (0.922)	0.049 (0.452)	−0.027 (0.680)	−0.078 (0.234)	−0.047 (0.468)
Net bond issues	−0.077 (0.236)	0.060 (0.355)	0.048 (0.460)	−0.120 (0.067)	0.077 (0.235)	−0.049 (0.454)
Net increase in debt	−0.228 (0.0004)	0.126 (0.053)	0.161 (0.013)	0.065 (0.321)	−0.029 (0.657)	−0.191 (0.003)
Development grants	0.221 (0.0007)	−0.084 (0.202)	−0.165 (0.011)	−0.062 (0.352)	0.003 (0.958)	0.192 (0.003)
Deferred taxes	0.061 (0.350)	−0.247 (0.0001)	0.047 (0.477)	0.195 (0.003)	−0.080 (0.222)	0.119 (0.068)

* Weighted by total sources. Number of observations: 234.

emerge. The correlations suggest that firms that rely on equity funding do not devote their resources in any significant way to any particular use. We can conclude that at least on average, firms do *not* issue stock to provide dividend income to incumbent shareholders.

Higher reliance on sources other than equity funding is significantly related to specific uses. Firms that rely on internal funds as well as government assistance invest larger portions of their funds in capital equipment and smaller portions in inventory and other working capital.[38] One interpretation of the positive relation between capital expenditure and government assistance is that government financing succeeds in promoting such expenditure. Alternatively, the results simply illustrate that capital intensive firms are more likely to become eligible for government aid. In either case, we cannot assess from these correlations whether such programs, that are designed to reduce the cost of capital to firms, mitigate capital market imperfections or induce "overinvestment" in fixed assets.

Firms that rely on debt invest less in equipment, pay out lower dividends, but devote a higher portion of their funds to inventory and working capital. These findings suggest that banks tend to provide credit to firms with tangible assets that are readily collateralizable, that is, inventories and securities, and less to firms undertaking long term capital investments. To summarize, firms go to the banks to fund the increase in

Table 6.8
Factors Affecting Year-by-Year 1990–1997 Flow of Funds: Sources*
(Each column is a GLS regression of the corresponding ratio to total sources using year-by-year firm-level data; t-statistics in parentheses)

	Internally generated cash	Net stock issues	Net bond issues	Net increase in debt	Development grants	Deferred taxes
Size (total assets—Dec. 1998 million NIS)	0.025 (2.183)	−0.062 (−7.466)	0.0004 (0.197)	0.038 (3.170)	0.004 (2.170)	−0.006 (−3.119)
Profitability (operating profits/sales)	0.609 (6.321)	−0.157 (−2.269)	0.002 (0.095)	−0.471 (−4.736)	−0.006 (−0.396)	0.025 (1.607)
Net profits/equity	0.105 (4.152)	−0.013 (−0.754)	−0.0012 (−0.246)	−0.086 (−3.311)	−0.004 (−1.054)	0.0011 (0.291)
Industry dummies	YES	YES	YES	YES	YES	YES
Year dummies	YES	YES	YES	YES	YES	YES
Greater Tel Aviv area**	−0.146 (−3.298)	0.016 (0.517)	0.040 (4.434)	0.080 (1.753)	0.008 (1.061)	0.0003 (0.054)
Development areas***	−0.115 (−2.946)	−0.001 (−0.064)	0.009 (1.108)	−0.047 (−1.166)	0.129 (19.058)	0.026 (4.180)
Multi-plant firms****	−0.078 (−1.675)	0.042 (1.253)	0.006 (0.651)	−0.016 (−0.343)	0.023 (2.903)	0.023 (3.054)
Age	0.006 (5.732)	−0.003 (−4.559)	−0.0005 (−2.458)	−0.0017 (−1.551)	−0.0002 (−1.366)	−0.0001 (−0.617)
Pre-IPO dummy	0.207 (3.773)	−0.253 (−6.394)	−0.021 (−1.911)	0.030 (0.543)	0.016 (1.696)	0.020 (2.334)
R^2	0.215	0.270	0.103	0.252	0.462	0.105

*Weighted by total sources. Number of observations: 1263.
**A dummy variable that equals 1 if firm is located in area codes 03, 09, and 0 otherwise.
***A dummy variable that equals 1 if firm is located in area codes 06, 07, and 0 otherwise.
****A dummy variable that equals 1 if firm has plants in more than one region, and 0 otherwise. Area codes 02, 04, 08 are the control region.

short-term assets, but expand their capital with the aid of internally generated funds or government assistance.[39]

The causality governing the relationship between capital expansion and internal funds is not unequivocally obvious: It could be that firms that want to spend a lot on new equipment must generate a lot of cash flow. Alternatively, it may be that firms that have a lot of new equipment (i.e., that spend a lot on fixed assets and less on securities, inventories, and working capital) succeed in generating a lot of cash flow.[40]

Some of the correlations described above (table 6.7) hold on a year-by-year basis as well (table 6.10). In a year-by-year analysis, firms that rely on internal sources and

Table 6.9
Factors Affecting Year-by-Year 1990–1997 Flow of Funds: Uses*
(Each column is a GLS regression of the corresponding ratio to total uses using year-by-year firm-level data; t-statistics in parentheses)

	Capital expenditure	Investment in inventory	Investment in working capital	Investment in securities	Investment in cash and cash equivalents	Dividends
Size (total assets—Dec. 1998 million NIS)	0.026 (3.191)	−0.006 (−0.823)	−0.017 (−1.954)	0.027 (3.675)	−0.033 (−3.047)	0.002 (0.481)
Profitability (operating profits/sales)	−0.175 (−2.561)	0.050 (0.822)	0.019 (0.260)	0.003 (0.044)	−0.108 (−1.203)	0.212 (5.515)
Net profits/equity	−0.009 (−0.545)	0.006 (0.412)	−0.005 (−0.250)	−0.001 (−0.079)	0.003 (0.141)	0.006 (0.594)
Industry dummies	YES	YES	YES	YES	YES	YES
Year dummies	YES	YES	YES	YES	YES	YES
Greater Tel Aviv area**	−0.033 (−1.043)	−0.042 (−1.509)	−0.013 (−0.389)	0.028 (1.001)	0.085 (2.074)	−0.026 (−1.476)
Development areas***	0.072 (2.595)	−0.029 (−1.197)	−0.049 (−1.665)	0.016 (0.668)	0.012 (0.348)	−0.023 (−1.489)
Multi-plant firms****	−0.010 (−0.319)	−0.015 (−0.509)	−0.066 (−1.885)	0.007 (0.226)	0.104 (2.393)	−0.019 (−1.018)
Age	0.0012 (1.602)	−0.000003 (−0.005)	0.0002 (0.364)	−0.001 (−2.421)	−0.0015 (−1.563)	0.0017 (4.001)
Pre-IPO dummy	0.092 (2.349)	0.057 (1.656)	0.051 (1.231)	0.019 (0.536)	−0.119 (−2.318)	−0.100 (−4.573)
R^2	0.230	0.056	0.057	0.049	0.126	0.115

*Weighted by total sources. Number of observations: 1263.
**A dummy variable that equals 1 if firm is located in area codes 03, 09, and 0 otherwise.
***A dummy variable that equals 1 if firm is located in area codes 06, 07, and 0 otherwise.
****A dummy variable that equals 1 if firm has plants in more than one region, and 0 otherwise. Area codes 02, 04, 08 are the control region.

government grants exhibit higher capital expenditure. Firms that rely on debt devote a large portion of their resources to inventory and working capital, similar to the findings using data averaged over time. However, some of the results in table 6.7 do not hold in the year-by-year analysis. For example, on a year-by-year basis firms that rely on equity offerings invest *less* in fixed assets and more in securities and cash. The interpretation is simple enough. Public equity offerings are discrete events, and their timing is often driven by market conditions, whereas investment programs are ongoing, and their timing and duration are often related to factors such as macroeconomic and industry conditions, adjustment costs, and so forth. Therefore, firms tend to increase disproportionately their cash holdings in the years that they issue

Table 6.10
Flow of Funds: Correlation of Sources and Uses, 1990–1997*
(Year-by-year firm-level data; P-values in parentheses)

	Capital expenditure	Investment in inventory	Investment in working capital	Investment in securities	Investment in cash and cash equivalents	Dividends
Internally generated cash	0.118 (0.0001)	−0.103 (0.0002)	−0.097 (0.0004)	0.012 (0.657)	0.032 (0.240)	0.153 (0.0001)
Net stock issues	−0.205 (0.0001)	0.028 (0.306)	−0.077 (0.005)	0.167 (0.0001)	0.141 (0.0001)	−0.090 (0.001)
Net bond issues	−0.072 (0.008)	0.002 (0.917)	0.034 (0.220)	0.029 (0.285)	0.007 (0.783)	−0.010 (0.709)
Net increase in debt	−0.010 (0.720)	0.090 (0.0010)	0.127 (0.0001)	−0.100 (0.0002)	−0.100 (0.0002)	−0.093 (0.0003)
Development grants	0.241 (0.0001)	−0.004 (0.884)	−0.115 (0.0001)	−0.057 (0.035)	−0.036 (0.185)	−0.016 (0.550)
Deferred taxes	−0.153 (0.0001)	−0.006 (0.833)	0.130 (0.0001)	0.040 (0.140)	−0.011 (0.673)	−0.045 (0.102)

*Number of observations: 1334.

equity. The analysis using time-averaged data confirms that this is a temporary "cash-hoarding" phenomenon, related to different timing of stock offerings and capital expenditure, that washes out over longer time horizons.

Our interpretation of the finding that, in the year-by-year analysis, there is a positive relation between reliance on bank debt and expenditure on inventory and working capital (and a negative relation with cash, securities, and dividends) is that, on a "daily basis," firms turn to their bankers, with whom they have long-standing relationships, for financing operations. By contrast, banks do not finance investment in equipment (see tables 6.7 and 6.10).[41]

Finally, it is apparent from table 6.10 that, on a year-by-year basis, firms that rely on equity financing pay out a lower percentage of their available funds as dividends. As can be seen in table 6.7, this correlation washes out over longer horizons. It could be that the legal impediments of using equity offering proceeds to fund dividends are indeed binding in the short term.

Determinants of Firm-level Capital Expenditure Some of the above results might convey the impression that stock market financing is not a central determinant of investment behavior, for example, the negative correlation of "net stock issues" and "capital expenditures" reported in table 6.10. This need not mean that firms are oblivious to capital market *conditions* when making investment decisions. In particular, many studies beginning with Tobin (1969) have argued that when stock prices are high, investment in fixed assets should increase. To evaluate the applicability of that proposition to the post-reform capital market in Israel, we perform a year-by-year GLS panel regression (weighted by existing capital stock) in which the dependent variable is the ratio of new investment in fixed assets during a calendar year to the existing capital stock.[42] The independent variables include size, age, profitability, industry, geographic and year dummies, and the previous year Tobin's q (table 6.11).[43] We try three types of specifications. In the first, the variables are included as levels (columns 1 and 2). In the second, we re-run the regressions adding interactive variables between Tobin's q and year dummies and age respectively (columns 3 and 4). This is because, as explained in the previous section, it is possible that Tobin's q, as calculated, might be influenced by differences over time between the CPI and the actual cost of replacing capital. In the third, the left-hand side variable (investment) as well as profitability and Tobin's q are calculated as differences from their mean over time (column 5). In this specification any firm-fixed effects wash out.[44]

The estimated coefficients of Tobin's q, in all specifications, are positive and statistically significant, suggesting that high stock prices enhance firms' investment in physical capital, as economic theory predicts. The interpretation of the magnitude of the coefficients on q is as follows: if q increases by 10 percentage points (for example, if it were to rise for a given firm from 1.0 to 1.1), the ratio of capital expenditures to the capital stock is predicted to increase, on average, by 1.32 percentage points relative to the previous year (see column 1 of table 6.11). Given that financial leverage is about 50 percent, a rise of, say, 20 percent in the market value of the company's stock is translated to a rise of 10 percent in q (that correspond to 10 percentage points if initially q is one). This entails a rise of 6 percent in capital expenditure because capital expenditures represents approximately 22 percent of the existing capital stock and, therefore, a 6 percent rise in capital expenditure is required to increase the ratio of capital expenditures to the capital stock by 1.32 percent ($0.22^{*}6 = 1.32$). Thus, the significance of the estimated coefficients as well as their magnitude are supportive of the q theory of investment.

Some of the other variables are also very significant in explaining investment. Firms in development towns increase their capital stock at a relatively more rapid pace, which is consistent with the positive correlation between government assistance and capital expenditure displayed in tables 6.7 and 6.10. In the specification reported in columns 1–4 we find that firms manufacturing textile and building materials tend to increase their capital stock at rates lower than in other industries such as electronics and chemicals.[45]

Table 6.11
Factors Affecting Year-by-year Firm-level Investment
(t-statistics in parentheses)*

	Dependent variable: Investment as a ratio of capital stock				
	Levels				Deviations from firm mean
Lagged size (total assets)	0.022 (2.841)	0.022 (2.877)	0.023 (3.036)	0.025 (3.175)	−0.143 (−3.612)
Lagged q	0.132 (6.499)	0.135 (6.617)	0.181 (7.582)	0.173 (7.309)	0.127 (4.941)
Profitability (operating profits/sales)	— —	−0.073 (0.035)	−0.075 (−2.178)	−0.073 (−2.092)	−0.208 (−2.236)
Net profits/equity	— —	0.0002 (0.0029)	0.002 (0.521)	−0.0005 (0.156)	−0.0001 (−0.040)
Year dummies	YES	YES	YES	YES	YES
Industry dummies	YES	YES	YES	YES	—
Greater Tel Aviv area**	0.043 (1.705)	0.045 (1.806)	0.040 (1.625)	0.040 (1.540)	— —
Development areas***	0.066 (2.772)	0.070 (2.905)	0.065 (2.756)	0.062 (2.576)	— —
Multi-plant firms****	0.070 (2.787)	0.074 (2.911)	0.060 (2.347)	0.056 (2.171)	— —
Age	−0.002 (−3.206)	−0.002 (−3.141)	−0.002 (−3.197)	0.0002 (0.288)	— —
Interaction: q with year dummies	—	—	YES	—	—
Interaction: q with age	—	—	—	YES	—
R^2	0.260	0.262	0.280	0.280	0.115

* Weighted by total sources. Number of observations: 984.
** A dummy variable that equals 1 if firm is located in area codes 03, 09, and 0 otherwise.
*** A dummy variable that equals 1 if firm is located in area codes 06, 07, and 0 otherwise.
**** A dummy variable that equals 1 if firm has plants in more than one region, and 0 otherwise. Area codes 02, 04, 08 are the control region.

Discussion: Macroeconomic Implications What are the implications of our empirical findings for investment in the economy as a whole? If Israel were a closed economy, aggregate investment would equal aggregate saving, and it could be argued that it really does not matter if equity issues contribute to investment for a particular group of firms because in the absence of a change in the rate of saving, overall investment remains unchanged. However, even in a closed economy, the rate of saving could change as a result of changes in financing patterns (although the direction is unclear). Moreover, even if aggregate savings and investment remained unchanged, the composition of investment may change. Perhaps, good projects which were previously not undertaken because of cash constraints become feasible, whereas other less profitable projects, previously funded by government-directed credit, are no longer undertaken. The poor productivity figures in the 1990s, however, raise some doubts about that possibility. Because Israel is an open economy, it is important to know how changes in funding affected the flow of funds into the country thereby affecting the overall level of investment.

Another issue with macroeconomic implications is the reliance of publicly traded firms on public equity versus bank funding. We found that during the 1992–1993 boom on TASE, publicly traded manufacturing firms relied very little on bank debt, whereas, as we know from other studies, Israeli firms that did not (or could not) raise money on the exchange during that period, continued to rely on bank debt. In 1995–1996, however, when the TASE went into a slump, publicly traded manufacturing firms increased their reliance on bank debt. We conclude that access to funding on a stock exchange can potentially mitigate credit crunches and reduce output volatility over the business cycle.

Notes

We thank Gil Avnimelech, Ravit Ben-David, Artur Lokomet, Renat Lokomet, and Josiah Rotenberg for excellent research assistance on various versions, Vladimir Lifshutz for invaluable support with the data, and Avi Ben-Bassat and Yishay Yafeh for detailed and most helpful comments on an earlier draft. The flow of funds data have been under construction for several years at the Research Department, Bank of Israel. Those who participated in that task include Avivit Bar-Eliezer, Daniel Radomsky, and Assaf Segal. Yosha gratefully acknowledges financial support from the Maurice Falk Institute for Economic Research and the Research Department, Bank of Israel. The material in section 2 draws on Yafeh and Yosha (1998) and Blass, Yafeh, and Yosha (1998).

1. Given that a separate chapter in this volume is dedicated to international capital flow liberalization, we will not address this topic.

2. One third of net equipment purchases were financed by equity issues between 1992 and 1994. See Yafeh and Yosha (1998) and Bank of Israel Annual Report, 1994, p. 61.

3. Although *aggregate* flow of funds tables have been constructed and analyzed in several countries in great detail, such data at the *firm-level* (in the U.S. and a few other OECD countries) are less comprehensive, focusing mostly on internal funds and capital expenditure, to the exclusion of other sources and uses.

4. Provident funds are long-term savings instruments, enjoying tax benefits, that can generally be redeemed after a period of no less than fifteen years.

5. Between 1977 and 1983, bank share prices quadrupled in real terms.

6. Blass, Yafeh, and Yosha (1998) write that "for the most part, [the government] has not interfered with bank operations (except for the appointment of senior managers and directors and in some debt restructuring plans)"; see also Blass and Grossman (1996).

7. For example, in 1990, the Herfindahl index of total bank assets was 0.24 in the Netherlands and 0.23 in Norway.

8. The model studied by Yosha (1995) highlights the following result: A multiproduct bank takes into account cross price effects between substitute products (e.g., long-term savings deposits and retirement provident funds) and will charge higher prices.

9. Indeed, this market power allowed the banks to manipulate their shares.

10. A similar but considerably less detailed table, for the period 1985–1994, was constructed by Yafeh and Yosha (1998). Their reported numbers differ from those reported here due to data updates, different data sources, different debt indexation methods, and, for some categories, less detailed data construction methods. The general flavor of the results remains, however.

11. Many shares on TASE are owned by other companies producing "double counting," but this does not affect the described time trends.

12. Whereas in 1988, government bonds accounted for over half of the overall volume of trade, the figure for 1994 was 16 percent (although the figure for 1996 is higher, close to 43 percent).

13. The Bank of Israel 1997 Annual Report refers to the growth of such firms as a central component of an overall structural change taking place in the manufacturing sector.

14. It is also possible that the success of such firms in raising funds on foreign exchanges has created competitive pressures that resulted in financial innovations on the TASE, thereby facilitating the access to local equity financing, and generated greater interest in Israeli firms among the international financial community.

15. Indeed, she finds, for a sample of Israeli firms, a positive association between firm accounting profitability and shareholding by banks or bank affiliates.

16. This finding is consistent with evidence on debt floatations in the United States. Most studies use pre-Glass-Steagall data—Ang and Richardson (1994), Kroszner and Rajan (1994, 1997), and Puri (1994, 1996)—whereas Gande et al. (1997) provide modern evidence exploiting the recent relaxation in the United States of Glass-Steagall restrictions regarding underwriting by commercial banks.

17. Of related interest is Blei (1998) who compares the (risk-adjusted) performance of bank-affiliated and nonaffiliated "flexible" mutual funds.

18. In the official TASE classification by industry, the category "manufacturing" includes venture capital firms and holding companies. To preserve the (relative) homogeneity of the sample, these firms are not included in the sample.

19. Approximately eighty Israeli firms are listed in the U.S. A minority of them is included in our sample.

20. The construction of the flow of funds tables is explained in more detail later.

21. In this procedure, we used four key variables—net profits, flows from investment activities, flows from financial activities, and flows from operations. A discrepancy of 5 percent (provided it is greater than 5000 December 1990 NIS) in one or more of these variables led to the removal of the firm-year observation from the sample.

22. Consider some ratio, x, compute the average of x over the sample years for a particular firm, and denote this average by x'. Repeat for all the firms in the sample, and compute the average of x' across firms, denoted x''. Firms for which x' minus x'' was larger than four standard deviations (of x'), for one or more source ratio, use ratio, or profitability ratio, were removed from the sample.

23. Consider some ratio, x, compute the average of x over the sample years for a particular firm, and denote this average by x'. Firm-year observations for which x minus x' was larger than four standard deviations (of x), for one or more source ratio, use ratio, or profitability ratio, are not included in the year-by-year analysis.

24. The usefulness of the international comparison should be tempered by the fact that the data in the OECD countries encompass the service sector as well as corporations not listed on the stock exchange, whereas the Israeli data are limited to the publicly listed manufacturing sector.

25. Convertible bonds are treated here as equity, even though the interest on such bonds appears as an expense (and not as a dividend payout).

26. Table 6.1 refers to the entire corporate sector (not only manufacturing) and includes bond issues by public utilities.

27. See Yafeh and Yosha (1998).

28. In 1990, deferred taxes were on average a *negative* source, as the amount of taxes deferred from previous years and due in 1990 exceeded the value of new deferrals to later years.

29. Table 6.2 provides information on some of these items for the entire manufacturing sector.

30. Certain expenses are disallowed, and firms do not receive rebates when losses are realized. This offsets the understatement of government assistance.

31. The latter is derived primarily from figures on imports of machines as well as aggregate construction figures, whereas the Industry and Crafts Surveys (published with a lag by the CBS) is derived, somewhat similarly to our data, from information reported by individual firms.

32. This trend is highly uniform across two-digit manufacturing subsectors, but for the minority of manufacturing firms holding relatively little equipment and large amounts of real estate, q might be overstated.

33. The price of equipment abroad generally increased less rapidly than other tradable goods, so the gap may be even greater.

34. Hubbard, Kashyap, and Whited (1995) is a prominent study in this field.

35. Because the regressors are the same in all the equations, there is no efficiency gain from estimating the equations as a system, and consequently, there is no need to deal with the fact that the left-hand side variables across equations sum to unity (or, alternatively, that the error terms across equations sum to zero).

36. Taken to the extreme, if we were to use daily data, even very profitable firms would exhibit negative total sources on payroll day, for example. Thus, the phenomenon of negative sources is in part due to short-term temporary effects that are smoothed out in the regressions using time-averaged data.

37. The industry dummies (not shown) also indicate that the textile industry relied heavily on debt and less on internal sources.

38. Also, firms that rely on internal sources and deferred taxes pay higher dividends.

39. In line with this, Blass and Yafeh (2001) find that Israeli banks are less likely to underwrite firms with hard to collateralize intangible assets.

40. Because internally generated funds include depreciation, firms with a lot of new equipment, ceteris paribus, will exhibit high cash flow. We regard this interpretation as less convincing.

41. This is probably not true for *privately* held companies.

42. The numerator of this ratio is not equal to the net increase of the capital stock because we ignore depreciation.

43. For a similar analysis for six OECD countries, see Kadapakkam, Kumar, and Riddick (1998).

44. We also tried both specifications, omitting the (potentially endogenous) profitability variable, and obtained virtually identical results.

45. The specification reported in columns 1–4 also indicates that large firms increase their capital stock at a relatively more rapid pace, although this effect is reversed in the specification used in column 5. We do not have a clear and intuitive interpretation for this result.

References

Ang, James S., and Terry Richardson. "The Underwriting Experience of Commercial Bank Affiliates prior to the Glass-Steagall Act: A Re-examination of Evidence for Passage of the Act." *Journal of Banking and Finance* 18 (March 1994): 351–395.

Asquith, Paul, and David W. Mullins Jr. "Equity Issues and Offering Dilution." *Journal of Financial Economics* 15 (Jan.–Feb. 1986): 61–89.

Ben-Bassat, Avraham. "Capital Market Reform in Israel." *Bank of Israel Economic Review* 65 (1993): 17–33.

Ber, Hedva. "Does the Identity of Large Shareholders Affect Corporate Control?" Jerusalem: Bank of Israel, 1998. Mimeo.

Ber, Hedva, Yishay Yafeh, and Oved Yosha. "Conflict of Interest in Universal Banking: Bank Lending, Stock Underwriting, and Fund Management." *Journal of Monetary Economics* 47 (February 2001): 189–218.

Blass, Asher A. "Performance and Market Structure of Provident Funds: 1987–1994." *The Economic Quarterly* 43 (1996): 260–279. (Hebrew)

Blass, Asher A. "Are Israeli Stock Prices Too High?" *Bank of Israel Economic Review* 71 (January 1999): 29–58.

Blass, Asher A., and Richard Grossman. "A Harmful Guarantee?" *International Review of Law and Economics* 16 (December 1996): 461–472.

Blass, Asher A., and Yishay Yafeh. "Vagabond Shoes Longing to Stray: Why Foreign Firms List in the United States." *Journal of Banking and Finance* 25 (March 2001): 555–572.

Blass, Asher A., Yishay Yafeh, and Oved Yosha. "Corporate Governance in an Emerging Market: The Case of Israel." *Journal of Applied Corporate Finance* 10 (1998): 79–89.

Blei, Sharon. "The Performance of Bank- and Non-Bank Affiliated Mutual Funds." Tel Aviv University, 1998. Mimeo.

Bufman, Gil, and Leonardo Leiderman. "Financial Reform in Israel: A Case for Gradualism." In *Financial Opening: Policy Lessons for Korea,* edited by Rudiger, Dornbusch, and Y. Park. Seoul: Korea Institute of Finance, 1995.

Gande, Amar et al. "Bank Underwriting of Debt Securities: Modern Evidence." *Review of Financial Studies* 10 (Winter 1997): 1175–1202.

Hubbard, Glenn, Anil Kashyap, and Toni Whited. "International Finance and Firm Investment." *Journal of Money, Credit and Banking* 27 (August 1995): 683–701.

Kadapakkam, Palani-Rajan, P. C. Kumar, and Lieght Riddick. "The Impact of Cash Flows and Firm Size on Investment: The International Evidence." *Journal of Banking and Finance* 22 (March 1998): 293–320.

Kroszner, Randall S., and Raghuram G. Rajan. "Is the Glass-Steagall Act Justified? A Study of the U.S. Experience with Universal Banking before 1933." *American Economic Review* 84 (June 1994): 810–832.

——— "Organization Structure and Credibility: Evidence from Commercial Bank Securities Activities before the Glass-Steagall Act." *Journal of Monetary Economics* 39 (August 1997): 475–516.

Puri, Manju. "The Long-Term Default Performance of Bank Underwritten Security Issues." *Journal of Banking and Finance* 18 (March 1994): 397–418.

——— "Commercial Banks in Investment Banking: Conflicts of Interest or Certification Role?" *Journal of Financial Economics* 40 (March 1996): 373–401.

Ribon, Sigal, and Oved Yosha. "Financial Liberalization and Competition in Banking: An Empirical Investigation." Tel Aviv University and Bank of Israel, 1999. Mimeo.

Sarnat, Marshall, and George Szpiro. "The Impact of a Financial Crisis on the Attitude to Risk." *Bank of Israel Banking Review* 3 (1992): 13–30.

Shin, Hyun-Han, and Rene M. Stulz. "Are Internal Capital Markets Efficient?" *Quarterly Journal of Economics* 113 (May 1998): 531–552.

Tobin, James. "A General Equilibrium Approach to Monetary Theory." *Journal of Money Credit and Banking* 1 (1969): 15–29.

Yafeh, Yishay, and Oved Yosha. "Financial Markets Reform, Patterns of Corporate Finance, and the Continued Dominance of Large Banks: Israel 1985–95." *Economic Systems* 22 (June 1998): 175–199.

Yosha, Oved. "Privatizing Multi-Product Banks." *Economic Journal* 105 (November 1995): 1435–1453.

7 The Pension Fund Reform

Avia Spivak

7.1 Introduction

Pension funds serve as major financial intermediaries in the Israeli economy. They collect 17.5 percent of the wages of insured and are responsible for supporting hundreds of thousands of pensioners. Thus, the stability and healthy performance of the funds are important policy goals for any government in Israel.

This chapter tells the story of Israel's pension-fund reform, paying attention to the institutional, legal, macroeconomic, and microeconomic aspects.

The reform began in March 1995, when the government resolved to restructure Israel's pension system. The resolution was adopted with the consent of the Histadrut, the owner of most pension funds. The immediate motive for the resolution was concern about the stability of the pension funds due to their large actuarial deficits. Under the resolution, existing funds were closed to new members and became "old pension funds," and new funds were established under new and different principles. The government assumed the old funds' liabilities to members and, by so doing, undertook to cover their actuarial deficits. The principles used in building the new funds assured that they would be free of actuarial deficits in the future.

There are two formal sources for government intervention in the pension-fund industry—labor laws that regulate employer-employee relations and income tax laws. The latter define pension funds as part of a larger set of long-term saving institutions that receive tax benefits—provident funds and, in respect to executive insurance plans, insurance companies. The Capital Market Division of the Ministry of Finance is the regulator of all these activities. This system, of course, underwent fundamental changes in the pension fund reform occasioned by the March 1995 government resolution. Government subsidization of pension funds, achieved by the sale of preferred-yield "earmarked" bonds to the funds, is another cornerstone of the institutional aspect. In this context, the pension fund reform should be considered part of the process of capital market reform elaborated upon elsewhere in this book.

The macroeconomic aspect deals with expected population aging in Israel and the concern that the national pie will not suffice for an economy populated in large measure by elderly retired people who depend on the working young. This is a global problem; to solve it, individuals must accumulate enough capital while young to finance their consumption in old age. A crucial institutional issue is the extent of pension coverage, the number of workers covered, and the fraction of wage that is pensionable, that is, covered by the pension plan. The extent of coverage is also important from the standpoint of the labor market, given that the economic environment is such that large structural changes and greater mobility among workplaces—and, therefore, greater uncertainty in employment—are expected. Below, we show that because pension plans have a beneficial effect on the accumulation of capital in the economy at large, expanding pension coverage is desirable.

The microeconomic aspect is the efficient structure of the pension-fund industry that ensures efficiency and good service for citizens. This matter is closely related to the structure of the funds' administrative and marketing expenditure. Central questions in this context are the desired extent of competition among funds, the optimum size and number of funds, and on what aspects the pension program should competition among funds focus. Another question concerns the relations between this industry and other financial intermediation industries, foremost insurance and banking.

The chapter begins with the story of the reform, describes the structure of the new pension funds, and discusses the macroeconomic implications of the reform and the question of the structure of this industry. The final part of the chapter evaluates the reform.

7.2 The Evolution of the Reform

Pension funds around the world are traditionally related to the establishment of trade unions and their concern for the disabled, widows, and orphans. Israel's pension funds are no exception. The state began to intervene in pension fund operations in the 1950s for two reasons—the need to safeguard the pension benefits of the insured and the wish to channel the funds' accrued savings to the needs of the state. The state was the main financial intermediary at that time; the capital market was nationalized for all practical purpose.[1] We now skip over the interesting history of the pension funds to the crisis that prompted the current reform. In the early 1990s, the pension system was typified by several basic facts:

1. Pension funds received preferred-yield earmarked bonds on the basis of a renewable annual agreement. The basic yield was 5.5 percent per annum, indexed to the Consumer Price Index.

2. The other long-term saving institutions, provident funds and insurance companies, stopped receiving earmarked bonds as part of a capital market reform that began with the provident funds in 1987.

3. The pensions are required to submit annual actuarial balance sheets as part of their reporting to the Capital Market Division. According to the balance-sheet assumptions, the funds had deficits of 30 percent of assets. However, this was not an immediate problem for most funds.[2]

4. The legislative framework for the funds' operations originated in the Income Tax Law, which defined provident funds as long-term saving institutions that are eligible for tax exemptions, and in the supervisory regulations promulgated by the Capital Market Division. Pension funds are considered a type of provident fund. To this day, a pension law has not been enacted in Israel.

The Finance Ministry wished to complete the capital-market reform and reduce the pension funds' subsidy. It was also concerned about the funds' deficits and their implications for the long-term stability of the capital market and for the benefits of the insured. Although the government had never formally undertook to guarantee the benefits of pension fund members, after it intervened in the 1983 bank share crisis and spared investors in these shares from large losses, it obviously could not stand aside in the event of a pension fund collapse.

Following Government Resolution 117 of September 8, 1992, the Fogel Committee was appointed to submit recommendations for a comprehensive policy and an immediate action plan in the field of pension saving. In its work, the committee was to address itself to the assurance of a minimum level of economic existence for every citizen and to make reference to the implications of the pension contributions on labor cost, labor mobility, channels of long-term investment, the capital market, and investment at large.

The committee presented its recommendations in June 1994. It spoke of "urgency—unless appropriate measures are taken promptly, the Israeli economy will not be able to withstand the burden of today's pension liabilities. The collapse of the set of defined-benefits (DB) pension funds is inevitable." The recommendations included "limiting the secondary level to up to three times the national average wage ... anchoring the terms of saving, state involvement, and rules of regularization and regulation in primary legislation ... phasing out budgetary pension countrywide ... [and] phased integration of secondary-level forms of saving, including pension plans, into the capital market."

Although the government did not adopt these recommendations, the committee's important infrastructure work undoubtedly became a basis for the negotiations and the decision-making process that followed. After negotiations with the Histadrut, another resolution was adopted, and on its basis, the pension fund reform was crafted. Before we take up the government resolution, it is worth noting that one of the stimuli for the resolution was the constitutional revolution that occurred in Israel when the Freedom of Occupation Law and the Human Dignity and Freedom Law were enacted. Pursuant to the passage of these Basic Laws, insurance companies petitioned the High Court of Justice for permission to receive preferred-yield earmarked bonds, as did the pension funds. The court instructed the government to reply to the insurance companies' demands in the form of a resolution. After several postponements, the deadline for the response was set for April 1, 1995. The government adopted its resolution in the last few days of March 1995, under deadline pressure and after hasty negotiations with the Histadrut.

Principles of the Reform as Expressed in the March 29, 1995 Government Resolution

The principles of the reform were based on experience. The giving of benefits without adequate actuarial coverage was the nightmare of the professional agencies that crafted the reform. They wished to design a system that would make the actuarial-economic consideration paramount in two senses: Pension funds would have to maintain overall actuarial balance, and rights would be accrued on an actuarial basis so that fund members, foremost the young, would have an appropriate incentive to save. The Finance Ministry and the Histadrut did not dispute this point, provided that the system assured reasonable benefits for Histadrut members. The Finance Ministry's wish to complete the capital-market reform ended with a compromise—investment of 30 percent of members' contributions in the free market and the rest in earmarked bonds. The compromise also limited the level of wage for which funds would be entitled to preferred-yield bonds, on the rationale, which we consider reasonable, that persons earning one hundred thousand NIS per month, for example, do not need a pension subsidy from the government. The principles are summarized below:

1. Existing funds are barred to new members as of January 1, 1995, and will henceforth be called "old funds." All new members of pension funds will be referred to "new funds" that will offer less generous terms.[3]

2. The government guarantees the benefits of members of old funds, although there will be some limits on the growth rate of the average wage, on which basis their pensions will be calculated, and each fund must implement a restructuring plan under the supervision of the Capital Market Division of the Ministry of Finance.

3. Old funds will continue to receive 5.5 percent earmarked bonds. New funds will invest only 70 percent of contributions in earmarked bonds that pay an effective yield of only 5.05 percent[4] and the remaining 30 percent in solid investments in the free market. The government undertakes to maintain a safety net against risks of these investments and against an aberrant increase in life expectancy.[5]

4. The wage insured by the new funds will be limited to twice the national average wage.

Following the resolution, the Finance Ministry issued guidelines for the creation and management of new pension funds, and new funds were established and began to operate after the Finance Ministry approved their statutes. However, the system has not yet equilibrated; the Histadrut and the Finance Ministry continue to struggle, each attempting to tug the arrangement in its own direction.

Attempts to Modify the Pension Arrangement: The Yellow Pad, the Brodet Committee, and the General Strike

The first side that sought to modify the agreement was the Histadrut, in a matter pertaining to members of old funds. The government resolution was eroded in two ways—an amendment to the resolution on April 28, 1996, and the "Yellow Pad" of May 10, 1996 (an agreement written on a yellow pad), both of which took place shortly before the elections. The first measure improved the interest rate for the portion of wage exceeding the national average wage limitation and changed the timing of determination of the wage base after generous countrywide wage increases in the civil service were negotiated. The second adjustment was less technical and therefore more radical: The lavish wage increases created a large differential between retirees insured under the "last-three-years" method, in which the pension is based on the last three years of wage, and retirees whose pension is computed on the basis of the "averages method," that is, the average wage in all years of labor. With a large pay hike, the pension using the former method is much larger. To avoid discrimination among workers, the Histadrut demanded compensation for the losers in the form of equalization of benefits.[6] On May 10, 1996, the Finance Minister succumbed to the Histadrut's pressure and agreed to compensate persons disadvantaged by the averages method by paying them 60 percent of the difference over the next five years.

Severe political turbulence occurred in 1996, following the assassination of Prime Minister Yitzhak Rabin on November 4, 1995, and the Likud's electoral victory with the election of Benjamin Netanyahu to the premiership. However, the Finance Ministry adhered to its stance. The new Finance Minister, Dan Meridor, named his director general, David Brodet, to chair a committee tasked with proposing capital-market reforms in response to shocks that were buffeting the Tel Aviv Stock Exchange.

The Brodet Committee report, submitted in September 1996, included recommendations concerning pension funds that were stern from the Histadrut's standpoint. For example, recommendation no. 1.1, *Retirement Saving*, stated the following: As part of the preference of retirement saving (comprehensive Old Age, Survivors, and Disability [OASD] pension), earmarked bonds should be issued to pension funds only, at a rate of 70 percent of assets, only for contributions from members' wages that do not exceed the ceiling of one time the national average wage.

According to data cited in the committee's report, 90 percent of the wage bill in Israel is below the ceiling of twice the national average wage, whereas only 70 percent is under the ceiling of the average wage itself. Lowering the ceiling would allow more pension savings to reach the capital market and would reduce the government subsidy implicit in the preferred interest rate paid on the earmarked bonds. Thus, the pension funds, as institutional investors that are interested in a long-term return, would move into the capital market and stabilize it.[7]

In the aftermath of the Brodet Committee report, the government resolved on March 13, 1997, to lower the insured wage ceiling of new pension funds from twice the national average wage to the national average wage. The government also reneged on the May 10, 1996, agreement.[8] After lengthy negotiations over these two points, during which the government and the new Histadrut made no progress toward agreement, the New Histadrut, chaired by Amir Peretz, declared labor sanctions that escalated into a general strike. The Histadrut's desiderata centered on pension issues, not wage demands. In the opinion of the Histadrut, the government had precipitated the strike by unilaterally breaching its agreements in pension affairs. The strike was a success from the Histadrut's standpoint as its two major demands were met. The Ministry of Finance, for its part, successfully abolished the safety net that it had given the pension funds for the yield on bonds in the free market and for the increase in life expectancy. In this respect, the funds advanced in the defined-contribution (DC) direction and moved away from DB.

The account of the reform leads to several conclusions, some of which transcend the particular Israeli time and place:

1. Because pension (and National Insurance) arrangements have a political dimension, they are prone to frequent change. In the United States, for example, income tax laws are being revised continually—for example, the establishment of long-term savings mechanisms such as 401k. And in the United Kingdom the pension system has undergone a comprehensive reform. Each side to the political debate attempts to modify the arrangement in accordance with its perspective and its political strength.

2. The foregoing case provides an example of the political hazard that pervades any intergenerational risk sharing.

3. Both parties in the agreement, and in the struggles, are symmetrical in terms of their willingness to adjust the agreement to their advantage at a propitious time.

4. It is evident that the arrangement is not the final word. The Brodet Committee report is the Finance Ministry's way of saying that it does not consider the existing situation a state of equilibrium. The arrangement should be viewed as an interim one in which future changes should be expected.

7.3 The Establishment of New Pension Funds

On September 20, 1995, the Commissioner of the Capital Market Insurance and Saving, who is also the Superintendant of Insurance, issued "Directives for the Establishment and Management of New Pension Funds." This document, on the basis of which the statutes of new pension funds were written, was revised on January 8, 1997, and will probably be revised again in the future.[9]

Management Company

Each new pension fund must be established within the contours of a limited liability corporation that will be its management company. This company must engage only in the management of pension funds and provident funds. Interestingly, the pension fund is required to attain a membership of at least fifteen hundred within two years. The capital requirement is truly minuscule—only five million NIS. The company must obtain an insurer's license from the Superintendent of Insurance and establish a Board of Directors and its committees, following the accepted practice in companies that deal with the public's money.

The fund may charge management fees of no more than 8 percent of contributions (employees' and employers') and 0.25 percent per annum of outstanding balance of inactive members. The management company receives only 6 percent of management fee revenue, with 0.75 percent being earmarked for a special actuarial reserve and 1.25 percent being kept in a reserve to cover expenses for payout of benefits to eligibles in the future. In other words, the fund may not charge a management fee for its pension payout expenses because this has already been collected via the contribution mechanism.

Principles of Pension Plans

The regulations speak of two types of funds: subsidized by earmarked bonds, and unsubsidized. We will focus on the subsidized plans, of course. The crux of the matter is as follows:

1. The fund must cover all risks—old age, survivors and disability.

2. Funds of two types may be established—defined-contribution and defined-benefits. Both are eligible for government subsidies. Because the DB type is dominant, our discussion focuses on it.

3. The old-age pension is calculated using the portions method: Each month, a numerical coefficient is calculated using an actuarial calculation on the basis of its

mortality tables and interest rate. The coefficient is multiplied by the monthly wage, and the product is the pension portion. This portion is pegged to the Consumer Price Index. The sum of all the portions is the old-age pension.

4. A survivor of an active member receives a pension on the basis of the member's expected eligibility, that is, the old-age pension that the member would have received had s/he lived to retirement age. The minimum pension for a widow is 50 percent of expected eligibility; the minimum benefit for an orphan is 25 percent thereof. Total benefits must not exceed 100 percent of the member's wage. Benefits for pensioners' survivors follow the same rule but are based on the pension actually paid.

Interestingly, a survivorless pensioner may request an increase in pension on account of reduction of risk to the pension fund—an option previously unavailable.

5. Disability pension is at least 40 percent of the expected old-age pension but no more than 75 percent of insured wage.

6. The pension fund has an actuarial equilibration mechanism that operates in the following way: Each year the fund draws up a detailed actuarial balance sheet that complies with the guidelines of the Commissioner of the Capital Market. Actuarial surpluses are transferred to a special-risks reserve. They can be used to boost the benefits of all members, whether they are contributing to the fund (active) and receiving pensions from the fund (pensioner) or have a balance on deposit with the fund but have stopped making contributions (inactive), provided that the reserve exceeds 4 percent of the fund's accumulated liabilities. In such a case, the fund may distribute only a reserve sum that exceeds 3 percent of its liabilities.[10]

However, a fund that has accumulated an actuarial deficit above a critical percentage value of accumulated liabilities must cover it. The sources for this coverage are the actuarial reserve, to which 0.75 percent of contributions from the firm's management fee are transferred; the special-risks reserve; and cutbacks in benefits. To reduce benefits, the fund must obtain the approval of the Commissioner of the Capital Market. The fund may invoke the equilibration mechanism at its discretion and *must* do so in either of two cases: if the cumulative actuarial deficit surpasses 3 percent of liabilities for three consecutive years or if it is greater than 5 percent in any given year.

It is important to note that *the management company does not use its own equity to cover its actuarial deficit*. The authors of the regulations treated the deficit as an objectivity that has nothing to do with management's behavior. However, the conservatism of a pension fund's actuarial assumptions is, among other things, based on decisions of the fund's management, and this structure of incentives does not take this factor into account. As we will see below, one explanation for the differences among funds in the structure of benefits is the difference in the degree of conservatism of their actuarial assumptions.

7. Members who withdraw their contributions receive their money in accordance with a formula in the income tax regulations known as the "surrender values formula."[11]

Remarks

1. The actuarial equilibration mechanism is designed to make new pension funds into DC funds of sorts, and the Ministry of Finance sometimes treats this as an unwritten rule. For example, if the return on a fund's investments in the free market—a return that has no safety net—slips below a stipulated level, members' benefits are decreased (with the approval of the commissioner of the capital market, as stated). If life expectancy increases in a way that finds expression in the actuarial balance sheet, a decrease in benefits is needed. Of course, this is not a true DC program, in which each individual maintains a balance in his/her own account and at retirement age converts this balance into a pension or receives it in a lump sum. In our case, the benefits vary commensurate with the fund's total accrual and total actuarial liabilities; therefore, this plan has a mutual insurance component that unalloyed DC plans lack.[12]

2. The old-age pension is computed in a totally new way, based on actuarial tables, giving the young an economic incentive to save for old age by joining pension funds. Using the expected old-age pension to derive survivors' and disability benefits is an accepted method that the old pension plans used as well. However, the share of pension given to widows and orphans of active members was increased.

3. The possibility of competition among funds exists: A fund managed by better managers (or that has better luck in its investments) will amass actuarial surpluses and may enhance members' rights and, thereby, attract more members. However, this competition may be a two-edged sword: Funds that compromise and admit members indiscriminately may suffer later on. If a pension fund has more disabled or long-lived members than its actuarial balance sheets assumed, it will build up a deficit and will have to reduce benefits. This gives the funds a motive to be selective in accepting new members—a phenomenon known as "creaming." Some competition may also occur in management fees; see below.

7.4 Macroeconomic Implications of the Reform: The Influence of Pension Funds on Capital Accumulation[13]

Pension funds (and provident funds) are instruments for long-term saving that the government rewards by means of tax benefits. However, the funds' influence on total

Table 7.1
Income, Consumption, and Saving by Age Cohorts (Latitudinal cross-section data)

Age	20–30	31–50	51–64	65+	Total
Income	1,564	1,819	2,132	2,071	1,904
Consumption	1,663	1,741	2,013	1,895	1,820
Saving	−99	78	118	178	84
Saving as pct. of disposable income	−5.9	4.5	5.9	9.3	4.6

Source: 1992/93 *Household Expenditure Survey.*

Table 7.2
Saving as Share of Total Disposable Income (Percent) by Age Quintiles

Quintile/Age	20–30	31–50	51–64	65+	Total
1	−22.9	−19.3	−23.9	−20.2	
2	−12.5	−8.0	−7.0	−13.7	
3	−11.5	−2.6	2.2	−0.9	
4	−6.1	5.1	6.6	3.5	
5	5.3	21.2	20.2	36.3	
Total	−5.9	4.5	5.9	9.3	4.6

Source: 1992/93 *Household Expenditure Survey.*

saving is not unequivocal. When individuals are forced to save with pension funds due to labor agreements, they may reduce their volitional long-term saving commensurably. If this occurs, total saving does not increase.

The conceptual framework for such behavior by individuals is the life-cycle theory. According to this theory, individuals plan their consumption and saving rationally, from an early age and for the rest of their lives, and have no liquidity limitations and can borrow on future income. If this theory holds true, we would expect individuals to consume at a constant level throughout their lives, to have negative saving in youth and in old age, and to have positive saving during most of their working years.

As table 7.1 shows, consumption is not constant across age cohorts, but rather adjusts itself to income. Another finding inconsistent with the life-cycle theory is the positive saving at retirement age (65+). We would expect individuals in that age cohort to consume their entire income and more by negative accumulation of property. (In the United States, for example, it is possible to take out a reverse mortgage, in which a bank pays individuals a fixed monthly sum for many years in return for which it takes title of their dwelling at the end of the term. Old-age homes in Israel use a similar arrangement.) Table 7.2, which itemizes saving by income groups, shows that most saving at retirement age is amassed by persons in the uppermost quintile.

Table 7.3
Income and Its Sources for Persons with and without Pension at Age 65+
(Current prices)

	Quintile	National Insurance benefits	National Insurance old-age pension	Pension	Home owners income	Other income	Labor	Total pretax income
Pension recipients	1	36	419	418	207	73	48	1200
	2	53	449	622	355	43	89	1611
	3	71	452	800	440	120	245	2129
	4	48	486	1201	567	224	303	2829
	5	59	517	1884	765	970	970	5164
	Total	54	465	**987**	467	287	332	**2591**
Pension nonrecipients	1	42	443	0	58	42	59	644
	2	61	435	0	192	165	104	955
	3	57	469	0	351	208	177	1263
	4	96	375	0	427	499	464	1860
	5	82	368	0	758	1968	1337	4512
	Total	68	418	0	358	578	429	**1851**
Total population		60	442	512	415	427	379	2235

Source: 1992/93 *Household Expenditure Survey.*

Saving at retirement age may be explained by the saver's motive—to build up an estate to bequeath or to be prudent, for example, to accumulate enough property to move into a nursing home. Both factors fall outside the boundaries of the classic life-cycle theory.

Table 7.3 allows a first glance at the question of saving. It compares the income of elderly persons, sorted by those eligible for pensions and those not, in 1992. The average monthly pension was NIS 987. Were the argument expressed by the life-cycle theory correct, the other income of those without pensions would be higher by exactly this sum, to compensate them for the lack of pension saving; in that case, persons with and without pensions would have the same total income. However, the income of pension recipients is NIS 2,591, NIS 740 higher than the income of pensionless persons. In other words, NIS 247 was offset for pension from the added increment of income, but the entire NIS 987 was not. This primitive offset coefficient is 247/987, that is, less than one-third.

At first glance, the offset coefficient seems to be biased downwards. We know that people with higher income are those who receive pensions, given that pension eligibility is more common among persons with regular jobs, skilled workers, white-collar workers, and so forth. This is the situation worldwide; Israel is no exception. To work out a more accurate pension coefficient, we used two alternative sources of data. One was macro-data on national saving and pension contributions in a time series, with which we examined the effect of total pension contributions on total saving. The other was a unique set of micro-data. The 1979 *Household Expenditure Survey*, and it alone, asked households about their pension contributions. For each household, saving was calculated as the difference between the income and the expenditure reported in the survey. Thus, one may determine the offsetting effect of pension saving on other saving for these households.

For the longitudinal cross-section, we used saving and pension contributions as a share of GDP, and we added the saving lag, S_{-1}, to determine the short- and long-term effects. The explanatory variables are the share of wage in GDP, WYD, and contributions to pension funds, SRP:

$$\underset{(2.3)}{S = 25.67} - \underset{(-4.2)}{1.13WYD} + \underset{(3.4)}{0.92WYD_{-1}} + \underset{(2.1)}{0.86SRP} + \underset{(2.1)}{0.33S_{-1}} \tag{7.1}$$

D.W. = 1.74

adj. $R^2 = 0.71$ LM test: $F = 0.44$, Prob. = .65, $p = 2$

Contributions to pension funds are 40 percent of total contributions to provident funds SR. Therefore, the short-term effect of SRP on S is only $0.4^*0.86 = 0.34$.[14] Thus, the correct equation is the following:

$$S = A + 0.34SR + 0.33S_{-1} \tag{7.2}$$

The long-term effect of SR on S is obtained by substituting in equation (7.2), $S = S_{-1}$. The result is a coefficient of 0.507.

In sum, the longitudinal study elicits an offset coefficient of approximately 0.50.

Results of the Latitudinal Cross-Section Study In the latitudinal cross-section study, 1,166 households appeared in the sample culled from the 1979 *Household Expenditure Survey*. In the article mentioned in note 13, several equations appear that were estimated, some in logarithmic form and some in polynomial form, that allow us to determine a marginal propensity to consume that varies with income. The following consumption equation is the simplest:

$$\ln C = \underset{(3.4)}{24.79} - \underset{(-1.9)}{0.021} \ln PEN + \underset{(36.7)}{0.773} \ln YD - \underset{(-5.5)}{0.111} \ln FAMS \underset{(-3.2)}{-3.12A}$$

$$\underset{(3.2)}{-0.16A^2} + \underset{(3.2)}{0.00005A^4} - \underset{(-3.1)}{0.0000002A^5} \quad \text{adj. } R^2 = 0.681 \tag{7.3}$$

Where:

$\ln PEN$ is a natural log of the pension contribution.

$\ln YD$ is a natural log of income per standardized person.

$\ln FAMS$ is a natural log of household size.

A is the age of head of household.

Computing the Marginal Effect of Pension Contributions on Consumption The regression findings allow us to calculate the marginal effect of pension contribution on consumption, via the relationship between elasticity, marginal value, and mean. A coefficient of a double logarithmic regression is elasticity, of course, and therefore, the elasticity in this case is 0.021. Elasticity = marginal value/average = 0.021. Because the pension contribution is 4 percent of consumption, the mean is 1/0.4 = 25. Hence, the marginal value is 0.5.

Below, we express this in more formal terms:

$$d \ln C/d \ln PEN = (dC/dPEN)/(C/PEN) \Rightarrow dC/dPEN$$
$$= d \ln C/d \ln PEN^{*} C/PEN$$

$$d \ln C/d \ln PEN = 0.021 \qquad PEN/C = 0.04 \Rightarrow C/PEN = 25 \Rightarrow dC/dPEN = 0.5$$

We thus obtain an offset coefficient of one-half in the cross-section study as well.

The Effect of Pension Funds on Capital Accumulation From a macroeconomic perspective, an increase in saving leads in the long term to an increase in investment. (Some investment in an open economy may evolve into an increase in assets abroad—e.g., if pension funds are allowed to invest abroad.) Therefore, if the pension funds collect several billion sheqels from employees, because the offset coefficient is only one-half, half of the sum collected represents a net increase in saving and capital accumulation. A compulsory pension arrangement for all employees will result in larger contributions to pension funds and, for this reason, in an increase in national saving. This has many advantages in long-term thinking about population aging, because the added capital will generate the product increase that is needed to finance the additional pension disbursements for the adult population. If the capital is invested abroad, the interest and payback on principal will serve to finance the added pension liability.

In contrast, *diverting the funds' investments from earmarked government bonds to alternative forms of investment, for example, shares, will not lead to added saving and economic growth.*

This result stems from aggregate national accounting identities. The change described does not increase net saving because this saving is determined institutionally. Therefore, the investment that is always equal to saving does not change. The effect on the capital market will be reflected in government bond sales—more in the free market and fewer in earmarked form to pension funds. For example, if the funds decide to continue investing their entire portfolio in government bonds, the only difference in the capital market will be *the lower interest rate that the government will pay on its debt.*[15] If some of the investment is made in shares, the equilibrium level of share prices will rise, and the yield on shares will fall. Basically, this change in relative yield occurs because total supply of saving for the unrestricted capital market has increased, and therefore, the price of capital—the rate of return—has declined. Assuming that the change is made skillfully, it may have a favorable effect on the efficiency of capital allocation in the Israeli economy. Thus, the referral of pension funds' money to the capital market should be examined in view of its effect on the stability of the funds and the return for savers, and according to its effect on the structure and performance of the capital market itself. Hence, the main impact is in market efficiency terms—microeconomic terms—but not in macroeconomic terms, in which there is no effect whatsoever.[16]

Government Subsidization

Spivak and Lavi (1996) calculated the level of government subsidization of pension funds, and found that the existing pension plans were being subsidized at about 0.5 percent of GDP. They also found that if a compulsory pension is introduced, the changeover will raise the subsidy rate to 1 percent of GDP, and national saving would increase by much more.

Practically speaking, the government subsidy insures against uncertainty in the return on capital. In the last section of this study, which discusses proposals for changes in the pension system, we address ourselves to this matter at greater length.

7.5 Structure of the Industry

The question of competition among pension funds is one of the most important issues in the current reform. The purpose of competition is to enhance service to the customer, assure correct management of members' money, and generate a range of pension plans tailored to the needs of diverse population groups.

Monitoring of developments in the pension-fund industry shows that competition does exist. As in all oligopolistic competition, in which there are only a few large

Table 7.4
Distribution of Members, Assets, and Accrued Capital in New Pension Funds (End of 1997, NIS millions)

	Members	Accrued capital	Share of members	Share of accrued capital
Mivtachim	136,474	1,065,866	59.4%	55.9%
Makefet	22,642	242,043	9.8%	12.7%
Meitavit	15,700	154,691	6.8%	8.1%
Atidit	8,266	50,534	3.6%	2.6%
Gilad	5,796	57,045	2.5%	3.0%
Teutza	5,740	68,160	2.5%	3.6%
Ahdut	5,134	17,037	2.2%	0.9%
Atudot	5,081	35,489	2.2%	1.9%
Yozma	4,636	21,601	2.0%	1.1%
Yuvalim	4,213	98,915	1.8%	5.2%
Netivot	4,097	47,742	1.8%	2.5%
Pisga	3,748	9,857	1.6%	0.5%
Adi	3,550	7,614	1.5%	0.4%
Amit	2,365	26,888	1.0%	1.4%
Magen Zahav	1,592	2,250	0.7%	0.1%
Shiluv (Menorah)	774	1,405	0.34%	0.1%
Total	229,808	1,904,890	100.0%	100.0%

Source: Balance sheets of the pension funds.

rivals, the aims in competition here are to establish market share and the name of the company (Mivtachim) or the plan ("Makefet Personal") as brand names by means of lavish advertising expenditure. The companies also use other direct-marketing mechanisms.[17] Additional indications of competition are the bids that groups of workers solicit among pension funds to obtain the best possible terms and various manuals that consulting companies issue to help people choose the most appropriate fund. There was no need for such manuals under the previous method, in which the individual had no say in choosing his/her pension fund because membership was arranged through the works committee.[18] Table 7.4 shows how the funds have apportioned the market and illuminates the centralized structure of the pension industry. Mivtachim, the leader, has more than a 50 percent market share, and the three largest pension funds have a market share of 76 percent.

It is interesting to compare competitiveness in the pension fund industry with that in another important sector in the Israeli economy—banking. To perform the comparison, we calculated Herfindahl indices for new and old pension funds. The Herfindahl index is expressed by the following formula:

$$H = \sum_i \alpha_i^2$$

Table 7.5
Indices of Pension-Fund Concentration

	Herfindahl, members	Herfindahl, accrued capital	CR4, members	CR4, accrued capital
Old funds, 1994	31%	34%	82%	87%
Old funds, 1995	27%	34%	80%	87%
Old funds, 1996	27%	34%	80%	87%
New funds, 1995	56%	31%	90%	83%
New funds, 1996	43%	34%	85%	82%
New funds, 1997	37%	34%	80%	82%

where α_i is the share of pension fund i in the grand total. The Herfindahl index fluctuates between $1/N$, in a case where all funds are identical in size, and 1 in the case of a monopoly. We also used the CR4 index, which expresses the percent share of the four largest funds in the total. The results are shown in table 7.5.

The table depicts a highly centralized industry. In comparison, the Herfindahl index for another Israeli financial industry, banking, was 27 percent in 1990—it, too, representing a higher level of concentration than in Western countries, where the median is 16 percent.

The table illuminates the dynamic of concentration: Among the new funds, the index for concentration of members is declining, but that of capital has been unchanged. This means that the small funds have attracted more members who, however, have brought in less capital.

What are the reasons for the concentration? They include high entrance barriers and a expenditure structure that carries scale economies. Examples of entrance barriers are workers' relations with old pension funds and the brand name Mivtachim or Makefet. The funds spend large sums on advertising in the media to strengthen the brand name or to modify it slightly, that is, "Makefet Personal." The relationship of labor unions with old funds and, through them, the continuation of this relationship with the new funds is, of course, an important asset for the established funds.

The two figures below illustrate the old funds' expenditure structure. Figure 7.1 represents expenditure among all funds and figure 7.2 focuses on small funds that have fewer than ten thousand members. As the figures show, average expenditure declines at the small funds and does not change significantly at the large funds. This is a natural expenditure structure: Pension funds have obvious scale economies, because they are administrative instruments for the collection of money and the payout of pensions.

Our data are culled from the old pension funds' balance sheets for 1995 and 1996. For this reason, each old fund appears twice. There is no point in reporting the new

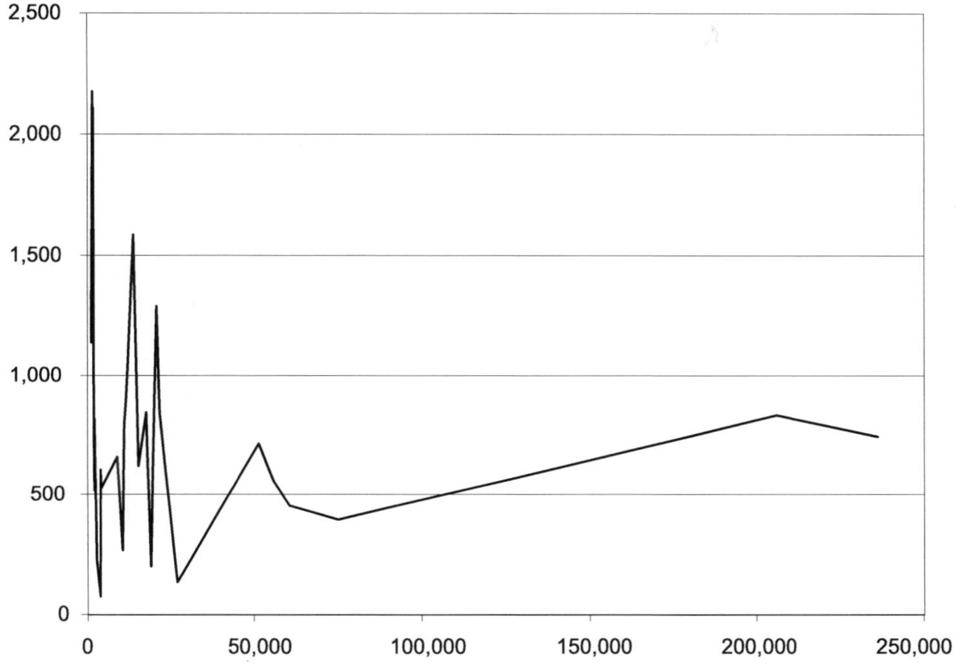

Figure 7.1
Average Expenditure, (NIS per year per member) All Funds, by Number of Members

funds' data; in most cases their balance sheets show expenditure at exactly 6 percent of collections, as their operating statutes allow. One should also assume that some expenditure of new funds that are outgrowths of old funds were loaded onto their parent funds in one way or another. This is one of the entrance barriers against new funds.

The expenditure structure and the entrance barriers present the regulatory agencies with a severe challenge: To maximize efficiency in caring for the insured, the public interest obviously indicates that competition should be maintained among a sufficiently large number of new pension funds. In the absence of adequate competition, the small number of insurers will be able to pressure the regulatory agencies and trust them to pull their chestnuts out of the fire (the too-big-to-fail syndrome). Furthermore, they would be too large to invest freely in the capital market.

To conclude our study, we present evidence from the Mivtachim pension fund Web site that illustrates factually how difficult it is to regulate large funds. The item in question, a clipping from the October 3, 1996, edition of the newspaper *Ma'ariv*,

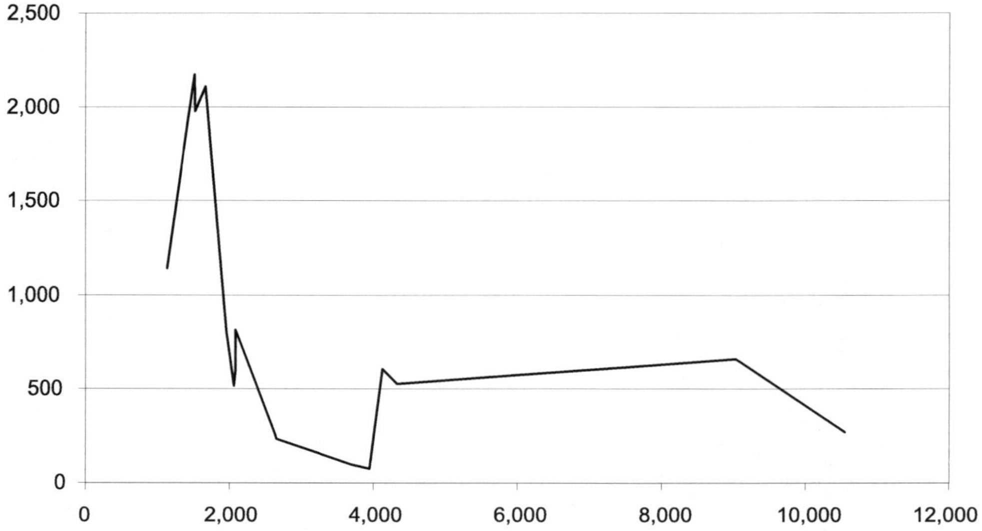

Figure 7.2
Average Expenditure, (NIS per year per member) Small Funds

carries the headline: "Prime Minister's Office will Recommend to [Antitrust Authority Director Yoram] Turbowicz to Declare Mivtachim Pension Fund a Monopoly." Thus, in the opinion of Mivtachim's advertising executives, instead of pondering the woes that await a monopoly, potential consumers will absorb the message that this is Israel's largest and most important pension fund.

7.5 Summary and Conclusions

This chapter surveyed the pension fund reform and described the political process that brought about the situation that exists today—the establishment of new pension funds, macroeconomic effects of the reform on saving and economic growth, and the structure of the pension fund industry, that is, a structure of new and old funds.

The new funds are hybrid entities that came into being by force of a compromise among different outlooks and amidst a political balance of forces—the Ministry of Finance on the one hand, which applies pressure to reduce government involvement and limit subsidization, and the New Histadrut on the other hand, which applies pressure to give pensioners social preference. Thus, the reform still appears to be in an interim phase. The Ministry of Finance will attempt to halt the subsidy and stop issuing the funds with earmarked bonds, and the Histadrut will attempt to broaden the pension coverage and improve its terms. The current balance of forces and the ideology that most shapers of public opinion makers accept do not augur well for workers for the time being.

A reasonable forecast is that the Finance Ministry will manage to reduce the implicit subsidy in the pension arrangement and will maintain the structure of new pension funds. The action that is termed "investment in the free market" will continue to constitute investment in solid assets—foremost, government bonds—to spare the funds from destabilization. An arrangement allowing some investment in international capital markets may materialize.

The following evaluation of the reform makes reference to two levels—its sponsors' immediate goals and an analysis of economic efficiency.

The reform managed to bring long-term stability to the pension industry, albeit at a steep price: The government undertook to cover the funds' actuarial deficits, leaving the Histadrut and the old funds' members almost totally absolved of this burden. The reform swept away the legal labyrinth that had prompted the High Court of Justice to intervene and allows any entity that wishes to enter the field to do so. Indeed, new pension funds have come into being and, to some extent, engage in competitive relations. The administrative framework of the new pension funds functions soundly under the regulation of the Capital Market Division of the Finance Ministry. In this sense, the reform has been quite successful. Furthermore, administrative expenses are much lower among pension funds than in alternative long-term saving institutions such as provident funds and insurance companies.

However, the promise to develop a comprehensive pension policy has not been kept, and main legislation for the pension industry has not passed.

The reform failed to provide solutions at both the microeconomic and the macroeconomic levels. The structure of the industry of new pension funds strongly resembles that of the old funds, although new players have entered the field. This structure makes the industry difficult to deregulate and threatens its efficiency and stability. From the macroeconomic standpoint, pension funds are an important source of national saving, and the prevention of shocks to the industry has kept the status quo intact. However, population aging entails the creation of additional saving, and the pension fund reform has made no significant contribution in this regard.

The macroeconomic perspective deserves broader attention. Population aging has created a problem for pilots of economic affairs in all countries, given that the productive segment of the economy must support rising numbers of dependents. In other words, the dependency ratio has risen. In terms of the old-generation and young-generation dichotomy, the young must set aside a larger share of income to support the old. To relieve the young of this burden, adults must generate more pension savings while they are young in order to overcome the increase in life expectancy. In macroeconomic terms, the increase in saving by the elderly expands the national pie by exactly the increment of their increased consumption, and the young are unscathed. The reform made no reference to this problem; it left the contribution rate unchanged at 17.5 percent of the insured wage. The change is that the increase in life expectancy will precipitate a decrease in pensioners' benefits. The pie will not grow, but the young will not be harmed because their share will not change. Instead of raising the rate of contributions, the population covered by pension plans or the share of wage insured could have been raised. These measures were also not taken.

One of the advantages of the new pension mechanism is its correct structure of incentives for the saver due to the principle of actuarial balance. However, this method rules out the possibility of an intergenerational division of risk, because all the risk—for example, an increase in life expectancy or of the rate of return—devolves on the elderly. However, the subsidized yield on earmarked bonds constitutes an intergenerational transfer that helps the older generation shoulder the risk.[19]

From the standpoint of economic efficiency, it is advisable for the generations to divide the risks. The challenge for the continuation of the pension reform is to find the right way to accomplish this.

Notes

I thank Avi Ben-Bassat, Moshe Justman, Tsippi Samet, Arik Almagor, Yishai Ashlag, and Gadi Hazak for their comments on an earlier version and Gadi Berko for his fine research assistance. As is accepted, responsibility for the contents of this chapter resides with the author alone.

1. In the 1950s, the Finance Ministry and the Histadrut waged a struggle over the pension fund money. For a fascinating account of these events, see Lev Greenberg (1993).

2. Some of the deficits are attributable to the funds' structure of entitlements, which allowed recent immigrants to accrue a reasonable pension after only ten years of work.

3. Subsequently, the High Court of Justice postponed the "debut" to March 1995.

4. The funds receive the bonds at a discount, but the nominal rate is 4.8 percent per annum.

5. The safety net was subsequently withdrawn; see below.

6. Interestingly, in previous cases of wage erosion that made the averages method more advantageous than the last-three-years method, there was a demand for a changeover to the averages method. This occurred at Kagam in the late 1980s.

7. This is an accepted characterization of pension funds as investors in the capital market. However, as we will see below, the funds must submit an annual actuarial balance sheet and revise downward their schedule of entitlements if a deficit is created. This gives them an incentive to behave, like short-term investors in the capital market.

8. The government also resolved to abolish the safety net—a minimum return on the funds' unrestricted investments, provided that these investments be made in government bonds, and coverage of the actuarial deficits that stem from an increase in life expectancy (paragraph 2b of the government resolution).

9. There was a significant difference between the two versions in respect to the length of time in which a member who had terminated his/her membership in an old fund might return to it. The period was six months according to the first version and twenty-four months according to the second.

10. Practically speaking, the method for apportioning rights on account of surpluses has not yet been stipulated; increases in rights were prohibited in 1997, and the criteria and terms for distribution of surplus balances will be determined later on.

11. In the popular lingo, the formula used for old funds was termed the "theft formula," due to the scanty return for those who withdrew their money in comparison with the funds' healthy yields.

12. In its original resolution, as we recall, the government undertook to compensate the funds for an increase in life expectancy by improving the terms of its earmarked bonds.

13. This section of the study draws extensively on "The Impact of Pension Schemes on Saving in Israel" (1999), co-authored with Yaakov Lavi of the Bank of Israel Research Department.

14. This is explained in greater detail in the article. The equation here appears in the article as equation 9.

15. The interest subsidy that the government gives the funds by means of its earmarked bonds conventionally ranges between 1 percent to 1.5 percent of the principal in the long term. The effective interest rate exceeds 5 percent; the long-term interest rate is 3.5 to 4 percent.

16. The same argument was raised in the debate surrounding the privatization of the American Social Security system. See Genakoplos et al. (1998).

17. It is interesting to note that insurance agents are not eager to market the pension funds. Because the funds' management fees are limited to 6 percent, agents earn a much lower commission for marketing pension funds than for marketing executive insurance plans. The agents use the aforementioned legal weaknesses of the pension funds, in which individuals do not hold ownership rights in their pensions and can discover that their pensions have been modified by a unilateral decision of the funds (with approval of the Ministry of Finance), to underscore the superiority of the plans that they sell. This is quite disingenuous, given that all new executive insurance plans are participatory insurance plans and are subject to no less uncertainty in regard to their yields.

18. In certain cases in which the works committees were independent (higher-learning institutions and high-tech enterprises), they were able to chooseamong funds. Pension consultants already did a thriving business back in the era of the old funds.

19. The overall rate of return on capital, in which people are willing to assume the risk, is much higher than the rate of return on government bonds. One may regard the preferred yield on bonds for pension funds as a return whose risk is partially borne by the young generation of taxpayers.

References

Abel, Andrew B. "The Aggregate Effects of Including Equities in the Social Security Trust Fund." The Wharton School and NBER, August 1998.

Commissioner of the Capital Market, Insurance, and Saving. *Annual Report* 1–2, 1996–1997, Jerusalem: Ministry of Finance, 1997. (Hebrew)

Diamond, Peter. "National Debt in a Neoclassical Growth Model." *American Economic Review* 55 (December 1965): 1126–1150.

Genakoplos, John, Olivia S. Mitchell, and Stephen P. Zeldes. "Would a Privatized Social Security System Really Pay a Higher Rate of Return?" NBER Research Paper no. W6713, August 1998.

Greenberg, Lev Louis. *The Histadrut Above All.* Jerusalem: Nevo Publishing, 1993. (Hebrew)

Lavi, Yaakov, and Avia Spivak. "Retirement Saving by Means of Pension and Provident Funds and Its Effect on Total Saving and the Capital Market: Alternative Scenarios." *Economics Quarterly* 2 (1996): 202–235. (Hebrew) See also Y. Lavi and A. Spivak: "The Impact of Pension Schemes on Saving in Israel." *Applied Economics* 31 (1999): 761–764.

Mitchell, Olivia S., James M. Poterba, Mark J. Warshawsky, and Jeffrey R. Brown. "New Evidence on the Money's Worth of Individual Annuities." *American Economic Review* 89 (December 1999): 1299–1318.

Mivtachim Web site. ⟨http://www.mivtachim.co.il⟩. (Hebrew)

Report of the Brodet Committee. Jerusalem, September 1996. (Hebrew)

Report of the Fogel Committee. Jerusalem, June 1994. (Hebrew)

Samuelson, Paul. "An Exact Consumption Loan Model of Interest with or without the Social Contrivance of Money." *Journal of Political Economy* 66 (December 1958): 467–482.

Smetters, Kent. "The Effect of Pay-When-Needed Benefit Guarantees on the Impact of Social Security Privatization." University of Pennsylvania, 1999.

Spivak, Avia. "The Pension-Fund Crisis in Israel: Conceptual Framework and Examination of Recommendations for a Solution." *Economics Quarterly* 41 (October 1994): 484–523. (Hebrew)

8 Liberalization in the Capital Account of the Balance of Payments

Daniel Gottlieb and Mario Blejer

8.1 Introduction

After a failed liberalization attempt in the late 1970s, the Israeli economy entered a process of gradual liberalization as part of an encompassing strategy of economic reforms since the successful stabilization of rapid inflation in July 1985.

Macroeconomic stabilization is a major prerequisite for any capital account liberalization. Though the Stabilization Plan of 1985 did reduce inflation radically, inflation still remained at a relatively high level—some 18 percent, which was about 14 percentage points above the rate prevailing in many Western trading partners. In light of this discrepancy, the pursuit of full integration of Israel into world financial markets still necessitated a continued strategy toward eliminating this inflation gap. The gradual reduction of the large public debt, a legacy of past excessive government deficits, constitutes another aspect of the relevant prerequisites for a sustainable liberalization. Other conditions, such as stability in the government's accounts and in the current account of the balance of payments were achieved already in the 1985 stabilization plan. During the late 1980s, in view of the lacking convergence of the inflation gap, policymakers adapted the strategy of liberalization in an important way: Instead of postponing liberalization after full price stability was achieved, a timing that was highly uncertain at the time, it was decided to seize any political opportunity that presented itself for a gradual liberalization, side by side with a continued gradual effort toward price stability.

International experience with liberalization attempts shows that the flexibility of the foreign exchange regime is crucial for the advance of liberalization in a high-inflation environment. The challenge facing policymakers was therefore, how to ensure a smooth transition from the fixed exchange regime, installed during the stabilization plan of 1985, to an increasingly flexible exchange regime, able to accommodate sharp exchange rate fluctuations in an environment of free international capital movements. The strategy of disinflation changed gradually but significantly over the years 1986 to 1999. In the second half of the 1980s, the exchange rate was supposed to anchor inflation at a low level, without much success: Inflation remained in the vicinity of 18 percent per year. In the process, the real exchange rate became appreciated. Time and again, this situation triggered pressure on Israel's official foreign exchange reserves, which, in turn, repeatedly forced policymakers to adjust the parameters of its foreign exchange policy. A horizontal exchange rate band was declared with an upper and lower boundary at +/−3% from the central rate for direct intervention in the foreign exchange market. This step enhanced exchange rate flexibility, though intervention was not limited to the boundaries. By the end of 1991, monetary policy began to change in a gradual process. Annual inflation targets were set and public awareness about them has been growing over time. The flexibility of the exchange regime was further strengthened by changing the (up to now) fixed boundaries to boundaries that change at a given rate of depreciation per day. This targeted depreciation was calculated as the difference between Israel's inflation target and its main trading partners' expected inflation for the year ahead. Particularly since the end of 1994, the Bank of Israel's official interest rate became increasingly focused on the achievement of the inflation target, as set by the government, and foreign exchange flexibility increased. Over the years 1995 to 1997, the exchange rate band was widened from +/−5% to a band of +/−15%. Since February 1996, the Bank of Israel stopped intervening directly in the foreign exchange market, except for defending the exchange rate at the boundaries, which has hardly been required since mid-1997. The increased potential exchange rate volatility enhanced the efficiency of the interest rate as a tool for monetary policy and thus allowed for a transition to a conventional anti-inflation policy. During the 1990s, several fundamental processes affected the Israeli economy—the wave of immigration in the early 1990s from the former Soviet Union, the peace process in the Middle East, which progressed within the context of worldwide geopolitical changes. The globalization of financial markets emphasized the growing importance of financial investors from Western countries, seeking investment opportunities in emerging markets. As a result, foreign investment in emerging markets, including Israel, grew. Israel continued to advance, albeit slowly, with economic reforms. These processes, together with a structural change in Israel's industry away from traditional branches, toward the expansion of high-tech intensive branches, caused a large inflow of capital. With this perspective in mind, the advance in the capital account liberalization needs to be seen as an investment in Israel's financial infrastructure. In the years 1998 and 1999, a further facet of the liberalization became emphasized. The opening of the capital account and the enhanced flexibility of the exchange regime brought about increased capital flows in both directions, and exchange rate volatility grew. The Israeli business sector and public, long accustomed to a managed exchange rate path and controlled capital (in)flows, did not appreciate these fluctuations, although they reflect the process of Israeli financial markets' integration in world financial markets. In the late 1990s, several Southeast Asian economies suffered contagious financial crises.[1] The crisis that hit Russia in August 1998 indicated a turning point for world financial markets, causing many foreign investors to pull—mainly financial—investments out of emerging economies, including Israel.

An important test of the success of a country's financial strategy, including its foreign exchange liberalization, is the degree to which the economy succeeds in absorbing external shocks and uncertainty at a minimal cost in the standard of living and in the economy's macroeconomic stability.

Viewed from an international perspective, liberalization processes were popular in the 70s and 80s among Western economies and during a large part of the 90s in many emerging economies. Until the outburst of the Southeast Asian (1997) and Russian (1998) financial crises, there had been a consensus in academic and governmental circles that foreign exchange controls are an inefficient tool for preventing capital flight over time.[2] Israeli policymakers learned this lesson the hard way in the first half of the 1980s, when tight capital controls did not prevent capital flight during the economic crisis. The evidence appeared as a leakage in foreign exchange reserves, accompanied by an unrecorded capital flight that was clearly reflected in the negative "errors and omissions" in the balance of payments. These had grown rapidly, from 1 to 4 percent of GDP, during the crisis (figure 2).

In recent years, a controversy regarding the costs and benefits of capital account liberalization has evolved.[3] One of the fundamental questions asked is whether a small open economy can choose the extent of its openness toward international financial markets once financial integration has started. Attempts to reduce the degree of openness in the capital account, especially for short-term flows, encounter many technical difficulties. An economy wishing to protect itself from the hazards of financial vulnerability[4] needs to secure financial stability of its banking sector and to strengthen and develop the market tools fit to cope with foreign exchange risk, such as the derivative markets. Macroeconomic policy must be disciplined in order to ascertain investors' confidence in the economy.

International financial organizations have been urging countries to reform their capital accounts in the balance of payments, in order to improve resource allocation and also to finance domestic investment by foreign savings. International financial flows tend to improve risk diversification of the households' portfolio and the functioning of financial markets. Financial markets in emerging economies often contain cartel arrangements. Capital account liberalizations act against this tendency by promoting competition in financial services. The control of international capital movements is similar to a protective tariff. Israeli experience suggests that it is much easier to reduce oligopoly power in the banking sector through capital account liberalization than through anticartel legislation or through legal requirements for split-ups of big banks into smaller units. The process of liberalization typically attracts less opposition from banks or trade unions.

8.2 The Liberalizations of 1977 and the late 1980s—From Failure to Success

The adopted policy can be compared to the recommendations derived from a framework of optimal policy. Such a framework belongs to the realm of "second-best theory." According to Johnston (1998), the liberalization path should be chosen such as to minimize risk caused by liberalization itself. It is widely accepted that a successful liberalization depends mainly on the achievement of macroeconomic stability, the strength of the economy's financial system, and the adequacy of financial supervision. According to this approach, the liberalization of the capital account should occur relatively late in the reform. An alternative approach, acknowledging the prevalence of "political economy" considerations, suggests that liberalization steps should be adopted whenever there is a political will to do so. A policy that postpones liberalization efforts due to insufficient fulfillment of the relevant preconditions may be postponed indefinitely. A pragmatic approach, therefore, calls for a gradual approach to liberalization.[5]

Israel has experienced two foreign exchange liberalizations: The first in October 1977[6]—of the "big bang" type—failed and was canceled in early 1979; the second, present one was gradual. It started about 1987 and was more or less completed in May 1998 with respect to the business sector, well advanced concerning households, and still incomplete regarding mutual funds, provident funds, and pension funds.

Precondition I—Macroeconomic Stability

Before the 1977 liberalization, inflation worsened by 7 percentage points, from an already high rate of 24 percent in the years 1970 to 1974 to 31 percent in the years 1975 and 1976 (see table 8.1). Inflation was high and exceeded that of Israel's major international trading partners' by about 20 percentage points. The public sector deficit was already very high during the years 1970 to 1974, which caused a rapid accumulation of Israel's public debt. In the second period, no steps were taken to improve the fiscal situation. On the contrary, the deficit was widened by another 3 percentage points of GDP, reaching 16 percent of GDP. During the years 1970 to 1977, the cumulative public sector deficit reached 110 percent of GDP, and obviously, this "fiscal policy" was unsustainable. The mismanagement was reflected in a high deficit in the current account of the balance of payments—about 13.5 percent in 1975 and 9 percent on average in the years 1975 and 1976. The liberalization was carried out in the form of a "big bang," thus intensifying the public's uncertainty about the effects of the reform and reducing the public's ability to prepare itself for the new situation. With the harmful economic background, the 1977 liberalization had hardly any

Table 8.1
Macroeconomic Conditions before the Liberalizations

	Inflation (p.a.)	Inflation differential with advanced countries	Public sector deficit (+)*	Current account deficit (+), balance of payments*	Exposure to foreign direct investment*
Difference between periods**—First liberalization	**7**	**4**	**3**	**2**	**−1.3**
1975 to 1976	31	20	15	9	0.2
1970 to 1974	24	16	13	7	1.5
Difference between periods**—Second liberalization	**−193**	**−121**	**−14**	**−5**	**−0.6**
1986 to 1987	18	14	−2	0	0.5
1976 to 1985	211	135	12	5	1.1

* GDP percent.
** Percentage points.

chance to succeed. Furthermore, it probably paved the way to Israel's macroeconomic crisis of the first half of the 1980s.

The stabilization plan of July 1985 improved macroeconomic conditions radically. Inflation dropped within months from about 500 percent to the vicinity of 20 percent per annum (p.a.). The public sector accounts moved from a huge multiyear deficit to a surplus in 1986/1987, and the current account in the balance of payments turned from a perilous deficit before the stabilization plan to a surplus.

The Israeli economy's exposure to world capital markets, as reflected in its share in foreign direct investment in emerging and developing economies, was negligible in both periods. Direct investment from abroad accounted for less than 1 percent of total direct investment in developing countries.[7]

Precondition II—The Stability of the Banking Sector

The Southeast Asian financial crisis in the second half of the 1990s focused attention on the relationship between liberalization and the stability of banking systems in emerging economies.[8] Unlike in previous financial crises, there was no major macroeconomic disarray in Southeast Asia. The basic macroeconomic indicators in the ASEAN-4 countries (Thailand, Indonesia, Philippines, and Malaysia) were good: Medium-term growth (average over the five years preceding the crisis) was 7 percent per year on average, and the average annual inflation was 6.5 percent. The current account deficit in the balance of payments was albeit large, but about 2.3 percentage points lower than the growth rate.[9] There is a wide consensus that the main weakness responsible for the crisis was the distorted structure of the national financial systems. Demirguc-Kunt and Detragiache (1998) analyzed the relationship between the banking systems, financial liberalization, and deregulation in a set of fifty-three countries during the period 1980 to 1995. They found that countries with a weak enforcement of law and contracts, which is characteristic of many developing countries with low per capita incomes, have a high probability of incurring a banking crisis following financial liberalization. They explain this finding by the decline in the franchise value of financial organizations, resulting from the reduction in oligopoly power during the liberalization process. The pressure on profitability pushes banks toward greater risk taking, especially if they believe that the government will bail them out in case of a crisis in the financial sector.

In the 1970s, the Israeli banking system enjoyed considerable oligopolistic power in the domestic financial market and—together with financial support from the U.S. government and other donations—it was also the major supplier of foreign exchange to the domestic economy. With the benefit of hindsight, the timing of the bank-share crisis in September 1983[10] may not be purely coincidental. It occurred but a few years after premature liberalization. The lack of transparency, particularly concerning the division of responsibility between the banks and official institutions, and the evaluation by decision makers in the banking sector that the banks would be bailed out should a crisis occur (which turned out to be correct) certainly created a favorable environment for the "stock price smoothing" that eventually caused the bank-share crash. This crisis had the important benefit of sharpening banking supervision in Israel thereafter. The financial deregulation, such as the elimination of credit and interest ceilings, was in fact accompanied by an intensified and improved banking supervision. This improvement in the standard of Israel's banking supervision probably added to the stability of Israel's financial system during the world financial crisis of 1997/1998.

The Sequence of Israel's Liberalization

The order of the liberalization can be analyzed in various ways. One that is commonly used is to divide them by (1) type and maturity, and (2) sectors—households, the business sector, foreign residents, exempted groups (e.g., new immigrants). Liberalization in Israel advanced gradually according to these principles. Israel preferred first to free long-term capital imports, then to move on to relax constraints on short-term capital imports, leaving the lifting of controls on capital exports to a later stage. This strategy is probably motivated by the belief that the major effect from the abolition of capital controls is the direct effect, that is, the belief that lifting capital import restrictions will mainly increase capital inflow. However, for several countries, the lifting of controls on capital exports did not bring about an increase in outflows, but on the contrary, caused a large inflow of capital. In the case of Israel, Israeli policymakers' determination to stick with the strategy of liberalization may be viewed as an "investment in infrastructure," in the sense that it paved the way for free capital movements. At first, there was little response. It took a couple of years to recognize the importance of timely liberalization: Capital began to flow into the country at a steadily increasing pace after the immigration wave had created expectations for high investment yields, and following the peace process in 1993.

The years of advance in liberalization[11]

By type of instrument and maturity

i) Medium-, Long-Term Capital Imports	1989, 1990
ii) Short-Term Capital Imports	1991
iii) Capital Exports	1992, 1994, 1995, 1996, 1997, 1998
iv) Derivatives (Futures, Options, etc.)	1998

By sector

i) Foreign residents	A basic preferential treatment existed before liberalization started. Every year from 1987 to 1998
ii) "Exempted citizens" (new immigrants) were by and large exempted from foreign exchange control throughout the 1980s and 1990s	
iii) Mutual funds, provident funds, and pension funds	1989, 1992, 1994, 1995, 1997, 1998
iv) Business sector	1987, 1989, 1990, 1991, 1992, 1995, 1997, 1998
v) Households	1987, 1988, 1990, 1991, 1992, 1993, 1994, 1995, 1996, 1997, 1998

An economy's potential of (short-term) capital outflow, the potential of "capital flight," is often considered an important indicator of that economy's financial stability. It is with this conception in mind that foreign exchange restrictions were first lifted on direct investment and long-term loans from abroad, which are viewed as more stable than other capital inflows. One of the first steps was to allow for inflows with shorter maturities, later on, the interest-rate ceiling was lifted. Indeed, the chronological order of the liberalization steps in Israel reveals a clear bias in favor of capital imports over capital exports and long-term flows over short-term flows. The delayed treatment of derivatives may partly have been due to their novelty for Israeli financial market participants and policymakers.

The liberalization encompassed all sectors, though somewhat favoring the business sector. By 1999, there were no more effective controls on the business sector's foreign exchange transactions. Other groups with preferential treatment were foreign residents and "exempted citizens" (mainly new immigrants). Financial investments and the holding of foreign exchange accounts by households remained restricted to later stages of the liberalization.

The Remaining Capital Controls[12]

From May 1998 onward, the exchange control regime was fundamentally altered: Until then the system was designed such that any foreign exchange transaction was a priori restricted, and therefore, any transactions that were allowed needed to be explicitly excluded from the (general) restriction. In the new instructions, effective since May 1998, any foreign exchange transaction is a priori permitted except for a list of certain transactions, which if requiring a special permit, this must be explicitly stated by the foreign exchange controller. The main restrictions still in place relate to investments in foreign currency denominated assets by Israeli institutional investors: Provident funds are still limited by a 5 percent ceiling of their total assets in foreign exchange. Moreover, they are not allowed to engage in "futures" transactions. They are also not allowed to be a party at interest in a foreign corporation.

Mutual funds, pension funds, and insurers are restricted in the purchase or receipt of foreign exchange from an Israeli citizen or in the execution of transactions of foreign exchange futures, securities, and other assets. Certain futures transactions between Israelis or Israeli banks and foreign residents are restricted.

The requirements for the reporting of foreign exchange transactions have generally been intensified. This is necessary for general monitoring purposes and also for fighting "money laundering."

8.3 Liberalization Effects on the Openness of Israel's Financial Markets

A successful liberalization should eventually lead to a tightening of the links between the capital market in the home economy and the major capital markets elsewhere in the world. A financial market that is well integrated with world financial markets will exhibit similar interest rates or at least similar movements in interest rates. Also, movements in domestic stock price indices are expected to resemble more closely those abroad the higher the degree of integration between domestic and world capital markets. Many liberalized economies experienced a sharp increase in capital imports in the early stage of the liberalization and an increased fluctuation of capital movements later on.[13] Another indicator of improved integration is enhanced access to international capital markets, which will typically show in an improved sovereign credit rating. Eventually, the improved capacity to finance investment activity at home with foreign funds should manifest itself in an investment rate that exceeds the domestic saving rate.

In this section, we test to what extent such links have indeed been strengthened during the years of intensified liberalization.

Private Capital Flows and Liberalization

Net capital imports to Israel grew like they did to other emerging economies that had liberalized their capital accounts. From the third quarter of 1993 to mid-1998, annualized net private capital imports reached about U.S.$ 2.7 billion (at constant prices of 1998), compared to U.S.$ 0.1 to 0.6 billion in the earlier periods. The rapid increase in capital movements began at the end of 1993 and raised not only net capital inflows but also gross capital flows in and out of the country. This indicates that liberalization acts as a kind of infrastructure, facilitating and encouraging capital movements in either direction. The expansion of net capital imports was affected by real factors, such as the immigration wave and the advancement in the peace process, which created financing needs for investment. Capital imports also increased in response to tight monetary policy, which was necessary for reducing inflation. This brought about an interest rate increase, enhanced by an artificial reduction in the foreign exchange risk premium. The latter was due to the effective limitation of exchange rate volatility, caused by the binding floor of the exchange rate band. Whereas the immigration wave and the peace process affected the expected real return on domestic investment positively, the combined effect of monetary and exchange rate policy and the limitations on the exchange rate band reduced the cost of capital import through the aforementioned reduction in the risk premium and through an increase in "creditor interest rates." We conclude that if the immigration wave or the peace process had happened against the background of a controlled capital account, it would have been much more difficult to finance the surge in real investment, and at least a part of the economy's growth opportunities would have been missed.

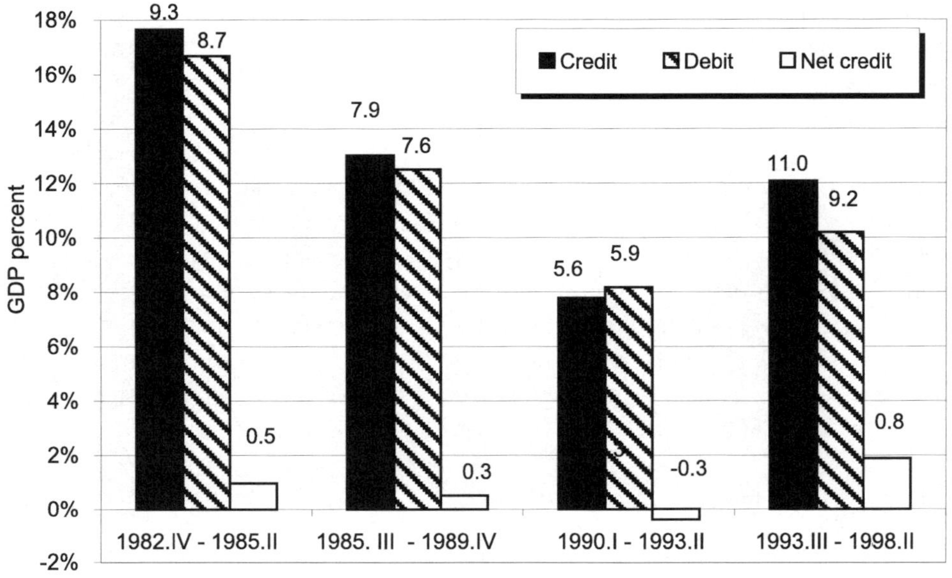

Figure 8.1
Recorded Capital Movements—Gross and Net Flows. Numbers above bars are GDP percent, based on 1998 prices

In the medium and long run, foreign exchange controls are eventually circumvented. This experience was also be observed in the Israeli context: "Net errors and omissions" in the balance of payments typically reflect to a large extent short-term capital flows that have not been recorded properly.[14] In a period of financial crisis, when the incentive for (illegal, short-term) capital flight is high, "errors and omissions" tend to be negative. See figures 8.1 and 8.2.

Capital controls turned out to be ineffective in the prevention of short-term capital flight due to currency substitution in times of rapid inflation and in the face of the rapidly revolving short-term foreign debt, due to the difficulty of longer-term debt financing. If the direct effect from liberalization were the main effect, then the sequence of liberalization chosen in Israel should have caused a gradual increase in the share of private short-term capital flows during the 1990s. Instead, figure 8.3 shows that the ratio of short- to longer-term capital movements dropped over time, in favor of longer-term capital movements.[15] Indeed, the abolition of capital controls affects potential rather than actual capital flows. The composition of capital flows by maturity in favor of long- and medium-term capital was probably affected mainly by Israel's improved international creditworthiness (due to the move in Israeli industry

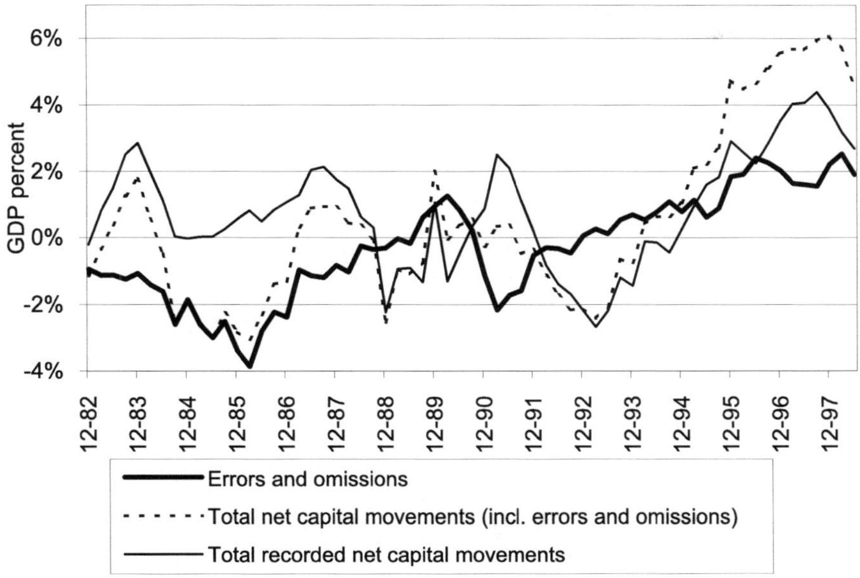

Figure 8.2
Recorded Net Capital Movements and "Errors and Omissions". Total net capital movements = Direct investment + short-, medium- and long-term loans and deposits + errors and omissions (as proxy for unregistered short term capital flows)
Source: Central Bureau of Statistics.

toward high-tech), the advancement in the peace process in the early 1990s, the successful absorption of the immigration wave, and the improvement in macroeconomic policy regarding fiscal and monetary stability in the late 1990s.

Net foreign direct investment in Israel, mostly originating in advanced economies, increased rapidly, mainly since 1995 (see figure 8.4). Part of the growth was due to a general interest in "emerging markets" by investors from advanced economies. Israel is included in the emerging economies, which are typically identified as fast-growing economies, pushing ahead with market-oriented economic reforms. Foreign direct investment, especially if led by well-established firms from abroad, tends to raise technological know-how and managerial ability in the investment-absorbing country.

A number of factors acted as stimuli of net foreign direct investment. The Oslo Agreement symbolized to the international business community a major breakthrough in the peace process. This encouraged many international business companies to breach the secondary Arab boycott, which until then had threatened noncomplying firms with sanctions. The loosening of the boycott raised the potential for Israeli

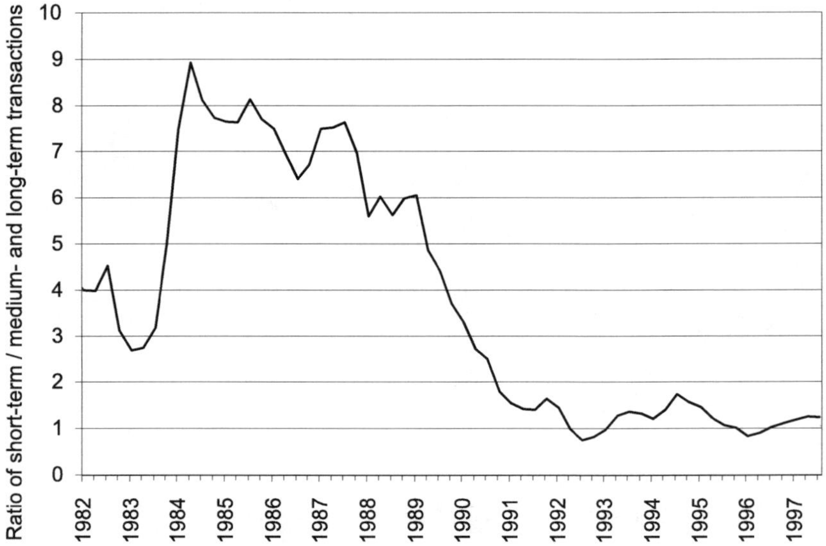

Figure 8.3
Ratio of Short term over Medium- and Long-Term Capital Transactions

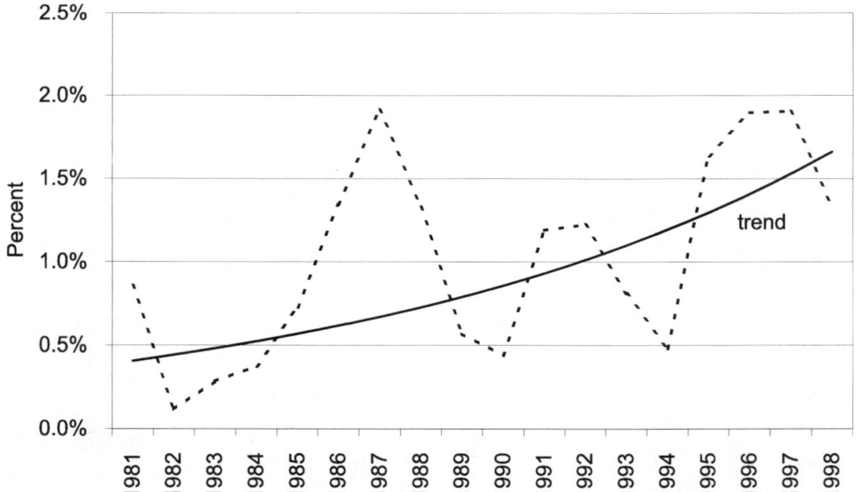

Figure 8.4
Foreign Direct Investment In Israel/FDI in Developing Countries
Sources: Bank of Israel; Institute of International Finance, Washington D.C.

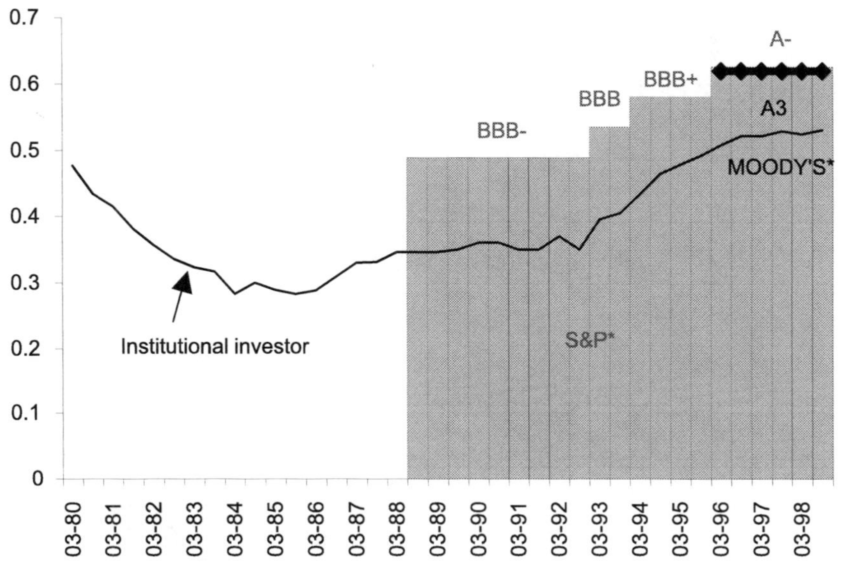

Figure 8.5
Israel's International Creditworthiness
* The ratings of S&P and Moody's are linearly transformed to fit the scale of the Institutional Investor.

exports at once and gave impetus to the structural change in Israeli industry, already underway, from traditional toward largely export-oriented high-tech intensive sectors. The immigration wave significantly raised the share of workers in the labor supply, with relatively high human capital. This created a downward pressure on wages and improved international competitiveness. These tendencies were further fortified by consistent macroeconomic policy encouraging fiscal and monetary stability and economic reforms.

An economy with a high yield of return on its investment in its capital stock and an internationally integrated capital market can maintain an investment ratio that exceeds the national saving ratio over time, thus accelerating its growth rate. Another advantage of openness in capital markets is the economy's ability to smooth national consumption with respect to temporary fluctuations in income streams.

Israel's Creditworthiness

A significant indicator of a successful liberalization is the change in attitude toward the liberalizing economy and its business sector by international credit-rating agencies and by major international investment funds (see figure 8.5). The economic monitoring of emerging economies by credit rating agencies influences the allocation of international investors' funds among the potential receivers of these funds. The rating industry's economic ranking of country risk influences both the availability and the cost of capital. Credit rating indices are calculated by firms such as Moody's, Standard and Poor's (S&P), or by the periodical *Institutional Investor*. S&P started rating industrial countries in 1959. Ratings of emerging economies started in the late 1970s (e.g., the rating of Venezuela by Moody's in 1977). The *Institutional Investor* started rating 130 to 140 countries, among them Israel, in September 1979.[16] Empirical analysis of country-risk rating shows a strong and significant relationship between fundamental macroeconomic variables and country risk. An analysis of Israel's creditworthiness shows that the major factors affecting it are the level of economic development as reflected in the trend of per capita GDP, the official international reserves as a ratio of imports or exports, and the GDP ratio of public debt and inflation.[17] As can be seen from studying the actual country-risk reports of major rating agencies, liberalization and other reform efforts importantly affect credit ratings although they are not easily observable in empirical country risk studies.

The Savings-Investment Ratio

In an economy that is closed to foreign capital markets, national savings and investment will be equal. Horioka and Feldstein (1980) found that investment ratios in twenty-one countries during 1960–1974 are largely explained by the saving ratio (coefficient of 0.89). A coefficient of 1.0 would indicate a closed economy. In an article by Bacchetta and Feldstein (1991), the coefficient for the period 1982–1991 was lower, about 0.62, thus indicating a move toward increased openness. An advance in liberalization should therefore increase the divergence of the coefficient from 1. The divergence may be positive or negative, depending on the economy's time preference. Comparing the Israeli savings-investment relationship for three subperiods (1980–1985, 1986–1989, 1990–1998) shows that according to this criterion, the last period is indeed the most open one, but the first is more "open" than the intermediate period, despite the fact that the economy's international credit standing improved much from its low point in the first period. See figure 8.6. The excessive deficits in the balance of payments in the crisis years (first half of the 1980s) were unsustainable and were mainly financed by official borrowing abroad. It would probably have been difficult for the private sector to finance the current account deficit satisfactorily. In contrast, the financing during the 1990s was mostly carried out by the private sector, reflecting its improved creditworthiness.

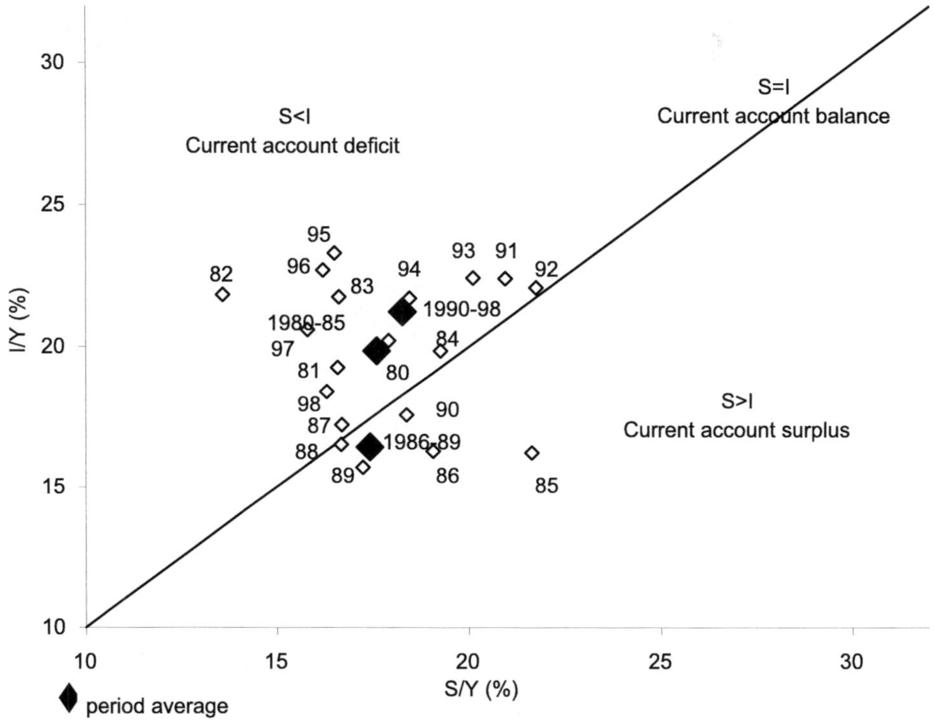

Figure 8.6
National Saving and Investment Ratios

Expected International Yield Parities

The effect of the liberalization of capital controls on the capital account of the balance of payments can be analyzed by observing the behavior of interest parities, both covered and uncovered. In an open economy, such differentials are supposed to vanish. If they persist, they indicate that some limitations still hamper the free flow of capital or else that domestic market participants have a "home bias."[18] Due to the lack of a well-developed risk insurance market for foreign exchange risk in Israel during the 1990s, covered interest arbitrage cannot be tested. We therefore focus only on testing uncovered interest differentials.[19] Several disadvantages should be kept in mind, however—first of all, the existence of the aforementioned home bias. Exchange rate expectations are unobservable and can only be quantified by approximation and will thus remain as a potential source of error. The risk premium needs to be dealt with individually for each type of transaction.

In order to test the hypothesis of uncovered interest parity, we estimated various equations, depending on the type of transaction and on the treatment of the risk factor.[20]

We estimated level equations and their first differences (Δ)[21] for each type of transaction:

Borrower-Borrower (*BB* and *BBr*, where *r* stands for the risk premium), Lender-Borrower (*LB* and *LBr*, respectively), Borrower-Lender (*BL* and *BLr*, respectively) and Lender-Lender (*LL* and *LLr*, respectively).

where $i =$ domestic interest rate, $i^* =$ comparable U.S. Dollar interest rate, $e =$ depreciation expectations, $\sigma =$ foreign exchange risk and $\varepsilon =$ residual.

Comparison between the prime rate on a domestic loan and on a loan denominated in U.S. dollars. Dollars without a risk premium:

$$i = \alpha_1 + \alpha_2[(1 + i^*)(1 + e)(1 + \sigma) - 1] + \varepsilon \tag{8.1}$$

$$\Delta i = \alpha_1 + \alpha_2 \Delta[(1 + i^*)(1 + e)(1 + \sigma) - 1] + \Delta\varepsilon \tag{8.1$'$}$$

A similar equation results from the combined transaction of borrowing abroad and depositing at home (interest on domestic deposits and the U.S. prime rate, *LB* denoting transactions without accounting for a risk premium and *LBr*, when the risk premium is included).

Borrowing at home and depositing in the U.S.—Prime rate at home and deposit rate abroad or, alternatively, depositing both at home and abroad:

$$i = \alpha_1 + \alpha_2[(1 + i^*)(1 + e)/(1 + \sigma) - 1] + \varepsilon \tag{8.2}$$

$$\Delta i = \alpha_2 \Delta[(1 + i^*)(1 + e)/(1 + \sigma) - 1] + \Delta\varepsilon \tag{8.2$'$}$$

The estimation has to deal with two major problems. First, the expectations variable is by nature unobservable. Any expectations-proxy based on nominal yields suffers from a technical simultaneity. Here, we used expectations calculated from the Israeli capital market.[22] Furthermore, there is also a simultaneity bias arising from the influence that interest rates can exert on depreciation expectations, whereas the model assumes only the effect of expectations on interest rates. For example, if the Central Bank raises its interest rate in order to reduce inflation, this will reduce inflation expectations and also depreciation expectations, which are closely linked with inflation expectations. This kind of simultaneity is dealt with here by use of the foreign interest rate and lags of the depreciation expectations as instrumental variables. We found the interest rate equation to be downward biased.[23] See table 8.2.

Table 8.2
Domestic Prime Rate versus Expected Yield Based on U.S. Prime Rate* (Observation period: January 1992–March 1999)

Dependent variable	Constant	Explanatory variables i^*, e	$\Delta(i^*, e)$	i^*, e, σ	$\Delta(i^*, e, \sigma)$	AR(1)	R^2	DW	Number of observations
i	0.01	1.07					0.64	0.62	87
	(0.9)	(12.3)					0.014		
	0.13	0.31				0.82	0.89	1.07	86
	(8.8)	(3.5)				(17.8)	0.007		
Δi	−0.00		0.26				0.09	1.00	86
	(−1.1)		(2.9)				0.008		
	−0.00		0.12			0.49	0.30	1.99	85
	(−0.3)		(1.9)			(5.5)	0.006		
i	0.005			1.08			0.74	0.84	78
	(0.4)			(14.6)			0.01		
	0.13			0.28		0.93	0.91	1.23	77
	(7.7)			(3.2)		(21.4)	0.007		
Δi	−0.00				0.26		0.11	1.26	77
	(−0.2)				(3.1)		0.007		
	0.00				0.15	0.40	0.24	1.95	76
	(0.08)				(2.3)	(3.9)	0.006		

*Numbers in brackets are t-values; the numbers below the R^2 are standard errors of the regressions.

We also made use of the depreciation expectations of Stein (1999). These expectations are developed from the price of options on the NIS/U.S. dollar rates, which are issued twice a week by the Bank of Israel.[24]

Confirming Bufman and Leiderman (1996), the results appear to show full openness of the capital market (e.g., first regression in table 8.2).

This regression is comparable to line 6 in table 8.2. The Null Hypothesis $\alpha_1 = 0$, $\alpha_2 = 1$ is not refuted. This equation was also estimated in logarithmic form, and the coefficients were similar. The unit roots were found to be of first order (I(1)). However, these results may be misleading for two reasons: (1) the equation may be miss-specified, given that it does not include a risk premium. (2) The residuals of the regression exhibit serial correlation (see Durbin-Watson test). Adjustment for serial correlation reduced the α_2-coefficient, thus indicating less than full integration of the Israeli and world stock markets. Estimates from the first difference equations also exhibit an integration coefficient α_2 below the value of 1. In order to decide whether the liberalization process has been successful over time, one should be able to observe a continued convergence of α_2 toward 1. We analyzed this hypothesis by testing the stability of the recursive coefficients. The results from these tests[25] show a more or less smooth convergence of α_1 and α_2 to their final values at the end of the observation period, though less so in the regressions of first differences. The parameter estimate for the integration coefficient (α_2) converged to a value of less than 1. We conclude that this test suggests that openness to world capital markets has increased over time but is not yet a full one. The tests (not all of them are showed here) indicate a high sensitivity of the level of α_2 to the type of transaction.

Competition in Financial Services

A consistent and permanent liberalization tends to reduce the domestic financial sector's monopolistic power. In an open capital market, domestic investors are not limited by the supply of funds from the domestic banking sector. They can opt for foreign finance through loans or issuances. Domestic savers can choose between investing their surplus at home or abroad. This process eventually reduces the interest differential of financial intermediaries.

As discussed in section 8.2, the process of relaxing controls on capital movements began with the lifting of the bias in favor of long- and medium-term loans and later on by relaxing limitations on issuances in stock markets. The liberalization in deposits was much slower, and transactions still need to be done through the domestic banking sector. Interestingly, when the equation is built on the Israeli deposit rate, then the convergence is slower, and the final coefficient value reaches only 0.7 to 0.8. The yield differentials shrink rapidly when the domestic interest rate in the equation is a debit rate. In a perfectly competitive environment at home and abroad, in the absence of tax distortions, there should be no difference between the various differences between coefficients.

According to figure 8.7, the link between the Israeli and the U.S. financial markets was strengthened in the last months of 1998, in line with the general tendency toward increased integration during much of the 1990s. The timing coincides with the world financial crisis that originated in the Russian debt default. This shock affected Western financial markets, particularly the high-yield market in the USA[26] and was the major cause of the sharp depreciation in the Israeli foreign exchange market that took place in October 1998.

In figure 8.8, we compare the difference between the regression coefficients obtained from equations using (Israeli) borrowing rates and deposit rates. This gap serves as an indicator of the extent of monopoly power exercised by the banking system. The speed of reduction of the gap, as well as its size at the end of the observation period, depend, among other things, on the risk premium. When the risk premium is included in the regressions, then the gap is largely eliminated by late 1994. This tim-

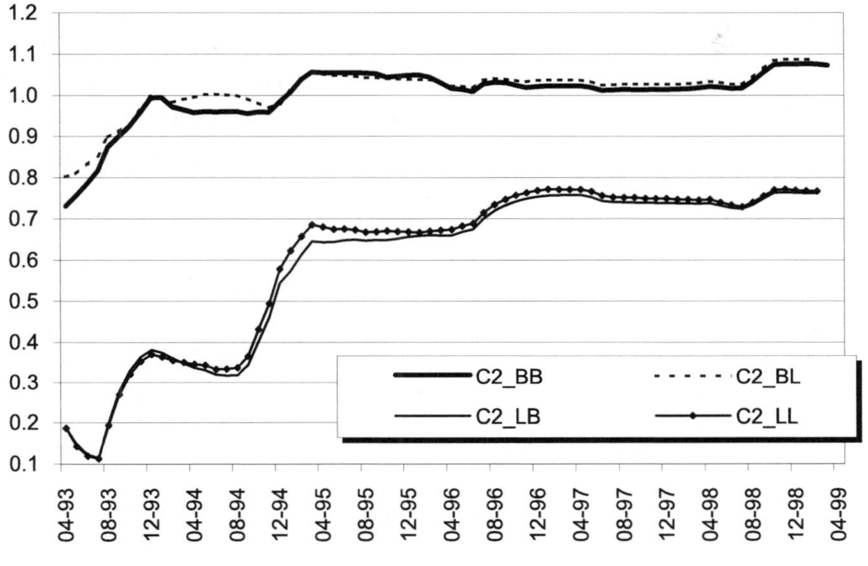

Figure 8.7
Recursive Regression Coefficients (α_2) of the Uncovered Yield-Differential

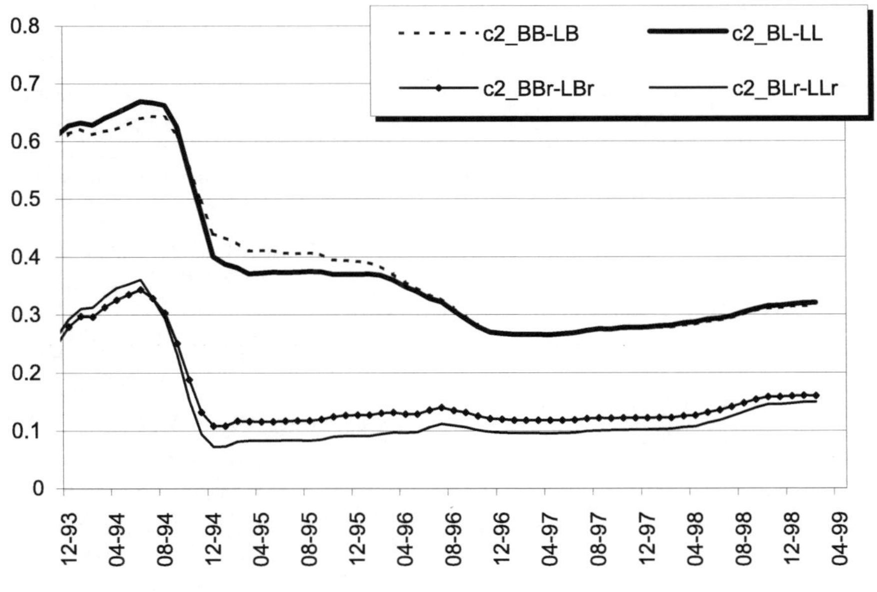

Figure 8.8
Difference between Recursive Regression Coefficients (α_2) of the uncovered "Borrowing-Lending" Gap

ing signals the large capital inflow in the wake of the widening gap between the domestic and foreign interest rates, following the anti-inflationary policy of monetary tightening. This, together with the improvement in Israel's creditworthiness, increased capital inflows and thus enhanced the relative importance of this source of finance. This shift toward more external finance weakened the oligopoly power of the domestic banking sector.

Throughout the whole period the gap between Israeli and U.S. interest rates is larger when the gap includes the domestic deposit rate. This result holds only for domestic, not foreign, deposit rates. This may be due to the fact that to date most international capital movements are still done through the domestic banking system.

International Integration of the Israeli Stock Market

A commonly used indicator of the integration of domestic and foreign capital markets is the correlation coefficient between domestic and foreign stock price indices. Following Mussa and Goldstein (1993), Bufman and Leiderman base their measure of the Israeli economy's openness on correlation coefficients between stock prices. The correlation coefficients reported in table 8.3 reveal that the strongest link exists between Israel and the European markets or the G5 countries.

However, this impression is not supported by the basic regression:

$$\mathrm{SPRIS} = \beta_1 + \beta_2 \mathrm{SPR}^* + \varepsilon \tag{8.3}$$

$$\Delta\mathrm{SPRIS} = \beta_2 \Delta\mathrm{SPR}^* + ?\varepsilon \tag{8.3'}$$

where *SPRIS* denotes the stock price index in real terms for Israel, and *SPR**, the index for other countries or groups of countries. ε denotes the error term of the equation.[27]

The regression approach is preferable because it allows for an analysis of statistically significant relationships of β_1 and β_2 over time. Regressions 1, 3, 5, 7, and 9 in table 8.4 indicate the presence of serial correlation (see D.W. test). After adjusting for serial correlation, the European aggregate stock price variable is not any more statistically significant. The indices for the U.S., the U.S. and Europe, and the G5 remain statistically significant. The first difference equations, which suffer much less from serial correlation than the level equations, allow also for a recursive procedure: The strongest relationship ($\beta_2 = 0.95$) is achieved with the combined U.S.-European index. Emerging economies' stock prices do not explain the behavior of Israel's stock prices.

Figure 8.9 (line C2_SPR) illustrates the integration of the Israeli stock market into world capital markets. The coefficient β_2 rises gradually from about 0.3 to 1. It seems

Table 8.3
Correlation Coefficients between Stock Market Indices in Israel and Abroad (Deflated by the respective Consumer Price Index, GDP weighted when combined index)

	Israel	U.S.	U.K.	Korea	Mexico	New Zealand	Germany	France	U.S. & Europe	Japan	Emerging Economies	G5 Countries	Europe
Israel	1												
USA	0.483	1											
UK	0.499	0.946	1										
Korea	−0.211	−0.483	−0.374	1									
Mexico	0.850	0.456	0.502	−0.087	1								
New Zealand	0.041	0.451	0.550	−0.519	0.064	1							
Germany	0.269	0.874	0.828	−0.540	0.231	0.537	1						
France	0.486	0.923	0.887	−0.380	0.415	0.359	0.911	1					
USA & Europe	0.475	0.997	0.949	−0.481	0.443	0.462	0.902	0.945	1				
Japan	−0.615	−0.574	−0.463	0.737	−0.545	−0.336	−0.412	−0.407	−0.549	1			
Emerging Economies	−0.205	−0.388	−0.247	0.959	−0.070	−0.365	−0.435	−0.292	−0.383	0.716	1		
G5	0.345	0.953	0.934	−0.313	0.331	0.419	0.896	0.947	0.964	−0.307	−0.208	1	
EUR	0.322	0.837	0.786	−0.517	0.250	0.493	0.934	0.893	0.864	−0.426	−0.427	0.848	1

Emerging Economies: Australia, Korea, Mexico, New Zealand.
U.S. and Europe: Includes U.S., U.K., France, and Germany; G5 includes also Japan.
Source: Stock market indices are from the International Financial Statistics (IFS), IMF, Washington D.C.

Table 8.4
Relationship between Israeli and Foreign Real Stock Price Indices (SPR—Countries)

Dependent variable	Explanatory variables: SPR—indices abroad	Const. β_1	β_2	AR(1)	R^2 (S.E. Reg)	DW	Number of observations	Observation period
SPR—Israel	SPR—total	42.5	0.9		0.20	0.04	153	1986:01
		(1.6)	(1.6)		(70.9)			1999:04
		86.6	0.77	0.97	0.96	1.8	149	1986:02
		(1.23)	(4.1)	(57.7)	(14.7)			1999:04
Δ(SPR—Israel)	Δ(SPR—total)	0.49	0.78		0.09	1.82	149	1986:02
		(0.4)	(4.03)		(5.99)			1999:04
SPR—Israel	SPR—U.S.	112.7	0.46		0.24	0.05	160	1986:01
		(8.18)	(7.0)		(68.1)			1999:04
		120.3	0.47	0.97	0.97	1.8	159	1986:02
		(1.97)	(3.17)	(55.8)	(14.9)			1999:04
Δ(SPR—Israel)	Δ(SPR—U.S.)	0.22	0.5		0.06	1.85	159	1986:02
		(0.17)	(3.1)		(15.0)			1999:04
SPR—Israel	G5	87.0	0.69		0.12	0.04	160	1986:01
		(3.5)	(4.7)		(72.9)			1999:04
		86.7	0.77	0.97	0.96	1.80	149	1986:02
		(1.23)	(4.08)	(57.7)	(14.8)			1999:04
Δ(SPR—Israel)	Δ(SPR—G5)	0.41	0.74		0.08	1.83	159	1986:02
		(0.3)	(3.6)		(14.8)			1999:04
SPR—Israel	SPR—U.S. & Europe	100.1	0.59		0.23	0.04	160	1986:01
		(6.4)	(6.8)		(68.4)			1999:04
		88.3	0.70	0.98	0.97	1.83	159	1986:02
		(1.4)	(4.1)	(57.3)	(14.6)			1999:04
Δ(SPR—Israel)	Δ(SPR—U.S. & Europe)	0.07	0.73		0.10	1.85	159	1986:02
		(0.07)	(4.1)		(14.6)			1999:04

SPR—Israel	SPR—Europe	110.6 (5.2)	0.87 (4.4)		0.11 (73.4)	0.07	160	1986:01 1999:04
		247.8 (3.4)	0.12 (1.5)	0.98 (61.7)	0.96 (15.2)	1.78	159	1986:02 1999:04
Δ(SPR—Israel)	Δ(SPR—Europe)	1.22 (1.01)	0.11 (1.4)		0.01 (15.3)	1.80	159	1986:02 1999:04
SPR—Israel	SPR—Emerging economies	270.4 (9.7)	−0.48 (−2.6)		0.04 (77.6)	0.05	153	1986:01 1999:04
		254.8 (2.6)	0.14 (1.3)	0.98 (61.9)	0.96 (15.5)	1.74	149	1986:02 1999:04
Δ(SPR—Israel)	Δ(SPR—Emerging economies)	1.38 (1.1)	0.14 (1.4)		0.01 (15.5)	1.76	149	1986:02 1999:04

Note: SPR-total: All countries listed, excluding Israel.

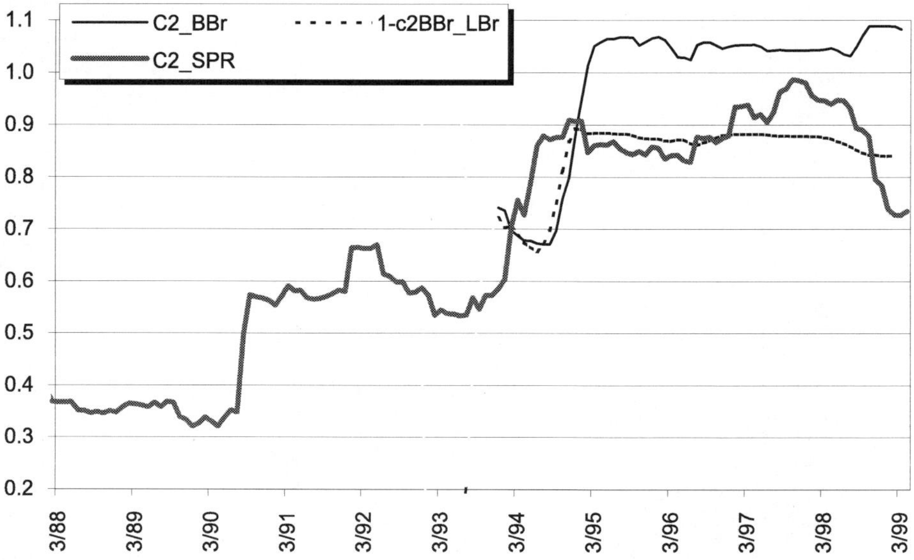

Figure 8.9
Indicators of Israel's Capital Market Integration into Capital Markets Abroad

that the presence of Japan in the G5 weakens the link with the Israeli stock market. As with the interest rate equations, the Russian financial crisis of 1998 also had an impact on the stock market equations.

All three indicators for capital market integration (figure 8.9) point to a similar conclusion: The links between financial markets in Israel and abroad have grown stronger during the 1990s. The coefficients α_2 and β_2 have become gradually larger. In both markets, there was a pronounced shift toward higher coefficients in the first half of the 1990s. However, the adjustment in the interest differentials preceded that of the stock markets, which rose mainly since 1996. The third indicator, which relates to the oligopoly power of the domestic banking system as reflected in the difference between domestic and foreign interest rates[28] also shows an improvement.

8.4 Economic Effects of Liberalization—Advantages and Disadvantages

The liberalization of capital flows aims at facilitating economic activity abroad of domestic citizens and vice versa. Independently, the process of globalization, reflecting increasing worldwide economic interdependence, has been progressing in the 1990s. This includes more than just capital markets; it includes production technology, telecommunication, entrepreneurship, management and marketing practices, and movement of workers across borders. The globalization process is gaining impetus. The more encompassing the liberalization, the wider the scope for Israel's participation in the wide spectrum of globalization. Given the economy's growing trade openness, the liberalization becomes increasingly irreversible.

The advantages of liberalization are emphasized when the return on capital in the domestic economy is above the world average. An economy with a liberal capital account policy will attract more capital than others. Such a situation arose in Israel in the beginning of the 1990s, when the peace process in the region and the immigration wave raised the expected return on capital. The demand for investment grew by some 76 percent in the years 1990–1991. It is hard to imagine how such a surge in investment could have been financed without referring to the world capital market. This example emphasizes the importance of improved international capital allocation and the extension of the sources of finance in excess of domestic savings. Furthermore, liberalization enhances the individual's freedom to manage his assets and liabilities. Given the difficulty to enforce capital controls, their absence also improves the standing of law enforcement in general. A somewhat related advantage is the reduction of bureaucratic power and its potential arbitrariness.

The following argument is both an advantage and a disadvantage. Globalization has significantly increased the financial vulnerability of emerging economies. The international financial markets' reaction to mistakes in a country's economic policy has become swift and amplified. Even in the absence of actual policy mistakes, a liberalized country bears a higher risk of contagion than a closed economy during a financial crisis, because market participants react not only to actual policy mistakes but also potential ones. This situation causes a constant threat for policymakers in economies with open capital markets. The more they adhere to macroeconomic self-discipline such as low inflation and balanced government budgets, the less they will be prone to contagion. Improved macroeconomic self-discipline eventually improves macroeconomic performance and the economy's international credit rating.

In the short run, the liberalization causes adjustment costs. The private sector, which after years of an overregulated foreign exchange market has become used to an artificial certainty of the exchange rate, will have to learn how to manage exchange rate risk, but also how to evaluate country risk and other risks relevant for economic activity in a globalized environment.

Liberalization, Monetary Policy, and Banking Supervision

In the second half of the 1980s, Israeli monetary policy was designed mainly to finance the balance of payments whereas the exchange rate was expected to act as an anchor on inflation. In times of downward pressure on the exchange rate, the interest rate was increased in order to raise the cost of purchasing foreign exchange from the Bank of Israel. Given the high inflation in Israel vis-à-vis the major trading partners, this situation brought about a sharp real appreciation and caused latent devaluation expectations and pressures on official international reserves. Exchange rate policy became torn between conflicting aims in the attempt to balance the tasks of nominal anchor and those of offsetting real appreciation. The surprising 10 percent depreciation in early 1987—the first since the stabilization plan—caused indeed a real depreciation, but at the same time, the public understood that there was no real commitment to use the exchange rate as a nominal anchor. The horizontal exchange rate band (1989–1991), whose parameters were adjusted four times, enabled a relatively smooth depreciation. The diagonal band, introduced at the end of 1991, considerably blurred the trade-off between the two tasks of the exchange rate. With the advance in the foreign exchange liberalization, the offset coefficient of monetary policy (the extent to which monetary policy is offset by international capital flows) increased, and the exchange rate regime became more flexible. The gradual reduction of the slope of the diagonal band, in line with the difference between the inflation target (introduced for the first time in 1992) and expected inflation abroad, was intended to help curb inflationary expectations regarding the yearly target set by the government. The change in strategy from a nominal anchor to inflation targets was gradual and eventually allowed for the use of the interest rate in the pursuit of the inflation target.

On the one hand (as shown in the previous section), the link between domestic and foreign interest rates was strengthened by the liberalization; on the other hand, the increased flexibility of the exchange rate allowed for enhanced independence of the monetary policy.[29]

There are important consequences for the design of the exchange rate regime to be drawn from liberalization in an environment of independent monetary policy. The existence of band limits tends to increase capital flows when these limits become unsustainable. This creates a need for sterilization. If the Central Bank smoothes the exchange rate on a steady path, this lowers the exchange rate risk artificially, and capital flows will be higher than in a regime with natural exchange rate volatility. Several liberalized economies with an independent monetary policy have accompanied liberalization by an increased flexibility of their exchange rate policy, sometimes even a floating exchange rate regime.[30]

In the wake of the Mexican economic crisis (1994–1995), the Southeast Asian crisis (in 1997) and the Russian debt default (1998) focused attention on the risks for the stability of the domestic financial sector that stem from free capital flows. It is argued that the shrinking oligopoly power (see above) pushes banks to compensate for the declining profitability by taking more risks.[31]

An unstable banking sector and incentives to take excessive risk are detrimental for any economy. It is unlikely that capital account liberalization should cause a financial crisis that would not have occurred otherwise. Although a crisis may be exacerbated or precipitated in an environment of free capital flows, it is unlikely that a healthy financial sector would incur a crisis because of the opening up of the capital account.

The financial crisis of the late 1990s has evoked a debate on the usefulness of controls on short-term capital, in order to limit the economy's vulnerability arising from its greater flexibility compared to capital imports with longer maturity. Chile, for example, imposed a tax on compulsory deposits at the Central Bank, which returns it after a year without paying interest. Capital imports will thus be more expensive the shorter the maturity of the debt. Although it did improve monetary autonomy for a short while, there was no significant lengthening of the maturity structure of the debt.[32] In October 1998, Chile decided to abolish the compulsory deposit.

8.5 Israel's Liberalization—An International Perspective

In 1996, the IMF calculated several indices on controls on member countries' international trade and capital movements in order to compare the extent of advance in foreign exchange liberalization among them. The "index of capital account controls" is calculated as the sum of the number of actual controls divided by the number of all existing controls—forty-seven as listed by the International Monetary Fund (IMF). See figure 8.10. The index varies from 0 to 1. A high index indicates that the country is heavily controlled. The index was calculated for forty-one countries (industrial, emerging, and developing economies). The Netherlands is the most freely operating country with an index of 0.0, Kazakhstan and Tunisia are the most constrained with an index of 0.83 and 0.87, respectively. As can be seen from chart 8.10, Israel's index was in the middle range, ranking as the seventeenth most constrained member country with an index of 0.43, meaning that in 1997, Israel maintained 43 percent of the total list of capital controls.

In 1998, Israel significantly accelerated liberalization (see section 8.2), and the index dropped to 0.15. The indices for other countries were not yet published at the time of writing this section, but it seems that 1998 was not a year of major advances in liberalization. The Southeast Asian crisis that evolved in 1997 and the Russian debt crisis in mid-1998 even brought about a retreat from liberalization in some

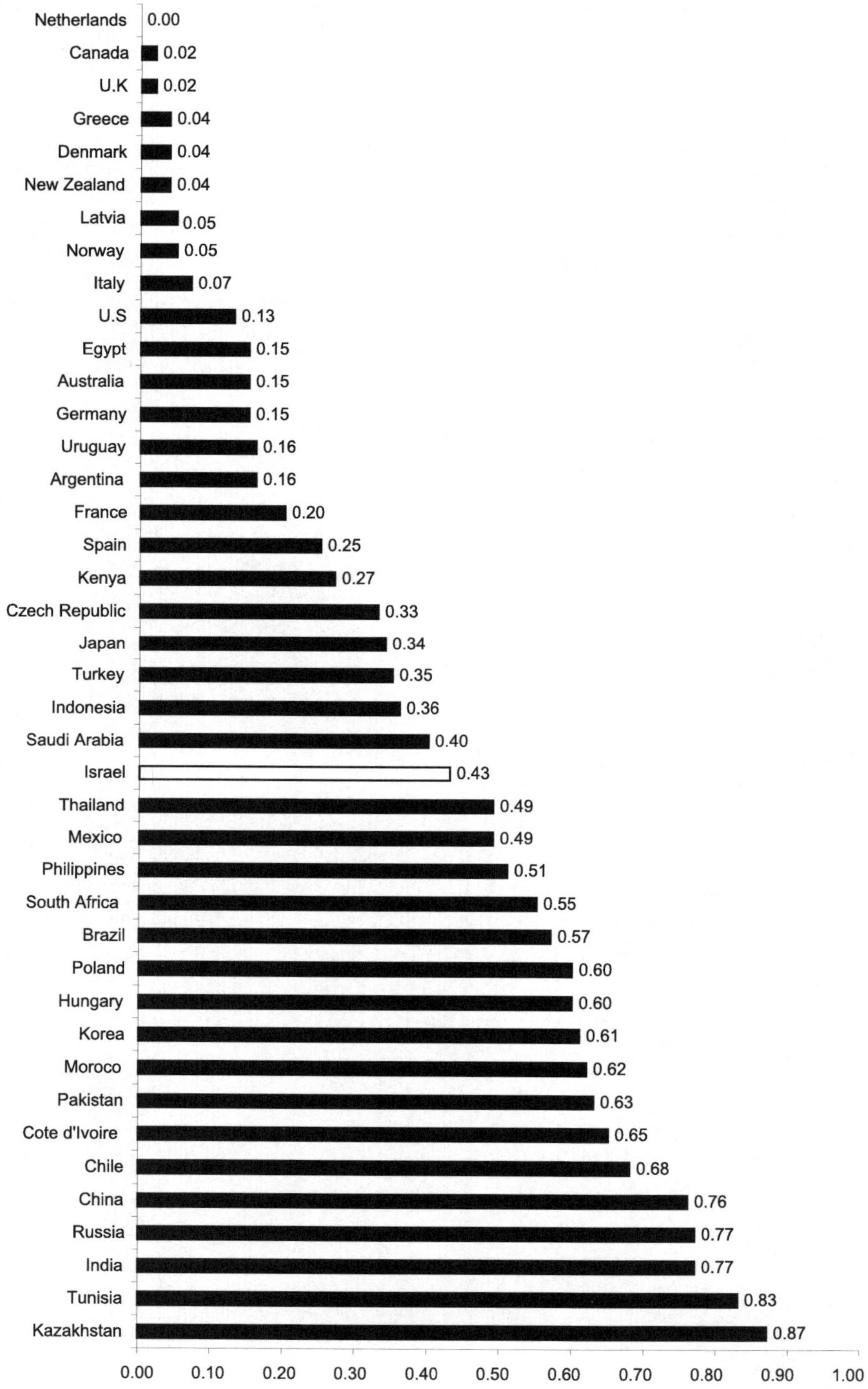

Figure 8.10
The Index of Capital Account Controls—International Comparison

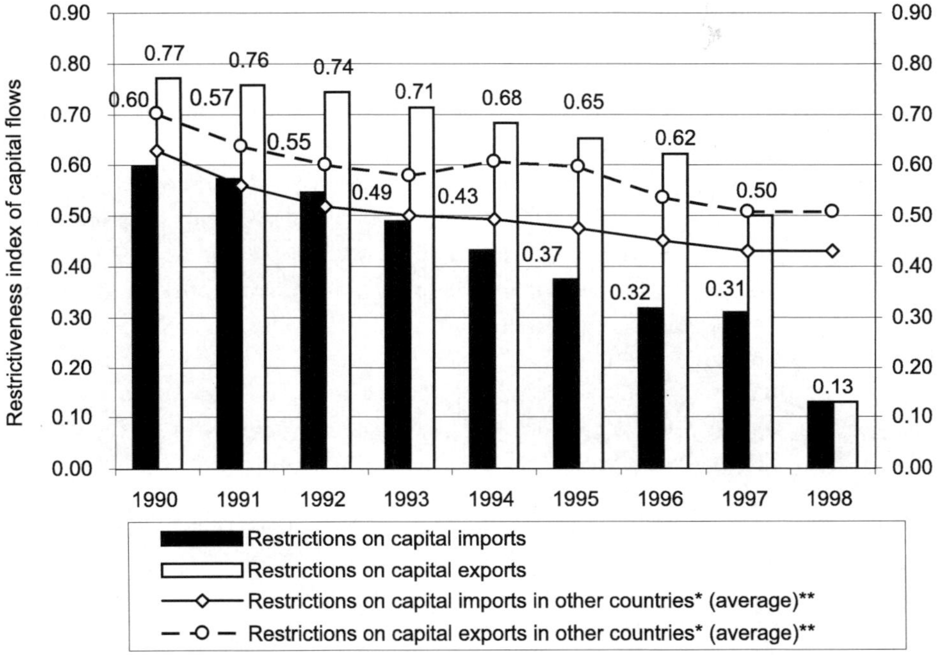

Figure 8.11
The Index of Capital Account Controls—A Comparison between Israel and Other Emerging Economies
*Other countries: Argentina, Brazil, Chile, Colombia, India, Indonesia, Korea, Malasia, Mexico, Peru, Philippines, South Africa, Thailand.
**Data for 1998—estimate.

countries (e.g., Malaysia). Comparing Israel's 1998 index to an unchanged index (from 1997 to 1998) for all other countries in figure 8.10, Israel's ranking would move up to the seventh rank, together with Australia, Egypt, and Germany.

The IMF also calculates separate indices for capital imports and exports. Figure 8.11 compares Israel with the average index of fourteen other countries. The figure confirms the conclusion from section 8.2, namely, that liberalization was more advanced in capital imports than in exports. However, in 1998, the liberalization of capital exports caught up with that of capital imports. The figure also shows that Israel's liberalization of capital exports was less advanced throughout most of the 1990s. It converged until 1997 toward the average index of the group of comparison, and it is likely that its liberalization efforts surpassed that of the other countries in 1998. Concerning capital imports, liberalization started out at a similar level, but since 1994, Israel liberalized more rapidly.

In 1998, liberalization faced a serious challenge. The move toward a liberal capital account in midst of the above-mentioned worldwide financial turmoil reflected a strategic choice. Indeed, the financial turmoil caused an outflow of financial capital of foreign residents in the last quarter of the year, but not so of Israeli holdings of foreign exchange deposits—despite the possibilities that had been opened up by the liberalization moves in May 1998. Furthermore, foreign direct investment continued to increase throughout the period. The flexibility of the exchange rate regime was comfortable, after the exchange rate band had been widened sharply in June 1997. At the time of the turmoil in the Israeli foreign exchange market, the band allowed for exchange rate fluctuations of 33 percent and functioned as a shock absorber.[33] The exchange rate surge was translated into a sharp jump in inflation and inflation expectations, after inflation had been low for about a year and expectations had been declining consistently. The swift monetary policy reaction (an increase in the Central Bank's interest rate by 4 percentage points) managed to restore price stability.

In April 1997, the Interim Committee of the International Monetary Fund decided to encourage the liberalization of international capital movements as one of its major tasks. It was agreed that the charter should be amended for that reason. A final decision depends on the acceptance of the formulation of this amendment by at least 85 percent of votes in the committee. It has been agreed already that liberalization should be orderly and adequately timed. The board of governors will accept delays in liberalization if they are warranted by defense needs, the need to develop the domestic capital market, or if the proposed steps would jeopardize the stability of the banking sector.

8.6 Summary and Conclusions

The Israeli economy is an exciting case for analyzing the process of capital account liberalization. After a failed liberalization in the late 1970s, Israel opted for a gradual approach, embedded in a wider strategy of reforms in several areas of the economy since the successful implementation of the macroeconomic stabilization plan of 1985. The Israeli experience stresses the paramount importance of macroeconomic stabilization as a fundamental precondition for the success of capital account liberalization. The stabilization plan reduced inflation radically compared to the past, but inflation remained too high and the public debt too large. This situation called for a gradual approach, leaving sufficient leeway for a further improvement in macroeconomic stability. The advance in liberalization was steadier than the progress in the achievement of macroeconomic stability, particularly the reduction in inflation. This policy coincided with two processes: (1) the rapid acceleration in globalization and (2) the search for investment opportunities in emerging economies, among them Israel, by the private sector in the highly developed economies. These capital movements, particularly the short-term component, considerably strained monetary policy, which increasingly focused on the achievement of price stability according to governmental inflation targets. With the benefit of hindsight, we conclude that in spite of temporary setbacks the strategy of gradual but adamant pursuit of liberalization-cum-stabilization has been a successful approach. The indicators used here to assess the extent of integration of the Israeli capital market in world capital markets are based on the analysis of capital flows and their structure, on yield differentials between the domestic currency and the U.S. dollar (adjusted for depreciation expectations and foreign exchange risk), on the spread between borrowing rates and deposit rates and on the relationship between Israeli and foreign stock price indices. All the indicators point to a growing international integration of the Israeli capital market during the 1990s. The analysis suggests that the convergence in the (expectations-adjusted) interest rates was faster than between stock prices. Stock price convergence became stronger only since late 1996. The indicator of oligopoly power of the banking sector suggests that liberalization has enhanced competition especially since late 1994, when capital imports intensified, due to a combination of high interest rate differentials and low foreign exchange risk due to the latter's prolonged artificial limitation by the lower limit of the exchange rate band.

Liberalization improves productivity in the economy, encourages cooperation with foreign companies, exposes the economy to technological advances, and strengthens the access to huge markets for Israeli products and services. However, in times of crisis and turmoil, it also exposes the economy to foreign shocks. In the short run, these shocks can be harmful to economic growth.

The negative effect of the crisis on an emerging economy will become amplified if the crisis affects the country's creditworthiness. Consequently, globalization requires macroeconomic policy to be geared, even more than before, toward stability as a response to the hazards of repercussion effects from international financial turmoil.

Notes

We thank Mimi Cohen and Erez Kapitolnik for excellent research assistance. The authors, of course, remain solely responsible for any mistakes.

1. See a thorough description in Corsetti et al. (1998a, b).

2. See Johnston and Ryan, 1994.

3. Articles critical of liberalization policy include Bhagwati (1998), Krugman (1998), and Rodrik (1997, 1998).

4. For financial vulnerability, see Milesi-Ferretti and Razin (1996), Berg and Patillo (1998), and Corsetti et al. (1998a).

5. See McKinnon (1973) (1991) and Johnston (1998).

6. In October 1977, the newly installed government decided on a reform package containing three areas:

a. A foreign exchange liberalization, abolishing the restrictions on foreign exchange loans from abroad, allowing for holdings of unlimited amounts of securities and deposits in foreign exchange, to be held in Israeli banks. Israeli businesses were allowed to hold foreign currency accounts for the conduct of international business. Controls on Israelis' purchase of assets abroad were not lifted. Services transactions related to tourism and unilateral transfers out of Israel were also simplified.

b. The multiple exchange rates, which had existed until then for various goods, services, and capital movements, were unified into a single exchange rate. However, most import tariffs remained in place, such that the effective exchange rate still varied for different international transactions in goods and services. It was only in the early 1990s that a gradual import tariff liberalization was implemented. The 1977 liberalization resulted in a 45 percent devaluation on capital transactions, which caused a sharp change in relative prices of the public's assets and liabilities portfolio.

c. The foreign exchange regime moved from a "crawling depreciation," implemented after the energy crisis in 1973, to a managed float.

7. See Pfeffermann et al. (1999).

8. See Corsetti et al., 1998a, b.

9. All the numbers are five-year averages (1992–1996) preceding the crisis year 1997.

10. In September 1983, the bank shares of several Israeli banks crashed and brought about their de facto nationalization (among them the three largest Israeli banks). It took a couple of years to start the tedious process of privatization. In the year 2001, this process was not yet completed.

11. For a detailed account, see the appendix in the Hebrew version.

12. For a detailed account, see the appendix in the Hebrew version.

13. See Johnston, Darbar, and Echeverria (1997).

14. Errors and omissions can also arise due to data problems concerning international trade in goods and services. Figure 8.2 is based on the assumption that errors and omissions arise solely from capital account problems.

15. The ratio is defined as following: The sum (four quarters) of the absolute value of credit and debit capital flows with a maturity of up to one year, divided by the same calculation for longer-term maturities.

16. This is a bi annual survey among approximately one hundred banks specializing in international lending/investment, which rank countries from one to one hundred, a high rank indicating a low probability of debt default. The survey answers are then weighted, based on the size of their lending in the bank's portfolio.

17. See Gottlieb (1989), Ben-Bassat and Gottlieb (1992).

18. See Bufman and Leiderman (1996, p. 85), in Hebrew.

19. Bufman and Leiderman (1996) estimate an approximation of the covered interest arbitrage between the NIS and the U.S. dollar by use of the differential between the domestic interest rate and the sum of the U.S. dollar interest rate and the risk premium on call options. They conclude that the hypothesis of yield equality cannot be rejected. However, the remaining strong serial correlation in the data question the validity of this conclusion.

20. This risk has been neglected by many researchers including Bufman and Leiderman.

21. Regressing first differences allows for the use of OLS after correcting for serial correlation.

22. We thank Miki Kahan from the Monetary Department of the Bank of Israel for providing us with a series of depreciation expectations. These were derived from the relationship between unindexed (nominal,

NIS denominated) Israeli government bonds and U.S.-dollar denominated Israeli government bonds of equal maturity. Gottlieb and Ribon, for example, calculate depreciation expectations from the position of the exchange rate within the existing exchange rate band parameters and from the accumulated real appreciation or depreciation since the last change in parameters. This implies that a future change in parameters will allow for a correction of the real appreciation or depreciation. Such an approach is independent of the interest rate but hinges on relatively strong assumptions.

23. $i = \underset{(-1.3)}{-.02} + \underset{(13.0)}{1.28}\,[(1+i^*)(1+e)]$

24. $i = \underset{(13.6)}{0.098} + \underset{(12.1)}{0.78}\,[(1+i^*)(1+e)].$

25. Only a small part of the tests is presented here.

26. The high-yield market is the medium through which firms, rated approximately BBB, can issue stocks and corporate bonds.

27. For detailed definitions and sources of variables, see appendix 8.1.

28. The series is a linear transformation (1-C_2BB_LB) of the indicator in figure 8.8; a reduction in the interest gap appears as an increase.

29. For an analysis of Israeli monetary policy from 1988 to 1997, see Gottlieb and Ribon (1997).

30. See Eichengreen et al. (1998).

31. See, for example, Goodhart (1985), Demirguc-Kunt and Detragiache (1998).

32. See Edwards (1998), Cardoso and Laurens (1998), and the discussion on errors and omissions in section 8.3.1 above.

33. Calculated from the center of the band.

References

Ben-Bassat, Avi, and Daniel Gottlieb. "Optimal International Reserves and Sovereign Risk." *Journal of International Economics* 33 (1992): 345–362.

Berg, Andrew, and Catherine Pattillo. "Are Currency Crises Predictable? A Test." IMF WP/98/154, November 1998.

Bhagwati, Jagdish. "The Capital Myth." *Foreign Affairs* 77 (May/June 1998).

Cardoso, Jaime, and Bernard Laurens. "The Effectiveness of Capital Controls on Inflows: Lessons from the Experience of Chile." Washington, D.C.: International Monetary Fund Working Paper, December 1998, WP/98/168.

Cooper, Richard N. "Should Capital-Account Be a World Objective?" In *Should the IMF Pursue Capital-Account Convertibility*? edited by S. Fischer et al. Essays in International Finance, no. 207, May 1998.

Corsetti, Giancarlo, Paolo Pesenti, and Nouriel Roubini. "What Caused the Asian Currency and Financial Crisis? Part I: A Macroeconomic Overview." NBER Working Paper no. 6833, December 1998a: 1–51.

Corsetti, Giancarlo, Paolo Pesenti, and Nouriel Roubini. "What Caused the Asian Currency and Financial Crisis? Part II: The Policy Debate." NBER Working Paper no. 6834, December 1998b: 1–41.

Demirguc-Kunt, Asli, and Enrica Detragiache. "Financial Liberalization and Financial Fragility." WP/97/106, 1998.

Dooley, Michael. "A Survey of Academic Literature on Controls of International Capital Transactions." IMF Working Paper 95/127, 1995.

Edwards, Sebastian. "Interest Rate Volatility, Contagion and Convergence: An Empirical Investigation of the Cases of Argentina, Chile, and Mexico." *Journal of Applied Economics* 1 (November 1998).

Eichengreen, Barry, et al. "Exit Strategies: Policy Options for Countries Seeking Greater Exchange Rate Flexibility." Occasional Paper no. 168, IMF, 1998.

Eichengreen, Barry, and Michael Mussa, "Capital Account Liberalization—Theoretical and Practical Aspects," Washington, D.C.: International Monetary Fund Occasional Paper 172, 1998.

Feldstein Martin, and Charles, Horioka. "Domestic Saving and International Capital Flows." *Economic Journal* 90 (June 1980): 314–329.

Goldstein, Morris, and Michael Mussa. "The Integration of World Capital Markets." Working paper WP/93/95. Washington, D.C.: IMF, December 1993.

Mathieson, Donald J., and Timothy Lane. "Determinants and Systemic Consequences of International Capital Flows." Occasional paper 77. Washington, D.C.: IMF, 1991.

Goodhart, Charles A. E. "The Evolution of Central Banks: A Natural Development?" London: London School of Economics, Suntory—Toyota International Center and Related Disciplines, 1985.

Gottlieb, Daniel. "On the Determinants of a Country's Creditworthiness: The Case of Israel, 1971 to 1983." *Journal of Economic Development* 14 (June 1989): 65–91.

Gottlieb, Daniel, and Sigal Ribon. "Capital Flows of the Private Sector and Monetary Policy in Israel—October 1988 to March 1997." *The Economic Quarterly* 46 (May 1999). (Hebrew): 136–174.

Johnston, R. Barry, and C. Ryan. "The Impact of Controls on Capital Movements on the Private Capital Accounts of Countries' Balance of Payments: Empirical Estimates and Policy Implications." Washington, D.C.: IMF Working Paper 94/78, 1994.

Johnston, R. Barry. "Sequencing Capital Account Liberalizations and Financial Sector Reform." PPAA/98/8. Washington, D.C.: IMF.

Johnston, R. Barry, Salim M. Darbar, and Claudia Echeverria. "Sequencing Capital Account Liberalization: Lessons from the Experiences in Chile, Indonesia, Korea and Thailand." Washington, D.C.: IMF Working Paper 97/157, 1997.

Johnston, R. Barry, and V. Sundararajan, eds. "Sequencing Financial Sector Reforms." Country Experiences and Issues. Washington, D.C.: IMF, 1999.

Klein, David. "Liberalization Cum Stabilization: The Israeli Experience." Jerusalem: Bank of Israel, September 1995. Unpublished manuscript.

Krugman, Paul. "What Happened to Asia." ⟨http://web.mit.edu/krugman/www/disinter.html⟩, September 1998.

———. "Saving Asia: It's Time to Get Radical." *Fortune Investor*. ⟨http://web.mit.edu/krugman/www/disinter.html⟩, September 1998.

Martin, R., and M. Selowsky. "Nascent Capital Flows, Learning, and Chilean-type Controls." In *Central Banking and Monetary Policy: Major Issues and Implications for Transition Economies*, edited by Mario I., Blejer, and M., Skreb. City: Kluwer Academic Publishers, forthcoming.

Mathieson, Donald J., and Liliana Rojas-Suarez. "Liberalization of the Capital Account." Washington, D.C.: IMF Working Paper, 92/46, 1992.

McKinnon, Ronald. *Money and Capital in Economic Development*. Washington: Brookings Institution, 1973.

———. *The Order of Economic Liberalization: Financial Control in the Transition to a Market Economy*. Baltimore, Maryland: John Hopkins University Press, 1991.

Milesi Ferretti, Gian Maria, and Assaf Razin. "Sustainability of Persistent Current Account Deficits." NBER no. 5467, 1996.

Montiel, Peter. "Capital Mobility in Developing Countries: Some Measurement Issues and Empirical Estimates." *World Bank Economic Review* 8 (1994): 311–350.

Obstfeld, Maurice, and Kenneth Rogoff. "The Intertemporal Approach to the Current Account." In *Handbook of International Economics*, edited by G. Grossman and K. Rogoff, Amsterdam, Holland: Elsevier Science Publishing, 1995.

Pfeffermann Guy P., Gregory V. Kisunko, and Mariusz A., Sumlinski. "Trends in Private Investment in Developing Countries—Statistics for 1970–97." Washington, D.C.: International Finance Corporation, Discussion Paper 37, 1999.

Reisen, Helmut, and H. Yeches. "Time Varying Estimates on the Openness of the Capital Account in Korea and Taiwan." OECD Development Center Technical Paper no. 42, August 1991.

Ribon, Sigal, and Oved Yosha. "Financial Liberalization and Competition in Banking: An Empirical Investigation." Bank of Israel Discussion Paper Series, May 1999.

Rodrik, Dani. "Has Globalization Gone Too Far?" Washington, D.C.: Institute for International Economics, March 1997.

———. "Who Needs Capital-Account Convertibility?" "Should the IMF Pursue Capital-Account Convertibility?" edited by S. Fischer et al. Essays in International Finance no. 207, International Finance Section, Princeton University, May 1998: 55–65.

Roubini, Nouriel. "The Case against Currency Boards: Debunking 10 Myths about Benefits of Currency Boards." ⟨www.stern.nyu.edu/globalmacro⟩.

Sabirin, S. "Capital Account Liberalization—The Indonesian Experience." In *Financial Sector Reforms in Asian and Latin American Countries: Lessons of Comparative Experience*, edited by S. Faruqi. EDI Seminar Series, World Bank (1993): 147–161.

Sokoler, Meir. "Extracting Information from Financial Markets for Monetary Policy Objectives: The Case of Israel." Manuscript prepared for the June 1998 workshop at the Centre for Central Banking Studies, Bank of England, 1998.

IV REFORMS IN THE GOODS AND SERVICES MARKETS

9 The Import-Liberalization and Abolition of Devaluation Substitutes Policy: Implications for the Israeli Economy

Yoram Gabai and Rafael Rob

9.1 Introduction

In 1985–1995, Israel continued to invoke its policy of opening its economy to international trade. This chapter analyzes the matter in two dimensions—the trade, policy, and its results, especially the positive impact of "trade creation"; and the positive impact of "trade diversion." During this time, Israel signed and completed several trade agreements with blocs of developed countries—foremost among them being the European Common Market (completion of the 1975 agreement), the United States (signing and completion starting in 1985), and the European Free Trade Association (EFTA) countries.[1] In the early 1990s, Israel unilaterally applied a policy of opening its economy to imports from "third countries." These trends led to greater trade between Israel and its trading partners and diverted trade by preferring blocs of countries with which Israel had trade accords over countries that lacked such agreements or toward which a policy of gradual lowering of barriers was applied.

In the policy dimension, we will attempt to examine the main policy measures taken during the years at issue, in two senses—mitigating or abolishing devaluation substitutes and lowering tariff and nontariff barriers vis-à-vis various blocs of countries—the European Common Market, the United States, EFTA, and the rest of the world. This discussion will also attempt to examine the principals who took action to expedite or impede the policies and the disagreements among the policymakers themselves. These conflicts of interest led to inconsistency in trade policy, especially in the second half of the 1980s.

As we look into the trade policy, we also examine the exchange-rate policy in reference to its devaluation-substitute components. Here, too, the policy was inconsistent and vague in the second half of the 1980s and devaluation substitutes were revoked consistently in the early 1990s. In this context, we will attempt to understand the factors at work in this field and to pinpoint trends.

The empirical part of the study asks whether the "results on the ground" correspond to the goal of the policy and the theoretical expectations. In this section, we present numerical data on consumer price levels and patterns of trade, with which we may investigate whether the Israeli economy is progressing toward the goals of the import liberalization as presented in the sections on theory and policy.

9.2 The Import Liberalization Policy, 1985–1995

General Remarks

The debate of values and politics over the openness or closedness of a domestic economy to cross-border flows of goods is almost as old as history. In the Middle Ages, governments tended to keep markets closed, protected, and apportioned; in the early modern era, the mercantilist and the liberal approaches vied with each other. Only toward the second half of the nineteenth century did the ideology gather strength that stressed the growth of the wealth of nations when countries open themselves to free trade.

However, the rhetorical and theoretical consensus about the advantages of free trade did not attenuate the acrid disagreements between the proponents and opponents of openness. In recent decades, opponents of free trade have been supporting their case by citing considerations of fledgling industries, employment, and balance of payments; their support of the free-trade theory is mostly a vision for the end of days. However, the collapse of the Soviet Union in the late 1980s severely weakened the arguments in favor of protection against competing imports, and various blocs of countries have become increasingly open to trade, albeit with many strings attached.

In its brief economic history, Israel has passed through various gradual phases of progress in trade liberalization. The early 1950s were noted mainly for tariff, quantity, and other barriers on a large scale, due to foreign-currency liquidity problems. At that time, officials even prepared foreign-currency balance sheets, that is, stipulated a foreign-currency source for every substantial expenditure. That era also featured ramified forms of protection for domestic manufacture and subsidization of exports.

In the 1960s and, especially, since the mid-1970s, Israel signed Free Trade Area (FTA) agreements with the developed countries (the European Common Market and the United States). The strategic premise that guided policymakers was that such agreements are advantageous from Israel's standpoint because they would allow Israeli exports to penetrate the developed markets, albeit at the price of exposing the domestic economy to tariff-free imports. This strategy was applied mainly vis-à-vis developed countries. In contrast, in regard to "third countries"—mainly developing countries, with which Israel had not concluded FTA agreements (generally, all countries except for the Common Market and the United States)—Israel raised its tariffs and erected even tougher quantitative and nontariff barriers against imports.

The leading policy in the 1970s and 1980s favored openness to imports only where Israeli exports receive preferential treatment. In all other cases, according to Israel, domestic manufacture should be protected in various and sundry ways—from tariffs and quotas to standards, procedures, and other restrictions.

After the Economic Stabilization Program in 1985, professionals gradually came around to the view that Israel should apply greater vigor in liberalizing imports from all countries of origin, including third countries. This, they believed, would have various salutary effects, including greater domestic competitiveness, lower consumer prices, prevention of waste of foreign currency occasioned by trade diversion, and greater domestic efficiency. In the second half of the 1980s, this model, promoted by the professional echelons at the Ministry of Finance and the Bank of Israel, collided with the views of the manufacturers and the Ministry of Industry and Trade. Therefore, the trends in liberalization were uneven and inconsistent.

A substantive change occurred in the first half of the 1990s. The policy of opening the domestic economy to imports gained the support of the political echelon, and the process of liberalizing imports from third countries, coupled with the elimination of various import duties, resulted in a large degree of openness vis-à-vis the entire world. In recent years, Israel has been completing the liberalization process in all fields of goods and services, including standards, agriculture, and personal imports, to name only three. However, since 1997, as the unemployment rate has risen slowly but steadily, demands to reinforce protection of domestic manufacture against imports from third countries have been voiced again. The rationales this time concern dumping and the effect of the Southeast Asia crisis. The government is being tested at this time: Should it complete the liberalization process or slow the pace of change? The results of the efficiency and liberalization process are more difficult to assess today, a time of economic slowdown, than in the boom years of the early 1990s, when unemployment rates fell gradually from 12 percent to 6.5 percent.

FTA Agreements with the European Common Market and the United States, 1975–1995

Israel made its first moves toward trade liberalization in the late 1950s and early 1960s. In the course of these efforts, it concluded an initial framework agreement with the European Common Market in 1965 that served as a basis for another partial agreement in 1970.

In May 1975, Israel and the Common Market signed their most comprehensive accord, which stipulated a phased reduction of tariffs on industrial products that the sides traded with each other. In this context, two classes of products were set forth. In one class (accounting for about 60 percent of import volume), made up mainly of raw materials, tariffs were applied at low rates that were lowered gradually to zero between July 1975 and January 1980. Products in the second class (some 40 percent of import volume), mainly final consumer goods, carried high tariffs that were lowered gradually between July 1975 and January 1989. (The graduated procedure was adopted chiefly to protect domestic manufacture and allow it to adjust to conditions of unrestricted competition.) In 1985, as the agreement with the Common Market was being implemented, Israel signed an FTA accord with the United States. Here, too, tariffs were gradually lowered to zero in a process that was completed in 1995. The two agreements are similar in many respects, although the rules of origin are different and arrangements pertaining to agricultural imports are more liberal (less protective policy) in the agreement with the U.S.

Concurrently, Israel was more adamant than ever in its policy of fending off imports from third countries. Although tariffs were not raised (and at times were reduced), standards barriers, quantity restrictions, and other limits, including purchase tax, were toughened. This integrated process—liberalization vis-à-vis the Common Market and the United States coupled with a proliferation of import restrictions vis-à-vis third countries (especially developing countries)—entailed continual monitoring of countries and rules of origin in order to minimize smuggling from third countries via FTA countries. In many cases, the effect of controls and supervision over countries of origin resulted in inefficiency.

Protection by Means of Devaluation Substitutes

Throughout Israel's economic history until the early 1990s, policy instruments that amounted to substitutes for currency devaluation were invoked. They included import duties or export premiums that were applied broadly and indiscriminately among countries and blocs of countries in respect to goods, services, and capital. These instruments were used not only to protect domestic manufacture and subsidize exports but also to attain fiscal, monetary, and other economic goals. Notably, because import taxes that were originally applied as devaluation substitutes eventually became "ordinary" budget revenue, they were difficult to abolish for budget reasons. It deserves emphasis that the devaluation substitutes were neither eliminated nor stipulated in a linear process. On certain occasions (in 1962 and 1997, for example), actions to unify rates and abolish devaluation substitutes were taken, but in the early 1980s, of all times, varied policy measures were invoked to combine the protection of domestic manufacture with devaluation substitutes and fiscal goals. Several important devaluation substitutes still existed in the second half of the 1980s:

1. A 2 percent *general import duty*, computed on the basis of total customs value on the tariff-free import prices of products.

2. A 1 percent *foreign-currency purchase duty*, 80 percent of which was collected on account of foreign-currency purchase for imports of goods and 20 percent for overseas travel and imports of services.

3. An *imported services duty*, imposed in July 1984. (At first, the tax also applied to foreign currency that businesses purchased for their operations abroad.) The duty, initially set at 15 percent, was lowered incrementally and the business sector was fully exempted from it in 1989.

Generally speaking, the business sector managed throughout that time to minimize and avoid its liabilities on account of this tax because assessors found it difficult to distinguish between activity abroad and activities originating in Israel.

4. A NIS 250 *foreign-travel duty*, imposed on every citizen who went abroad. From April 1987 until the duty was abolished in the early 1990s, it was held at this level.

5. A 3 percent *foreign-currency credit duty*, collected between August 1987 and September 1988. Its main purpose makes foreign credit less advantageous. The main motive for this measure had to do with spreads between domestic inflation rates and exchange-rate changes, which resulted in sizable nominal interest spreads between Israel and abroad and, consequently, foreign-currency inflows that might endanger monetary stability.

Administrative and Other Nontariff Barriers

In the 1980s, following its historical tendency, Israel considered it legitimate to use standards and administrative decisions to protect domestic manufacture. According to this mindset, the distinction between the policy goals of consumer protection (for reasons of public safety and health) and protection of domestic manufacture was blurry. Many measures related to standards were applied by means of the Standards Institution and the manufacturers, and the considerations behind their decisions embraced quite a few aspects, as stated. The Ministry of Industry and Trade also believed at this time that standards should be used to protect domestic manufacture and even considered this legal and valid in terms of Israel's relations with third countries (unlike trade with the Common Market and the United States, in which this use of standards was explicitly prohibited). Notably, many government ministries (Health and Communications, to name only two) have standards mechanisms. Their decisions, too, were informed by a combination of considerations—protection of consumers, domestic manufacture, and at times, even sole importers.

In sum, amidst actions to stimulate competition and liberalize imports, Israel applied formal and informal systems of protection that constituted "affirmative action" for both domestic manufacture and imports from the United States and the Common Market.

The Overall Impact of Trade Policy in the 1980s

Trade policy was typically uneven in the 1980s. On the one hand, the Free Trade Area agreements with the Common Market and the United States were expanded and implemented and tariffs on imports from the rest of the world were lowered. Concurrently, administrative and nontariff barriers were raised, and administrative import restrictions were put to greater use, chiefly to protect domestic manufacture. Below, we attempt to profile the extent of use of nontariff barriers in quantitative terms and to generalize about the overall direction of import policy in the 1980s.

Quantitative Import Barriers In the 1980s, increased use of administrative barriers offset the effects of the lowering of tariffs on imports from all blocs of countries. The main characteristic of the nontariff protection policy was reflected in the fact that the number of restricted customs items increased by about 60 percent during that decade. An empirical analysis of the findings shows that Israel limited and impeded imports in numerous and diverse ways.[2] Table 9.1 sorts these findings by types of restrictions.

At that time, the authority to issue import licenses was vested with the Minister of Industry and Trade, who, under the Import-Export Ordinance, 1979, issued a "Unrestricted Import Order." The order had two appendices pertaining to barriers: (1) "Goods Not Authorized for Import," for which imports were prohibited in the absence of an import license, and (2) "Goods Conditionally Authorized for Import," including a list of customs items and the terms for the issuance of an import license. Occasionally—every year or two—an amendment to the order was gazetted.

The figures shown above pertain to customs items that were subjected to the foregoing restrictions. In the 1980s, the list grew with a celerity that points to a substantive

Table 9.1
Charges in Custom Restrictions, 1980–1988

	Number of restricted customs items		
	1980	1988	Percent change
Compulsory licensing	444	733	65
Material printed in Hebrew	21	85	305
Special permission	210	327	56
Standards certification	181	294	62
Compulsory marking in Hebrew	75	122	63

shift toward import barriers that were meant largely to protect domestic manufacture. Below, we examine the essence of each restriction and its principal target, by products and countries of origin (Common Market/U.S. and the rest of the world).

Compulsory Licensing Compulsory licensing was applied to "Goods Not Authorized for Import." As stated, the growth rate of customs items listed in this part of the Order included nearly two-thirds of the 289 items to which compulsory licensing was imposed. Some 134 items were absolved of this requirement if they originated in the Common Market, and thirty-four were also excused if they originated in the United States. The exemption applied only to products for which the licensing requirement was added in the 1980s; ostensibly, it facilitated some import activity from Common Market countries and the United States. With respect to items that came under compulsory licensing and originated only in third countries, protection of domestic manufacture was the obvious purpose. Because even Israel understood that it could not present the Common Market and the U.S. with a more convincing argument, it refrained from imposing licensing on them, too. However, Israel took frequent action to limit imports even from blocs of countries with which it had FTA agreements (increases of 30 percent vis-à-vis the Common Market and 37 percent vis-à-vis the United States), although the arguments in favor of licensing may be varied and sincere and not solely for protection of domestic manufacture.

Some eliminations and cutbacks in compulsory licensing occurred at this time, but their share in the total was marginal. Policymakers placed special emphasis on reinforcing protection of the printing industry against material printed in Hebrew abroad.

The identity of products for which the licensing requirement was expanded or imposed also shows that protection of domestic manufacture was the main consideration in this policy. The industries most strongly affected were wood and wood products, knitwear and other clothing, footwear, glass and glass products, dried fruit and walnuts. Domestic manufacturers who exerted pressure for tougher protection operated extensively in all these fields.

Special Permit As a barrier, special permit essentially resembled compulsory licensing except that it usually pertained to ministries other than Industry and Trade, that is, Transport, Communications, and Agriculture. The figures point to an increase of more than 50 percent in this item. Although the special-permit requirement was abolished for thirty-two items, it was replaced by binding standards in most of those cases.

Standards Certification In the standards requirement, a manufacturer is typically required to meet the requisites of an official or Israeli standard and the terms of a specific specification of supply. During the period at issue, 139 customs items were added to the list and 26 were deleted. Four of the added items were exempt from standards certification if imported from the Common Market; twenty-one were also exempt if imported from the United States. The standards-certification requirement was broadened not only to show concern for consumers but to protect domestic manufacture. In the course of the expansion, products such as toys, sporting gear, and electrical machinery and equipment, to name only a few, were included.

Compulsory Marking in Hebrew Because this requirement is applied at the import phase, it is invoked before the goods are shipped from abroad. The list grew from seventy-five customs items in 1980 to 122 in 1988, as fifty-two items were added and five were delisted. The nature of the products shows clearly that this requirement was meant to protect domestic manufacture. It was imposed on industries such as furniture, knitwear, other clothing, and leather products, in which the component of domestic manufacture was relatively large.

Because Israel revised its customs classifications significantly in the middle of 1988, it is difficult to assess the policy between 1988 and 1991. A partial examination of products shows that most delisted items were in fuel because of the reform in that industry; in the other fields, the requirement actually became tougher and more items were affected.

In sum, the 1980s—an era of decreasing tariffs—witnessed a bolstering of protection of "sensitive" domestically manufactured products for which manufacturers were able to apply considerable pressure. The main industries in this regard, recurring in all types of prohibitions and quantity restrictions, were textiles, clothing, furniture, toys, glass, and printing. The barrier policy mitigated the possibility of imports in many product groups and, in some cases, destroyed it altogether.

In 1990, industrial imports from the "rest of the world" (areas from which imports were restricted) were only 7.6 percent of total industrial imports.[3] However, it should borne in mind that the barriers often thwarted all imports. In 1990, more than one-third of items protected by licensing and one-fourth of imported items from the "rest of the world" were not imported at all. Thus, the quantity barriers had two effects: In some items, protection against cheap imports sufficed to secure the entire domestic market for Israeli industry; in others, the main effect was the diversion of imports from inexpensive sources to more expensive ones in the Common Market or the United States. As a rule, the nontariff protection was much more powerful than the tariff protection, which was steadily declining.

The findings for 1991 (shortly before imports from third countries were liberalized) show that nontariff barriers provided an average effective protection rate of 57 percent as against average tariff protection of only 21 percent.[4] The disparities were most conspicuous in textiles, where nontariff barriers achieved an 87 percent effective protection rate, while tariff protection provided less than 6 percent. In clothing, the effective nontariff protection verged on 1,500 percent as against 8 percent in tariff protection. Metals also showed a significant spread (60 percent versus 5 percent).

The Net Effect of Trade Policy in the 1980s As stated, the 1980s were typified by vagueness in regard to trade policy. The Bank of Israel and the Ministry of Finance were inclined at this time, as before, to promote import liberalization as part of trade agreements that had substantially lowered tariffs. Concurrently, the Ministry of Industry and Trade, other special-purpose ministries, and the Standards Institution furthered (deliberately or not) the goal of protecting domestic manufacture by means of nontariff barriers.

Overall, the main effects of the policy were two—exacerbation of economic distortions and vast empowerment of the professional and political bureaucracy to prefer domestic manufacturers and importers and to enrich close and less-close associates by providing favored parties with import licenses at no charge—licenses that at times were "sold" afterwards to importers for a steep price, commensurate with the rent created by the import quota.

Generally speaking, the empirical findings show that the overall rate of protection of industry was rather stable in the 1980s; that is, that the increase in nontariff barriers roughly offset the effect of the decreases in tariffs. The rate of effective tariff protection declined from 28.2 percent in 1982 to 15.7 percent in 1987, but the substitution factor made the net change marginal at best.[5]

Data from the Central Bureau of Statistics[6] show that in industry at large, the share of competing imports in total domestic sales hardly changed in the 1980s and held steady at 25–26 percent between 1977 and 1990. The share of imports actually increased in several "protected" fields, as the nontariff protection attenuated the process but did not change the trend. For example, the share of competing imports in domestic textile sales climbed from 28 percent in 1977 to 39 percent in 1990 and even more steeply in rubber products, from 14 percent to 54 percent in the respective years.

An additional empirical study[7] confirms the sense that the 1980s were an era of general status quo in protection of domestic manufacture. It shows that total effective tariff and nontariff protection declined gently in 1982–1985 but climbed again in the second half of the decade, mainly by nontariff means, so that the end-of-decade level resembled that at the beginning of the decade.

The Transition to Liberalization and Nearly Total Exposure of Domestic Manufacture to Competing Imports, 1990–1995

The hallmark development in the second half of the 1980s was a political and economic struggle between proponents of protection of domestic manufacture and supporters of the import-liberalization policy. In the early 1990s, the disagreements were essentially resolved in favor of the latter. Between 1989 and 1995, the Ministry of Finance, in concert with the Bank of Israel, oversaw the adoption of a lengthy series of proliberalization decisions, and in the 1990s, the Ministry of Industry and Trade subscribed to the goal of opening the Israeli economy to competition from all sources, even without reciprocity. As the proliberalization forces coalesced, the manufacturers became increasingly fragmented. Some manufacturers favored the process because it would lower the costs of imported raw materials and intermediates; others adhered to the traditional approach of maintaining the status quo—openness toward developed countries and closedness toward the rest of the world.

The pro-openness forces won the day in various dimensions of activity:

Elimination of Devaluation Substitutes The leading approach at the Ministry of Finance and the Bank of Israel favored the elimination of all devaluation substitutes in goods and services, on both the import and the export sides, as a prerequisite in making the sheqel convertible and eliminating the distortions occasioned by the substitutability of sheqals sold at the formal exchange rate and sheqals sold at the rate including taxation. Accordingly, (1) in April 1990, the 1 percent foreign-currency purchase duty was abolished and (2) in January 1993, the rest of the devaluation substitutes were abolished, including the imported services duty (which had been lowered from 7.5 percent to 4.5 percent in December 1990), the foreign-travel duty (which rested at NIS 250 per passenger at that time), and the 2 percent import duty. Israel culminated this process by joining the international agreement of the International Monetary Fund, which prohibits import duties of all types, including any form of export premium, direct or indirect.

As the devaluation substitutes were abolished, the exchange-rate system was refined and adjusted to needs. The new system was based on a theoretical "midpoint" that climbs at a predetermined slope along with trading bands that straddle this rate. As a rule, the change in the midpoint was based on the principle of maintaining a real exchange rate, that is, the expected spread between inflation in Israel's trading partners and in Israel. During this time, the midpoint was occasionally adjusted and the diagonal slopes and the trading bands were realigned.[8] When these adjustments were made—especially when raising the midpoint was expected to stimulate inflation by creating an effective currency devaluation—the import duties and exchange-rate insurance that offset the foreseen impact of the exchange-rate change on import prices and exporters' return were reduced.

Elimination of Protection by Purchase Tax In 1987–1988, the governments of the U.S. and the Common Market countries demanded that Israel correct all violations of agreements that it had allegedly perpetrated by means of purchase tax. They accused Israel of having protected domestic manufacture by applying a purchase tax that, theoretically, applied at a uniform rate on imports and domestic manufacture in ways that discriminated against imports. The empirical findings confirm the Common Market and U.S. allegations;[9] in the 1980s, Israel did apply purchase tax to protect domestic manufacture. This was especially conspicuous at times when Israel carried out substantial reductions in tariffs—which raised the sums of purchase tax and the rates of the percent-quota supplement—both for fiscal reasons and to protect domestic manufacture.

Liberalization of Imports from Third Countries

Although Israel's trade agreements with the European Common Market and the United States led to an increase in trade with these countries, they diverted trade from third countries to the countries stipulated in the agreements. Furthermore, the lowering of tariffs with the agreement countries was sometimes accompanied by the imposition of additional nontariff stringencies and standards with respect to trade with third countries, and the trade-diversion process actually worsened. The more important the third countries became in global trade, the more detrimental the trade diversion was and the more severely Israel suffered from its failure to exploit these countries' comparative advantages in its trade relations.

Trade diversion has numerous and diverse effects, including higher consumer prices, loss of foreign currency, and prevention of greater efficiency in the domestic business sector. Therefore, the Ministry of Finance, the Bank of Israel, and the Ministry of Industry and Trade decided in 1990/1991 to introduce a policy of liberalizing imports from third countries within the ambit of policy on prices, foreign currency, and enhancement of domestic economic efficiency. Awareness of the urgent need for liberalization became much stronger when mass immigration from the former Soviet Union ensued, due to fears that the newly landed manpower would be taken in by weak and inefficient industries and would thereby create grave economic problems in the future.

The authors of the liberalization policy presumed that it would be impossible to conclude bilateral trade accords with dozens of countries separately. Thus, they decided to invoke a unilateral liberalization vis-à-vis the General Agreement on Tariffs and Trade (GATT) countries without insisting on reciprocity. The presumption was that the existing situation was costing Israel dearly and should be corrected. The liberalization model was based both on the comparative-advantage theory and on comprehensive empirical findings from countries that had undergone such a process. The conclusion in respect to these countries was that a rapid and "cold turkey" liberalization confers many advantages in terms of prices, foreign currency, efficiencies, and even employment in the industries exposed.

The theory and the empirical findings were compatible. Obviously, the elimination of trade diversions saves foreign currency, and lowering prices enhances economic efficiency. It also stood to reason that exposing domestic raw materials and intermediates to competition would stimulate employment because the exposed industry would be able to compete with imports and export at lower cost. It was assumed, for example, that liberalizing imports of wood from third countries might harm the domestic wood-products industry but would allow the domestic furniture industry to manufacture at lower cost and compete with imported furniture, which was exempt from customs (when it originated in an agreement country) and would also enable this industry to export more. A similar assumption was made in regard to textiles, clothing, and other industries. Thus, policymakers assume that excluding temporary and local difficulties, liberalization amidst mass immigration would stimulate domestic employment, in addition to its other economic advantages. Moreover, at a time of mass immigration, it was crucial to place the new workers in competitive industries in order to prevent economic hardships in the longer term.

Liberalization of Imports from Third Countries: The Phased Approach

In September 1990, the government adopted a policy of exposing the domestic economy to imports from third countries. The ministerial team that was empowered to determine how to implement the policy was composed of the ministers of Finance, Industry and Trade, Justice, and Economics. The team drew up the implementation principles in April 1991 and chose to begin the liberalization process on September 1, 1991. The main principle was the elimination of nontariff barriers, including import licensing and all quantity restrictions, and the imposition of protective tariffs that would be lowered incrementally over a 5–7 year period to a uniform and very low rate (8–12 percent).

The ministers also agreed that firms that had to and were willing to begin adjusting to the new conditions should receive assistance. The import liberalization was applied unilaterally, and no demand for reciprocity was made, it being assumed that bilateral agreements with most countries could not be concluded.

General Decrease in Israel's Import-Tax Burden

In the 1990s, the culmination of agreements with the Common Market and the United States, coupled with the liberalization of imports from third countries, led to a substantial decrease in import taxes, especially in several product groups (foremost, machinery and equipment).

Data on total import taxes (including customs, purchase tax, and compulsory payments)[10] show that the average rate of taxation declined from 11 percent in 1990 to 8.1 percent in 1998. The declines were most conspicuous in intermediates (from 4 percent to 1.7 percent) and machinery and equipment (from 8 percent to 2.4 percent). Gentler decreases were observed in other fields—from 22 percent to 20.8 percent in current consumption goods, from 69 percent for 49.8 percent in durable goods, and from 65 percent to 61.3 percent in transport vehicles.

These aggregate figures show that Israel acted continually to lower its import taxes even when these taxes did not serve entirely to protect domestic manufacture. Thus, it applied the overall process of opening up its economy ubiquitously and at all levels.

9.3 Import Liberalization in Other Fields

Nearly all the liberalization process took place with regard to manufacturing. As the process neared its end, effective protection rates in this field were very low. However, liberalization was also reflected in other fields, several of which are examined below.

Agriculture

GATT, in coordination with the United States Government, applied stiff pressure to all members in 1994–1996 to liberalize agricultural imports as part of the Uruguay Round. A comprehensive agreement in this matter, pertaining mainly to a gradual process of exposing agriculture to imports, was signed in 1996. The basic mechanism set forth in the agreement was the phaseout of nontariff barriers against agricultural imports—including licensing, quotas, and the minimum prices—and the replacement of these arrangements with declining tariffs. It was agreed, however, that countries could protect especially sensitive products by means of import quotas. Because the agreement defined Israel as a "developing" country, Israel was allowed to maintain especially high levels of protection. For quite some time, the ministries of Industry and Trade and Agriculture invoked this prerogative vigorously.

As the agreement was being signed, the two aforementioned ministries, prodded by the Ministry of Finance, agreed to carry out the liberalization with greater celerity than the agreement required, but without renouncing the option of backtracking to the trajectory set forth in the agreement.

The accelerated liberalization was applied in the agriculture and processed-food industries. It stipulated a faster pace of tariff reduction in fresh produce and processed foods, in accordance with various criteria, and a total phaseout of tariffs and licensing requirements at an earlier point in time than the agreement entailed. Maximum fixed-rate tariffs in domestic currency were to be replaced with percent ceilings. Terms were set forth for tariff reduction even at times of "shortage." Again, however, the possibility of a subsequent retreat to the original downward path was retained.

Although Israel's liberalization process was faster than the international agreements required, it left high rates of protection in place and gave the bureaucracy sweeping withdrawal powers. The test for agriculture would be reflected at the level of performance and in the political system's willingness to apply its authority to expedite the process.

Standards

The standards policy was gradually liberalized in 1985–1998, and the trends in this regard corresponded with those relating to the protection of industrial imports (protection of domestic manufacture from competing imports). In the second half of the 1980s, the trend in standards liberalization corresponded to that in protection, as the Ministry of Finance strove to abolish protective standards while the Ministry of Industry and Trade and the manufacturers regarded them as a legitimate protection tool. In the early 1990s, government ministries reached a consensus in favor of terminating the use of standards for nontariff protection purposes. However, since the manufacturers and the Standards Institution continued to apply pressure for such protection (importantly, manufacturers participated in the professional standards committees), the overall result was vague. Not until the second half of the 1990s did the Ministry of Industry and Trade invoke a consistent policy of abolishing protection by means of standards, and it took until November 1998 to complete the official reform in this field. The principles of the reform were as follows:

1. Adoption of international standards to abolish artificial protection of domestic manufacture by means of standards.

2. An explicit statement to the effect that standards should assure public safety and health, protect the environment, provide consumers with information, and assure compatibility and substitutability, and that official standards for any purpose outside these goals should be removed.

3. A decision by the Ministry of Industry and Trade to eliminate the "official" status of half of the official binding standards (approx. 270 of 500—140 pertaining to food and 130 in other fields).

The process of adopting international standards and abolishing standards previously used to protect domestic manufacture caused the import liberalization process to advance to a more effective stage. As the 1990s drew to a close, Israel became one of the most advanced countries in this respect, combining nearly total exposure of domestic manufacture to competing imports with genuine consumer protection.

Expected Effects of the Liberalization Process on Economic Indicators

Israel's liberalization policy in the 1980s and 1990s was typified by the specific goal of exposing domestic manufacture to imports. The process vis-à-vis the European Common Market and the United States was applied consistently and explicitly from the mid-1970s to the first half of 1990; that involving third countries began in the first half of the 1990s and accelerated significantly in the second half of that decade. In view of the theoretical model used above to describe the policy, we would expect the following results:

1. Exposure of the domestic economy to competition in goods and services should lower the prices of tradeable goods relative to nontradeable goods in the domestic market; the liberalization policy should be reflected chiefly in relative prices to the consumer.

2. The general goal in trade policy between the second half of the 1980s and the first half of the 1990s was the preference of imports from the European Common Market and the U.S. relative to third countries. Therefore, we would expect to see the proportion of imports from these two blocs increase relative to imports from the rest of the world.

3. The process trade diversion should continue in the 1990–1993 period. This is because in the first phase of liberalization of imports from third countries (especially September 1991–September 1992), the rates of protection against third-country imports stabilized and actually increased, whereas the elimination of the "third appendix" and the corrections to the percent-quota supplement accelerated openness to

imports from the Common Market and the U.S., especially in industries such as clothing, footwear, leather and leather products, and the like. In the first year of the liberalization program, tariffs were raised very vigorously and the effective protection rate climbed as well.[11]

4. However, imports from third countries should increase substantially even in the early 1990s. The elimination of quantity restrictions facilitated imports of some products considerably, albeit at high rates of tariff protection.

5. In the mid-1990s and the second half of that decade, the appreciable and steady decline in effective rates of protection against imports should lead to an improvement in trade diversion.

6. The process of liberalizing imports from third countries should have no effect of substance on relative employment in the industries exposed. This hypothesis, which corresponded to experience in the West, traces to the various effects of imports on prices and costs of various products. In any product for which the customs barrier is lowered more quickly in the final product than in intermediates, employment in that industry may decrease. In contrast, a substantial reduction in tariffs on imported raw materials and intermediates would make this product better able to compete with imports and exports from the Common Market and the United States, and would enhance employment.

7. The penetration of imports in manufacturing industries should accelerate in the 1990s; for this reason, the share of competing imports in the total activity in each industry should climb.

8. Israeli manufacturing should become less centralized. This should occur relative to the 1980s as a result of opening the economy to the Common Market in the U.S., and in the 1990s due to the completion of the process with the FTA agreement countries and the onset of competing imports from third countries.

The upshot of all these variables is that the ongoing process of trade creation, coupled with an expected decrease in trade diversion, should improve domestic economic efficiency, bring down costs, and enhance consumer welfare.

9.4 The Empirical Model

To examine the effect of Israel's international trade agreements on its trend in foreign trade and determine whether these agreements caused trade diversion, we should not only focus on the changes that occurred in Israeli imports but also survey the fluctuations in global trade all told.

The following empirical analysis examines trends in trade among blocs of countries and Israel's place in these processes, including the effects of the trade policy. The period reviewed is 1975–1997. To perform the examination, we divided the world into the following groups:

- Japan
- United States
- other industrialized countries, including the European Common Market, Canada, Australia, and New Zealand
- Israel
- the rest of the world

This division corresponds mainly to levels of development and industrialization; it isolates Japan from the rest of the "developed" group.

The trends are illustrated in graphic form in figure 9.1, which shows changes in the proportions of imports from various countries in Israel's total imports. The abrupt turnabout that began in 1990 is clearly visible: The share of "other industrialized countries" climbed to 60 percent while that of the "rest of the world" declined to 18 percent, a level that it has maintained to this day. The shares of Japan and the United States remained stable.

For a more detailed examination of the effect of the liberalization policy, we looked into its impact on domestic prices of goods and the changes that occurred in imports of specific products in 1990–1996.

The main goal in exposing the domestic economy to competing imports from third countries was to stimulate competition and, thereby, to lower relative prices. Domestic industries that specialized in manufacturing for the domestic market and had benefited from nontariff protection were subjected to international competition and had to streamline, lower their prices, and expand their exports. To attenuate the effect of the liberalization on the domestic economy, we performed several empirical tests. Table 9.2 contrasts the rates of change in prices of tradeable goods in the Consumer Price Index to the change in the overall CPI in 1991–1997 (the import-liberalization years). During that time, the prices of tradeable goods included in the CPI declined by 2.1 percent per year on average and by 20 percent in cumulative terms. At first glance, these figures correspond to the expectations of the liberalization process.

A restrictive remark is in order: During the years at issue, the global prices of some products included in the liberalization declined steadily. Prices of tradeable goods also declined due to other macroeconomic changes in both the global and the domestic markets (e.g., a change in the composition of domestic production and

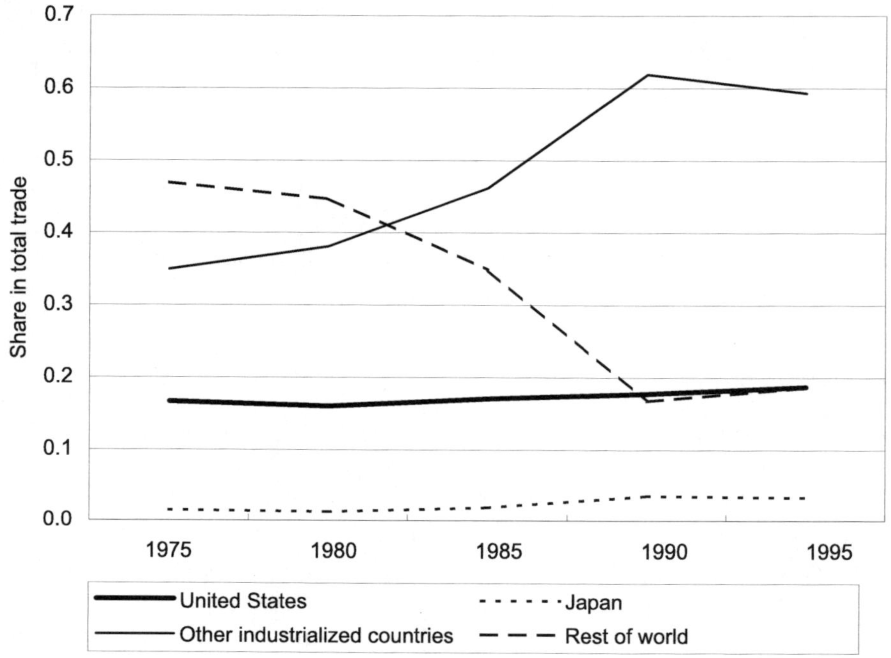

Figure 9.1
Trend in Israeli Imports by Origin, 1975–1995

Table 9.2
Prices of Tradeable Goods vs. CPI, 1991–1997 (Annual percent change)

	Consumer Price Index	Index of tradeable goods within CPI	Pct. change
1991	18	13.3	−4.1
1992	11.9	10.9	−0.9
1993	10.9	7.3	−3.3
1994	12.3	7.8	−4.2
1995	10	8.1	−1.8
1996	11.3	9	−2.1
1997	9	7	−1.9
Average	11.9	9.1	−2.1
Cumulative multiannual	119.4	83.2	19.8

Source: Bank of Israel, *Annual Reports*, 1991–1997.

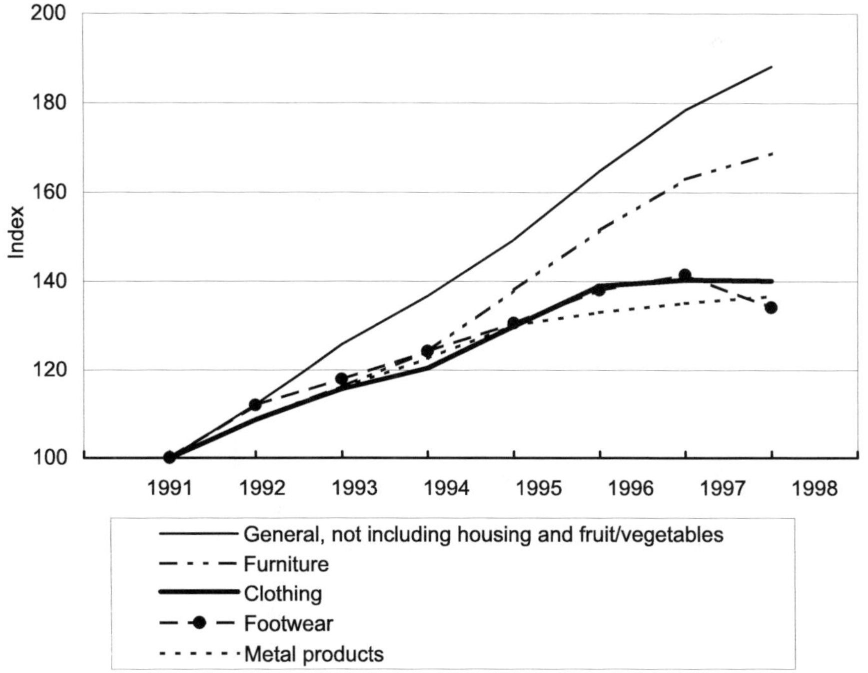

Figure 9.2
Consumer Price Index, Main Industry Groups, 1991–1998

imports and changes in the exchange rate). Were it not for these factors, the effect of the liberalization policy in lowering the prices of tradeable goods would probably have been gentler.

During the period 1991–1998 we could see the relative price effect on salient industries that were exposed to competing imports. During that time, domestic prices (excluding housing and fruit/vegetables) climbed by 88 percent while prices in import-liberalized industries rose more gently—furniture by 68 percent, clothing by 40 percent, footwear by 34 percent, and metal by 36 percent. Consequently, prices in these industries decreased by 12–40 percent in real terms. Figure 9.2 and table 9.3 show this trend. These figures definitely support the claim that the liberalization process lowered real domestic prices.

We also examine the behavior of the wholesale price index of industrial output for domestic use in salient industries that were "exposed" in 1991–1998. This index actually monitors the trend in GDP prices only in relevant industries that may be

Table 9.3
Consumer Price Index, Main Industry Groups, 1991–1998

	Metal products	Footwear	Clothing	Furniture	General, excl. housing and fruit/vegetables
1991	100.00	100.00	100.00	100.00	100.00
1992	108.35	111.78	108.53	108.61	111.93
1993	115.97	117.91	115.63	116.16	125.83
1994	122.69	124.28	120.49	124.29	136.78
1995	130.23	130.65	129.97	138.11	149.37
1996	133.13	138.08	138.99	151.47	164.84
1997	135.22	141.50	140.37	162.97	178.43
1998	136.72	134.18	140.14	168.78	188.25

Source: Central Bureau of Statistics, *Price Statistics Quarterly*, 1991–1998.

import substitutes. Here, too, a trend of real price decrease is visible. The general index climbed by 71 percent during this time, but textile prices rose by 48 percent, footwear and leather products by 44 percent, and metal products by 64 percent. However, prices of furniture climbed by 95 percent, reflecting a substantial increase in real terms. This aberration may be attributable to a tendency to divide up the domestic furniture market, with imports gravitating to the market for simpler and cheaper furniture and domestic manufacturing focusing on higher quality and prestige products. Growth in the domestic furniture market at large and structural changes in the lumber and plywood industry may also explain the outrider.

In sum, the import liberalization policy attained one of its main goals, a significant relative decrease in prices of tradeable goods in the domestic market and, for this reason, the enhancement of consumer welfare. The trend is also reflected in saving in foreign currency due to lower prices of imported sources.

Additional significant findings with regard to the results of the policy may be seen in tables 9.4 and 9.5, which show the rates of competing import penetration and centralization in main industry groups in 1980–1994.[12] The assumptions, as stated, are that imports made large inroads in manufacturing in the 1990s and that the liberalization of imports from all countries of origin during the period at issue should reduce centralization.

The most noteworthy industries are wood and wood products, in which the import penetration rate climbed from 12 percent in 1982 to 20 percent in 1994, leather (from 24 percent to 40 percent), and textiles (23 percent to 45 percent). Food (meat, fish, oil, and dairy) remained stable, reflecting continuity in the protection policy. The centralization rate, too—the share of the three largest establishments in each indus-

Table 9.4
Penetration of Competing Imports, Main Industry Groups, Percent (Current prices)

	1980/81	1982/83	1985/86	1988	1990	1992	1994
Total	22.1	21.2	21.6	24.9	25.0	26.8	30
Meat, fish, oil, and dairy	13.1	11.6	9.7	9.5	10.1	9.9	12.4
Textiles	23.3	27.0	33.6	38.4	39.1	40.8	45.5
Leather and leather products	23.9	32.3	24.9	35.4	34.7	33.6	40
Wood and wood products	12.2	12.1	12.3	12.2	15.0	13.7	20
Metal products	17.4	13.0	20.8	20.4	19.8	20.1	21.2

Table 9.5
Centralization Rates, Main Industry Groups (Current prices)

	1980/81	1982/83	1985/86	1988	1990	1992	1994
Total	40.6	42.7	39.76	35.82	33.79	31.2	29
Meat, fish, oil, and dairy	49.79	52.54	45.48	45.76	52.95	50.5	51.3
Textiles	32.48	38.07	34.5	29.41	22.22	16.9	15
Leather and leather products	25.81	25.09	23.94	21.78	19.88	17.5	11.9
Wood and wood products	34.88	28.48	27.68	26.24	23.79	22.4	19.5
Metal products	41.13	43.85	34.53	34.66	31.76	24.9	20.4

try in the total market—has declined markedly since the early 1980s and with increasing momentum strength in the 1990s. Between 1981 and 1994, centralization rates declined from 32 percent to 15 percent in textiles, from 26 percent to 12 percent in leather products, from 35 percent to 19 percent in wood products, and from 41 percent to 20 percent in metal products. Centralization in the food industry remained stable during this time, evidently due to a high and stable level of protection. These findings are consistent with the import liberalization policy, which was applied in an incomplete manner in the 1980s (in the form of substitution among ways of protecting domestic manufacture) and more effectively in the 1990s. Both the tables and figures 9.3 and 9.4 illuminate the rising share of competing imports in the domestic market—a trend that had been vague in the 1980s but gathered much momentum in the 1990s.

Another aspect of the liberalization process concerns the value of imports and average taxes paid by importers between 1991 and 1998. Our hypothesis here is that import taxes declined gradually from the Common Market and the U.S. and, gradually, from third countries, even though in the early 1990s, import barriers from

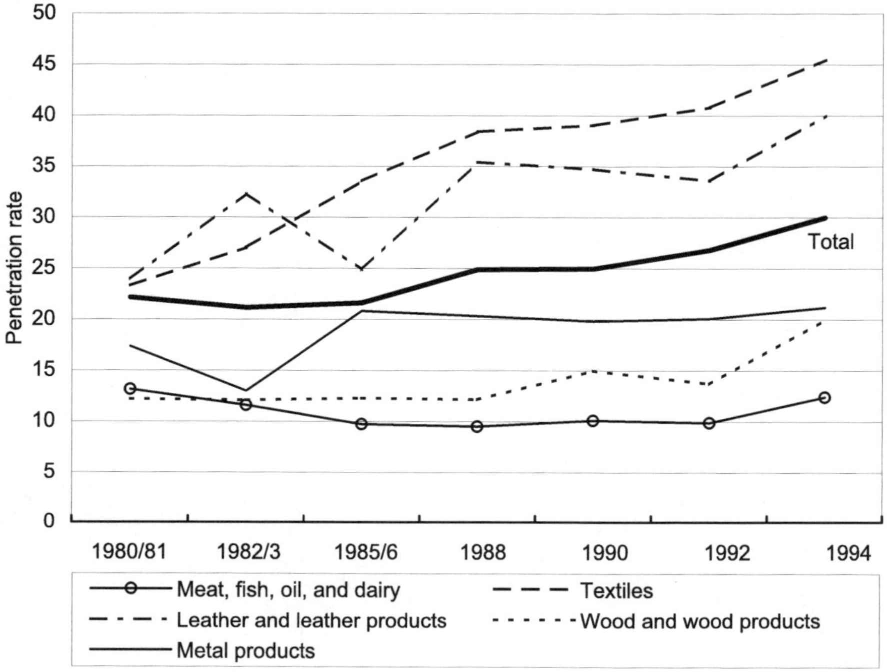

Figure 9.3
Penetration of Competing Imports, Main Industry Groups, 1980–1994

third countries were eliminated and the tariff rates were actually raised (foremost in clothing and footwear). In this table, we examined the trend in total current-consumption imports and taxes paid on their account, and probed the trajectory of these trends in two salient industry groups that were exposed to competing imports during those years—clothing and footwear, and furniture and household appliances. The total value of these imported consumption goods climbed by 300 percent; total taxes paid on account of them rose by 265 percent; and total customs paid on account of them increased by only 76 percent. In clothing and footwear, however, import value climbed by 687 percent, total taxes paid climbed by only 31 percent, and total customs paid climbed by 518 percent. In furniture and household appliances, import value climbed by 330 percent, total taxes by 93 percent, and customs by 82 percent.

In imports of current consumption goods, both the share of total taxes and that of the customs component declined perceptibly. In clothing and footwear, however, a decline in the share of noncustoms import taxes, that is, purchase taxes, is clearly

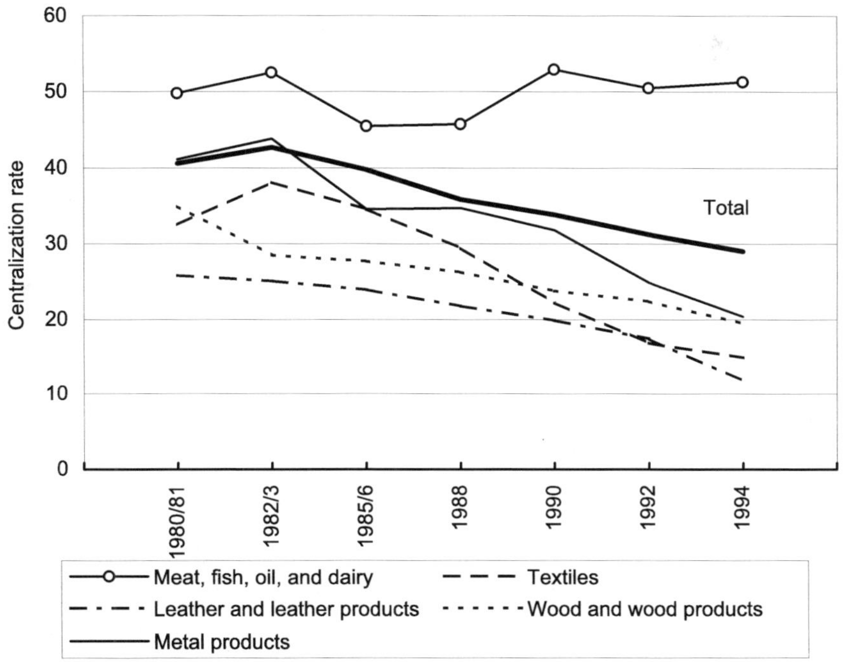

Figure 9.4
Centralization Rates, Main Industry Groups, 1980–1994

evident. Practically speaking, purchase taxes on clothing and footwear have been revoked since 1993. In furniture and household appliances, the share of total taxes including customs declined in parallel fashion. Another salient figure is the significant increase in the share of clothing and footwear in total current-consumption imports—from 10 percent in 1991 to 22 percent in 1996. Customs receipts on account of these products increased in proportional terms because the liberalization policy abolished administrative and quantity barriers and replaced them, in part, with tariffs.

In sum, the gradual liberalization of imports from all country blocs was reflected in a significant decrease in tariffs, except in industries for which tariffs were used as a substitute for previous nontariff barriers. Concurrently, devaluation substitutes in imports were eliminated in an accelerated process.

Table 9.6 charts the trend in state revenues from devaluation substitutes and their share in total revenues of the Customs and Value Added Tax Division in 1985–1993. The proportional decline in revenues from devaluation substitutes went from 27.4 percent of total Division revenues in 1985 to only 4.2 percent in 1993. This provides

Table 9.6
Total Revenues from Devaluation Substitutes, 1985–1993 (NIS millions, constant prices)

	Total revenues		Share of devaluation substitutes in total revenues
	Devaluation substitutes	Customs and VAT Division	
1985	433.7	1,582.0	0.27
1986	1,042.4	6,750.0	0.15
1987	1,425.0	9,786.6	0.15
1988	1,323.3	10,605.3	0.12
1989	1,080.5	11,229.0	0.10
1990	1,103.7	13,978.9	0.08
1991	1,327.0	19,554.0	0.07
1992	1,600.0	25,000.0	0.06
1993	1,151.0	27,337.0	0.04

Source: Reports of the State Revenues Administration, 1985–1993.

unequivocal evidence of the efficacy of the liberalization policy in the additional respect of eliminating devaluation substitutes, as figure 9.5 shows in graphic form.

As the devaluation substitutes were being abolished, tariffs on imports from the Common Market and the United States, which account for most of Israel's imports, were steadily phased out. In imports from the "rest of the world," the process was more complex. Until the liberalization began in 1991, tariffs were in the low to medium range (0–35 percent) but came with quantitative and other restrictions. In the course of liberalization, tariffs were raised steeply (as the quantity restrictions were eliminated), and their spread was widened considerably. In 1992, the rates (including the fixed domestic-currency tariff) ranged from 0 percent to more than 100 percent and the mode was 0–65 percent. Since the tariffs were gradually lowered, the tariff spread also narrowed, and by September 1998, tariffs on imports from third countries fell to a 0–12 percent range except in clothing and footwear, in which the 20 percent tariff was to decline to 8–12 percent in 2000. In sum, tariffs and deviation from the mean are very low today. Thus, a unification of rates has occurred in customs, too. See figure 9.5.

The figures show, as stated, that Israel attained its goal of abolishing devaluation substitutes in the mid-1990s, making it possible to complete the processes of foreign-currency liberalization.

9.5 Summary and Prognosis

As we have seen, the 1990s were decisive years in the trajectory of Israel's economic liberalization and global integration. The historical decision that made this possible

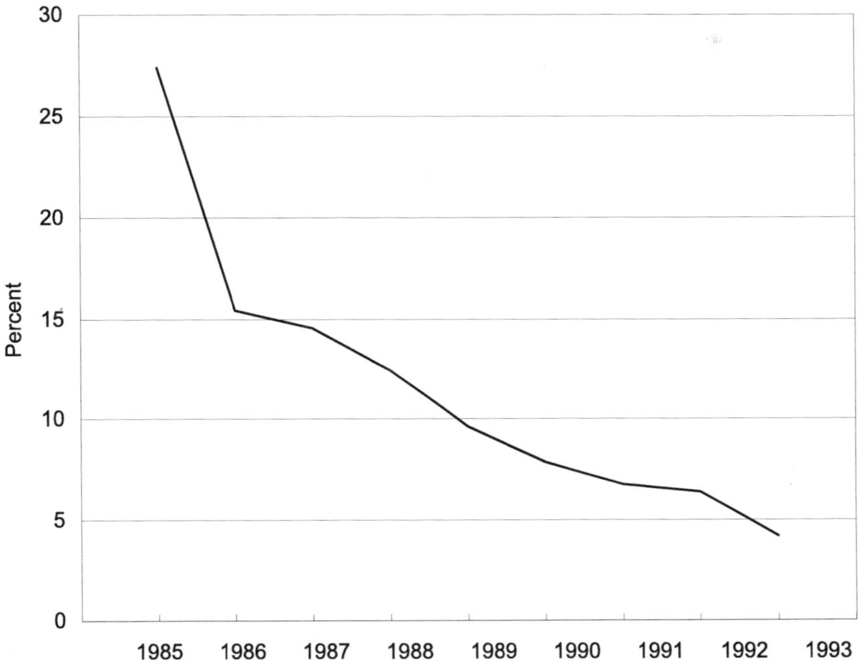

Figure 9.5
Share of Import Devaluation Substitutes in Customs and VAT Division Revenues, 1985–1993

had far-reaching and highly favorable results from the standpoint of the Israeli consumer and economy. The range of available goods expanded greatly, prices of tradeable goods declined substantially, and economic centralization diminished. This process slowly but steadily mitigated trade diversions and, consequently, led to savings in foreign currency.

Because Israel invoked its import liberalization at a time of mass immigration from the former Soviet Union, its economy absorbed the extra increment of labor in industries that were making efficiency efforts. The liberalization and immigration processes converged, and unemployment rates declined from 12 percent to 6 percent and the additional labor integrated into all industries. In the first half of the decade, the employment growth occurred in all industries—those exposed to competing imports and others as well.[13] For example, most employment growth in the first half of the 1990s took place in an "exposed" industry, furniture, and a similar process occurred in plastic and rubber products. Employment expanded even more swiftly in these industries than in those that had always been tradeable, such as electronic communications equipment, electronic components, and electrical motors. The trend changed in the second half of the decade;[14] at that time, the increase in employment became more perceptible in industries that required sophisticated personnel and were more open, as opposed to those already exposed to competing imports and defined as less sophisticated.

In the final reckoning, the liberalization processes as such did not seem to affect domestic employment trends adversely. Thus, the rates of unemployment and employment were modified by other macroeconomic conditions. During those years, Israel completed the process of opening its economy and became one of the most open economies in the world, in which its comparative-advantage industries would blossom. Complementary liberalization measures are still needed in several fields, such as agriculture, pharmaceuticals, state tenders, and domestic competition. However, the main liberalization measures have already been completed or will have been completed by 2000. Israel has created competitive conditions for greater economic efficiency. Complementary policy action in investments, education, infrastructure, and R&D will allow the Israeli economy to realize its comparative advantages fully, to the benefit of the wealth and welfare of the Israeli consumer and worker.

Notes

The authors thank Eldad Brick for his assistance.

1. Iceland, Liechtenstein, Norway, and Switzerland.
2. Tsippi Galyam, unpublished internal material, Bank of Israel Research Department.
3. Halevi (1994), p. 13.
4. Halevi (1994), p. 14.
5. Halevi (1994), p. 15.
6. Halevi (1994), pp. 15–16.
7. Eini (1994), pp. 92–93.
8. Ben-Bassat (1995).
9. Pelzmann (1994), p. 57.
10. Bank of Israel, *Annual Report*, 1998, p. 314.
11. Halevi and Bartov (1993), p. 122.
12. Regev and Bar Eliezer (1994) and updates for 1992–1994.
13. Israel Democracy Institute (1999), p. 189.
14. Bank of Israel, *Annual Report*, 1998, p. 119.

References

Bank of Israel, *Annual Report* (1991–1997).

Ben-Bassat, Avi. "The Exchange-Rate Regime, the Monetary Policy, and the Inflation Target." *Bank of Israel Research Department*, Discussion Article 95.10, Jerusalem, September 1995.

Eini, Dalida. "Nominal and Effective Protection of Israeli Industry." In *The Import Policy and Exposure of Israeli Industry [to Competing Imports]*, edited by Nadav Halevi (pp. 59–95). Jerusalem: The Maurice Falk Institute for Economic Research in Israel, 1994.

Halevi, Nadav. "General Survey." In *The Import Policy and Exposure of Israeli Industry [to Competing Imports]*, edited by Nadav Halevi (pp. 1–18). Jerusalem: The Maurice Falk Institute for Economic Research in Israel, 1994.

——— and Bartov Hedva. "The September 1991 Import Liberalization Policy and Its Effects in the First Year," In Halevi, ed. 1994.

Israel Democracy Institute (1999). "Integration of Israel into the Global Economy," p. 189, part of "The Growth-Resumption Policy," the Sixth Economic Conference, June 1998.

Papageorgiou, Demetris, Michael Michaely, and Armeane M. Choski, eds. *Liberalizing Foreign Trade*, vol. 7, Lessons of Experience in the Developing World. Washington, D.C.: IBRD, Blackwell, 1991.

Pelzmann, Yosef. "Domestic Taxes as a Substitute for Foreign-Trade Policy." In Halevi, ed. (pp. 43–58), 1994.

Regev, Chaim, and Simha Bar-Eliezer. "Control of the Domestic Economy and Economic Functioning in Israel Industry." Jerusalem: The Maurice Falk Institute for Economic Research in Israel, Discussion Article 94.05 (and updates for 1992–1994), 1994.

10 Structural Changes in Israeli Public Utilities—The Reform That Never Was

Reuben Gronau

10.1 Introduction

The Israeli economy emerged from the inflationary crisis of the mid-1980s with the awareness that the economy requires, beyond the immediate macroeconomic solutions, a thorough structural change to uproot the hard core of inflation, and open the pass to sustainable growth. The required structural changes encompassed the labor and capital markets, manufacturing, agriculture, banking, and government services. A key role in these changes was to be played by the public utilities. The lively discussion during the last decade concerning the structural changes in the public utilities may seem surprising given the little interest in the topic during the first four decades of Israel's existence. The prime contributors to the awakened interest were the winds of deregulation and reforms blowing from the outside, the recognition that the present structure of the industry impedes the development of the infrastructure industries and the growth of the rest of the economy, and the recognition that the reduction of the government's intervention in the economy involves the privatization of these industries.

This chapter will describe the successes and failures in introducing the desired structural changes and other reforms in the public utilities industries. The industries discussed are electricity, communication, public transport, ports, and fuel.[1] Common to all these industries is their monopolistic structure, and the focus of the discussion are the attempts to open them to competition.

10.2 The Public Utilities Industries—Institutional Background

Traditionally, public utilities are associated with returns to scale giving rise to natural monopolies (Crew and Klindorfer, 1979). If the creation of the monopolies in the public utility industry in Israel can be explained by economic forces (returns to scale and market size), there is little in the economic development since their creation to explain the preservation of their monopolistic power. This explanation can only be found in the political sphere—in the explanation of government behavior.

The electric company and the refineries were established as private companies, receiving at their birth (1926 and 1933) a seventy-year franchise from the British government. The franchise gave the electric company exclusivity in the supply of electric power in Palestine. (In the case of the refineries, it assured the company some tax breaks and property rights on its site, but did not assure exclusivity.) Both companies were bought by the Israeli government in the 1950s (in 1953 and 1959, respectively), when the original owners tried to disassociate themselves from the new state.

Phone services, ports, and railroads were governmental departments under the British mandate, and continued to be so under the Israeli government. To allow them more flexibility, they were given different levels of autonomy: ports became an independent authority in 1961, and a special law assured the authority monopoly power on all Israeli shores (the only exception being the oil port in Ashkelon). In 1988 the Port Authority took over the Israeli Railroads Company. The phone services, which were part of the Transport Ministry, and later the Ministry of Communication, were handed over in 1984 to a government company "Bezek—the Israeli Communication Company," which had by law exclusive rights to all communication services in the state.

The only nongovernment owned industry is the bus service industry. The industry is dominated by two major cooperatives—one serving the Tel Aviv metropolitan area and the other the rest of the country.[2] These companies were created by a series of mergers. Because the operation of regular bus services required a permit by the Ministry of Transport, the companies used their political clout to prevent any new entrants into the industry.

The concentration of public utilities in government hands was accompanied by the establishment of various organs to regulate their tariffs. Regulation was split between the various ministries supervising the operation of the companies (the Ministry of Energy oversaw electricity rates, the Ministry of Communication, phone rates, etc.). The parliament (Knesset) reserved the right to be the final arbitrator of all public utility rates. But also in this case, the authority was split between various parliamentary committees. The multitude of regulating bodies resulted in a hodgepodge system characterized mostly by perfect pass-through of costs.

Things got even worse in the late 1970s following the oil crisis and the accelerated inflation. The Ministry of Finance, which played a key role in setting the public utility rates, attempted frequently to postpone the rate adjustment with the hope that it would decelerate price increases in the economy. As a result of the multitude of bodies responsible for the rate setting, the rate system emerged from the period of three-digit inflation lacking any resemblance to the underlying cost structure. At the same time, government ownership, monopoly power, lack of supervision, and inflation resulted in gross inefficiencies that plagued the industry.

10.3 The Implications of the Monopolistic Structure for the Public Utilities

The classical monopoly is assumed to increase its profits by curtailing output and raising prices. This model of behavior clearly does not describe the activities of the government-owned monopolies in the public utilities in the 1970s and the 1980s. Even if the owner aimed for higher profits, it is doubtful that he possessed the transmission and enforcement mechanisms to make the companies' management follow his wishes. But the government intentionally gave up profits to attain other targets—social aims in the sphere of income distribution, the encouragement of certain industries (e.g., agriculture) or certain activities (e.g., exports), and the slowing down of inflation. Relinquishing the profit motive led to a series of misallocations affecting the industries efficiency, wages, and relative prices.

Government-owned companies are popularly associated with inefficiency. There is little systematic research in Israel to support this claim. Ben-Ishai (1996) examined four companies that were privatized during the period 1986–1989. Only in one company, he found, was privatization associated with increased profitability. Though systematic research is scarce, there is, however, an abundance of anecdotal evidence to support this claim.

Inefficiency can take many forms: a nonoptimum investment policy, excess manpower, and delays in the adoption of technological innovations. Most public utilities are capital intensive. The size and timing of investment, therefore, play a crucial role in determining the firm's cost. Government ownership secured for the companies an easy access to cheap funding, but involved a cumbersome decision process. The effect of government ownership on the timing of investment is, therefore, indeterminate. Excess investment in ports (Ganot, 1985), the shift from cheap to expensive buses (Gronau, 1997), and the speed of replacement of analogue by digital exchanges in the phone service are examples of premature investments. The delay in the introduction of coal in the production of electricity is an example of the second kind of inefficiency.

Whereas the excess capacity of capital is hard to detect, surplus manpower is widely reported. The production processes of many of the public utilities underwent significant technological changes in the last thirty years—coal-operated turbines in electricity generation, digital exchanges in phone service, containerization in ports; and electronic control processes in electricity, phone service, and the refining industry. The common feature of all these innovations is their labor-saving aspect. The downscaling of the labor force is usually a slow process. It has been slowed down even further by strong labor unions and government ownership. The slow adjustment hurt less fast-growing firms, but became especially apparent in firms that suffered from slower growth rates. An international comparison, for example, showed that the output per worker in the Israeli refineries is only 60 percent of the European standard (Gronau, 1996).

Wages in Public Utilities

Monopolistic status and government ownership contributed to the creation of a rent-sharing mechanism, whose main beneficiaries were the providers of the factors of production. Suppliers of machines and equipment to the government monopolies enjoyed generous markups (the profits of the domestic suppliers of the phone and electricity companies can bear witness to this), and the monopolies' labor force enjoyed inflated wages.

The high wages paid by the phone company and the public transport companies result in communication and transport industries' wages exceeding the average wage in the economy by 15 to 30 percent (with the gap widening over the years). The water and electricity industries already enjoyed in the early 1960s wages that exceeded the national average by 60 percent. By the 1990s, the gap was more than 100 percent.[3] Klinov (1998), who standardized these wages by the measured quality of workers (using a Mincer wage function) found industry premiums ranging between 13 to 28 percent compared to wages in trade.

Real wages increases offset any attempt to reduce labor costs by reducing the labor force over the period 1993–1997. The phone company was successful in shedding 17 percent of its workers, but this effort was invalidated by an increase of 18 percent of real wages (wages in the business sector grew during that period by only 4 percent). In the period 1991–1995, the refineries reduced their labor force by 14 percent, but at the same time real wages grew by 39 percent (six times the growth of industrial wages, and 1.5 times the growth of government employees). The ports were able to reduce their labor force during the period 1985–1993 by 10 percent, only to see their wage bill growing by 62 percent as a result of a 81 percent wage hike.

To an outside observer, it may look like wage hikes were the price paid by management in order to buy the insiders' consent to labor force contractions. This must have been a very short-sighted policy to follow.

A special place in this landscape of inflated wages is reserved for the wages of cooperative members in public transport. In the early 1990s, wages constituted over 60 percent of the cost of that industry (Gronau, 1997a). Cooperative members contributed over two-thirds of the wage bill. Their wages were already in the early 1960s 2.6 times the average wage in the economy and this gap was preserved throughout the 1970s and the 1980s.

The wage of cooperative members is supposed to compensate them for their labor as well as capital and managerial inputs. Their wages were throughout the period more than twice that of nonmember employees of their companies. A standardization by occupation shows that the ownership premium constituted two-thirds of the nonmembers' wages.

A series of agreements signed in the 1970s between government and the cooperatives governing bus rates and subsidies were intended to erode the wage of cooperative members. The government, however, never tried to enforce this part of the agreement. In 1991, cooperative member wages exceeded by 40 percent the agreed wage, and the gap for noncooperative employees was 20 percent (Gronau, 1997a). These wage increases were the major sources of cost increases in the 1970s and 1980s. The government subsidy instead of constraining wage growth—inflamed it. Subsidies were determined by wage increases, and fare revenue played an ever-decreasing role in the cooperative wage policy.

The sharp increase in bus costs (over 50 percent) in the 1970s and 1980s is especially noteworthy given the stagnant market in which the companies operated. Bus-km did not increase during the period, and the revenue in constant bus prices from scheduled service (a proxy for passenger-kms) even declined by one quarter (Gronau, 1997a). The cooperatives were able to maintain, with government's cooperation, their monopoly on the scheduled service, but lost their hold on the market for nonscheduled bus services (tourist tours, special busing to places of work, school busing, etc.) Private companies specializing in these services who owned only seven hundred buses in 1971 owned five times that number in 1991, and accounted for 40 percent of total bus-km. The labor cost per km, which was in the cooperatives two and a half times that of the private companies, was a major contributor to the flourishing of the private bus sector.

The Tariff Structure in the 80s—Cross-Subsidization

A common feature of public utilities is the large fixed component in their costs. This component confronts management with a major problem when it sets its service rates: how to establish rates that will yield right signals to users about the real cost of the service, and allow the coverage of the fixed costs. Most companies failed this test. Their rate structure barely reflected costs, and mirrored mostly the special interests of the bodies involved in the rate setting. A main feature of the public utility rates was cross-subsidization. The patterns of cross-subsidy differed from one service to the next, and therefore, require separate discussions.

Electricity Fluctuations in electricity rates reflected primarily fluctuation in oil prices. These were affected by world prices and the government's policy of subsidizing fuel oil (the main fuel used in electricity generation until the early 1980s). The economy benefited from the decline in oil prices in the 1960s and early 1970s (leading to a reduction of electricity rates (in real terms) of over 40 percent). When oil prices started to increase after the first oil crisis, the government tried to mitigate the increase in electricity rates by subsidizing fuel oil prices (Barkai, 1986). This policy was abandoned after the second oil crisis. Only in 1982 was coal introduced as the base source of energy, severing the tie between oil prices and electricity rates.

Throughout the period, the rate structure was characterized by tariff discrimination. Households paid a rate that was almost twice the rate paid by industry, which in turn paid a rate higher than water pumping. In the early 1990s, the rate consisted of three components—a monthly fixed charge, an energy charge, and a charge dependent on the daily maximum consumption (a "peak-demand" charge). The latter was introduced as an incentive to reduce demand fluctuations. These components varied by the user's industry branch. In 1982, the electricity company introduced peak-load pricing covering large industrial consumers and water pumping. This system was expanded in the early nineties to cover almost half of annual consumption, but the company preserved the "peak-demand" component and the sectorial differentiation.

It is hard to discern the patterns of cross-subsidization in such a complex system, but it seems that the variation in sectorial prices declined during the 1980s.

Phone The phone network consists of two parts—the connection of the customer's premise to the exchange, and the interexchange network. The first part ("the private loop") is reserved for the exclusive use of the customer, whereas the second part is like a public thoroughfare. In a fare structure based on costs, the cost associated with the first section (which are a prerequisite for obtaining the service) should be covered by a fixed payment (a monthly charge or installation costs), and the payment for the use of the second part should depend on the traffic generated by the customers. The high cost of a new line (the private loop constitutes about 40 percent of the cost of the network) and the reluctance of rate makers to set such high fixed charges, resulted in a system where traffic rates (domestic and international) are significantly higher than their costs, and the differences cover the "access deficit." According to the Meidan Committee, which investigated the phone rate structure in 1988 and 1992, monthly charges and installation rates covered only 15 percent of the costs of access. This created a system in which heavy users (e.g., the business sector) subsidized low-volume users (e.g., the household sector).[4]

Ports The port tariff structure has always been based on the discriminatory principle of "what the traffic can bear." To cover the investment in the breakwater and the deepening of the anchorage, the port authority established a "wharfage fee" based on the value of the freight. The high wharfage fee allowed for low stevedoring and porterage charges and for low vessel charges, giving the wrong signals to both shippers and ship companies.

In contrast to other public utilities in which cross-subsidization was disguised, tariff discrimination was the port authority's official policy. Whereas imports had to pay a 2 percent wharfage fee, exports were exempt. Export loading charges were only 30–70 percent of the unloading charges of identical import items. In this system, 10 percent of the import freight contributed half of the wharfage fee revenue, which, in turn, constituted half of the port authority's total revenues.

Fuel The prices of the different oil products were determined by government. Some of these products (most notably, gasoline) were subject to a fuel tax, and some were exempt. To mitigate the fluctuations in oil prices, the government established an "equalization fund." However, as the years passed, the fund abandoned its original aim and was used as an additional taxation tool, and a channel through which gasoline taxes were diverted to subsidize diesel oil.

Gasoline taxes were always a major source of tax revenue. In the 1960s, they constituted 5.0–6.5 percent of government income (1.6–2.6 percent of GDP). The income from this source allowed the generous subsidization of other fuels, most notably, diesel oil and fuel oil. In the 1950s and 1960s, the retail price of gasoline was 3.5–6 times that of diesel oil, though their price at the refinery gate was almost equal (Barkai, 1986).

Following the first oil crisis, the government tried to mitigate the hike in oil prices (absorbing over half of the world price increase) by lowering tax rates. The lower gasoline tax rates and the shift of an ever-increasing number of commercial vehicles from gasoline to diesel oil brought a revaluation of the government subsidy policies and a reduction in the gasoline-diesel oil price ratio.

The outbreak of inflation in 1977 and the second oil crisis led to dramatic changes in the government's tax policy. In an attempt to insulate the economy from the oil price increases, gasoline taxes were slashed drastically (with the government absorbing 80 percent of the price increase). In four years, 1975–1979, fuel taxation turned from a source of income (of about 2 percent of GDP) into a source of expenditures (the net subsidy accounting for 0.5 percent of GDP). The attempt to postpone oil price and electricity rate increases forced the government to accelerate the increase in the subsidy rate. In 1982, oil subsidies rose to a level of 1.7 percent of GDP. Gasoline tax rates shrank to their lowest level (40 percent), as did the gasoline/diesel oil price ratio (Barkai, 1986).

The erosion of the gasoline tax base (a decline in absorption of 4.2 percent of GDP) had an important role in increasing the government's budget deficit and in inflaming inflation. Only in 1982 did the government abandon this futile policy and raise fuel taxes.

Public Transport Whereas in most public utilities (electricity, phone service, ports) cross-subsidization was an outgrowth of the need to cover large fixed costs, this motive does not exist in the case of public transport, where inputs are highly divisible and fixed costs are small. In this case, cross-subsidization was a direct outcome of the government's subsidy policy.

The subsidy of public transport was initiated in 1968, as part of the government social policy. The income elasticity of bus service is less than unitary (Sadka, 1985), and subsidizing this service, as part of government's subsidy policy of basic goods and services, was intended to improve resource distribution. The late 1970s witnessed an expansion of the policy's aims—a prime aim became the mitigation of price increases during the inflation period.

The increase in fuel costs and wages increased the real costs of bus service during the period 1971–1984 by over 50 percent. The cost rise did not affect tariffs, which remained unchanged and even declined in real terms (Gronau, 1997). To cover this gap, government had to increase its subsidy eightfold. The subsidy, which initially contributed only about 15 percent to the companies' revenue from scheduled service, constituted over 60 percent in the early 1980s (and was the source of over one-half of total bus revenue).

Also in this case, the drain of government resources forced it to abandon this policy. In the years 1984–1986, subsidy was slashed by one third, and bus rates increased (in real terms) by 80 percent.

In contrast to other goods receiving a government subsidy, the bus subsidy was never determined on the basis of output, and took the form of a fixed payment to the service provider. The subsidy to the individual line was, therefore, determined by their cost of operation and the rate set by the Ministry of Transport. It is not surprising that in this scheme the intrinsic cross-subsidization served neither distributional nor allocative aims.

Bloom (1980) investigated the rate structure of the major provider and compared the rates with the cost per passenger, where costs are affected by speed of travel and the load factors. According to his calculations, only 15 percent of the lines were profitable. These were the heavily traveled intercity express lines. In the lightly traveled regional lines, revenues covered barely half the costs. A similar coverage rate was found for the urban lines, due to low speed and slow turnover time. The urban lines contributed two thirds of the company's losses.

10.4 The Reform That Happened and Did Not Happen

The containment of the inflationary wave in 1985 was accompanied by a call for a reduction in government's involvement in the economy, and especially, its direct activity in the business sector. The call for privatization, originating abroad, was enforced by the government's need for additional funds that it hoped to raise through the sale of assets, and by the belief that the transfer of firms from government to private ownership would raise their efficiency.

The distinction between the privatization of natural monopolies and other government owned firms was established already in the first discussions of this topic both in government and academic circles (*Economic Quarterly*, 1998). There was an agreement that in the case of monopolies (a group that includes the electricity, phone, and water companies as well as the refineries), privatization has to be preceded by regulation and liberalization. Privatization without liberalization, it was argued, creates insurmountable obstacles to any structural change in the future. The need for liberalization became especially acute for those monopolies whose seventy-year franchise was running out. Consequently, government reform efforts proceeded on two parallel tracks—liberalization and regulation. The story of the public utilities reforms is the story of progress (or lack of progress) on these two tracks.

The Reform That Did Not Happen—Structural Changes in the Electricity Company

The seventy-year franchise assuring the Israeli Electric Company (IEC) monopoly power in the electricity market was to expire in March 1996. In January 1992, the government appointed a committee (the Vardi Committee) to examine the implications of the extension of the franchise. The committee examined a number of questions: should the franchise be extended, or should it be replaced by a series of limited permits? Should the IEC's exclusivity in the market be extended? Should the company be split into separate companies, each responsible for a different stage of the production process (generation, transmission and distribution)? What should be the role of independent power producers (IPPs) in the future market?

The committee concluded that the main principle to guide the government's decisions should be increased efficiency, while maintaining a balance of the interests between the different actors—customers, the company and its owners, and other potential producers. It was argued that the existing structure of the IEC constitutes an obstacle to competition and increased efficiency. The committee recognized that the returns to scale in production are confined to the transmission stage, and that given the present market size, the company exhausted the returns to scale in the power generation and the distribution stages, but it stopped short of recommending a split-up of the company according to the different stages of the production processes. It recommended that the franchise be replaced by a series of permits for each of the separate activities involved in the production process, and that none of these permits should assure the company the continuity of exclusivity it had enjoyed for the past seventy years. Each of the company's units should be run as a separate profit center.

The Minister of Energy was asked to establish rules to encourage the entry of new competitors in the field. These independent producers would be allowed to sell either to the national transmission network or to large consumers directly. The committee recommended that the regulatory responsibilities should be split: The right of granting permits and determining and enforcing quality standards should be left with government, and the responsibility of setting tariffs, accounting rules, and serving as consumer protector, should be transferred to a newly established Public Utility Commission (PUC).

An implementation committee (the Czamanski Committee) that had been asked to set the detailed rules to govern the activities of the government and the company in the future went even further in its recommendation—a complete split-up of the company, and the privatization of the production and distribution stages. According to this scenario, only the transmission company should remain in government ownership after the year 2000.

The Minister of Energy rejected the recommendations of the Czamanski Committee, and the new law preserved all the rights the IEC had in the past. The only change was a replacement of the franchise by a ten-year permit. The proposed new law also preserved all the regulatory responsibilities in the Ministry of Energy, and the PUC was, according to the proposal, supposed to be part of the Ministry. Independent power producers were restricted to sell the energy to the IEC during the first ten years of the law.

The Finance Ministry backed the Ministry of Energy in its objection to a split-up of the company but tried, unsuccessfully, to shorten the duration of the permit. It was more successful in its fight to make the PUC an independent agency, and allow the independent producers to sell directly to large customers.[5] The new law introduced in March 1996 was vague about the body responsible for quality standards (according to the law, these responsibilities were held both by the Ministry of Energy and the PUC).

The new law postponed all structural change for a decade. The Ministry of Energy, which fought any attempt of liberalization, tried to undermine even the few liberalizing elements incorporated in the new law. In the first bid for an independent power producer, it forbade the direct sell to customers, and had to withdraw only after the intervention of the court.

Communication The attempt to liberalize the electricity market is definitely the most resounding defeat in the attempt to bring structural change to the public utilities. The communication market is clearly the most shining success. These two services are the fastest growing public utilities in terms of output,[6] and their liberalization had, therefore, the most far-reaching long-run implications for the industry and the economy. The differences in the outcomes of the two reforms cannot be traced to economic factors, but rather to political ones. The reform in the electricity market was forced on the political level by an outside timetable, that is, the expiration of the IEC franchise. The failure of the reform is closely tied with the rejection by the political level (the Minister of Energy) of the recommendations made by the administrative level. The reform in the communication market also originated in the proposals of the administrative level in the Ministry of Communication. But these were warmly embraced by the Ministers of Communication.

The 1982 Communication Law granted Bezeq—the Israeli communication company—exclusiveness in all communication services provided in Israel. In 1989, the government decided to examine ways to encourage competition in the communication market. It took three years and two government committees for the 1982 law to be changed, and it took another two years (and another committee) for it to be implemented.

The new law granted Bezeq a general permit, which allowed it to continue and offer infrastructure, phone, and auxiliary service, but forced it to transfer all its cellular phone services, international calls, equipment sales, and installation services to subsidiary companies. The permit maintained Bezeq's monopoly in the regular domestic phone market, but allowed the opening of all other markets (served by Bezeq's subsidiaries) to competition.

The first step, and in many respects, the most important one, was the opening to competition of the cellular phone market in 1994. The main criterion for the choice of winner in the public bid for the second competitor in this market (besides the Bezeq subsidiary) was the rates asked for the service. The winner offered to sell his services at a rate (3¢) which was one fourth to one third of the European and the U.S. rates. The new competitor's fast penetration into the market forced the incumbents to reduce their rates by over one third.

The fall in rates changed the whole nature of the cellular phone market. The cellular phone was transformed from an exclusive luxury item, characterized by a high-income elasticity, into a mass product good, within everyone's reach. The growth rates of the Israeli cellular phone market have few equals in the world, and few equals in the Israeli durable market. In January 1995, the number of cellular phones was about 130 thousand. Within three and a half years, it reached 1.9 million subscribers. Within five years (by the year 2000), the number of cellular phones exceeded the number of regular phones, and its penetration rate came close to 50 percent.

In 1997, competition was expanded. This time, the criterion for the winning bid was the size of royalties paid to the government. The winner was ready to pay 390 million dollars. The introduction of an improved technology (GSM) by the new competitor, led to an upgrading of the other two networks, and an additional reduction in rates. The economy benefited not only from an improvement of service at lower prices, but also from a stream of new investment—investment in the new networks adding up to 1.7 billion dollars.

The fast growth of the cellular market resulted, naturally, in a slowdown of the growth of the regular phone market. The diversion of calls from regular to cellular phones affected the growth of traffic between regular phones (LTL—land-to-land calls). But the new options of calling from or to a mobile destination resulted in a growth of overall calls (measured in minutes). Because the destination of over a third of all cellular phone calls is a regular phone (mobile to land [MTL]), and because a third of all calls terminating in a mobile phone originate in a regular phone (land to mobile [LTM]), the loss of LTL calls was offset by an increase in calls between the markets (LTM and MTL).

The cellular phone, despite its impressive penetration rate, is far from endangering the dominant position of Bezeq in the vocal phone market. At the end of 1998, the number of mobile phones was three quarters that of Bezeq's regular lines. But the number of call-minutes originating in mobile phones was less than a fifth. Differences in service quality and, more importantly, phone rates explain this gap.

The second turning point in the opening of the communication market to competition was the liberalization of the international calls market. Following the changes in Bezeq's general permit, the government issued in October 1995 a bid for two additional providers (besides the Bezeq subsidiary) of international calls. The Ministry of Communication also adopted in this case the criterion of low rates as the main criterion for the choice of winners. The government promised as part of the bid not to allow any additional competitors into the market for the next seven years.

International calls have always been a source of cross-subsidization of other phone services (and a major source for the coverage of the "access deficit"). The impact of competition was dramatic. International call rates dropped by 70 percent, and the market share of the incumbent was slashed, within a few months, by half. The outgoing traffic grew by 70 percent, but a major part of the growth came at the expense of the incoming calls, total traffic growing by only 15–20 percent. As the share of the incumbent dropped under 60 percent, the regulative rules were changed. Minimum prices that were established to prevent dumping, were replaced by maximum rates.

It is worth noting that the opening of the international market to competition did not go without a fight. On the eve of the bid, Bezeq's management asked for compensation, saying that the loss of this revenue source would prevent it from covering the access deficit. These demands were backed by Bezeq's workers' union, which declared a strike. The combined pressure was successful, the government agreeing to reduce Bezeq's royalties, slow down the phone rate reduction, and impose a special tax on the new competitors (in the form of increased interconnect charges) in order to preserve Bezeq's "financial stability."

According to the reform timetable, the year 1999 was supposed to be the year of the final step of the liberalization—the opening of the domestic phone market to competition. Two government committees worked out the details of this step. The major two problems they faced had to do with the question of whether the competition should be facility-based competition (with each provider providing its own network) or whether it should be based on the unbundling of the incumbent's facilities. Another question concerned the scope of services and geographical coverage of each provider. The recommendations allowed new entrants to provide only partial service (in terms of variety and geographical coverage), preserving Bezeq's role as universal provider. The original recommendation was that each entrant would have to provide its own facilities, but this recommendation was later altered. The date of opening the domestic market for competition was postponed under Bezeq's union pressure time after time, and by 2001, the prospect of reform and the future shape of this market were still unclear.

The Ports Whereas most of the attempted reforms were forced on the public utility companies from the outside (usually by the Ministry of Finance and the regulating Ministry), the port reform proposals were worked out jointly by the government and the Port Authority's management. The management regarded the reforms as a way for attaining the operative flexibility it lacked as a governmental authority. Moreover, it saw in the reform a solution to the constant drain of resources created by the annexation of the railroad in 1988. The railroad required ever-increasing investments in order to transform it from a backward freight to a modern suburban passenger rail system, and these investments cut sharply into the funds available for investment in the ports themselves. In 1995, the Port Authority planned to build two new ports, adjacent to the two existing ones (in Haifa and Ashdod), and it felt it will not be able to finance them unless it got rid of the railroad. The Ministry of Finance was ready to resume the financing of the rail investment, but made its consent conditional on structural reforms.

A report prepared for the Port Authority's management recommended changing from a government authority to a publicly owned holding company that would operate the ports as subsidiaries. The ports would be operated by the authority and private contractors and, eventually, would be allowed to compete with each other.

The report prepared for the Ministry of Transport was more far-reaching in its implications. Its author (Raanan, 1997) discusses the costs to the Israeli economy resulting from the Authority's inefficiency—delays in loading and unloading (at an annual cost to the economy of about eighty million dollars), congestion charges on marine freight, increased costs of transshipment, and inflated overhead costs (in the years 1961–1996, the manpower at the Authority's headquarters increased two and a half fold, while manpower at the ports themselves shrunk by 40 percent).

Raanan recommends competition and privatization as the sole remedy to the authority's ailments. Based on the examples of ports in Chile, Malaysia, New Zealand, and the United Kingdom, he proposed the dismantling of the central authority and the operation of the ports as independent entities. These entities, financed by public and private funds, would buy the ports' structures and equipment and rent the infrastructure. Some of the services offered by the ports should be privatized (with the employees' partial participation), and new services will be offered on the basis of "Build and Operate" (BOT). The regulatory responsibilities will be transferred from the Port Authority to the Ministry of Transport. The split-up of the Authority was approved by the Ministry of Finance in 1996, but was blocked by opposition from the workers' union.

The Refineries Since the establishment of the State of Israel, and in particular, after the first oil crisis, oil imports were regarded by policymakers differently than any other good. Oil was defined as a "strategic" good immune to economic consideration. Given the risk of oil supply interruptions, due to Arab countries' pressures, the government became the central actor in the oil market, delegating the refineries, the infrastructure companies, and the marketing companies to the role of subsidiary agents. The price of oil products was determined by the Ministry of Finance, and the marketing profits were divided between the companies involved according to fixed formula, independent of costs and market shares. (The same formula was used during the British Mandate period.)

The peace treaty with Egypt that formalized the oil imports from that country, the signing of long-term contracts with Norway and Mexico, the disintegration of OPEC following the Iran-Iraq War, and the increased importance of the spot market resulted in a reevaluation of the government role in the oil market. This economic examination pointed out the inefficiencies and excess profits created by the close association of the government and the marketing companies, by pricing based on perfect cost pass-through, and by a system of profit-distribution that is adverse to efficiency.

The reform in the oil market initiated in 1988 was intended to break the unofficial cartel arrangements governing the market, and establish a pricing system independent of the activities of the local players.

The reform focused in its initial stages on the wholesale segment of the nontransport fuels market (fuel oil, naphtha, kerosene, and nontransport diesel oil). The sale of these fuel products does not require expensive marketing channels, and the barriers to entry are, therefore, relatively low. The success of the reform in this sector was swift and dramatic. The removal of administrative barriers to trade led to a sharp decline in markups.

The reform failed in its attempt to erase the high marketing markups in the retail fuel market. In this market, there exist two main marketing channels—gas stations selling transport fuels (gasoline and diesel oil) and door-to-door delivery of propane gas sold in containers. The markups on these fuel products declined in the early 1990s, but stabilized in the second half of the decade. Given the decline in crude oil prices, and the decline in refinery prices, the share of the marketing markup relative to the refinery price increased over the decade. In mid-1996, the markup of transport fuels was almost equal to their refinery prices, and the markup on propane gas exceeded the refinery price by a wide margin (Gronau, 1996).

The marketing markup consists of two parts: A small part (about 10 percent) covers land transport, handling and storage costs, and the larger part covers the cost and rents of gas companies and gas station owners. The estimate of the second component in 1995 was 415 million dollars—an average of 730 thousand dollars per station. These high rents are explained by average sales that are among the highest in the world and markup rates that are significantly higher than in Europe. The division of these rents between the gas company and the gas station operator depends on the ownership of the station (sometimes the station is owned by the company and sometimes by the operators). The attempts to reduce the markup took several forms—modifications in the long-term contractual agreements between the three marketing companies and the station operators, and encouraging entry of new gas stations and additional marketing companies. Until now, these attempts had only a very modest success.[7]

Attempts to open the propane gas market to competition were also only partly successful. The removal of price controls in 1988 led to an increase in markups of almost 50 percent. It took almost two years until the entry of new competitors led to a reduction in markups. But after four years, the trend reversed again. The share of the markup in the retail price in 1996 was higher than in the prereform era. Increased markup is the main source of the increase in retail price (Gronau, 1996).

Genuine competition in the retail market is clearly the top priority on the reform's short- and medium-term agenda. In the long run, once this target is attained, the reform has to tackle the problem created by the monopoly upstream. Maintaining a monopoly in the refinery sector jeopardizes the reform achievements downstream.

One of the aims of the 1988 reforms was reduced direct intervention of the government in the fuel market. Prior to this reform, the government was the sole purchaser of fuel, the marketing companies and the refinery company serving merely as agents. The attempts to reduce the government's involvement in the market succeeded more than expected, but into the void created by the government withdrawal stepped the refinery company. The company, which played only a minor role prior to 1988, became, following the reform, a key actor governing a strategic crossroad in the market.

The reform plan distinguished between two segments of the crude oil market—the "contractual" segment and the "open market" segment. The contractual segment, which constituted initially about 60 percent of the crude oil imports, covered that part of the imports subject to long-term purchases agreements (agreements with Egypt, Mexico, and Norway). The reform plan retained the marketing companies' position as the sole importer of this oil (prespecifying their market shares), and delegated the refineries to the role of agent working for a fixed (government set) fee. The refineries were allowed to operate as an importer (along with other large oil consumers) only in the open spot market, but only up to a quota of one-third of the spot market imports (i.e., 13 percent of all imports).

The built-in advantage of the refineries in the purchase of crude oil, the new price policy, and the changes in the world oil market resulted in drastic changes in the shares of the two segments. The weakening of OPEC, the expansion of the open market, and the opening of new import sources cheaper and closer to home led to a constant shrinkage of the contractual segment. The marketing companies discovered that at the new price, they are better off buying the oil products from the refineries directly, rather than import the crude oil and pay the refineries a fixed refining fee. The companies withdrew gradually from the crude oil import market, leaving the refineries as the sole player in this market in the triple role of producer, importer, and exporter.

The huge investment required for the building of a new refinery, excess capacity, and environmental considerations rule out the building of new refineries as a way of introducing competition in this market. The natural solution in this case is the splitting of ownership of the two refinery sites in Haifa and Ashdod. The discussion of the advantages and disadvantages of a split-up gained momentum as the expiration of the refineries' franchise in 2003 drew close. It was the topic of several studies during the period 1989–1996. All the studies agreed about the inefficiency of the refineries, but disagreed about the solution. The refineries' management claimed that the cost of a split-up exceeds by far its benefits, and that the opening of another port for oil products, and the resulting competition with imports, will lead to a gradual decline in the refineries' manpower and increased efficiency.

The reform supporters disagreed with this scenario. A team appointed by the Ministries of Energy and Finance (Gronau, 1996) concluded that the cost of inefficiency to the economy is 60–80 million dollars. Inefficiency characterizes almost every aspect of the company's operation—excess manpower and high wages, wasteful use of energy, excess capacity, and inefficient allocation of production between the two sites. The team rejected the solution suggested by the refineries' management of increased competition with imports, arguing that the local refineries have a built-in advantage in terms of transport costs, supply flexibility, and taxation. An importer will have great difficulties in overcoming these disadvantages, in particular, if he faces a monopolist who can threaten buyers with disruption of supply.

According to the team, the synergism between the two refineries is limited, and can be overcome with relatively small investments. The Haifa refinery, the larger of the two, has an advantage in terms of size, the complexity of its production process, and the proximity of the petrochemical plants that assure it of an immediate outlet to some of its products. The comparative advantage of the Ashdod refinery lies in its proximity to the centers of consumption in central and southern Israel (including the Tel Aviv metropolitan area), and its proximity to crude oil port in Ashkelon.

The team could not rule out the possibility that a split-up will give rise to a duopoly, splitting the market and preventing competition, but argued that this is a low probability scenario. At present, the Haifa refinery is exporting a large fraction of its output at a loss. When the market opens to competition, it is expected to try to dislodge Ashdod's hold of the profitable domestic market by undercutting prices. The large excess capacity at Haifa will encourage this tendency.

The years 1994–1998 were bad years for the Israeli refineries. The shrinking of the European refining mark-ups and the increases in labor costs resulted in declining profits and even losses. The team proposed a complete overhaul of the fuel market. It proposed that the refineries be split up and the present horizontal stratification be replaced by vertical integration. According to this model, the refineries will be allowed to expand downstream and develop their own marketing channels (the refineries are currently prohibited from owning a marketing company or gas stations). Vertical integration, the prevalent structure abroad, will reduce the refineries' vulnerability to the fluctuation of oil price without harming competition.

The team's 1996 proposal was adopted by the government, but in spite of the formal resolution, the government never tried to implement it. On the reform's tenth birthday, one can conclude that it was only partially successful in its attempt to reduce government's involvement in the fuel market. It changed the government's form of involvement, but did not lead to its complete withdrawal. The government moved from the role of leading actor to the role of regulator. Its attempt to replace regulation by competition fell short of its expectations. The government deregulated wholesale prices, but maintained the regulation of refinery prices and most retail transport-fuel prices. The price of propane gas was deregulated, but the government resumed its regulation when it discovered that competition failed, and that the increase in markups pushed the retail price upward.

The expectation that the reform will lead to increased efficiency was also only partially attained. The increased competition triggered drastic moves by the private marketing companies to become more efficient. Their labor force was reduced by one-third, wages were cut, and the companies changed their whole mode of operation by diversifying into new fields (real estate, car imports, oil exploration, and more). The government sector was much slower in moving in this direction. In 1992, the refineries agreed to reduce their labor force, but the process was slow and offset by wage hikes. Consequently, the cost of labor per unit of output increased rather than declined (Gronau, 1996).

Public Transport The year 1985 was a turning point in the relations between government and the public transport bus companies. As in the past, government policy was hardly affected by transport consideration, and its motivation was merely macroeconomic: Whereas the pre-1985 policy subsidy was instigated by an attempt to ameliorate fare hikes and slowdown inflation, the post-1985 policy was motivated by the drive to cut the budget deficit. The 1985 stabilization policy led to a 40 percent cut in transport subsidies, but the cut proved to be only temporary—within four years, it bounced back to a level only 80 percent of what it was in its heyday. The attempt to find a long-term solution to the subsidy, accompanied by the recognition that a major part of the subsidy went to pay for the inflated cooperative members' salaries and that the lack of competition affects the cooperatives' efficiency, led to a renewed evaluation of government's role in this market. A team consisting of representatives of the Ministries of Transport and Finance proposed in 1991 that the public transport market be divided into three parts: (1) The profitable intercity and regional lines should be opened to competition, and the government fare regulation be removed. (2) The profitable urban and metropolitan lines will be divided into clusters. Each cluster will be operated for a limited period (3–5 years) by an exclusive operator chosen in a bid. The fares in this sector will be regulated but not subsidized. (3) The unprofitable urban and regional lines will also be divided into clusters, but in this case, the operator will continue to receive subsidies. The rate of subsidization shall be the main criterion for the choice of the franchise owner. To encourage the use of public transport, it was recommended that the government expand the network of bus express lanes, and limit the use of private cars through road use charges and a reduction in car allowances (which are an important part of public service salaries).

The recommendations were presented to the Minister of Transport, but it took seven years (and two more ministers) before they were brought to government approval. In 1998, the government started its liberalization policy, putting out a bid for the first cluster. After a lengthy court battle, and after the Supreme Court turned down the cooperatives' claim that they have an inherent right to the lines they serve, the way was opened for competition. According to an agreement between government and the cooperatives, cooperatives were precluded from participating in the bids in their first stages. The winner in these bids were private companies who had specialized before in nonscheduled service, and who were ready to offer their services at much lower rates than the current (subsidized) fare.

A factor that may slow down the drive for competition is the ownership of most urban central bus stations by the cooperatives' subsidiaries. Another factor that may affect future competition is the fast development of suburban trains in the late 1990s.

The Reform That Was—Price Regulation in the Public Utilities

To an outside viewer, the competitive landscape in the late 1990s may not look significantly different from the landscape in the mid-1980s. With the exception of the communication market, most structural reforms are still at the drawing-board stage. Against this background, it is worth noting the progress that has taken place in the sphere of rate regulation. A series of public committees established the mechanisms of rate setting in the communication and electricity markets. An external mechanism determines the wholesale product prices at the refinery gate. The government tightened its grip on public transport tariffs and subsidies, and by the end of the decade, the port was the only public utility whose rates escaped regulations and rationalization. The common thread passing through all these reforms is the creation of incentive mechanisms to encourage efficiency. The establishment of these normative mechanisms freed the rate setting to a large extent from exterior considerations and political intervention.

The struggle to turn the price mechanism into a efficiency-promoting device required the breakup of the old perfect pass-through system, and the search for new "objective" yardsticks for the computation of normative costs. The attempt to reduce the damage caused by the cross-subsidization required the building of a rate structure based on costs. This attempt was often hindered by the asymmetry of information, that is, the different knowledge levels of the regulated company and the regulator. But even worse is the case of a "symmetry of ignorance." Years of a perfect pass-through system, in which average rates were determined by the company's average costs and individual service prices were set arbitrarily, led to a neglect of modern supervisory cost mechanisms and, in particular, to a lack of appropriate accounting tools. The absence of modern information systems was often the result of managerial neglect, but was so widespread that one is tempted to wonder if it were not sometimes intentional, motivated by "what I don't know—I cannot tell." The reluctance to adopt detailed accounting procedures based on profit centers (ironically) gained stimulus when reformers called for the companies' split-up as a way to enhance competition (as in the examples of the electricity company and the refineries). For example, Bezeq, the phone company, started developing a detailed cost accounting system only after it had to admit publicly, on the front page of its stock trade offer, that its management did not possess the tools to evaluate the profitability of its individual services, and estimate the effect of rate change on its overall profitability. It can be safely assumed that many other governmental companies escaped such an embarrassment by avoiding the stock market and relying on government funds. The Port Authority, for example, started developing its cost accounting only in the mid-1990s.

The Finance Ministry has to bear the blame for much of the misconstruction of the rate structure in the 1970s and early 1980s. During these years, it often sacrificed efficiency in a futile attempt to achieve macroeconomic goals (i.e., the suppression of inflation). The same ministry went through a change of heart and became the major factor in the normalization of the rates structure in the 1990s. The success of the Finance Ministry depended, often crucially, on the cooperation of the ministry in charge of the public utility. The different regulating schemes established in the different markets reflect, therefore, not only differences in the production processes, but also differences in the political-economic environment—the levels of resistance of the regulated industry to change, and the support that the reform received from the regulating ministry.

Oil Prices The reform in the price structure of oil products was, in many respects, the most far-reaching of the regulatory reforms. In the prereform era, the government joined forces with the private (or semiprivate) marketing companies and with the government-owned refineries, to establish a completely artificial price structure. In an industry characterized by sharp fluctuations in the prices of crude oil and fuel products, the government bore all the risks and its "partners" enjoyed riskless fixed fees. The close ties between government officials and the marketing companies' management resulted in a very generous fee structure, which in turn led to excess manpower, generous wage contracts, and inefficiency downstream. The fuel tax was often adapted in order to isolate the Israeli consumer from the vagaries of world markets.

A central element of the 1988 oil-sector reform was the establishment of objective criteria for price setting. This stranglehold exerted by the refineries on the Haifa fuel port[8] made imports a purely theoretical option. The reform circumvented this difficulty by making normative import prices the yardstick for domestic wholesale oil-product prices. In the absence of imports, prices were based on the North Italian price (the price at the oil port of Lavera, near Genoa). To overcome the resistance of the market companies, the government allowed a surcharge of 4.8 dollars per ton of light fuel products and 4.6 dollars for fuel oil. The price set according to the formula CIF Lavera + 4.8 was adjusted monthly on the base of the exchange rate and the European oil price fluctuations. The government succumbed to the pressure of local propane gas and naphtha consumers, and established lower markups on these two distillates, leading to a lengthy quarrel between consumers and the refinery concerning the unobstructed supply of these products.

The reform that was adopted in spite of the vehement resistance of the marketing companies tied for the first time the local refining market with those in Europe. Fortunately, for the oil industry (and the reform), the first years of the reform witnessed increasing markups in Europe, translating into increased profits for the local refineries. This increase in profitability was taken advantage of by the regulators to cut the surcharge from 4.8 to 2.8 dollars in 1994. The trend in oil markups was reversed in 1994. The decline in the refineries' profitability was worsened by the exit of the marketing companies from the crude oil import market. The latter discovered that they are better off buying the distillates from the refineries rather than importing the crude oil and employing the refineries as a contractor at a preset fee (Gronau, 1996).

The late 1990s became, therefore, a testing ground for the reform's resilience. The decline in revenues and increased costs turned refining from a highly profitable activity into a loss-bearing activity. In the prereform era, these losses would have led most probably to increased wholesale prices. The success of the reform is reflected in a continuing decline in wholesale and retail product prices.[9]

It took seven years to establish similar principles in the pricing of the oil infrastructure services (the oil port, pipelines, and storage facilities). In 1995, a government committee established new rules for the pricing of these services. The new rates (replacing perfect pass-through) were intended to prevent cross-subsidization and encourage efficiency. The pipeline service rates were for the first time based on distances (and not merely volume), and the rates were supposed to decline at an annual rate of 2.6 percent.

The only infrastructure company exempt from this rule is the crude oil pipeline company, which enjoys the benefits of a specific franchise (originally signed to gain the cooperation and partnership of the Iranian Shah). As a result, the pipeline pumping rate from Ashkelon to Ashdod (a distance of 20 km) is the same as that to Haifa (a distance of 150 km). Because the Ashkelon port is exempt from wharfage fee, the Haifa refinery finds it profitable to unload its crude oil in Ashkelon and pump it 150 kilometer northward, rather than unloading it in the adjacent Haifa port.

Phone Rates Years of rampant inflation followed by a price freeze, imposed as part of the inflation containment policy, left the public utilities' rate structure in shambles. The erosion of profits led to the monopolies' request for a complete overhaul of their rate structure. In contrast to the refining industry, where a common technology is used to produce a set of homogeneous goods, and where one can adopt yardsticks based on the experience abroad, the other public utilities are characterized by a diversity of technologies and a heterogeneity of service qualities. Service prices abroad can serve, in this case, only as crude indicators for normative domestic costs. The import option does not exist for these services, and regulators cannot rely on notional import prices for price setting.

The procedure employed in the setting of phone rates in 1989 has become the standard procedure (with few modifications and improvements) for rate setting in the other public utilities industries. The new procedure differs from the previous ones in three crucial respects—the body recommending the new rate structure, the rate base, and its updating over time. To isolate the rate setting from any considerations alien to consumers' welfare and the industry's efficiency, the authority to recommend a new rate base was moved from the government's regulatory ministry (suspected of being a captive of the regulated company) to an independent public committee. The committees included representatives of the Finance Ministry and the regulatory ministry, and independent experts. The independence of these committees from government intervention grew over time. This is reflected both in their composition and chairmanship. The number of independent experts serving in these committees grew over time, the regulated company that had its representatives in the early committees lost its seat later on, and the chairmanship of the committees was delegated from the representative of the Ministry of Finance to an independent expert.

The choice of rate base and the updating process reflect the information constraints facing the regulator. The committees recognized the important role of the rate mechanism as an engine of increased efficiency and rejected, therefore, the existing pass-through system as a base for the new rate base. The regulatory bodies and the committees lacked the detailed information required to estimate the monopolies' normative costs of production. Because of differences in technology and network size, they could not rely on the experience abroad, and had no choice but to accept (with few modifications) the companies' reports on current costs. Hence, the only normative component in the rate base was the cost of capital and, specifically, the rate of return on equity. This rate reflected the evaluation of the committees of the low-risk premium involved in the financing of these monopolies. However, whereas the rate base was dominated by the companies' actual costs, the updating process was based on criteria independent of the companies' activities. The price cap system called for the updating of rates according to the Consumers' Price Index,[10] allowing for a deduction reflecting returns to scale, expected reductions in equipment prices, expected technological improvements and increased productivity. Rates were set for a period of 4–5 years, during which the company was allowed to keep any excess profits.

The committees were aware of the damage caused by cross-subsidization, but lacked the detailed information required to correct it. Their recommendations in this area, however, contributed to the simplification of the rate structure.

The first of the committees, establishing this new mode of rate setting, was the Fogel Committee, which was charged with the setting of phone rates. The committee, headed by the head of the Bureau of the Budget at the Ministry of Finance, delivered its recommendations in September 1989. It allowed for a return on equity capital of 8.5 percent, and recommended that rates be increased at the beginning of the following year by 15 percent.[11] The rates were set for four years: During the first half of this period, rates should be reduced (in real terms) at an annual rate of 3 percent, a rate to be increased to 3.5 percent during the second half of the period.

As the first rate period drew to a close, a new committee (the Shorer Committee) was established to set the rates for the second period. Building on the experience gained in the first period, the new committee's recommendations were much more far-reaching. In setting the rate base, the committee distinguished between costs on which the phone company had little discretion (royalties, payment to phone companies abroad, finance costs) and costs that were under the company's discretion (wages and operating costs). The committee noticed that the company made a major effort to reduce the latter during the first two years of the rate period, but relinquished this effort toward the end of the period, as if to inflate the new base rate. The committee estimated that if the drive for increased efficiency would have continued, the company's unit costs would have been 16 percent lower than actual unit costs. Consequently, it recommended a 10 percent cost in phone rates.

Its recommendations for future rate reductions were no less drastic. The committee estimated that inefficient operation, inflated equipment costs, future technological changes, and returns to scale would allow the company to reduce its unit costs at an annual rate of 6.5 percent. The phone company had done very little to comply with the Fogel Committee's recommendation to reduce cross-subsidization. A special committee (the Meidan Committee) appointed to examine the size of these subsidies concluded that they account for almost 40 percent of the company's income. To stop these subsidies, fixed-user changes would have to be increased by a factor of six, which would allow a reduction of domestic phone call rates by 33–40 percent, and a reduction in international call rates by 10–30 percent. The Shorer Committee recommended a gradual increase in the fixed user charges, accompanied by an identical reduction in call rates. The new rate period would last five years.

The Ministry of Communication and the government approved the new rules with only slight modification (the rate reductions during the first two years were confined to 6 percent), but later, on the eve of the opening of the international calls market to competition, succumbed to the employees' pressure, and cut the annual reduction to 3.5 percent.

The new rate system had far-reaching implications for the phone company's rate structure: Over the following rate period, the average real rate declined at an accumulated rate of over 30 percent, and the fixed user charge doubled. The rates of international calls and wide-band services underwent even sharper cuts, the company trying to discourage new entrants into these markets (Gronau, 1998).

The last phase in this process was the Gronau Committee, which was charged with devising the rate structure for the period starting in January 1999. The new rate structure became of special importance, given the fast growth of the competing cellular phone market, and the government's plan to open the domestic market for competition.

The examination of the phone company's cost structure revealed the familiar pattern. The company made a great effort to shear costs in the first two years of the previous rate base period. The large rate reductions during those years (1995–1996) forced the company to reduce its labor force, press its suppliers for lower prices, and economize. During these years, the company succeeded in increasing the output by a quarter with hardly any change in costs. But once the government agreed to lower rate reductions (3.5 instead of 6.5 percent), the effort to economize slackened, and unit costs increased. The fast growth in output led to increased profits. The committee agreed (given the new competitive environment) to increase the company's rate of return on equity capital to 10.5 percent, but found that a return to normative costs and profits requires a rate reduction of 10.5 percent. The annual rate reduction for the next four years was set at 7 percent.

The changes in the rate structure during the second rate base period (1995–1999) resulted in significant reductions in the cross-subsidies. The committee recognized that the continuation of these subsidies in a competitive environment endangers the stability of the incumbent provider. The fear that new entrants will capture the profitable segments of the market, leaving the incumbent with the loss-making part, called for an immediate solution to the "access deficit" problem. According to its calculations, about one third of the company's normative costs are common costs (i.e., costs that, given the current accounting system, the committee could not allocate to any specific service). The committee charged each service for these common costs at a rate proportionate to its direct costs, but exempted the access services from these charges. As a result, access rates (fixed monthly charges) were increased slightly, and domestic call rates were cut by a third. The new rates were based on the committee's estimates of the long-run incremental cost, and for the first time, the cross-subsidies were eliminated.[12]

Finally, the fast growth of the mobile phone market and the opening of the international calls market to competition resulted in an ever-increasing share of the incumbent's revenue coming from "interconnect" services (calls originating or terminating in the incumbent's network). The interconnect rates were only slightly lower than regular call rates. Consequently, the shift of calls from the incumbent to its competitors hardly affected the incumbent's revenue. The interconnect rates, instead of reflecting the company's costs, reflected its monopolistic position as the gatekeeper of 2.8 million clients. The committee (similar to other committees abroad) regarded these rates as an obstacle to competition. It did not see a reason why the competitors' subscribers should be charged the same overhead as the incumbents' subscribers (i.e., participate equally in the coverage of the access overhead charges). Lower overhead charges allowed a cut in the interconnect charges of two-thirds to a level recommended by the OECD.

The committee's recommendations were delivered to the Ministers of Communication and Finance in September 1998. The recommendations ran into stiff opposition from the phone company's management and workers' union but were finally approved in March 1999.

Parallel to the working of the rate committees, the government considered the establishment of an independent regulatory body to take over the regulatory responsibilities of the Ministry of Communication. The government decided in May 1996 to start the appropriate legal proceedings, but the decision has never been implemented.

The Electricity Rates In contrast to the communication market, which is characterized by a large variety of services, the electricity market is characterized by one homogeneous good kilowatt-hours (KWH). The cost of this service depends on the time of production (determining the marginal costs of production), transport costs (i.e., the costs of transmission), and distribution costs. In essence, the setting of price for this service is much simpler than that of the communication services.[13]

The Fogel Committee for the setting of electricity prices (1999)[14] adopted with slight modifications the principles established by the communication rates committee. It distinguished four cost components—fuel (36 percent of total costs), capital (32 percent), operating and maintenance (32 percent), and purchases from independent power producers (negligible). It assumed that the appropriate capital structure is two-thirds debt, one-third equity (the same as the phone company); that the interest the monopolist faces is 4.25 percent; and that the adequate rate of return on equity is 7.5 percent (making for an average price of capital of 5.33 percent). The fuel component in costs was adjusted according to the regulated refinery prices, and the other components according to the CPI. The rates were reduced at a rate of 1.5 percent for the first two years of the period, and 2 percent later. The committee did a lot to simplify the rate structure: The "peak demand" component was removed from the peak-load rates, and the number of special rate schedules was reduced from 11 to 4.

The inclusion of a normative capital cost component in the rates required an increase in electricity rates of 8.2 percent when the new rate was introduced (October 1991).[15]

The establishment of the Public Utility Commission had only a minor effect on rates. In the absence of information, it adopted in 1997 the Fogel Committee formula with slight modifications (it raised the interest rate on debt to 4.5 percent and lowered the return on equity to 6.5 percent, for an average of 5.17 percent). The PUC planned to introduce a new rate formula in 1999 but had to postpone it until 2001. Though the formula has not changed, two of the PUC's decisions had a crucial effect on the rates: The first related to arrears payments to the workers' pension fund, which, according to the 1996 law, were to be covered by the new tariffs (requiring an 8 percent increase in rates); the second was the PUC's decision to provide the IEC with exchange-rate hedging services on its foreign debt. The second decision raised the average cost of capital effectively from 5.17 to 6.17 percent, and linked 40 percent of the capital costs component to the rate of exchange.

In the period 1991–1996, electricity rates declined (in real terms) by 18 percent. The PUC's decisions (and the 1998 devaluation) changed this trend for the first time in six years. Despite the sharp drop in oil prices during the 1997–1998 period (a decline of 25 percent), electricity prices did not decline.

Port Charges In 1993, the port tariffs were reexamined in order to establish a new cost based rate structure. The examination was taken up jointly by the Port Authority and the Ministries of Finance and Transportation, the Port Authority realizing that the prevailing cross-subsidies were detrimental to the ports' operation.

The wharfage fee had been reduced a year earlier from 2 to 1.5 percent. The reduction was not part of a move toward an improved rate structure, but rather the result of heavy U.S. pressure, the U.S. regarding this tariff as discriminatory. The 1993 examination showed that despite this reduction the cross-subsidies continued to be sizeable. Using newly available cost accounting data, it showed that the 1992 capital costs of infrastructure were less than one fourth the revenue from the wharfage fee. The operating costs exceeded the revenue from freight handling (e.g., stevedoring and portage charges) by 50 percent. This gap created a complex system of cross-subsidies, by which expensive freight subsidizes cheap freight, and imports subsidize exports.

It was suggested that shippers bear the total cost of freight handling (given that they are responsible for packaging, an important determinant of these costs), and that the shipping companies be responsible for the vessel costs. Vessel charges should be raised substantially (almost fourfold) to reflect the high cost of the piers and congestion, and should replace the wharfage fee as the main tool for the coverage of infrastructure costs.[16] Vessel charges are based on ship length. But whereas in the current system they increase progressively with length, favoring small old vessels, it was recommended they change proportionally, encouraging large modern ships, and allowing for a more efficient use of the pier anchorage.

It was also suggested that port tariffs be reduced annually (similarly to other public utilities rates). The reduction was set at 2.5 percent during the first two years of the arrangement, and 2.75 percent thereafter. The recommendations were accepted by the heads of the Ministries of Finance and Transport but were not approved by their ministers. Because by law the authority to recommend tariff changes rests with the Board of the Port Authority, in which there is a strong port-users' representation, the recommendations were never implemented.

Still the wharfage fee was reduced from 1.5 to 1.3 percent, and for the first time, exporters had to bear the fee, though at a reduced rate (0.2 percent).

Public Transport The public transport tariff policy is a classic example of "the tail that wags the dog." Instead of transport policy dictating the bus (and taxi) tariffs, and the tariffs, in turn, determining the appropriate subsidies, the subsidies determined the transport policy. The 1985 budgetary cuts resulted in a 40 percent cut in subsidies (in real terms) but they rebounded at a rate of 35 percent over the following four years. Only in 1990 did the Finance Ministry succeed in controlling the subsidies, lowering them (in real terms) in the following years. The erosion of subsidies was accompanied by a constant increase in bus tariffs. Real tariffs jumped 80 percent over the years 1984–1986, and increased by another 50 percent over the following decade (Gronau, 1997).

No attempt was made to replace the global subsidies by a set of specific subsidies depending on the number of urban and interurban travelers. Though congestion, which is perhaps the greatest transportation problem, affects mainly urban transport, urban bus rates increased faster than interurban rates (100 vs. 60 percent, respectively).

The reduction in subsidies, a gradual reduction in the number of high wage cooperative members (financed in part by the government's contributions to their severance and pension funds), and their replacement by cheaper salary employees, brought to a halt the wage increases, and resulted in a reduction in the cost of bus-km over the period 1990–1995 (Gronau, 1997).

10.5 The (Almost) Lost Decade—Summary and Lessons

It is over a decade since the word "privatization" entered the Israeli public discourse.[17] The discussion of privatization strengthened the call for a reduction of government involvement in the economic activity. It breathed a new life into the discussion of structural changes in the public utilities. The staggering growth rates and stubborn inflation rates, which refused to decline beyond the 15–20 percent step, strengthened the feeling that a revolutionary move was required to increase the competitive drive and the efficiency of the public utilities and other infrastructure industries. Privatization that precedes liberalization was conceived as a threat to this important move. At the end of the decade, one can conclude that the government accomplishments in introducing structural change in this field have been quite modest, and if there were any successes, they were mostly in introducing a more systematic regulatory system to govern the companies' activities. The failure cannot be explained by a lack of effort in the administrative ranks; it is traced rather to lukewarm political backing.

The failure of the structural reform was significantly affected by the fact that its timing and priorities were dictated to the government from the outside. The reform that had to be tackled first was the organizational structure of the electricity company. The government did not choose this order, which was forced on it by the expiration of the IEC franchise in 1996. Selecting as the first target the oldest and best-entrenched monopoly, the company with the best organized and the strongest workers' union, brought the whole process of reforms to a halt. The lengthy and well-publicized discussions in the various committees, which dragged out to the eve of the 1996 election, cooled the fervor of the politician for any additional structural reforms in this field.

Confronting an externally imposed deadline, the politicians decided to shelve the problem for the next ten years. At the point of decision, there were not enough power groups to balance the pressure of the workers' union for a continuation of the status quo. The public discussions of the reforms in other sectors were much less detailed, and received only little media attention. The political level's decision to postpone the reforms was received almost offhand.

In this dim landscape, the success of the communication sector reform shines brightly. Partners to this success were technological, economic, and institutional factors. One of the major features of the last decade was the communication technology revolution. New technologies allowed the opening of new channels (e.g., wireless) into the customer's premise, circumventing the bottleneck of the copper wire governed by the monopoly. New inventions in fiber optics and computer technologies increased the efficiency of the interexchange transmission of calls tenfold. These improvements contributed to the expansion of new services provided through the telecommunication network (the most notable, of course, being, the Internet). These sweeping technological changes played a key role in the opening of the communication industry to competition.

The development of a new technology, the cellular phone, circumventing the traditional access channels, led to the first breach in the monopolistic wall. The success of the new competitor highlights the importance of a new technology in the process of structural change. A new competitor will find it difficult to compete with a well-entrenched monopoly when he is forced to employ the same technology that the incumbent has been using for years—in particular, if this technology is characterized by returns to scale. His way is going to be much easier when the accumulated experience cannot serve as an entry barrier into the industry because all competitors use a new technology. The entry of the new competitor into the cellular phone market was helped by the small share of this market in the monopolistic revenues (less than a tenth in 1994). The phone company's management and workers' protest in 1992 against changes in the general permit was motivated more by their fear of the precedence of the loss of exclusivity, than by their fear of sharing the small cellular phone market with another competitor.

The revolutionary change in the cellular phone market, as the result of competition, eased, indirectly, the implementation of the second stage of reform—the introduction of competition in the international calls market. This time the fight was over a market that was far from negligible, contributing 30 percent of the incumbent's gross revenue and a fifth of its net revenue (after the deduction of payments to foreign companies). This time, the profitability of this market segment worked, ironically, to the incumbent's disadvantage. The cross-subsidies, which turned this market into a source of gigantic profits, and the low technological and economic barriers to entry put this market high on the acquisition list of any potential rival. It is not surprising that there were six participants in the international bid. Placing a low tariff as the major criterion for the choice of the winner provided the public an immediate demonstration of the benefits of competition.

Against the background of the modest achievements in the fields of structural reforms, the accomplishments of the regulatory reforms stand out. The oil prices reform, and the new regulatory rules concerning communication and electricity rates that followed it, are the best examples in this field. The decline in real prices in these sectors is a living demonstration of the reform's success. In the years 1987–1997, the relative prices of propane gas and kerosene for domestic use, phone, and electricity declined by 18 percent compared with other goods included in the CPI. In spite of this small share in the CPI (4.2 percent in 1997), the reform contributed to a decline of one percent in the CPI. The success of the reform is, in particular, noteworthy compared with the rise in public utility rates of sectors where the reform failed—the public transport and water (for home use) rates. Their relative prices increased by over 30 percent, offsetting the achievements of the reform.

Price reduction is only one aspect of increased efficiency in the public utilities (for which the phone company is, perhaps, the best example). The reduction of rates forced the companies for the first time to employ their economic power, and force their suppliers to lower their markups. International bids for equipment and tougher bargaining led to an erosion of the excessive profits of the phone and electricity companies' domestic suppliers, and led to increased efficiency of the cable, transformers, and phone exchange industries.

Increased efficiency takes many forms, many of which the reformer could have never predicted. For example, the pressure applied by the phone company on its suppliers resulted in the reorganization of one of them, which then became one of the leading electronic producers in the economy. The other producer, which delayed its reorganization, reached the brink of bankruptcy.[18] The international bids employed by the electricity company to lower its costs forced the leading electric transformers' producer in Israel to change its marketing strategy—reduce the inefficient production of transformers, and specialize in the production of air conditioners. The change in strategy made this producer within five years one of the leading air-conditioning producers in Europe. The competition in the cable producers' industry, after their loss of their dominant position as suppliers of the phone and electricity monopolies, forced them to become more efficient, and resulted in a diversion of a large fraction of their output to the export market. The oil marketing companies reacted to the erosion of their profits (in particular, in the wholesale market) by diversifying into real estate, car imports, and more.

It is only natural to ask why did the regulatory reform succeed whereas the structural reform failed? The explanation lies, most probably, in the level of resistance and support of the two reforms. The structural reform was regarded by the monopoly and its workers as an "existential" threat—a threat to the management's freedom of operation in a world without comparative yardsticks and a threat to the workers' employment and excessive wages. The regulation of tariffs reduces profitability but does not constitute an existentialist threat. One has to remember that the approval of the first two rate structures (the Fogel Committees for the phone and electricity rates) led to increased rates, and a recovery of the monopolies' profitability, and that the price-cap system allowed the monopoly to retain its profits during the tariff period. The refusal of the electric workers' union to cooperate with the Public Utility Commission and the strike of phone workers against the implementation of the recommendation of the latest phone rates committee indicate that this attitude is changing as management and workers are beginning to understand the long-term implications of the regulatory reforms.

The second difference lies in the support centers for the reform. "Structural reform" is an abstract term. The implications of the split-up of the refineries, competition between the ports, and competition in electricity generation are not immediate. The case of the communication market, in which the demonstration of the advantages of competition fed into the success of the next stage, is the exception rather than the rule. On the other side, a rate reduction is concrete, and the welfare improvement to the customers is immediate.

The struggle for reform is fought on the political battlefield, and the outcome depends on the political power of the two sides. The reforms affect several groups—consumers, monopoly owners, potential competitors, the regulator, the monopoly's management and workers. In this struggle, the main potential benefactors—the public and the business community—played only a passive role. They hardly participated in the public debate, and the business sector rather than pressing for the opening of new opportunities for entrepreneurial initiatives, tried to preserve its protected positions as suppliers to the monopoly (e.g., the cable producers industry) or benefactors of favorite rates (e.g., the port users). The monopolies' management and workers' union headed the opposition to any reform. In contrast to previous stages of organizational change (the transformation of the ports and the phone company from government units to independent entities) in which the risks to employment were balanced by the chance of greater managerial flexibility and higher wages, the reform was perceived as a threat to workers' unions past wage achievements. The workers, with the support of the general workers' union (the Histradrut), spearheaded the fight against reform.

The ownership of most public utilities monopolies is concentrated in government hands. In the few cases in which ownership was private, one can discern two tendencies: In the case of profitable monopolists (e.g., the oil marketing companies), the owners did everything they could to subvert the reform; but in those cases in which the operation of the monopoly had become only marginally profitable (e.g., the bus cooperatives or the refineries), the owners were ready to yield their monopolistic rights for a right price, and sell their stocks to the government.

The government itself spoke in many tongues. The administrative level was not united. The Government Companies Authority, the informal owner of the companies, played only a secondary role in the reform process. Its main interest in the last decade was the privatization of the companies, but it recognized the importance of liberalization preceding privatization, and the long-run risks in privatizing the monopolies in their present state. However, the Authority had no power to lead the reforms. This role was left to the heads of the Ministry of Finance and the Bureau of the Budget in this Ministry.

The containment of inflation in 1985 returned the Bureau of the Budget to its natural playground—that of microeconomic reforms. After eight years during which it was forced to deal with macroeconomic problems and futile attempts to block the inflation, the Bureau workers were happy to try and remedy some of the injuries imposed by the inflation on the economy. With the support of the research department at the Bank of Israel, the Antitrust Authority, and academia, the Bureau of the Budget led both the structural and the regulatory reforms. Its success, however, depended crucially on the cooperation of the regulatory ministry. The success of the reforms in the oil and communication industries is a direct result of the cooperation of the Ministry of Finance economists with those of the Ministries of Energy and Communication, respectively. The objection of the Ministry of Energy contributed to the failure of the reform in the electricity industry. The weakness of the administrative level in the Ministry of Transport weakened the attempts to reform the ports and public transports.

But by the end of the day, the factor that separated success from failure was the commitment and tenacity of the political level. Most of the Ministries of Finance in the last decade backed the reform recommendations of their subordinates. (The objection in 1996 to the electricity reform, and their continuous objection to the reform in public transport are the exceptions.) But also at the political level the success depended on the support of the ministers in charge of the regulatory ministry. Their commitment explains the success of the oil and communication industries reforms, and their weakness or objection led to the failure of the electricity, public transport, and ports reform.

The number of observations is too small to reach any generalities concerning the factors determining the readiness of the political level to adopt the reform recommendations. The personality of the minister and his ideology clearly play an important role in this process, but not less important is his party affiliation. It seems that the distinguishing feature is not the party's declared ideology and its place in the political spectrum (right vs. left), but rather its size. Throughout the period, the Ministry of Finance was headed by one of the two big parties, but the reform's success depended on the party affiliation of the minister in charge of this regulatory ministry. When this minister belonged to one of the two big parties, the reform was destined to failure.[19] The requirement for success is the affiliation of the minister with a small party.

The readiness to adopt the reforms can be explained by the balance of forces supporting and resisting the reform and their access to the minister. The resistance was headed by the workers' union and the companies' managements. The union and the Histadrut were always the stronghold of one of the two big parties, but also had close connection with the other. The introduction of primaries in the two parties to elect their representatives to parliament increased the power of the unions and their pressure on the big party ministers. On the other hand, the reliance of the small parties (and in particular, the religious parties) on the unions was minimal, which allowed their representatives much more freedom in carrying out the reforms.

Another obstacle on the road to reform are political appointments. Political appointees in the management and board of directors of the government-owned monopolies became the faithful spokesmen of their companies. The close relations between the appointing minister and his appointees strengthen the forces opposing the reforms. Experience shows that this factor is less important in the case of ministers affiliated with small parties compared to the big ones.

At the end of a decade of reforms, it seems that reform in the public utilities lags behind its sisters—reform in the capital market and liberalization of imports. If we are to learn a lesson from the other reforms and from the few successes of the public utilities reform, it might seem that the reformers tried to achieve too much in too little time. The reforms in the capital market and in trade succeeded after a long period of absorption and maturing. In both cases, there was close cooperation between the government organs responsible (the Bank of Israel and the Ministry of Finance, in the case of the capital market reform, and the Ministry of Industry and Trade and the Ministry of Finance in the case of the import reform), and in both the progress was gradual. The public utilities reform tried to advance on a wide front, without a clear definition of priorities.

It seems that structural changes should be preceded by regulatory reforms. Only when the stage of liberalization is finished should the privatization option be examined.

The committees that set the rates for electricity and phone services did a lot for the increased efficiency of these two industries. The regulation of port tariffs and the tariffs of public transport are delayed for too long. In both industries, service rates are disconnected with the cost structure, and cross-subsidies prevail. The finishing of the regulatory reforms in these two areas should rank high among the reform priorities.

The public committees contributed a lot to the regulatory reform. Their shortcoming is lack of continuity. An independent body, free of political pressures, is required to balance the economic and political power of the monopolies. The Public Utilities Commission is a first step in this direction, and it is still struggling to find its way. The government decision to establish a similar authority in the communication market is delayed. Similar bodies are required in the ports and pubic transport industries.

It is sometimes suggested that all regulatory responsibilities be awarded to one authority. On the other hand, an increase in the number of regulatory bodies should increase the competition among them, and make their capture by the regulated monopolies more difficult. One of the first tasks of the new regulatory bodies is the establishment of modern cost accounting systems in the regulated companies, to allow a cost-based rate system. A sophisticated accounting system based on a profit center is an important step on the road to structural change.

The opening of the public transport market to competition has just begun. Increased efficiency and coordination between the newly developed rail system and the bus network are necessary conditions to arrest the deterioration of public transport, and are a prerequisite to any solution to the urban congestion problem. The recent changes in the private ownership of the refineries and the fuel marketing companies creates a window of opportunity for the split-up of the refineries, and a structural change in that industry. An acceleration in the opening of the electricity market to independent power producers is a prerequisite for long-term changes in this field.

Experience indicates that the secret of success lies in gradual progress, with each reform weakening the opposition at the next stage. The success of regulatory reform should ease the way to structural reform. The opening of public transport and the ports to competition will serve as ammunition in the fight over the electricity market reform.

In the long run, the greatest incentive for efficiency is not the regulator, regardless of how competent he may be, but competition. Only the first steps in this direction have been made in the opening of the cellular phone market and the international calls market for competition. But these steps demonstrate the potential for increased welfare. The dramatic change in these markets could never have been achieved by a regulator. The markets were perhaps not in equilibrium to begin with (given their high profitability and low entry barriers), and may not be in equilibrium even now, so that they may not be indicative of the outcomes of structural reforms in other markets (refineries, electricity, ports, and public transport). But the accumulation of inefficiency in these markets is still so widespread that competition will enhance welfare in a way that the more evolutionary treatment of the regulator can never expect to achieve.

Notes

1. The public utilities include also the water supply industry. Because of the complexity of the problems associated with the industry, given the major role it plays in the profitability of agriculture, reforms in the water industry are not discussed in this chapter. However, in general, the reform in this industry meshes well with the story of the other public utility reforms.

2. The public transport market in the Mandate period was characterized by a large number of regional companies. These companies merged in the early fifties into three companies. The final stage in this concentration process occurred in 1967 when the large intercity transport company, Egged, merged (with government encouragement) with the Jerusalem metropolitan company.

3. Due to confidentiality requirements, the Central Bureau of Statistics (CBS) publishes only the data on the average wage in the whole industry. The public utility employees constitute only 15–50 percent of the corresponding industry labor force.

4. Given that high phone rates can be assumed to affect firms' prices, the final incidence of the cross-subsidy is, of course, unknown.

5. The Ministry of Finance was supported in its fight for the independence of public utilities commission by the chairman of the Parliament's Finance Committee. The chairman succeeded single-handedly to pass the amendments to the law against the vehement opposition of the IEC union representatives. His vote cost him his seat in parliament. The law was passed on the eve of the elections, and his party did not put him up for reelection.

6. Over the last fifty years, electricity consumption grew at a rate 40 percent faster than GDP, while communication exceeded it by more than two thirds.

7. See the symposium in the May 1999 issue of the *Economic Quarterly*.

8. Haifa is the only port for oil products. It was operated by the refinery company's employees.

9. The price of oil products in the mid-1990s was on average only 60 percent of the price at the beginning of that decade.

10. The only two exceptions were the cost of international incoming calls (in the phone rate), which was linked to the exchange rate, and the cost of fuels (in the electricity rate), which was linked to their regulated refinery prices.

11. The inflation and the following price freeze resulted in the erosion of the phone company's profits to a level way beyond the newly approved rate of return on equity. The recognition that the company is entitled to an adequate rate of return explains the initial rate increase.

12. Throughout the period, the phone services subsidized the other services provided by the company (broadcasting, wideband, etc.).

13. The only complications rose from some special institutional arrangements, e.g., the government's debt to the workers pension fund.

14. Aharon Fogel, who was the head of the Bureau of the Budget at the Ministry of Finance at the time, headed both the phone rates and the electricity rates committees.

15. As in the case of the phone rates (see n. 11), the recognition that IEC is entitled to a fixed rate of return on its equity explains this price increase.

16. In the present system, the handling charges are divided between the shippers (who bears the portage charge) and the shipping companies (who are responsible for the stevedoring charge). The wharfage charge is paid by shippers, and the vessel charges by the shipping company. The recommendations attempted to keep constant the shares of shippers and shipping companies in the total charges.

17. At the time, there did not exist a Hebrew word for *privatization*. The popularity gained by the term led the Academy for the Hebrew Language to introduce a new word in the Hebrew vocabulary.

18. A third producer, whose attempts to sell to the phone company blocked by the first two producers, had to compete abroad and became, as a result, one of the leading communication equipment producers in Israel.

19. The only exceptions to this rule are the reform in the oil industry and the recent (1997–1998) reforms in communication. In both cases, the ministers involved were affiliated with big parties. It is noteworthy that the same person who led the oil reform tried to block the reforms in communication and electricity. In both cases, the ministers' support can be explained by their junior status in their party. They may have perceived, correctly, that the reforms would enhance their standing with their voters.

References

Barkai, Haim. "The Energy Sector in the 1960s and 1970s." In *The Israeli Economy—Maturing through Crisis*, edited by Yoram Ben Porath. Cambridge: Harvard University Press, 1986.

Ben-Ishai, Guy. "Post-Privatization Efficiency Increases in Israeli Government Firms," The Falk Institute Discussion Papers, January 1996. (Hebrew)

Berglas, Eitan, et al. "Privatization—Necessity or Fashion?—A Symposium," *The Economic Quarterly* 39 (April 1988): 135–136. (Hebrew)

Blass, Asher A. "Contracts as Barriers to Entry in Gasoline Retailing in Israel," *The Economic Quarterly* 46:1 (May 1998): 22–48. (Hebrew)

Bloom, Kalman. "The Desired Rate Structure and Subsidies in the Scheduled Bus Lines in Israel." October 1980, Mimeo. (Hebrew)

Czamanski, Daniel. The Reorganization of the Israeli Electricity Market—Interim Report, July 1994. (Hebrew)

Crew, M. A., and P. R. Kleindorfer. *The Economics of Public Utility Regulation*. Cambridge, MA: The MIT Press, 1987.

Eckstein, Zvi, and Menachem Perlman. "Supply Agreements in the Motor Gasoline Market and the Public Good," *The Economic Quarterly* 46:1 (May 1999): 65–92. (Hebrew)

Fogel, Aharon. The Report of the Committee for the Setting of the Phone Rates, September 1989. (Hebrew)

———. The Report of the Committee for the Setting of the Electricity Rates, October 1991. (Hebrew)

Ganoth, Zvi, Samuel Bulmash, and Dan Schlesinger. "Investment and Developmet Strategy of the Israel Ports Authority," *The Economic Quarterly* 127 (December 1985): 373–384. (Hebrew)

Gronau, Reuben. The Report of the Team for the Examination of the Structure of the Refinery Industry in Israel, November 1996. (Hebrew)

———. "Intervention and Competition in the Israeli Ground Transport Market: III. Bus Subsidies and the Intervention in the Cab Market." Falk Institute Discussion Paper 97:03 iii, June 1997a. (Hebrew)

———. "Public Transport Policy in Israel, 1970–1995." *The Economic Quarterly* 44:4 (December 1997b): 609–628. (Hebrew)

———. The Report of the Committee for the Setting of Phone Rates, September 1998. (Hebrew)

Klinov, R. "Why Have Wage Disparities Increased? Israel, 1972–1995," November 1998, Mimeo.

Miedan, Israel. The Report on the Costs and Cross Subsidies in the Phone Services—Final Report, September 1993. (Hebrew)

Muller, Eitan. "Exclusive Vertical Agreements and Horizontal Competition in the Israeli Petrol Market," *The Economic Quarterly* 46:1 (May 1999): 49–64. (Hebrew)

Raanan, Zvi. "Reforms in the Israeli Ports," The Vidra Institute for Research of Shipping and Aviation, 1996, Mimeo. (Hebrew)

———. "Competition in Israeli Ports," The Vidra Institute for Research of Ports and Aviation, May 1997, Mimeo. (Hebrew)

Sague, Eli. "Barriers to Competitiveness in the Israeli Economy—Fuel Supply," *The Economic Quarterly* 46:1 (May 1999): 18–21. (Hebrew)

Shorer, Doron. The Report of the Committee for the Setting of Phone Rates. (1993).

Vardi, Joseph. The Report of the Committee Examining the Electricity Company's Franchise, December 1992. (Hebrew)

V IMMIGRATION AND THE LABOR MARKET

11 The Integration of Immigrants from the Former Soviet Union in the Israeli Labor Market

Zvi Eckstein and Yoram Weiss

11.1 Introduction

The mass immigration of Jews from the former Soviet Union to Israel, which began toward the end of 1989, amounted to a total of about 711 thousand immigrants between 1990 and the end of 1997 (see table 11.1). The Israeli population at the end of 1989 was 4.56 million, and the premigration population growth rate during the 1980s was between 1.4 percent and 1.8 percent per annum. The 1990–1991 wave of immigration increased the population almost instantly by 7.6 percent. The flow from 1992 to 1995 stabilized at about sixty-four to sixty-eight thousand, and declined to about fifty-five thousand in 1997, contributing almost one percent to the annual rate of growth of the population. The accumulated flow of immigrants from the former Soviet Union during the period 1990–1997 constitutes about 16 percent of the labor force of the premigration population of Israel.

An important characteristic of this wave of immigration is the immigrants' exceptionally high level of education and their prior experience in academic jobs (see table 11.1). Those who arrived before the end of 1993 possessed an average of 14.5 years of schooling, and half of them had held academic and managerial positions before immigrating. Of those, 57,400 defined themselves as engineers and 12,200 as medical doctors, compared with 30,200 engineers and 15,600 doctors in Israel in 1989. The large entry rates of highly skilled immigrants generated a gradual adjustment process, whereby immigrants first worked at low skill occupations and then climbed up the occupational ladder as they became more familiar with the Israeli labor market and found jobs that matched their skills.

We have chosen to focus our analysis on the time patterns of aggregate and individual wages and examine three interrelated features of the assimilation process—the rise in the productive capacity of immigrants as they gradually adapt to the Israeli labor market, the rising rewards that immigrants receive for their imported skills, and the role of the family in facilitating the acquisition of local skills. Our purpose is to provide an integrative view of the wage dynamics, putting aside other important features that have been discussed elsewhere.[1] Section 2 provides a summary of the aggregate time series evidence on the link between immigration, economic growth, employment, and wages. These aggregate patterns are linked with the microeconomic analysis that follows. It is shown that the estimated individual wage profiles can be used to create a quality-adjusted labor aggregate that maintains a fixed aggregate capital labor ratio, during the period of mass immigration. This allows us to reconcile the stable average wage of Israelis and the rising wages of immigrants

Table 11.1
Total Immigrants and Immigrants from Former USSR by Year of Immigration and Occupation Abroad (Total immigrants in parentheses)

	1990		1991		1992		1993	
	Number	%	Number	%	Number	%	Number	%
Total Arrivals	185,227		147,839		65,093		66,145	
	(199,516)		(176,456)		(77,057)		(76,805)	
Aged 15+	142,944		117,395		52,037		52,569	
	(153,395)		(133,987)		(60,451)		(60,607)	
Worked Abroad			79,743	100.0	33,696	100.0	33,141	100.0
	(100,720)	(100.0)	(84,694)	(100.0)	(36,948)	(100.0)	(36,128)	(100.0)
Occupation* Abroad								
1			31,693	39.7	12,242	36.3	10,214	30.8
	(43,315)	(43.0)	(33,078)	(39.1)	(13,179)	(35.7)	(11,219)	(31.1)
2			26,021	32.6	10,872	32.3	10,736	32.4
	(34,443)	(34.2)	(27,321)	(32.3)	(11,631)	(31.5)	(11,658)	(32.3)
3			22,029	27.6	10,582	31.4	12,191	36.8
	(22,962)	(22.8)	(24,294)	(28.7)	(12,138)	(32.9)	(13,251)	(36.7)

*Occupation 1: Academic professionals and managers. Occupation 2: Associate professionals and technicians. Occupation 3: Other skilled and unskilled workers.
Source: Israeli Central Bureau of Statistics, *Statistical Abstracts*, 1990–1995; Israeli Central Bureau of Statistics, *Annual Statistics*, 1997–1998.

during the period 1990–1995, which was characterized by a large inflow of labor and a corresponding, but delayed, increase in capital.

Section 3, which is based on Eckstein and Weiss (1998), analyzes individual wage growth for immigrants of different skills. The general pattern is an initial low wage compared with Israelis of similar skills, followed by a sharp increase with time spent in Israel. For instance, the average hourly wage of a highly skilled immigrant who arrived in the cohort 1990–1991 at the age of thirty is predicted to be 60 percent of the wage of an equivalent native Israeli. The estimated equation predicts that this immigrant will reach at age fifty-five a wage that is about 84 percent of the equivalent native. On the average, real wages of immigrants grow at a rate of 6.4 percent a year during the five years following the arrival. Rising prices for imported skills, mainly schooling and work experience, account for one half of this rise. As the price of imported skills rise, immigrants become more differentiated, and their wage become less equal.

Section 4 compares the impact of marital status on the wages and labor force participation of immigrants and native Israelis. For immigrants, we find a large initial marriage premium of 8.1 percent for males and 11.5 percent for females. This

Table 11.1 (continued)

1994		1995		1996		1997		Total 1990–1997	
Number	%	Number	%	Number	%	Number	%	Number	%
68,079 (79,844)		64,847 (76,361)		59,049 (70,919)		54,591 (66,000)		710,870 (822,958)	
54,706 (63,615)		52,382 (61,031)		47,960 (56,852)		44,536 (53,124)		564,529 (643,062)	
35,145 (39,232)	100.0 (100.0)	36,338 (41,230)	100.0 (100.0)	32,009 (36,943)	100.0 (100.0)	31,026 (35,877)	100.0 (100.0)	281,098 (411,772)	100.0 (100.0)
11,563 (13,086)	32.9 (33.4)	11,089 (12,514)	30.5 (30.4)	10,771 (12,277)	33.6 (33.2)	9,926 (11,589)	32.0 (32.3)	97,498 (150,257)	34.7 (36.5)
11,748 (13,179)	33.4 (33.6)	11,272 (12,593)	31.0 (30.5)	10,220 (11,680)	31.9 (31.6)	9,856 (11,181)	31.8 (31.2)	90,725 (133,687)	32.4 (32.7)
11,834 (12,967)	33.7 (33.1)	13,977 (16,123)	38.5 (39.1)	11,018 (12,986)	34.4 (35.2)	11,244 (13,107)	36.2 (36.5)	92,875 (127,828)	33.0 (31.0)

gap between married persons and singles rises during the first fifteen years in Israel and then narrows down. In contrast, among native Israelis, we find a small and insignificant marriage premium. We interpret this difference as evidence for stronger family coordination of work activities among immigrants. This coordination allows married immigrants to enjoy a higher wage level and a higher wage growth than single immigrants.

11.2 Aggregate Aspects

Ben-Porath (1986) provides a detailed description of the growth of population and output in Israel from 1922 to 1982 and notes the positive correlation between immigration and growth. Table 11.2 updates his table up to 1997 and reveals that this pattern continued in the 1990s, despite the lower growth rates in later years. In particular, consumption per capita rises during periods of mass immigration. This was made possible through investments that were triggered by the immigration shocks. As seen in table 11.2, the capital stock keeps up with the increase in employment after some delay. This is true for both productive capital and residential capital. There is also some evidence that the rate of capital utilization increased initially after the mass immigration began.[2]

Table 11.2
Annual Growth Rates of Population, Production and Capital, 1922–1997

Years	Population	GNP	GNP per capita	Capital Stock	Housing Stock	Consumption per capita	Immigration Rate
1922–1932	8.0%	17.6%	7.8%	13.7%			8.2%
1932–1947	8.4%	11.2%	3.0%	9.8%			6.4%
1947–1950	31.9%	11.2%	3.0%	9.8%			19.8%
1950–1951	20.0%	29.7%	10.0%				13.2%
1951–1964	4.0%	9.1%	4.9%	12.3%	11.6%	12.8%	2.2%
1964–1972	3.0%	8.9%	5.5%	8.4%	7.7%	8.7%	1.3%
1972–1982	2.1%	3.2%	0.8%	6.7%	7.7%	6.1%	0.9%
1982–1989	1.4%	3.4%	1.7%	3.3%	1.6%	2.6%	0.4%
1982–1986	1.5%	3.0%	1.2%	3.5%	−3.2%	2.4%	0.4%
1986–1989	1.3%	4.0%	2.3%	3.0%	8.4%	2.8%	0.4%
1989–1997	2.9%	5.3%	2.0%	5.4%	9.2%	3.4%	2.3%
1989–1993	3.8%	5.8%	1.9%	3.7%	10.1%	3.0%	2.8%
1993–1997	2.1%	4.9%	2.2%	7.2%	8.2%	3.7%	1.7%

Sources: Israeli Central Bureau of Statistics, *Statistical Abstracts*, 1960–1997 and Ben-Porath (1986).

Razin and Sadka (1993) and Sussman (1998) use a simple aggregate model with Cobb-Douglas production function to describe the comovements of population, GDP, employment, wages, and capital. An implication of this technology is that under competitive conditions, the wage rate is proportional to the output per worker and, therefore, the continued rise in GNP per capita is an indication that the mass immigration was accompanied by a corresponding increase in other inputs and in productivity, without a substantial negative impact on the wages and employment opportunities of native Israelis.

Figure 11.1 shows the movements in real wages in the public and the business sectors from 1980 to 1997. Following the beginning of the mass immigration in 1990, there is an initial small decrease in average wages followed by a subsequent increase. The temporary reduction in wages occurred mainly in the business sector, while public sector wages continued to grow. The different patterns of adjustment by sector reflect the importance of collective bargaining in the public sector (see Sussman and Zakai, 1998). The large and unexpected immigration wave, and the increase by 11.6 percent in the working population, aged 15+ during 1990–1992, caused no discernible break in the time pattern of the average wage.

Separate time patterns in the real hourly wages for natives and immigrants during 1991–1997 (see Eckstein and Weiss, 1999) show that the wage of *both* groups tended to *rise* during the period, with higher proportional wage growth among immigrants. In particular, the wage of natives with 16+ years of schooling remained flat during

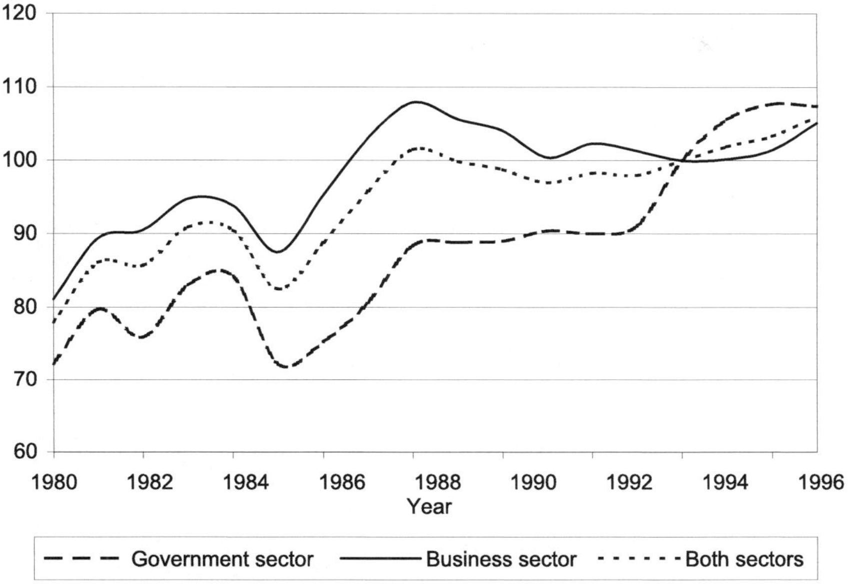

Figure 11.1
Indices of the Real Wage in the Government and Business Sectors, 1980–1997, (1994 = 100)
Source: Bank of Israel, *Annual Report*, 1998.

1991–1994 and then began to rise slightly. The average wage of such workers declined as more immigrants joined the 16+ group, because their wage is about half the wage of natives. Thus, the decline in average wages mainly reflects the entry of immigrants into low-paying jobs, and does not imply that natives suffered a wage loss. Freidberg (1996) provides additional evidence showing a small impact of the mass immigrants on the wages of native Israelis. This accumulated evidence is consistent with the literature on the impact of immigrants on wages of native workers (see Altonji and Card, 1991; Lalonde and Topel, 1991). We note that the U.S. studies examined the impact of immigration on wages of natives in *local* labor markets. Local wages can be unaffected because native workers move out as immigrants enter (see Freidberg and Hunt, 1995). In contrast, we report the absence of countrywide wage affects, where labor mobility is not operative. Instead, capital inflow and its effect on the aggregate capital labor ratio maintain wage stability.[3]

The aggregate employment data misrepresents the time changes in the aggregate labor input and, consequently, in the aggregate capital labor ratio, because immigrants are treated as perfect substitutes to natives. In fact, as we show in detail, immi-

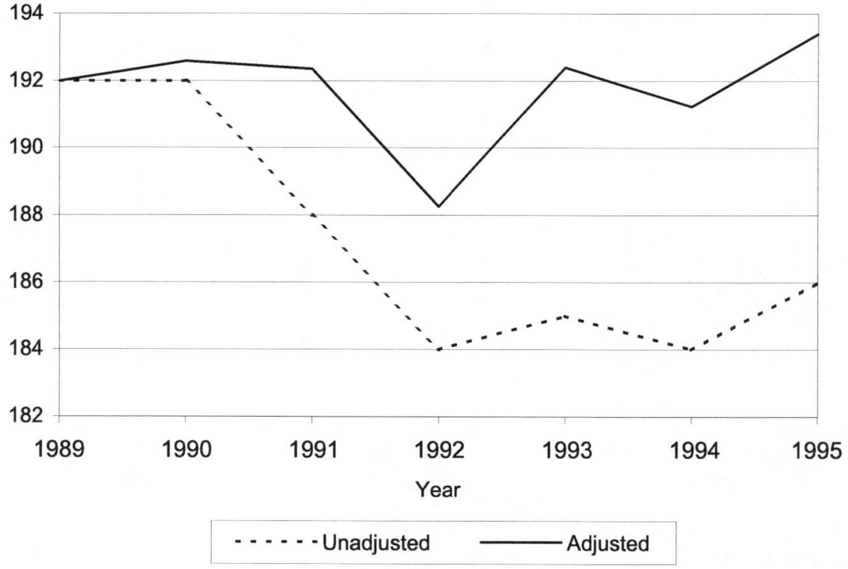

Figure 11.2
Adjusted and Unadjusted Capital—Labor Ratio
Sources: The unadjusted capital labor ratio is from the Bank of Israel Report, 1998. The adjusted capital labor ratio is obtained using the adjustment factor from table 3 in Eckstein and Weiss (1999).

grants adapt *gradually* to the Israeli labor market and become closer substitutes to comparable Israeli workers with similar schooling and work experience as they spend more time in Israel. This process is reflected in the initially low wages of immigrants, about half the wages of comparable natives, followed by a sharp increase in wages with time spent in Israel.

Following Jorgenson and Griliches (1967), we propose a simple method for quality adjustment based on the relative wages of immigrants and natives (a detailed description of these adjustments appears in the Appendix). The implied adjustments in the capital labor ratio are shown in figure 11.2. As seen, the adjustments imply that the aggregate capital labor ratio remained roughly constant during the period of mass immigration. Under constant returns to scale technology and competitive conditions, this implies that the growth in inputs has no effect on wages. The only sources for growth in average wages are quality changes, reflecting shifts in composition of the labor force toward more productive workers, and growth in total factor productivity. Among immigrants, there is a 20 percent increase in quality during 1990–1995, compared with only 2 percent among Israelis. In this respect, the aggregate data, properly interpreted, is consistent with a stable average wage for native workers and rising average wages for immigrants.

11.3 Analysis of the Convergence of Immigrant Wages

A Framework for Analysis

An immigrant brings with him a fixed set of marketable skills such as schooling, occupation, and work experience acquired abroad. As time passes, these skills are gradually adapted to the Israeli market, and their quality and market value rises. The immigrant may also augment his skills or acquire new skills in Israel. The acquisition of new skills requires some sacrifice of current earning. Thus, each immigrant is faced with an investment problem in which he compares the benefits from investment in terms of higher future earnings to the costs in terms of foregone current earnings. The investment decisions interact with the changes in the market value of the immigrant's skills and together determine his earning growth. An Israeli worker faces a similar investment problem, except that he does not have skills that were acquired abroad.

We distinguish three sources of wage growth for immigrants: (1) the rise of the return to imported human capital, (2) the impact of accumulated experience and investments on the job in the host country, and (3) the mobility up the occupational ladder in the host country.[4] We provide a simple framework, based on human capital theory, to explain the connections between rising prices of skills and investment in human capital and describe the conditions under which the earnings of immigrants will converge with the earnings of comparable natives. We use two basic results from human capital theory: Investment declines as the individual becomes older and approaches the end of his working career, and current investment is higher if the individual expects an increase in the price of skills. The first result follows from the fact that the value of human capital depends on the expected period of utilization. The second result follows from the observation that investment in human capital involves a sacrifice of current earning capacity in favor of increased future earning capacity. Based on this framework, we formulate a nonlinear model, which is estimated using repeated cross-section data that includes immigrants with different duration of time in Israel, observed in the years 1991 to 1995. The estimation is done in two steps: First, a wage equation is estimated for Israelis, and the estimated coefficients are used to predict earnings for immigrants. Then, imported skills and their interaction with time spent in Israel explain the difference between actual and predicted earnings for immigrants.

Data on Wages

Hourly wages are constructed from data on earnings and hours, reported in the CBS Income Surveys for the years 1991 to 1995, which are random annual surveys of the entire Israeli population. Using these data, we construct two subsamples—a sample of native-born Israelis and a sample of immigrants from the former USSR who were older than thirteen upon arrival. The two subsamples include only Jewish men of ages twenty-six to sixty-five who worked more than two weeks during the last month and more than twenty-five hours per week. We also exclude all individuals with no information on age, no information on the number of years of schooling and with more than thirty-one years of schooling. For immigrants, we can break the number of years of schooling and work experience into those acquired in the former Soviet Union and those accumulated in Israel.

From the summary statistics for the two subsamples from the Income Survey, we learn that on the average, immigrants earn about 64 percent of the monthly wage of Israelis (and 66 percent of their hourly wage). Immigrants are about three years older than Israelis and have one year more of education. The occupational distribution of working immigrants is quite similar to the occupational distribution of working Israelis. The immigration flows from the former USSR were concentrated in two time periods; about 20 percent of the immigrants, observed in 1991–1995 arrived in the early wave of 1970–1979, and 62 percent arrived in the later wave of 1989–1992. Seventy-five percent of the immigrants in the sample were newly arrived and had been in Israel for less than six years.

Implementation

We follow a simple two-stage estimation procedure. We first use a sample of Israeli natives to estimate a wage equation for Israeli workers. We use these estimates to predict what each immigrant would earn in Israel if he could sell his observed skills for the same price as native Israelis. We then form the differences between actual and predicted earning for immigrants and estimate a second regression equation, with the objective of identifying the effect of changing prices of skills as a function of time spent in Israel.[5] We allow for cohort effects and for the possibility that immigrants who are "trapped" in low-skill occupations receive a lower return for schooling acquired abroad.

The observed imported skills in this analysis are schooling and experience acquired abroad. Schooling is measured simply by the total time spent in school. However, experience is not simply the accumulated time spent at work, but rather the amount of human capital or skills accumulated in work. This quantity is given by the expression

$$\left[b\,exp - \frac{c\,exp^2}{2}\right],$$

where *exp* denotes experience, defined in the usual way (age-schooling-6-military service). We normalize by setting the price (in terms of log earnings) paid to Israelis for their "true" experience to unity. We shall *define* the "true" work experience that immigrant import as

$$\left[b\,exp_0 - \frac{c\,exp_0^2}{2}\right],$$

using the values for b and c as for Israelis.[6] We then estimate the time pattern of the price that immigrants receive for this quantity. The prices of unobserved skills are represented by the time patterns of the occupational specific constants.

Regression Results for Israelis

Table 11.3 presents the estimation results of the wage equation for Israelis. The yearly dummies represent the difference from the wage in 1995. We find that despite the mass immigration, the wage per hour for Israelis *increased* during the period. Controlling for schooling, occupation, and experience, the hourly wage in 1991 is about six percent lower than in 1995 (1992 is an exception with wage per hour almost equal to that in 1995). The wages in occupation 1 and occupation 2 are, respectively,

Table 11.3
Wage Regression for Israeli Men, Aged 25–65, Years 1991–1995

Variable	Coefficient	Standard Deviation
Constant	1.2726	0.0360
1991	−0.0614	0.0160
1992	−0.0083	0.0162
1993	−0.0437	0.0167
1994	−0.0223	0.0162
Occupation 1	0.2718	0.0165
Occupation 2	0.2150	0.0170
Experience	0.0451	0.0018
Experience^2	−0.0007	0.00004
Schooling	0.0728	0.0022
R^2	0.3215	
No. of obs.	8,186	

about 27 and 22 percent higher than in occupation 3. There is a 4.5 percent increase of the hourly wage with the first year of experience and about 7 percent increase of the hourly wage with a year of education.[7]

We use this equation as the benchmark for studying the convergence of the wages of immigrants to native Israelis, as described in the model above.

Regression Results for Immigrants

To estimate the convergence parameters, we use as a dependent variable the difference between the observed log wage of each immigrant and his predicted log wage, using the estimated parameters in table 11.3. The explanatory variables are schooling acquired abroad (interacted with occupation), experience acquired abroad, and occupation in Israel. The effect of each of these variables (including the constant) is allowed to interact with time since arrival to Israel. To isolate the impact of mass immigration in 1990–1991, we distinguish three cohorts—immigrants who arrived before 1990, during 1990–1991 and during 1992–1995—and allow them to affect the constant. Specifically, we estimate the nonlinear regression

$$\begin{aligned} D_i = {} & b + b_{<90}c_{<90} + b_{92\text{–}95}c_{92\text{–}95} + de^{-\lambda(t-t_{0i})} \\ & + [b_{occ1} + d_{occ1}e^{-\lambda(t-t_{0i})}] \cdot occ1 + [b_{occ2} + d_{occ2}e^{-\lambda(t-t_{0i})}] \cdot occ2 \\ & + [b_{exp} + d_{exp}e^{-\lambda(t-t_{0i})}] \cdot [(.045 - .0007\, exp_{0i}) \cdot exp_{0i}] \\ & + [b_{s\_occ1\&2}(occ1 + occ2) + b_{s\_occ3}occ3 + d_s e^{-\lambda(t-t_{0i})}] \cdot s_{0i} + \varepsilon_i, \end{aligned} \tag{11.1}$$

where D_i is the residual from the first stage, $t - t_{0i}$ is potential experience in Israel, exp_{0i} is potential experience in former USSR, s_{0i} is the number of years of schooling in the USSR, $occ1_i$ and $occ2_i$ are dummies that take the value 1 if the immigrant works in occupations 1 or 2, respectively (occupation 3 is the reference group), and $c_{<90}$ and $c_{92\text{–}95}$ are dummy variables that take the value 1 if the immigrant entered Israel before 1990 and between 1992 and 1995, respectively. The value of $[(.045 - .0007\, exp_{0i}) \cdot exp_{0i}]$ is the accumulated human capital associated with the market labor experience that the immigrant imported, using the estimated coefficients for experience and experience squared for Israelis in table 11.3.

The effects of occupation schooling and experience interact with time spent in Israel, where each effect has the form $b + de^{-\lambda(t-t_{0i})}$. The first part, denoted by b, describes the *long-run* difference in the effect between Israelis and immigrants. The second term, denoted by $de^{-\lambda(t-t_{0i})}$, describes the adjustment process and $d + b$ is the *immediate* impact. Note that the same speed of adjustment, λ, is assumed for the

Table 11.4
Nonlinear Regression on Residuals for Male Immigrants, Age at Arrival >25, Years 1991–1995

	Without occupation-schooling interaction		With occupation-schooling interaction	
Coefficient	Estimate	St. Dev.	Estimate	St. Dev.
b_{cons}	0.3917	0.2114	0.4233	0.2103
$b_{cohort<90}$	0.0625	0.0468	0.0621	0.0467
$b_{cohort\ 92-95}$	−0.0562	0.0274	−0.0574	0.0274
d_{cons}	0.5743	0.2582	0.5766	0.2565
λ	0.0941	0.0344	0.0953	0.0348
$b_{con\_occ\ 1}$	0.3679	0.0851	0.1062	0.1595
$d_{con\_occ\ 1}$	−0.2426	0.1151	−0.2513	0.1146
$b_{con\_occ\ 2}$	0.2116	0.0980	−0.0209	0.1550
$d_{con\_occ\ 2}$	−0.1553	0.1359	−0.1734	0.1357
b_{exp}	−0.2372	0.2618	−0.2333	0.2605
d_{exp}	−1.0013	0.2879	−1.0142	0.2858
b_{school}	−0.0423	0.0119	—	—
$b_{school\_occ\ 1\ \&\ occ\ 2}$	—	—	−0.0290	0.0136
$b_{school\_occ\ 3}$	—	—	−0.0455	0.0119
d_{school}	−0.0371	0.0141	−0.0359	0.0139
Mean dependent var.	−0.6106	0.4822	−0.6106	0.4822
Sum of sq. residuals	234.307		233.799	
Log-likelihood	−724.262		−722.369	
R^2	0.7780		0.7767	
No. of obs.	1,744		1,744	

Dependent Variable: Residuals from Wage Regression in Table 11.3.

effects of schooling experience and occupation. The estimated parameters for this nonlinear regression are presented in table 11.4.

The estimated speed of adjustment, λ, is .0953 per year, implying that within a period of ten years each price is adjusted by 62 percent of the initial distance from its long-run value. However, convergence also depends on the long-term difference between the prices that Israelis and immigrants obtain for their skills. We shall, therefore, discuss each of the prices for schooling, experience, and unobserved skills separately.

The initial difference, upon arrival, in the price (rate of return) of schooling between immigrants and Israelis is $b_{s\_occ1\&2} + d_s = -.0290 - .0359 = -.0649$ in occupations 1 and 2 and $b_{s\_occ1\&2} = d_s = -.0455 - .0359 = -.0814$ in occupation 3. Given the estimated rate of return of .0728 for native Israelis, the initial reward for schooling is slightly positive for an immigrant working in occupation 1 or 2 and slightly negative (but not significantly different from zero) for an immigrant working in occupation 3. The long-run difference in the rate of return for schooling in occupations 1 and 2 is

$b_{s\_occ1\&2} = -.0290$ and $b_{s\_occ3} = -.0455$ in occupation 3. Hence, the rate of return that immigrants can expect in the long run is only $.0728 - .0290 = .0438$ in occupations 1 and 2 and $.0728 - .0455 = .0273$ in occupation 3. This substantial gap between natives and immigrants suggests that schooling acquired in the former USSR is not fully transferable to Israel, either because of differences in quality or informational frictions that cause immigrants to "give up" in their search for better jobs (see Weiss et al., 1999).

The initial difference, upon arrival, in the value of experience acquired abroad is $b_{exp} + d_{exp} = -.233 - 1.014 = -1.247$. Because the price of accumulated experience that Israelis obtain is normalized to one, this means that the initial return for accumulated experience is $1 - 1.247 = -.247$. This means that, initially, experience accumulated in the former USSR has negative value in the Israeli labor market. With time, however, the price rises to $1 - b_{exp} = 1 - .233 = .767$, which, given the high standard error on b_{exp}, is not significantly different from 1. Thus, we cannot reject the hypothesis that in the long run, immigrants obtain the same rate of return for experience as native Israelis.

The occupational dummies show that immigrants who work in the high-skill occupations 1 and 2, obtain higher premia (relative to occupation 3) than comparable Israeli workers. Using the specification without a schooling-occupation interaction, these premia are in the short run $.272 + (.368 - .242) = .398$ and $.215 + (.212 - .155) = .272$ in occupations 1 and 2, respectively. In the long run, these premia are even higher—$.272 + .368 = .640$ and $.215 + .212 = .427$. However, a large part of these occupational effects is a consequence of the lower rate of return for schooling in occupation 3. When a schooling-occupation interaction is added, it is seen that the occupational effects are reduced to .127 and .021, in the short run and to .378 and .194 in the long run. The remaining occupational effects suggest that, in the long run, workers who were lucky to find jobs in the high-skill occupations, or had some unobserved characteristic that made them more suitable for employment there, fare substantially better than those immigrants who remain in low-skill occupations.

We now turn to the discussion of the constant terms that summarize the *average* impact of unmeasured characteristics of immigrants. As seen in table 11.4, for both specifications, the coefficients b and d are positive and large, indicating that in the short run, there is not much to distinguish between immigrants with different human capital indicators. However, with time, the constant term declines and more weight is shifted to observable characteristics, given that their prices rise.

The cohort dummies indicate a reduction in the unmeasured quality of immigrants. Holding measured characteristics constant, immigrants who came before

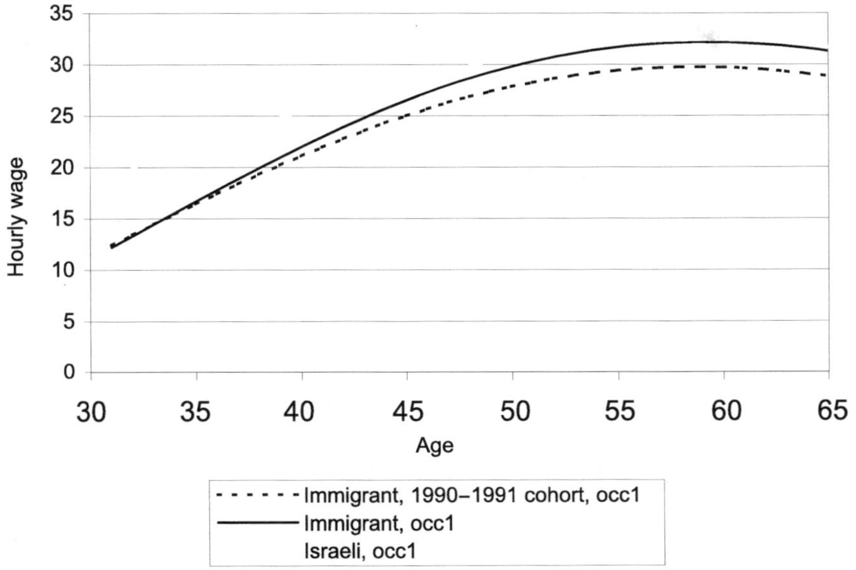

Figure 11.3
Simulated Wage-Age Profiles in Occupation 1 for an Israeli and an Immigrant, with and without Cohort Effects, Schooling = 16, Age at Migration = 30*
* Wage per hour in 1991 NIS, based on the regressions in tables 11.3 and 11.4.

1990 earn 6.2 percent more than immigrants who came in 1990–1991 (the omitted group), who earn 5.7 percent more than immigrants who came in 1992–1995. This pattern is consistent with the observed reduction in measured quality in terms of schooling and academic occupation (see table 11.1).

The (Non) Convergence of Wages within Occupations

The estimated regressions allow us to compare the simulated life-cycle wages for immigrants and natives. Figures 11.3, 11.4, and 11.5 show the predicted wage-age profiles for an immigrant with sixteen years of schooling who arrived in Israel during the period 1990–1991 at the age of thirty, and for an equivalent native Israeli. We consider three such comparisons, one for each occupational category.

As seen in these figures, the immigrant's wage-age profile is generally below that of the native Israeli. In occupation 1, convergence is predicted for the *average* immigrant, but not for members of the recent immigration wave. In occupations 2 and 3, wages of immigrants with sixteen years of schooling do not converge to those of a comparable Israeli, but rather to the wages of an Israeli with the average level of

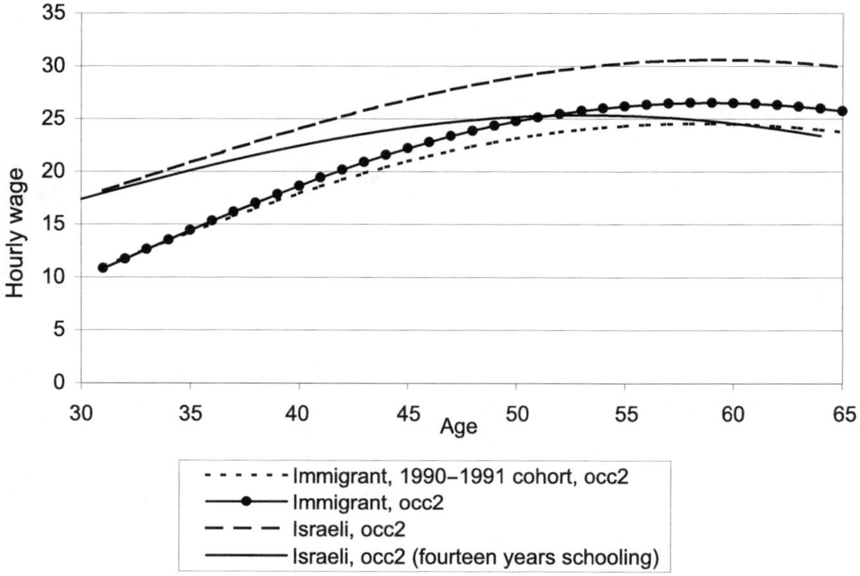

Figure 11.4
Simulated Wage-Age Profiles in Occupation 2 for an Israeli and an Immigrant, with and without Cohort Effects, Schooling = 16, Age at Migration = 30*
* Wage per hour in 1991 NIS, based on the regressions in tables 11.3 and 11.4.

schooling in these occupations, fourteen and twelve years, respectively.[8] The predicted wage gaps between immigrants and Israelis with sixteen years schooling at age fifty-five for the 1990–1991 cohort are 8 percent, 20 percent, and 34 percent in occupations 1, 2, and 3, respectively.

The (Non) Convergence of Average Wages

As we have seen, the occupation at which an immigrant is employed has a strong impact on his wages. Therefore, the rate at which immigrants find jobs in the high-skill occupations is an important determinant of wage growth. Because of market frictions and lack of information, immigrants do not immediately find jobs that suit their qualifications and skills. Instead, they start at the bottom of the occupational ladder and gradually climb up. Weiss and Eckstein (1998) and Weiss et al. (1999) provide a detailed description of this process. We shall provide here only a brief description of occupational transitions.

Table 11.5 shows the occupational distribution of immigrants by years in Israel for two age groups; those who arrived at age twenty-six to forty and those who arrived

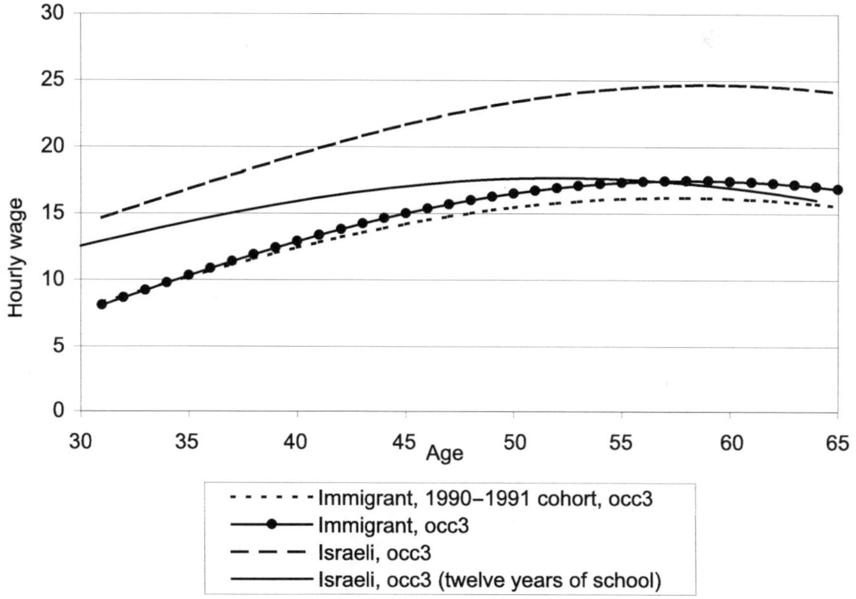

Figure 11.5
Simulated Wage-Age Profiles in Occupation 3 for an Israeli and an Immigrant, with and without Cohort Effects, Schooling = 16, Age at Migration = 30*
*Wage per hour in 1991 NIS, based on the regressions in tables 11.3 and 11.4.

at age forty-one to fifty-five. These figures show a sharp increase in the proportion employed in academic jobs, especially among immigrants who arrived at a young age. Among those with more than sixteen years of schooling, only 20 percent are employed in academic jobs upon arrival. After four years in Israel, this percentage rises to 36 percent and 28 percent among the young and old, respectively. Among those who had been in Israel for five to fifteen years, the corresponding figures are 54 percent and 37 percent. By way of comparison, the percentage of Israelis with 16+ years of schooling who work in occupation 1 is 63 percent. Using simple Logit estimation, it is expected that the occupational gap between recent immigrants and comparable Israelis will narrow substantially with time spent in Israel.[9]

We now bring together our results on wage dynamics and the dynamics of occupational transitions by immigrants, and examine the convergence of the average wage, unconditioned on occupation. Figure 11.6 presents wage-age profiles, averaged over occupations, for an immigrant with sixteen years of schooling, who arrived in Israel at age thirty and a comparable Israeli. Figure 11.6 shows that the wage dif-

Table 11.5
Occupational Distribution of Male Immigrants (Percent)

	After 1 year		After 2 years		After 3 years		After 4 years		After 5–15 years		After 15+ years	
Occupation	All	Sch 16+	All	Sch 16+	All	Sch 16+	All	Sch 16+	All	Sch 16+	All	Sch 16+
Age upon arrival 26–40												
1	6.94	20.77	12.05	24.79	16.35	34.65	17.06	36.50	21.05	54.26	23.79	58.40
2	6.20	10.38	8.18	8.97	9.31	10.09	11.57	13.50	11.18	13.45	11.37	12.18
3	65.93	45.36	67.73	51.71	67.30	45.61	65.58	46.00	63.29	28.70	58.30	26.05
Not working	20.93	23.50	12.05	14.53	7.04	9.65	5.79	4.00	4.47	3.59	6.54	3.36
Num. of obs.	951	183	880	234	795	228	674	200	760	223	765	238
Age upon arrival 41–55												
1	6.82	19.16	9.41	18.91	11.03	21.46	14.00	28.22	18.81	37.42	25.75	75.00
2	3.48	3.27	5.26	6.30	6.21	8.68	8.32	10.40	8.26	6.75	7.78	2.50
3	66.48	47.20	68.74	54.20	72.76	58.90	69.78	50.99	67.20	49.69	60.48	12.50
Not working	23.23	30.37	16.59	20.59	10.00	10.96	7.91	10.40	5.73	6.13	5.99	10.00
Num. of obs.	719	214	627	238	580	219	439	202	436	163	167	40

Source: CBS Labour Force Surveys, 1991–1995.

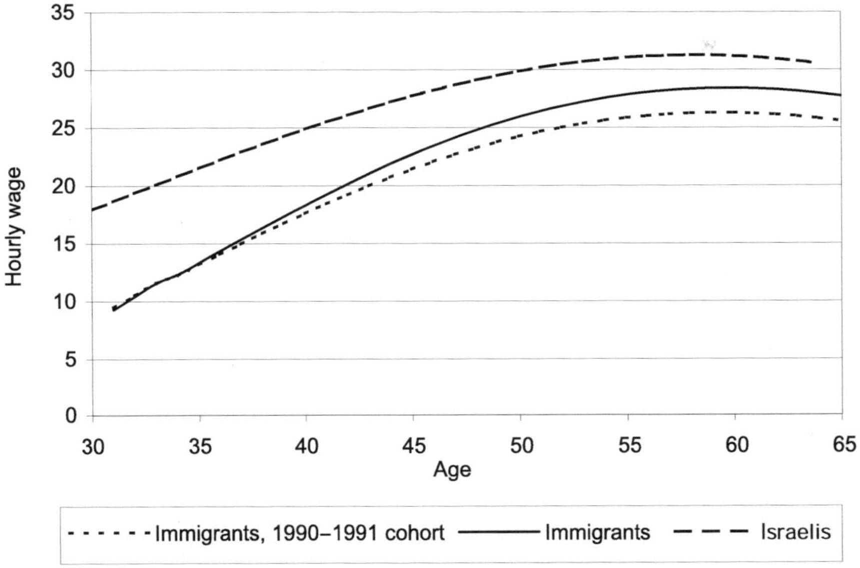

Figure 11.6
Simulated Wage-Age Profiles Averaged over Occupations, for an Israeli Worker and Immigrant, with and without Cohort Effects, Schooling = 16, Age at Migration = 30*
* Wage per hour in 1991 NIS, based on the regressions in tables 3 and 4.

ferential between immigrants and comparable native Israelis narrows substantially with time spent in Israel. An immigrant who arrives at age thirty with 16+ years of schooling earns on average only 52 percent of the wage of a comparable Israeli. After five years in Israel, the same immigrant earns a wage that is 62 percent of the wage of a comparable Israeli and after twenty years this proportion rises to 80 percent. The growth in early years is mainly due to the rise in the returns for imported skills. The growth in later years is mainly due to occupational switches, reflected in the narrowing of the occupational differences between immigrants and native Israelis. However, convergence is slow, and full convergence is not attained, because of incomplete convergence in the occupational structure and the lack of convergence within occupations.[10]

11.4 Family Effects

Immigrants arrive to Israel as single or married, with small or large families. Family structure has a marked effect on the labor market integration and the wages of immigrants. Wages of married immigrants tend to be higher and grow at a faster rate. These patterns reflect the coordination of work activities between immigrating spouses. In this section, we outline the main features and consequences of this coordination.

Data on the Family

The data source that we use to assess the impact of family structure on wages is the 1995 Israeli Census of Population. We extracted from the 1995 census all the available data on immigrants from the former USSR. For purpose of comparison, we have also drawn a random sample of the similar size of native Israelis from the 1995 census. Immigrants from the former USSR include only those who entered Israel at ages between twenty-six to fifty-five and who were sixty-five or younger in 1995. Native Israelis are included only if their age falls in the range twenty-six to sixty-five.[11] These restrictions give us samples of 14,384 male and 17,737 female native Israelis and on 14,719 male and 18,223 female immigrants from the former USSR. The sample means are reported in Eckstein and Weiss (1999).

We focus on the wage of "full time" workers who had worked more than ten hours in the census week and positive hours a week before. Workers with less than eleven hours per week are counted as unemployed. The "hourly wage" is available only for workers who reported monthly gross salary (in September 1995) and weekly hours of work.[12] Many sampled individuals have no wage data, despite being of working age, because they had no work or failed to report wages and hours. We use the term *participation* to indicate the availability of wage data on the individual and that the individual worked more than ten hours a week.

There are some important differences in family structure between native Israelis and immigrants. The immigrants are older by about five years on average and have fewer and older children (.07 aged one to five and .55 aged six to fourteen vs. .60 and .80, respectively, among Israelis). There are more singles, especially single women, among the immigrants. Only 12 percent of the males immigrants are single vis-à-vis 25 percent of the female immigrants. The corresponding figures for native Israelis are 9 percent and 13 percent, respectively. Participation rates among married Israelis and immigrants are almost the same. Single immigrants have a lower labor participation rate. Immigrants have higher unemployment rate, and their hourly wages are much lower than those of Israelis, despite their higher average schooling. Male immigrants earn an hourly wage of 18.5 IS, compared with 32.8 IS for male Israelis, and female immigrants earn an hourly wage of 15.5 IS, compared with 27.2 IS for female Israelis. The lower average wage and the higher unemployment rate of immigrants reflect the short duration in Israel for most immigrants in the sample, about five years on average.

The average wages per hour are the same among married and single immigrants, but male Israelis who are married earn an hourly wage which is 16 percent higher than singles. Although the raw means seem to indicate that there is no marriage premium among immigrants, as we shall now show, there is in fact a large premium when we compare married and single immigrants with the same characteristics, using a wage regression corrected for selection.

Wage Regressions with Family Effects

We allow marital status to affect both the wage and participation functions, reflecting the division of labor between spouses.[13] As we have seen in section 3, wages of immigrants tend to be lower than those of comparable natives, but grow at a faster rate. We, therefore, introduce interactions of marital status with experience and time in Israel, allowing marital status to affect both the level and growth in participation and wages. We use children as instruments that affect participation but not wages.

In Table 11.6, we report the results of estimating the wage regressions for male and female immigrants with and without Heckman's correction for employment selectivity bias. In table 11.7, we report the corresponding results for Israelis. There is a clear pattern of *positive* interaction between the schooling level of the two spouses. Among married immigrant men, an increase in the wife's schooling raises the husband's wage by 1.8 percent. Among married immigrant women, an increase in the husband's schooling by a year raises her wage by 2.5 percent. We find the same patterns with almost the same estimates (1.9 percent and 2.2 percent) for Israelis in table 11.7. These strong positive interactions reflect the matching process in the "marriage market" and are consistent with positive assortative mating based on schooling (the correlation in schooling among spouses is generally high, about .5; see Weiss and Willis, 1997). Although each person can only market his own characteristics, the high education of the spouse indicates that the person has unobserved marketable characteristics that make him attractive to potential mates and employers.[14]

Recent studies (Baker and Benjamin, 1997 and Duleep et al., 1999) have addressed the question whether wives support investment activities by their husbands via increased participation at reduced wages, at the early stage after migration. The data on immigrants from the USSR to Israel is consistent with a more symmetric view. Marital status helps *both* husbands and wives. This is reflected in the higher participation rates and the higher wage level and wage growth for married immigrants of both sexes during the early years in Israel, relative to comparable singles.

As seen in figure 11.7, the initial growth rate in wages for single male immigrants is 8.1 percent a year, whereas married male immigrants enjoy an initial growth of 10.7 percent. There is a positive and significant initial marriage premium of 8.1 percent

Table 11.6
Hourly Wage and Participation Regressions for Immigrants

	Heckman				Log-Linear			
	Men		Women		Men		Women	
Variables	Coef.	Std. Err.	Coef.	Std. Err.	Coef.	Std. Err.	Coef.	Std. Err.
Wage regression								
Age at migration	0.0307	0.0063	0.0734	0.0078	0.0157	0.0058	0.0110	0.0069
Age at migration^2	−0.0005	0.0001	−0.0012	0.0001	−0.0003	0.0001	−0.0002	0.0001
Years of schooling	0.0568	0.0018	0.0786	0.0021	0.0490	0.0016	0.0603	0.0019
Husb-wife school. diff.	−0.0179	0.0020	0.0252	0.0023	−0.0127	0.0019	0.0202	0.0020
Husb-wife age diff.	−0.0027	0.0014	−0.0051	0.0016	−0.0033	0.0013	−0.0035	0.0014
Years since migr.	0.0804	0.0098	0.1299	0.0094	0.0643	0.0094	0.0602	0.0088
Years since migr.^{2}	−0.0026	0.0004	−0.0042	0.0004	−0.0015	0.0004	−0.0009	0.0004
Married	0.0816	0.0364	0.1155	0.0364	−0.0131	0.0350	−0.0523	0.0344
Married*ysm	0.0256	0.0105	0.0243	0.0106	0.0155	0.0100	0.0318	0.0099
Married*ysm^2	−0.0008	0.0004	−0.0010	0.0005	−0.0005	0.0004	−0.0012	0.0004
Constant	1.0951	0.1304	−0.4929	0.1579	1.7125	0.1189	1.3471	0.1379
Probit regression								
Age at migration	0.0705	0.0161	0.1438	0.0132				
Age at migration^2	−0.0012	0.0002	−0.0023	0.0002				
Years of schooling	0.0654	0.0042	0.0893	0.0035				
Husb-wife school. diff.	−0.0333	0.0050	0.0253	0.0040				
Husb-wife age diff.	0.0025	0.0034	−0.0078	0.0027				
Single's ch. <6	−0.1310	0.1836	−0.4492	0.0776				
Single's ch. 6–14	0.1434	0.0754	0.0994	0.0277				
Married's ch. <6	−0.0342	0.0423	−0.1543	0.0351				
Married's ch. 6–14	0.0044	0.0186	−0.0374	0.0143				
Years since migr.	0.0872	0.0198	0.2334	0.0146				
Years since migr.^{2}	−0.0044	0.0008	−0.0097	0.0006				
Married	0.4057	0.0762	0.4624	0.0598				
Married*ysm	0.0723	0.0217	−0.0116	0.0169				
Married*ysm^2	−0.0031	0.0009	−0.0002	0.0007				
Constant	−1.7556	0.3275	−3.8687	0.2704				
Rho	0.7937		0.9181					
Sigma	0.5017		0.6227					
Lambda	0.3982	0.0102	0.5717	0.0079				
Number of obs.	12873		16333		9840		9163	
R-squared					0.2184		0.2442	
Log likelihood	−12003.7353		−15149.6682					

Source: 25% sample from the 1995 census.
Note: Dependent variable—log hourly wage in 1991 IS.

Table 11.7
Hourly Wage and Participation Regressions for Israelis

	Heckman				Log-Linear			
	Men		Women		Men		Women	
Variables	Coef.	Std. Err.	Coef.	Std. Err.	Coef.	Std. Err.	Coef.	Std. Err.
Wage regression								
Years of schooling	0.0955	0.0022	0.1208	0.0030	0.1080	0.0020	0.1144	0.0019
Husb-wife school. diff.	−0.0188	0.0024	0.0223	0.0020	−0.0245	0.0022	0.0208	0.0019
Husb-wife age diff.	−0.0116	0.0017	−0.0011	0.0016	−0.0126	0.0016	−0.0006	0.0016
Experience	0.0287	0.0061	0.0324	0.0043	0.0308	0.0058	0.0310	0.0042
Experience^2	−0.0003	0.0002	−0.0004	0.0001	−0.0004	0.0001	−0.0004	0.0001
Married	0.0283	0.0522	0.1442	0.0446	0.0331	0.0487	0.1547	0.0442
Married*experience	0.0023	0.0065	−0.0073	0.0047	0.0105	0.0061	−0.0082	0.0047
Married*experience^2	0.0000	0.0002	0.0001	0.0001	−0.0001	0.0002	0.0001	0.0001
Constant	1.7984	0.0601	1.0259	0.0725	1.4153	0.0543	1.1670	0.0507
Probit regression								
Years of schooling	0.0740	0.0053	0.1301	0.0045				
Husb-wife school. diff.	−0.0326	0.0056	0.0273	0.0043				
Husb-wife age diff.	−0.0047	0.0040	−0.0108	0.0032				
Single's ch. <6	0.0419	0.0880	−0.4013	0.0640				
Single's ch. 6–14	0.3742	0.0848	−0.0651	0.0403				
Married's ch. <6	−0.0607	0.0174	−0.2875	0.0163				
Married's ch. 6–14	−0.0278	0.0142	−0.0967	0.0122				
Experience	−0.0113	0.0122	0.0264	0.0101				
Experience^2	0.0001	0.0003	−0.0008	0.0002				
Married	−0.0356	0.1143	0.0884	0.1173				
Married*experience	0.0637	0.0133	0.0117	0.0112				
Married*experience^2	−0.0013	0.0003	−0.0005	0.0002				
Constant	−0.4158	0.1303	−1.2963	0.1268				
Rho	−0.7558		0.1870					
Sigma	0.5541		0.4680					
Lambda	−0.4188	0.0146	0.0875	0.0319				
Number of obs.	12542		15933		9873		9675	
R-squared					0.2789		0.2772	
Log likelihood	−13022.2910		−15916.4530					

Source: 25% sample from the 1995 census.
Note: Dependent variable—log hourly wage in 1991 IS.

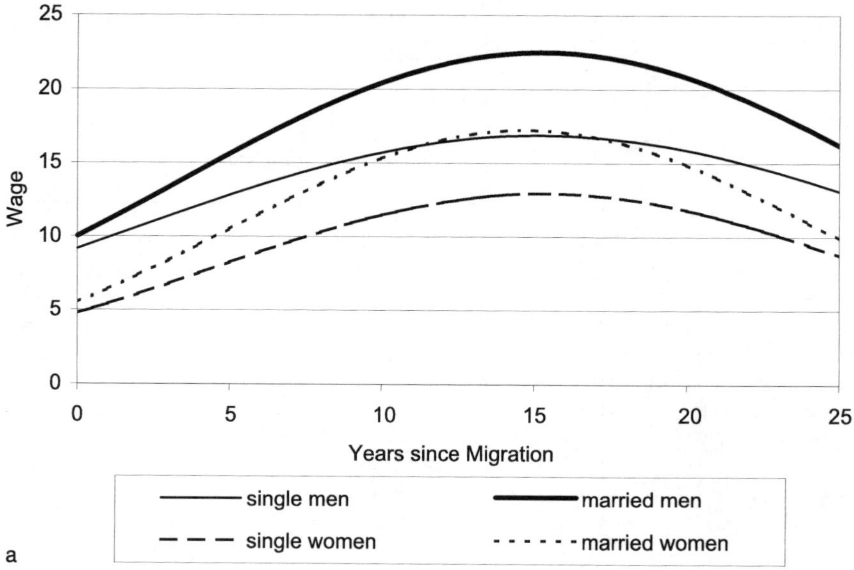

a

b

Figure 11.7
Simulated Wage and Participation of Immigrants

for males and 11.5 percent for females. This gap between married and singles rises during the first fifteen years in Israel and than narrows down. For female immigrants, the difference in the initial growth rate between married and single is also positive (15.5 vs. 13 percent, respectively), and the pattern over time is very similar to that of males.

In contrast to the positive marriage gap among immigrants, the marriage premium among Israeli men is very small, controlling for measured attributes and accounting for the differences in participation. Comparing immigrants who have been in Israel for ten years with Israelis who had ten years of market experience, we see that married immigrant males obtain a large (15 to 20 percent) marriage premium for both males and females, whereas for Israelis the corresponding premia are essentially zero. This large "difference in differences" provides strong evidence for the presence of complementarities in the development of wages of married immigrants. It seems that being married provides a substantial advantage for married couples in the absorption into the Israeli labor market.

The higher participation and wage growth among married immigrants can be either an outcome of different behavior, for example, coordination of work activities, or different attributes of married couples. It is very difficult to separate these effects from a single cross section. Let us note, however, that the husband-wife interactions in schooling and age follow the same pattern as among married Israelis, suggesting that selection by attributes operates in a similar way for the two groups and that the difference in wage growth between married and single is probably due to coordination. One indication for coordination is that the wage differences between married and single immigrants tend to vanish after a long stay in Israel. Among Israelis, we do not see any change in the differences between married and singles, suggesting that the differences mainly reflect assortative mating. Another indication for coordination is the fact that among immigrants females, the married participate (and work) more than the single, whereas among Israeli females, the single work more (see figure 11.6 and figure 10 in Eckstein and Weiss, 1999).

For both Israelis and immigrants, one can observe a clear *positive* correlation between the husband's and wife's participation in the labor market. That is, one is more likely to participate if the spouse is participating. This pattern survives after one controls for personal attributes, such as age and schooling, and for the number of children (see figures 11.8 and 11.9). This somewhat surprising pattern has been noted in other studies (Davis et al., 1992, and Giannelli and Micklewright, 1995) and is usually attributed to unobserved common factors that influence the labor supply of both husband and wife and incentives created by the welfare system. Comparing these differences across groups, we see that immigrating husbands are influenced by

Figure 11.8
Participation Rates of Immigrants by Spouse Employment States Data

the participation of their wives to a lesser degree than comparable Israeli husbands, whereas immigrating wives are more influenced by the participation of their husbands than comparable Israeli wives. In addition, there is a smaller difference between the participation rate of husbands and wives among immigrants than among Israelis.

Three are two possible explanations for these findings. First, among immigrants, an important common factor for married partners is their joint time of arrival to Israel. Second, because of their low initial income, immigrants are entitled to welfare transfers in the form of "income augmentation," based on *family* income. Because husbands have higher wages, the family strategy is for the husband to work and for the wife to adjust to his employment status. If he does not work, the family is eligible. Therefore, she does not work and the family collects benefits. If he works, she is inclined to work too, because the family is no more eligible. Among natives, who have higher family income, the welfare transfers are more in the form of unemployment benefits, which are based on *individual* income and employment status. Therefore, coordination is less important, and the positive correlation primarily reflects sorting.

Figure 11.9
Participation Rates of Immigrants by Spouse Employment States Probit Prediction

Appendix

This appendix describes a simple procedure for adjusting the quality of employed natives and immigrants, based on the wage regressions reported in this paper.

Consider a constant returns to scale production function $Y_t = A_t F(K_t, L_t^*)$, where Y_t is GNP, K_t is aggregate capital and L_t^* is the aggregate *quality-adjusted* supply of labor, and A_t is an index of total factor productivity. Let there be J types of labor where L_{jt} is the quantity of each type and w_{jt} is the wage of each type in year t. Then $L_t = \sum L_{jt}$ is the unadjusted aggregate and $w_t = \sum w_{jt} L_{jt}/L_t$ the average wage in year t. We define the quality-adjusted index as $L_t^* = \sum_{j=1}^{J} \gamma_j L_{jt}$, where γ_j is a *fixed* positive weight of labor of type j. These weights are defined as the wage of type of labor j relative to the average wage in some base year, $t = 0$, that is, $\gamma_j = w_{j0}/w_0$. By construction, with this choice of weights, the unadjusted and adjusted indices coincide in the base year, that is, $L_0^* = L_0$. Recall that under constant returns to scale, the marginal product of labor $A_t F_L(K_t, L_t^*)$ depends only on the adjusted capital labor ratio K_t/L_t^*. Under competitive conditions, the linear aggregation rule implies $w_{jt} = \gamma_j A_t F_L(K_t, L_t^*)$ and $w_t = A_t F_L(K_t, L_t^*)(L_t^*/L_t)$. Setting, $A_0 = 1$, the average wage equals the marginal product of labor in year 0. Notice that if labor quality rises, because of shift toward more productive workers, average wage may grow even if the adjusted capital labor ratio is constant and no technical change occurs.

Into this simple framework, we now introduce immigrants. We divide the population between immigrants and natives, and each of the two groups is cross-classified by four levels of schooling—0–8, 9–12, 13–15, 16+; there are three occupational groups—academic, white collar, and blue collar; and six levels of experience—0–4, 5–10, 11–20, 21–30, 31–40, 40+, a total of seventy-two cells. Within each cell, immigrants are further classified by year since migration, $1, 2, \dots, 6$, and by cohort 1990–91 or 1992–1995.

We assume that immigrants who came before 1990 can be treated as Israelis. Immigrants in each occupation, j, are distinguished by their cohort, c, and time in Israel, τ. For $t = 1990, 1991, \dots, 1995$, let $N^o_{jt}(\tau, c)$ be the number of working immigrants with τ years since migration and of cohort c in year t, and let $w^o_{jt}(\tau, c)$ be their wage. We transform immigrants into equivalent Israelis in the cell by using *relative wages* as weights. Thus, the adjusted number of working immigrants in each year, $N^{o^*}_{jt}$, is

$$N^{o^*}_{jt} = \frac{\sum_{c=0}^{2} \sum_{\tau=0}^{5} w^o_{jt}(\tau, c) N^o_{jt}(\tau, c)}{w^n_{jt}},$$

where w^n_{jt} is the wage of native Israelis in cell j in year t. The total number of "Israeli equivalent" workers in each cell is $L_{jt} = N^n_{jt} + N^{o^*}_{jt}$, where N^n_{jt} is the number of Israelis working as type j at year t. We define the weights for each type of labor, j, based on the relative wages of *Israelis* in 1991, that is, $\gamma_j = w^n_{j0}/w^n_0$, where w^n_{j0} and w^n_0 are the wage of natives of type j and the average wage of natives in 1991, respectively.

A restrictive assumption behind this procedure is that the *relative* wages of Israeli workers of different types do not change over the period under analysis. We allow, however, the weights for immigrants relative to Israelis to change over time, because immigrants of different skills may adapt at different rates. An alternative log-linear specification

$$L^*_t = \exp\left(\sum_{j=1}^{J} \gamma_j \ln(L_{jt})\right),$$

where γ_j are labor shares at the base year, can be used to allow for changes in relative wages (see Young, 1995).

The wages w_j^n and $w_{jt}^o(\tau, c)$ are calculated using the predicted wages from the regressions reported in the text, based on the income surveys for 1991–1995. We use the mid-point in the cell for the conditioning variables. For example, for the schooling cell of thirteen to fifteen years of schooling we used the year fourteen. The average wages, $w_{average}^n$ and $w_{t,average}^n$ are the average predicted wage of native Israelis, using the regression reported in table 11.4. The number of workers for each cell of natives and immigrants is taken from the labor force surveys for the years 1990–1995.

We assume that the labor force survey is a representative sample of all cells in the population. Within each survey, we estimate the ratio L_t^*/L_t separately for immigrants and natives for the years 1990–1995. We then use aggregate data on employed immigrants and natives, as reported by the CBS annual reports, multiply it by the corresponding adjustment factors, and add over the natives and immigrants to get the total adjusted labor force. The results are given in table 3 of Eckstein and Weiss (1999).

Because we have estimated regressions only for male workers, *relative* wage differentials between male natives and male immigrants were imputed to females. We ignored the within-group gender differences in wages. Based on cross-section data from the 1995 census, female workers earn about 20 percent less than males, adjusting for observed characteristics, and among immigrants, this difference is almost 40 percent. Because the proportion of employed females is larger among immigrants, we underestimate the quality adjustment required for immigrants. Our procedure can be extended to include further adjustment for male and female workers, but this would require more work than we could complete for this study.

Notes

This paper is prepared for special volume in memory of Michael Bruno on "Structural Changes in the Israeli Economy During the last Decade." We thank Karnit Flug and Michael Beenstock for their comments and Evgeny Agronin and Maria Tripolski for their excellent research assistance. Financial support for this project was received from National Institute of Child Care and Human Development Grant Number 5 R01 HD34671-03 and the Falk Institute.

The authors can be reached at ⟨eckstein@econ.tau.ac.il⟩ and ⟨weiss@post.tau.ac.il⟩.

1. Sikron and Leshem (1998) provide a comprehensive collection of papers that describe many other aspects of the recent immigration wave from the former USSR to Israel. Papers that discuss wage and occupational dynamics include Eckstein and Weiss (1998), Weiss et al. (1999), and Friedberg (1996) and (1999).

2. We do not have good aggregate measure of capital utilization; however, we know that some production plants initially moved to more shifts and that the number of households and individuals per apartment increased significantly.

3. Another potential mechanism, which would operate even if relative factor endowment change, is factor price equalization through trade. A recent paper by Gendal et al. (1999) shows that substantial growth in

exports, high-tech products in particular, have absorbed much of the impact of increased supply of high-skilled and moderately-skilled workers. See also Beenstock and Fisher (1997).

4. We use three occupations as follows: Occupation 1 includes engineers, physicians, professors, other professionals with an academic degree, and managers; occupation 2 includes teachers, technicians, nurses, artists, and other professionals; occupation 3 includes blue collar and unskilled occupations.

5. The two-stage procedure allows us to incorporate in a simple way the identifying restriction that the time effects, reflecting a common rental rate for human capital that may vary over time, are the same for immigrants and natives.

6. If both the parameters *b* and *c* differ between Israelis and immigrants, one cannot separate "quantity" from "price." It is possible, however, for one parameter, to differ across these groups. We have estimated the model, allowing the coefficient *c* to differ. We found that this coefficient was $-.00061$ for immigrants and $-.00066$ for Israelis. The difference between the two estimates is statistically insignificant.

7. These estimates and the fit ($R^2 = 0.32$) of the model are similar to those obtained in other application of Mincer's wage function. The only nonstandard feature is that we allow occupation to have separate effect on wages, beyond schooling. This is mainly done to allow comparability with immigrants, for whom occupational transitions play an important role.

8. The widening gap in occupation 3 between immigrants and Israelis with sixteen years of schooling suggests that immigrants who stay in occupation 3 for a long time are of increasingly lower quality, compared with the Israelis who stay.

9. The data source for occupational transitions of immigrants is the CBS Labor Force Survey, from which the Income Survey is drawn (both surveys report occupation, but only the Income Survey has wage data). This is a relatively large sample with almost ten thousand observations. The logits estimated for natives control for schooling and age. The logits for immigrants control for schooling, age at arrival, cohort and time in Israel.

10. In contrast, Friedberg (1999) reports that the wages of immigrants from the USSR who arrived to Israel before 1983, do converge to those of native Israelis. Earlier immigration from the USSR was of a much smaller scale.

11. We also exclude observations with age difference between husband and wife of more than thirty years in absolute value; years of schooling difference between husband and wife of more than sixteen years in absolute value; wage per hour of less than five or more than 99 IS; no information on hours or wages; no information on the labor market activity; employed workers who did not work a full month.

12. Because the wage is constructed, we treat as unknown hourly wages that appear too low (less than four sheqels) or too high (more than one hundred sheqels).

13. We use the term *participation* to include individuals that are working more than ten hours a week. Nonworkers include both unemployed and nonparticipant individuals. Workers with no information on hours or wages are dropped from the regression analysis.

14. Weaker interactions can be noted in the age of the two spouses. An increase in the wife's age by one year raises the husband's wage by 0.3 percent. The effect of the husband's age on his wife's wage is negative, small, and insignificant.

References

Altonji, J. G., and D. Card. "The Effects of Immigration on the Labor Market Outcomes of Less-Skilled Natives." In *Immigration, Trade and the Labor Market*, edited by J. M. Abowd and R. B. Freeman. Chicago: University of Chicago Press, 1991.

Baker, M., and D. Benjamin. "The Role of the Family in Immigrants' Labor Market Activity: An Evaluation of Alternative Explanations." *American Economic Review* 87.4 (1997): 705–727.

Beenstock, M., and J. Fisher. "The Macroeconomic Effects of Immigration: Israel in the 1990s." *Welt-wirtschaftliches-Archiv* 133 (1997): 330–358.

Ben-Porath, Y. "The Entwined Growth of Population and Product, 1922–1982." In *The Israeli Economy: Maturing through Crisis*, edited by Yoram Ben-Porath. Cambridge, MA: Harvard University Press, 1986.

Borjas, G. J. "Assimilation, Changes in Cohort Quality, and the Earnings of Immigrants." *Journal of labor Economics* 3 (1985): 463–489.

Davis, R., P. Elias, and R. Penn. "The Relationship Between a Husband's Unemployment and his Wife's Participation in the Labor Force." *Oxford Bulletin of Economics and Statistics* 54 (1992): 145–171.

Duleep, H., M. Reget, and S. Sanders. "A New Look at the Human Capital Investment: A Study of Asian Immigrants and their Family Ties." Kalamazoo, MI: Upjohn Institute of Economic Research, 1999.

Eckstein, Z., and Y. Weiss. "The Absorption of Highly Skilled Immigrants: Israel 1990–1995." Foerder Institute Working Paper (1998): 3–98.

Eckstein, Z., and Y. Weiss. "The Integration of Immigrants from the Former Soviet Union in the Israeli Labor Market." Foerder Institute Working Paper (1999): 33–99.

Freidberg, R. "The Impact of Mass Migration on the Israeli Labor Market." Brown University Department of Economics Working Paper 96/28, 1996.

Freidberg, R. "You Can't Take It With You? Immigrant Assimilation and the Portability of Human Capital." *Journal of Labor Economics* (1999), forthcoming.

Freidberg, R., and J. Hunt. "Immigration and the Labor Market." *Journal of Economic-Perspectives* 9 (1995): 23–44.

Gandal, N., G. Hanson, and M. Slaughter. "Rybczynski Effects and Adjustments to Immigration in Israel." Policy School, Tel-Aviv University, 1999.

Giannelli, G., and J. Micklewright. "Why Do Women Married to Unemployed Men Have Low Participation Rates?" *Oxford Bulletin of Economics and Statistics* 57 (1995): 471–486.

Jorgenson, D., and Z. Griliches. "The Explanation of Productivity Change." *Review of Economic Studies* 34 (1967): 249–283.

LaLonde, R., and R. Topel. "Immigrants in the American Labor Market: Quality, Assimilation and Distributional Effects." *American Economic Review* 81 (1991): 297–302.

Sikron, M., and E. Leshem. *Profile of an Immigration Wave: The Absorption Process of Immigrants from the Former Soviet Union, 1990–1995*. Jerusalem: The Magnes Press, The Hebrew University, 1998.

Sussman, Z. "Impact of the Immigration on the Economic Situation of the Veteran Population." In *Profile of an Immigration Wave: The Absorption Process of Immigrants from the Former Soviet Union, 1990–1995*, edited by M. Sikron and E. Leshem. Jerusalem: The Magnes Press, The Hebrew University, 1998.

Sussman, Z., and D. Zakai. "The Mass Immigration of Physicians to Israel and the Steep Rise in Wages of Veterans in Israel: A Paradox?" Research Department, Bank of Israel, 1998.

Razin, A., and E. Sadka. (1993), *The Economy of Modern Israel: Malaise and Promise.* Chicago: University of Chicago Press, 1998.

Weiss, Y., and R. Willis. "Match Quality, New Information and Marital Dissolution." *Journal of Labor Economics* 15 (1, part 2) (1997): s293–s229.

Weiss, Y., R. Sauer, and M. Gotlibovski. "Immigration, Search and Loss of Skill." Foerder Institute Working Paper no. 26–99, 1999.

Young, A. "The Tyranny of Numbers: Confronting the Statistical Realities of the East Asian Growth Experience." *Quarterly Journal of Economics*, CX (1995): 641–680.

12 The Flexibility of the Israeli Labor Market

Yael Artstein

12.1 Introduction

The Israeli labor market of the late 1990s differs from that of the mid-1980s in several respects—first, in the composition of employment between native Israelis, immigrants, workers from the territories, and foreign workers, as well as in the occupational and industrial distribution of the employed; second, in employment patterns, between collective agreements, personal contracts, and the use of employment agencies; and third, in labor market institutions like the cost-of-living allowance agreement, the minimum wage, other labor costs, and so forth. These changes took place in response to several exogenous shocks to the economy and to economic processes that evolved thereafter.

The main shocks were the July 1985 Economic Stabilization Program, the mass immigration from the former USSR since 1990, and political events in the region that caused the employment of workers from the territories to diminish and led to extensive use of foreign labor. These shocks, and an increase in the openness of the domestic economy to international trade and foreign capital markets, induced long-term adjustment processes in the labor market—processes that evidently have not run their full course.

In the mid-1980s, after the Economic Stabilization Program arrested inflation and slashed budget deficits, many government-supported organizations embarked on rationalization plans that in several cases eventually led to privatization. In the 1990s, pursuant to the arrival of masses of highly educated immigrants, the production and exports of schooling-intensive industries expanded, a trend that was subsequently reinforced by the peace-making process. At the same time, as the economy was increasingly exposed to competition from abroad, the share of traditional industries in economic activity declined. All this was accompanied by an increase in employment under personal labor contract and through employment agencies—a development reinforced by the weakening of the Histadrut in the course of this period.

All the important labor market institutions were modified during the period. Cost-of-Living Allowance (COLA) provisions were adjusted in several ways, the minimum-wage agreement was replaced with legislation, employers' contribution rates to social security were lowered, eligibility criteria for unemployment benefits were revised, and pension arrangements were reformulated. The policy measures in the labor market were not components of a comprehensive reform; they evolved in response to specific problems that surfaced during that era or to various pressures. This is in contrast to other areas, in which comprehensive reforms have been planned since 1985 and were phased in subsequently. These include a foreign currency liberalization, exposure to competing imports, and reforms in the financial and capital markets, as discussed in other chapters of this volume. Yet, given that the structure and operation of the labor market changed so much during these years, we ask how this entirety affected the performance of this market.

The present study examines the changes since 1985 in the composition of the labor force, employment patterns, and labor market institutions. These changes meant greater flexibility in hiring and compensation at the individual-employer level and could have been translated, in principle, to greater labor market flexibility at the macroeconomic level as well. We ask whether this has in fact happened, and in particular, whether the response to exogenous events in the 1990s exhibits stronger competitive forces and weaker inertia elements than in the past. If so, we ask whether one may associate such differences with the many changes that the labor market experienced throughout this period.

The aggregate data do point to a change in the response of the labor market to exogenous shocks. In contrast to the inflexible response of real wages to the shocks created by the 1985 stabilization program, real wage per employee declined substantially and employment expanded vigorously in the early 1990s in response to mass immigration. Examination of wage trends by industry in the 1990s shows that employment expanded mainly in industries with flexible labor markets and below-average wages, where the intake of immigrants drove wages even lower. The decline in the national average wage in the early 1990s is largely the result of the change in the industrial composition of product and employment. Also, the intake of immigrants in 1989–1994 did not reduce the wages of veteran workers (Friedberg, 1997). The macroeconomic wage flexibility in the early 1990s is thus mainly a reflection of the smooth adjustment of product markets, and the increase in demand for labor in industries that paid low average wages. Wages themselves were also more flexible in the 1990s than in the mid-1980s, but here the exception is their inflexibility after the stabilization program. Previous studies (Artstein, 1997; Beenstock and Ribon, 1993) show that the Israeli labor market had been relatively flexible in the past as well; escalating inflation supported this flexibility before 1985 and rapid growth did so in the first half of the 1990s.

The general conclusion of this study is that the higher microeconomic flexibility in the 1990s is not the main explanation for the better macroeconomic adjustment to shocks in those years. This conclusion is supported by developments in the labor market in the second half of the 1990s. The economic slowdown, which began in 1996, intensified in 1997, and turned into a recession in 1998, was not accompanied by a parallel deceleration of real average wages but by their increase, along with rising unemployment. Here, too, the explanation lies mainly in the composition of employment—this time in the arresting of employment growth that ended the moderating effect of the influx of newly hired workers on wages.

It seems that increasing labor market flexibility is a lengthy process, the results of which prevail only years later. This conclusion is consistent with the findings of similar studies in other countries. A study on labor market flexibility in Great Britain (Standing, 1986), for instance, describes in detail numerous flexibility-enhancing measures that had no perceptible mitigating effect on unemployment after they were adopted. It took several additional years for unemployment in Britain to ebb, but today, wage increases there are moderate, and unemployment is low. Policy measures aiming at the same goal were also taken in the Netherlands (de Neubourg, 1990) throughout the 1980s, yet this country still had in the late 1980s one of the highest unemployment rates in Europe. Today, the unemployment rate in the Netherlands is particularly low. A cross-country study (Organization for Economic Cooperation and Development [OECD], 1997) of twenty-one OECD countries found no significant differences between the 1980s and the 1990s in the response of average wages to an increase in unemployment, despite many changes in policies and institutions in these countries' labor markets. The authors of the study believe that because some countries implemented their flexibility-enhancing measures only in the early 1990s, it is too early to expect an impact on wage-setting patterns. This may be the situation in Israel as well, particularly since the Israeli labor market is already more flexible than most European labor markets.

Finally, we discuss the conflict between improving the performance of the labor market and promoting a more equal income distribution. In this context, we wonder whether greater flexibility of the Israeli labor market should at all be desired. Technological change in the past two decades, which has increased relative demand for skilled workers at the expense of their low-skilled counterparts, has aggravated income inequality in flexible labor markets, while in less flexible markets, it has increased unemployment among the unskilled. This involves a difficult choice for policymaking, especially given that inequality in Israel is already among the highest in the Western world.

The structure of this study is as follows: In part 12.2, we draw a distinction between macro and micro (enterprise-level) labor market flexibility. In part 12.3, we describe the changes (since 1985) in employment patterns, labor market institutions, and the demographic composition of employment, and discuss the relationship between these changes and wage flexibility at the enterprise level. In part 12.4, we address wage flexibility at the macroeconomic level, using a wage-setting model for Israel that refers explicitly to the main labor market institutions. Part 12.5 is a discussion of employment flexibility, and part 12.6 concerns wages and employment in the public sector. In part 12.7 we assess the impact of changes in the composition of employment on changes in the average wage and discuss the relationship between these factors and the rate of economic growth. In part 12.8, we present an international comparison of wage flexibility and the relationship between labor market institutions, the market's flexibility, and economic performance. Part 12.9 is a discussion of the relationship between flexibility and income inequality, and part 12.10 is a conclusion.

12.2 Flexibility

The term "labor market flexibility" expresses the extent to which wages and employment adjust to changes in economic conditions. There is more than one way to define this flexibility, and we distinguish between macroeconomic flexibility, discussed below, and flexibility at the level of the individual employer, which is discussed later in this section.

Theoretically, the labor market is considered flexible if the response of wages and employment to demand and supply shocks is close to that of a competitive market. When labor demand contracts, for example, after a negative shock to the product market, a flexible labor market responds by lowering real wages, thereby mitigating the negative effect on employment. A shock that increases labor supply also results in lower real wages in a flexible labor market, allowing employment to grow, whereas an inflexible labor market exhibits a weak response of wages that leads to a rise in unemployment. Overall, the more flexible real wages are, the more the adjustment of employment approximates that of a competitive market. Accordingly, the macroeconomic discussion emphasizes the flexibility of real *wages*.

In the second half of 1985, real wages decreased, as the economic stabilization program had intended, but shortly afterwards—in 1986 and 1987—real wages increased vigorously and were inconsistent with other forces at work during those years. Wage rigidity at that time contributed to the economy's slowdown thereafter. In the early 1990s, when another major shock hit the economy, the labor market adjusted much better. The large increase in labor supply, which initially outpaced the rise in labor demand, translated into a protracted decline in real wages coupled with an expansion of employment. Thus, the general impression from macroeconomic data is of a relatively inflexible labor market in the mid-1980s and a more flexible one in the first half of the 1990s.

Less aggregate data reveals a more complex picture. Several studies in recent years show that the various sectors of the economy respond to shocks in different ways—some with greater flexibility and others with more rigidity. Artstein and Sussman

(1992) found that the limited flexibility of wages after 1985 originated in strong interdependencies among wage increases in different industries. Although those interrelations were rooted in many years of high inflation, they persisted even after inflation was arrested. In another study, Artstein (1997) identified two types of industries in the Israeli labor market, unionized industries in which wages were less flexible, and competitive ones, with more flexible wages, and strong interrelations among wages in industries of both types.

The Bank of Israel reports for 1988–1990 also sort industries into two sectors. There, the distinction is between the tradeable sector and the nontradeable sector, and it is shown how reasonable wage increases in nontradeable industries were translated into unsustainable wage increases in the tradeable sector. This is because price rises in tradeable industries are limited by prices in other countries, whereas in nontradeable industries prices rise according to supply and demand. After the stabilization program, the relatively mild wage rises in the nontradeable sector spilled over into the tradeable sector, where they became large increases in real wage cost to employer, at the expense of profitability and employment.

Another kind of dichotomy, a matter of salient importance in recent years, is between skill-intensive industries and those intensive in unskilled labor. The 1997 Bank of Israel Report compares the industrial exports of these two sectors. Skill-intensive exports, which have been rapidly expanding for two decades, especially in the 1990s, are characterized by relatively flexible labor markets. In the traditional sector, on the other hand, wages are less flexible, and the globalization process of the recent years has impaired profitability and led to layoffs.

Disaggregate data on wages and employment thus reveal several submarkets, some of which are more flexible and others less so, and they are all strongly interrelated, and affect the overall flexibility of the labor market.

As for labor market flexibility at the *microeconomic* level, that of the individual enterprise, here one can distinguish among several components of flexibility, relating to the quantity and composition of labor input and to its price. A study on wage and employment flexibility at the enterprise level (OECD, 1989) found that enterprise level flexibility in several OECD countries took five forms:

1. "External" flexibility, by which a firm adjusts its number of employees to its needs by shifting from collective agreements and permanent jobs to short-term contracts, temporary posts, and simplification of dismissal procedures.

2. Outsourcing of the production process. This is another way to replace rigid employment contracts with arrangements that do not protect workers' rights. It includes subcontracting, hiring via employment agencies, and use of freelancers.

3. Adjusting work hours to the employer's needs, including shift work.

4. "Functional" flexibility, that is, switching employees among jobs within the enterprise. This is appropriate mainly for large organizations with multiskilled employees, which by adopting this practice can redeploy resources without layoffs.

5. Wage flexibility, which can be attained by shifting gradually from a structure of standard wage scales and seniority raises to a system that links remuneration to employee performance.

The relative importance of each component of enterprise level flexibility varies from one country to another, of course, because countries differ in their systems of labor relations, the role of trade unions, and their institutional and legal setups.

12.3 Structural and Institutional Changes in the Labor Market

Changes in the structure and operation of the labor market affect its wage-setting and employment patterns, and therefore, they have an impact on the market's flexibility. The changes in Israel since 1985 fall into three categories:

1. Changes in the *demographic composition* of the labor force—Israelis versus workers from the territories and foreign workers, native Israelis versus immigrants, all of whom also differ in level of schooling and vocational skill.

2. Changes in *employment patterns*—the decline of the Histadrut and the rise in power of separate trade unions, especially in the public sector; privatization; collective agreements; personal contracts, and employment agencies.

3. Changes in *labor market institutions*—Cost-of-Living Allowance (COLA) agreements, minimum wage, unemployment benefits, other labor cost components, and the pension system.

Labor Supply and Its Composition

Over the past decade, there have been two major changes in labor supply: (1) an increase in the employment of non-Israeli workers, consisting of a decline in workers from the territories and a large influx of foreign workers; (2) a steep increase in labor supply since the onset of mass immigration from the former Soviet Union, particularly of highly skilled labor.

Workers from the territories have been employed in Israel since 1968, their numbers gradually increasing to 109,000 in 1987 (table 12.1). They were employed mainly in agriculture and construction but also in manufacturing and in some services. They

Table 12.1
Employment and Labor Force

	Civilian Labor Force (Israeli)			Employment			
	Total	Non-immigrants	Immigrants	Total	Israelis	Workers from the Territories	Foreign workers
1975	1147.8			1178.8	1112.5	66.3	
1980	1318.0			1329.5	1254.4	75.1	
1985	1466.8			1457.3	1368.3	89.0	
1987	1494.1			1512.6	1403.7	108.9	
1989	1603.3			1565.7	1460.8	104.9	
1990	1649.9	1628.0	21.9	1602.1	1491.9	107.7	2.5
1991	1770.3	1673.9	96.4	1689.9	1583.1	97.8	9.0
1992	1857.8	1704.0	153.8	1782.4	1650.2	115.6	16.6
1993	1946.1	1753.4	192.7	1864.7	1751.1	84.0	29.6
1994	2029.7	1801.1	228.6	1993.0	1871.4	70.0	51.6
1995	2110.0	1849.6	260.4	2120.1	1968.1	60.0	92.0
1996	2156.9	1861.0	296.0	2191.2	2012.8	41.0	137.4
1997	2210.1	1882.6	327.3	2231.2	2040.2	48.0	143.0
1998	2271.6	1919.8	351.8	2269.8	2076.6	53.0	140.2

Source: Bank of Israel, *Annual Report*, 1998.

had a moderating effect on domestic wages due to their flexible supply, their job mobility, and their low wages. Their employment declined when the "Intifada" began in December 1987, decreased further during the Gulf War (1991), expanded in 1992 because of an exceptional rise in the demand for housing, and contracted again beginning in 1993 as a consequence of severe terrorist attacks.

Former Soviet immigrants joined the labor force at high rates, but in spite of the large share of the highly educated among them, finding work in their occupations was difficult, and many had to accept low-skill jobs, at least temporarily (see the chapter on immigrants in this volume). In manufacturing and services, immigrants replaced workers from the territories, but in industries that the immigrants did not tend to join, like agriculture and construction, excess demand for labor built up, and since 1993, the government has allowed the employment of documented (licensed) foreign workers. Pressure from employers led to protracted growth in quotas of foreign workers, who were then joined by many undocumented aliens. (The figures in table 12.1 are for licensed workers only.)

How were these changes in the composition of the labor force expected to affect labor market flexibility at the enterprise level? The natural increase in native Israeli workers has been boosted since the 1970s by three groups of workers, each at a different time—first, workers from the territories, later, immigrants, and then, foreign workers. Each group, by joining the labor market at the bottom of the wage scale, pushed the veteran employees up the occupational hierarchy. Workers from the territories and foreign workers remained at the bottom of the wage scale, but for immigrants, the situation was different; the economic growth that was reinforced by the expansion of high-tech investments, eventually enabled many of the newcomers to move into better paying professional jobs.

Union Membership and Employment Patterns

The arrest of rapid inflation in 1985 exposed financial crises in many Histadrut (labor unions) related entities, and the Histadrut's standing in the economy has been weakened since then. Indicators of this decline are the termination of Histadrut control of several large enterprises, the development of a dependency on government funding in agriculture and the General Health Fund, and revelations about huge actuarial deficits in Histadrut-owned pension funds. Additionally, the National Health Insurance Law went into effect in 1995, allowing residents to separate their membership in the Histadrut from their eligibility for health services.

Due to the historical structure of the Histadrut, in which anyone who subscribed to the health insurance services of the General Health Fund automatically became a Histadrut member, Israel does not have data on union density. Indicators for 1994 (Nathanson and Zisser, 1996) point to an average membership rate of 44 percent countrywide and only 24 percent in the business sector, excluding Histadrut and state-owned enterprises. These rates represent a decline from previous levels and are much lower than the corporative image of the Israeli labor market in the past would suggest. Financial crises erupted in the aftermath of the 1985 stabilization in government-controlled companies as well, leading to rationalization processes that entailed layoffs and, in some cases, privatization. The changes in ownership often resulted in changes in employment patterns—a transition from collective agreements to personal contracts, use of employment agencies, and use of subcontractors.

As for wage accords, the weakening of the Histadrut core made the separate trade unions more powerful but reduced the share of unionized labor and collective agreements. The strengthening of the separate trade unions was evident in public-sector unions and large monopolies, while union presence in most of the business sector in the mid-1990s was quite weak (Nathanson and Zisser, 1996). Union presence is especially low at the two extremes of the occupational distribution—the upper end (high-tech industries) and the lower end (personal and other services), where union density has also been low in the past, as in other countries.

Theoretically, the focusing of wage negotiations at the industry or occupational union, instead of at the national level, may result in excessive wage increases. Empirical evidence of such a phenomenon was found in the well-known study of Calmfors and Driffill (1988). The reason for the excessive wage rises is that the separate unions have enough power to obtain substantial wage increases, but unlike a national organization, they lack the perspective of the economy at large, and do not internalize the price increases that follow such wage increases. In Israel such a phenomenon may be aggravated by a wage-spillover mechanism among industries, according to which wage increases obtained in one industry quickly induce similar increases in others (Artstein and Sussman, 1989, 1992).

The other effect of the decline of the Histadrut—contraction of the share of unionized labor at large—is reflected in the increased incidence of personal wage contracts, the use of employment agencies, and outsourcing. We briefly describe the evolution of these employment patterns in Israel.

Personal wage contracts have become increasingly common, both in workplaces governed by collective agreements and in those that have no workers' committees or collective bargaining at all (Sussman, 1995). Here, too, data is scarce. Nonunionized workplaces, as stated, are either small employers in miscellaneous services, which were always nonunionized, or the high-tech industries, which expanded vigorously in the 1990s. The spread of employment under personal contracts to unionized workplaces in the 1980s and 1990s was enhanced by the privatization of large businesses formerly owned by the public sector and the Histadrut (Bezeq, Koor, banks, etc.). In the public services themselves, employment under personal contract expanded tremendously in the 1990s (Sussman and Zakai, 1994). There are two major types of contracts in this sector—one for low-wage temporary work and the other for people at the top of the scale, where higher wages compensate for no tenure and fewer social benefits.

Employment agencies also expanded greatly in the 1990s. In this temporary employment pattern, agencies provide a third party with personnel and maintain the employer-employee relationship themselves. Information on the extent of this phenomenon is scanty, because the employment data categorize employees by the industries in which they work. An attempt to estimate the extent of this practice in 1995–1997 shows (Achdut, Sulla, and Eisenbach, 1998) that about 5 percent of all Israeli employees were employed in this fashion in 1997. This is a much higher rate than the Western norm (1–2.5 percent), but its attributes are similar—overrepresentation of young people, women, and low-skill workers; employment of a severely temporary nature; and high employee turnover. Partial indicators for this type of employment before 1995 point to a steep and steady increase since 1989.

The two employment patterns, personal labor contracts and the use of employment agencies, give employers greater flexibility in adjusting wages and employment in response to changes in the demand for goods. Under these employment patterns, workers receive currently the entire remuneration for their labor but lose job security and some social benefits.

Outsourcing is another change in corporate management that has become popular in recent years. According to this strategy, the organization focuses only on its core business, and other functions are outsourced. Outsourcing has been spreading steadily in Israel, and like the other methods described, it helps employers make flexible adjustments to changing conditions in an era of rapid technological change and escalating competition. The public sector also outsources extensively, because it allows circumventing the set of collective agreements and standard personnel slots. According to partial data on municipal government services, 30–70 percent of various services are outsourced (Galin, 1998). Galin's analysis of this phenomenon points to advantages in organizational efficiency and cutting of production costs. Yet alongside the advantages of outsourcing, there has recently been a growing awareness of its limitations, mainly loss of control of parts of the system, severe dependency on subcontractors, and a detriment to employee loyalty and commitment to the workplace.

The flexibility obtained by the three patterns described above is microeconomic, enterprise-level flexibility, which facilitates adjusting wages and employment in response to adverse shocks. Do companies that adopt these employment patterns lower wages to avoid cutbacks in employment? This has not been analyzed in Israel yet. High-tech companies, which make especially widespread use of personal contracts, have been expanding rapidly in the past decade and wages have been rising; thus, their response to a slowdown in activity has not yet been put to the test in Israel. However, research on this question in the most flexible labor market of all, that of the United States, elicited a conclusion that may be surprising:

In a recent microeconomic study based on hundreds of interviews with employers in the northeastern U.S., Bewley (1998) asked why employers tend to refrain from cutting wages even when the state of the business warrants such cuts. His unequivocal answer is that this way of cutting expenses costs more than the savings from lower pay. Though the unemployed are very flexible in their wage demands, employers consider a cut in wages seriously detrimental to employee morale, and therefore more harmful to their labor productivity and future recruiting than layoffs would be.

Labor Market Institutions

The first *cost-of-living allowance* agreement dates back to the 1940s, and since then, it has undergone many modifications. A major reform in the COLA mechanism in 1975 introduced the principle of partial compensation for price increases. When inflation accelerated, the rate and frequency of compensation were increased, and after the 1985 stabilization, both features were downscaled in several steps. A fundamental change in the COLA agreement was instituted in 1989, when economic activity slumped. The new COLA, to be paid every six months, stipulated no compensation for the first 3 percent of inflation during that period, and an 85 percent compensation for the rest. The idea was to allow a decline in real wages wherever warranted and at the same time to assure that such a decrease was limited to a predetermined level. Declining inflation since 1992 led to two modifications of the agreement, in 1996 and in 1998. According to the current agreement, COLA is paid once a year, there is no compensation for the first 4.25 percent of annual inflation and a 90 percent compensation for the rest. The changes in the COLA accord lowered the effective rate of compensation from 70 percent of price rises in the early 1980s to only 40 percent in the late 1990s (figure 12.1).

Did these changes affect wage flexibility? Ostensibly, low automatic compensation for price increases leaves room for additional differential wage increases that match the state of profitability in each industry and establishment. However, COLA is only one of several wage adjustment mechanisms in Israel, because many years of high

Figure 12.1
Ratio of COLA to CPI increase, 1976–1997
(Percent)

inflation with partial COLAs led to the assimilation of additional compensation mechanisms in the wage system. Studies on this topic point to substitution between COLA and other wage increases: Undercompensation by the COLA mechanism is taken into account when wage agreements are signed and affects the other wage adjustments. Kleiman (1989) found that in 1968–1982, as the economy shifted from price stability to rapid inflation, when compensation via COLA contracted, other compensation mechanisms developed and allowed wages to rise in real terms. Artstein (1997) pointed to the existence of strong effective indexation of wages to prices throughout 1975–1993, even during periods of severe undercompensation by the formal COLA arrangement. Thus, it seems that the COLA arrangements, although part of the institutional system, are largely endogenous, so that the effect of the formal arrangement on wage flexibility is limited.

Israel has had a statutory *minimum wage* since April 1987; it was preceded by a minimum wage agreement between the Histadrut and employers' organizations that was renewed from time to time. Protracted inflationary erosion of the minimum wage led to social pressure to enshrine the minimum wage in legislation. The 1987 law set the minimum wage at 45 percent of the national average wage and created an adjustment mechanism in which full adjustment to the 45 percent of the average wage was made every two years and partial adjustments were made annually and whenever a COLA was paid. In April 1997, the rate was raised to 47.5 percent of the national average wage, and full adjustment to this rate became annual.

Subminimum wage earners are entitled by law to a wage supplement, paid automatically by their employers. Only the base wage is taken into account for this purpose, whereas miscellaneous increments (for seniority, family, shift work, etc.) are excluded. Thus, even workers whose total wage surpasses the minimum may receive an income supplement if their wage net of those increments is subminimum.

When the Minimum Wage Law was enacted, there was concern that it would boost low wages and spill over into higher-wage levels, causing a general wage increase, layoffs among low-wage earners, and a shift to unorganized labor. The few studies on the topic show that these fears were exaggerated, probably because of low compliance with the minimum wage law, due to the absence of an enforcement mechanism; compliance is not monitored regularly but rather in response to workers' complaints, which are few. Flug and Kasir (1994) found poor compliance with the minimum wage agreement in the business sector, which increased only slightly after the law went into effect.

In contrast to the labor market changes discussed thus far, which were intended to enhance wage flexibility, the Minimum Wage Law is expected to have the opposite effect, imposing at the low end of the wage spectrum higher wages than market con-

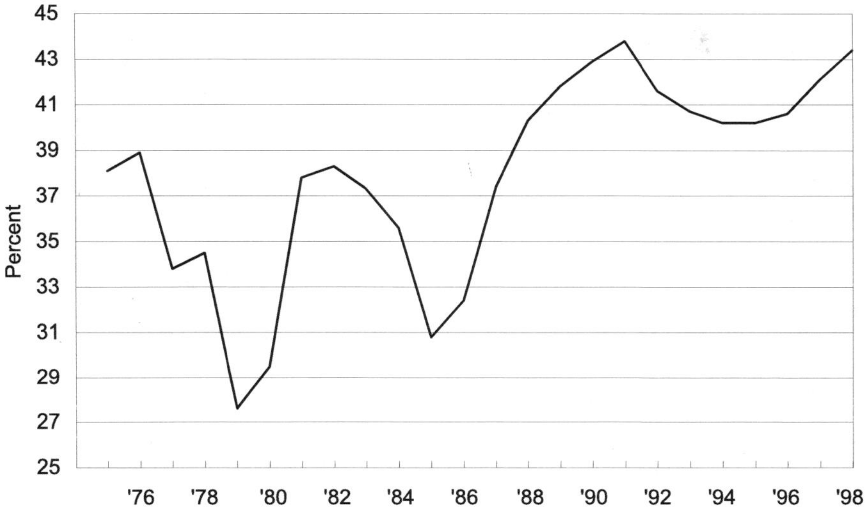

Figure 12.2
Ratio of Minimum Wage to Average Wage, 1975–1998
(Percent)

ditions support. The direct effect in a competitive market is a contraction in employment, though in the absence of perfect competition, other effects are possible.

The ratio of the minimum wage to the average wage, shown in figure 12.2, ranged between 40 and 43 percent in the 1990s. In most OECD countries, this proportion has been declining, but it is still higher than in Israel (except for Spain). The ratio is lower than Israel's in North America and even lower in developing countries (OECD, 1997, 1998).

Unemployment benefits are paid by law to persons who have lost their jobs, built up insurance entitlements by contributions from wages before dismissal, and showed a willingness to accept alternative work but were not offered suitable jobs by the labor exchange. Unemployment benefits are paid for up to 138 days, after a five-day waiting period, and are based on the claimant's predismissal wage relative to national average wage, using a formula in which the marginal benefits decline in several steps, as the ratio of predismissal wage to average wage increases. In 1991–1994, various aspects of the law were toughened to reduce abuse, and to mitigate the disincentive to work that the law created, though the quantitative effect of these measures seems to be minimal.

Figure 12.3 shows the replacement rate, the ratio of unemployment benefits to average wage. This rate is lower in Israel than in most OECD countries, and the

Figure 12.3
Replacement Rate,* 1975–1998
(Percent)
* Ratio of average unemployment benefits to average wage.

duration of compensation is also especially short. Figure 12.3 demonstrates the inflationary erosion of unemployment benefits in the 1970s, a corrective adjustment of benefits to price increases in 1980, renewed erosion afterwards, and an increase in the replacement rate following the 1985 stabilization.

Labor taxes and other labor costs are also considered institutional arrangements here because they create a wedge between employer's labor cost and the employee's wage. Changes in these parameters thus affect profitability and employment and, in turn, labor market flexibility. The main elements here are direct taxes on wages—income tax and the employee's National Insurance (social security) contributions—and labor taxes paid by the employer—payroll tax and the employer's contribution to National Insurance. Additional types of labor costs are contributions to various funds (severance, pension etc.), which affect wage flexibility just as labor taxes do.

As inflation accelerated, Israel's income tax provisions were modified in several ways, especially through recurrent adjustments of tax brackets, but their erosion was not eliminated, and effective tax rates rose. The disinflation since mid-1985 set an opposite trend in motion—a substantial broadening of tax brackets and a decline in effective tax rates. Additional changes were made in 1987 and 1994, and an immigrant-absorption surtax of 5 percent of income tax was charged in 1991–1994.

Employers' contributions to National Insurance were reduced in several steps in order to reduce production costs and stimulate growth in employment and product. Since 1995, Israel has had a national health insurance law, and a health tax is deducted from wages, replacing previous voluntary health-fund dues. A payroll tax on employers' wage expenses was imposed in 1975, partially waived in 1980, gradually lowered since 1987, and abolished (except on public services) in 1992.

Overall, a policy of lowering total taxes on labor was invoked between 1985 and 1995. Since then, however, some retreat has taken place. Cutting taxes on labor contributes to a more flexible labor market, because its effects are shared by employee and employer, as in the standard analysis of the effect of a tax on prices. Thus, the lowering of tax rates would be reflected in higher net wages as well as in higher producer profits and an increase in employment. The dominant effect in Israel, as noted below, is on employment.

In sum, the steep increase in labor supply in the 1990, as immigrants and foreign workers joined the labor force, led to strong employment growth and a flow of the newly employed to rather poorly paying jobs in the more flexible industries. All this happened against the background of processes of rationalization and privatization that had begun earlier, and of changes in labor market institutions.

12.4 Macroeconomic Wage Flexibility

The many changes in the structure and behavioral rules of the labor market since 1985 gave employers greater latitude in setting wages, determining employment, and adjusting both parameters to changes in labor supply and demand. In the next sections, we examine whether this greater microeconomic flexibility was translated into greater flexibility at the macro level. The current section focuses on *wage* flexibility at the macro level from a long-run perspective and explores the main factors that affect it. The analysis is based on a wage-setting model developed by Artstein (1997), in which the main Israeli labor market institutions are taken into account. In this model, wages are set at the industry level, and interdependencies among wage trends in different industries are examined.

The Theoretical Model

The model draws a distinction between two kinds of wage-setting behavior, resulting in two types of industries—those in which workers belong to trade unions and others where labor is unorganized and wages are determined by labor supply and demand. In this model, wages in a unionized industry are set in an optimization process, in which the union maximizes its members' expected utility, with regard to their alternatives and to labor demand in that industry. After wages in the industry have been set, firms determine the number of employees.

Once wages and employment in the unionized industries have been determined, this also determines labor supply for the nonunionized sector of the market, which in fact is a residual market that absorbs excess supply of labor in the unionized industries. It is assumed that not all excess labor supply in the unionized sector is translated into labor supply for the competitive sector, due to workers' eligibility for unemployment benefits and to their concern that accepting a job in a nonunionized industry inflicts a stigma that reduces their chances of future employment in the unionized industries. The total supply of labor for the nonunionized sector, coupled with demand for labor in this sector, then determines the levels of wages and employment in this part of the market.

The labor market is thus composed of two interrelated submarkets, a primary unionized market and a secondary competitive one. It differs from other studies on dual labor markets in its emphasis on wage setting at the industry level, which renders a richer set of interrelations among wages in the various industries.

This framework yields two types of wage equations. Wages in a unionized industry are determined by workers' expected alternative income and by shocks to that industry. The alternative income is a weighted average of expected wages in other industries and the unemployment benefits for which laid-off employees in the industry are eligible. The shocks are changes in labor productivity, relative prices, and taxes on labor. Assuming optimal prediction of shocks by workers, and rational expectations with regard to their alternative income, expected values can be translated into lagged values of these variables and of wages in the industry itself. (For the detailed assumptions concerning expectations and optimal forecasting and the full derivation of the equations, see part II of Artstein, 1997.)

The wage equation for a nonunionized industry is different: In such an industry, wages are set by labor supply and demand after wages and employment have been determined in the unionized industries, and the shocks have become known. The explanatory variables of the equation in this case are therefore expressed in current terms; these are wages in unionized industries, average unemployment benefits, the labor force, and shocks to the industry itself and to the unionized industries.

The model describes the setting of net *real* wages, that is, net wage per employee deflated by the Consumer Price Index, and prices are exogenous. The fact that inflation is unknown when wage accords are signed, and the partial indexation of the COLA arrangement, were factored in by adding unexpected inflation to the wage equations. The model was further expanded to include (1) a possible effect of minimum wages and (2) outside intervention in wage-setting patterns during the stabilization program of 1985. (For further details, see Artstein, ibid.)

Model Estimation and Main Conclusions

The model was estimated for the 1975–1993 period, using annual panel data for the main economic branches (industries). The competitive sector of the labor market includes agriculture and personal services, which are characterized by a large number of small businesses, a large share of unskilled labor, and low union density. Wage per employee in these two industries is the lowest in the economy. The unionized industries are all others—manufacturing, construction, commerce, restaurants and hotels, transport and communications, financing and business services, and public services. (Because these industries also have subindustries with low union density, the attribution of entire industries to the unionized sector is somewhat arbitrary; however, the available data do not allow estimation at the subindustry level, and agriculture and personal services are at the bottom of the industrial hierarchy anyway.) We note that although the use of personal contracts has expanded in the past decade to unionized industries, for most of the estimation period, collective agreements were the common employment pattern.

The equations for all industries were estimated together, and their being of two types was of course reflected in the method of estimation, which is not detailed here. The equations were estimated in logarithmic form so that the coefficients are short-term wage elasticities. The equations below are followed by a discussion of the main results.

Equation of industry i in the unionized sector:

$$w_{i,t} = 0.19w_{i,t-1} + 0.59(0.25w_{M-i,t-1} + 0.50w_{O,t-1} + 0.25b_{i,t-1}) + 0.16a_{i,t-1} - 0.05(1+\pi_t^{ne}) + 0.06D86 + c_i$$

Equation for industry j in the non-unionized sector:

$$w_{j,t} = 0.34w_{M,t} + 0.18b_t - 0.30l_t + 0.25a_{j,t} + 0.96a_{M,t} - 0.27\theta_{j,t} - 0.05(1+\pi_t^{ne}) + c_j$$

The notation is as follows: the unionized sector is marked by index M and the nonunionized sector by index O. w_i is the real wage in industry i of the unionized sector, w_j is the real wage in industry j of the nonunionized sector, w_M is the average real wage in the unionized sector, w_O is the real average wage in the nonunionized sector, and w_{M-i} is the real average wage in the unionized sector exclusive of industry i. All of these are *net* wages. b_i is real unemployment benefits for a person dismissed from industry i, b is real average unemployment benefits in the economy, a_i is real product per person employed in industry i, a_M is real average product per person in the unionized sector, θ_j is the ratio of labor cost to net wage (the wedge) in industry j, π^{ne} is unexpected inflation, l is the labor force, D86 is a dummy variable for 1986, and c_i and c_j are the constants of the equations, which vary among industries. All coefficients are significant, and the adjusted R^2 is 0.98.

The estimation results support the theoretical framework of a dual labor market. In primary sector (unionized) industries, wages in the previous year were found to be of decisive influence: The wage elasticity of workers' alternative income (composed of lagged wages in all other industries and of unemployment benefits for those dismissed from the industry) was almost 0.60, and lagged wages in the industry itself received a coefficient of 0.20. Product per employed person in the industry was significant, but its short-run elasticity was only 0.16. This relatively low elasticity conforms to previous studies on wages in Israel.

Wages in nonunionized industries depend, as noted, on current year variables, and here the elasticities were 0.34 for the average wage in the unionized sector, negative at 0.30 for the labor force, and 0.18 for average unemployment benefits. The short-run elasticity with respect to productivity in the industry was 0.25, and elasticity with respect to average productivity in the unionized sector was close to unity. The elasticity with respect to relative-price shocks and taxes on labor (the wedge) was negative in this case, whereas in the equations for primary sector industries, this variable was insignificant in all the versions examined.

Real-wage erosion due to unexpected inflation turned out to have only a minor effect on real wages in both sectors, suggesting strong built-in compensation mechanisms in Israeli wages. The model allows us to examine the hypothesis that adjustments in the COLA agreement during the period changed the effective rate of indexation of wages to prices, but this hypothesis was rejected.

In the second half of 1985, wage increases were held to predetermined rates by administrative measures, which were lifted in March 1986. One would therefore expect a negative effect of these measures on wages in 1985 and compensating wage rises in 1986. The equations, however, point to a different story: A dummy variable for 1986 received a significant and positive coefficient of 0.06, whereas a dummy variable for 1985 was insignificant, both with the 1986 dummy variable and without it. This suggests that the decrease in real wages in 1985, though imposed by the stabilization program, was consistent with the wage-setting patterns for the entire period, whereas the renewed wage increase in 1986 deviated from these patterns considerably.

The short-run elasticities of the equations allow us to compute long-run wage elasticities that reflect the interdependencies between wages in different industries and the lag structure of wages. These calculations show that the long-run effect of shocks to primary sector wages is approximately twice as strong as the immediate effect, whereas the cumulative effect of shocks to secondary sector wages exceeds the original shock by only about 25 percent.

The main conclusions of the study are the following:

1. There is substantial underlying *inertia* in real wages in the unionized industries, whereas wages in the competitive sector are influenced almost entirely by contemporary variables. However, due to the strong interactions between wages in the two sectors, the unionized sector's wage inertia affects wages in the other sector, and by the same token, the competitive sector's wage setting mitigates wage inertia in the unionized sector. This wage inertia is reflected, inter alia, in the disparities between short-run and long-run wage elasticities with respect to shocks.

2. Wage elasticity with respect to *labor productivity* in the primary sector is low in the short run, in which only about one-sixth (0.16) of the increase in productivity is translated into a wage increase, but this elasticity climbs to 0.90 in the long run. The reason is that an increase in productivity increases not only wages but profits as well, and therefore also product and employment in the industry; consequently, wages in the secondary sector also rise, followed by another rise in wages in the primary sector, and so forth. In the secondary sector, wage elasticity with respect to productivity is higher in the short run, at 0.25, but much lower in the long run.

3. The formulation of the equations assumes that the *wage elasticities* do not change along the period. Yet the findings for the 1985 and 1986 dummy variables show that real-wage increases in 1986 strongly deviated from previous patterns. In response to the mass immigration that has taken place since 1990, in contrast, the equations accurately describe wage trends throughout the immigrants' integration into the labor market.

4. *Unemployment benefits* were found to have a substantial impact on wages in all industries, a 0.18 elasticity in the short run, and twice that level in the long run. This finding supports the Israeli practice of a short eligibility for such benefits (unlike Europe, for example) because extended eligibility would intensify wage inertia and impair wage flexibility.

5. *Taxes and other labor costs* had the (predictable) effect of lowering net wages in the nonunionized sector, though for the unionized sector this variable was insignificant. Thus, in the unionized sector, changes in these taxes and costs are borne

entirely by the firms and induce changes in employment, whereas in the non-unionized sector, they also affect net wages. This finding supports the policy of enhancing employment by reducing labor costs, as has been the practice since the mid-1980s.

6. *COLA* was not factored into the model directly. However, the effect of unexpected inflation on real wages, which is negative and significant but small, suggests that effective wage indexation is high. Even when the formal COLA arrangement stipulated severe undercompensation, the adjustment of wages to price rises was sustained in a multitude of other channels, as previous studies had also shown.

7. The *minimum wage* was not found to have an effect on the average wage. Theoretically, the minimum wage should receive a positive coefficient in the wage equation, varying among industries, and larger in low-wage industries. Our model does not identify such an effect. This finding conforms to findings about the effect of minimum wages in other countries, and the low compliance rate in Israel.

8. Wages are more flexible in Israel than in *European countries* for which similar studies are available, including the U.K. For an extended international comparison, see Artstein (1997), the main findings of which are presented in part 12.8 below.

To sum up, the Israeli data for the past two decades support a labor market model with two types of industries—unionized industries that respond to exogenous shocks with a time lag and slowdown the response of the average wage to exogenous developments, and a competitive sector that responds quickly to shocks and contributes to a more flexible wage system. The existence of a competitive sector, even a small one, affects the behavior of the entire labor market in the short run as well as in the long run.

Additional Tests

The model presented above allows us to test for changes in wage elasticities during the period by estimating the same model for subperiods. Were it possible to add data for the late 1990s, we could reestimate the model and test whether its coefficients for the 1990s were different than those for the earlier period. Unfortunately, the data cannot be extended in this fashion, due to an industrial reclassification introduced by the Central Bureau of Statistics in 1995.

To address the question partially, the era was split into two subperiods, 1975–1989 and 1990–1993, and the model was reestimated with dummy variables for the subperiods. No significant differences between the coefficients in the two subperiods were found. This should not be surprising, given that changes in behavioral patterns of the labor market are long-term processes, and even if a change has began, it would probably take several more years to identify it in wage equations. This conclusion is consistent with the findings of a study on wage setting in OECD countries in the 1990s. There too, many institutional changes in the labor markets took place in the 1980s and the 1990s, and the study (OECD, 1997; surveyed in part 12.8 below) asked whether the relationship between wage increases and unemployment in the 1990s was different than it was earlier. The general conclusion is that there is no evidence of a significant change at the macroeconomic level.

In another study on Israel—Artstein and Sussman (1992), cited above—elasticities were not calculated directly, but findings also point to wage rigidity in the period following the 1985 stabilization program, and greater flexibility thereafter. This study, based on quarterly wage data for fifty-four subindustries, identified a wage-spillover mechanism among subindustries, in which wage increases in some industries quickly spilled into others and led to a spiral of wage rises. Such wage spillovers originated in the period of rapid inflation, in an attempt to prevent real-wage erosion, but later became an accepted norm in wage bargaining. The study found that the wage-spillover mechanism continued to operate even after stabilization: It was temporarily arrested when the stabilization program was implemented but resumed in early 1986. The mechanism that protected real wages from inflationary erosion, thus, turned into a system in which attempts to change relative wages led to across-the-board wage rises that impaired further disinflation.

Estimates of the intensity of the wage-spillover phenomenon show that it was powerful in 1986 and 1987 but lost some ground in late 1988. However, the various trade unions in the public sector reactivated the wage-spillover mechanism in 1993–1994 (part 12.6 below) but with almost no spillover into the business sector.

Other Indicators of Wage Rigidity

Several indicators of wage rigidity that were developed in the 1980s were based on Phillips curves, for instance, Grubb et al. (1983) and Coe (1985). The indicator of *real*-wage rigidity in these studies is the increase in the unemployment rate required to offset the long-term inflationary effect of a real shock. A quantitative estimate of real-wage rigidity is then derived from the coefficients of the Phillips curve. A major problem in these indicators of wage rigidity is the dependence of the estimate on the specific formulation of the Phillips curve. Coe's estimates (1985) demonstrate how adding variables (productivity, for example) to the Phillips curve affects the coefficients of the equation and radically changes the derived rigidity.

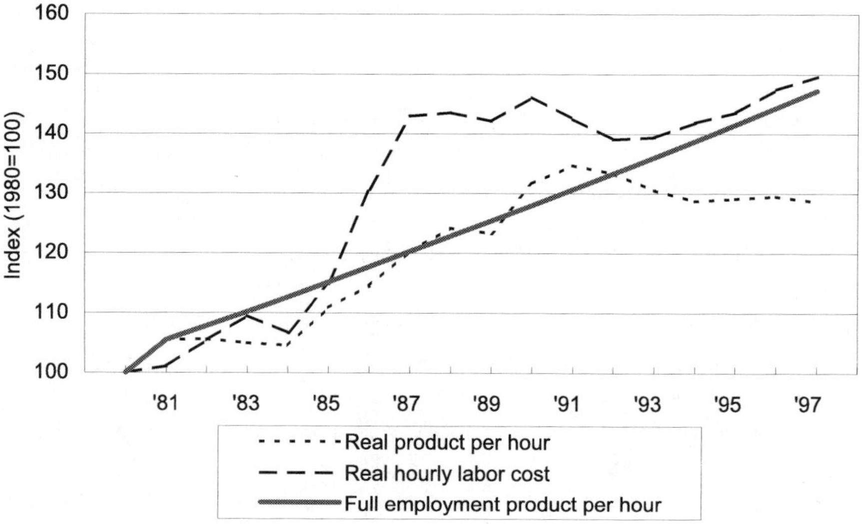

Figure 12.4
"Wage Gap" in the Business Sector, 1980–1997
(Index, 1980 = 100)

A different type of indicator of real-wage rigidity is obtained by comparing the trend of wage per hour with that of product per hour in the business sector. Here, one compares the change in real labor cost with the change that is "justified" by the increase in labor productivity, that is, the change that would maintain unit labor cost.

Figure 12.4 presents indices of real labor cost per hour and of product per hour in the business sector in 1980–1997. As shown, these two indices rose at similar moderate rates in the first half of the 1980s, but in 1986–1987, real labor cost climbed much faster than real product, which means a strong rise in unit labor cost. Unit labor cost then receded but has been increasing again since 1993.

If we replace actual product per hour in the comparison by full employment product per hour, that is, if we smooth business cycle fluctuations, we obtain an indicator of the "wage gap." This concept was suggested by Bruno and Sachs (1985), who also calculated wage gaps for several industrial countries for 1973–1981. Conceptually, a widening of the wage gap points to insufficient flexibility in the adjustment of wages to changes in labor productivity. Calculations of full employment product per hour for Israel in 1980–1997, under several alternative assumptions (one of which is shown in figure 12.4), reveal the following picture: The wage gap fluctuated in both directions in 1980–1984, widened severely in 1986–1987, gradually narrowed again between 1988 and 1993, and stabilized at approximately the 1980 level thereafter. This indicator, like those described above, points to relative wage flexibility in the early 1980s, wage rigidity following the stabilization program, and a resumption of flexibility in the 1990s.

It is worth noting that both the simple comparison of wage and productivity trends and calculations of the wage gap are aggregate indicators for the business sector at large. When great structural changes take place, and productivity grows vigorously in some industries and contracts in others, an aggregate indicator masks different trends in separate industries. In part 12.7, we address this issue.

12.5 Employment Flexibility

The more flexible real wages are, the stronger does employment adjust to shocks, and the closer is its response to that of a competitive labor market. Following the mass immigration in the 1990s, employment increased rapidly, far exceeding all predictions. Business-sector employment grew by 35 percent between 1991 and 1995, an average annual growth of more than 6 percent (table 12.1). The unemployment rate, which had climbed in the early 1990s, swiftly retreated afterwards and stood at only 6.7 percent in 1996, much lower than the 8.9 percent rate before the onset of immigration, and also much lower than earlier forecasts. Labor demand thus proved to be substantially more flexible than the early estimates assumed, and the policy of encouraging the business sector to absorb the additional labor supply was successful.

Beenstock and Ribon (1993) estimated a model of the Israeli labor market, consisting of five behavioral equations, using annual data for 1960–1989. In this model, labor demand is derived from a production function that is nonseparable in labor and capital, and employment is a function of the capital stock, its change, the ratio of domestic demand to the capital stock, and real business-sector wage cost. Labor demand elasticity with respect to real wages obtained there was negative at 0.53. Wage setting followed some type of a Phillips curve, in which wages were affected by the deviation of the actual from the natural rate of unemployment. Simulations using this model show the following:

1. An exogenous increase in labor supply immediately raises unemployment to a rate exceeding the natural rate. Consequently, real wages decline, leading to an increase in employment and a retreat in unemployment in the following year.

2. An increase in investment and in capital stock boosts employment and lowers unemployment in the short term; later on, however, it translates mainly into a wage increase while changes in employment and unemployment are small.

3. Unemployment benefits have a substantial effect on wages and, in turn, on employment and unemployment.
4. The main effects of shocks disappear within the first two years.

Generally, the model finds that labor supply in Israel is quite flexible and that the labor market clears quite rapidly after shocks, with a sizeable effect on employment. This is in line with the wage flexibility presented in part 12.4.

12.6 The Public Sector

The public sector in Israel is highly unionized and its budget constraint is softer than the profitability constraints of the business sector. Furthermore, the employer here negotiates wages not with one trade union but with several unions that compete with each other on their achievements regarding wage rises. In the long run, however, public sector wages are also affected by basic economic forces such as excess demand for or supply of workers in certain occupations and workers' alternatives elsewhere in the economy.

Sussman and Zakai (1996), in a survey of twenty years of public-sector wage policy (1974–1994), found that wage-restraining policy during most of that period resulted in various (some odd) mechanisms to offset the wage erosion that this policy entailed. Consequently, the public sector shifted gradually from centralized wage setting with across-the-board wage increases to separate negotiations with each union and differential wage increases, which led to a widening of wage gaps between different groups of workers. The shift in negotiating focus from general framework agreements to lower negotiating echelons modified the wage structure: Most wage changes were implemented in a proliferation of wage supplements and accelerated promotion on the wage scale. Initially, these differential wage increases created a more flexible wage structure that could respond better to market supply and demand forces. Later, however, the wage supplements spilled over indiscriminately to additional groups of workers, thereby losing their original function and damaging the wage system.

Most of these changes occurred between the mid-1970s and 1985, when labor tried to protect its real wages from inflationary erosion. After the stabilization program, public-sector real wages declined stronger than business-sector wages, but later on they rose again, and between 1989 and 1992, the average wage gap between the sectors was closed (figure 12.5). This average wage rise was not uniform; some unions earned real increases, and others recorded real decreases. As a result, the wage spillover mechanism was reactivated in 1993: Several unions demanded to correct the

Figure 12.5
Real Wage in Business and Public sectors, 1975–1998
(Index, 1975 = 100)

erosion in their relative wages; following several strikes, the government gave in, and soon had to grant similar wage increases across the board.

An (extreme) example of disruption of the relationship between excess labor supply and wage changes is the exceptional wage increase that physicians in the public sector received in the 1990s even though the supply of immigrant doctors grew vigorously. Sussman and Zakai (1998) investigate how the Israel Medical Association managed to secure such an exceptional increase in the wages of its veteran members alongside an expansion of doctors' employment and a cooperation of veteran doctors in the absorption of their immigrant colleagues.

The study emphasized the strength of the doctors' union, and identified three main factors that made this paradox possible: (1) a fierce struggle, in which sanctions and strikes were used, to raise wages and to increase the number of positions beyond the increase of the demand for medical services; (2) easing of the competition from immigrant doctors by a lengthy training process in which the veteran doctors serve as instructors, and placement of the immigrants who obtained licenses at the bottom of the occupational scale; and (3) a differential wage increase, in which senior physicians received large raises and occupational promotions due to the expansion of the system.

12.7 Structural Change

The strong response of the average wage to the macroeconomic shocks of the early 1990s, compared to its inflexible response to the shock of 1985, may be due to two types of factors. One is the changes in employment patterns and labor market institutions discussed in part 12.3 above that allow greater flexibility at the microlevel. The other is the change in the industrial composition of employment, due to the structural change on the production side. We first focus on the latter factor, which was especially powerful in the 1990s.

Immigration from the former Soviet Union increased the labor force by one third between the beginning of the decade and 1996. This large influx of labor was accompanied by a big change in the industrial composition of employment and wages because (a) so many immigrants joined industries that paid relatively low average wages and (b) their inflow caused wages in these industries to decline further. Upon their arrival, the immigrants created additional demand for basic goods and enhanced demand for labor in the industries that produce them. Although most immigrants had a much higher occupational profile, relatively few found employment in their occupations and the others had to accept, at least temporarily, unskilled jobs in low-wage industries. Because newly employed workers are paid less than veterans, the immigrants who flowed to these particular industries lowered average wages in them even when no veteran employee took a wage cut. The real decline in the national average wage in the early 1990s is thus the result of the strong expansion of low-wage industries and the further decline of wages there. We calculate the first of these effects and then discuss the second.

Average wages vary widely among industries, already at the level of main industry groups (table 12.A1), and even more so at the subindustry level. The subindustries that absorbed most of the increase in employment between 1989 in 1994 were business and legal services, in which wages were about 80 percent of the national average; education, in which the average wage was similar; general contracting, subcontracting, and other retail trade, in which the average wage was also below the national average; and welfare and nursing, food services, and mixed farming, with wages that were only half the national average. Relative employment actually declined in especially well-paying subindustries—electricity and water, financial institutions, certain subindustries of transport and communications, and manufacturing subindustries like mining and quarrying, chemical and petroleum products, electrical and electronic equipment, and transport vehicles.

The quantitative effect of this structural change in the first half of the 1990s is calculated in part A of table 12.2. There, we compare the increase in the national

Table 12.2
Change in Average Wage for Fixed Industrial Distribution of Employees, 1990–1998 (Percent)

	Business sector			Economy at large		
	Actual change vs. previous year	Computed change for employee distribution of previous year	Difference*	Actual change vs. previous year	Computed change for employee distribution of previous year	Difference**
	(1)	(2)	(3)	(4)	(5)	(6)
a. 1990–1994						
1990	−1.35	−0.77	−0.58	−0.91	−0.25	−0.67
1991	−5.23	−3.01	−2.29	−3.06	−1.45	−1.63
1992	1.84	2.69	−0.83	1.23	2.02	−0.78
1993	0.26	0.92	−0.65	0.54	1.17	−0.62
1994	−0.52	0.08	−0.60	2.47	3.03	−0.54
Cumulative***	−5.04	−0.76	−4.31	0.18	4.37	−4.02
b. 1995–1998						
1995	0.39	1.42	−1.02	1.95	2.80	−0.83
1996	1.28	1.01	0.27	1.42	1.41	0.01
1997	3.97	4.02	−0.05	2.60	2.82	−0.21
1998	3.06	2.89	0.17	2.21	2.35	−0.14
Cumulative****	8.53	8.04	0.45	6.36	6.62	−0.24

*Computation of difference: (3) = {[100 + (1)]/[100 + (2)] − 1} × 100.
**Computation of difference: (6) = {[100 + (4)]/[100 + (5)] − 1} × 100.
***Rate of change of 1994 vs. 1989.
****Rate of change of 1998 vs. 1995.

average wage that would have prevailed in each of the years 1990–1994 had the distribution of employee posts among the subindustries remained unchanged from the previous year (column 2) to the actual increase in the average wage (column 1). These calculations, based on wage increases in the subindustries, were carried out once for the business sector (forty-six subindustries) and again for the economy at large (fifty-four subindustries, eight of which belong to the public sector).

Table 12.2 shows that in each of the years 1990 to 1994, the actual average wage change was smaller than the change under a fixed industrial distribution of workers. Turning to the cumulative gap, by computing the average wage for 1994 for the industrial distribution of workers in 1989, a difference of 4.3 percent is obtained: Actual average wage in the business sector declined by 5 percent during those five years, and this decline was almost entirely due to the change in the composition of employment; for a *fixed* composition of workers, the cumulative wage decline was less than one percent. Similar calculations for the economy at large reveal similar gaps: Although the actual total change in the average wage was negligible, this aggregate masks a cumulative increase of over 4 percent in an unchanged labor composition, and a parallel decline prompted entirely by changes in the workers' industrial distribution.

Similar calculations for the 1995–1998 period, based on the new industrial reclassification (part B of table 12.2), show that the same trend continued in 1995: The actual wage increase was about 1 percent lower than that for a fixed composition of employee posts. The picture is different for subsequent years (1996, 1997, and 1998): The gap between the actual change and the fixed-distribution change is negligible at both the annual and the three-year cumulative levels. This is because the rapid growth of the economy was halted in mid-1996, so that hiring diminished, and the industrial composition of labor stopped changing. The moderating effect of the change in industrial composition on wages was then halted as well, and real wages resumed their upward trend.

These findings mean that the sizable decline in business-sector average wages in the first half of the 1990s, which could have been interpreted as an increase in macroeconomic wage flexibility, largely reflects the flexibility of the product markets, and the adjustment of employment to changes in labor demand.

To discuss the decline in average wages within an industry while it is absorbing many new workers, we turn to the findings of Friedberg (1997), who asked whether a large concentration of immigrants in a given occupation has a negative impact on the employment or wages of native Israelis in that occupation. Although Friedberg's classification is by occupation and not by subindustry, her findings conform well to the foregoing industry-level investigation. Friedberg found that when estimating OLS (Ordinary Least Squares) wage equations for native Israelis, the higher the share of immigrants in the occupation, the smaller the wage increase for native Israelis in that occupation in 1989–1994. In contrast, when one accounts for the possibility that the occupational distribution of immigrants is not independent of conditions in the Israeli labor market, that is, estimates 2SLS (2 Stage Least Squares) equations with the same specifications, the negative effect reported above disappears. Thus, the hypothesis that the influx of immigrants had no effect on native Israelis' wages is not rejected. The negative effect of immigrants on native Israelis' wages in the OLS equations is then due to immigrants' massive entry to the low-wage occupations.

As the immigrants' experience in Israel increased, the share of highly skilled immigrants who found work in schooling-intensive occupations rose, and their wages rose as well. One explanation of this phenomenon is offered by Eckstein and Weiss (this volume). According to their study, immigrants are not rewarded for their imported skills upon arrival, but later on their wage rises outpace those of comparable native Israelis. The three sources of this wage rise are an increase in the return on the immigrants' imported schooling, their occupational experience in Israel, and their mobility up the occupational ladder.

Following each of the two major shocks to the economy, the 1985 stabilization program and the early 1990s immigration, major structural changes were required. After 1985, rapid disinflation revealed inefficiencies in many production systems, and they needed restructuring in adjustment to poststabilization conditions. In the early 1990s, changes in production were needed twice—first, to meet the immediate needs of the masses of immigrants, and later on, to provide jobs that would put the high skills of the immigrants to use.

As expected, it was easier to restructure production amidst a general state of rising demand than during an economic slowdown, when structural change causes layoffs. The structural change of the 1990s induced a general expansion in product and employment, so that employment did not decline even in industries that lost proportional ground. The post-1985 structural change, in contrast, entailed a stage of production cuts and layoffs in many enterprises, and the difficulty to reduce wages under these circumstances reflects real-wage rigidity.

This inflexibility of real wage in the post-1985 period is different not only from the response of wages to shocks in the 1990s, but also from their response to shocks in the decade that preceded stabilization—foremost, the two fuel crises in the 1970s. Then, too, real wage declined only in the short term and resumed its upward trend afterwards, but this was a reaction to government policy at that time. Government attempted, on the one hand, to erode real wages through frequent currency depreciation and, on the other hand, absorbed most of the increase in the labor force to the public sector, thereby avoiding the unemployment that would have supported the decrease in real wages. The shocks of the 1970s were actually absorbed by the public sector, causing repeated price increases and thereby setting an inflationary spiral in motion. In this sense, the rise of real wage in the 1970s was not due to rigidities in wage setting or labor market institutions.

The foregoing discussion points to relative labor market flexibility at times of rapid economic growth (the first half of the 1990s and also up to 1972, a period that is not analyzed here) and, as noted, in periods of accelerating inflation (1974–1985). In contrast, when overall growth is low and inflation is in retreat, and parts of the economy warrant a microlevel wage decrease, wages exhibited rigidity at the macroeconomic level as well. We thus reiterate our general conclusion: One may attribute only part of the greater wage flexibility in the 1990s to the many changes in patterns of employment and institutions. Labor market developments in the late 1990s, when the economy slowed down, further support this conclusion. Had the greater flexibility of wage in the first half of the 1990s reflected mainly a change in the *patterns* of wage-setting, the turnabout in the late 1990s should have been accompanied by more moderate rises in wage and unemployment. This did not happen; as shown in table 12.2, in the absence of the moderating effect of the influx of newcomers, real wages increased in 1996, 1997, and 1998, even though the demand for labor has declined.

12.8 International Comparison

Most OECD countries have taken measures to introduce greater flexibility to their labor markets during the past two decades. These actions followed escalating unemployment rates in the 1970s, after the fuel crises, which were blamed on rigidities in these countries' labor markets. The various countries had very diverse unemployment rates in the 1970s and 1980s, and a rich literature has developed in an attempt to explain the differences. One of the main lines of research addressed the relationship between the institutional structure of the labor market, including wage-setting patterns, and the performance of this market and of the economy at large. The scope of the present study leaves no room to describe the diverse measures that the various countries took in order to strengthen the response of the labor market to economic incentives and to mitigate institutional rigidities. Yet we briefly survey several studies that estimated wage flexibility and that explored the correspondence between labor market flexibility and economic performance, and between labor market institutions and the flexibility of this market.

Estimates of Real-Wage Flexibility

In comparing real-wage flexibility in Israel (Artstein, 1997) to findings for other countries, we address only models of similar type, that is, models in which wage is determined by an optimizing labor union, as in the model for Israel. The studies for the various countries vary by data aggregation and by the research question that led to the choice of the specific model.

In a study on the United Kingdom (Lee and Pesaran, 1993), the authors conclude that the wage system is an important mechanism in the diffusion of industry-level shocks across the economy. They estimated separate wage equations for each of sixteen industries in the business sector in 1954–1990 and found substantial wage inertia, larger than in Israel. The effect of industry-level productivity was slightly lower than the one obtained for Israel, and the services were found to be more sensitive than other industries to exogenous factors, similar to the finding for Israel.

A study on the Norwegian labor market (Johansen, 1996), derived from data on subindustries in manufacturing and service for 1966–1987, found that the most important effect on the industry wage is wage outside that industry, with a 0.80 elasticity, and that industry-level product had a long-term elasticity of only 0.20. Compared to Israel, wages in the rest of the Norwegian economy exert a stronger influence and industry-level productivity, a weaker one.

A comparative study of five countries—Sweden, Norway, Finland, Germany, and the United States (Holmlund and Zetterberg, 1991)—also investigated the extent to which wages respond to industry-level factors as against macroeconomic factors. Using a model for 1960–1985, with an identical specification for all five countries, the study found, predictably, that industry level wages in the United States were the most sensitive to industry-level productivity and relative price shocks, whereas in northern Europe, where wage bargaining is centralized, the elasticity with respect to wages outside the industry was closer to 1 in the long run (against only 0.7 in the United States).

Comparisons of studies that estimated *aggregate* wage equations with the findings for Israel are more problematic, because these studies lack interindustry dynamics. The wage inertia that they portray is therefore lower and the derived long run elasticity higher than in disaggregate models.

An aggregate model for the Swedish business sector in 1960–1986 (Calmfors and Forslund, 1991) found that the long-run effect of shocks on wages was more than twice their short-run effect. The magnitude of this effect was similar to the one obtained for Israel's primary sector using the industry-level model. A dual sector aggregate model for the U.K. business sector (Holly and Smith, 1987) found a leading sector (manufacturing) that was less flexible than Israel's primary sector, and a secondary sector in which wage flexibility resembled that of Israel's secondary sector. A model of aggregate wage setting for the Finnish manufacturing sector (Holm et al., 1994) found long-term wage elasticity to be roughly twice the level of short-term elasticity, similar to findings of aggregate models for the other northern countries. An aggregate model of wage and employment in Denmark (Andersen and Risager, 1991) showed that long-term wage elasticities there were slightly higher than in the industry-level study for Israel.

Summing up, our comparison of industry level equations in the countries mentioned with those of the Israeli model shows that wages are more flexible in Israel than in Great Britain and northern Europe. In aggregate models, one loses interindustry wage dynamics, so that their findings also point to greater wage flexibility in Israel.

The Framework of Wage Bargaining

An influential article by Calmfors and Driffill (1988) points to a nonmonotonous relationship between economic performance and the degree of centralization in wage negotiations: Superior economic performance and lower unemployment rates prevail in the two extreme cases, centralized national bargaining and highly decentralized systems with firm-level wage setting, as against an intermediate degree of centralization at the level of separate trade unions. The reason is that unions operating at the firm-level have limited market power, given that wages are constrained by competition in the market for the firm's products; a national-level union also prevents excessive wage increases, because it internalizes the negative effect of a wage increase on inflation and on total employment. In intermediate cases of separate trade unions, in contrast, unions have some market power but ignore macroeconomic implications of their actions, and this is reflected in excessive wage increases and inferior macroeconomic performance. All this leads to a hump-shaped curve between the degree of centralization in wage bargaining and real wage (and between centralization and unemployment).

More recent studies, including different estimates of centralization in wage bargaining, additional indicators of economic performance, and data for additional years, elicited some results that support the original hump-shaped curve and others that contradict it. Danthine and Hunt (1994), for example, show in a theoretical study that the hump-shaped curve flattens out as international integration accelerates, because greater competition in product markets reduces union power.

Collective bargaining institutions in several OECD countries have undergone substantial change over the past decade (OECD, 1997). Decentralization of bargaining gathered momentum in Great Britain and New Zealand, and Sweden replaced centralized-level by industry-level wage accords. Norway and Portugal, on the other hand, moved toward more centralized bargaining. In Australia, wage bargaining centralized until 1987 and then reverted to enterprise-level agreements. The opposite pattern evolved in Denmark—decentralization in the 1980s and centralization later on. The same is true for Italy. In the OECD report, the Calmfors and Driffill analysis was extended to cover the 1986–1996 period. It found only weak evidence of inferior economic performance in countries that were in the intermediate degree of centralization, even when the model was expanded to take account of additional variables such as union density. Comparing the 1980s with the 1990s, there was some support for the hypothesis that countries that moved toward less centralized or less coordinated bargaining experienced larger declines in employment than other countries. However, the only unequivocal finding in this study is the correspondence with inequality: Earnings inequality is lower in countries with more centralized or coordinated bargaining than in others.

Labor Market Institutions and Economic Performance

The International Labor Organization sponsored a series of studies on the relationship between unemployment and labor market flexibility in several countries—Great Britain (1986), Sweden (1988), Finland (1990), the Netherlands (1990), Austria (1991), Spain (1984), and Italy. These studies discuss each country's particular institutional setting and evaluate its effect on labor-market flexibility and on changes in unemployment in the 1970s and 1980s. The authors' concept of flexibility varies slightly among countries, but as a rule, the authors conclude that labor market institutions have an effect but are not the main factor in the rise in unemployment. The study on Austria (Walterskirchen, 1991), the country usually considered the most corporative, argues that labor market rigidities do not explain any increase in the unemployment rate. In the study on Great Britain (Standing, 1986), greater labor market flexibility is defined in view of its results—an increase in the number of jobs. The author notes that the measures adopted in Great Britain were accompanied by a decline in job security, a widening of wage gaps, and segmentation of the labor market. When the study was published, unemployment in Great Britain was still very high at over 10 percent.

The study on Sweden (Standing, 1988) was conducted while the Swedish economic model was still considered a successful blend of capitalism and social consensus, and the author noted an impressive structural change beginning in the 1970s that did not result in greater unemployment. In regard to Finland, the authors (Lilja et al., 1990) believed that the country's economic policy of social consensus was the reason of its successful response to exogenous shocks. The Netherlands case (de Neubourg, 1990) was studied at a time of very high unemployment (12 percent) and its labor market ranked at the rigid end in comparative studies. Here, too, the author's conclusion was that labor market rigidities were not the main cause of the country's high unemployment, yet he recommended flexibility-enhancing measures.

The situation in these countries was very different in the late 1990s. Unemployment was low in Great Britain and in the Netherlands, whereas in Sweden and in Finland the egalitarian model broke down and unemployment rates climbed steeply.

A main lesson from this collection of studies is the importance of the time dimension, which is particularly long in the labor market.

The 1997 OECD report offers another way to investigate the effect of the many changes in labor market institutions on the performance of this market. After surveying the changes that various countries made in their labor market institutions and policies in the 1990s, the authors asked whether these changes affected the sensitivity of the average wage to unemployment. They estimated augmented Phillips curves for the 1970–1995 period, a separate curve for each of twenty-one OECD countries, and used the estimates to test for a change in the relationship between average wage changes and unemployment. The authors found no support for the hypothesis that the response of the average wage to increasing unemployment in the 1990s was milder than in the past. They noted that given that some changes in institutions and policies did not take place until the 1990s, it could be too early to look for an impact on wage setting patterns.

In a recent study on the relationship between labor market institutions and the performance of these markets in OECD countries (Nickell and Layard, 1999), the authors ask which labor market institutions are really bad for unemployment and growth, and which are not. They present a wage-setting model and derive an equilibrium unemployment equation, to be estimated from cross-country data. Five groups of labor market institutions were expected to influence the rates of unemployment and economic growth—labor taxes, employment protection laws, trade union activity and minimum wages, unemployment benefits and active labor market policy, and education and skill formation. The regressions were based on two cross-sections dated 1983–1988 and 1989–1994, for twenty OECD countries, altogether forty observations.

Based on the findings of the regressions, the authors conclude that a policy to reduce unemployment and enhance growth should focus on two institutions only—trade unions and social security systems. Enhancing competition in product markets is a key policy to mitigate the negative effect of unions, and for social security, the key policies are a benefit reform coupled with active labor market policies to move people from welfare to work. The authors see no reason to worry about labor market regulations, employment protection, or minimum wages.

12.9 Flexibility and Inequality

Technological change in the past two decades, coupled with increasing openness to international trade, have increased the skill premium in industrialized countries, and led to decreasing demand for unskilled labor and a widening gap in unemployment rates between skilled and unskilled labor. In the United States and Britain, wage gaps between these two groups of workers have also widened substantially. Do flexibility-enhancing policies aggravate wage gaps and income inequality?

According to Krugman (1994), in countries such as the United States, where government intervention in the labor market is rather low, the change in relative demand for skilled labor caused an increase in income inequality and growing poverty. In continental Europe, with its generous welfare system and less flexible labor markets, the outcome was increasing unemployment and a decline in participation rates of unskilled workers.

Nickell and Layard (1999) analyze unemployment and wage data for various schooling groups in OECD countries, and examine changes in the demand for skilled labor relative to the demand for the unskilled, and the relative supply of these two groups of workers. According to their analysis, the fact that relative demand has outstripped relative supply much more in Britain and the United States than elsewhere helps to explain why relative wages of the skilled have risen by far more in these two countries. They also found that the compressed earnings distributions in some OECD countries were due to equally compressed skill distributions.

Israel has also experienced skill-biased growth, at least since the mid-1970s, with a rapid expansion in the share of skill intensive exports (Bank of Israel, 1997). In the following two decades, income inequality has displayed a general uptrend that is consistent with a labor market that, for most of that time, has been quite flexible. Similar correspondence was found in subperiods as well: Between the mid-1970s and the mid-1980s, when wages were relatively flexible, income inequality rose substantially (Dahan and Ben-Porath, 1997), and unemployment remained low. In the post-stabilization years, when wages were inflexible, inequality declined, and with some delay, unemployment climbed to 9 percent. In the 1990s, the labor market was more flexible again, wage gaps widened, and after an initial rise, unemployment quickly retreated.

Wage inequality has followed a similar trend to that of total income inequality, and it, too, has increased significantly since the early 1990s. Dahan (in this volume) attributes the link between mass immigration in the 1990s and the widening of labor market inequality to the erosion of the immigrants' human capital in their move to Israel. According to Dahan, changes in the return on schooling and education gaps explain only one third of the change in wage inequality. The remaining two thirds, inequality among individuals with identical measurable traits, are actually the segment of inequality that strongly increased in the 1990s. Dahan found that the labor market assigns immigrants' occupational experience a lower price than it does to the experience of native Israelis, and when this is factored into the wage equations, the unexplained portion of inequality in the 1990s contracts. However, wage inequality among native Israelis also rose significantly in the 1990s, and here, the increase in the return on schooling played a central role.

Sussman's (1998) discussion of wage gaps in the 1990s also emphasizes the widening of wage gaps among native Israelis, between academic occupations and blue collar and unskilled workers. One explanation for this is that when immigrants arrived, they were still unable to compete for jobs that required university degrees; thus, they turned to unskilled jobs, and reduced wages in that sector. Later on, when they increased labor supply for academic occupations, demand for such jobs had also risen, due to additional investments in the meantime, so that the increase in supply did not erode the veterans' wages.

In sum, the growth of high-tech at the expense of traditional industries has been manifested in Israel, as elsewhere, in a long-term rise in inequality, which reversed temporarily after 1985, but worsened again in the 1990s, as the immigrants integrated into the labor market. This trend in inequality in the 1980s and 1990s provides additional support to the claim that the Israeli labor market was quite flexible during most of that time.

12.10 Summary and Conclusions

The period following the 1985 economic stabilization program was characterized by real wage rigidity, though from a long-term perspective, this was exceptional: Greater flexibility was the rule in the decade before the stabilization and in the decade after it. The long-term trend in income inequality supports this assessment. The Israeli labor market is also more flexible than its counterparts in many European countries.

The relatively slow response of labor markets to shocks, compared to that of product markets, is due to long-term wage contracts, various institutional arrangements, the power of "insiders," and efficiency-wage considerations. Changing behavioral norms in wage setting and employment is a long process, even at a time of privatization and increasing use of personal contracts and subcontracting. Therefore, it is not surprising to discover that even though most labor market institutions have become more flexible, the decline in the average wage in the first half of the 1990s traces mainly to the rapid economic growth and the changing industrial composition of labor, and not to enhanced wage flexibility. The wages of veteran workers were hardly affected during those years and actually rose in many occupations. The rise in real average wage in the late 1990s, despite economic slowdown and higher unemployment, also supports the assessment that the changes in labor market institutions of the past decade have not yet been translated into a significant increase in macroeconomic wage flexibility.

This does not mean that the many changes in Israel's labor market since 1985 had no effect on the determination of wages and employment. Studies on labor market flexibility in other countries emphasize the long delay between measures to ease institutional barriers in this market and their effect on wage moderation. Nickell and Layard (1999), quoted in part 12.8, found that only two institutional arrangements had important effects on economic performance in OECD countries—the existence of strong trade unions and the unemployment benefit system. Total labor taxes were also found to have a considerable impact on labor cost and unemployment. The influence of unions is expected to contract as product markets become more competitive, and the adverse effect of unemployment benefits may be eased by a benefit reform and an active labor market policy.

Do these conclusions apply to the Israeli economy as well?

Competition in product markets did accelerate in the 1990s. The very competitive high-tech sector, where personal labor contracts are widespread, grew vigorously. The traditional sector has also become more competitive, through exposure to competing imports (Gabai and Rob, this volume) and due to privatization (Gronau, this volume). Concurrently, the trade unions have lost power. All these developments are expected to have a moderating effect on wages.

The unemployment benefit system was found to have a substantial effect on wages in Israel, as in other countries, though unemployment compensation in Israel is quite modest compared to most European countries; this is one of the explanations for the greater basic wage flexibility in Israel. As for the effect of taxes on labor, it seems to be quite large in Israel, though in Israel tax reductions do more to boost employment than to raise workers' net wages.

The issue of widening wage gaps in Israel is also linked to labor market flexibility. The choice between greater labor market flexibility, to improve the economy's performance, and one of its painful results, an increase in income inequality, is not merely an economic question but an important social choice. The long-term trends of a growing high-tech sector and a relative decline in the traditional industries that employ unskilled labor have increased wage and income gaps, and the absorption of the immigrants in the labor market strengthened this trend. As the immigrants integrate and climb the occupational ladder, their effect on inequality is expected to reverse.

Technological change, with its negative impact on unskilled labor, in contrast, is expected to continue, and in the absence of a supportive policy, these workers are increasingly exposed to unemployment and may gradually leave the labor force. Enhancing the ability of weak population groups to cope with the rapidly changing labor market requires investment in upgrading their occupational skills. The policy to be followed should include vocational retraining for the labor force and for those who left it in despair, and extended schooling for the young at all levels of education. In the long run, participating in the labor market strongly depends on skill formation, as does the ability to attain the combination of a relatively flexible labor market and a more equal income distribution.

Appendix

Table 12.A1
Relative Wage (wage per employee post in industry relative to national average wage), 1975–1994

	Agriculture	Manufacturing	Electricity and water	Construction	Trade, food, and hotels	Transport and communications	Financial and business services	Public services	Personal services
1975	0.689	1.046	1.773	0.969	0.865	1.463	1.114	0.935	0.678
1976	0.685	1.090	1.730	1.026	0.884	1.450	1.118	0.887	0.726
1977	0.648	1.047	1.996	0.917	0.851	1.451	1.128	0.937	0.704
1978	0.660	1.062	2.099	0.909	0.869	1.499	1.102	0.916	0.719
1979	0.630	1.061	1.887	0.872	0.839	1.432	1.069	0.963	0.718
1980	0.638	1.096	1.983	0.891	0.832	1.499	1.119	0.913	0.709
1981	0.621	1.111	2.172	0.878	0.840	1.478	1.110	0.911	0.666
1982	0.635	1.138	2.079	0.926	0.884	1.475	1.108	0.871	0.723
1983	0.619	1.133	2.112	0.868	0.850	1.418	1.120	0.898	0.731
1984	0.621	1.159	1.978	0.830	0.843	1.443	1.045	0.914	0.693
1985	0.617	1.180	2.014	0.824	0.912	1.470	1.093	0.861	0.689
1986	0.629	1.171	1.876	0.863	0.940	1.489	1.127	0.834	0.750
1987	0.634	1.162	1.972	0.931	0.938	1.519	1.097	0.827	0.803
1988	0.623	1.136	1.961	0.908	0.935	1.484	1.119	0.856	0.807
1989	0.626	1.161	2.019	0.899	0.922	1.453	1.079	0.870	0.775
1990	0.601	1.172	2.002	0.867	0.907	1.468	1.080	0.880	0.756
1991	0.580	1.162	2.067	0.860	0.905	1.524	1.046	0.915	0.747
1992	0.585	1.171	2.141	0.933	0.906	1.509	1.044	0.900	0.749
1993	0.589	1.183	2.094	0.941	0.914	1.504	1.040	0.914	0.756
1994	0.592	1.152	2.043	0.960	0.878	1.461	0.997	0.981	0.789

Source: Central Bureau of Statistics.

Table 12.A1 (continued)
Relative Wage, Reclassification, 1994–1998

	1994	1995	1996	1997	1998
Agriculture	0.56	0.56	0.57	0.58	0.59
Manufacturing	1.15	1.17	1.18	1.23	1.26
Electricity and water	2.02	2.10	2.15	2.15	2.16
Construction	0.94	0.91	0.85	0.86	0.87
Wholesale and retail trade	0.96	0.95	0.95	0.94	0.95
Accommodation and restaurants	0.56	0.54	0.54	0.53	0.53
Transport and communications	1.40	1.37	1.33	1.34	1.33
Banking, insurance, and other finance	1.75	1.65	1.72	1.81	1.73
Business activities	0.81	0.80	0.83	0.84	0.85
Public administration	1.31	1.39	1.43	1.38	1.39
Education	0.82	0.87	0.87	0.85	0.85
Health, welfare, and social work services	0.96	0.96	0.94	0.91	0.88
Community, social, and personal services	0.78	0.78	0.77	0.75	0.75

Source: Central Bureau of Statistics.

References

Achdut, Lea, Victor Sulla, and Zvi Eisenbach. "Employment of Workers by Means of Employment Agencies: The Extent and Characteristics of the Phenomenon." Social and Economic Research Institute of the Histadrut, May 1998. (Hebrew)

Andersen, Torben M., and Ole Risager. "A Wage Bargaining Model for Denmark." *Applied Economics* 23 (April 1991): 567–578.

Artstein, Yael. "Wage Rigidity in Israel: Institutions vs. Market Forces." *Working Paper no. 35-97*, The Eitan Berglas School of Economics, Tel Aviv University, 1997.

Artstein, Yael, and Zvi Sussman. "Wage Policy During Disinflation: The Israeli Stabilization Program of 1985." *The Economic Quarterly* 139, (January 1989). (Hebrew)

———. "Wage Dynamics in Israel: Market Forces and Spillover Effects." *Applied Economics* 24 (September 1992): 969–979.

Bank of Israel. *Annual Reports* for 1988, 1989, 1990, 1996, and 1997.

Beenstock, Michael, and Sigal Ribon. "The Market for Labor in Israel." *Applied Economics* 25 (July 1993): 971–982.

Bewley, Truman F. "Why Not Cut Pay?" *European Economic Review* 42 (May 1998): 459–490.

Bruno, Michael, and Jeffrey D. Sachs. *Economics of Worldwide Stagflation.* Cambridge, Massachusetts: Harvard University Press, 1985.

Calmfors, Lars, and John Driffill. "Centralization of Wage Bargaining." *Economic Policy* no. 6 (April 1988): 13–61.

Calmfors, Lars, and Andres Forslund. "Real Wage Determination and Labor Market Policies: The Swedish Experience." *The Economic Journal* 101 (September 1991): 1130–1148.

Coe, David T. "Nominal Wages, the NAIRU and Wage Flexibility." *OECD Economic Studies* (Paris) no. 5 (1985): 87–126.

Dahan, Momi, and Ori Ben-Porath. "Mass Immigration and Income Distribution." *The Economic Quarterly* 44 (1997): 351–372. (Hebrew)

Danthine, Jean-Pierre, and Jennifer Hunt. "Wage Bargaining Structure, Employment and Economic Integration." *The Economic Journal* 104 (May 1994): 528–541.

Flug, Karnit, and Nitza Kasir. "Compliance with the Minimum Wage Law in the Business Sector." Bank of Israel, Research Department, Discussion Paper 94.12, 1994. (Hebrew)

Friedberg, Rachel. "The Impact of Mass Migration on the Israeli Labor Market." PSTC Working Paper no. 97-11, Brown University, 1997.

Galin, Amira. "Outsourcing." Research Report no. 14/98, Faculty of Management, Tel Aviv University, 1998. (Hebrew)

Grubb, Dennis, Richard Jackman, and Richard Layard. "Wage Rigidity and Unemployment in OECD Countries." *European Economic Review* 21 (1983): 11–39.

Holly, Sean, and Peter Smith. "A Two Sector Analysis of the UK Labor Market." *Oxford Bulletin of Economics and Statistics* 49 (1987): 79–102.

Holm, Pasi, Seppo Honkapoja, and Erkki Koskela. "A Monopoly-Union Model of Wage Determination with Capital and Taxes, an Empirical Application to the Finnish Manufacturing." *European Economic Review* 38 (1994): 1009–1034.

Holmlund, Bertil, and Johnny Zetterberg. "Insider Effects in Wage Determination, Evidence from Five Countries." *European Economic Review* 35 (1991): 285–303.

Johansen, Kore. "Insider Forces, Asymmetries, and Outsider Ineffectiveness: Empirical Evidence for Norwegian Industries." *Oxford Economic Papers* 48 (1996): 89–104.

Kleiman, Ephraim. "Indexation in the Labor Market." In *The Israeli Economy, Maturing through Crises,* edited by Yoram Ben-Porath, Cambridge, Mass.: Harvard University Press, 1986.

Krugman, Paul. "Past and Prospective Causes of Unemployment." In *Reducing Unemployment: Current Issues and Policy Options,* Proceedings of a Symposium in Jackson Hole, Wyoming. The Federal Reserve Bank of Kansas City, 1994.

Lee, Kevin C., and M. Hashem Pesaran. "The Role of Sectoral Interactions in Wage Determination in the UK Economy." *The Economic Journal* 103 (January 1993): 21–55.

Lilja, Reija, Santamaki Tuire, and Guy Standing. *Unemployment and Labour Market Flexibility: Finland.* Geneva: International Labour Office, 1990.

Nathanson, Roby, and Guy Zisser. "The Influence of Trade Unions on Wage and the Labor Market: An Empirical Analysis." In *The New World of Work in an Era of Economic Change.* Ministry of Economics and Planning, 1996. (Hebrew)

de Neubourg, Chris. *Unemployment and Labour Market Flexibility: The Netherlands.* Geneva: International Labour Office, 1990.

Nickell, Stephen, and Richard Layard. "Labour Market Institutions and Economic Performance." In *Handbook of Labor Economics,* volume 3C, edited by Orley Ashenfelter and David Card. Amsterdam. North Holland (1999): 3029–3084.

OECD. *Labour Market Flexibility—Trends in Enterprises.* Paris, 1989.

———. *Employment Outlook.* Paris, July 1997.

———. *Employment Outlook.* Paris, July 1998.

Ribon, Sigal. "Factors Influencing the Duration of Unemployment of Individuals Eligible for Unemployment Compensation." Bank of Israel, Research Department, Discussion Paper 90.09, 1990. (Hebrew)

Standing, Guy. *Unemployment and Labour Market Flexibility: The United Kingdom.* Geneva: International Labour Office, 1986.

———. *Unemployment and Labour Market Flexibility: Sweden.* Geneva: International Labour Office, 1988.

Sussman, Zvi. "From Collective Agreements to Personal Contracts: Wages, Labor Relations and the Histadrut." *The Economic Quarterly* 42 (April 1995). (Hebrew).

Sussman, Zvi. "The Impact of the Immigration on the Economic Situation of the Veteran Population in Israel." In *Profile of an Immigration Wave*, edited by Moshe Sicron and Elazar Leshem. Jerusalem: The Magnes Press, The Hebrew University of Jerusalem, 1998. (Hebrew)

Sussman, Zvi, and Dan Zakai. "Wage Restraint Policy and Compensatory Mechanisms—The Public Sector, 1974–1994." Bank of Israel, 1994. Mimeo. (Hebrew)

———. "The Decentralization of Collective Bargaining and Changes in the Compensation Structure in Israel's Public Sector." Bank of Israel, Research Department, Discussion Paper no. 96.04, 1996.

———. "The Mass Immigration of Physicians and the Steep Rise of Wages of Veterans in Israel: A Paradox?" *The Economic Quarterly* 45 (1998). (Hebrew)

Walterskirchen, Ewald. *Unemployment and Labour Market Flexibility: Austria.* Geneva: International Labour Office, 1991.

VI GROWTH, BRANCH STRUCTURE, AND INCOME DISTRIBUTION

13 Capital Accumulation, Productivity and Growth in the Israeli Economy

Zvi Hercowitz

13.1 Introduction

This paper addresses capital accumulation and total factor productivity (TFP) in the Israeli business sector. The two topics are related, partly because of the common factors affecting both capital accumulation and TFP growth, and partly because of the possible link between capital accumulation and temporary productivity losses.

To provide an overview of the relative importance of TFP growth and accumulation of inputs for growth, let us start with the following computation, as in Helpman (1998), for the 1960–1997 period. Business-sector output grew 9.2 times during this period, while weighted (capital and labor) inputs and productivity grew 4 and 2.3 times, respectively. The relative importance of these two factors, however, differ dramatically across subperiods. During the 1960–1975 subperiod, the corresponding figures are 3.5 for output, 2 for inputs and 1.75 for TFP. Hence, in this early period the contribution of productivity is not much smaller than that of input growth. In the 1975–1989 subperiod, output grew 1.6 times, while inputs grew 1.3 times. Hence, the relative contribution of productivity growth significantly declined. In the subperiod 1989–1997, influenced by the immigration influx from the former Soviet Union, output and inputs both grew about 1.6 times, and hence, the contribution of productivity is nil.

These sharp differences across different subperiods motivates the preliminary discussion in section 13.2, which focuses on the behavior of investment and its relative price, two key variables, over the entire 1960–1997 period. The view presented is that the first part of the period (until about 1975) is dominated by increasing returns to scale stemming from the process of constructing a new economy, whereas thereafter the economy is closer to a typical growing pattern.

Section 13.3 presents the basic framework of analysis, including the theoretical considerations and the empirical formulation. There are two forms of technological progress—neutral technological change, affecting production through TFP, and investment-specific technological change, embodied in new equipment goods. The estimation of investment equations for equipment and structures separately is reported in section 13.4. Given the interpretation presented in section 13.2, the shorter sample 1975–1997 is used. The main results are the following: A measure of investment-specific technological change, embodied in new equipment, and immigration, has important effects on investment per capita of both types. Inflation, taxation, and credit subsidies are found to have significant effects on investment in structures but not on equipment.

In section 13.5, we turn to the implications of capital accumulation and other macroeconomic factors for TFP. The focus of the analysis is the productivity stagnation in the 1990s. The main hypothesis is that the adoption of new equipment and the new technologies embodied in it entails an initial period of low productivity. This section borrows from Hercowitz, Lavi, and Melnick (1998).

Section 13.6 addresses human capital accumulation, in the form of formal schooling and R&D, as sources of long-run neutral technological change and TFP growth. It is found that during the sample period these factors behave very similarly to a linear upward trend.

13.2 Real Investment and Its Relative Price: Overview of the 1960–1997 Period

This section is devoted to the behavior of investment and its relative price over the 1960–1997 sample, in an attempt to provide a general interpretation of the pattern observed.

Figure 13.1 portrays I/Y, the ratio of real fixed business investment to real gross business product (GBP). The 1990s are characterized by a sharp increase in invest-

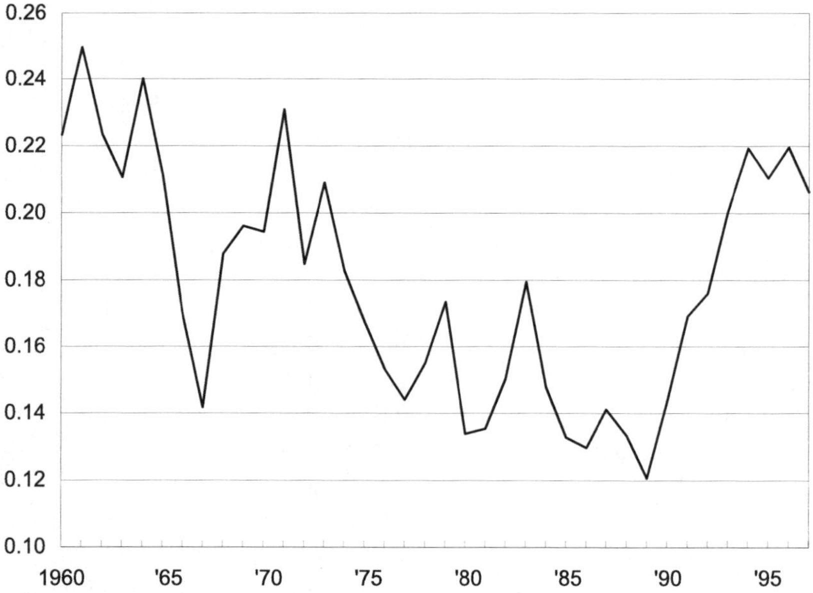

Figure 13.1
Investment-Output Ratio

ment due to the immigration influx, whereas prior to 1990, the investment/GBP ratio has a declining trend. The relative price of investment, P_i—the ratio of the investment deflator—is shown in figure 13.2. From 1960 to 1975, the relative price of investment increases 2 percent per year; from 1976 to 1985, 1 percent per year; and from then onwards, it declines.

The declining relative price of investment in the latter part of the sample can be explained by investment-specific technological change, which lowers the relative price of new investment goods. This is a typical long-run phenomenon due to technological change being biased toward investment goods.[1]

The prolonged increase in the relative price of investment, mainly until the middle 1970s, is less typical. Investment has a larger component of tradeable goods, which have exogenous foreign-exchange prices, than total output. Hence, P_i resembles a real exchange rate. The relatively low P_i at the beginning of the sample, when the Israeli economy was relatively underdeveloped, implies that domestic production was then relatively inefficient: The price of domestic production was high relative to imported investment goods. The relative expensive nature of production in the early Israeli economy is also suggested by comparing P_i in figure 13.2 to its U.S. counter-

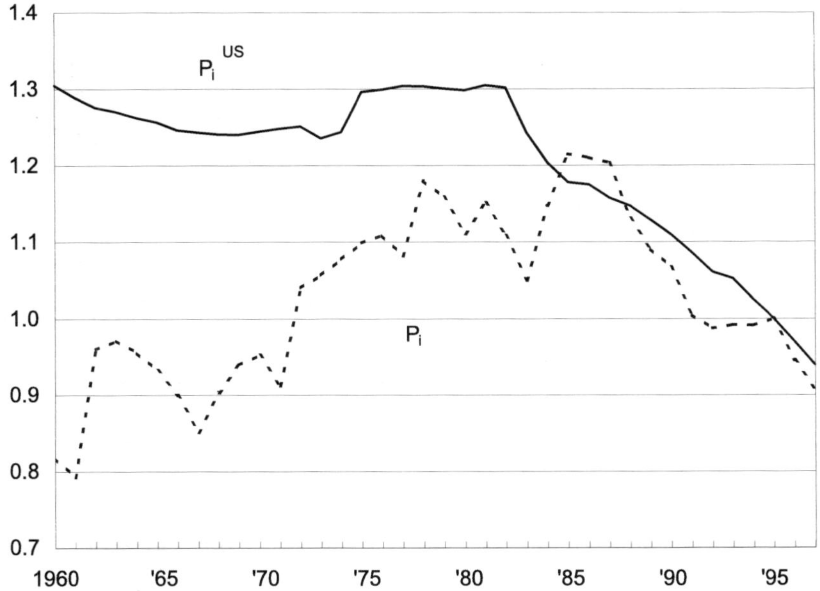

Figure 13.2
Relative Price of Investment—Israel and the U.S.

Table 13.1
Dependent Variable: log P_I; sample: 1961–1997

Variable	Coefficient	t-statistic
Constant	−2.149	−3.012
log A	0.368	2.978
log P_i^{US}	0.852	3.296
$AR(1)$	0.601	4.200
$R^2 = 0.782$		S.E. = 0.051
Adj. $R^2 = 0.762$		D.W. = 1.832

part, P_i^{us}.[2] The high rates of investment in the early period, the 1960s and early 1970s, can be related to the relatively low price of domestic investment in the early Israeli economy.

The increase in P_i (or real depreciation) during the first part of the sample is consistent with a gradual development of the new economy, including opening and thickening of new markets. The process may have involved increasing returns to scale and fast productivity growth in domestic production.

From the considerations above, the behavior of the relative price of investment over the sample may be characterized by two opposite forces. One is overall efficiency growth, which slows down the GBP deflator (the denominator in the relative price ratio) and thus tends to generate a real depreciation, or upward-trending relative price. The other is investment-specific technological progress, which slows down the investment deflator. The first effect strongly dominates during the earlier stages of the construction of the Israeli economy, say, until 1975, and it becomes weaker later on, as the economy converges to a typical long-run pattern.

The regression reported in table 13.1 is an attempt to confront this interpretation with the data. The relative price of investment, P_i is regressed on total factor productivity, A, (defined in section 13.3) and on the U.S. counterpart of the relative price, P_i^{us}, capturing the normal long-run behavior of this relative price. The A variable represents overall productivity growth, and it is expected to enter with a positive coefficient. P_i^{us} reflects investment-specific technological change (as elaborated in section 13.3); its decline captures the increasing efficiency of new capital per unit of output spent in investment. Hence, P_i^{us} should enter with a positive coefficient of magnitude 1. Two versions of the regressions, without and with adjustment for serial correlation of the residual, yield positive coefficients on both A and P_i^{us}, with the coefficient of the latter being close to 1.[3]

As shown in figure 13.3, A increases rapidly until the early 1970s and then slows down. In figure 13.2, P_i^{us} has a general declining trend. Hence, both the signs of the

Figure 13.3
Relative Price of Investment and TFP

coefficients in table 13.1 and the behavior of the two variables in figures 13.2 and 13.3 seem consistent with the story that overall productivity change is dominant in the first part of the sample.

The conclusion from the discussion above is the following. The data until the middle 1970s seem to be dominated by the unique process of building a new economy. Given that the rest of the paper focuses on the later period, the 1990s in particular, and on policy analysis that is intended to be relevant for the future, the observations prior to 1975 are not included in the following empirical work. This conclusion is not based on a formal econometric criterion. The informal criterion adopted is that the combined phenomena of real depreciation and fast TFP growth until the middle 1970s, as shown in figure 13.3, distinguish this period from the rest of the sample.[4]

13.3 The Basic Framework

Theoretical Considerations

This section sketches the theoretical background of the paper. Consider an open-economy version of the neoclassical growth framework. The domestic economy specializes in the production of good y, which is also exported, and imports productive equipment and consumption goods. The terms of trade, or the relative price of y in the world market relative to imports, are given from abroad at a constant level. From the domestic producer's point of view, the relative price of y in terms of imports differs from the terms of trade, given a nonlinear transformation of y production into exports in the world market. The economy faces a constant real rate of interest and perfect capital flows. Technological progress is exogenous and of two types—neutral and investment-specific.

The production function for the domestic good has the constant-returns form

$$Y_t = A_t K_{et}^{\alpha_e} K_{st}^{\alpha_s} L_t^{1-\alpha_e-\alpha_s}, \qquad 0 < \alpha_e,\ \alpha_s < 1,\ \alpha_e + \alpha_s < 1, \tag{13.1}$$

where Y_t is output, A_t is TFP, K_{et} is the stock of equipment, K_{st} is the stock of structures and L_t is labor input. TFP obeys the relationship

$$\log A_t = \sum_i \lambda_i X_{ti} + e_t^a \tag{13.2}$$

The Xs are observed exogenous variables, and e^a is an unobserved stochastic residual. The Xs include Z, Hicks or Harrod, neutral exogenous technological change.

The two capital stocks evolve according to the standard form

$$K_{et+1} = K_{et}(1 - \delta_e) + I_{et}, \qquad 0 < \delta_e < 1,$$

$$K_{st+1} = K_{st}(1 - \delta_s) + I_{st}, \qquad 0 < \delta_s < 1,$$

where I_e and I_s represent gross investment in equipment and structures, respectively, and δ_e, δ_s are the corresponding depreciation rates. Equipment investment differs from investment in structures in two respects: (1) I_e is imported, while I_s is produced domestically, (2) equipment quality improves over time, whereas the quality of structures is assumed to be constant. I_e represents "real" equipment investment; that is, it is adjusted for quality. This is the notion used, in principle, in national income accounts. Equipment investment can be written as

$$I_{et} = I_{et}^* Q_t, \tag{13.3}$$

where I_e^* is expressed in foreign output cost units, and Q is exogenous quality improvement, or investment-specific technological change. The foreign firms selling equipment maximize the profits: $\{I_{et}^* Q_t P_{et}^* - I_{et}^*\}$, where P_{et}^* is the foreign price of a quality-unit of equipment in terms of foreign output. The optimization over I_e^* implies that $Q_t = 1/P_{et}^*$; that is, the foreign relative price of equipment in terms of output reveals investment-specific technological change.

The resource constraint for good y is

$$Y_t = I_{st} + C_t + F(E_t), \tag{13.4}$$

where C is consumption of good y (private and public), E is exports, and $F(\cdot)$, $F(\cdot)' > 0$, $F''(\cdot) > 0$, represents the transformation of domestic production into goods in the world market (transportation and marketing costs). Total consumption, which includes also imported goods, and investment of the two types are assumed to be determined by intertemporal optimization, given the exogenous rate of interest, terms of trade, and technological change.

The composition of consumption—C and imports—depends on the domestic relative price of consumption imports in terms of good y. Likewise, the composition of investment, structures and equipment, depends on the relative price of equipment in terms of y, P_e. Both relative prices are two forms of the "real exchange rate." The relationship between P_e and the relative price of consumption imports is dictated by the world goods markets. The variable that adjusts to satisfy equation 13.4 is the real exchange rate (either P_e or the relative price of consumption imports).

The components of the vector X are exogenous or predetermined, and the focus of the following analysis is on the effects of X on capital accumulation, I_e and I_s, and on TFP, A. Given that the marginal productivity of capital of the two types is affected by A, all the variables affecting A should, in principle, affect capital accumulation. The relationship between capital accumulation and TFP is not constrained in the present analysis to their joint dependency on X; the short-run implications of capital accumulation for TFP via adoption of new capital goods are also investigated, and they constitute the focus of the TFP analysis.

Empirical Formulation

Here, the components of the exogenous vector X that are chosen for the empirical analysis are introduced. The mechanisms of effect of each component on I_e I_s, and A are elaborated in the next two sections, which are devoted to capital accumulation and TFP growth. Details about the data used are given in the data appendix.

- *CS*: credit subsidy (ratio to GDP).
- *KT*: capital transfers (ratio to GDP), which are direct subsidies to investment expenditure.
- dP^{20+}, dP^{20-}: inflation rates higher and lower than 20 percent per year, respectively. Inflation reflects both the role of real balances in production and/or macroeconomic instability.

- τ: tax rate (total taxation as a ratio to GDP).
- $K_r/INPUT$: ratio of the stock of roads infrastructure to weighted inputs, where $INPUT \equiv K_e^{\alpha_e} K_s^{\alpha_s} L^{1-\alpha_e \alpha_s}$ captures the level of economic activity.

Technological variables include

- t: time, capturing Z, neutral technological change.
- Q: equipment-specific technological change. It corresponds to $1/P_e^*$, where P_e^* is matched to the relative price of equipment in the U.S.

Another variable is

- $OLIM$: ratio of immigrants to population.

13.4 Determinants of Capital Accumulation

This section is devoted to the macroeconomic factors affecting the accumulation of capital in equipment and structures. As mentioned in section 13.2, given the likelihood that the early part of the 1960–1997 sample is dominated by the process of constructing a new economy, the sample used in what follows is 1975–1997.

The analysis consists in estimating separately investment equations for equipment and structures, considered reduced forms. The two equations estimated are

$$\log \frac{I_e}{POP} = \beta_0^e + \beta_1^e CS + \beta_2^e KT + \beta_3^e \, dP^{20+} + \beta_4^e \, dP^{20-} + \beta_5^e \tau$$

$$+ \beta_6^e \log \frac{K_r}{INPUT} + \beta_7^e t + \beta_8^e \log Q + \beta_9^e OLIM + e^e, \tag{13.5}$$

$$\log \frac{I_s}{POP} = \beta_0^s + \beta_1^s CS + \beta_2^s KT + \beta_3^s \, dP^{20+} + \beta_4^s \, dP^{20-} + \beta_5^s \tau$$

$$+ \beta_6^s \log \frac{K_r}{INPUT} + \beta_7^s t + \beta_8^s \log Q + \beta_9^s OLIM + e^s, \tag{13.6}$$

where POP is the population size, and e^e, e^s are error terms. The expected signs of the coefficients are

- CS: credit subsidy (ratio to GDP). It lowers the interest rate faced by private agents; $\beta_1^e, \beta_1^s > 0$.
- KT: capital transfers (ratio to GDP), which are direct subsidies to investment. They lower the private cost of investment projects; hence, $\beta_2^e, \beta_2^s > 0$.

• dP^{20+}, dP^{20-}: inflation rates higher and lower than 20 percent per year. Inflation reduces real balances held by firms, and if liquidity services are included in A, inflation reduces the marginal productivity of capital. Inflation may also reflect the negative effect of macroeconomic instability. The separation between high and low inflation rates allows for a nonlinear effect; $\beta_3^e, \beta_3^s, \beta_4^e, \beta_4^s < 0$.

• τ: tax rate (total taxation as a ratio to GDP). Taxation reduces the private return on capital, and thus, it should have a negative effect on investment. Taxation may have an additional negative effect on investment through human capital accumulation and the quality of labor (i.e., via A); $\beta_5^e, \beta_5^s < 0$.

• $K_r/INPUT$ represents the productive role of roads infrastructure, affecting investment through A; $\beta_6^e, \beta_6^s > 0$.

• t: time, capturing Z, neutral technological change, affects investment through A; $\beta_\tau^e, \beta_\tau^s > 0$.

• Q: equipment-specific technological change, measured as the inverse of the relative price of equipment in the U.S. Higher Q implies a lower cost of an efficiency unit of equipment investment; hence, $\beta_8^e > 0$. Given complementarity between the two capital stocks (equation (1)), higher Q induces more I_s as well, although to a lower extent; $\beta_8^e > \beta_8^s > 0$.

• $OLIM$: ratio of immigrants to population. Immigration should have a temporary positive effect on investment in order to restore the capital/labor ratio; $\beta_9^e, \beta_9^s > 0$.

The estimation is carried out as follows. First, all the explanatory variables in equations 13.5 and 13.6 are included.[5] Then, the variables with t-statistics below 1 are deleted.[6] The estimated equations are reported in tables 13.2 and 13.3, on which the following discussion concentrates.

For equipment, table 13.2, the most important explanatory variable is Q. As technology embodied in equipment improves, equipment investment increases with an elasticity of 1.7. Another significant coefficient for equipment investment is $OLIM$

Table 13.2
Dependent Variable: $\log(I_e/POP)$; sample: 1975–1995

Variable	Coefficient	t-statistic
Constant	1.220	13.885
KT	6.001	1.827
$\log Q$	1.729	10.376
$OLIM(-4)$	6.267	2.666
$R^2 = 0.855$		S.E. = 0.111
Adj. $R^2 = 0.867$		D.W. = 2.032

Table 13.3
Dependent Variable: $\log(I_s/POP)$; sample: 1975–1995

Variable	Coefficient	t-statistic
Constant	1.281	2.740
CS	8.634	3.802
KT	6.248	1.971
dP^{20+}	−0.364	−4.055
dP^{20-}	−2.117	−2.807
τ	−3.051	−3.063
$\log Q$	2.324	6.003
$OLIM(-3)$	5.494	1.981
$OLIM(-4)$	5.507	1.942
$R^2 = 0.946$		S.E. = 0.102
Adj. $R^2 = 0.915$		D.W. = 2.100

lagged four years. For each percentage point increase in the immigration/population ratio, investment/per capita in equipment goes up by 6.3 percent after four years. Substituting $OLIM_{t-4}$ with $OLIM_{t-3}$—which is insignificant when $OLIM_{t-4}$ is included—yields also a positive and significant coefficient. Capital transfers, KT, has a positive and significant coefficient, as expected, but credit subsidies CS, turns out to have an insignificant effect.

Table 13.3 reports the estimation of the I_s equation. The variables CS, KT, dP^{20-}, dP^{20+}, τ, Q, and $OLIM$ enter with significant coefficients of expected signs. Credit subsidies and inflation appear to have strong effects on structures, although not on equipment. For each 10 percentage points of inflation above 20 percent, investment in structures is reduced by 4 percent, and for inflation below 20 percent, the corresponding figure is 21 percent. Equipment-specific technical change has also a large coefficient, 2.3, which is even higher than the coefficient on I_e, 1.7, contradicting the prediction that the effect of Q on structures should be weaker. Hence, it is likely that Q captures also the effect of Z (t, however, is insignificant). Taxes are found to have a negative effect, with a 3 percent decline for each percentage point of taxation.

As elaborated in the next section, the results for total factor productivity raise the suspicion of endogeneity of KT. Given the reduced-form interpretation of the regressions—based on the exogeneity assumption regarding X—the equations are reestimated excluding capital transfers. The results, shown in tables 13.4 and 13.5 remain similar to those in tables 13.2 and 13.3. The main difference is that $OLIM_{t-3}$ replaces $OLIM_{t-4}$ as the most relevant OLIM variable.

One of the interesting results is the negative effect on inflation, high and low, on investment in structures. However, note that these equation are estimated with twenty-three observations and only 16 to 19 degrees of freedom. In any event, when the sam-

Table 13.4
Dependent Variable: $\log(I_e/POP)$; sample: 1975–1995

Variable	Coefficient	t-statistic
Constant	1.343	23.182
log Q	1.722	0.693
$OLIM(-3)$	5.997	2.407
$R^2 = 0.865$		S.E. = 0.118
Adj. $R^2 = 0.852$		D.W. = 1.675

Table 13.5
Dependent Variable: $\log(I_s/POP)$; sample: 1975–1995

Variable	Coefficient	t-statistic
Constant	2.379	5.370
CS	7.054	3.487
dP^{20+}	−0.520	−5.867
dP^{20-}	−3.743	−4.538
τ	−4.893	−5.199
log Q	2.190	7.322
$OLIM(-3)$	7.610	2.579
$AR(1)$	−0.439	−1.783
$AR(2)$	−0.359	−1.805
$R^2 = 0.931$		S.E. = 0.115
Adj. $R^2 = 0.892$		D.W. = 2.294

ple is extended to the 1970–1997 period, the results in tables 13.2 through 13.5 remain very similar, including the negative and significant coefficient of low inflation.[7]

13.5 Determinants of Total Factor Productivity

As shown in figure 13.3, total factor productivity undergoes a dramatic slowdown in the 1990s, which is even more pronounced than the well-known slowdown after 1973. This section analyzes the macroeconomic factors affecting TFP, with an emphasis on explaining its evolution during the 1990s. The analysis is based on Hercowitz, Lavi, and Melnick (1998). Here, a shorter sample is used, 1975–1997, instead of 1960–1996 in that study. The main hypothesis is that the productivity slowdown in the 1990s is related to the massive absorption of new equipment, embodying new technologies, which took place during this period.

Given the temporary, dynamic nature of the main hypothesis, the error-correction framework is adopted in this section: productivity levels are described in a first equation, and the dynamics around these levels in a second equation of growth rates, with error-correction. Because of the short sample, the usual interpretation of the level equation as the long-run relationship is not appropriate here. A preferable interpretation in the present context is that it addresses a lower frequency than the growth rate equation.

The level equation is specified similarly as those of investment in the previous section. However, given that this equation describes the low frequency, the *OLIM* variables, which represent temporary immigration waves, are excluded. Correspondingly, *OLIM* and capital accumulation variables—which also reflect temporary capital stock adjustments—are included in the growth rate equation. Additionally the Q-type technological change does not belong in the level's relationship because Q is embodied in K_e (while A is the residual that is not captured by labor and capital inputs). The level equation, corresponding to equation (2), is thus specified as follows:

$$\log A = \lambda_0 + \lambda_1 CS + \lambda_2 KT + \lambda_3\, dP^{20+} + \lambda_4\, dP^{20-} + \lambda_5 \tau + \lambda_6 \log\left(\frac{K_r}{INPUT}\right) + \lambda_7 t + e^a. \tag{13.7}$$

A is computed using equation 13.1, with $\alpha_e = 0.18$, $\alpha_s = 0.12$ (from Greenwood, Hercowitz and Krusell (1997)). The expected signs of the coefficients are

- CS, KT: credit subsidies and capital transfers, respectively. If the demand for the domestic good is stochastic and capital utilization is in general partial, these subsidies encourage firms to increase the buffer stock of capital, and thus lower measured productivity; $\lambda_1, \lambda_2 < 0$.
- dP^{20+}, dP^{20-}: inflation captures the role of real balances in production; $\lambda_3, \lambda_4 > 0$. Similarly, as in the previous section, the separation between rates higher and lower than 20 percent allows for a nonlinear relationship.
- The tax rate, τ, should generate negative incentives for human capital accumulation and work effort (given hours of work). Hence, $\lambda_5 < 0$.
- $K_r/INPUT$ ($INPUT \equiv K_e^{\alpha_e} K_s^{\alpha_s} L^{1-\alpha_e\alpha_s}$) represents the productive role of the roads infrastructure relative to economic activity; $\lambda_6 > 0$.
- t: Hicks neutral technological change; $\lambda_7 > 0$. This variable is thought of as capturing R&D accumulation and increasing average quality of human capital. Approximating these factors by a linear trend is discussed below in section 6.

The regression with all the variables in equation 13.7 is reported in the appendix, table 13.9. Credit subsidies, CS, have a negative coefficient as expected, but surpris-

Table 13.6
Dependent Variable: log *A*; sample: 1975–1996

Variable	Coefficient	t-statistic
Constant	−4.865	−0.998
CS	−1.612	−3.682
dP^{20+}	−0.057	−4.742
τ	−0.306	−1.643
$\log(K_r/INPUT)$	0.592	3.158
t	0.004	1.565
$R^2 = 0.978$		S.E. = 0.021
Adj. $R^2 = 0.972$		D.W. = 1.415

ingly, *KT* have a positive coefficient. This suggests the possibility of reverse causality: Capital transfers may react positively to changes in tax revenues, which are related to cyclical changes in factor utilization and, thus, in measured TFP. To check this possibility, KT_t was replaced with KT_{t+1}. The resulting coefficient is even larger than with KT_t. This is consistent with the possibility of reverse causality: Higher economic activity is likely to translate into higher tax collection with a delay, making funds available for capital transfers in the following year.[8] Given the reduced form interpretation of equation 13.7—following from the assumption that the variables in the vector *X* are exogenous—capital transfers are excluded from the rest of the analysis. The final level's equation, excluding dP^{20-} that has a *t*-statistic less than 1, is reported in table 13.6.

The coefficient of *t* is 0.4 percent per year, which is too low for trend productivity increase. The technical reason for this low coefficient seems to be that $K_r/INPUT$ is also trended, and it picks up part of the long-run increase. The coefficient of $K_r/INPUT$ is 0.59, larger than the similar estimates obtained in the literature (e.g. Aschauer, 1989), which are in the order of magnitude of 0.3–0.4. Inflation higher than 20 percent, dP^{20+} has a significant negative coefficient. According to this estimate, for every ten percentage points of inflation above 20 percent, the productivity level is lower by 0.57 percent.[9] Credit subsidies, *CS*, have a negative coefficient: Increasing these subsidies by one percentage point of GDP lowers productivity by 1.6 percent, which seems a strong effect. Note, however, that one percentage point of GDP is more than one third of the average credit subsidy/GDP ratio in the 1975–1997 sample (0.027).

The dynamic equation includes the first differences of the relevant variables in *X*, as well as the rate of change in the stock of equipment, K_e. The main hypothesis is that the new technologies embodied in equipment require a process of adoption and learning that are costly in terms of productivity. The equation is formulated as follows (d indicates first-difference, and $PLUS20$ is a dummy variable for years with inflation rates higher than 20 percent):

$$d \log A_t = \omega_0 + \omega_1 \, d(\log K_{et}) + \omega_2 \, d(CS_t) + \omega_3 \, ddP_t \times PLUS20 + \omega_4 \, ddP_t \times (1 - PLUS20) + \omega_5 \, d\tau_t + \omega_6 \, d\left[\log\left(\frac{K_{rt}}{INPUT_t}\right)\right] - \phi e^a_{t-1} + u_t. \tag{13.8}$$

The expected signs of the coefficients are the following:

- $\omega_1 < 0$: this coefficient captures the main hypothesis regarding new equipment. The possibility that $d \log K_e$ captures capital accumulation in general (i.e., that productivity losses are not related to new technologies) and/or immigration, is also analyzed.
- $1 > \phi > 0$: "error correction" coefficient. It is required for convergence to the low frequency level described in equation 13.7.
- The rest of the variables appear in levels also in equation 13.7, and their coefficients should reflect the same considerations.

In the estimation of equation 13.8, e^a_{t-2} was also added, given that e^a_{t-1} was insignificant. The results excluding the insignificant variables are shown in table 13.7. The coefficient of $d \log K_e$ is 0.26, which implies that a 9 percent annual increase in the stock of equipment—the average over the 1991–1997 period—lowers productivity growth by about $2\frac{1}{4}$ percent per year, consistent with a dramatic slowdown. The error-correction mechanism, as estimated, starts working after two years, and from then onwards, the impact declines at the rate of 75 percent per year, which is a fairly fast pace.

Table 13.7
Dependent Variable: $d(\log A)$; sample: 1977–1997

Variable	Coefficient	t-statistic
Constant	0.019	3.173
$d(\log K_e)$	−0.263	−2.980
$d(CS)$	−1.433	−2.551
$ddP \times (1 - PLUS20)$	−0.230	−3.246
$e^a(-2)$	−0.751	−3.404
$R^2 = 0.697$		S.E. = 0.155
Adj. $R^2 = 0.623$		D.W. = 2.079

The coefficient of credit subsidies, CS, is negative, as in the levels equation, but of somewhat smaller magnitude (−1.43 here and −1.62 in the levels equation). In fact, one could expect that the impact of CS should be much smaller in the short run, because the process of increasing the buffer-stock of capital should take time.[10]

It turns out that only when inflation is *lower* than 20 percent do changes in the inflation rate have a negative (significant) coefficient. This stands in contrast with the results for the productivity level (table 13.6), where only high inflation is found to have a significant effect. These results may be interpreted as follows. High inflation, which should be strongly related to monetary growth, does not affect productivity immediately. For example, real balances held by firms are not adjusted right away, given planned production levels. The adjustment takes place over time, and therefore, high inflation should enter only in the low-frequency equation. Low inflation is likely to reflect, more than high inflation, real shocks. Accordingly, the immediate effect of low inflation on productivity growth can be interpreted as capturing the impact of temporary productivity shocks.

The coefficient of $d \log K_e$ may capture capital accumulation in general, rather than technology adoption. Increasing the capital stock may be accompanied by short-term disruption of production and thus lower productivity. To explore this possibility, the rate of change in the stock of structures was added to the equation. The results, shown in table 13.8, indicate that $d \log K_s$ does not contribute to explaining productivity changes.

Equipment growth is also correlated with immigration flows, and thus, it may capture the decline in productivity as immigrants workers learn domestic-specific and language skills. To test this possibility, $OLIM$ variables are added to the equation. Surprisingly, the only two significant lags, $OLIM_t$ and $OLIM_{t-4}$, have *positive* coefficients, and the coefficient on $d \log K_e$ becomes larger (−0.4 compared to −0.26).[11]

Table 13.8
Dependent Variable: $d(\log A)$; sample: 1977–1997

Variable	Coefficient	t-statistic
Constant	0.017	2.503
$d(\log K_e)$	−0.357	−2.453
$d(CS)$	−1.585	−2.653
$ddP \times (1 - PLUS20)$	−0.256	−3.275
$d(\log K_s)$	0.190	0.818
$e^a(-2)$	−0.828	−3.420
$R^2 = 0.710$		S.E. = 0.016
Adj. $R^2 = 0.614$		D.W. = 2.042

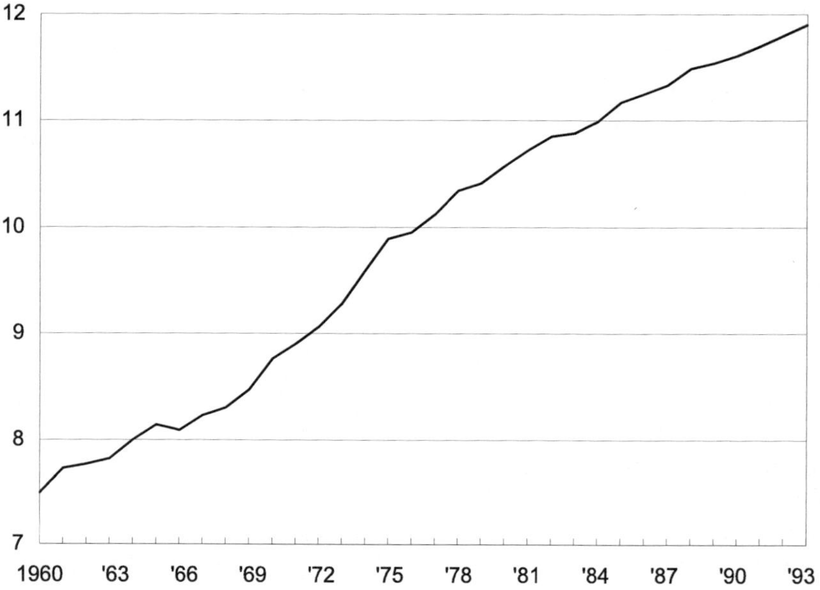

Figure 13.4
Average Years of Schooling of Employees

13.6 Human Capital Accumulation and R&D

In the previous analysis, neutral technological change, Z, was approximated by a time trend. Obviously, the evolution of Z over time reflects underlying factors such as human capital accumulation and R&D. The aim of this section is to address these two factors, attempting to assess the extent to which using a time trend is a good approximation.

An important component of human capital is formal education. Harari and Tamari (1993) computed the average years of schooling of employees for the 1960–1992 sample. Figure 13.4 shows that this variable has increased quite smoothly since 1975. The regression of years of schooling on a linear time trend in the 1975–1992 sample yields an R^2 of 0.99. Hence, the time trend should capture well the effects of labor's schooling level on productivity.

Research and development expenditures increased dramatically during the sample period. R&D expenditures in 1996 were 8.6 higher than in 1975. For comparison, the gross business product went up only 2.6 times during this period. The channels of effect of R&D on growth can be characterized, in the context of this paper, as

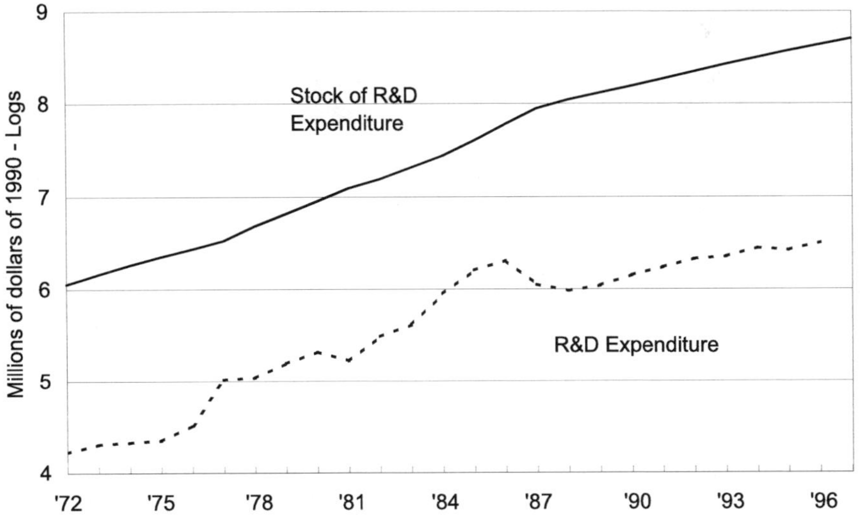

Figure 13.5
R&D Expenditure and R&D Stock
(log of millions of 1990 U.S. dollars)

working through Z (i.e., via A) and Q. Given that a measure of Q is included in the analysis, the remaining channel is total factor productivity.

To quantify the accumulated productive implications of R&D, one can apply the perpetual inventory methodology on the R&D flows, similarly as in the computation of physical capital stocks. This procedure was followed by Coe and Helpman (1995) in the context of a multicountry study of R&D effects on productivity. Another possibility is to apply the same procedure to a measure of *output* of R&D activities. Trajtenberg (1999) compiled data on Israeli patents in the U.S., which can be used in this context. Correspondingly, two stocks are computed. One is the stock of R&D expenditures and the other is the stock of patents. Following Coe and Helpman, the initial stock for each series is taken as $K_0 = X_0/(g + \delta)$, where X_0 is the flow in the first available observation, g is the average growth rate of the flow, and δ is the depreciation rate.

Figure 13.5 displays (in logs) the flows of current R&D expenditure in 1990 prices for the 1972–1996 sample (from Griliches and Regev (1999), table VIII)[12] and the resulting stocks. The stocks are computed using $g = 0.11$ (the average growth rate of R&D expenditure over the sample) and $\delta = 0.05$ (the depreciation rate used by Coe and Helpman). Both the flow and the stock display a short acceleration starting in

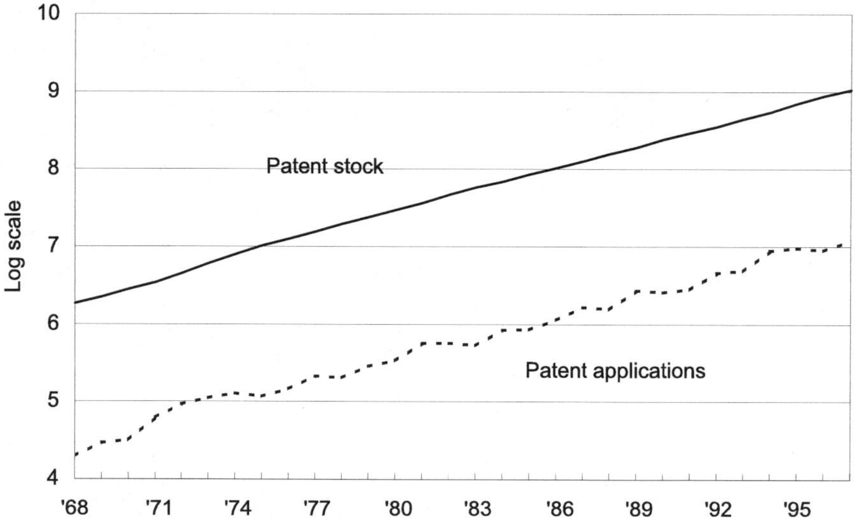

Figure 13.6
Patent Applications in the U.S. and Patent Stock (logs)
Source: Trajtenberg (1999), table 1.

1984/1985 and a slowdown afterwards. The average growth rate of the R&D stock is 11.3 percent over the 1972–1997 sample, but only 7.5 percent since 1987. From 1985, the average growth rate is 8.5 percent.

Figure 13.6 displays the similar figures, using the flow of patents applications from Trajtenberg (1999, table 1) for the 1968–1997 sample. The stocks here are computed with $g = 0.091$ and the same $\delta = 0.05$ as above. Remarkably, patents applications and thus the patent stock behave very close to linear trends; in other words, the growth rates are close to being constant.[13]

Using Trajtenberg's data on patents actually issued, the behavior of the stock is very similar to that in figure 13.6, although the average growth rate of patents issued is slightly lower—8.8 percent—and there is some more variation around a linear trend than in patent applications.

Looking at patents in the present context rather than at R&D expenditures has two advantages. One is that they measure output of R&D activities, rather than input, and thus they are closer to the variable which should actually affect production performance. The other advantage has to do with the computation of the accumulated stocks. R&D expenditures underwent large swings during the sample. In this situation, the first observation available has large ex-ante variance. Given that the value of the first observation affects significantly the behavior of the computed stock series, the resulting pattern of the stock can be considered less reliable than in the case of patents.

Obviously, the implications of education and R&D activities for productivity are important issues to investigate. Also, it may be interesting to analyze the link between the input of R&D expenditure, which is volatile, and output in the form of patents, which grow very smoothly. In the present context, however, that focuses on investment and the dynamics of productivity, it seems that a time trend is a reasonable approximation of neutral technological progress.

Appendix

Table 13.9
Dependent Variable: log A; sample: 1975–1996

Variable	Coefficient	t-statistic
Constant	−7.933	−1.641
CS	−1.627	−3.665
KT	1.584	2.497
dP^{20+}	−0.033	−2.026
dP^{20-}	0.223	1.684
τ	−0.148	−0.858
$\log(K_r/INPUT)$	0.273	1.284
t	0.006	2.325
$R^2 = 0.986$		S.E. = 0.018
Adj. $R^2 = 0.979$		D.W. = 1.800

Data
All Data is Annual, from 1960 to 1997

U.S. data

P_i^{us}: (Deflator of gross private fixed nonresidential investment)/(deflator of business sector GDP).

P_e^{us}: (Deflator of gross producer durable equipment investment)/(deflator of business sector GDP).

$Q = 1/P_e^{us}$: Equipment-specific technological change.

Source: Economic Report of the President, 1997 and 1998, tables B1 and B2. The base year of the deflators was changed to 1995 (from 1992) for comparison with Israeli data.

Israeli data

National Income Accounts (business sector, 1995 prices):

I_e: Gross equipment investment (machinery and transport vehicles).

I_s: Gross construction investment (excluding roads).

I: Total gross investment (including roads).

K_e: Net stock of equipment.

K_s: Net stock of structures (excluding roads).

K_r: Net stock of roads.

Y: Gross domestic product of the business sector (GBP).

P_i: Total investment deflator/GBP deflator.

dP: Annual rate of change of the GBP deflator.

Other data

L: Total hours worked in the business sector (weekly averages)

OLIM: Ratio of immigrants to total population

POP: Total population

τ: Ratio of total tax revenues to GDP

CS: Ratio of credit subsidies (Hebrew: hatavot ashrai) to GDP

KT: Ratio of capital transfers (Hebrew: maanakim al heshbon hon) to GDP

Notes

This paper was prepared for the Conference on Research in memory of Professor Michael Bruno. I thank Michel Strawczynski and participants in the Interim Conference for helpful comments.

1. Given that investment goods have a large tradeable component, the behavior of the relative price of investment is related to the "Balassa-Samuelson" effect, i.e., a typical long-run real appreciation due to technological change being biased towards tradeable goods.

2. Figure 13.2 also shows that the declining trend in the U.S. relative price of investment is interrupted following the oil shocks of the 1970s. This may be related to higher investment demand, as part of the existing capital stock becomes obsolete at the higher energy prices.

3. The relationship estimated in table 1 cannot be interpreted as a structural one, given that the returns to scale effect should vanish over time, and A is endogenous.

4. The process until the middle 1970s can be visualized in an aggregate supply-aggregate demand diagram with the price of domestic goods, relative to imports, on the vertical axis. Rapid productivity growth shifts the aggregate supply schedule to the right, generating a decline in the relative price of domestic good—or, alternatively, a real depreciation. Of, course, other factors are also at work during the same period, which affect the aggregate demand and supply schedules. However, the outcome of a declining relative price

along with high growth rates of output indicates that rightward shifts in the supply schedule constitute the dominant force during this period.

5. The variable *OLIM* is included lagged three and four years, which are the only lags that turned out to be significant in at least one version of the equations.

6. Lack of significance of roads infrastructure was also obtained by Lavi and Strawczynski (1998) in the context of total business investment. The time trend in I_s, which in contrast to the theory, has a negative coefficient, is also deleted although it was significant. Apparently, colinearity with Q produces a negative coefficient on t and a much larger—and implausible (see below)—coefficient on Q. When Q is deleted, the coefficient on t becomes positive and significant.

7. Lavi (1990) finds a negative effect of the short-run real interest rate, which is affected by monetary policy, on investment. The present analysis, which abstracts from monetary factors, is based on the setup of a small open economy facing a constant interest rate and perfect capital flows.

8. The phenomenon of higher spending and tax revenues lagging after higher economic activity was found in OECD countries. See Hercowitz and Strawczynski (1999).

9. The corresponding direct productivity loss of ten percentage points of constant inflation, in present value, is about 10 percent of GDP (assuming a 5 percent real interest rate and an infinite horizon).

10. Credit subsidies may have an additional negative effect on capacity utilization, and thus, on measured productivity. This mechanism works as follows. Credit subsidization reduces the private real interest rate, and thus increases the desired capital stock. If utilization involves higher depreciation—the "user cost"—increasing the capital stock can be achieved also by lower utilization, reflected in lower measured productivity.

11. The contemporaneous effect seems to correspond to the increase in capacity utilization during the very early 1990s, as recent immigrants worked additional shifts. The four-year lagged variable could be explained by positive effects of immigrants following successful absorption.

12. Prior to 1987, the years 1971/1972, 1972/1973, ..., are taken as 1972, 1973, ... Missing figures for two years, 1973/1974 and 1983/1984, were interpolated from the adjacent years.

13. The R^2 in a regression of the log of patent applications on time is 0.99; in a regression of the log of the stocks on time, the R^2 is 0.999.

References

Aschauer, David A. "Is Public Expenditure Productive?" *Journal of Monetary Economics* 23 (1989): 177–200.

Coe, David T., and Elhanan Helpman. "International R&D Spillovers." *European Economic Review* 39 (1995): 859–887.

Greenwood, Jeremy, Zvi Hercowitz, and Per Krusell. "Long-Run Implications of Investment-Specific Technological Change." *American Economic Review* 87 (1997): 342–362.

Griliches, Zvi, and Haim Regev. "R&D, Government Subsidies and Productivity of Industry Plants in Israel, 1975–1994." *The Economic Quarterly* 46 (Hebrew) (1999): 335–356.

Harari, Batia, and Ephraim Tamari, eds. "The Labor Market in Israel." Jerusalem: Ministry of Economy and Planning, 1993. (Hebrew).

Helpman, Elhanan. "Israeli Growth: International Comparison." Based on lecture at the Israeli Economic Association meeting, 1998. Mimeo.

Hercowitz, Zvi, Yaakov Lavi, and Rafi Melnick. "The Impact of Macroeconomic Factors on Productivity in Israel: 1960–1996." *Bank of Israel Economic Review* 72 (1998): 103–124.

Hercowitz, Zvi, and Michel Strawczynski. "Cyclical Ratcheting in Government Spending: Evidence from the OECD," 2001. Mimeo.

Lavi, Yaakov. "The Effect of Interest Rates on Investment in the Business Sector of the Israeli Economy: 1962–1988." *The Economic Quarterly* 143 (Hebrew) (1990): 343–368.

Lavi, Yaakov, and Michel Strawczynski. "The Effect of Policy Variables and Immigration on the Supply of Output and Its Components, Factors of Production and Productivity: Israel, 1960–1995," 1998. Mimeo. (Hebrew).

Trajtenberg, Manuel. "Innovation in Israel, 1968–1997: A Comparative Analysis Using Patent Data." *The Economic Quarterly* 46 (Hebrew) (1999): 285–322.

14 Structural Change and the Emergence of Israel's High-Tech Sector

Moshe Justman

14.1 Introduction

Some of the structural changes that the Israeli economy experienced in the fifteen years after the stabilization program of 1985 were typical outcomes of the usual course of economic development—characteristic changes in supply and demand deriving from rising incomes and the assimilation of improved technologies. Other changes, however, were shaped by deliberate government initiatives aimed at reducing the role of the public sector in the economy, removing institutional barriers, and strengthening the forces of competition; these initiatives prepared the ground for the country's renewed growth in the 1990s. The structural changes that the Israeli economy underwent after 1985 were thus partly the effect and partly the cause of its economic development.[1]

Figure 14.1 describes the aggregate development of Israel's business sector since 1985—its growing share in gross domestic product (GDP) at constant prices, and the falling relative price of its output.[2] These trends reflect the impact of extensive cutbacks in public sector spending, which figured prominently in the stabilization program and its aftermath, as well as important institutional changes that strengthened the business sector and improved its efficiency. Nonetheless, the share of the public sector in Israel's domestic product remains disproportionately large, approximately double that of Germany, Britain, or the United States (Bar Eliezer, 1998, table 1). Differences in defense expenditures explain only half of the disparity; the remaining gap indicates extensive scope for further change.

Changes in the industrial structure of the business sector at the one-digit industry level (figure 14.2) continued earlier trends familiar from the experience of other countries, and it is now generally similar to that of most advanced industrial countries.[3] Agriculture continued its secular decline, as did manufacturing, after reaching its peak in the 1970s, while the share of the service sector continued to rise, its increase contributing two thirds of the increase in employment of Israelis in the business sector between 1985–1998. These structural trends largely reflect long-term changes in the composition of demand stemming from rising incomes and differences in the income elasticities of different product categories, and differential rates of technological progress that affect the conditions of supply.

The construction industry is the notable exception to this pattern of continuity, swinging sharply from bust to boom. In the years immediately following stabilization, it experienced deep cutbacks as a result of reduced government spending, high real interest rates, and the general economic slowdown. This was then dramatically

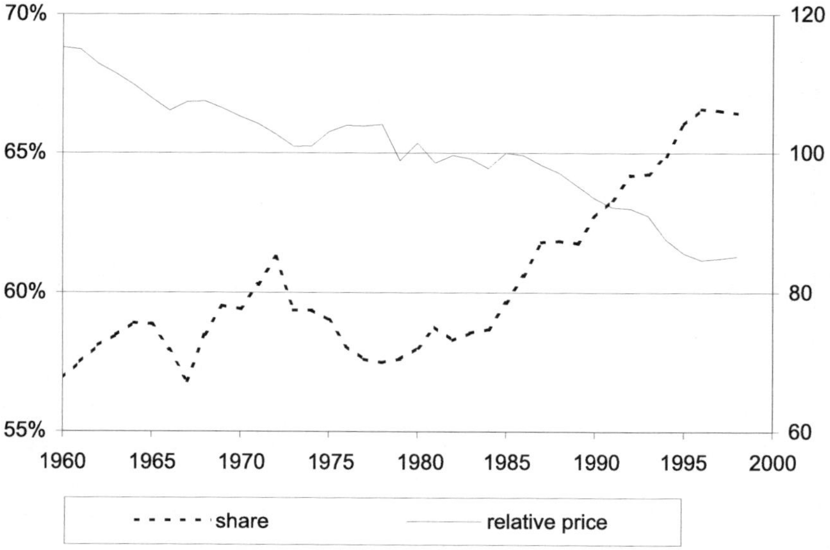

Figure 14.1
The Share of the Business Sector in GDP (1997 prices) and the Relative Price of Business Sector Output (1985 = 100)
Source: Bank of Israel, *Annual Report*, 1998.

reversed as building activity rapidly expanded after 1990, initially to accommodate the large numbers of newly arrived immigrants, and then in response to renewed growth and increased public investment in infrastrucure.

Other major structural changes in Israel's business sector took place *within* these one-digit industries. The most important of these was the high-tech revolution, which placed Israel at the forefront of economic activity in the information technology sector, especially in communications equipment and software. This revolution is not immediately apparent from the aggregate data, as it did not halt the downward trend in the share of manufacturing in the business sector, nor of the share of technologically advanced industries in manufacturing (see table 14.3); nor was there an increase in the share of research and development (R&D) expenditures in the country's GDP (in constant prices) until the late 1990s (Central Bureau of Statistics, 1999). This is because Israel's high-tech revolution was in large measure a shift of economic resources from a technologically advanced but commercially unprofitable defense sector to civilian manufacturing based on similar technologies. A deliberate reduction in domestic defense procurement after 1985 released tens of thousands of skilled workers into the labor market, providing an abundant supply of skilled labor for an

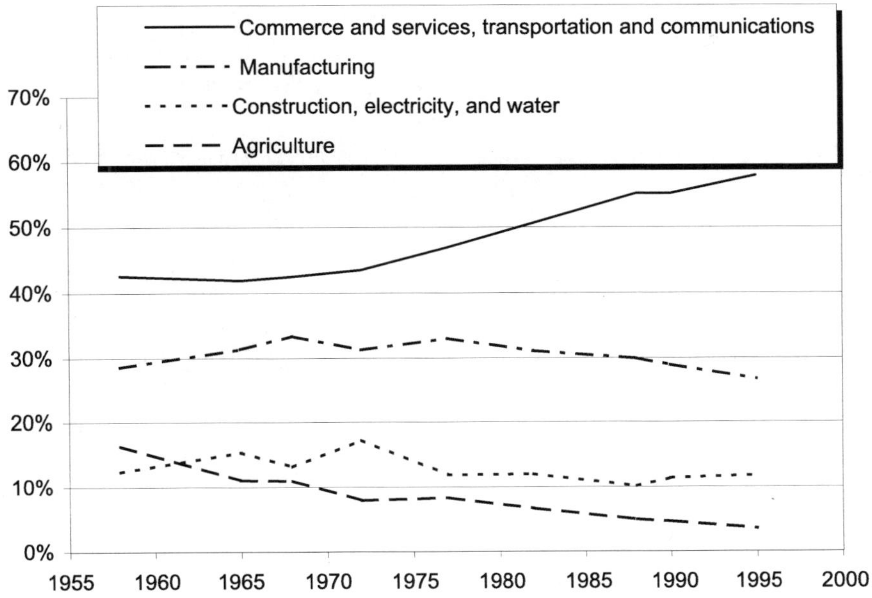

Figure 14.2
The Composition of Business Sector Output (current prices)
Source: Bar-Eliezer, 1998.

emerging private high-tech sector and allowing more efficient exploitation of the commercial potential of Israeli R&D.[4] More surprisingly, perhaps, the high-tech revolution did not leave its mark on the measured productivity of the business sector, which did not seem to increase at all in this period, despite the obvious surge in technological progress and the country's greatly improved competitiveness on world markets. We look into this "productivity puzzle" more carefully in the penultimate section.

The remainder of this chapter provides a chronological description of the process of structural change that the economy has undergone since 1985, a more detailed description of internal developments within each of the one-digit industries, a discussion of the "productivity puzzle," and some concluding remarks.

14.2 A Brief History of Time

The changes in the structure of the business product between 1985–1998 suggest an internal division of the period into three subperiods: 1985–1989, 1990–1995, and

1996–1998. The initial shakeout in the wake of the stabilization plan in the first period was followed by a surge of growth triggered by the large wave of immigration from the former Soviet Union in the second period, which was then followed by a slowdown that began in the second half of 1996.

Ideological and conceptual changes played a key role in the structural changes that began to take shape in the first years after the stabilization plan, and the most important of these was a new recognition of the economic advantages of competitive markets.[5] The huge economic and social cost inflicted by hyperinflation in the "lost decade" of the Israeli economy led to a general appreciation of the efficiency of the market mechanism, and of the need to reduce public involvement in the economy. This recognition was the result not only of reasoned economic analysis, but also of Israeli society shifting from a collectivist to an individualistic ethos, as the formative experiences of holocaust and the struggle for independence grew more and more distant. This new attitude, which paralleled similar changes of sentiment in other countries—"Thatcherism" in Britain, "Reaganism" in the United States—informed the policies of all Israeli governments throughout the period, at both the political and administrative levels.

Stabilization also restored meaningful economic measurement, which triple-digit inflation had undermined. Grave distortions that had been hidden in the mist of hyperinflation were now exposed to the light of day, and could be addressed. There began a Schumpeterian process of "creative destruction," in which government no longer automatically bailed out businesses in financial distress, thus enabling the market to eliminate less efficient economic activities and release valuable resources for more productive uses.

Cuts in domestic purchases of defense goods and services (excluding salaries) were especially severe, reflecting the urgent need to reduce the government's deficit (Tischler and Rotem, 1995). Their share in GDP dropped from 9.1 percent of GDP in 1982 to 6.1 percent in 1987, and then dropped further to 3.5 percent—its current level—after discontinuation of the Lavie project (figure 14.3). At the same time, world demand for military equipment also declined, a by-product of the end of the Cold War, causing Israel's miltary exports to decline by half (Arens, 1995); and the defense industry's efforts to find alternate civilian markets were only partially successful (Galai and Shachar, 1993; Halperin and Tsiddon, 1993; Dvir et al., 1998). These developments are clearly reflected in table 14.1, which presents data collected by Simcha Bar-Eliezer of the Central Bureau of Statistics on twenty-nine manufacturing companies that supply at least 10 percent of their produce to the defense sector. Their combined share in manufacturing output fell from 33 percent in 1985/1986 to 17 percent in 1996, while their share of industrial exports declined from 36 percent to 23

Table 14.1
Defense Sector Firms

	1985/86	1987	1991	1994	1996
Share in manufacturing					
Product (value added)	33.1%	24.4%	21.3%	17.2%	17.1%
Sales	23.3%	17.2%	15.8%	13.1%	12.8%
Exports	36.4%	32.3%	31.9%	25.6%	23.0%
Investments	30.0%	17.0%	13.9%	10.1%	11.1%
Labor force	23.5%	18.1%	15.8%	11.7%	10.9%
Exports, 1998 U.S.$ mill.		2,968	3,772	3,365	3,080
Employees, thousands	70.4	55.9	49.4	41.1	38.2

* Twenty-nine firms with 10% or more of local sales made to the defense sector.
This table is based on data especially prepared for this chapter by Simha Bar-Eliezer of the Central Bureau of Statistics.

percent. A steep drop in the defense industry's labor force was unavoidable. Within five years—by 1990—these twenty-nine companies had let go twenty thousand employees, and another ten thousand followed in the next five years. Of these, seven thousand workers were laid off from Israel Aircraft Industry alone, and a further four thousand from the Israel Military Industries (Sadeh, 1995).

These widespread layoffs in companies that had traditionally enjoyed strong political backing and were presumed to be immune from drastic cuts in employment sent a clear message to the business community as a whole: Companies in distress could no longer depend on the government to bail them out.[6] The demise of the Atta textile company, despite the dramatic efforts of its workers to mobilize government aid that could prevent, or at least postpone, the company's closedown, vividly illustrated this change in government policy, which sharply reduced preferred credit and direct subsidies for manufacturing and agricultural production, as a share of GDP (figure 14.3).

The sector that was hardest hit, both by cutbacks in government support and by the rise in real interest rates that followed stabilization, was agriculture. Many moshavim and kibbutzim (cooperative and communal settlements) were suddenly plunged deeply into debt with no economic solution in sight. However, they still retained some of their considerable political influence. Special laws were passed that erased some of their debts, and other debts were covered by the rezoning and sale of agricultural land for housing construction, though a large portion of the debt remains to be settled. The economic crisis precipitated a social and political crisis that continues to threaten the continued existence of many kibbutzim and Moshavim. Moreover, although agricultural product continued to grow in real terms at a rate similar to that of the business sector as a whole, its relative price and its profitability

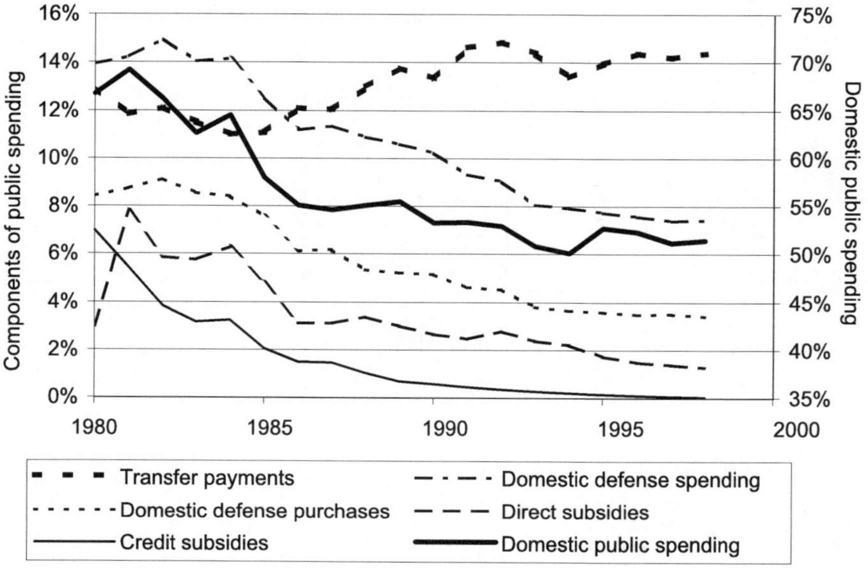

Figure 14.3
Components of Public Spending (percent of GDP)
Source: Bank of Israel, *Annual Report*, 1998.

declined, and with it the the number of self-employed farmers, as the industry became more and more dependent on cheap foreign labor.

The recession of 1988–1989 marked the trough of the economy's decline. Manufacturing output decreased in real terms for two consecutive years. The average return on net capital fell to under 7 percent, and investments sank to a low of 12.1 percent of the business-sector product. The uprising in the West Bank and Gaza Strip (the "intifada") added to the feeling of uncertainty, and Israel's economic future seemed less and less promising. In the words of Moshe Syrquin (1986, p. 72): "The next decade will tell if the proper reference group in a future international comparison will be Scandinavia, as long term trends indicate, or South America, as the recent past suggests."

The answer to this question was not long in coming. The collapse of the Soviet Union and the massive immigration that followed in its wake drew the economy out of its depression in one fell swoop. Macroeconomic stabilization, the sharp reduction in the government deficit, and new initiatives for structural reform, notably in the financial sector, prepared the ground for the surge in economic activity that followed. Increased demand, arising from the pressing needs of the new immigrants, quickly absorbed the increased supply of labor and capital, triggering a boom such as the country had not experienced for over twenty years. The strongest and most immediate effect of these developments was felt in construction and in the manufacturing industries that supply it, as well as in food production and other categories of consumption. However, export markets also expanded, as the demise of the Soviet Union led to an improvement in political relations between Israel and many second and third world countries that opened up new opportunities for trade. Nonetheless, the force of the domestic expansion was such that the ratio of exports to domestic uses fell, and the growth rate of the export share in manufacturing output declined.

This dual expansion of demand was coupled with a large influx of labor. The drastic reduction in domestic defense spending released thousands of skilled workers into the workforce (see table 14.1) and greatly increased the pool of potential entrepreneurs.[7] These were joined by the large influx of scientists and engineers from the former Soviet Union, by the surge of new graduates from Israeli universities and colleges, and by a growing trickle of expatriate Israelis returning to Israel after accumulating valuable experience in the United States high-tech sector. The increase in labor supply caused real wages to drop, and combined with the expansion of demand, sharply raised profits. The return on capital more than doubled from its previous low, reaching a level of 15 percent in 1992, while the share of gross investment in business sector output rose to over 20 percent in 1993.

This increase in investment was made possible by far-reaching changes in Israel's capital markets, which enabled it to take part in the worldwide trend toward globalization of financial markets, and opened up new channels for foreign investment (see Blass and Yosha, in this volume, for an extensive discussion of these capital market reforms). The reduction of the strategic threat to Israel's existence, the relative contraction of the external debt, United States loan guarantees in the order of ten billion dollars, and perceived progress in the peace process all contributed to Israel's increasing lure as a target for foreign investment. Large sums were raised by floating new issues in foreign stock markets, and by early 1999, the combined market value of "Israeli" companies traded on United States stock markets amounted to over thirty billion dollars (table 14.2).[8] The new technological entrepreneurs were highly successful in raising funds in Israel, too. New issues on the Tel Aviv Stock Exchange amounted to about seven billion dollars in 1992–1994 (in 1998 prices). In addition, a new venture-capital sector emerged, attracting nearly three billion dollars in 1993–1998 from domestic and foreign sources, of which it had invested about 70 percent by early 1999 (*Ha'aretz*; May 25, 1999). Capital that had accumulated in real estate deals, construction, and traditional manufacturing and service industries sought new opportunities for investment, while trust funds and holding companies redirected

Table 14.2
Aggregate Data on Israeli Shares Traded in the U.S. (Early January, U.S.$ million at current prices)

	1992	1993	1994	1995	1996	1997	1998	1999
Sales	4,008	4,408	5,504	5,729	10,470	12,524	14,396	16,291
Profits	243	355	438	321	495	584	272	844
Equity	1,602	2,466	3,549	4,303	5,721	7,325	8,453	9,820
Market value	5,018	10,272	11,846	8,711	15,287	22,058	23,507	32,942

Source: '*Ha'aretz*' daily newspaper, various issues; author's calculations.

more and more of their capital to the high-tech sector. Strategic partnerships between leading Israeli companies and major international concerns were formed in almost all areas of economic activity, as more and more Israeli companies began to plan their business activities with a global outlook.

The government played an important role in this high-tech revolution not only in its essential reform of the capital market, but also by explicitly encouraging the establishment of the new venture-capital companies, and by providing matching grants for industrial innovation through the Office of the Chief Scientist (OCS) in the Ministry of Industry and Trade.[9] The result was a tide of technologically intensive industrial activity, partly based on the intangible technological assets of the defense sector, which underwent a process of spontaneous conversion to nonmilitary uses. The equity of this process, which freely transferred valuable, though intangible, public assets to private hands has been called into question, but its efficiency is beyond doubt. It has created market value in new companies that far exceeds the value of the defense industry as a whole, and has brought Israeli companies to the forefront of economic-technological achievement in information technologies.

At the same time, the government also began selling off some of the business enterprises it had come to own. In financial terms, the largest privatization initiative was the sale of government-held bankshares. While the direct, immediate effect of this sale on banking activity appears to have been limited, it does seem to have increased the level of competition in the economy, as the banks were required to sell off large portions of their concentrated real holdings. With regard to manufacturing, the sale of Israel Chemicals was the government's main achievement. Selling off the large defense-sector manufacturing enterprises is still a long way away; many of them continue to accumulate large losses, and would need to be reorganized before they could be placed on the market.

Arguably, the most important privatization-cum-liberalization of government assets occurred in the communications sector, broadly defined. For the first time, private investors were allowed to compete with Bezeq, the government-owned telephone monopoly. Frequency bandwiths were sold to three cellular operators, and two new suppliers of international communications services were allowed to enter the market. The government also relinquished its monopoly in television and radio. Bandwaves were tendered to a large number of new regional radio stations; cable television networks and a satellite network were licensed to operate throughout the country; and a second broadcast television channel divided its airtime between private franchises. However, efforts to privatize the supply of electricity and water were stymied by organized labor (privatization of the infrastructure is discussed extensively by Gronau in this volume).

Other important institutional changes further reinforced the market mechanism by circumscribing more clearly the scope of political involvement in the market, and by ensuring that newly acquired market power was not abused. Existing institutions such as the State Comptroller, the Securities Authority, and the Antitrust Authority were given new powers, and came out in determined defense of the market against the powerful economic and political forces that threatened to undermine its efficient workings. These efforts were shaped by the key personalities that headed these agencies, but the aggregate scope of change indicates a phenomenon that transcends the influence of one individual or another. They were able to withstand the pressures that were brought to bear by the commercial interests that suffered from their scrutiny because they enjoyed strong public support and the unreserved backing of the judicial system.

Recent years have witnessed a slowdown in market activity, though more moderate than that of a decade ago and not as universally damaging. Construction slowed down in relative terms, as did the industries supplying it with merchandise and services; and some of the defense industries continued their downward trend, although Israel Aircraft Industry began to show signs of recovery. However, the civilian high-tech sector continued to grow at an accelerated pace, especially software and communications equipment, and impressive growth was also evident in communications and other services. These signs indicate that the structural changes that began in the wake of the 1985 stabilization are continuing. It suggests that the apparent slowdown is more than a cyclical correction, and also reflects the costs of adjustment to a new economic structure.

In the following pages, we examine these developments in greater detail, industry by industry.

14.3 Manufacturing

From 1985–1998 manufacturing output grew by 74 percent in real terms, which was less than the growth in business-sector product as a whole—it doubled in the same period—so that the share of manufacturing in business-sector product at constant prices declined, like its share in current prices (figure 14.2). Comparing the growth in manufacturing product with the increase in industry inputs indicates a modest rise in total factor productivity, less than one percent per annum on average. However, the capital-labor ratio increased by more than 50 percent, demonstrating the industry's ability to attract new investments. Its internal structure underwent extensive changes. Electronic communications equipment, Israel's principal high-tech manufacturing industry, greatly increased its share in manufacturing ouput (software is classified as a service industry), as did nonmetallic minerals and wood products, following the growth in construction, while the cutbacks in domestic defense purchasing caused a decline in the share of transportation equipment (which includes the aircraft industry) and metal products. The private sector increased its share in manufacturing product at the expense of the government and of the Histadrut, Israel's association of trade unions. The average number of employees per plant declined in almost all industries, and concentration ratios fell while exposure to imports increased. In the following pages we examine in further detail the changing industrial composition of manufacturing, its increasing globalization, its improved ability to commercialize new technologies, the declining involvement of the public sector, and the heightened level of competition within manufacturing industries.

Industry Composition

Table 14.3 presents the composition of manufacturing product by two-digit industries at current prices for the years 1983, 1989, and 1994. In the category of advanced industries—identified by the share of highly skilled labor in the workforce, and including electrical and electronic equipment, machinery, transportation equipment, and chemical and petroleum products—the outstanding trends were the sharp rise in the share of electronic communications equipment and the decline in transportation equipment. In the aggregate, production in advanced industries did not increase, as these two trends canceled each other out, highlighting the nature of Israel's high-tech revolution as a transfer of resources from government-owned high-tech defense-sector firms to private-sector high-tech firms producing largely for civilian markets. Similar trends characterize manufacturing exports, which grew at a similar rate to exports in general, but changed their composition. The main change was the dramatic growth in the share of electronics in manufacturing exports, which doubled between 1985–1998, in constant prices, leading to a rise in the share of advanced manufacturing in manufacturing exports, despite the relative decline in exports of machinery and transportation equipment.

Table 14.3
Composition of Manufacturing Product, Current Prices

Code	Industrial branch	1983	1989	1994
25	Electrical and electronic equipment	13.6	17.5	22.3
24	Machinery	3.6	3.2	4.5
26	Transport equipment	8.4	6.8	5.7
20	Oil and chemical products	9.9	10.7	9.9
19	Rubber and plastic products	5.8	5.1	5.3
22, 23	Metal and metal products	20.7	15.4	12.5
21	Mining and quarrying	3.7	2.9	2.7
10, 16	Nonmetallic mineral and wood products	6.6	6.5	8.0
18	Printing and publishing	3.0	5.4	5.6
17	Paper and paper products	2.0	2.4	2.2
11–12	Food, beverages, and tobacco	11.4	12.2	12.7
13–15	Textiles, clothing, and leather	9.0	9.2	6.7
27	Miscellaneous	2.3	2.7	1.8

Source: Simha Bar-Eliezer, Central Bureau of Statistics, personal communication.

Among the less advanced manufacturing industries, nonmetallic mineral products and wood products increased their share of manufacturing output in 1989–1994, as a result of the increase in construction, while the share of textiles and clothing fell as the result of continued trade liberalization, which exposed them to competition from cheap imports (see Gabai and Rob, in this volume, for a detailed discussion of Israel's trade liberalization). The printing and publishing industry almost doubled its share of manufacturing product at current prices during this period, though its share at constant prices showed almost no change. This may reflect the difficulty in separating price changes from quality changes, in a period of dramatic progess in printing technology.

Globalization

Capital market liberalization, increased profitability, and the improvement in Israel's geopolitical situation attracted direct foreign investments in both advanced and conventional manufacturing enterprises. Some strategic partnerships, between leading Israeli companies and prominent international concerns, were aimed at bolstering the Israeli partner's position in the domestic market through the know-how, name brand, and financial resources of the foreign partner. Other partnerships, in technology-intensive fields, were intended to combine Israeli scientific and technological skills with the foreign partner's complementary assets in production, marketing, and finance (Shachar and Zuscovitch, 1993). In yet other strategic partnerships, Israeli companies played a leading role. An Israeli clothing manufacturer might typically design the product in Israel; purchase the cotton and spin the yarn in Egypt; return to Israel for weaving, dyeing, and finishing; farm out cutting and sewing to subcontractors in Jordan, Egypt, or Romania; and return again to Israel for quality control, packaging and delivery. Marketing of the product—in the United States, Western Europe, and Japan—would then be carried out by domestic retail chains in those countries that maintain long-term strategic ties with the Israeli producer, and are involved in the manufacturing process from the design stage.[10]

Technology

From the outset, Israel has had exceptional technological and scientific capabilities in relation to its size and resources, but until the last decade, these capabilities were predominantly directed to public objectives, most of all, defense. The Israeli military-industrial complex has attained impressive achievements in nuclear engineering, aeronautical engineering, avionics, electronic intelligence, and so forth, which gave Israel's military capability a qualitative edge. These capabilities also formed the basis for a substantial defense export business, which began its expansion in the 1970s, rising from less than one percent of GDP before 1973 to about three percent in the late 1970s. However, application of these technologies to civilian products was limited during this period (Teubal, 1993).

In the early 1980s, the emergence of several private-sector civilian high-tech companies signaled the potential of Israel's high-tech sector, but it took almost another decade before conditions were ready for it to take off. We reviewed these conditions in the preceding section—deep cutbacks in domestic defense purchases, capital market reforms, the sustained boom of the United States economy, immigration from the Soviet Union, expansion of tertiary education, the improvement in Israel's international standing, and improvements in its relations with its neighbors. All of these released a tide of technologically intensive manufacturing activity, which produced enormous economic value much of which is reflected in table 14.2.

The shift from military to civilian applications is evident in the sharp decline in the share of military equipment in manufacturing R&D subsidies allocated by the Ministry of Industry and Trade, which dropped from 25 percent in 1987 to only 8 percent in 1994 (Justman et al., 1999). Data on Israeli patents registered in the United States analyzed by Trajtenberg (2000) illustrate the increasingly global orientation of Israel's high-tech industry. It shows a doubling in their number between 1991–1995, a substantial increase in the share of patents held by commercial enterprises, and the high quality of Israeli patents, especially in communications equipment, software, and biotechnology. In Israel, too, the share of Israeli patents increased substantially from less than one quarter of total registered patents in the mid-1980s to over one third a decade later.

The reduction in defense spending may have been the most important contribution of fiscal policy to the development of Israel's high-tech industry, but other fiscal initiatives also played a key role. Over the last thirty years, Israel's industrial R&D susbsidy program, administered by the Office of the Chief Scientist in the Ministry of Industry and Trade, has provided contingent matching grants to approved projects against royalties from sales if the project succeeds. When this program was first implemented over thirty years ago, it was unique in the "neutral," reactive nature of its support. It did not target specific industries for preferred treatment, and thus allowed the market to play a leading role in setting directions. This large-scale program provided essential financial liquidity to many private investors, and had a hand in the majority of technological and commercial success stories in Israel's high-tech sector in the last decade.[11]

Public Ownership

The share of the public sector—the government and the Histadrut (trade union association)—in manufacturing output declined from just under 50 percent in 1985 to 35 percent in 1994. This reduction was the combined result of cutbacks in government-owned defense suppliers and some privatization (table 14.4). Among government-owned firms, the sale of Israel Chemicals stood out as the main achievement, whereas efforts to privatize defense firms have yet to bear fruit. In contrast, the extreme economic difficulties in which the Histadrut found itself, especially after nationalization of its sick fund, greatly expedited the transfer of its firms to private hands. Political entities have inherent difficulties in running business concerns, and the Histadrut's problems were exacerbated by its dual role of employer and workers' representative. Realizing it was unable to take the necessary steps to turn around a difficult situation, it privatized virtually all of its manufacturing holdings. Figure 14.4 illustrates something of the dynamics of privatization in Israeli manufacturing. Traditional manufacturing has always been dominated by the private sector; mid-tech industries were split between the private and public sectors, and it is in this category

Table 14.4
Privatization of government companies, excluding banks (U.S.$ million, current prices)

Year	1986–1989	1990	1991	1992	1993	1994	1995	1996	1997
Sum	333	94	163	268	550	98	536	41	310

Source: State-Owned-Enterprises Authority, *Annual Report*, 1998.

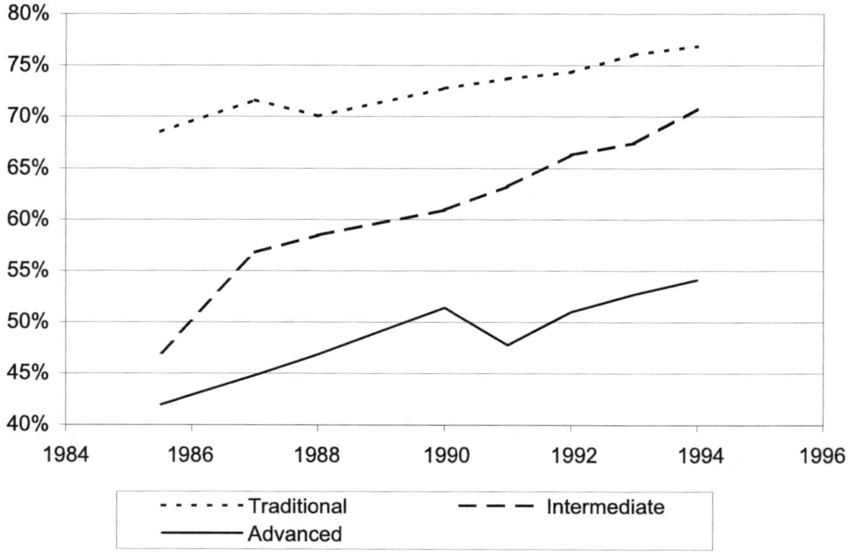

Figure 14.4
Percentage of Manufacturing Output Produced by the Private Sector, by Type of Industry
Source: Industry and Crafts Survey, various years.

that most of the privatization has taken place; and much advanced manufacturing output is still produced by government-owned defense-sector firms.

Competition

The structural changes that took place after 1985 increased competition in manufacturing in three ways: It reduced average plant size, increased exposure to competing imports, and increased regulatory supervision. The decline in average plant size (table 14.5) affected almost all industries in the years immediately following stabilization. It was a result of cutbacks in some of the very large plants and the emergence of many small, young enterprises. Small-scale entrepreneurship was seen as an important element in the absorption of new immigration, and received generous encouragement through various channels, including designated entrepreneurship centers, the technological incubators program, the mentor program, and so forth (Bar, 1994).

Increased competition was also achieved through the direct intervention of Israel's Antitrust Authority, whose powers were increased by legislation in 1989. Previously, it had been geared to regulating anticompetitive agreements and controlling prices

Table 14.5
Percentage Change in the Number of Employees per firm

Industrial branch	1985/6–1990	1990–1994
Mining and quarrying	−28%	4%
Nonmetallic mineral products	−11%	2%
Food, beverages, and tobacco	−22%	7%
Textile, clothing, and leather	−23%	−5%
Wood, paper, and printing	−15%	3%
Plastic and rubber products	11%	12%
Chemical and oil products	13%	−9%
Basic metals	−31%	22%
Metal products	−20%	−9%
Machinery	−37%	0%
Electric and electronic equipment	−24%	−11%
Transport equipment	−56%	−21%
Miscellaneous	−25%	−2%

Source: Industry and Crafts Survey, 1985/1986, 1990, 1994.

in monopolized industries. The new legislation also gave it the authority to prevent undesirable mergers. No less important, it was given the necessary resources for enforcement. These changes, in combination with increased exposure to imports (described in detail by Gabai and Rob, in this volume) reduced the degree of concentration in manufacturing (table 14.6).

14.4 Agriculture

Agricultural output grew 85 percent (in real terms) in 1985–1998, slightly less than the growth in business-sector output in that period, reducing its share in business-sector output at constant prices by 0.4 percentage points. At the same time, its relative price declined sharply, so that the drop in its share of business sector output at current prices was even steeper (figure 14.2). Labor input continued a secular declining trend, reducing agriculture's share of the labor force from 5.1 percent in 1985 to 2.7 percent in 1997, and investment declined below replacement levels so that the industry's capital stock began an unprecedented decline in 1985 that lasted until the mid-1990s. This increase in real output despite declines in both capital and labor inputs was made possible by an increase in total factor productivity that exceeded that of all other one-digit industries. However, profitability suffered both from the relative fall in agricultural prices and from the sharp cutbacks in preferred credit and direct subsidies, plunging the agricultural sector into a prolonged crisis that profoundly changed its internal structure.

Table 14.6
Import Shares and Concentration Ratios in Manufacturing Industries

Year	Import share	Concentration ratio, C_3
1965	10%	45%
1977	24%	37%
1982	21%	43%
1988	25%	36%
1990	25%	34%
1992	27%	31%
1994	30%	29%

Source: Bank of Israel, *Annual Report*, 1994; Regev and Bar Eliezer, 1994; Bar Eliezer, 1998.

The economic dimension of this crisis and its social, political, and ideological dimensions, which were certainly no less important, mutually reinforced each other (Schwartz, 1995). In the past, agriculture was at the forefront of the Zionist movement, epitomizing the Jewish people's renewed physical connection to the land and defining the borders of its emerging national entity. The communal and cooperative settlements—the kibbutzim and moshavim—that comprised the bulk of the agricultural sector carried a unique message of collective solidarity, egalitarianism, and a reliance on one's own (rather than hired) labor; and their contribution to public service, especially defense, greatly exceeded their relative share in the population. For all of these reasons, the pre-1985 agricultural sector enjoyed extensive preferential treatment, operating in a protective bubble in which water prices and quantities, the allocation of land and land rents, production quotas, and marketing channels both at home and abroad were all centrally controlled by agricultural interests. After 1985, this protective bubble began to disintegrate.

A number of factors caused this to happen. The national goals to which agricultural settlement was directed were no longer as important as they had once been, nor were the kibbutzim and moshavim immune to the new emphasis on personal achievement over social commitment. Moreover, stabilization of the currency dispelled the hyperinflationary fog that had obscured both the extent of the economic crisis in agriculture and the huge susbsidies that were needed to keep it afloat. The sharp rise in real interest rates in the aftermath of stabilization further intensified the crisis. Large numbers of cooperative and communal settlements had accumulated debts that totalled billions of dollars, and had to turn to the public sector to stave off imminent insolvency, which further undermined their moral standing and weakened their political influence, setting off a vicious cycle of economic and political decline.

The generous price supports and input subsidies that agriculture had enjoyed in the past were drastically reduced, first in 1985 and then again in 1986 (table 14.7).

Table 14.7
Total Fiscal Support for Agriculture
(Fiscal years; NIS million, 1986 prices)

Year	1980	1981	1982	1983	1984	1985	1986
Sum	636	1,601	1,554	1,831	3,869	1,472	370

Source: State Comptroller, *Annual Report*, no. 38, 1986/1987, p. 360.

Broiler subsidies fell from a peak rate of 96 percent of their retail price to 27 percent, egg subsidies from 90 percent to 16 percent, and milk subsidies from 72 percent to 15 percent (State Comptroller's Annual Report no. 38). The marketing boards that administered the quota systems ensuring high, stable price levels were almost all dismantled. The economy was partially opened to agricultural imports, especially from the Palestinian Authority. Agricultural product prices rose by 165 percent between 1986–1997, considerably less than the 245 percent increase in agricultural factor prices in the same period, or the 335 percent increase in the consumer price index. Agricultural income in CPI-deflated constant prices reached its peak in 1981, and has since fallen by one third, despite a growth of 75 percent in agricultural product (Kislev and Vaxine, 1998).

Without its protective bubble, the agricultural sector had to change its mode of operation. Foreign labor—initially Palestinian, later Thai and other—replaced self-employment. The absolute number and share of self-employed agricultural labor followed a downward trend throughout the period (figure 14.5). Official data from the National Insurance Institute and the Employment Service's Payments Authority show a rising trend in the number of foreign laborers employed in agriculture, but are certainly downwardly biased, as many of them are not legally resident in the country (table 14.8).

The large majority of agricultural land is leased from the government for token rents that account for less than one percent of total production expenditures. However, the supply of agricultural land is increasingly affected by its rising shadow price, especially in the center of the country where demand for new residential areas has been strong. Rezoning and sale of this land is playing a central role in discharging the large remaining debts of the kibbutzim and moshavim. As Israel's central region becomes more and more crowded and the profitability of agriculture continues to fall, real estate development becomes an increasingly important source of income for the agricultural sector.

Water is a severe limiting factor for agricultural development in Israel. It has traditionally been controlled by a quota system rather than through prices, which have always been much lower for agriculture than for other uses. This, too, is gradually

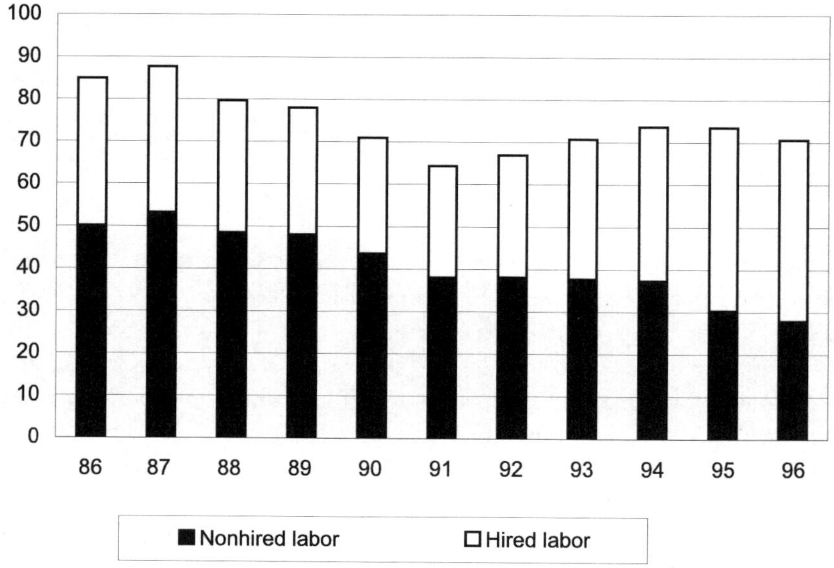

Figure 14.5
Composition of the Workforce in Agriculture
Source: Statistical Abstract of Israel, 1998.

Table 14.8
Foreign Workers as a Percentage of Employees in Agriculture (Official data)

	From the Territories and southern Lebanon	From other locations	Total
1994	12.0%	9.6%	21.6%
1995	8.0%	18.5%	26.5%
1996	5.5%	22.7%	28.2%
1997	7.0%	24.4%	31.4%

Source: Statistical Abstract of Israel, 1998.

Table 14.9
Composition of Sales and Exports in Agriculture, Selected Categories (Percent)

	1990	1991	1992	1993	1994	1995	1996	1997	1998
Sales revenues									
Cotton fibres	2.5	1.1	1.2	1.5	1.6	2.3	2.6	2.4	2.8
Citrus fruits	12.6	8.8	7.3	6.8	6.4	8.3	7.4	6.4	6.4
Flowers, etc.	8.1	9.9	8.9	10.6	10.4	10.2	10.6	10.6	10.2
Total crops	60.5	58.5	57.2	56.9	58.0	58.4	57.4	56.3	57.8
Total livestock	39.5	41.5	42.8	43.1	42.0	41.6	42.6	43.7	42.2
Exports									
Cotton fibre	10.4	3.7	5.2	6.6	6.9	9.1	10.0	10.1	11.1
Citrus fruits	32.7	24.8	21.5	17.0	18.4	24.0	20.2	18.7	20.2
Flowers, etc.	25.1	33.0	32.6	34.4	35.5	32.5	31.9	32.5	29.1
Total crops	95.9	94.3	93.5	91.3	91.0	94.1	94.6	93.0	93.7
Total livestock	4.1	5.7	6.5	8.7	9.0	5.9	5.4	7.0	6.3
Exports/revenues, %	20.2	19.7	17.5	18.9	18.5	20.7	21.8	20.4	20.9

Source: Bank of Israel, *Annual Report*, 1998.

changing. The price of water for agriculture increased by 356 percent between 1986–1997, much more than the average price increase in agricultural inputs, and even more than the cost of living index. Nonetheless, water still accounts for only 7.5 percent of agricultural production costs, and the rise in the cost of water has had less of an impact than reductions in quotas. The amount of fresh water allotted to agriculture is constantly being reduced as the total supply of fresh water is more or less constant whereas high-priority industrial and residential needs are constantly growing. Consequently, a succession of drought years dramatically reduces the amount of water available for agriculture, as happened in 1991. This especially reduced cotton production, which recovered only by changing over to recycled water. Increasing claims on common water resources by the Palestinian Authority and the Kingdom of Jordan can also be expected to reduce available fresh water in the near future. It is generally accepted that in the long run the solution to Israel's water needs will combine large-scale desalination with a price-based allocation system.

Some of the structural changes that agriculture has undergone in the last decade are reflected in the changing composition of agricultural production and exports (table 14.9). Approximately 20 percent of agricultural output is designated for export. This share fell slightly during the peak immigration years, but then climbed back to above its level at the beginning of the decade. As trade liberalization continues to exert competitive pressure on domestic prices that reduces profitability from domestic sales, the industry's dependence on foreign markets is likely to increase in the future. The recent experience of densely populated, heavily industrialized countries in

Table 14.10
Deviation of Annual Growth Rates and Correlation between Industrial Changes and Changes in Business Product

	Deviation			Correlation with business product		
	1961–1984	1985–1998	Change	1961–1984	1985–1998	Change
Business sector	5.4	2.9	−3.5	1.00	1.00	0
Construction	10.9	10.4	−0.5	0.84	0.52	−0.32
Transportation and communication	6.2	3.0	−3.2	0.92	0.58	−0.34
Electricity and water	3.6	2.7	−0.9	0.88	0.70	−0.18
Commerce and services	4.7	3.0	−1.7	0.87	0.85	−0.02
Industry	6.9	3.4	−3.5	0.92	0.92	0
Agriculture	4.5	6.6	2.1	−0.08	0.50	0.58

Source: Bank of Israel, *Annual Report*, 1998 and author's calculations.

Western Europe suggests that, in future, Israeli agriculture may rely increasingly on publicly funded landscaping and ecological projects.

Of course, competitive pressures also exist in export markets, especially in the citrus industry in which Israel competes with other Mediterranean countries. This competitive pressure, along with new opportunities to rezone agricultural land for more lucrative residential and commercial uses, has caused the uprooting of many orchards in the center of the country. Though some of these have been replaced by new orchards in the northern Negev, flowers have superseded citrus fruit as Israel's main agricultural export. Flowers need little land, use foreign labor intensively, and allow precise differentiation of the final product with regard to variety, quality, and timing. This differentiation is supported by large-scale government research on agricultural technology aimed at constantly developing new species.

A different manifestation of the profound changes that the industry experienced after 1985 is illustrated in table 14.10. The dispersion in the annual rates of change of agricultural product grew in 1985–1998, compared to 1961–1984, while falling in other industries. Moreover, the correlation between annual changes in agricultural product and in total business-sector product increased, while that of construction, transport, and communications declined.[12] A possible explanation for this phenomenon is that the industrialization of agriculture—extensive investments in automated drip irrigation systems and greenhouses, the use of pesticides, and heavy investments in R&D—reduced its dependence on natural conditions; another explanation is that trade liberalization, sharply reduced subsidies, and the dismantling of the marketing boards with their production quotas removed the protective shield that insulated the agricultural sector from economic fluctuations in the past, rendering it more similar

Table 14.11
Construction Starts, Area in Thousands of Square Meters

	Total buildings	Public buildings	Industrial and commercial	Residential	Public residential	Roads
1975	6,296	528	742	4,700		1,396
1980	4,930	361	618	3,750		1,060
1985	3,870	327	621	2,780		917
1986	3,725	313	589	2,730	270	707
1987	4,360	360	773	3,235	260	722
1988	4,830	447	651	3,420	310	1,196
1989	4,210	361	761	3,110	350	1,275
1990	7,030	526	913	5,610	1,800	1,556
1991	10,260	461	1,303	8,730	5,080	1,751
1992	7,870	583	1,942	5,750	1,895	1,559
1993	7,990	568	2,671	5,220	670	2,806
1994	10,040	686	2,830	6,380	1,045	2,035
1995	12,990	602	2,794	9,270	2,875	4,269
1996	11,585	698	2,555	7,940	2,060	3,367
1997	10,745	615	1,828	7,475	1,630	2,118
1998	8,945	571	742	6,660		

Source: Bank of Israel, *Annual Report*, 1998, and *Statistical Abstract of Israel*, 1999.

to the rest of the business sector. These two explanations are not mutually exclusive, although the second explanation corresponds more closely to the increase in the dispersion of annual growth rates after 1985.

14.5 Construction

The construction industry is generally given to large fluctuations, but in 1985–1998, these fluctuations were especially pronounced. At the beginning of the period, the rise in real interest rates and the general uncertainty that pervaded the economy reduced private demand for both business and residential construction, and cutbacks in government spending reduced public construction as well (table 14.11). The trough in construction activity continued for about two years, but full recovery only came with the wave of immigration from the former Soviet Union: in one year, 1990, new residential construction increased by 80 percent, mostly through public initiatives. Growth continued in 1991, which was a peak year for housing starts, and again, the public sector played a central role: It was the only year in which the public sector accounted for the majority of new residential construction. In the following years, residential construction, especially by the public sector, was substantially reduced, while industrial and commercial construction expanded as a result of strong economic growth, and government spending on road construction increased. Housing starts and new investments in roads peaked again in 1995, and, as in 1991, the public sector played a major role.[13] Public sector housing starts grew by 180 percent over the previous year, and investment in new roads doubled, while private industrial and commercial construction remained at its high level and private housing starts increased by 15 percent. The subsequent peak in industry output in 1996 was followed by a slowdown that could be postponed but not avoided. Private housing demand eased up as the wave of immigration subsided and the general slowing of the economy weakened demand for commercial construction; public investment had already reached an unprecedented level that could not be sustained, let alone increased. Nonetheless, even in the slowdown, industry output was still more than double its level in the 1980s.

These large fluctuations in demand were accompanied by large changes in the composition of the industry's workforce (table 14.12). The late 1980s saw continued growth in the number of Palestinian workers replacing Israeli labor, their share in the industry's workforce peaking at 46 percent in 1990. However, in the years that

Table 14.12
Product, Capital, and Labor, and Workforce Composition, in Construction

Year	Industry product index	Capital/ product ratio	Capital/ employee index	Employees, thousands	Israeli workers	Workers from the Territories	Foreign workers
1980	124	0.51	108	115.7	68%	32%	—
1981	124	0.52	108	118.3	66%	34%	—
1982	121	0.53	101	124.2	64%	36%	—
1983	120	0.52	94	131.8	65%	35%	—
1984	109	0.57	99	124.9	63%	37%	—
1985	100	0.59	100	116.5	62%	38%	—
1986	99	0.55	98	109.4	56%	44%	—
1987	110	0.46	85	117.4	58%	42%	—
1988	112	0.45	77	127.8	58%	42%	—
1989	116	0.42	76	127.6	56%	44%	—
1990	133	0.36	66	139.9	54%	46%	—
1991	179	0.27	58	163.1	59%	41%	—
1992	195	0.30	60	193.5	56%	44%	—
1993	190	0.35	71	183.0	64%	33%	2%
1994	206	0.38	81	188.0	66%	26%	7%
1995	230	0.40	78	235.0	61%	18%	20%
1996	257	0.43	89	247.0	61%	11%	28%
1997	253	0.50	101	247.0	59%	13%	28%
1998	242	0.58	119	233.0	56%	15%	29%

Source: Bank of Israel, *Annual Report*, 1998.

followed, the Palestinian uprising and Israel's frequent temporary closures of its pre-1967 borders to Palestinian entry led to a gradual displacement of Palestinian workers, initially by Israelis and later by foreign workers from various countries. In 1996, as the internal security situation improved, the share of Palestinian workers in the industry increased, again displacing Israeli workers. The plentiful supply of cheap foreign labor delayed the adoption of industrialized construction methods and slowed capital investment in the industry. Total factor productivity grew at an average annual rate of 0.5 percent over the period as a whole, capital-labor and capital-output ratios hardly changed, and construction times were not shortened.

14.6 Electricity and Water

In the past thirty years, the combined share of electricity and water in business-sector output has remained within a narrow range, between 1.9 percent to 2.2 percent, as a result of two opposite trends canceling each other out: The water supply declined in relative terms while electricity production increased. Annual fresh water production peaked at about 2,000 million cubic meters (mcm) per annum in the mid-1980s, a level beyond which it cannot be increased in the long term; the supply of recycled water is still limited, about 250 mcm in 1997; and desalination is yet to be implemented on a significant scale. Electricity production, in contrast, rose by 134 percent between 1985–1997, considerably more than the doubling of business-sector output. Consequently, the combined output of the electricity and water industry increased by 105 percent between 1985–1998, while labor input increased by 77 percent and the capital stock by 81 percent, implying an average annual increase in total factor productivity of 1.1 percent. The supply of both electricity and water is controlled by government-owned monopolies. Israel Electric Company controls access to the nation's electric grid, and Mekorot, Israel's national water company, supplies nearly two thirds of the country's water. The rents that derive from their monopoly power accrue in large part to the labor unions that control them, which seem to have tightened their hold in recent years. Average salaries in the combined industry are consistently the highest of all one-digit industries, and higher than all two-digit industries except electronic communications equipment. Moreover, the gap has widened over time: In 1986, industry salaries were 85 percent higher than the average wage in the economy, whereas in 1997, they were 115 percent higher.

The need for structural change in the water market is particularly urgent. With sources of fresh water fully exploited, and the population growing at a steady pace, a gradual but sustained decline in the routine allocation of fresh water for agriculture is unavoidable, punctuated by temporary drastic cutbacks when a sequence of drought years deplete the country's natural reservoirs. Building new purification plants and expanding existing ones can increase the supply of recycled waste water for some agricultural uses, but all forecasts indicate that investment in desalination will be necessary in the near future. Timing remains a subject of public debate, with some arguing that a target date as far away as 2020 would be optimal, provided framers are required to pay the full cost of the water they use, and the Palestinian share of water resources does not increase (Kislev and Rosenthal, 1999). Others, doubting that either of these conditions is likely to be met, argue that early desalination of hundreds of mcm annually could serve as a lever for promoting better neighborly relations, and point out that large-scale desalination has an additional advantage for the economy, apart from the direct increase in water supply. It transforms water from a natural resource in fixed supply, much like land, to a "manufactured" good produced from tradeable inputs, the supply of which is perfectly flexible over a moderate time span. This transformation can speed up the dismantling of the water quota system, currently the primary instrument of water management in Israel, and allow its replacement by a system of consumption prices and extraction taxes that would contribute to a more efficient use of existing water sources. Efforts to privatize the water and electricity industries are discussed in further detail by Gronau, in this volume.

14.7 Transportation and Communications

The transportation and communications industry increased in real terms at a rate of 134 percent between 1985–1998, more than any other industry apart from construction; and total factor productivity increased at an average annual rate of 2.8 percent, more than any other industry apart from agriculture. This combination of strong growth and increased productivity mostly reflects giant strides in communications services, which increased by 265 percent in real terms between 1986–1998, increasing their share in the combined one-digit industry from 24 percent to 39 percent at current prices despite a decline of 35 percent in the CPI deflated price of communications services between 1988–1998 (table 14.13). These giant strides were the joint result of dramatic technological progress in communications coupled with institutional reforms. Bezeq, the government-owned national telephone company, was forced to relinquish its absolute monopoly position, and compete with two rival suppliers of international telephone services and three cellular phone companies. Cable and satellite televison companies were licensed to compete with the government's broadcast television channel, and a second broadcast channel was established and its airtime auctioned off to private companies. However, there remain major

Table 14.13
Price Indices in Transportation and Communication, in Relation to the Consumer Price Index

Year	Land transport	Bus	Taxi	Truck	Train	Sea transport	Air transport	Commu-nication
1986	100	100	100	100	100	100	100	100
1987	108	109	115	106	97	93	90	110
1988	105	107	107	104	91	86	89	109
1989	102	114	108	95	83	80	89	100
1990	98	126	114	84	92	73	86	100
1991	98	129	114	79	92	72	91	103
1992	100	138	115	78	92	74	88	98
1993	96	147	118	74	92	69	89	90
1994	87	145	110	66	82	65	80	79
1995	87	151	110	64	84	60	76	75
1996	85	148	109	60	85	58	70	73
1997	86	156	109	59	81	56	70	72
1998	82	151	104	56	74	53	74	65

Source: Bank of Israel, *Annual Report*, 1998.

structural reforms in the industry that have yet to be implemented, for instance, the privatization of Bezeq itself, reform of the Postal Authority, and further shaping of the competitive structure of broadcast, cable, and satellite television (reforms in the communications industry are discussed in detail by Gronau, in this volume).

In contrast, transportation output increased by only 51 percent between 1986 and 1998. Expansion and efficiency gains are noticeable in international transport, with air and sea travel prices dropping considerably in comparison to the consumer price index (table 14.13), while turnover doubled in real terms. However, land transportation deteriorated, as inadequate investments in infrastructure failed to keep up with growing demand. Accelerated population growth through immigration, rising living standards (cars per capita increased by 39 percent between 1986–1997), and cuts in subsidies for public transport that raised bus ticket prices by 50 percent in real terms since 1986, all contributed to increased congestion. A surge in investment in roads and intersections in the mid-1990s provided only temporary relief, as improvements in travel times encouraged further construction and further use of private vehicles, until congestion built up again. Alternative, rail-based systems of mass transportation have not been developed significantly, and train travel continued to account for a miniscule fraction of land travel (table 14.14). The planning authorities generally recognize that road congestion can only be alleviated by a combination of vigorous measures that include the use of toll roads, expansion of the railroad system, and development of the less-populated Beer Sheva area as an alternative focal point for metropolitan growth, and have integrated these elements in statutory national

Table 14.14
Structure of the Transportation Sector
(Revenues at constant prices)

Year	Sea and air transport	Land transport				
		Total	Bus	Taxi	Truck	Train
1986	30%	59%	39%	8%	11%	0%
1987	32%	57%	37%	8%	11%	0%
1988	33%	56%	35%	8%	12%	0%
1989	34%	55%	33%	9%	13%	1%
1990	36%	52%	30%	9%	13%	1%
1991	37%	52%	29%	9%	14%	1%
1992	37%	52%	28%	9%	14%	1%
1993	37%	51%	26%	10%	15%	1%
1994	38%	49%	24%	10%	15%	1%
1995	39%	47%	22%	10%	15%	1%
1996	38%	46%	20%	10%	15%	1%
1997	38%	45%	20%	10%	15%	1%
1998	39%	44%	20%	10%	15%	1%

Source: Bank of Israel, *Annual Report*, 1998.

planning documents. However, their implementation depends on the allocation of the necessary funds through the political process, which proceeds slowly.

14.8 Commerce and Services

Commerce and services industry is the largest of the one-digit industries in the business sector, accounting for almost half its output, and continues to increase its share. Between 1985–1998, its product increased by 124 percent, slightly more than the growth in both its labor and capital inputs, indicating an annual rise of approximately 1 percent in labor productivity and 0.7 percent in total factor productivity. This modest increase may reflect the difficulty in measuring real changes in service output stemming from an innate difficulty in quantifying improvements in service quality. However, the industry's significant contribution to employment growth is abundantly clear. Between 1985–1998, it supplied approximately 340,000 new jobs for Israeli workers, accounting for approximately 70 percent of the overall increase in employment of Israelis in the business sector as a whole.

The industry includes a wide variety of economic activities, and the many structural changes it has undergone in recent years can only be described briefly in this limited space. Moreover, even if space were not a limiting factor, the available data would not support a detailed investigation. Until very recently, a socialist tradition

Table 14.15
The Structure of Industry Product in Commerce and Services, 1995 Prices

Year	Retail and wholesale trade	Hotels and restaurants	Financial and business services	Private health and education	Personal services, etc.
1989	33.5	7.4	49.2	5.7	4.2
1990	34.3	6.7	49.0	6.0	4.1
1991	34.6	6.5	49.0	5.8	4.1
1992	34.4	6.7	48.7	6.1	4.0
1993	34.7	6.7	48.2	6.1	4.3
1994	35.0	6.5	47.6	6.4	4.5
1995	35.3	6.3	47.1	6.8	4.5
1996	34.6	6.4	47.3	7.1	4.6
1997	34.3	6.8	46.8	7.4	4.7
1998	33.8	6.8	47.4	7.5	4.5

Source: Bank of Israel, *Annual Report*, 1998.

that emphasized agriculture and manufacturing as core economic activities and viewed services as their derivative, was also reflected in the meager statistical data on the service sector. Only in the last few years has this been rectified in some measure, and the scope of data collection on services widened, in large part based on VAT data. The principal trends are indicated in table 14.15, which describes the composition of industry product in commerce and services among five subcategories. It indicates stability in the share of retail and wholesale trade in industry output, some counter-cyclical fluctuations in the share of hotel and restaurant services, a relative decline in financial and business services, a marked rise in the share of private health and education services, and a modest rise in personal and other services.

The stability of the share of retail and wholesale trade hides substantial changes in the structure of retail trade. Small, individual shops in urban centers have been replaced by much larger stores clustered in shopping centers and open malls, many of them located on the outskirts of cities and at road junctions—a universal phenomenon accompanying the process of suburbanization and the diffusion of car ownership. These new shopping centers offer a variety of retail outlets, as well as food and entertainment services. An indirect indication of this changeover is the 150 percent increase in the scope of consumer goods sold in chain stores and department stores between 1985–1997, which far exceeded the rate of growth in retail and wholesale trade as a whole (Statistical Abstract of Israel 1998, table 17.1). Another indirect indication is the increase in the number of multiscreen cinemas, from nineteen in 1989 to sixty in 1994, at a time when the overall number of cinemas dropped (Raviv, 1996).

Table 14.16
The Hotel Industry

	Tourist bed-nights (millions)	Israelis bed-nights (millions)	Total bed-nights (millions)	Employees (thousands)	Rooms (thousands)	Average occupancy rate
1988	6.9	6.1	13.0	22.4	32.3	53%
1989	6.8	5.7	12.5	21.7	32.1	51%
1990	6.0	6.1	12.0	19.5	31.3	51%
1991	4.5	6.1	10.6	19.3	28.4	49%
1992	7.9	5.6	13.4	21.9	28.4	61%
1993	8.3	5.9	14.1	24.1	29.8	60%
1994	8.7	6.2	14.9	26.7	32.3	58%
1995	9.8	6.7	16.5	28.1	34.4	61%
1996	9.2	7.5	16.6	27.8	35.8	58%
1997	8.4	8.1	16.5	27.9	37.6	54%
1998	7.9	9.1	17.1	27.8	39.4	59%

Source: Bank of Israel, *Annual Report*, 1998.

Changes in the level and composition of demand in the hotel industry are presented in table 14.16. Tourist demand was adversely affected by political developments, especially by the Gulf War in 1991 and by more recent reversals in the peace process. However, this was more than offset by a secular rise in domestic demand since 1992. The net result has been a gradual increase in the aggregate number of bed-nights, as well as an increase in the number of employees in the industry. This, and the anticipation of increased religious tourism at the turn of the millenium, has motivated recent investments in enlarging hotel capacity.

Turnover in financial and business services—of which 63 percent were business services and 37 percent banking and insurance services (at 1998 prices)—increased at an average real annual rate of 8.6 percent between 1995–1998. The composition of business services is presented in table 14.17. The high-tech revolution is reflected in the rapid rise of computer services and R&D services. Most other business services also show impressive real growth, with declines only in architecture and engineering, following the slowdown in construction, and in photography. The accelerated growth in business services has continued in recent years despite the slow growth of the economy as a whole, suggesting that the economy is not experiencing an ordinary cyclical downturn but rather a period of structural change. The specific growth of business services reflects the growing importance of the business sector and the strengthening of market forces.

Globalization of business services is apparent from increased cooperation between Israeli suppliers of business services and leading multinational companies. Advertis-

Table 14.17
Business Services: Composition of Sales by Subbranch

	Percentage of sales		
	1995	1998	Revenue growth 1998, %
Computer services	14	25	29
Research and development	3	4	19
Employment agencies	9	8	11
Security and cleaning	9	8	5
Lawyers and notaries	12	10	9
Accounting and bookkeeping	9	7	10
Financial consulting	4	5	20
Engineering and architecture	25	20	−4
Advertising and public relations	11	8	3
Photocopying	2	2	−1
Other financial services	4	4	14

Source: Bank of Israel, *Annual Report*, 1998, Table 20b.

ing leads this trend, with almost all major Israeli advertising firms forging alliances with leading foreign companies.[14] Moreover, mergers between foreign partners of Israeli companies induced concomitant mergers in Israel, thus increasing the degree of industry concentration: The four leading advertising companies currently account for one quarter of industry sales, according to Dun and Bradstreet. Similar trends can be observed in accounting and consulting.[15]

The revolution in information technology, and the institutional changes that it induced, had a far-reaching affect on business services in general. Its direct influence is apparent in the accelerated growth of computer and software services that generated nine hundred million dollars of exports in 1998, and drew billions more in investments. Other business services were affected through their heavy involvement in the processing and distribution of information. Advertising has been dramatically influenced by the introduction of commercial television, which contributed approximately 25 percent of industry income in 1998. Technological developments in printing and publication, which improved production quality and lowered costs, have also contributed to advertising growth, although their long-term impact on profitability is ambiguous inasmuch as they lower entry barriers. Similar effects are evident in other business services, too. Thus, computerized legal databases may initially favor large law firms, which are more easily able to absorb the fixed cost of absorbing a new technology, but past experience indicates that once the technology matures and becomes available in standardized form, it is rapidly diffused to smaller firms, which benefit from it disproportionately.[16] At the same time, the increasing complexity

Table 14.18
Government Bankholdings (Percentage of ownership)

	December 1992	December 1998
Bank Hamizrahi	97.0%	6.7%
Israel Discount Bank	87.0%	60.0%
Bank Leumi	95.0%	54.1%
Bank Hapoalim	99.9%	24.3%
Union Bank	58.0%	19.5%

Source: The Israeli Banking Sector, 1997, 1998.

of the legal environment, due to such factors as the globalization of business activity, the deregulation of financial markets and appearance of new financial instruments, the growing importance of intangible assets, and so forth, favors larger, diversified law firms able to offer a broad spectrum of legal expertise under one roof.

The banking industry has changed greatly in the last two decades, as a result of both internal changes in ownership structure and external change in the business environment. The change in ownership was initially precipitated by the bank share crisis of 1983, to which the government responded by bailing out small shareholders and buying their holdings at above-market prices. This gave the government a controlling interest in all but one of Israel's major banks, which it wisely refrained from exercising directly. Instead, it created a public commission, which appointed the banks' boards of directors on a professional basis. In the early 1990s, the government took the logical next step and began a process of privatization, selling the bankshares back to the private sector. This has proved a lengthier process than was expected—vetting potential buyers, determining the terms of sale, divesting the banks of some of their real holdings, coming to terms with the trade unions—and though considerable progress has been made, it is still far from complete (table 14.18).

The stabilization of the sheqel and reduction of the government deficit allowed the banks gradually to shift their assets from foreign currencies to the sheqel, and to increase the share of credit extended to the public while reducing the share of government credit (table 14.19). Within the sheqel-denominated sector, banks shifted from index-linked to nonlinked assets and liabilities, which increased from one half of sheqel activity in 1991 to two thirds in 1997. Profit margins in the nonlinked sector are much greater, so that despite a significant erosion in nonlinked interest rate spreads—from over 15 percent in 1986–1988, to 10 percent in 1990–1991, and then to 5 percent from 1993 on—the overall profitability of the banks greatly increased. The after-tax return on capital increased from an average of 3.1 percent in 1988–1991, to an average of 9.1 percent in 1992–1997. The share of equity in total assets

Table 14.19
Composition of Aggregate Balance Sheets of Israeli Banking Institutions, Current Prices

	1985	1997
Assets		
Sheqel denominated	56%	74%
of which, credit to the govt	51%	7%
In foreign currencies	44%	26%
of which, credit to the public	27%	57%
Liabilities		
Sheqel denominated	58%	74%
In foreign currencies	42%	26%

Source: Statistical Abstract of Israel, 1998.

more than doubled between 1985 and 1997, and total assets deflated by the consumer price index increased by 31 percent in the same period. In addition, mortgage banks significantly increased their activity due to the construction boom and the increase in mortgage sizes. Their activity more than doubled between 1992–1997, while maintaining an average annual return on capital of over 13 percent. The influence of information technology on the industry is evident from the diffusion of automatic teller machines, which increased from 555 in 1987 to 1,241 in 1998 while the number of bank branches hardly changed (*Israel's Banking Sector, 1987 and 1998*). Other indications are the increased use of banking by phone and through the Internet, which can be expected to grow increasingly widespread and reduce both direct banking costs and securities trading fees, as it has done in the United States.

Finally, we note the accelerated growth of private education and health services, at an average annual rate of over 10 percent between 1989–1998. As a result of this rapid growth, their share in total national spending on health and education grew from 10 percent to almost 14 percent between 1990–1996. This increase reflects the gradual privatization of health and education services, which parallels the privatization of government holdings in the business sector. The scope of private education and health services is still limited, but the trend is clear, and its social implications are certainly no less important than the privatization of factories or banks.

14.9 Israel's Productivity Puzzle

Data on overall productivity in the business sector in 1985–1998 indicate a fall in productivity in the very years in which the economy seemed to have been doing best. Dividing the period between 1985–1998 into two equal subperiods, we find in 1985–1991 an impressive average annual increase of over 3 percent in business-sector total

Table 14.20
Total Factor Productivity in the Business Sector
(Average annual increase)

	Aggregate data	Industrial branch data
1985–1987	4.0%	2.6%
1988–1989	0.7%	−1.2%
1990–1991	4.4%	3.8%
1985–1991	3.2%	1.8%
1992–1995	−0.4%	1.1%
1996–1998	−0.5%	0.6%
1992–1998	−0.4%	0.9%

Source: Bank of Israel, *Annual Report*, 1998.

Table 14.21
Annual Growth Rate in Business Sector Output: Comparison of Sources

	Aggregate data				Industrial branch data			
	1995 BoIR	1996 BoIR	1997 BoIR	1998 BoIR	1995 BoIR	1996 BoIR	1997 BoIR	1998 BoIR
1995 growth rate	8.6	8.9	8.8	8.7	9.9	10.5	10.5	10.1
1996 growth rate		5.0	5.2	5.6		6.2	6.4	7.7
1997 growth rate			1.5	2.6			2.6	2.8
1998 growth rate				1.8				3.1

Source: Bank of Israel, *Annual Reports*, 1995–1998.

factor productivity (TFP) computed from aggregate data, compared to an average annual decline of 0.4 percent in 1992–1998 (table 14.20). This, in contrast to the dismal performance of the economy in the earlier period, and the many signs indicating substantial technological progress in almost all sectors of the economy in the latter period, including an explosion of innovation in the high-tech sector, the improved competitiveness of Israeli exports, and apparent improvements in the quality and variety of financial and business services. This marked contrast between direct observation and conventionally measured TFP is Israel's productivity puzzle.[17]

The answer offered here to this puzzle comes in several parts. First, it must be appreciated that growth rates are statistical estimates that are sensitive to their underlying assumptions. This is evident from table 14.21, which presents annual business sector growth rates for four years, published by the Bank of Israel in four annual reports. Two numbers are taken for each of four years from each of the annual reports, based on two principal methods of calculation, one using aggregate data directly and the other building an aggregate estimate from separate industry

Table 14.22
Annual TFP Growth in the Business Sector: Comparison of Sources

	Aggregate data				Industrial branch data			
	1995 BoIR	1996 BoIR	1997 BoIR	1998 BoIR	1995 BoIR	1996 BoIR	1997 BoIR	1998 BoIR
1995 growth rate	0.8	0.5	0.9	0.8	2.1	3.5	2.5	2.1
1996 growth rate		−0.2	0.4	−0.3		1.9	1.5	1.8
1997 growth rate			−2.4	−1.4			−1.4	−1.1
1998 growth rate				0.0				1.2

Source: Bank of Israel, *Annual Reports*, 1995–1998.

Table 14.23
Total Factor Productivity in the Business Sector by Industry

	Industry	Agriculture	Transportation and communication	Construction	Commerce and services	Water and electricity
1985–1987	1.1%	3.2%	2.5%	5.3%	2.8%	2.6%
1988–1989	−2.9%	2.1%	3.8%	−0.4%	−2.1%	−3.9%
1990–1991	2.9%	11.7%	2.1%	9.8%	1.6%	0.3%
1985–1991	0.4%	5.2%	2.8%	4.9%	1.0%	0.0%
1992–1995	1.5%	5.0%	3.5%	−7.1%	2.0%	1.9%
1996–1998	0.4%	5.4%	2.0%	−0.8%	−2.1%	2.8%
1992–1998	1.0%	5.2%	2.8%	−4.4%	0.2%	2.3%

Source: Bank of Israel, *Annual Reports*, 1998.

estimates. There are substantial differences between the two modes of calculation, and also differences from year to year, due to repeated revisions of the estimates. These differences are not so great as to change long-term growth trends. However, they are large enough to substantially affect the corresponding measures of total factor productivity presented in table 14.22. Thus, for example, the Bank's measure of TFP growth in 1995 varies from a low of 0.8 percent to a high of 3.5 percent.

Further examination of industry-level data suggests that the productivity puzzle is not present in all segments of the business sector (table 14.23). Thus, measured productivity in agriculture, in the transportation and communications industries, and in the electricity and water industries registered impressive gains in recent years. The sharp productivity decline in construction may be attributed to special difficulties in measuring construction product in recent years because of the difficulty in separating construction profits, which are part of industry product, from profits resulting from rising land values, which are not; and because of wide fluctuations in the distribution of new housing units by sector, type of building, size of unit, quality of finish, and so forth. In addition, measurement of labor input in the industry, which increasingly uses illegal immigrant labor, must also be extremely inaccurate. The very modest rise in productivity in commerce and services may be attributed to well-known difficulties in the measurement of quality improvement in services, and the consequent difficulty of measuring output independently of inputs; and to inadequate detail in the available statistical data on services.[18]

All of the above focuses our attention on the modest rise in manufacturing TFP—despite apparently large technological advances in recent years. A partial answer may be found in the growing importance of intangible capital—human capital, technological know-how, reputation, business networks—and its implications for national accounting (Johnson and Kaplan, 1987). Current accounting procedures are not equipped to deal with this change. Investment in intangible assets is expensed forthwith, and therefore does not add to national product.[19] This method of calculation reduces measured productivity in the year in which the investment is made, and increases it in future years, when it bears fruit, introducing a systematic bias in the timing of productivity gains. In years of economic prosperity, increased investment in intangibles moderates productivity growth, and in years of economic slowdown, the reduction in investment in nontangible capital adds to measured productivity.[20]

These effects pertain to measured productivity in a closed economy. In an open economy, the international transfer of intangible assets may introduce a further bias. In Israel, a significant share of the intangible capital that the country produced in recent years was not recorded as adding to GDP because it was "exported" by selling equity in the companies that produced it, rather than through actual product or service sales. This introduced a negative bias in measured industrial product and consequently in measured productivity. The commercial success of the software company Mirabilis illustrates the nature and potential scope of such biases. This privately held company developed a unique product, ICQ, at a cost of a few million dollars, and distributed it gratis to millions of users through the Internet. Based on this user base, the five owners sold their company to America Online (AOL) for approximately four-hundred million dollars, in return for which AOL received control of the ICQ software and user base. Mirabilis had no revenues, only costs; hence, both its added value and its productivity were negative, as measured by generally accepted methods, and yet the company produced assets that were demonstrably worth hundreds of millions of dollars at negligible cost. The widespread publicity surrounding the sale led to an exception being made in the way the sale was recorded in Israel's national accounts. A fraction (about two thirds) of the revenues from the sale of equity was recorded as having been produced in 1997 and exported in 1998. A single correction of this magnitude—and there have been many such cases in recent years—can raise measured manufacturing output by over 1 percent, and business sector output by several tenths of one percent. Some indication of the aggregate scope of this phenomenon can be derived from the increase in the difference between market and book value of Israeli companies traded in New York: it grew by approximately twenty billion dollars in 1992–1999 (table 14.2, above), a sum equal to over 3 percent of Israel's GDP in that period.[21] Clearly, measuring this intangible capital poses significant methodological difficulties, and yet ignoring it entirely must be misleading.[22]

Beyond this "productivity puzzle," there is another source of bias in measuring domestic product, which has an opposite effect on productivity. Israel's national accounts, like almost all others, ignore the effect of economic activity on overcrowding, pollution and the depletion of natural resources. Alternative methods of "green accounting," by explicitly treating natural resources as national assets, can contribute to a more efficient dynamic and spatial allocation of resources. Clean air, pure water, and open spaces may have as much an affect on our "standard of living" as many of the traded products and services that comprise domestic product. There can be little doubt that the importance of green accounting for a country as densely populated as Israel, will only increase with time.

14.10 Concluding Remarks

The gloomy prognoses for the Israeli economy in the late 1980s, when it was thought to be headed for an economic decline of South American proportions and duration, highlight the enormous strides it has made since then. The dramatic turnaround it experienced at the beginning of the 1990s was entirely unexpected. Fortuitous external developments beyond the country's control clearly played a key role—the huge wave of immigration from the former Soviet Union, an improved geopolitical situation, an extended boom in the United States. However, the opportunities opened up by these developments could not have been realized without the earlier macroeconomic stabilization of the economy and without the introduction of essential structural reforms. Capital market reform allowed domestic entrepreneurs to mobilize new sources of funds both at home and abroad. Domestic defense spending was sharply reduced, precipitating extensive layoffs of highly skilled workers in technologically intensive, defense-oriented manufacturing firms. Credit subsidies and direct support for agriculture and manufacturing were curtailed, allowing the forces of creative destruction to reallocate scarce resources from less efficient to more efficient uses. And a general reduction in the involvement of the public sector in the economy coupled with much-needed regulatory reforms strengthened the market mechanism. This combination of factors triggered and sustained a high-tech revolution in manufacturing and software, and generally increased the share of the business sector in the economy. It raised the economy to a level of industrial development and material well being comparable to that of all but the wealthiest Western economies.

The slowdown of recent years demonstrates all too clearly that past achievements are no guarantee of future performance. The government's role in the economy, though reduced, continues to exceed that of almost all industrialized economies, and the process of structural reform is far from complete; more needs to be done. Ironically, a reduction in the government's involvement in the economy can only be achieved through vigorous initiatives on its part. It must take on vested interests that have a stake in the status quo, which it can only do with broad public support. In 1985, a crisis environment allowed a national unity government to mobilize public support for the necessary reforms. As time passes and past crises recede from memory, the case for further reform must be made again and again. Growth in per capita output is an important enabling condition for reform as it allows resources to be allocated to new goals without reducing previous funding levels, but it is not sufficient in itself. The recent changes that have strengthened market forces have also widened the gap between "winners" and "losers" in the new economy. Wide support for the continued structural change that is essential for sustained economic development will also depend on an equitable division of the fruits of growth—allowing those who pay the price of change to reap a fair share of its benefits.

Notes

Thanks to Simha Bar-Eliezer for the data she prepared for this chapter and for her extensive comments on the manufacturing data; to Avi Ben-Bassat, Tuvia Blumenthal, Gadi Hazak, Joram Meyshar, Yossi Mualem, Yehuda Porath, Avia Spivak, Morris Teubal, and Manuel Trajtenberg for their helpful comments; and to Amit Yatov, David Lombrozo, and Yaron Buchnik for their excellent research assistance.

1. See Justman and Teubal (1991) for a general discussion of the reciprocal relation between technological progress and structural change.

2. The decline in the relative price of business-sector output was slightly stronger than the relative increase in its real output, so that the share of the business sector in GDP in current prices declined slightly.

3. See Chenery et al. (1986) for an extensive discussion of these trends from an international perspective, and Syrquin (1986) for a analysis of Israel's structural development until the mid-1980s.

4. Bregman and Marom (1998) found that the social rate of return on investments in R&D in Israel was double the rate on investments in physical capital.

5. Cf. Gerschenkron (1962) and Rostow (1972) on the essential role of the ideological dimension in historical transitions to modern economic growth.

6. Histadrut-owned manufacturing companies underwent a similar process.

7. At the time, the preponderance of opinion seemed to be that expansion of the defense sector was an important lever of growth, yet there were those who saw it as a hindering factor, which by absorbing huge amounts of technologically skilled labor was crowding out civilian, private-sector high-tech manufacturing (Halperin and Teubal, 1986; Berman and Halperin, 1990).

8. One of the results of globalization is a blurring of the national identity of firms whose investor base and workforce span several countries. Table 14.2 sums the market value of all firms listed under the heading "Israelis in New York" in the *Ha'aretz* daily stock listings. This poses a special difficulty for national accounts, a point discussed in the penultimate section on Israel's productivity puzzle.

9. In recent years, the OCS has disbursed in the vicinity of three hundred to four hundred million dollar annually.

10. This latter element of cooperation is an important channel for transferring technological and commercial business skills to Israeli manufacturers, as it has been in other industrializing economies, such as Taiwan, that similarly have learned by exporting (Pack and Page, 1994). Another important channel for absorbing foreign technology is by importing capital equipment. Argentina's and Brazil's past efforts to protect domestic equipment manufacturers from foreign competition undermined the competitiveness of other domestic industries (Nelson, 1993).

11. Between 1987 and 1994, fifteen hundred firms received from OCS $1,400 million in support of $3,500 of approved R&D (in 1996 prices), generating estimated sales of $31,600 million, which created 260,000 job years (Justman et al., 1999). Griliches and Regev (1999) found that the return to R&D in firms receiving OCS support was higher than the return to firms that did not receive support. The greatly improved access of Israeli high-tech firms to international capital markets suggests that these funds are less important today than they were in the past, except for smaller firms. The government also played an important catalytic role in the development of Israel's venture capital sector by establishing the Yozma fund in 1992, which was soon privatized.

12. From 1961 to 1984, there was no correlation between agricultural output and business-sector output, while other one-digit industries were closely correlated with it, but after 1985 agriculture's correlation grew considerably—the only industry in which it grew.

13. Both 1991 and 1995 were preelection years.

14. Among the foreign companies partnered with Israeli firms are Saatchi and Saatchi, J. Walter Thompson, McCann-Ericson, DDB Needham, BBDO, Ogilvy-Mather, etc.

15. Multinational accounting and consulting firms partnered with Israeli offices include PriceWaterhouse-Coopers, Ernst and Young, Arthur Andersen, KPMG, Deloitte Touche Tohmatsu, etc.

16. This is similar to patterns of technological convergence and vertical disintegration that characterized the early development of the machine tool industry in the United States (Rosenberg, 1963).

17. Cf. Young (1995) on the lack of measured productivity growth despite stellar industrial development in East Asia, and Greenwood and Yorukoglu (1997) on productivity slowdowns at the beginning of industrial revolutions.

18. Another source of bias is the use of the same labor and capital weights for all industries, though they clearly vary in their degree of labor and capital intensities.

19. The contrast between national accounting methods and the economic rationale is evident in the different way they treat R&D spending. In the national accounts, it is treated as an expense whereas empirical economic studies on R&D (e.g., Griliches and Regev, 1999; Bregman and Marom, 1998; Justman et al., 1999) treat it as an investment in R&D capital, which must be depreciated over a number of years.

20. The absorption of large numbers of new immigrants in the early 1990s is a case in point. From an economic standpoint, the enormous costs of absorption should have been treated as investment in human capital and amortized over a long time frame. Over longer time spans, the timing effects average out, and if there is a bias in measured productivity, it derives from a difference between the rate of investment in intangible capital and the rate of increase in labor productivity.

21. This is, of course, only a very rough indication.

References

Arens, Moshe. "The Development of the Military Industries." In *Israel's Defense Industries*, pp. 3–8. Ramat Gan, Israel: Bar-Ilan University Begin-Sadat Center for Strategic Studies, 1995. (Hebrew)

Bank of Israel, *Annual Report*. Jerusalem, 1994–1998.

Bank of Israel, *Israel's Banking Sector*. Jerusalem, 1997, 1998. (Hebrew)

Bar, Aryeh. "Industrial Policy in Support of Small Businesses in Israel." In *Renewal and Growth in the Small Business Sector*, edited by Moshe Justman, pp. 105–118. Jerusalem: Jerusalem Institute for Israel Studies, 1994. (Hebrew)

Bar-Eliezer, Simha. *Jubilee Publication no. 4*. Jerusalem: Central Bureau of Statistics, 1998. (Hebrew)

Bar-Eliezer, Simha. Personal correspondence, 1999.

Berman, Eli, and Ariel Halperin. "Skilled Manpower, Security and Growth." In *An Industry Technology Policy for Israel*, edited by David Brodet, Moshe Justman, and Morris Teubal, pp. 147–182. Jerusalem: Jerusalem Institute for Israel Studies, 1990. (Hebrew)

Blass, Asher A., and Oved Yosha. "Reform in the Israeli Financial System and the Flow of Funds of Publicly Traded Manufacturing Firms." Chapter 6 in this volume.

Bregman, Aryeh, and Aryeh Marom. "Productivity in Israeli Manufacturing and its Sources, 1960–1996." Working Paper 98.03. Jerusalem: Bank of Israel, 1998. (Hebrew)

Gerschenkron, Alexander. *Economic Backwardness in Historical Perspective*. Cambridge, Mass.: Harvard University Press, 1962.

Central Bureau of Statistics. *Industry and Crafts Surveys*. Jerusalem, 1985/86, 1990, 1994.

Central Bureau of Statistics. *Statistical Abstract of Israel.* Jerusalem, 1999.

Central Bureau of Statistics. *National Expenditure on Civilian Research and Development, 1989–98*. Jerusalem, 1999.

Chenery, Hollis B., Sherwin Robinson, and Moshe Syrquin. *Industrialization and Growth*. Oxford: Oxford University Press, 1986.

Dun and Bradstreet. *Israel Business Guide*. Tel Aviv, various years. (Hebrew)

Dvir, Dov, et al. "Demilitarization of Military Technologies in Israel." *Economic Quarterly* (Riv'on leKalkala) 45, no. 2 (1998): 358–370. (Hebrew)

Gabai, Yoram, and Rafael Rob. "Import-Liberalization and Abolition of Devaluation Substitutes Policy: Implications for the Israeli Economy." Chapter 9 in this volume.

Galai, Dan, and Joseph Shachar. "Technology Transfer and Demilitarization of Projects in Israel's Defense Industry." Jerusalem: Israel Democracy Institute, 1993. (Hebrew)

Griliches, Zvi, and Haim Regev. "R&D, Government Support and the Productivity of Manufacturing Plants in Israel, 1975–1994," Sapir Forum. Jerusalem: Hebrew University, 1999. (Hebrew)

Greenwood, Jeremy, and Mehmet Yorukoglu. "1974." *Carnegie-Rochester Conference Series on Public Policy* 46 (1997): 49–96.

Gronau, Reuben. "Structural Changes in Israeli Public Utilities—The Reform That Never Was." Chapter 10 in this volume.

Halperin, Ariel, and Morris Teubal. "Government Policy and Capability Creating Resources in Economic Growth," Maurice Falk Institute for Economic Research. Jerusalem: Hebrew University, 1986.

Halperin, Ariel, and Daniel Tsiddon. "Conversion of Defense Industries in Israel: The Labor Market." *Economic Quarterly* (Riv'on leKalkala) 40, no. 1 (1993): 7–30. (Hebrew)

Johnson, H. Thomas, and Robert S. Kaplan. *Relevance Lost*. Cambridge, MA: Harvard University Press, 1987.

Justman, Moshe, and Morris Teubal. "Technological Infrastructure Policy: Creating Capabilities and Building Markets." *Research Policy* 24 (1995): 259–281.

———. "A Structuralist Perspective on the Role of Technology in Industrial Development." *World Development* 19 (1991): 1167–1183.

Justman, Moshe, et al. *Benfits from R&D Supported by the Office of the Chief Scientist*. Jerusalem, Ministry of Industry and Trade, 1999. (Hebrew)

Kislev, Yoav, and Gadi Rosenthal. "The Water Divide." *Economic Quarterly* (Riv'on leKalkala) 46, no. 1 (1999): 106–135. (Hebrew)

Kislev, Yoav, and Evgenia Vaxine. *A Statistical Atlas of Israeli Agriculture*. Rehovoth, Israel: Agricultural Economics Research Center, 1998. (Hebrew)

Nelson, Richard R., ed. *National Innovation Systems*. Oxford: Oxford University Press, 1993.

Pack, Howard, and John M. Page, Jr. "Accumulation, Exports, and Growth in the High-Performing Asian Economies." *Carnegie-Rochester Conference Series on Public Policy* 40 (1994): 199–236.

Raviv, Merav. "An Economic Analysis of the Movie-House Industry," MA thesis, Ben Gurion University, 1996. (Hebrew)

Rosenberg, Nathan. "Technological Change in the Machine Tool Industry, 1840–1910." *Journal of Economic History* 23 (1963): 414–446.

Rostow, Walter W. *The Stages of Economic Growth: A Non-Communist Manifesto*, 2d ed. Cambridge: Cambridge University Press, 1972.

Sadeh, Sharon. "The Rehabilitation of the Defense Industries." In *Israel's Defense Industries*. Ramat Gan, Israel: Bar-Ilan University BESA Center, 1995, 15–23. (Hebrew)

Schwartz, Moshe. *Unlimited Liability*. Beer Sheva: Ben-Gurion University Press, 1995. (Hebrew)

Shachar, Muriel, and Ehud Zuscovitch. "Industrial-Technological Joint Ventures: A Business Economic Analysis." In *An Industry and Technology Policy for Renewed Growth*, edited by Moshe Justman, Ehud Zuscovitch, and Morris Teubal, pp. 52–83. Jerusalem: Jerusalem Institute for Israel Studies, 1994. (Hebrew)

Syrquin, Moshe. "Economic Growth and Structural Change: An International Perspective." In *The Israeli Economy: Maturing through Crises*, edited by Yoram Ben-Porath, pp. 42–74. Cambridge, MA: Harvard University Press, 1986.

Teubal, Morris. "Israel's National System of Innovation." In *National Innovation Systems*, edited by Richard R. Nelson, pp. 476–502. Oxford: Oxford University Press, 1993.

Tischler, Asher, and Zeev Rotem. "The Sources of Israel's Defense Industries' International Success." *Economic Quarterly* (Riv'on leKalkala) 42 (1995): 468–496. (Hebrew)

Trajtenberg, Manuel. "Innovation in Israel, 1968–97: A Comparative Analysis Using Patent Data." *Research Policy* 30 (2001): 363–389.

Young, Allan. "The Tyranny of Numbers: Confronting the Statistical Realities of the East Asian Growth Experience." *Quarterly Journal of Economics* 110 (1995): 641–680.

15 The Rise of Earning Inequality

Momi Dahan

This work is composed of two parts. The first presents an overview of income inequality in Israel, focusing on the factors that determine income inequality. We describe the main findings concerning the effect of government intervention on income inequality and in particular the effect of transfer payments and direct taxes. We also discuss macroeconomic factors that affect income inequality.

Earning inequality in Israel is considerable and has been rising for almost three decades. The key element of earning inequality is inequality in the labor market. Whereas in the second part of this chapter, we probe the trend in wage inequality, in this part, we trace the origins of the rise in wage inequality over the past two decades, focusing on questions such as the following: Does the rise in inequality reflect a widening of schooling disparities? (Surprisingly, the effect of the Israeli education system on earnings inequality has not been researched.) Has the return on schooling changed significantly? How has immigrant absorption affected the structure of return on human capital?

15.1 An Overview

The Rising Tide of Earning Inequality

A glance at figure 15.1, which covers the years 1965–1997, reveals a clear trend of widening economic disparities in Israeli society since the mid-1970s, as measured in terms of inequality in total income among households headed by employees.[1] There is a perceptible overlap between macroeconomic events and the trend in income inequality. Inequality increased as the economy tumbled into a deep recession in 1967 and contracted immediately after the recession ended. Income inequality grew when the economy shifted into hyperinflation in the mid-1980s and contracted (although not fully) immediately after inflation was checked. Inequality rises again (this time to record levels) with the advent of mass immigration in the 1990s.

Table 15.1 presents inequality data for a shorter period, from 1979 to 1997, during which definitions were more uniform. The table shows that the earning inequality created by market forces, measured by a Gini index for inequality in earnings, has attained a troubling level and has been climbing steadily since 1980.[2] Israel's level of earnings inequality, before the effect of transfer payments and direct taxes is mechanically factored in, surpasses that of the United States (table 15.6) and brings to mind countries that have blatant economic disparities, such as Brazil and Guatemala.

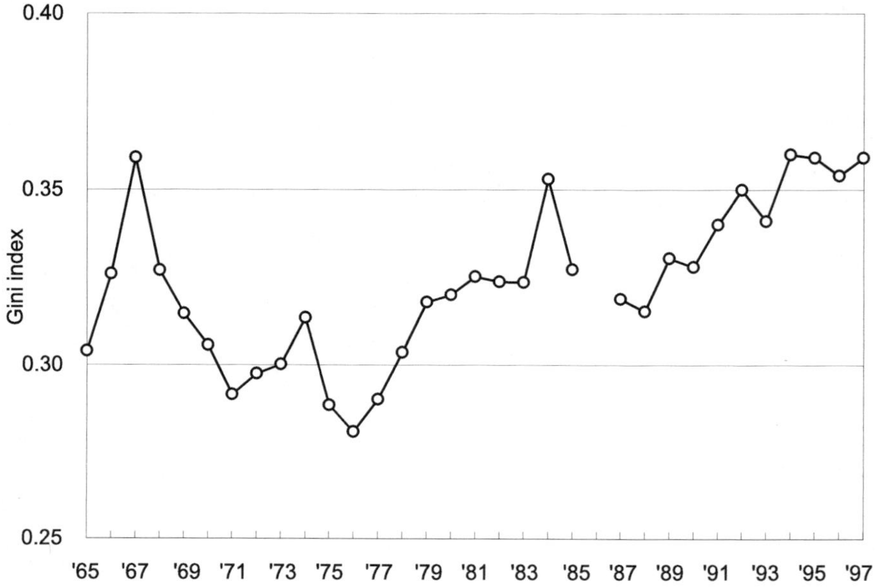

Figure 15.1
Inequality in Israel, 1965–1997*
* Gini index for total income inequality among employee-headed households.

Despite the differences in data-gathering methods, demographic structure, and other attributes, an international comparison may be instructive. In 1999, the Inter-American Development Bank released figures on inequality in South American countries. They portray Latin America as the continent with the highest inequality in the world (IABD, 1999). According to this publication, the Gini index for income inequality in Latin America ranged from 0.43 in Uruguay to 0.59 in Brazil. Given that the rate of transfer payments in South American countries is negligible, these give an approximation of inequality in earnings. In comparison, in 1997, the Gini index for earnings inequality in Israel was 0.533 while inequality in labor income in Israel was even greater at 0.585 (table 15.1). Clearly, the labor market "produces" considerable inequality, which is translated into earnings inequality. (The second part of this study is devoted entirely to the origins of labor-market inequality.)

Government involvement by means of transfer payments and taxes reduces economic disparities in Israeli society to the common European level. The Gini index for net-income inequality was 0.372 in 1997 and 0.333 after standard-person adjustment. (Notably, however, the inequality index for net income is flawed, as we show in the next section.)

Table 15.1
Gini Index for Income inequality among Households, Population at Large, 1979–1997

	Labor income	Earning	Total income	Net income	Private consumption
1979	N/A	N/A	N/A	N/A	N/A
1980	0.544	N/A	0.411	0.361	No survey
1981	0.538	N/A	0.410	0.354	No survey
1982	0.559	N/A	0.413	0.352	No survey
1983	N/A	N/A	N/A	N/A	No survey
1984	N/A	N/A	N/A	N/A	No survey
1985	0.560	0.504	0.419	0.356	No survey
1986	No survey	No survey	No survey	No survey	0.328
1987	0.559	0.498	0.414	0.361	No survey
1988	0.555	0.496	0.408	0.358	No survey
1989	0.568	0.513	0.421	0.367	No survey
1990	0.576	0.516	0.417	0.366	No survey
1991	0.586	0.524	0.423	0.373	No survey
1992	0.585	0.529	0.432	0.378	0.321
1993	0.579	0.526	0.422	0.368	No survey
1994	0.588	0.535	0.440	0.385	No survey
1995	0.579	0.527	0.432	0.372	No survey
1996	0.586	0.532	0.432	0.375	No survey
1997	0.585	0.533	0.432	0.372	N/A

Inequality in standard of living, measured on the basis of the Gini index for private consumption, is even smaller than inequality in net income. Many tend to think that this measure provides the best summarizing indicator of standard-of-living inequality. Additionally, this index does not have the flaws that impair the net-income inequality index. Inequality in well-being is even smaller after taking into account additional factors that affect household well-being, such as number of children, amount of leisure time, and consumption of public services (table 15.2).

Another difference stands out in table 15.1—the long-term trend in earnings inequality relative to net-income inequality. Whereas earnings inequality has worsened considerably, net-income inequality has increased only slightly.

The next section shows that the degree of transfer-payment intervention needed to offset the increase in earning inequality is rising. To reduce the inequality brought about by forces in the market, especially the labor market, high tax rates are needed to finance transfer payments for disadvantaged population groups. As we see below, such involvement may also be one of the factors in Israel's high earnings inequality.

Table 15.2
Distribution of Income and Standard of Living, Population at Large, 1992/1993 (Percent)

	Decile									
	Lowest	2	3	4	5	6	7	8	9	Uppermost
Earning	0.4	1.6	3.2	5.2	6.9	9.2	11.3	13.7	17.9	30.6
Total income	2.1	3.7	5.0	5.8	6.9	9.1	10.7	12.9	15.7	28.1
Net income	2.6	4.5	5.9	6.8	7.8	9.6	11.0	12.9	15.1	23.8
Consumption	3.4	5.1	5.9	7.3	8.6	9.5	10.7	12.8	15.4	21.2
Educ. & health*	13.5	13.3	12.2	11.0	10.0	9.6	8.9	8.7	8.1	4.7
No. of children**	1.3	1.3	2.0	1.9	1.9	2.2	2.1	2.1	2.0	2.2
Leisure hrs/week**	96.9	87.4	84.5	80.3	79.5	76.1	76.0	73.5	71.4	70.5

* The share of each decile in education and health services was computed on the basis of net income deciles per standard adult.
** Number of children and hours of leisure time were computed among households in which the head of households was aged 30–44, in accordance with net income deciles of the population at large in the Income Survey (without adjustment for and standard adult).
Sources: income and private consumption—Central Bureau of Statistics, *Household Expenditure Survey 1992/93*. No adjustment for standard adult is made. Education and Health—Central Bureau of Statistics, Publication 1049 and *Household Expenditure Survey 1992/1993*.

Effect of Government Policy Measures on Income Inequality

Government intervention affects inequality in various ways, which can be sorted into several categories: (1) the effect of the distribution of ownership of tangible assets, that is, physical capital—for example, the sale of public housing at subsidized prices; (2) the effect of the distribution of intangible assets, that is, human capital—for example, the provision free public education; (3) the effect on the structure of return on tangible and intangible capital—for example, progressive income tax; (4) current public support—for example, old-age pensions; and (5) regulations and laws that do not have budget implications—for example, government regulations to protect monopolies.

There is no information on the overall effect of government on the distribution of ownership of tangible assets. Even reasonable information about the distribution of capital in Israel is lacking. Unfortunately, this important topic is still shrouded in darkness. According to conventional wisdom based on findings in other countries, wealth is more unequally distributed than labor income. Due to the lack of data on the distribution of wealth, one cannot estimate, for example, the effect of government policy on the distribution of wealth in Israel. Similarly, we cannot estimate the effect of monetary policy on wealth inequality.

Government action may affect income inequality even if it has no budget implications. Government regulations that give a private entity a monopoly—imports of electrical appliances, for example—do not entail budget expenditure but benefit the monopoly holders, who receive a windfall. In Israel, no comprehensive study has been done that could estimate the impact of monopoly- and cartel-friendly regulations on income inequality.

The Effect of Direct Taxes and Transfer Payments The Central Bureau of Statistics (CBS) surveys provide reliable information on the distribution of ownership of human capital. Reliable data also exist on income from labor, income from public support, and direct tax remittances. The data in the Household Income Survey pertain only to households headed by employees; income of the self-employed is not sufficiently reliable and is not published.

The National Insurance Institute presents an annual survey on the effect of transfer payments and direct taxes on poverty and income inequality. To estimate the effect of the policy measures, a Gini index for inequality in earnings income is compared to total income (earning plus transfer payments) and net income.

As table 15.3 shows, inequality is smaller in total income per standard person than in earnings inequality. In 1997, the Gini index earnings inequality, was 0.505 per standard person. The inclusion of transfer payments in income lowered the inequality to 0.395, a 21.8 percent decrease. Inclusion of the effect of direct taxes lowered the index of net-income inequality by another 12.3 percent. This calculation might be interpreted as if transfer payments are much more effective than direct taxes in reducing inequality. Furthermore, the rate of contraction of inequality by transfer payments has been increasing over time. This does not prove that the transfer payments are becoming more efficient, given that the rate of transfer payments has also been rising. In direct taxes, too, one cannot point to such a clear trend, but the effect was greater in 1997 (the end of the period investigated) than in the early 1980s. In regard to taxes, too, these results imply nothing about efficacy. Practically speaking, this method does not provide information on the effectiveness of the policy measures.

The estimation of the effect of these policy measures on inequality, following the approach described above, suffers from several problems, and therefore, caution is warranted. First, the data on transfer payments and direct taxes (unlike those on labor and capital income) are not obtained from interviews with respondents; instead, they are computed by officials at the Central Bureau of Statistics.[3] Below is a quotation from a CBS publication that explains how the data in the Household Income Survey are gathered and processed:

> The material at the individual level is subjected to various computations and corrections, such as ... computation of child allowances at the National Insurance rates; imputation of other benefits wherever reporting is incomplete; ... computation of total income for cases in which

Table 15.3
Effect of Transfer Payments and Direct Taxes on Inequality, 1979–1997

	earnings*	Gini index Total income*	net income*	Percent of decrease resulting from transfer payments	Percent of decrease resulting from direct taxes
1979	0.432	0.366	0.318	15.2	11.1
1980	0.434	0.369	0.324	14.9	10.4
1981	0.439	0.372	0.319	15.4	12.1
1982	0.444	0.367	0.312	17.3	12.4
1983	0.439	0.360	0.301	17.9	13.6
1984	0.472	0.398	0.327	15.8	15.1
1985	0.468	0.372	0.312	20.2	13.1
1986	No survey	No survey	No survey	No survey	No survey
1987	N/A	N/A	N/A	N/A	N/A
1988	0.457	0.370	0.322	19.1	10.5
1989	0.474	0.378	0.325	20.3	11.1
1990	0.480	0.376	0.326	21.7	10.3
1991	0.490	0.377	0.327	23.1	10.2
1992	0.498	0.393	0.339	21.1	10.7
1993	0.494	0.383	0.329	22.5	10.9
1994	0.502	0.399	0.344	20.4	11.0
1995	0.497	0.397	0.337	20.2	12.1
1996	0.496	0.387	0.329	22.0	11.8
1997	0.505	0.395	0.333	21.8	12.3

*The Gini index for net income is adjusted to standard persons.
Source: National Insurance Institute, *Annual Survey*, 1997/98.

net income or a sum paid is reported; [and] computation of direct taxes on the basis of the income tax and National Insurance tables. (CBS, *Household Income Survey*, 1992, 1993, Special Publication 993)

Thus, the evaluation of the effect of policy measures on inequality assumes that direct taxes are collected by the book (and that households realize all benefits they are entitled to) and are not based on income tax and National Insurance contributions actually paid and benefits actually received. The foregoing estimates of the effect of transfer payments and direct taxes are biased to the extent that tax evasion and incomplete takeup of entitlements exist.

Second, the computation may be biased even if all individuals pay taxes by the book and invoke their full eligibility for benefits. This is because this approach assumes that individuals cannot adjust their labor supply in response to changes in tax rates and generosity of benefits.

Finally, a budget action usually has implications for both the expenditure and the revenue sides of the budget. When we measure the effect of transfer payments on inequality using the method described above, we answer the following question: How do transfer payments affect inequality if we disregard the way the budget sources are raised? This information should not be used to assess the effect of budget package. Raising the rate of Value Added Tax (VAT) would almost certainly be regressive if we ignore the uses to which the added revenues are put, but we might reach but the opposite conclusion if the added tax revenues were used to increase progressively distributed transfer payments.

The Effect of Indirect Taxes on Inequality Gabai (1996), investigating the effect of indirect taxes on income-distribution inequality, found that they have a positive effect on income inequality. However, the assessment of the impact of indirect taxes failed to take account of individuals' responses to the imposition of taxes. Additionally, because indirect taxes apply to goods and services and not to individuals, and therefore it is difficult to identify who bear the burden. The indirect-tax burden is shared between consumers and producers depends on supply and demand elasticity. Indirect taxes affect also the real wage rate of the workers who may be the very same consumers or the consumers of other products. This makes it even more complex to gauge the impact of indirect taxes on income inequality.

In contrast, the effect of indirect taxes on the distribution of private consumption is very easy to estimate if the taxes are applied to all products at the same rate, as in the case of VAT in Israel: VAT is neutral in its effect on consumption inequality.

Distribution of Public Services by Income Levels Individuals also benefit from public education and health and social services. In measuring the effect of government on income inequality, one must add public services to transfer payments and taxes. In a special publication, the Central Bureau of Statistics (1997) estimates the distribution of public education and health services (in king income) by income deciles.[4]

According to the estimate in table 15.4, central government provides disadvantaged population groups with more education and health services than it does high income deciles. Education services is 47 percent of net (mean) household income in the lowest decile as against only 9 percent of net household income in the top decile. The government effect is progressive in transfer payments, direct taxes, and the main public services (education and health). Earnings are twelve times higher in the top decile than in the lowest decile. The ratio falls to approximately 5.3 when transfer payments and direct taxes income are included and to 3.7 when the monetary value of education and health services is included. In fact, social services are distributed more equally than are transfer payments.

Table 15.4
Education and Health Services, by Net Income Deciles* (per standard adult), 1992/1993

	Decile									
	Lowest	2	3	4	5	6	7	8	9	Highest
Econ. income	1,020	2,051	2,703	3,514	3,996	5,097	6,186	7,654	9,628	12,541
Transfers	919	913	829	748	678	610	523	489	516	625
Direct taxes	58	178	270	464	531	766	1,077	1,514	2,243	3,223
Net income	1,881	2,786	3,262	3,768	4,143	4,941	5,632	6,629	7,901	9,943
Educ. and health	880	868	798	715	653	626	578	569	525	306

* Monthly household income (NIS).
Source: Central Bureau of Statistics (1997).

Minimum Wage and Inequality Another policy measure designed to reduce inequality among workers is the minimum wage. A collective agreement concluded between the Coordinating Bureau of Economic Organizations ("organized management") and the Histadrut (General Federation of Labor) in 1972 assured every worker in Israel a minimum income pegged at 44 percent of the national average wage. Over the years, the minimum wage relative to the national average wage eroded because it was adjusted mainly according to the Cost-of-Living Allowance (COLA) agreement. In April 1987, this arrangement became law, and the minimum wage was set at 45 percent of the national average wage.

The effect of the Minimum Wage Law on inequality, assuming full compliance with the law, is reflected in cutting the left-hand tail of the distribution and in a change in the wage scale of persons who previously received a near-minimum wage. Dahan (1995) found no support that the level of minimum wage affects inequality in total-income distribution among employee-headed households. This finding is not sensitive regardless of whether the 1972–April 1987 period is treated as if there were a law, or whether one treats the minimum wage until the law was enacted as zero. This apparently reflects the low level of compliance with both the agreement (Yaniv, 1986) and the law (Flug and Kasir, 1993).

This result may also trace to the lack of a stipulation in the Minimum Wage Law requiring consideration of household income. Theoretically, the Minimum Wage Law may reduce inequality among workers but not among households due to the structure of breadwinners in the household. This would occur even with a high rate of compliance and even if the law had a negligible (negative) effect on employment.

Inequality and Macroeconomic Factors

Unemployment and Inequality The unemployment rate climbed rather quickly, from 3.3 percent of the civilian labor force in 1979 to 8.9 percent in 1989, and in

1997, rested at 8.7 percent. It is difficult to believe that this volatility reflects only employment changes that are typical of the business cycle, the type that naturally tends to disappear over time. For this reason, the relationship between unemployment and inequality is important beyond the usual question of smoothing business cycles in economic activity and employment.

Several studies have shown a strong positive correlation between the unemployment rate and income inequality among households headed by working employees in Israel.[5] A rising unemployment rate has an expansionary effect on inequality and has been one of the main explanatory factors in Israel's inequality trend in the past thirty years. In other words, when unemployment worsens, so does the relative situation of people in the lower income deciles.[6]

No discussion of the effect of the unemployment rate on income inequality among employees would be adequate without reference to the unemployed. The more unemployed there are, the more people there are whose incomes were zero before the Unemployment Benefits Law was enacted and remained paltry afterwards. An increase in the unemployment rate causes greater inequality if the unemployed earned low wages during their term of employment. According to the CBS Labor Survey, unemployment is more prevalent among those with a low level of schooling. The rise in unemployment rate exacerbated inequality not only among employed households but also among the population large.[7]

One of the main factors in the upturn in inequality in the late 1980s and early 1990s was the rising unemployment rate, which reflects the crowding out of part of the population—foremost, members of disadvantaged groups—from employment. A low level of schooling allows their employers to pay them even less, and, thereby, exacerbates wage disparities.[8]

Inflation and Inequality Empirical research in Israel also shows a significant positive correlation between the inflation rate and income inequality,[9] indicating that the lower deciles are unable to evade the relative erosion of their income. This finding is consistent with Artstein and Sussman (1991), who found that the standard deviation of wage changes rose tandem with the escalation of inflation in 1984 and 1985 and contracted after the Economic Stabilization Program was applied. The finding also supports Sussman and Zakkai (1983), who showed that the wage structure in general government became less equal as the inflation rate rose.

This finding is surprising given the COLA agreement. For a long time, the agreement included a wage ceiling beyond which a COLA would not be paid. Thus, in de facto terms, high wages were indexed at a lower rate than that declared (Leviathan, 1982). This is because the trade unions deliberately skewed the COLA agreement progressively to fight inequality as the inflation rate rose. This progressive skewing, however, was not translated into practice, and inflation served as a regressive tax. One way to explain this, perhaps, is to note that for low-wage earners, the COLA agreement was a major factor in wage increases—under which circumstances only part of the real wage erosion was compensated—whereas wage changes among high wage earners were dictated more by contracts, which were better protected against inflation.

These findings are important in an overall evaluation of fiscal and monetary policy that may affect both the unemployment rate and the inflation rate. In the short term, of course, sustained high (low) inflation and low (high) unemployment for a short time may be substitutable. The discussion above allows us to add the aspect of income distribution to the set of considerations. To obtain a deeper understanding of this issue, research is needed on the direct effects of monetary policy on income distribution through changes in interest rate. One presumes that individuals at the bottom of the income scale are net borrowers and that those at the top are mostly lenders. Changes in the Bank of Israel key rate may have at least a short-term effect on income inequality.

Immigration and Inequality The mass immigration that began in late 1989 exacerbated the uptrend in income inequality in the first half of the 1990s (Dahan and Ben-Porat, 1997). The main transmission mechanism between immigration and income disparities was the escalation of unemployment to a rate surpassing that observed in 1966. This aggravated the erosion of the bargaining power of nonimmigrant Israeli workers in low income deciles. The flow of immigrants to unskilled jobs also took a toll on the bargaining power of low-wage workers. Consequently, the relative wage of low-wage workers declined, and economic disparities widened.

Even though a high proportion of immigrants are in low deciles, the fraction of immigrants in the population was not found to have a significant effect on inequality in the 1990s. As stated, the main impact occurred via the increase in the unemployment rate. The inconsistency between the findings of cross-section data with those based on a time series is typical of many studies in labor economics.

Israel from a Global Perspective

The World Bank has built a database of income inequality that includes most countries around the globe.[10] To assure a satisfactory level of uniformity and reliability, countries were included in the database only if their inequality data met several criteria. One of the criteria was full coverage of the population, and Israel was excluded from the sample on this account. The CBS Income Surveys omitted small localities that, before 1995, were home to about 20 percent of the population. In 1995, the

Table 15.5
Inequality and Economic Development ($)

No. of countries	GDP range	Avg. per-capita GDP	Gini index
21	9,843–17,594	13,351	34.8
21	4,027–9,238	6,086	40.9
21	1,974–3,942	2,820	43.1
25	482–1,913	1,107	43.9
Israel 1992	9,843	9,843	33.9

Source: The Gini index is from Deininger and Squire (1996) and per-capita GDP from Summers and Heston (1984). The figures for Israel pertain to net-income inequality among households.

coverage rate climbed to 90 percent. Here, with the warranted degree of caution, we attempt to put Israel's inequality in an international perspective.

Much has been written about the empirical relationship between economic development and inequality, especially in the context of the Kuznets curve. The positive correlation between inequality and per-capita GDP, as an indicator of economic development, stands out in table 15.5. A glance at the data shows that no developed country whatsoever has severe inequality (the variance among developed countries is actually rather small) but that some developing countries have rather small inequality. This is the source behind the relationship that is known as the Kuznets Curve.

International comparison gives us a yardstick with which we may determine Israel's place. Israel rests at the bottom of the group of affluent countries (the first column in table 15.5), and its level of inequality in net income inequality resembles that in those countries. In other words, Israel's level of net income inequality is not exceptional given its level of economic development. As mentioned above, however, earnings inequality in Israel resembles that of South America.

Israel is not unique in evidencing an upturn in earnings inequality. Economic research around the globe can help (to a limited degree) to identify additional factors that may be responsible for the increase in inequality in Israel, given that the Israeli economy is exposed to economic processes that resemble those sweeping the global economy. In the 1980s, inequality increased in most industrialized countries except for Germany and Italy (Gottschalk and Smeeding, 1997). Escalating inequality, especially in the United States, has attracted much attention that gave rise to documentation of the trends and attempts to explain them.

The main explanations for the increase in inequality (mainly in the United States) are the increasing openness of industrial economies to flows of goods, services, and capital; skilled-biased technological changes; and the waning power of trade unions. These factors are interrelated, and there is no consensus about the relative

Table 15.6
Gini Index of Inequality among Households, U.S. and Israel, 1985–1997

	Earning income		Total income		Net income	
	Israel	U.S.	Israel	U.S.	Israel	U.S.
1985	0.504	0.471	0.419	0.418	0.356	0.410
1986	No survey	0.476	No survey	0.423	No survey	0.434
1987	0.498	0.477	0.414	0.424	0.361	0.408
1988	0.496	0.477	0.408	0.425	0.358	0.411
1989	0.513	0.481	0.421	0.429	0.367	0.415
1990	0.516	0.480	0.417	0.426	0.366	0.410
1991	0.524	0.483	0.423	0.425	0.373	0.410
1992	0.529	0.490	0.432	0.430	0.378	0.415
1993	0.526	0.508	0.422	0.448	0.368	0.430
1994	0.535	0.510	0.440	0.450	0.385	0.431
1995	0.527	0.503	0.432	0.444	0.372	0.424
1996	0.532	0.505	0.432	0.447	0.375	0.429
1997	0.533	0.504	0.432	0.448	0.372	0.431

Sources: Israel—Table 15.1; U.S.—United States Bureau of the Census.

contribution of each to the increase in inequality. A recent study attempted to examine the effect of these factors on inequality in Israel.[11]

The lowering of import tariffs, a process that accelerated in 1987, made the domestic economy more receptive to inflows of goods and services. This openness advanced more vigorously, in relative terms, vis-à-vis countries less intensive than Israel in human capital. In the 1990s, the Israeli labor market also became increasingly exposed to the entry of foreign workers. In practice, the economy was opened asymmetrically; most of those who came possessed a low level of human capital. This policy brought wage pressure on workers at the bottom of the wage scale and may be partly responsible for the increase in inequality.

The attenuation of trade unions' power is undoubted even though systematic documentation of this trend is lacking. A trade union affects labor-market inequality in two main ways. First, like any social guild, a union wishes to widen wage disparities between organized workers and the unorganized and unemployed.[12] Second, to unify the ranks, a union strives to attain for a uniform wage formula that corresponds to its members' personal characteristics. Naturally, the wage formula is based on observable traits such as years of schooling and experience. These conditions leave employers with little leeway in rewarding workers for the quality of their schooling and (innate) personal attributes. This explains why this factor helps reduce (conditioned) inequality.

Additionally, wage disparities may occur among members of the trade union in accordance with the relative strength of groups within the union. Labor at the Israel Electric Corp., Mekorot, and Bezeq can disrupt Israelis' lives gravely. This ability is translated into a high relative wage with the union's support. In return, the trade union acquires an important platform for struggle against employers to improve the wages of all members.

From an empirical point of view, a strong trade union enhances the explanatory power of measurable traits such as schooling and age, and as a result, the unexplained remainder contracts. The long-term decline of the Histadrut has had a downward effect on inequality among "equals." However, as the foregoing discussion showed, the contraction of a trade union's power does not necessarily reduce labor-market inequality.

Another factor that has attracted some research attention is the winner-take-all phenomenon, described (although not for the first time) in Cook and Frank's American bestseller (1995). According to this explanation, the upturn in inequality is rooted in technological and social changes that allow star performers in services (especially in entertainment) to command astronomical wages. Some support for this view is the dramatic increase in the relative wages of executives, as we describe in the second part of this study. Admittedly, the increase in inequality has been affected significantly by the ascent of the wages of individuals at the top of the pyramid, but the explanatory potency of that argument is unclear.

In terms of similarity, Israel's inequality trend has several unique factors. First, inequality in the United States began to increase in the late 1960s, whereas in Israel the process got under way in the late 1970s. Second, our survey of research on inequality in Israel shows that inflation, which climbed to three-digit levels in the 1980s, had an expansionary effect on income-distribution inequality. This inequality contracted after inflation was checked in 1985 and rose again in the early 1990s.

Third, the widening of inequality in the early 1990s coincided with mass immigrant absorption. No Western country has experienced such a process. The influx of foreign workers at that time may also have exacerbated economic disparities. The coincidence of the increase in inequality and immigrant absorption (along with the admission of foreign workers) and the findings of previous studies illuminate the importance of this factor in explaining the upturn in inequality.

Fourth, Israel's unemployment rate has doubled since the late 1970s, and several studies have shown this to be a major a factor in the increase in inequality. Because unemployment did not increase in the United States, the upturn in inequality there cannot be traced to this factor.

An additional factor, difficult to measure but evidently active in the background, is the process of social atomization in Israel. It is difficult to state exactly when the process began, but by the late 1970s, one could sense the change in Israel's social climate by observing its reflection in the change in the parliamentary balance of forces. In the 1980s, values such as cooperation, mutual assurance, and economic egalitarianism did not always pass the test in leading institutions such as kibbutzim, moshavim, and the Histadrut. The erosion of these values seems to have "rewritten" unwritten rules that had formerly imposed wage restraint. In the absence of these rules, executives at the top of the pyramid were able to secure mammoth salaries.

15.2 The Rise of Labor-Market Inequality

Introduction

In the previous section, we saw that earnings inequality among households has been rising in Israel since the late 1970s and that the distribution of labor income has a key role in this development.

This work explores the sources of the increase in labor-market inequality between 1980 and 1996. It focuses on three factors that may be responsible for the widening of wage disparities. The first is a change in the structure of return on human capital. The second possible factor is a change in the distribution of human capital. Obviously, these two factors are not independent of each other. The third possible candidate is a change in inequality among "equals," that is, wage disparities among workers who have identical measurable traits, where these disparities are not explained by inequalities in return on various dimensions of human capital or by disparities in schooling.

This allows us to discuss earnings inequality in terms of prices (return on human capital) and quantities (ownership of human capital) that are less evasive in terms of systematic economic analysis. One can identify the channels along which economic events, such as disinflation and mass immigration, affect inequality in the labor market. For example, one may examine whether the shift to hyperinflation or the steep increase in labor supply affected income inequality via prices, quantities, inequality among "equals," or any combination of these.

The Data

This work is based on the Central Bureau of Statistics Labor and Income Surveys for 1980–1996. Each year, the CBS conducts four manpower surveys, in which one-fourth of respondents are also asked about their income. The figures on these respondents are published each year as part of the Household Income Survey. These surveys provide information about 80 percent of Israel's employee population, on the basis of a sample of six thousand households that contain about twenty thousand individuals. The rate of coverage increased in 1995, especially with respect to the proportion of non-Jews in the sample. The information includes a comprehensive coverage of sources of income—among which labor income is central—and particulars about individuals' characteristics such as schooling, age, year of immigration, nationality, and labor patterns. This work focuses on the wages of full-time employed men, the number of whom in the 1996 survey was approximately two thousand eight hundred. (Their numbers range from two thousand to three thousand during the period reviewed.) The next section explains why this population group was chosen.

In this work, I used aggregate years of schooling even in years for which detailed information on this indicator is available. I made this compromise to maintain uniformity of the variable that expresses one of the most important dimensions of human capital. This uniformity allows us to compare the regression coefficients over time. The information on the last type of school that the worker attended, a possible indicator of schooling quality, could not be used because it is available for some years only.

The Rise of Labor-Market Inequality

This part of the study focuses on inequality in the labor market. The research population in this study is composed of men aged twenty-five to sixty-five who are employed full-time. The variance of the natural logarithm of wage per hour worked in this population serves here as an indicator of labor-market inequality.

The population chosen reflects a trade-off between coverage and quality of the data. The labor-force participation rate of women increased significantly during the period reviewed. Men were chosen in order to control for changes in inequality that are not related to the changes in women's working patterns. Full-time employed were chosen because the wage per hour of part-time employees is susceptible to relatively large volatility and measurement errors.

Even if one accepts the considerations that informed the choice of population, one may ask (justifiably) about the degree of correspondence between inequality in wage per hour worked of full-time employed men and accepted indicators of inequality in household income. Table 15.7 shows correlation coefficients for variance in the natural logarithm of wage per hour worked among full-timed employed men and Gini

Table 15.7
Correlation among Indicators of Inequality: 1980–1996*

	Gini index			Variance of wage per hour worked
	Earnings	Total income	Net income	
Gini index of earnings	1	—	—	—
Gini index of total income	0.82 (5.27)	1	—	—
Gini index of net income	0.77 (4.56)	0.85 (6.06)	1	—
Variance of wage per hour worked among full-time employed working-age men	0.69 (3.69)	0.78 (4.7)	0.44 (2.09)	1

* The t values are shown in parentheses under the partial correlation coefficients.

indices for earnings inequality, total income, and net income of employee-headed families. The table shows a rather strong correlation between the indicator that this study uses to express labor-market inequality (variance) and the inequality indices (Gini coefficients) for the different definitions of income. In 1980–1996, there was a rather strong correlation (roughly 0.8) between the variance of (the natural logarithm) labor wage and the Gini index for the earnings distribution of household. This finding alludes to the existence of a strong correlation between a man's income and that of his spouse, and with capital income. Consequently, inequality among men is transmitted and maintained, to a large extent, among households as well.

Figure 15.2 illustrates the inequality in wage distribution per hour worked among full-time employed men in 1980–1996. Labor-market inequality increased steadily between 1980 and 1985, as the economy shifted from high inflation to hyperinflation. Labor-market inequality contracted after the successful Economic Stabilization Program was applied. Inflation settled at approximately 20 percent, but, concurrently, the unemployment rate climbed to about 9 percent in 1989, almost twice the rate in 1980. Wage disparities widened again in 1990 and subsequent years, concurrent with the absorption of mass integration. Inequality narrowed in 1996 but remained much higher than the 1980 level. What are the factors to which the increase in labor-market inequality between 1980 and 1996 should be traced?

Sources of the Increase in Labor-Market Inequality

We see that the upturn in labor-market inequality was translated into a similar trend of earnings inequality among households. In this part of the study, we present a method that allows us to identify the factors responsible for the increase in inequality

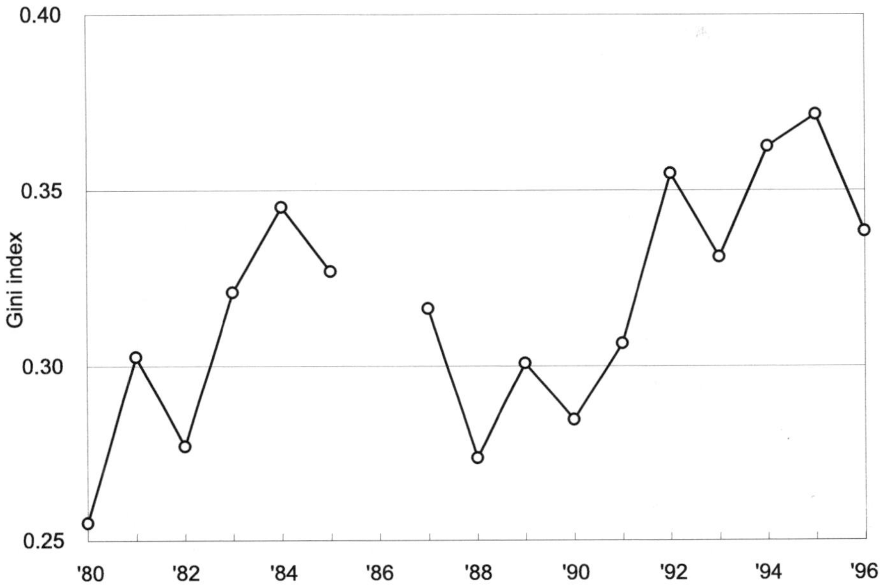

Figure 15.2
Inequality in the Labor Market, 1980–1996

in the labor market.[13] The method points to four sources of inequality: (1) inequality resulting from inequality in ownership of human capital, such as schooling and occupational experience; (2) inequality stemming from differences in the return on human capital; (3) the product of these two factors; and (4) inequality that the observable variables cannot explain.

The central feature of this method is a conventional regression of the human-capital equation (Mincer's equation), in view of which the natural logarithm of wage per hour worked is explained by variables that represent different aspects of the level of a worker's human capital. The change in variance of the explained variable (wage per hour worked) may flow from changes in this variance that reflect the distribution of ownership of human capital, changes in the regression coefficients that express the market price of the human capital, and changes in the variance of the unexplained residual that represents inequality among "equals."

A formal phrasing of the human-capital equation follows:

$$y_{i,t} = X_{i,t}\beta_t + \varepsilon_{i,t}, \tag{15.1}$$

where $y_{i,t}$ is the wage of individual i in year t; $X_{i,t}$ is a vector of several observable variables that represent different indicators of human capital, such as schooling and experience; and β_t is a vector of regression coefficients for the observable variables, by means of which the value of ownership of physical quantities of human capital may be translated into monetary income. ε_i expresses the disparity between the actual wage of individual i and his or her wage as measured for an assumed degree of ownership of human capital and the observed prices of human capital.

Below, we write an identical equation for period $t-1$:

$$y_{i,t-1} = X_{i,t-1}\beta_{t-1} + \varepsilon_{i,t-1} \qquad (15.2)$$

We use the two equations to calculate the long-term change in wage variance (in log terms) after several simple manipulations:

$$V(y_{i,t}) - V(y_{i,t-1}) = A + B - C + D, \qquad (15.3)$$

where:

$$A = [V(X_{i,t}) - V(X_{i,t-1})]\beta_t^2$$

$$B = V(X_{i,t})(\beta_t^{2-} B_{t-1}^2)$$

$$C = [V(X_{i,t}) - V(X_{i,t-1})](\beta_t^{2-} B_{t-1}^2)$$

$$D = V(\varepsilon_{i,t}) - V(\varepsilon_{i,t-1})$$

Equation 15.3 includes the four components that make up the variance in wage per hour worked (in log terms), that represents labor-market inequality in this study. The first factor, A, expresses the change in the distribution of quantities of the explained variable (human capital), which is composed of the sum of changes in variance of the various indicators of human capital and the correlation among them.

The second factor, B, reflects the effect of long-term changes in prices of human capital on inequality given the distribution of quantities of human capital in the current period (which corresponds to a price index according to Laspeyres).[14] Equation 15.3 may also be presented in terms of quantities of the previous period (which corresponds to a price index according to Paasche) or any combination thereof. The third factor, C, is the product of the change in both of the two before-mentioned factors; it is expected to have a small quantitative effect on inequality.

The fourth factor, D, reflects the effect of changes in variance of the unexplained residual on wage inequality. These are the wage disparities that are not explained by differences in years of schooling, experience, or other observable traits included in the regression. In this study, we use the term "inequality among equals" to represent these unexplained wage disparities. Because this term represents a linguistic "short cut" only, we place the word "equals" in quotation marks. "Equals" expresses quality in measured traits. Obviously, other traits may affect wage level even if we lack information on them.

Results

A human-capital equation was estimated for each of the years from 1980 to 1996, including potential experience, potential experience squared, dummy variables for five categories of reported years of schooling,[15] dummy variables for seven groups of occupations,[16] a dummy variable for household status (married is assigned the value of 1; others are 0), and a dummy variable for nationality (a Jew is assigned the value of 1; others are 0). These regressions provide a time series of regression coefficients and annual variance of the unexplained residual. The regression does not include industry branches in which the workers are employed in order to avoid mixing between changes originating in labor demand and changes in labor supply. Averages of the explanatory variables appear in table 15.8.

Table 15.8
Mean Values of Explanatory Variables

	1980–1981 Population at large	1995–1996 Nonimmigrants	1995–1996 Population at large
Potential experience (years)	29.6	28.4	28.3
Married (%)	91.8	84.7	85.1
Jewish (%)	96.4	83.0	84.9
Years of schooling (%)			
0–4	6.6	1.8	1.9
5–8	24.6	12.0	10.5
9–10	14.9	12.4	12.5
11–12	26.8	36.8	33.8
13–15	12.0	17.3	20.2
16+	15.1	19.6	21.1
Occupation (%)			
Academic	9.5	11.5	11.7
Liberal	9.8	8.7	8.6
Managerial	6.6	8.9	7.6
White-collar	17.0	11.1	9.8
Sales	9.8	12.6	11.4
Agricultural	1.6	1.3	1.3
Industrial	38.4	39.2	41.4
Unskilled	7.3	6.8	8.2
Immigrants (%)	0	0	17.1

Table 15.9
Wage Regressions, 1980–1996a*

	1980	1981	1982	1983	1984	1985	1987
Constant	**3.246**	**1.707**	**2.749**	**1.481**	**5.607**	**−0.319**	**0.352**
Potential experience	**0.036**	**0.036**	**0.036**	**0.036**	**0.031**	**0.049**	**0.051**
Experience squared	**−0.0005**	**−0.0005**	**−0.0005**	**−0.0005**	**−0.0004**	**−0.0007**	**−0.0007**
Married	**0.230**	**0.292**	**0.193**	**0.170**	**0.087**	**0.158**	**0.114**
Jewish	**0.207**	**0.244**	0.121	**0.212**	0.331	**0.251**	**0.177**
Yrs. of schooling							
5–8	**0.213**	**0.113**	**0.141**	**0.145**	0.043	0.118	**0.207**
9–10	**0.363**	**0.261**	**0.247**	**0.271**	**0.196**	**0.242**	**0.372**
11–12	**0.467**	**0.407**	**0.388**	**0.454**	**0.339**	**0.366**	**0.532**
13–15	**0.570**	**0.504**	**0.507**	**0.613**	**0.459**	**0.544**	**0.722**
16+	**0.625**	**0.616**	**0.580**	**0.655**	**0.552**	**0.627**	**0.800**
Occupation							
Academic	**0.245**	**0.271**	**0.326**	**0.207**	**0.348**	**0.339**	0.157
Liberal	**0.171**	**0.300**	**0.244**	**0.198**	**0.209**	**0.333**	0.150
Managerial	**0.260**	**0.333**	**0.350**	**0.332**	**0.423**	**0.484**	**0.227**
White-collar	0.055	**0.157**	0.104	0.036	0.089	**0.204**	0.043
Sales	**−0.127**	−0.035	**−0.128**	−0.101	0.002	0.031	−0.154
Agricultural	0.015	−0.112	0.014	−0.227	−0.097	−0.081	−0.153
Industrial	0.021	**0.107**	**0.097**	0.068	0.101	**0.158**	0.057
Total variance:	0.255	0.303	0.277	0.321	0.345	0.327	0.316
Unexplained	0.182	0.215	0.201	0.235	0.268	0.232	0.218
No. of observations	2,357	2,301	2,266	2,105	2,101	2,153	1,942

* Numbers in bold denote 1% significance; underlined numbers denote 5% significance.

Table 15.9 presents the results of the regression for the entire period investigated (1980–1996). The table shows that a one-year increase in potential experience (for an individual with zero experience) leads to an annual wage increase of 4.1 percent (on average over the entire period). Over the course of the period, the market price of a year of experience is quite volatile. The return on a year's experience climbed from 3.6 percent in 1980 to a peak of 5.5 percent in 1990 and slipped to 3.2 percent in 1996.

In contrast, the trend in the return on schooling is clear, albeit with year-on-year fluctuations. Table 15.9 presents the regression coefficients of five schooling categories; the value of the coefficients of each schooling group reflects an annual percent wage increase relative to the wage of workers with zero to four years of schooling. In 1996, for example, a worker with sixteen or more years of schooling earned 60 percent more than a worker with zero to four years of schooling but possessing the same characteristics (among the characteristics included in the regression). Sixteen or more years of schooling provided a smaller return in 1995 and 1996 than in the early

Table 15.9 (continued)

1988	1989	1990	1991	1992	1993	1994	1995	1996
0.767	**1.073**	**0.959**	**1.227**	**1.316**	**1.544**	**1.427**	**1.640**	**1.754**
0.045	**0.044**	**0.055**	**0.045**	**0.045**	**0.038**	**0.038**	**0.037**	**0.032**
−0.0006	**−0.0006**	**−0.0007**	**−0.0006**	**−0.0006**	**−0.0005**	**−0.0005**	**−0.0004**	**−0.0004**
0.116	**0.120**	**0.105**	**0.150**	**0.094**	0.078	**0.156**	**0.148**	**0.109**
0.144	0.104	0.104	0.014	0.103	0.086	0.091	**0.090**	**0.106**
0.112	0.062	**0.191**	**0.193**	0.137	0.060	0.148	0.002	0.280
0.294	**0.175**	**0.309**	**0.242**	0.196	0.102	0.236	0.143	0.276
0.375	**0.314**	**0.413**	**0.365**	**0.364**	**0.234**	**0.386**	**0.247**	**0.419**
0.520	**0.463**	**0.595**	**0.463**	**0.340**	0.223	**0.364**	**0.229**	**0.458**
0.593	**0.610**	**0.673**	**0.543**	**0.542**	**0.299**	**0.505**	**0.359**	**0.592**
0.291	**0.197**	**0.184**	**0.417**	**0.391**	**0.608**	**0.637**	**0.782**	**0.631**
0.232	**0.167**	0.135	**0.327**	**0.458**	**0.516**	**0.591**	**0.542**	**0.465**
0.313	**0.373**	**0.276**	**0.536**	**0.588**	**0.729**	**0.864**	**0.826**	**0.794**
0.113	0.028	−0.019	**0.215**	**0.267**	**0.414**	**0.410**	**0.457**	**0.413**
−0.072	−0.068	−0.086	−0.026	−0.007	0.134	**0.234**	**0.351**	**0.241**
−0.114	−0.193	−0.199	0.056	−0.129	−0.134	0.024	0.088	−0.040
0.086	0.039	0.021	0.083	0.110	**0.160**	**0.215**	**0.224**	**0.165**
0.274	0.301	0.284	0.306	0.355	0.331	0.362	0.372	0.338
0.194	0.207	0.204	0.215	0.255	0.242	0.251	0.250	0.226
1,983	2,136	2,205	2,427	2,325	2,101	2,335	2,776	2,816

1980s. However, the added increment of highly schooled workers who had just reached the country at that time may have skewed the returned on higher schooling significantly.

Seven occupational groups were included in the regression. The occupation of "unskilled worker" was omitted, and each coefficient expresses an annual percent wage increase in the occupations that appear in the regression in comparison with unskilled workers. The results of the regression show, predictably, that managers occupy the top of the wage scale. The relative wages of academic and managers rose meteorically between the early 1980s and the 1990s.

The return on marriage sank from a relatively high level of more than 20 percent in the early 1980s to 10 percent in the mid-1980s and remained on that plane for most of the period. This shows that marriage is not what it used to be.... On average, for the years 1980 to 1996, Jewish workers earned 14 percent more than non-Jewish workers.[17] This "premium" was greater in most of the 1980s and declined to 10 percent in the first half of the 1990s. Furthermore, in the 1990s, this wage premium was not always significant to the accepted extent.

Table 15.10
Factors in the Increase in Labor-Market Inequality (1990–1996 mean vs. 1980)

	Total population without dummy variable for immigrants	Total population with dummy variable for immigrants	Nonimmigrants only
Change in inequality	8.1	8.1	6.9
Unexplained portion	5.6	2.1	2.8
Structure of human-capital return	3.6	**	3.4
Ownership of human capital	0.4	**	0.9
Ownership and structure of return	2.8	6.0	4.1

Table 15.10 (the column farthest to the right) shows the estimated effect of these factors on labor-market inequality. The impact of the changes on the structure of human-capital return are obtained by multiplying the prices—the estimated annual regression coefficients for each of the human-capital traits that were included in the regression—by the inequality in quantities (i.e., the ownership of these traits) in 1996. In other words, changes in this component may originate only in changes in the regression coefficients, commensurate with their relative importance.

A similar computation was performed to estimate the effect on wage inequality of inequality in ownership of quantities of various human-capital traits. Inequality in the various indicators of human capital, such as years of schooling and experience (and the variance shared by all indicators), measured for each year, was multiplied by the prices of the indicators as estimated for 1996.

On average, labor-wage inequality was 0.336 in 1990–1996 as compared to 0.255 in 1980.[18] About 65 percent of the upturn in wage inequality among full-time employed men stems from an increase in inequality among "equals," which was measured by the variance of the residuals. The change in prices (i.e., the structure of return on human capital) explains almost the rest of the increase in inequality. The growth of inequality in quantities (i.e., changes in inequality in ownership of indicators of human capital) had a negligible impact on labor-market inequality (table 15.10). The specific contribution of changes in return on human capital (prices) as against changes in inequality in human-capital ownership (quantities) are only slightly sensitive to the choice of base year.[19]

There were no significant year-on-year fluctuations in the effect of quantity distribution and structural changes in human-capital return on wage inequality. Predictably, price volatility is greater than quantity volatility. Given that owning various indicators of human capital is somewhat like owning an inventory, one expects distribution of human-capital quantities to shift slowly. Prices, however, may change

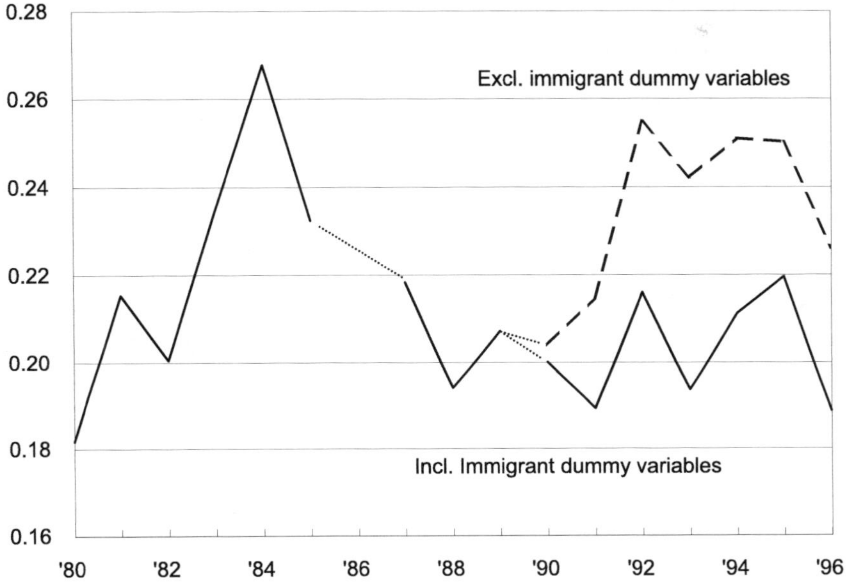

Figure 15.3
Unexplained Portion of Labor-Market Inequality: The Contribution of Immigration

sharply. In 1995, there was a relatively steep relative increase (although not an absolute increase) in the contribution of quantity distribution. This occurred because the coverage rate of the Arab population increased in the income survey for 1995, as reflected in a significant upturn in variance of the nationality dummy variable.[20]

Figure 15.3 illustrates the contribution of inequality among "equals" to wage inequality, as measured by the variance of the residuals. The upper curve in the figure almost perfectly mirrors the wage-inequality trend shown in figure 15.2. Inequality among "equals" increased when high inflation moved into hyperinflation in the mid-1980s, contracted immediately after inflation was checked, and rose again with the onset of mass immigration in the 1990s. The point estimate for a regression coefficient is single-variable; the variance of the residuals appears on the right-hand side, and the wage variance is positioned on the left-hand side and is roughly equal to 1.

The correlation between inflation and inequality corresponds to previous studies surveyed in part A. The findings here are novel in that they show the channel along which the effects of inflation are transmitted. The results here suggest that inflation acts mainly to increase the random component in wage and has a negligible effect on the return on schooling.

In the early 1990s, the narrowing of wage disparities after the Economic Stabilization Program was halted, and labor-market inequality began to expand again. The coincidence of the widening of two forms of inequality—labor-wage and unexplained inequality—and the onset of mass immigration suggests that the two are correlated. The next section of the study investigates how the massive influx of labor in the 1990s affected labor-market inequality.

The Effect of Mass Immigration[21]

The indicators of immigrants' human capital are different from those of non-immigrants. This may hurt the predictive power of observable variables such as years of schooling and (potential) experience, which are reflected in an upturn in a rise in inequality among "equals." Practically speaking, human capital is measured in this study, as in many other studies, on the basis of reported years of schooling and potential experience.

The use of years of schooling fails to take account of disparities among workers in quality of schooling; consequently, the quality of the wage disparity prediction is impaired. The quality of schooling acquired outside of Israel is different from that acquired by the Israel-born in the Israeli education system.[22] The loss of schooling (those elements of schooling that are specific to the Soviet economy) upon immigration to Israel, the lack of fluency in Hebrew, and other acculturation difficulties make it hard for immigrants to fulfill the earning potential that the reported schooling may reflect. The transition from the Former Soviet Union to Israel also eroded the human capital that is reflected in experience. The Israeli market may price the human capital of the immigrant workers differently, and this may explain the increase in the 1990s in the unexplained portion of labor-market inequality.

Table 15.11 presents regressions for 1990–1996 that make special reference to immigrants (workers who reached Israel after 1989). The estimated wage equation expresses the (possible) different effect of years of schooling and years of (potential) experience on the wages of immigrants, along with variables of interaction between these variables and the immigrants' dummy variables. It is clear that the market prices the immigrants' experience differently. The coefficient of the variable of interaction between experience and an immigrant (AGE_IM) reflects a reality in which, in the 1990s, an additional year of experience (in the first year) gives a nonimmigrant Israeli worker a 5 percent increase and an immigrant worker only 3 percent. This coefficient is significant at the accepted level throughout the period of immigration intake.

In contrast, there is no unequivocal indication that immigrants' schooling is less rewarded than nonimmigrant workers' schooling. The interaction coefficients between schooling and the dummy variable for immigrants is not significant in most of the 1990s. However, in years when these coefficients were significant, they indicate a substantial negative effect on the immigrants' wages. Moreover, the dummy variable for immigration (with no interaction whatsoever) is not significant in most immigrant-intake years after the special pricing of immigrants' schooling and occupational experience is taken into account. Strangely, this coefficient was positive and significant in 1994. This result underscores the importance of explicit representation of the channel that makes immigrants' wages different from those of nonimmigrants.

Figure 15.3 sketches the path of the unexplained component of inequality according to two different formulations of the wage equation—with and without special reference to immigrants. The variance of the residuals in the wage equation in table 15.9 were compared with the corresponding figure elicited by the wage equation in table 15.11. The figure points clearly to the absorption of immigrants in the labor market as the cause of the increase in the unexplained fraction of inequality in the 1990s.

The analytical framework set forth above does not allow us to distinguish between prices and quantities because the wage equation does not maintain a constant form over time. As table 15.11 shows, the wage equation for 1990–1996 includes variables that, for obvious reasons, were not included in the 1980–1989 wage equation in table 15.9. In other words, in the transition from 1989 to 1990, a variable that affected both quantities and prices came into play. It is possible to isolate the effects of prices (or quantities) only when one can hold one of the factors constant. Furthermore, the significance of several variables in table 15.11 is quite unstable. These sharp fluctuations make it impossible to apply a uniform equation over time because the methodology of this study assigns an insignificant coefficient the value of 0.

Much of the increase in labor-market inequality in the 1990s traces to changes in the distribution of ownership of human capital and the structure of return on human capital (table 15.10). However, as stated, the specific contribution of each of these factors cannot be estimated. The increase in the unexplained portion also played a role in the upturn in inequality in the 1990s relative to the early 1980s. However, the effect of this factor is smaller than that estimated on the basis of a wage equation that does not take immigrants into account.

This analysis leaves several important questions unanswered. For example, did the labor-market inequality increase because nonimmigrants obtained a higher return on higher schooling? Did the increase in inequality originate in a widening of disparities in nonimmigrants' schooling? Did the inequality widen because immigrants congregated at the bottom of the wage scale? Did it expand due to relatively severe inequality among the immigrants themselves?

Table 15.11
Wage Regressions, 1990–1996*

	1990	1991	1992	1993	1994	1995	1996
Constant	0.942	1.212	1.243	1.347	1.286	1.553	1.651
Potential experience	0.055	0.048	0.050	0.052	0.045	0.048	0.045
Experience squared	−0.0007	−0.0006	−0.0006	−0.0007	−0.0005	−0.0006	−0.0005
Married	0.109	0.159	0.086	0.072	0.149	0.139	0.092
Jewish	0.107	0.028	0.121	0.142	0.113	0.133	0.149
Yrs. of schooling							
5–8	0.190	0.188	0.177	0.076	0.211	−0.060	0.200
9–10	0.316	0.279	0.303	0.199	0.363	0.137	0.259
11–12	0.416	0.404	0.458	0.318	0.531	0.254	0.422
13–15	0.612	0.617	0.613	0.523	0.695	0.386	0.625
16+	0.674	0.657	0.808	0.666	0.815	0.523	0.776
Occupation							
Academic	0.205	0.302	0.172	0.302	0.434	0.610	0.404
Liberal	0.133	0.195	0.235	0.225	0.362	0.376	0.265
Managerial	0.276	0.373	0.339	0.381	0.573	0.584	0.526
White-collar	−0.018	0.094	0.072	0.184	0.194	0.288	0.220
Sales	−0.080	−0.102	−0.097	−0.002	0.111	0.224	0.095
Agricultural	−0.197	−0.048	−0.196	−0.083	−0.038	0.028	−0.089
Industrial	0.030	0.030	0.058	0.082	0.140	0.175	0.104
Immigrant*5–8	n.a.	0.397	−0.125	0.306	−0.237	0.154	0.264
Immig.*9–10	−1.400	0.060	−0.438	0.097	−0.448	0.022	0.203
Immig*11–12	−1.389	0.151	−0.364	0.090	−0.501	−0.044	0.076
Immig*13–15	−2.196	−0.077	−0.569	−0.123	−0.674	−0.123	−0.073
Immig.*16+	−1.467	−0.019	−0.733	−0.308	−0.690	−0.137	−0.091
Immig.*exp.	−0.030	−0.015	−0.017	−0.020	−0.014	−0.019	−0.020
Immigrant	2.174	−0.037	0.610	0.294	0.623	0.394	0.306
Total variance	0.284	0.306	0.355	0.331	0.362	0.372	0.338
Unexplained	0.200	0.189	0.216	0.193	0.211	0.220	0.189
No. of observations	2,205	2,427	2,325	2,101	2,335	2,776	2,816

* Numbers in bold denote 1% significance; underlined numbers denote 5% significance.

To answer some of these questions, a wage equation was estimated for a sample composed solely of full-time employed nonimmigrants. As before, we estimated wage inequality among nonimmigrants by measuring the variance of the natural logarithm of wage. Figure 15.4 shows that the increase in inequality documented for the entire working population is also typical of nonimmigrant working Israelis.

By excluding immigrants from the sample, we may investigate the trend in inequality among nonimmigrants without having to rephrase the wage equation. Of course, inequality among nonimmigrants is not independent of the impact of immigrant absorption in the labor market. Table 15.12 presents the results of the regressions for 1990–1996. The effects of the changes in the distribution of human-capital

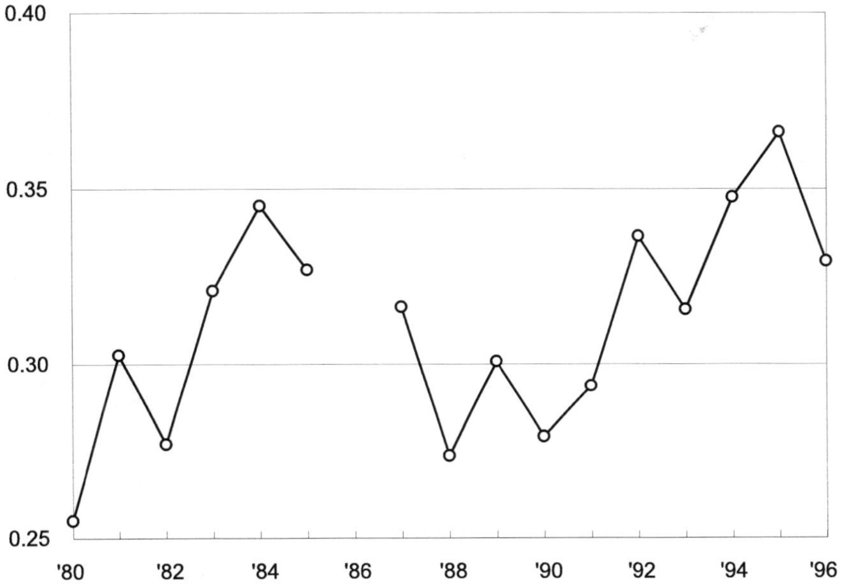

Figure 15.4
Inequality in the Labor Market: Nonimmigrants Only

ownership, return on human capital, and the unexplained inequality were computed on the basis of these regressions.

Table 15.10 summarizes the specific effects of the three sources of increase in inequality among working nonimmigrants. It shows that the changes in the structure of return on human capital were central in the increase in inequality among working nonimmigrants. Figure 15.5 points to a substantial increase, starting with the advent of mass immigration, in the specific contribution of price changes to the upturn in inequality. The significant increase in the relative wages of managers and academic posts was especially striking. Managers earned 42.5 percent more than unskilled workers with the same observable traits (e.g., experience) in 1990–1996 against 26 percent in 1980. The return on schooling for persons with thirteen or more years of study increased in the 1990s relative to the early 1980s, and the return for those with twelve years of study or less declined.

Changes in unobserved inequality also played a role in the increase in inequality in the 1990s among working nonimmigrant Israelis. In contrast, changes in the distribution of ownership of human capital had a negligible impact.

Table 15.12
Wage Regressions, 1990–1996*
(Immigrants excluded from sample)

	1990	1991	1992	1993	1994	1995	1996
Constant	0.929	1.189	1.215	1.288	1.236	1.504	1.618
Potential experience	0.056	0.051	0.053	0.056	0.048	0.051	0.050
Experience squared	−0.0007	−0.0006	−0.0007	−0.0007	−0.0006	−0.0006	−0.0006
Married	0.107	0.154	0.097	0.088	0.148	0.143	0.062
Jewish	0.107	0.031	0.103	0.121	0.113	0.143	0.144
Yrs. of schooling							
5–8	0.189	0.184	0.174	0.069	0.207	−0.077	0.194
9–10	0.315	0.275	0.304	0.193	0.356	0.116	0.255
11–12	0.415	0.403	0.462	0.317	0.529	0.236	0.421
13–15	0.612	0.622	0.620	0.530	0.707	0.383	0.630
16+	0.679	0.678	0.829	0.674	0.834	0.542	0.790
Occupation							
Academic	0.198	0.243	0.135	0.316	0.415	0.552	0.370
Liberal	0.138	0.165	0.229	0.234	0.343	0.350	0.250
Managerial	0.277	0.344	0.327	0.388	0.568	0.571	0.502
White-collar	−0.014	0.075	0.067	0.212	0.201	0.293	0.205
Sales	−0.070	−0.124	−0.088	0.029	0.134	0.234	0.096
Agricultural	−0.192	−0.065	−0.142	−0.082	−0.116	0.021	−0.047
Industrial	0.033	0.015	0.051	0.112	0.164	0.189	0.092
Total variance	0.279	0.294	0.337	0.316	0.348	0.366	0.329
Unexplained	0.197	0.193	0.227	0.227	0.220	0.227	0.197
No. of observations	2,185	2,245	2,050	1,758	1,966	2,303	2,331

* Numbers in bold denote 1% significance; underlined numbers denote 5% significance.

Inequality among "Equals"

The human-capital equation estimated in this study explains only about one-third of the wage disparities in the labor market. This is due to limitations in our information about workers' traits, places of work, and occupational attributes. In a certain sense, our inquiry is reminiscent of the man who lost his key under a streetlight (although the search *should* begin under the light). One may point to several factors about which information is limited (or wholly absent) that may create wage disparities among workers with identical reported traits (such as schooling and occupational experience): measuring problems, differences in innate aptitudes, racism and discrimination, and differences in the quality of the human capital.

Most of the aforementioned factors are responsible for the large extent of inequality among "equals" at a given point in time, but one cannot know which of them was the main factor in the upturn in unobserved inequality. The prime candidate to explain this finding, it seems, is a possible widening of disparities in schooling

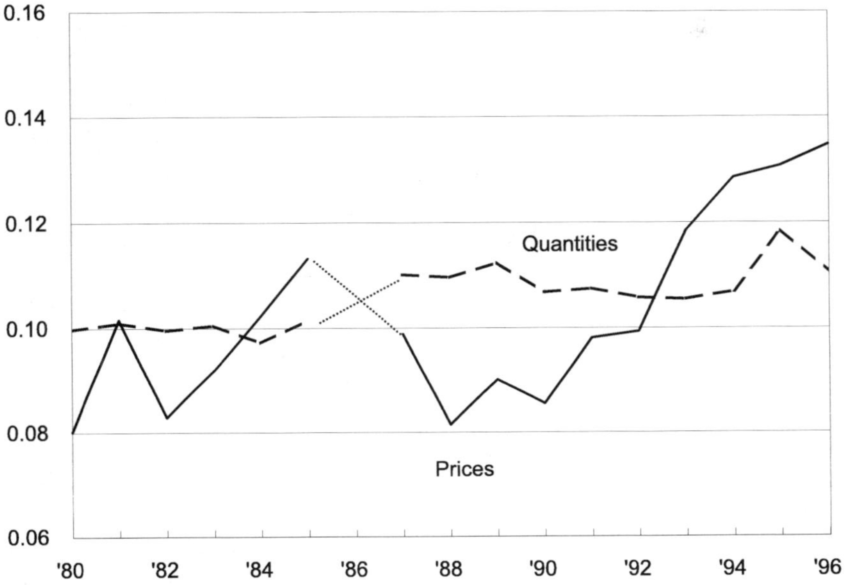

Figure 15.5
The Effect of Human Capital: Nonimmigrants Only

quality. We possess raw information only on workers' actual level of schooling and occupational experience. Years of schooling and potential years of experience mask possible disparities in the quality of the human capital. As we have seen, immigrants provide a marked example of this. The *haredim* ("ultra-orthodox") are another population group for which it is difficult to predict labor wage on the basis of years of schooling. The schooling delivered by *haredi* education institutions is intrinsically different from that acquired by other Israelis in the public and academic education system.[23]

Substantial disparities in schooling quality may be discovered among nonharedi nonimmigrant Israelis as well. The quality of human capital of workers who report having completed twelve years of study and received matriculation certificates does not resemble that of someone who completed twelve years of study in a vocational school and did not earned a matriculation certificate. The same may be said about the quality of schooling of teachers' college graduates as against university graduates. The increase in inequality among "equals" is consistent with disparities in the quality of schooling delivered by the education system to the Israeli public. This finding points to the need to subject the public education system that purports to provide universal schooling at a uniform level of quality to thorough research.

Conclusion

Inequality in the labor market, measured in terms of the labor wage of full-time employed men, widened by 32 percent between the early 1980s and the 1990s. In view of the tendency of inequality indices to change at a snail's pace, this is a significant increase. The rise in inequality is the result of a change in the structure of the return on human capital and an increase in inequality among individuals who have the same reported characteristics. Hardly any of the upturn traces to greater inequality in ownership of various indicators of human capital.

Wages of persons with higher schooling (thirteen years of study or more) climbed steeply relative to those of the poorly schooled. In the early 1980s, workers with sixteen or more years of schooling earned 62 percent more than those with very little schooling; in some years in the 1990s, the gap widened to 83 percent. Managers are another group that has benefited from a dramatic increase in relative wage. In the early 1980s, managers had a premium of 26 percent, and it escalated to a peak of 57 percent in 1995.

One-fourth to one-half of the wage gap is explained by variables that represent different dimensions of human capital. The empty half of the glass is the fact that the causes of much of the wage disparity are still shrouded in fog. This study shows that inequality among "equals" is also important in explaining the trend in labor-market inequality; this factor explains much of the increase in inequality in the 1990s relative to the early 1980s. In the United States, the upturn in inequality among "equals" was believed to reflect increase in demand for skilled workers; some have applied this explanation to the Israeli case as well. However, this result may reflect a widening of gaps in schooling quality in Israel.

The increase in return on human capital among the highly schooled (thirteen plus years) coincided with an increase in the proportion of persons with higher schooling. This is an indication of a more rapid growth of demand for human-capital-intensive workers. To some extent, one may construe increase in the unexplained fraction as further evidence of a swift growth (relative to supply) of demand for skilled workers.

Notes

I thank the School of Public Policy, The Hebrew University, Leah Achdut, Avi Ben-Bassat, Elhanan Ben-Porath, Shlomo Yitzhaki, Joram Mayshar, and Daniel Tsiddon for their useful remarks. I also thank the participants in the Bank of Israel seminar for their useful remarks. Special gratitude is reserved for Gilli Fernandez for his important contribution in preparing this study.

1. The Gini index for total-income inequality is an updated version of data in Dahan (1995). Dahan (1995) presents a detailed survey of changes in definitions in the income surveys and their implications for the quality of comparisons over the years. One can probably use these data with all due caution. Unfortunately, there is no sufficiently lengthy series of inequality data for the other definitions of income.

2. This remark does not refer to the perfect action of market forces. Earning inequality is affected by the use of transfer payments and direct taxes (see discussion below). Moreover, the government provides public education that affects labor income.

3. Other Western countries also behave similarly (Gottschalk and Smeeding, 1997).

4. "Influence of In-Kind Transfers on Income Distribution," Publication 1049.

5. Dahan (1995), Achdut (1996), Silber and Zilberfarb (1994).

6. A similar result was obtained in the United States (Blinder and Esaki, 1978), United Kingdom (Nolan, 1988), the Philippines (Blejer and Guerrero, 1990), and Sweden (Bjorklund, 1991).

7. Awwad (1998) found that unemployment has a regressive effect on inequality in the population at large.

8. Pressure on the wages of the disadvantaged also mounted due to the arrival of foreign workers (beginning in late 1993), primarily in occupations that pay low wages. It also has a negative effect on the relative wages of workers with a low level of schooling.

9. Use of a shorter period of years than that used by Dahan (1995) and Silber and Zilberfarb (1994) shows that inflation is not econometrically stable in its impact on inequality (Achdut, 1996; Awwad, 1998).

10. Deininger and Squire (1996).

11. Klinov (1999) found no support for skilled-biased technological changes. However, she found indication of changes in the bargaining power of trade unions as a source of the rise in inequality.

12. Sussman and Zakkai (1997) identify another way in which a trade union may aggravate inequality. These researchers document the fascinating story of the Israel Medical Association, which took action in the 1990s to widen wage disparities between nonimmigrant Israeli and newly landed immigrant physicians.

13. Juhn, Murphy, and Pierce (1993) used a similar method to examine the sources of the increase in U.S. inequality in 1963–1989.

14. Inconsideration of the degree of significance of the regression coefficients is one of the drawbacks of this method.

15. The six schooling groups are zero to four, five to eight, nine to ten, eleven to twelve, thirteen to fifteen, and sixteen plus. The zero-to-four group was omitted from the regression. The Income Survey for 1996 makes it possible to compare the explanatory power of the total regression on the basis of an exact number of years of schooling as against schooling groups as an explained variable. It was found that the availability of precise data on years of schooling improves the explanatory power of a regression only slightly.

16. The eight occupation groups are academic worker; liberal and technical professionals; managers; white-collar workers; agents, salespeople, and service workers; skilled farm workers; skilled industrial and construction workers; and unskilled workers. The group of unskilled workers was omitted from the regression. A more refined division of occupations (sixteen groups) elicits similar results, and most occupation dummy variables are not significant at an accepted level.

17. This finding may be consistent with discrimination against Arab workers, but the wage disparity between Jewish and non-Jewish workers does not necessarily trace to discrimination. This is because the regression does not include all characteristics of workers, such as quality of schooling; especially, it does not take account of possible differences in the attributes and location of the worker's job. This doubt comes up because it is difficult to presume the existence of discrimination against singles, widowers, and divorcees as opposed to married persons, even though a married man earns more than an unmarried man with identical observable traits.

18. A wage equation was also estimated with use made of a sample that unifies all observations in 1990–1996. Here it was found that the main regression coefficients do not change substantially from the average of the coefficients estimated for each year. The small number of years illustrates with greater emphasis the need to present the data for each year separately. In view of the negligible differences in the size of the coefficients, I preferred to maintain consistency in presenting the single-year data.

19. Notice that according to the method used here, each year is compared with the base year chosen (and not with the year preceding it).

20. The variance of the dummy variable (which we mark with a V) that receives the value of 1 or 0 equals $V = a(I - a)^2 + a^2(1 - a)$, where a is the mean of the dummy value. This mean is equal to the proportion of observations that receives the value 1. It may readily be seen that the variance of the dummy variable is a negative function of a if a is greater than 0.5.

21. Dahan and Ben-Porath (1997) found that immigration plays an important role in the upturn in household-income inequality. For a thorough analysis of the intake of immigrants in the labor market, see Eckstein and Weiss (1998a,b).

22. Several studies have estimated the human capital loss occasioned by migration: Friedberg (1992), Flug, Kasir, and Ofer (1992), Eckstein and Shachar (1995), Beenstock and Ben-Menachem (1995), Weiss and Gotlibovski (1995).

23. Dahan (1998), Berman and Klinov (1997), and Berman (1998) noted the differences between haredi and general schooling. The information does not allow me to refer specially to the haredi population for the whole period.

References

Artstein, Yael, and Zvi Sussman. "A Dynamic of Wage Increases in Israel: Market Forces and Inter-Industry Comparisons." Bank of Israel, Research Department, Discussion Article 91.02, 1991. (Hebrew)

Awwad, Yasser. "The Effect of Macroeconomic Variables on Poverty and Income Distribution in Israel." National Insurance Institute, *Annual Survey, 1997/98*, 1998. (Hebrew)

Bjorklund, A. "Unemployment and Income Distribution: Time-Series Evidence from Sweden." *Scandinavian Journal of Economics* 93(3) (1991): 457–465.

Blejer, Mario I., and Isabel Guerrero. "The Impact of Macroeconomic Policies on Income Distribution: An Empirical Study of the Philippines." *The Review of Economics and Statistics* 72 (August 1991): 414–423.

Blinder, Alan, and Howard Esaki. "Macroeconomic Activity and Income Distribution in the Postwar United States." *The Review of Economics and Statistics* 60 (November 1978): 604–609.

Central Bureau of Statistics. "Influence of In-Kind Transfers on Income Distribution." Publication 1049, March 1997. (Hebrew)

Cook, J. Philip, and Robert H. Frank. *The Winner-Take-All Society: Why the Few at the Top Get So Much.* New York, London, and Toronto: Simon and Schuster, Free Press, Martin Kessler Books, 1995.

Dahan, Momi. "The Effects of Macroeconomic Variables on Income Distribution in Israel." *Bank of Israel Survey* 69 (1995): 21–48. (Hebrew)

——— and Ori Ben-Porath. "The Immigration Wave and Income Inequality." *Economics Quarterly* 44 (November 1995): 351–172. (Hebrew)

Deininger, K., and L. Squire. "Measuring Income Inequality: A New Data Base." *The World Bank Economic Review* 10 (1996): 565–591.

Eckstein, Zvi, and Ron Shachar. "On the Transition to Work of New Immigrants, 1990–92." Jerusalem: The Maurice Falk Institute for Economic Research in Israel, Discussion Paper no. 95.04, 1995.

Eckstein, Zvi, and Yoram Weiss. "The Absorption of Highly Skilled Immigrants: Israel, 1990–1995." 1998a. Mimeo.

———. "The Integration of Immigrants from the Former Soviet Union in the Israeli Labor Market," 1998b. Mimeo.

Flug, Karnit, Nitsa Kasir, and Gur Ofer. "The Absorption of Soviet Immigrants into the Labor Market from 1990 Onwards: Aspects of Occupational Substitution and Retention." Jerusalem: Bank of Israel Discussion Paper no. 92.13, 1992.

Flug, Karnit, and Nitsa Kasir. "Compliance with the Minimum Wage Law in the Business Sector." Bank of Israel, Research Department, Discussion Paper 94.12, 1993. (Hebrew)

Friedberg, Rachel. "You Can't Take It With You? Immigrant Assimilation and Portability of Human Capital: Evidence from Israel." Jerusalem: The Maurice Falk Institute for Economic Research in Israel, Discussion Paper no. 95.02, 1992.

Gabai, Yosef. "Influence of Fiscal Policy on Income-Distribution Inequality in Israel, *Economics Quarterly* 43 (April 1996): 53–95. (Hebrew)

Gottschalk, Peter, and Timothy M. Smeeding. "Cross-National Comparison of Earning and Income Inequality." *Journal of Economic Literature* 35 (June 1997): 633–687.

Inter-American Development Bank (IADB). *Facing Up To Inequality in Latin America*, Economic and Social Progress in Latin America, 1998–1999 Report.

Juhn, Chinhui, Kevin Murphy, and Pierce Brooks. "Wage Inequality and the Rise in the Return to Skills." *Journal of Political Economy* 101 (1993): 410–442.

Klinov, Ruth. "Changes in the Wage Structure—An Overview: Israel 1972–1995." 1999. Mimeo.

Leviathan, Oded. "Development of the Cost-of-Living Allowance Arrangement and Other Wage Clauses." *Economics Quarterly* 115 (December 1982): 753–943. (Hebrew)

National Insurance Institute. *Annual Survey, 1997/98*, 1998. (Hebrew)

Nolan, Brian. "Macroeconomic Conditions and the Size Distribution of Income: Evidence from the United Kingdom." *Journal of Post Keynesian Economics*, 11 (Winter 1988–1989): 196–221.

Silber, Jacques, and Ben-Zion Zilberfarb. "The Effect of Anticipated and Unanticipated Inflation on Income Distribution: The Israeli Case." *Journal of Income Distribution* 4(1) (1994): 41–50.

Summers Robert, and Alan Heston. "Penn World Table (Mark 5.6)." 1994.

Sussman, Zvi, and Dan Zakkai. "Changes in Wage Structure in General Government during the Rising Inflation Period 1974–1981." Bank of Israel, Research Department, 1983. (Hebrew)

———. "Paradox: Large Supply of Immigrant Doctors and Steep Increase in Nonimmigrants' Wages, 1990 to 1995." Bank of Israel, Research Department, Discussion Article 97.06, 1997. (Hebrew)

Weiss, Yoram, and Menachem Gotlibovski. "Immigration, Search and Loss of Skill." Tel Aviv: Foerder Institute Working Paper 34-95, 1995.

Yaniv, Gideon. "Noncompliance with the Minimum Wage [Law]: Theoretical Aspects and Implications for the Israeli Economy." National Insurance Institute, Research and Planning Division, Study no. 35, 1986.

Index

Academic wages, 511. *See also* Wages
Access deficit, 320–321, 333
Actuarial considerations, 224–225, 228–229
Agriculture
  import liberalization, 293–294
  structural change, 449–450, 459–465
Arab conflicts, 63–64, 78
Argentina, inflation policy, 169–170, 173–175, 178–179
Artstein, Yael
  labor market flexibility, 380–385, 392
  wages, 379–416
Ashdod refinery, 325
Auctions
  commercial bank deposits at the Bank of Israel, 95, 101, 104–106
  and monetary loans, 93–95, 104–106
Averages method, pension computation, 225
Average wages, 352–355, 404–406. *See also* Wages

Balance of payments, 38–42. *See also* Capital account liberalization
Bank credit and monetary aggregates
  analysis interpretation, 116–117
  evolution analysis, 107–111
Bank debt, 202
Bank Hapoalim, 196
Bank of Israel
  commercial bank deposit auctions, 93–95, 101, 106
  disinflation strategy, 183
  interest rates, 147–148
  monetary loan, 93–95
  monetary policy, 89–90, 93–101, 134
  net creditor to net debtor, 115
  nominal anchor, 89, 96, 132
  portfolio shifts and vulnerability, 143–147
  sterilized intervention, 96–100, 102, 118
Bank share crisis, 192, 223, 248
Banking system, 192–193. *See also* Bank of Israel
  Brodet Committee recommendations, 196
  capital market and, 118–123
  competition, 16–18, 195–196
  credit allocation role, 197–198
  Herfindahl index, 193, 236
  holdings in nonfinancial firms, 196–197
  interest rates, 118–123, 147–148
  monopoly power, 260–262
  stability, 247–248
  structural change, 474–475
  supervision and capital account, 267–269
Bezeq
  cost accounting, 328
  market competition, 310, 319–321
  structural change, 468–469
Big bang liberalization, 246–247
Blass, Asher A., 193–195, 197–198
BoI. *See* Bank of Israel
Bonds. *See also* Corporate bond market; Government bonds
  earmarked for pension funds, 221–222, 225
  government policy, 10
Brazil, inflation policy, 169–170, 173–175, 178–179
Brodet Committee
  banks' conflict of interest, 196
  pension fund, 225–226
Budget deficit
  capital market structure, 89–93
  decline, 64–65, 180, 193
  inflation, 159, 161
  law of diminishing, 6, 14 (*see also* Budget Deficit Reduction Law)
Budget Deficit Reduction Law, 65, 131, 138–139, 167, 180 (*see also* Budget deficit, law of diminishing)
Budget policy reform, 3–7, 53
Bureau of the Budget, Finance Ministry, 340
Business sector growth, 5–7, 52
Business sector trends, 445–483
  agricultural industry, 459–465
  commerce and services industry, 470–475
  construction industry, 465–467
  electricity market, 467
  general, 445–447
  industries' structural change, 447–453
  manufacturing industry, 453–459
  productivity contradiction, 475–479
  transportation and communications industry, 468–470
  water market, 467–468
Business services structural change, 472
Business subsidy reduction, 62, 70–71, 79
Bus service industry, 310, 313, 326–327

Cable producers' industry, 339–340
Calmfors, Lars, 387, 409–410
Capital account controls, 248–250, 252
Capital account controls index, 269–271
Capital account liberalization, 91, 243–273
  banking system, 247–248, 260–262
  capital flows, 91, 251–255
  creditworthiness, 255–256
  general, 243–245
  international comparison, 269–272
  macroeconomic stability, 243, 246–247

Capital account liberalization (cont.)
monetary policy and banking supervision, 267–269
savings-investment ratio, 256–257
stock market international integration, 262–266
strategy, 243, 248–250
uncovered interest parities, 257–260
Capital accumulation
determinants, 430–433
pension fund influence, 229–234
Capital accumulation and productivity, 423–444
determinants, 430–437
general, 423–424
human capital, 438–441
neoclassical growth analysis, 427–430
real investment and relative price, 423–427
Capital expenditure, manufacturing firms
analysis, 202–204
flow of funds, 212–214
Capital imports and exports, 271
Capital Investments Law, 23
Capital-labor ratio, 353–354
Capital market, 54
bank involvement, 118–123, 196–197
competitiveness, 197–198
government involvement, 7–14, 90, 189–192
international integration analysis, 262–266
monetary instruments and, 93–96
reform (*see* Capital market reform)
structural change, 89–92
underdevelopment, 87–89
Capital Market Commission, 227–229
Capital Market Division, Finance Ministry, 221–224
Capital market reform, 12–14
business sector trends, 451–452
pension fund subsidy, 223–224
Capital movements
financial market and, 251–255
during inflation, 178, 181
liberalization, 14–15, 91–92, 101–102
Capital sources, manufacturing firms, 200–202
Capital uses, manufacturing firms, 202–204
Cellular phone market, 319–320, 337–338. *See also* Communications
Central Bank. *See* Bank of Israel
Centralization rate, industry, 300–301
Chemanski Committee, 318
Chile
compulsory deposits, 269
inflation policy, 171, 173–175, 177–179
COLA. *See* Cost-of-living allowance
Colombia, inflation policy, 172–173, 176–178
Commerce industry structural change, 470–475
Commercial banks. *See also* Banking system
deposits auctions, 93–95, 101, 106
financial system dominance, 192–193, 197
Communications
electronics, 454
price regulation, 330–334
privatization, 452–453
reform, 337–338
structural change, 318–321
technological progress, 468–469
Communications Law, 319
Communications Ministry, 319–320, 332–333, 341
Competition
banking system, 16–18, 121, 195–196
communications, 468–469
financial services, 260–262
labor market, 393–398
manufacturing, 458–459
pension industry, 234–239
public utility, 343
Compulsory licensing, 28, 287
Compulsory marking in Hebrew, 288
Concentration, pension fund, 234–237
Construction industry structural change, 445–446, 465–467
Consumption
boom, 161
import trends, 302–303
savings and, 229–234
Cooperative member wages, 312–313, 336. *See also* Wages
Corporate bond market, 13, 200–202. *See also* Bonds; Government bonds
Corporation equity, 193–195, 196–197
Cost accounting, 328, 335, 342
Cost-of-living allowance
income inequality and, 493–494
labor market restructuring, 26, 388–390
wage-setting model, 393–401
Crawling exchange rate band, 16
inflation plateau, 167
monetary policy and, 97–99
Creaming, 229
Credibility, stabilization program, 160–161
Credit market, 189–192
Creditworthiness, international, 255–256
Critical mass approach, disinflation process, 139–141
Croatia, inflation policy, 169–170, 173–176, 178
Cross-subsidies, public utility, 30, 313–316
Crude oil market, 324, 326, 330
Custom restrictions, 286–290

Dahan, Momi, 139, 142
Defense expenditure analysis, 62, 70, 72–75
Defense sector change, 37, 448–449, 456–457
Deficit. *See* Budget deficit
Defined benefits and contribution funds, 227–229
Demand pressures, 160–161, 163
Demographics
  immigrant, 349–351, 366, 384–386
  labor market composition, 384–386
Denmark, wage elasticity, 409
Dependency ratio, pension fund, 239–240
Depreciation and capital accounts, 268
Desalinization, 468
Devaluation, 141–147
  expectations, 96–97
  substitutes, 281, 284–285, 290–291, 303–304
Development area/towns, 50
  firms vs. Tel Aviv firms, 206–207
  manufacturing firms, 213, 284–285
Development grants, manufacturing firms, 202
Direct tax, 489–491
Directed credit, 11, 49, 87
Disability pension, 227–229
Disinflation
  international comparison, 169–179
  Israel's experience, 179–182
  stabilization program, 159–160
Disinflation process, 129–153. *See also* Inflation
  analysis, 135–137
  costs, 148–150
  critical mass approach, 139–141
  declining trend, 130–135
  inflation break (1992), 138–140
  inflation break (1997), 140–147
  inflation step (1985–1991), 137
  monetary policy, 147–148
  slow rate, 133–135
  strategy, 182–184
Dividend smoothing, manufacturing firms, 204
Doctors' union, 403. *See also* Unions
Double-digit inflation period, 137, 160–168
Driffill, John, 387, 410
Dual labor market, 396
Dukas database, 198–199
Duties and taxes, 28, 284–285

Earmarked bonds, 221–222, 225
Earnings. *See* Wages
Earnings inequality. *See* Income inequality
Eckstein, Zvi
  family structure and wages, 366, 371
  occupational transitions, 362
  wage growth, 350, 352
Economic change, stabilization program, 447–453
Economic development, income inequality
  impacts, 494–495
Economic disparities. *See* Income inequality
Economic growth. *See* Growth
Economic indicators, import liberalization, 295–296
Economic model, industrial countries, 132–133
Economic stabilization program. *See* Stabilization program
Economy, closed vs. open, 215
Education. *See also* Schooling, rate of return
  income inequality impacts, 491–492
  productivity and, 438
  structural change, 475
Egypt, inflation policy, 171, 173–175
Elasticity, wage, 397–398
Electric company
  price regulation, 334–335
  structural change, 317–319, 337, 467
  tariff structure, 313–314
Electronic communications equipment, 454
Emerging markets indicators, 253–255
Employment
  agencies, 387–388
  flexibility, 401–402
  industrial composition, 404–406
  patterns, 386–388
Energy Ministry, 318–319, 341
Enterprise-level flexibility, 383–384, 388
Entrance barriers, pension fund, 236–237
Equalization fund, 315
Equilibration mechanism, pension fund, 228
Equity, manufacturing firms, 193–195, 196–197, 200
European Common Market, 283–284, 291
Exchange Control Regime, 250
Exchange rate, inflationary period, 159, 161, 166, 173–178
Exchange rate regime
  capital account, 243–244, 267–268, 272
  changes in, 96–97, 99
  development, 16
  disinflation process, 178, 181
  monetary policy and targets, 96–101
Expenditure and income, government, 61, 66–68
Expenditure structure, pension fund, 236–237
Experience rate of return, 360
Exports, 40–41
  agriculture, 463–464
  subsidies, 28
External shock, 182. *See also* Shock, disinflation process

Family structure and wages, 365–372
Finance Ministry
electric company, 318
oil product prices, 321
pension fund, 221, 223–225, 238–239
phone rates, 330–331
price regulation, 328
public transport, 336
public utility, 341
rail investment, 321
Financial intermediation sector, 93–96
Financial market, 250–266
capital flows, 251–255
financial services competition, 260–262
international analysis, 262–266
international creditworthiness, 255–256
reform, 9–14
savings-investment ratio, 256–257
uncovered interest parities, 257–260
Financial repression, 87–88
Financial services structural change, 472
Financial system reform
banking competition, 16–22, 195–196
goals, 189
government intervention, 9–11
post-reform research, 193–198
pre-reform, 189–193
Finland, labor market flexibility, 409, 411
Fiscal consolidation, 133, 139
Fiscal deficit. *See* Budget deficit
Fiscal discipline
disinflation process, 130–132
government size and, 61, 65–68, 78–79
Fiscal impulse, 139, 142
Fiscal policy
disinflation strategy, 184
public expenditure, 63–66, 68–72, 78–79
Fiscal retrenchment law, 180
Flow of funds, manufacturing firms
financing and investing analysis, 205–215
sources and ratios, 198–205
Flow statements, manufacturing firms, 199
Fogel Committee
electricity prices, 334–335, 339
pension saving, 223
phone rates, 331–332, 339
Foreign currency market reform, 14–22
Foreign duties and taxes, 28, 284–285
Foreign exchange market
capital account and, 243–245
sterilized intervention and, 96–100, 102, 118
Foreign investment trends, 451–452
Foreign workers, 25–27, 384–385, 497
Former Soviet Union immigrants. *See* Mass immigration, former Soviet Union
Free Trade Area agreements, 282–284
Friedberg, Rachel, 380, 406
Fuel market, 322–326
Fuel tariffs and cross-subsidies, 315

Gasoline tax, 315
GDP, growth and composition, 34–36
General import duty, 284
Gini index, 485, 500
Globalization process
business services, 472–474
capital account, 266–267
manufacturing, 455–456
Goals, financial system reform, 189
Goods and services market reform, 27–31
Government bonds, 190–191. *See also* Bonds; Corporate bond market
Government Companies Authority, 340
Government expenditure and income analysis, 61, 66–68
Government investment grants, manufacturing firms, 202
Government involvement
capital and credit markets, 189–192
financial system reform, 9–11
income inequality, 488–492
public utility, 340–341
Government-owned monopolies. *See* Public utility industries
Government size, 3–6, 61–81, 124
business subsidy, 62, 70–71, 79
defense expenditure, 62, 70, 72–75
fiscal discipline, 61, 65–68, 78–79
fiscal policy, 61, 63–66, 78–79, 124
welfare transfers, 62, 75–79
Government subsidization, pension fund, 234
Gradualism, 48–49
Great Britain, labor market flexibility, 381, 411
Greece, inflation policy, 171, 173, 176–177, 179
Green accounting, 479
Gronau, Reuben
cooperative members' wages, 312–313
fuel market, 323–326, 329
phone rates, 332
public transport, 311, 316, 336
Gronau Committee, 332–333
Growth. *See also* GDP growth and composition
immigration and, 351–352, 450–451
pre-stabilization, 158–159
rate and fiscal policy, 63–64

Haifa refinery, 325, 329–330
Health services
income inequality impact, 491–492
structural change, 475
Herfindahl index
banking, 193
pension funds, 235–236
High Court of Justice, 223, 239
High technology revolution
commercialization, 456–457
government's role, 452
productivity, 446–447
Histadrut, 50
decline, 25–26, 386–387, 457
income inequality, 496–497
pension fund reform, 221, 223–226, 239
public utility, 341
Horizontal exchange rate band
exchange rate regime, 16
and monetary policy, 97–99
Hotel industry structural change, 472
Household Expenditure Survey, 232
Household Income Survey, 499
Human capital
ownership of, 501–502, 506, 509–511
rate of return, 498, 501–502
regression, 501–503
theory, 355
Hungary, inflation policy, 172–173, 176–178

IEC (Israeli Electric Company), 317–319, 337
IMF (International Monetary Fund), 269–272
Immigrant integration, labor market, 349–377
aggregate time patterns wage analysis, 351–355
general, 349–351
marital status effect, 365–372
wage convergence analysis (*see* Immigrant wage convergence analysis)
Immigrants. *See also* Mass immigration, former Soviet Union
demographics, 349–351, 366
wages, 352–355
Immigrant wage convergence analysis, 355–365
equations, 356–357
framework, 355
Israeli regression results, 357–358
occupational impact, 361–365
regression results, 358–361
wage data, 356
Immigration. *See also* Immigrant integration, labor market
economic growth and, 351–352, 450–451
income inequality, 494
shock, 138
Imported services duty, 285
Import-Export Ordinance, 286–287
Import liberalization, 27–29, 281–306
agriculture, 293–294
devaluation substitute protection, 284–285
domestic price of goods, 296–304
economic indicators, 295–296
Free Trade Area agreements, 283–284
general, 281
manufacturing exposure, 290–291
nontariff barriers, 285–290
standards policy, 294–295
trade diversion and third countries, 291–293
Import tariffs, 293
Income and expenditure, government, 61, 66–68
Income inequality, 485–498
indirect tax, 491
international comparison, 485–486, 494–498
labor market flexibility, 412–414
macroeconomic factors, 492–494
minimum wage effect, 492
public services distribution, 491–492
transfer payments and direct tax, 489–491
Incomes policy, 159, 181
Income tax laws and pension funds, 221
Index
capital account controls, 269–271
Gini, 485, 500
Indirect tax, 491
Industrial composition, manufacturing, 454–455
Industry structure, pension funds, 234–238
Industry and Trade Ministry, 283
import liberalization, 290–292
standards policy, 294–295
trade protection, 285, 289
Inequality
income (*see* Income inequality)
labor market (*see* Labor market inequality)
Inflation, 42–45, 157–186. *See also* Disinflation process
break (1992), 138–140
break (1997), 140–147
declining trend, 130–135
disinflation analysis, 179–182
double-digit period, 137, 160–168
history, 157–160
inertia, 173
international comparison, 169–179
monetary policy and, 159, 161, 167–168, 182–184
single-digit period, 168–169, 179–180
steps theory, 135–147
strategy, 182–184

Inflation policy, international
Argentina, 169–170, 173–175, 178–179
Brazil, 169–170, 173–175, 178–179
Chile, 171, 173–175, 177–179
Colombia, 172–173, 176–178
Croatia, 169–170, 173–176, 178
Egypt, 171, 173–175
Greece, 173, 176–177, 179
Hungary, 172–173, 176–178
Mexico, 172–173, 176–179
Inflation rate, income inequality and, 493–494
Inflation target, 16
disinflation strategy, 180–181, 183–184
monetary policy and, 97–99, 101
Information technology, 473–474
Infrastructure investment, 7
Infrastructure services, monopoly, 29–30
Initial Public Offerings, 193–195, 197
Institutional investors, 12–13
Institutions, labor market, 388–393
Insurance companies, earmarked bonds, 223–224
Intangible capital, 478–479
Interest parity, 257–260
Interest rate
monetary policy, 111–118
post-1992 period, 147–148
spreads, 18–22, 111–118
Intergenerational division of risk, 239–240
International calls market, 320–321, 338. *See also* Communications
International capital account integration analysis, 262–266
International comparison
capital account, 269–272
disinflation, 169–179
income inequality, 485–486, 494–498
labor market, 408–412
public sector size, 65–66
structural reform, 45–46
International creditworthiness, 255–256
International inflation policy. *See* Inflation policy, international
International Labor Organization, 411
International Monetary Fund, 269–272
International trade. *See* Import liberalization
International yield parity, 257–260
Inventory investment, manufacturing firms, 204
Investments, 451
behavior and relative price, 423–427
ratio, savings-, 256–257
restrictions, 193
Investment-specific technology progress, 423–426, 428
IPOs (Initial Public Offerings), 193–195, 197
Israeli Electric Company, 317–319, 337
Israelis, native
labor market inequality, 510–511
wages, 352–355
Israel Medical Association, 403

Johansen Cointegration test, 67–68

Kuznets Curve, 495

Labor market, 379–416
competition, 393–398
demographic composition, 384–386
employment flexibility, 401–402
employment patterns and union membership, 386–388
flexibility, 380–385, 414–416
general, 379–382
immigrant integration (*see* Immigrant integration, labor market)
income inequality, 412–414
inequality (*see* Labor market inequality)
institutions, 388–393
institutions, and economic performance, 411–412
international comparison, 408–412
macroeconomic and microeconomic flexibilities, 382–384
model of trade unions and unorganized labor, 393–401
public sector wages and employment, 402–403
restructuring, 24–27
structural change, 54, 404–408
Labor market inequality, 412–414, 498–513
analysis, 503–508
data, 498–499
human-capital equation, 501–503
mass immigration effect, 508–511
sources of, 499–503
unexplained component, 498, 501–503, 506–509, 512–513
Labor productivity, 388, 394, 397, 400
Labor ratio, capital-, 353–354
Labor supply composition, 384–386
Labor tax, 392–393, 397
Lavi, Yaakov, 138, 141, 150, 153–155
Law of No Printing, 65. *See also* Money printing
Layard, Richard, 412–413, 415
Liberalization
capital account (*see* Capital account liberalization)
monetary policy, 89–92, 101–102, 116, 121
1977 and late 1980s, 246–250
public utility, 317–321, 336

Licensing, compulsory, 28, 287
Life-cycle theory, 230–234
Liquidity, 11, 86
Liquidization process, 123–124
Liviatan, Nissan, 135–136, 139

Macroeconomics
capital account liberalization, 246–247
capital accumulation, 430–433
income inequality and, 492–494
labor market flexibility, 382–384
pension reform, 229–234
population aging, 221–222, 239–240
total factor productivity, 433–437
wage flexibility, 393–401
Makam, 94–95, 105–106
Management company, new pension funds, 227–229
Manager wages, 511. *See also* Wages
Manufacturing
structural change, 453–459
trade protections, 285–291, 294–295
Manufacturing firm analysis
capital expenditure determinants, 212–214
capital sources and uses correlations, 208–211
large and profitable firms, 206–207
Tel Aviv vs. development area, 206–207
Marital status effect, 365–372
Marriage premium, 367–372
Mass immigration, former Soviet Union. *See also* Immigrant integration, labor market
economic boom, 163
education and experience, 349
family structure regressions, 365–372
general, 31–33
labor force component, 384–386, 404
labor market inequality, 508–511
Meidan Committee, 314, 332
Melnick, Rafi, 135–136, 139
Mexico, inflation policy, 172–173, 176–179
Microeconomics
labor market flexibility, 382–384, 388
pension fund industry, 222
Military-industrial complex, 456
Mincer's equation, 501
Minimum wage, 26
income inequality impact, 492
labor market institution, 390–391, 398
Mirabilis, 478
Mivtachim pension fund, 235, 237–238
Mobile phones. *See* Cellular phone market
Monetary aggregates and bank credit
analysis interpretation, 116–117
evolution analysis, 107–111
Monetary auction, Bank of Israel, 93–95, 101, 106
Monetary base, 106–107, 116–117
Monetary instruments, 102–118
capital market and, 93–96
commercial bank deposit auctions, 93–95, 101, 106
monetary loans (*see* Monetary loan)
quantitative analysis, 103–106
in the stabilization era, 88–89
treasury bills (Makam), 94–95, 105–106
Monetary loan
discount window and auction, 93–95
evolution analysis, 103–105, 115–116
interest rate, 112
interest rate estimation, 118–121
Monetary policy, 53, 85–128
budget deficit, 89–93
exchange rate regime, 96–101
financial intermediation sector, 93–96
inflation and, 159, 161, 167–168, 182–184
interest rates and interest rate spreads, 111–118
liberalization and, 267–269
monetary instruments (*see* Monetary instruments)
monetary loan econometric estimation, 118–121
post-1992 period, 147–148
stabilization era, 87–89
treasury bills (Makam), 94–95, 105–106
Monetary tightening, 116–118
Money market reform, 11, 89–92
Money printing, 90, 101, 124. *See also* Law of No Printing
Monopoly, public utility. *See also* Public utility industries
characteristics, 309–311
cross-subsidization patterns, 313–316
general, 29–31, 50–51
wages, 312–313

NASDAQ, Israeli listings, 194–195
National accounts
pension fund, 234
productivity, 37
National Insurance contributions, 26, 392–393
National saving, 229–234, 239
Neoclassical growth analysis (capital accumulation and productivity), 427–430
Netherlands, labor market flexibility, 381, 411
New Histadrut, 226, 238–239. *See also* Histadrut
New pension funds. *See also* Pension fund reform
competition and concentration, 234–237
creation, 224–225
subsidized funds principles, 227–229
Nickell, Stephen, 412–413, 415
Nominal anchor, 132, 159, 161, 167

Nontariff barriers
import liberalization, 27–29
trade policy effect, 285–290
Nontradeable industries and wages, 383
Nontransport fuels market, 323
Nonunionized market, wage equation, 393–398
No Printing, Law of, 65
Norway, wage study, 409

Occupational groups, 505
Occupational transition dynamics, 362–365
OECD. *See* Organization for Economic Cooperation and Development
Oil market structure and rate reform, 322–326, 329–330
Old-age pension, 227–229
Old pension funds, 221, 224–225. *See also* Pension fund reform
Open vs. closed economy, 215
Organization for Economic Cooperation and Development
collective bargaining institutions and performance study, 381, 410, 412
low inflation standards, 132–133
wage and employment flexibility study, 383
Oslo Agreement, 253
Outsourcing, 388. *See also* Privatization
Ownership, human capital, 506
distribution, 509–511
inequality source, 501–502

Parities, 257–260
Pass-through system
definition, 328
pricing, 323, 330–331
Patam, 10–11
Patents, 440–441, 456–457
Peace process
economic impact, 33–34
government size and, 78
Pension fund reform, 13–14, 221–242
evaluation, 238–240
evolution, 221–226
new funds establishment, 227–229
principles, 224–225
savings impact, 229–234
Pension funds
administrative expenses, 239
deficits, 223
industry structure, 234–239
Personal labor contracts, 387–388
Phillips curve
inflation break, 138–139, 142
wage rigidity, 399

Phone
cellular service, 319–320, 337–338
rates, 321, 330–334
service (*see* Communications)
Political appointments, public utility, 341–342
Population aging, 221–222, 239–240
Port Authority, 321–322, 328
Port charges, 335–336
Portfolio shifts, capital inflow, 143–147
Ports structure and rate reform, 314–315, 321–322, 335–336
Preferred-yield earmarked bonds, 221–224
Price
domestic goods, 296–304
human capital, 498, 501–502, 506
investment behavior and relative, 423–427
Price regulation
electricity rates, 334–335
oil market, 329–330
phone rates, 330–334
port charges, 335–336
public utilities, 313–316
Privatization, 7
public sector decline, 66
public utility, 311, 317, 322, 336
state-owned enterprises, 31, 452, 457
Productivity, 37–38, 423. *See also* Capital accumulation and productivity
determinants, 433–437
labor, 388, 394, 397, 400
puzzle, 475–479
research and development, 438–441
Profitability ratios, manufacturing firms, 204–205
Protective barriers, 27–28. *See also* Import liberalization
compulsory licensing, 287
compulsory marking in Hebrew, 288–289
devaluation substitutes, 284–285
nontariff barriers, 285–286
quantitative import barriers, 286–287
special permit, 287
standards certification, 287–288
Provident funds
capital controls and, 250
definition, 223
investment opportunities, 193–194
performance and structure, 197–198
saving instruments, 221–223, 229
Public employees, 29–30
Public expenditure decline, 78–79
components, 68–72
general trends, 63–66
Public ownership in manufacturing, 457–458

Public sector
deficit, 61–62, 65 (*see also* Budget deficit)
wages and employment, 402–403
Public services
changes, 29–31
distribution by income levels, 491–492
Public transport
structure and rate reform, 316, 326–327, 336
tariff policy, 336
Public Utility Commission (PUC), 318, 334–335, 339, 342
Public utility industries, 309–345
background, 309–310
communications market structure and rate reform, 318–321, 330–334, 337–338
electric company structure and rate reform, 317–318, 334–335, 337
lessons learned, 336–343
monopoly characteristics, 309–316
oil market structure and rate reform, 322–326, 329–330
ports structure and rate reform, 321–322, 335–336
public transport structure and rate reform, 326–327, 336, 343
tariff structure, 313–316
worker wages, 312–313
Purchase tax, 28–29, 291

Q theory of investment, manufacturing firms, 213
Quantitative import barriers, 286–287

Railroads, 321
Rate of return
experience, 360
human capital, 498, 501–502, 506
marriage, 505
schooling, 504–505 (*see also* Education)
Rate regulation, public utility, 313–316, 338
Ratios (source, use and profitability), manufacturing firms, 204–206
Real investment and relative price, 423–427
Real-wage flexibility, international comparison, 408–410
Real wages
flexibility, 407–408
inflation and, 161, 180
macroeconomic flexibility, 382–383
Recession, 137
Refineries structure and rate reform, 322
Regime change, government, 68, 73
Relative price and real investment behavior, 423–427
Research and development (productivity), 438–441
Reserve requirements, 92–95, 116
Retail fuel market, 323–324, 326
Retail trade structural change, 471
Retirement age savings and income, 230–231
Retirement funds. *See* Pension fund reform
Returns to scale, public utility, 309, 317
Risk premium, 118

Safety net, pension, 224, 226, 229
Savings and consumption, life-cycle theory, 229–234
Savings-investment ratio, 256–257
Schooling, rate of return, 359–360
Securities investment, manufacturing firms, 204
Services industry structural change, 470–475
Shock, disinflation process, 178–179, 181–182
Shorer Committee, 331–332
Single-digit inflation period, 168–169, 179–180
Skill-intensive industries and wages, 383, 413
Social atomization, 498
Social security, 26, 392–393
Source ratios, capital
analysis, 205–212
manufacturing firms, 204–206
Soviet bloc mass immigration. *See* Mass immigration, former Soviet Union
Spain, disinflation process, 135
Special permit requirement, 287
Stabilization program, 247
disinflation measures, 159–160
economic results, 130–131
exchange rate regime, 96–101
monetary policy, 87–89
Standard-of-living inequality, 487
Standards
certification requirement, 287–288
liberalization, 294–295
mechanisms, 285–286
Statistics, manufacturing firms, 199–200
Sterilized intervention
foreign exchange market, 96–100, 102, 118
inflation break (1997), 143–147
Stochastic properties, inflation rate, 136–137
Stock market
crash, 89
international integration, 262–266
Stock price, manufacturing firms, 199
Stock price bubble, 198, 215
Strategic partnerships, manufacturing, 455–456
Strawczynski, Michel, 139, 142
Structural reforms, 1–3, 54–55. *See also* Capital market reform
communications market, 318–321
disinflation process, 178–179, 181–182

Structural reforms (cont.)
electric company, 317–318
financial success indicators, 18–22
financial system, 9–14
foreign currency market, 14–18
goods and services market, 27–31
international comparison, 45–46
labor market, 24–27
ports, 321–322
public transport, 326–327
public utilities, 336–339
refineries, 322–326
taxation and subsidization of production goods, 23–24
Subsidization, production, 23–24
Subsidy. *See* Transfer payments
Subsidy reduction, business, 62, 70–71, 79
Survivors pension, 227–229
Sussman, Nathan, 138–139, 141, 150, 153–155
Sussman, Zvi, 382, 399, 402–403, 414
Sweden, wage study, 409

Target zone, 16, 97–99, 101
Tariff structure, public utility, 313–316
TASE. *See* Tel Aviv Stock Exchange
Tax
direct, 489–491
discrimination, 92, 102
fiscal policy and, 66
indirect, 491
production subsidization and, 23–24
Taylor model, central bank policy, 138–139, 150, 153–155
Technological progress, 423–426, 428, 435
Tel Aviv area manufacturing firms, 206
Tel Aviv Stock Exchange
1980s situation, 192
stock price bubble, 198, 215
Telephone service. *See* Communications
Third countries
import liberalization, 291–293
nontariff barriers, 27–29, 281–282, 284
Tight money, 139, 148, 152–153
Tobin's q, manufacturing firms, 205, 213
Tobin-tax, 118, 124
Total factor productivity, 37. *See also* Capital accumulation and productivity
determinants, 433–437
puzzle, 475–478
Tradeable industries and wages, 383
Trade diversion, 291–292
Trade liberalization, 28–29. *See also* Import liberalization
Trade policy, 286–291. *See also* Import liberalization
Trade unions, 496–497
Trading trends, 296–304
Transfer payments, 489–491. *See also* Business subsidy reduction; Welfare transfers
Transportation industry structural change, 468–470
Transport fuels, 323
Transport Ministry
ports and public transport, 341
public utility reform, 322, 326–327, 335
Treasury bills (Makam), 88, 91, 94–95, 100, 104–106

Uncovered interest parities, 257–260
Unemployment
benefits, 26, 391–392, 397, 415
disinflation process, 153
income inequality and, 492–493
rate, 27
Unexplained inequality, labor market, 501–503, 506–509, 512–513
Unionized market, wage equation, 393–398
Unions
income inequality, 496–497
membership, 386–388
United Kingdom, wage flexibility, 409
United States
fiscal deficit aid, 160
Free Trade Area agreements, 283–284
income inequality comparison, 495, 497
loan guarantee, 138
negative accumulation of property, 230
personal labor contract study, 388
port tariffs, 335
Uruguay Round, 293–294
Use ratios, capital
analysis, 204–206
manufacturing firms, 205–212

Vardi Committee, 317–318

Wage and price freezes, 173
Wage bargaining, international, 410–411
Wage convergence analysis, 355–365
Wage differential, 362–365
Wage elasticity, 397–398, 409
Wage equation, 356–357
Wage equation, unionized and nonunionized sectors, 393–398
Wage gap, 400–401, 415
Wage indexation, 159, 173

Wage inequality, 498–513
Wage inertia, 397
Wage rigidity, 382, 399–401, 407, 414
Wages
 average, 352–355
 convergence analysis, 355–365
 convergence of average, 362–365
 convergence within occupations, 361–362
 family effects regression, 367–372
 inflation and, 159, 161, 163, 180–181
 life-cycle for immigrants and natives, 361–362
 macroeconomic flexibility, 393–401
 monopoly industry, 29–30
 public utility, 312–313
Wage-setting model, 393–401
Wage-spillover mechanism, 399, 402
Water
 agricultural development and, 461–463
 industry structural change, 467–468
Weiss, Yoram
 family structure and wages, 366, 371
 occupational transitions, 362
 wage growth, 350, 352
Welfare transfers
 immigrant integration, 372
 increase, 62, 75–79
Wharfage fee, 314–315, 330, 335–336
Workers' union, public utility, 341
Working capital, manufacturing firms, 204

Yafeh, Yishay, 194–195, 197
Yellow Pad, 225
Yosha, Oved, 194–195, 197–198
Young vs. old, pension saving, 239–240

Zakai, Dan, 387, 402–403

Made in United States
Orlando, FL
04 November 2026

90219983R00302